Why Growth Rates Differ

EDWARD F. DENISON

Assisted by Jean-Pierre Poullier

Why Growth Rates Differ

Postwar Experience in Nine Western Countries

THE BROOKINGS INSTITUTION
Washington, D.C.

THE BROOKINGS INSTITUTION

*is an independent organization devoted to nonpartisan research, education, and publication
in economics, government, foreign policy, and the social sciences generally.
Its principal purposes are to aid in the development of sound public policies and to promote
public understanding of issues of national importance.
The Institution was founded on December 8, 1927, to merge the activities of the Institute
for Government Research, founded in 1916, the Institute of Economics, founded in 1922,
and the Robert Brookings Graduate School of Economics and Government, founded in 1924.
The general administration of the Institution is the responsibility of a self-perpetuating
Board of Trustees. The trustees are likewise charged with maintaining the independence of the staff
and fostering the most favorable conditions for creative research and education.
The immediate direction of the policies, program, and staff of the Institution is vested
in the President, assisted by an advisory council
chosen from the staff of the Institution.
In publishing a study, the Institution presents it as a competent treatment of a subject
worthy of public consideration. The interpretations and conclusions in such publications
are those of the author or authors and do not purport to represent the views of the other
staff members, officers, or trustees of the Brookings Institution.*

Foreword

This volume presents the results of Edward F. Denison's analysis of the economic growth record of eight West European countries and the United States in the postwar years. It represents an application to the European experience of the point of view and methodology of the author's earlier study, *The Sources of Economic Growth in the United States and the Alternatives Before Us*. That study, widely recognized as a pathbreaking and significant contribution to economic growth analysis, is extended in the present volume to include detailed comparisons of European and United States growth experience.

The author estimates the contributions to growth of key variables which he identifies as determining the rate and pattern of economic development. His results do not directly indicate the best public policy mix to increase the rate of economic growth in each case. However, the analysis does help to identify the areas of greatest promise if growth performance is to be improved and to determine the factors which have retarded growth. Some of these factors are largely beyond the reach of public policy; others, however, may be affected by the policy choices made.

To achieve his purpose, Dr. Denison found it necessary to compile and analyze data from a wide variety of European sources. In 1963, he was joined by Jean-Pierre Poullier, who became his invaluable collaborator. Mr. Poullier's important contribution is gratefully acknowledged by the author, and is reflected on the title page.

This study would have been impossible without the assistance of many organizations and individuals who provided help in assembling the mass of data required for the analyses. Special mention must be made of the generous cooperation of government statistical agencies, particularly those responsible for the national accounts, in all nine countries. The library of the International Monetary Fund and the European Community Information Service were also very helpful. National accounts statistics used in this volume were those available to the author as of October 1966.

Helpful advice and suggestions were received from Robert M. Solow, D. J. Daly, and Moses Abramovitz, each of whom carefully reviewed the original manuscript. In addition, Jack Alterman, Odd Aukrust, Kjeld Bjerke, Geoffrey Dean, Solomon Fabricant, Victor Fuchs, George Jaszi, Albert Kervyn de Lettenhove, Rolf Krengel, Edmond Malinvaud, and Robert J. Myers offered valuable comments. Many individuals made suggestions and provided help on particular chapters. The author acknowledges many of these contributions at the relevant points in the volume. The book is a product of the Economic Studies Program under the direction of Joseph A. Pechman. Constance L. Grant provided efficient secretarial services throughout the project and typed the manuscript. The volume was edited by Barbara P. Haskins, assisted by Susan Gilbert, and the index was prepared by Florence Robinson.

This study was made possible by a special grant from the Ford Foundation. The views expressed, however, are those of the author and do not purport to represent the views of the staff members, officers, or trustees of the Brookings Institution or the Ford Foundation.

KERMIT GORDON
President

July 1967
Washington, D. C.

Contents

Appendixes

Text Tables

Appendix Tables

Why Growth Rates Differ

The Purpose and Plan of the Study

This is a book about the sources of postwar growth in nine advanced countries. Changes in a large number of determinants of national income are measured. The contribution of each to the growth rate is estimated. Countries are compared. That this is a hazardous and speculative undertaking scarcely needs stating. That some topics can be better dealt with than others the reader will soon discover. Some can be treated only very inadequately, and it might seem that they were better ignored. But the subject of economic growth is inherently comprehensive and quantitative. The author is persuaded that it will not advance far without both comprehensiveness and quantitative measurement.

Economic growth has become a national goal almost everywhere. Fortunately, peoples and governments of the countries examined in this study have not elevated a high growth rate to the position of an *overriding* national goal that takes precedence over all others. None of these countries is willing to sacrifice what are regarded as fundamental liberties for growth. Even within this limitation, none is willing to push growth regardless of cost. The people of no nation do everything possible to obtain the highest possible growth rate. Nowhere does everyone work as hard as he possibly can and al-

ways at the job where his contribution to output is greatest. No democratic country deliberately holds the level of consumption to the bare minimum required for working efficiency and devotes all the remainder of its output to investment, research, and education so as to increase future output. None forsakes compassion expressed in social welfare programs to accelerate growth. There is at least tacit recognition that most actions that raise the growth rate impose costs of one sort or another, and that the higher income obtained may or may not be worth the cost.

It is precisely *because* steps to increase the growth rate usually involve costs that systematic study of growth in quantitative terms is necessary and rewarding. It is often possible to judge rather easily whether a contemplated change will add to or subtract from national income and hence to or from the growth rate. For example, additional investment, if sensibly allocated, will almost always contribute to future output. But rational decision-making requires estimation of the *amount* of additional growth that a given amount of additional investment will yield so that benefits can be compared with costs. If additional investment means less current consumption, a real cost to society is incurred.

Particular steps to increase investment, moreover, usually have other effects. Special provisions in tax laws designed to stimulate investment, for example, are almost always at the expense of equity in taxation, and usually also make the tax structure less progressive or more regressive.

Governments in all countries make decisions directly affecting growth. They also adopt policies that influence individual decisions that affect growth. They must somehow compare the total advantages and disadvantages of their policies, including both effects on growth and all other effects, good or bad.

In a study published by the Committee for Economic Development in 1962, I tried to contribute to objective and quantitative thinking about growth and ways of altering the growth rate in the United States.[1] The amount by which any income determinant would have to be changed to raise the national income twenty years in the future sufficiently —just over 2 percent—to add an extra one-tenth of a percentage point to the growth rate over a twenty-year period was estimated. I estimated, for example, that one-tenth of a point would be added to the growth rate if an additional 1 percent of national income were invested in business structures, equipment, and inventories throughout the twenty-year period; or if half the deaths that would otherwise occur among individuals less than 65 years of age were prevented and the survivors were kept in average health; or if working time were extended one hour a week beyond what it would otherwise be; or if one and one-half years were added to the average time spent in school by all those completing school during the period; or if the rate at which knowledge relevant to production advances were raised by one-eighth. Most of the thirty-one possibilities considered turned out not to have a potential large enough to raise the growth rate by 0.1 percentage points over a twenty-year period, and I estimated the maximum contribution that could theoretically be obtained. For example, the complete elimination of the misallocation of resources resulting from private monopoly in product markets or the complete

elimination of crime and the rehabilitation of all criminals would contribute 0.03 percentage points to the growth rate over a twenty-year period.[2] The estimates were, of course, approximations, and some of them required the acceptance of assumptions whose validity could not be firmly established. But I believe that they provided reasonable approximations.

The techniques that provided these estimates were also applied to the past to arrive at the contribution of changes in each of the variables that determine income to the growth rate in the past.[3] This required that past changes in each variable be approximated. I thus arrived at an allocation of the past growth rate of total real national income, and of real national income per person employed, among the sources of growth. This was done for the period from 1929 to 1957 and (in slightly less detail) for the period from 1909 to 1929. These calculations shared the difficulties that were encountered in estimating the effects of changes on the future growth rate, and in addition required further information —knowledge about past changes in the capital stock, in education, and the like—that could only be approximate.[4]

Many readers of that study were surprised that the changes required to add, say, one-tenth of a percentage point to the growth rate were as large as I found them to be. To some extent this was due to insufficient appreciation that even one-tenth of a point in the growth rate is rather a large amount. One-tenth of a point is over 3 percent of the long-term United States rate of growth of total national income (which has been about 3 percent per annum since 1929 or 1909) and over 6 percent of the long-term rate of growth of national income per person employed. It is enough to increase the national income after twenty years by more than 2 percent; in

1. Denison, *The Sources of Economic Growth in the United States and the Alternatives Before Us;* hereinafter referred to as *Sources of Economic Growth* [B25]. Further information on citations is given in *List of Sources*, p. 449.

2. See *ibid.,* Chapter 24, for the full list of alternatives examined.
3. The techniques were generally similar to those followed and described in the present study.
4. The situation with respect to the important source of growth labeled "advances of knowledge," for which no direct method of measurement could be devised, was different. Its contribution to the past growth rate was measured by deducting from the growth rate of national income the estimated contributions of all other growth sources. The estimate from the past was then used to judge the contribution that would be made by accelerating advances of knowledge in the future.

1980 this would amount to tens of billions of dollars a year. There may also have been insufficient appreciation that the changes that had occurred in the past to produce the historic 3 percent growth rate were as large as they were.

It would have been difficult to argue that *on the average* my estimates overstated or understated the requirements for altering the growth rate. The techniques used to measure these requirements and those used to measure the results of past changes were consistent, and the amounts allocated in the past to the various sources of growth exhausted the growth rate that was actually achieved. But advocates of the particular efficacy of some factor or other (usually capital, education, or technological progress) do believe that I understated the gains from changes in their field of interest and similarly overstated gains from changes in other fields.

That study raised an intriguing question. If it is as difficult as I estimated to raise the *United States* growth rate by whole percentage points, how is it that some other countries have achieved much higher growth rates than the United States in the postwar period? It was easy to suggest explanations that *might* be correct, but the facts that would be needed to assess what *had* been taking place had not been assembled.

Purpose and Scope

An attempt to measure the sources of growth in the United States and in each of eight European countries during the period from 1950 to 1962 and two subperiods provides the main unifying theme of the present study. The growth rate actually achieved by each country in each time period is allocated among the contributions made by over twenty sources of growth, each of which is examined in some detail.

If conducted for even a single country, an investigation of growth sources provides an appraisal of what has and has not been important in its past growth experience. It enables the contributions of sources that have contributed greatly but ephemerally to growth during a short span of years to be distinguished from the contributions of more persistent growth sources, a distinction that has obvious implications for the future. Far greater possibilities for generalization are afforded by comparisons of nine countries over two time spans, based on a common classification of growth sources and the application of uniform procedures.

The broadest generalization emerging from the study is that there are many sources of growth and these vary greatly in importance from time to time and from place to place. Although attempts are sometimes made to explain growth by dealing explicitly with only three or four of the many determinants of the growth rate, the use of so restricted a list of sources is grossly inadequate to do so. By focusing attention exclusively on the few variables selected, that procedure may also be seriously misleading. In this study I try to give explicit consideration to the largest possible number of factors affecting growth even though information for some is scant. This seems to me preferable to simply implying the insignificance of some sources by omission. Although not every possible growth source is discussed, and the effect of changes in some that are discussed utterly defied quantification, I believe it fair to say that I have tried to appraise, and particularly to measure the effect of changes in, more growth determinants than has any previous study attempting international comparisons.

The estimates of sources of growth provide much of the information needed to answer the question raised by the title of this book: Why did growth rates differ? The experience of the nine countries was very diverse, yet a number of interesting patterns emerge. Among the most illuminating are those relating to reallocation of resources, gains from advances of knowledge and their application to production, education, and economies of scale. But many others will also be traced.

The study also had two quite specific purposes. One was to test how well the methodology previously used to analyze the sources of American growth and to estimate the requirements for altering the future American growth rate could explain the wide divergence of growth rates among countries and time periods. If experience in other countries was incompatible with the implications of this methodology, some amendment of the estimated requirements for altering American growth might be suggested. If not, confidence in these estimates might be somewhat strengthened.

A second specific purpose was to try to establish whether or not European countries obtaining higher growth rates did so because they were doing more than the United States to obtain growth. This question is given a central place in the investigation; it is explored in connection with every growth source for which it has meaning. Alternative explanations for higher growth rates in these European countries are that they had opportunities for growth not present in the United States, or that the same kinds of causes resulted in larger percentage increases in national income under European conditions, including the much lower level of income in Europe. These possibilities are also explored. This phase of the investigation leads to an assessment of the growth performance of the American economy against the background of European experience. In addition, it further contributes to answering the question: Why did growth rates differ?

Because my primary interest is in American economic growth and economic policy, the discussion focuses on comparisons of the European countries with the United States. But comparisons among European countries are equally possible from the tables presented, and are by no means ignored in the text discussion.

In a study with the specific objectives stated there is little point in trying to compare countries at very different economic levels, and comparisons of countries with radically different economic and social systems would compound the difficulties of comparison. The nine countries covered in this study include all of the large and several of the small Western nations that have attained high levels of national income per person employed. There is, unfortunately, no country really comparable in this respect to the United States, which has much the highest level. Belgium, Denmark, France, Germany, the Netherlands, Norway, and the United Kingdom have levels of national income per person employed that are close to one another but much below the United States. Italy is much lower still. Postwar growth rates in the nine countries cover a wide range.

Canada and Sweden, the two countries closest to the United States in income per person employed, unfortunately had to be omitted from this book. However, the Economic Council of Canada is conducting a study that closely parallels this one, and comparisons between Canada and the nine countries covered in this study should become possible.[5]

This study is confined to the postwar period because that is the period when the rapid growth rates that require explanation were experienced. Years before 1950 are not included because the earlier postwar period was too much dominated by recovery from wartime conditions to repay analysis. Even the early 1950's had strong recovery elements that distort usual relationships in some countries and make analysis difficult, and the 1950–62 period is therefore divided into two subperiods at 1955. Even the period after 1955 was not, of course, free of recovery elements, but these do not appear to be crucial deterrents to the type of analysis undertaken. The period reviewed in detail ends with 1962. Requisite detailed data become available on something approaching a final basis only with a long time lag and many details for later years were still lacking when the statistical work for the study was completed. Growth rates themselves and some collateral data are given through 1964.

Providing Perspective on Growth

A review of postwar growth in any country is of greater interest if it can be placed in broader perspective. Comparisons of changes in the United States with those in the eight European countries, or more generally of each of the countries with the other eight, is intended to provide such perspective.

For the United States, however, this is not sufficient. Not only is the level of national income per person employed in the United States far above that in any of the European countries, but also levels of capital per worker, education per worker, and average hours worked, the cost of misallocation of resources, and most of the other income determinants examined are different in the United States and Europe. Comparisons of the United States and Europe with respect to changes over time can be better interpreted if positions at a point in time with re-

5. D. J. Daly and Dorothy Walters plan to report partial results of this investigation in a paper to be presented at the August 1967 meeting of the International Association for Research in Income and Wealth.

spect to each income determinant can also be compared. Such comparisons of levels are attempted. In addition to an analysis of the sources of growth in each of the nine countries, a corresponding analysis is made of the sources of difference in level of national income per person employed in 1960.

Some comparisons between Northwest Europe (defined as the European area covered except Italy) in 1960 and the United States in the mid-twenties, when national income per person employed was at about the 1960 Northwest European level, are also attempted. The purpose of this comparison is to learn whether Northwest Europe was obtaining its 1960 output in the same way that the United States obtained the same level of output per man in 1925.

From the author's standpoint, the decision to attempt level comparisons among countries was hazardous. In almost every way they are less satisfactory than the comparisons of the sources of growth over time. International differences in the exact definition and scope of statistical series that have a negligible effect on their movement over time sometimes become significant when data for countries are compared directly. Even more important, it is often possible after examination to assume, rightly, that over a brief time span within a country something that cannot be statistically quantified has not changed significantly, but the assumption that it does not differ significantly among countries may be dubious.

I therefore make this plea to the reader. Judge the time series estimates and the international comparisons of levels separately. If the level comparisons for some factor or other appear unsatisfactory, do not automatically reject the time series for this reason but appraise the two sets of comparisons independently. Remember that the main purpose of the level comparisons is to place the time series in better perspective. I believe most of the level comparisons do this sufficiently well to make the attempt rewarding, but clearly the degree of reliability is much lower.

Another way to gain perspective is to compare postwar growth in a country with its own history over a longer period. This approach is being used in a study sponsored by the Social Science Research Council, which is analyzing economic growth in the United States, France, Germany, United Kingdom,

Italy, Sweden, and Japan.[6] In the present study I shall not attempt long-term comparisons but the reader should be aware that the high postwar growth rates obtained by some European countries far exceed the long-term rates in those countries. Growth rates of both total national income and national income per capita have been higher in the United States than in most of the other countries included in this study over the past century, or over the period since 1900, and not more than fractionally below any of them. The reader should also understand that the ranking of the European countries by growth rates since 1950 in no way corresponds to their ranking by growth rates computed from 1938, 1929, or earlier dates.

Meaning of Sources of Growth

By "sources of growth" I mean the changes that caused national income to increase from one date to another. These may be divided very broadly between changes in the resources used to produce the national product (changes in factor inputs) and changes that affect output per unit of input.

Contribution of Inputs

Inputs include the labor, capital, and land used in production. An index of total input is calculated by combining separate indexes of the various types of input. Marginal products are used as weights. Insofar as is possible and appropriate, relative earnings are used to measure relative marginal products. If, on the average, one employed male 35 to 44 years old who completed college and works 2,000 hours a year, three employed females 25 to 34 years old who completed high school and work 1,800 hours a year, one building that would have cost $120,000 to build in 1958, and ten machine tools of a type that would have cost $12,000 a year to produce in 1958, all have equal marginal products, they

6. The first five of these countries are among the nine analyzed in the present study. I regard the present study, that of the Social Science Research Council, and that of the Economic Council of Canada, as complementary, and believe that the three studies together can make a cumulative contribution to our knowledge of the process of economic growth in advanced countries.

are considered to represent the same amount of input.

It obviously would be unsatisfactory to measure broad categories of inputs like labor, capital, and land by such crude counts of magnitudes as the number of workers or man-hours worked, the total number of structures and machines of all types, and the number of acres. Either a classification of inputs so detailed that units within each category can be regarded as homogeneous must be adopted or some other way to allow for changes in composition of broad categories must be found. The procedures actually followed use both techniques.

In measuring labor input, I consider the significant and measurable characteristics of employed persons to be the hours they work (which affect both the total number of hours worked and the efficiency of an hour's work), their sex, their age (used as a substitute for experience and vigor), and their educational background. To treat the individuals with each package of characteristics as a separate factor of production would require cross-classification of the employed labor force at various dates by all these characteristics simultaneously, and computation of indexes for the numbers in each cell. This cannot be done directly. Age-sex groups are treated in this way, but otherwise the same result has been approximated by measuring each of the characteristics in sequence. Certain additional aspects of labor, including health and intensity of work, are discussed but not incorporated in the measure of labor input. Natural ability is, of course, an important characteristic of labor but, in general, it can be ignored on the assumption that the distribution of talent at birth is the same at different dates in the same country and among the countries compared. It must be explicitly introduced in measuring the effects of changes in education, however, since segments of the labor force with different amounts of education also differ with respect to natural ability.

Capital is divided among dwellings, nonresidential structures and equipment, inventories, and international assets, each of which is treated as a separate factor of production. Within the "nonresidential structures and equipment" and "inventory" components, different types of capital goods are weighted by their relative sales price or production

cost at a point in time. A machine that costs ten times as much as another represents ten times as much capital because it is presumed to yield the same rate of return and to have ten times as large a net marginal product. The contributions of the services of dwellings and of international assets to growth rates are measured directly without use of an input measure. Land in this classification includes natural resources.

As the reader progresses through the first half of this book, I hope that it will become clear to him that there is no difference between the labor and capital input indexes with respect to the kinds of "quality adjustment" that are allowed for. Both take account of changes in composition. Neither considers an increase over time in marginal product that results from advances in technical or organizational knowledge to be an increase in input.

In the case of labor it is statistically necessary to start with the number of persons employed and to adjust for changes in the composition of employment; these adjustments are often referred to as quality adjustments. If it were necessary in the case of capital in the form of structures and equipment to start with a count of the total number of items of capital goods, similar adjustments for changes in composition would be required. Only the happenstance that other investigators have already compiled series for the capital stock that weight its components by value makes this unnecessary.[7]

---

7. An example may be helpful. Suppose there were ten workers and ten items of structures and equipment in the capital stock of a country in both 1950 and 1962. Suppose that in 1950 three of the workers were college graduates and seven were elementary school graduates, and in 1962 these figures were reversed. Suppose also that in 1950 three of the items in the capital stock were steel mills and seven were hammers, and in 1962 these figures were reversed. Then, the indexes of labor and capital input would both rise because *at a point in time* the marginal product of college graduates is greater than that of elementary school graduates and the marginal product of steel mills is greater than that of hammers. Neither would rise because technological innovations or new methods of business organization made it possible for workers with the same amount of education, and for capital goods whose production requires the same use of resources at a point in time, to produce more output in 1962 than in 1950. This is so whether or not it was necessary, in order to take advantage of the innovation, that the content of education be changed or that the design of the capital goods be changed. The growth sources, "advances of knowledge" and "change in the lag in the application of knowledge" together account for the entire contribution of new technological and managerial knowledge whether or not so-called "embodiment" in labor or capital is required.

The analysis leads to an estimate of the contribution that was made to the growth rate of each country by changes in labor input, subdivided among changes in employment, in hours of work, in the age-sex composition of total man-hours worked, and in education; by changes in capital input, subdivided among residences (including sites), other structures and equipment, inventories, and international assets; and by changes in land input (excluding residential sites). Contributions to growth rates of both total national income and national income per person employed are presented.

Contribution of Output per Unit of Input

Output per unit of input changes for five principal groups of reasons.

1. Advances in technological and managerial knowledge, including business organization, permit more product to be produced with the same inputs. For various reasons the average of actual practice followed by enterprises is always behind the best known. Hence the contribution of knowledge as such may be distinguished from that of changes in the lag of actual practice behind the best known.

2. At any given time there is some allocation of resources that would yield a maximum national product. This allocation would be such that every input—each individual worker in the case of labor—is used where the value of its marginal product is greatest. It would always prevail if the owner of every resource used it where its earnings would be greatest, and if earnings were always proportional to marginal product. The actual allocation will always be such as to yield a lower national product.

One reason is that the actual distribution of resources is never the same as the equilibrium distribution. Since the equilibrium distribution is always changing, and changes cannot be accurately foreseen, the actual distribution always reflects the equilibrium distributions of past periods. The size of the divergence between the actual and equilibrium distributions depends on the amount and speed of changes in the equilibrium distribution and the mobility of resources.

A second reason is that the equilibrium distribution itself does not coincide with the distribution that would yield the largest national income.

One cause is that the owners of resources do not always wish to use them where their earnings are greatest. A worker considers many aspects of a job other than earnings in his choice of a position. An entrepreneur may prefer to run his own business even though he could earn more by investing his capital in an enterprise run by others and accepting salaried employment. Such examples imply no misallocation of resources; they are consistent with maximum welfare though not with maximum national income. A second cause is that various institutional conditions may drive wedges between maximum obtainable marginal product and maximum obtainable earnings. These conditions include laws (tariffs, farm price supports) and private institutional arrangements (such as restrictions on entry into an occupation or business).

If the actual distribution of resources moves closer to or farther from the distribution that would yield a maximum national product, this will add to or subtract from the growth rate during the transition period. In this study contributions to growth are computed for three aspects of reallocation. These concern the reduction in importance of agriculture, contraction of nonfarm self-employment, and lowering of barriers to international trade. I find that much of the difference among countries in growth rates is due to these sources.

3. Obstacles may be deliberately imposed by governments, business, or labor unions against the most efficient utilization of resources in the use to which they are put. Changes in these restrictions may affect the growth rate. However, separate estimates are not attempted.

4. Enlargement of markets makes possible the reduction of unit costs by greater specialization and thus increases output per unit of input. The size of these gains depends greatly upon the distribution of increased expenditures among products as per capita expenditures rise, and shifting consumption patterns have a great deal to do with observed differences in postwar growth rates.

Insofar as markets grow because inputs are increased or because changes other than economies of scale increase output per unit of input, one might wish to impute gains from economies of scale back to the source causing the increase in the size of markets and consider them an addition to the contribution to growth made by that source. I have preferred to retain "economies of scale" as a separate source of growth but no matter of principle is involved.

5. The purpose of a study such as this, which focuses on the "supply" rather than the "demand" side of the determinants of actual output, is to analyze the source of changes in a nation's ability to produce when resources are utilized with the same intensity. But a nation's actual national income may also change from one date to another because of changes in the extent to which its available resources are used.

In my United States study I circumvented this difficulty by comparing years in which resource utilization appeared to be about equal so that changes in intensity of resource utilization were absent or unimportant. The years compared were also far enough apart so that even if they were not strictly comparable, the incomparability would have only a negligible effect upon the growth rate over the intervening time span.

This approach could not be used in the present study, which is confined to a short and disturbed period and deals with nine countries in which the timing and amplitude of cyclical phases and of recovery from war were not uniform. Neither did it appear feasible to adjust all the data to the situation that would have existed if use of resources had been equally full in each year compared. The following expedient was therefore adopted. Initially, I measure changes in actual national income, actual inputs (except that the stock of capital is not adjusted for cyclical variations in intensity of use), and actual changes in the other factors, not the changes that would have taken place if the rate of resource utilization remained unchanged. I then try to appraise the effect upon output per unit of input (as measured) of differences between the years compared in the rate of resource utilization. For five of the nine countries I conclude there was no significant effect. For the other four the difference in the intensity of utilization of employed resources is treated as a separate "source of growth" of output per unit of input between the dates compared. (The brevity of the time periods examined makes the contribution of this "source" to growth rates regrettably sensitive to errors in the resource utilization adjust-

ments for the years compared. It also makes the analysis more sensitive to errors in the national income estimates themselves than would be the case with longer time spans.) This procedure provides a breakdown of the sources of growth of national income per person employed, though not of total national income, that is substantially the same (if this special component is eliminated) as adjustment of all the data to eliminate the effects of different rates of resource use would provide.[8]

In measuring the contribution of each source to growth, a certain *ceteris paribus* condition is, of course, imposed. Thus, if it is estimated that the increase in the stock of nonresidential structures and equipment contributed 0.6 percentage points, or the increase in the education of the labor force contributed 0.5 percentage points, to the growth rate of a country in some period, this means the average percentage increase in national income would have been this much lower if, year by year, the stock of capital or the education of the labor force had not changed while other income-determining factors had changed as they actually did.

The classification of sources of growth that emerges in this study is, I believe, a useful one, well adapted for appraisal of policy actions and the effects of various indirect influences. However, such appraisals are not attempted in this study. For example, I estimate the amount by which capital stock in the form of nonresidential structures and equipment increased in each country, and the amount that this contributed to the growth rate, but I do not try to explain why the capital stock increased at the rate it did and no other, nor to estimate how much the increase in capital stock would have differed if a country had followed different policies. I do not seek to decide whether indicative planning in France or its absence in Germany was more conducive to growth, to establish the effect on the growth rate of maintaining a stronger or weaker pressure of demand or of one exchange rate rather

8. In five of the nine countries irregular fluctuations in farm output due to weather and similar conditions also significantly affected growth rates between the years compared. The amounts are estimated and, like the effects of differences in intensity of resource utilization, treated as a separate "source of growth" between the dates compared whose contribution can be eliminated for the study of more basic growth sources.

than another, to study the consequences of changes in the tax structure, or to examine the effects of the British "stop-go" cycle that originates in balance of payments crises. But such appraisals are aided by estimates of the type attempted here, and indeed could hardly be made without them. If French planning, for example, affects growth it must do so by influencing the quantity or quality of one or more inputs, their allocation, or the efficiency with which they are used. To appraise the effect of planning on the growth rate, its effect on each of these income determinants and the effect of a change in each of these determinants on national income would have to be established. For example, if one of the consequences of planning is acceleration of the growth of the capital stock, it is necessary to know not only by how much planning has increased the capital stock but also the contribution that the increase in capital stock has made to the growth rate. Thus I believe the present study will help to provide information necessary for studies that are more directly policy oriented.

Difficulties Encountered in International Comparisons

In addition to the problem of business fluctuations, several other difficulties were encountered in the comparison of experience in nine countries that were absent, or at least less intense, in my American study.

1. The quantity and quality of statistical information available for the European countries varies widely, but in most countries data are less suitable for the purposes of this study than those available for the United States. They are often more adequate for the later than for the earlier years covered.

Since comparison of countries is the heart of the study, every effort had to be made to locate comparable statistical series for the nine countries, and where this was not possible to adjust available series to make them comparable. This meant that the task of compiling series for nine countries required more effort than would have been required by nine separate country studies.

At the inception of this investigation, I had feared that nothing might be available in some

countries for certain types of required information and had hoped that compilations by the international agencies would provide a useful guide to the information that *is* available. Compilations by the international agencies turned out to be less suitable for this purpose than expected but after recourse to national sources, including some unpublished estimates, gaps in important series proved to be rare. The task of exploring national statistical sources to obtain the best possible series and comparisons was time-consuming but interesting. In this book, sources and adjustments of statistics are sufficiently described to enable the reader to appraise the degree of success in securing appropriate and comparable data, and to make substitutions if he should find a basis for further improving comparability. The chapters provide enough description to indicate the general quality of the information and the broad procedures followed, and the details are given in the appendixes.

2. In my United States study I had the advantage of familiarity not only with the economic statistics but also with the economy of the country analyzed and therefore had some basis to express judgments about the importance of changes of one type or another that could not be statistically measured. One individual could hardly have equal familiarity with nine countries, and certainly the author does not. The association of Jean-Pierre Poullier with the project has been very helpful in this as in all other matters, and so have the comments of friends and colleagues at home and abroad. But the danger of poor judgments arising from insufficient familiarity with local conditions is present. It is also likely that better informed individuals could arrive at useful appraisals where I have declined to express opinions.[9]

9. A large group project could obviate the difficulty of unfamiliarity with several countries, but that solution faces what may be even greater problems. A series of country studies has great difficulties in maintaining comparability of methodology, data, and judgments, whereas in an agreed group report the need for compromise to obtain consensus almost inevitably leads to the dilution of challenging and controversial ideas.

The Social Science Research Council project to which reference has already been made consists of a group of country studies, coordinated as closely as possible to provide information on a reasonably comparable basis, which will be followed by a summary report written by Simon Kuznets and Moses Abramovitz. This is a promising attempt to surmount both difficulties.

3. It was not possible to examine carefully for each of nine countries every one of the detailed topics discussed in my United States study. Some of the presumably less important potential sources of growth have had to be merely mentioned in passing or even ignored.

4. My classification of growth sources is such that if a condition that affects the size of national income is found not to have changed from one date to another, its contribution to the growth rate usually can be immediately set at zero. Many, even most, of the potential sources of growth examined in my United States study were judged to fall into this category. Not surprisingly, it is clear that some of these same conditions have changed in one or more of the European countries and added to or subtracted from the growth rate. In some cases I have tried to quantify the effect. In others, either information or technique was so totally inadequate for even an informed guess of its magnitude to be attempted that I have had to content myself with noting the probable direction and significance of the change.

5. The nine countries studied in the present investigation have much in common, including democratic political institutions and primary reliance upon consumer choice and the market mechanism to determine the allocation of output among products and the distribution of resources among activities. To a degree they have a common cultural heritage. To the outside world they appear as a rather homogeneous group. But in fact there are significant, though diminishing, differences among them in the general environment within which growth takes place—in political institutions; the general framework of law and of business and financial organization; prevailing attitudes of individuals toward income, work, and provision for the future; religious beliefs; and standards of conduct governing dealings among individuals. Changes in the general environment within a country may also influence growth. The general environment cannot be adequately examined here but attention is drawn to certain aspects of special importance.

The United States is a much larger country than any of the others considered. The European countries are more comparable in size to United States

regions or states than to the United States as a whole. As I pointed out in my American study, growth rates vary widely even among the eight broad regions of the United States. From 1929 to 1957 growth rates of total national product ranged from 2.0 percent in New England to 4.4 in the Far West, and growth rates of per capita national product from 1.2 in the Mideast to 2.7 in the Far West. National growth rates—2.9 in total product and 1.7 in per capita product—summarized these very divergent rates. It would have been illuminating to compare the sources of growth in the eight American regions and the eight European countries rather than to deal with the United States only as a single unit, but this was not feasible. However, the reader would do well to bear in mind the natural averaging effect of dealing with a country as large and diverse as the United States. I am confident he will also bear in mind without prompting the fact that the United States is not only the largest but also the richest of the countries studied, and the implications of this fact will recur at various points in the study.

The general methodology that was used in my study of United States growth has been retained in the present study. Certain broad assumptions have also been retained. The principal assumptions concerned (1) the relationship between hours worked and output per hour; (2) the fraction of income differentials between individuals with different amounts of education that is *due* to differences in education as distinguished from associated characteristics; and (3) the importance of economies of scale. They have been adapted as well as possible to provide consistent assumptions for the European countries and the United States.

The estimates of the sources of United States growth in the 1950–62 period are not, however, exactly comparable to those presented in the earlier study for the 1909–29 and 1929–57 periods. The main reason is that the availability of more detailed data for the period since 1950 than was available in earlier years has permitted more refined procedures to be adopted. A number of small improvements in methodology resulting from further reflection rather than better data have also been introduced. Some changes, particularly in the choice of statistical series, were made in the interest of improving comparability between American and European data.

Significant departures from procedures used in the earlier study are noted.

I have already referred repeatedly to my study of American growth and the reader will find an embarrassingly large number of additional references in future chapters. This is immodest but scarcely avoidable. The present study draws upon and supplements the earlier publication; in no way does it replace it. Material is repeated to the extent required to enable the present book to stand alone but, for fuller discussion of many points, reference must be made to the earlier study.

CHAPTER TWO

Growth Rates and Output Levels

Growth rates have varied widely during the postwar period. Among the nine countries covered in this study, the United States stood seventh in growth of total national income, eighth in growth of national income per person employed, and ninth in growth of national income per capita, both from 1950 to 1962 and from 1950 to 1964. However, the level of national income per person employed is far higher in the United States than in Europe and the differential has not been reduced since 1950 in absolute, as distinguished from percentage, terms. This chapter presents the rates of growth and levels of production that will be analyzed in the remainder of the book.

A nation's production or output is measured in this study by its national income or, as the same series is also called, its net national product valued at factor cost. These terms will be used interchangeably. Measurement is, of course, in constant prices.

National Income To Measure Production

The selection of national income from the various comprehensive measures of output that are, or readily can be, constructed from the national accounts implies three decisions: to analyze net rather than gross product, to analyze national rather than domestic product, and to value product at factor cost rather than at market prices.

Net National Product Rather Than Gross National Product

The decision to analyze net rather than gross national product is the most important. Net product measures the amount a nation consumes plus the addition it makes to its capital stock. Stated in another way, it is the amount of its output that a nation could consume without changing its stock of capital. Insofar as a large output is a proper goal of society and objective of policy, it is net product that measures the degree of success in achieving this goal. Gross product is larger by the value of capital consumption. There is no more reason to wish to maximize capital consumption—the quantity of capital goods used up in production—than there is to maximize the quantity of any other intermediate product used up in production, such as, say, the metal used in making television sets. It is the television sets, not the metal or machine tools used up in production, that is the objective of the production process.[1]

Growth rates of net national product and gross national product are only moderately different in most cases (see Table 2–1), so that one might suppose the choice between them is not really very important. But it is, in fact, fundamental in a study of the *sources* of growth even when growth rates of net product and gross product are identical. An increase in depreciation must be regarded as a contribution to GNP growth that is entirely ascribable to capital. Unless growth is due only to increases in capital, capital will therefore always be responsible for a larger fraction of the growth rate of gross product than of net product if the value of depreciation increases at all. Depreciation did increase in each time period in every country covered in this study. Whatever method is used to judge the contribution of capital to the growth of net product, its contribution to gross product must be greater, usually much greater.

With disturbing frequency, policy conclusions concerning the importance and desirability of contemplated actions to promote growth are drawn from analyses of gross product. This procedure must assume either that maximization of gross product is itself a policy goal or else that the same conclusions would be reached concerning the sources of growth of, and the possibilities of raising, net product and gross product. Neither assumption is correct.[2]

2. National Rather Than Domestic Product

The decision to analyze national rather than domestic product is also related to goals. In my view,

maximization of the income of its residents is a more appropriate and important goal for a country than maximization of the production carried on within its geographic boundaries. To measure success in achieving this goal inclusion of net earnings from abroad is as necessary as the inclusion of every domestic industry. If measurement were not comprehensive, diversion of investment from a covered to an omitted sector, whether domestic or foreign, would reduce the output measure even if the return on investment were increased. From the borrower's standpoint, failure to deduct the earnings of foreign investors would overstate the gains from borrowing. Similarly, to include the earnings of American investors in Norway as part of Norwegian rather than American national income would distort a comparison of the two countries. The contribution made by net income from international investment will, however, be shown as a separate item in the analysis both of the sources of growth and of the sources of differences among countries in national income levels.

3. Factor Cost Rather Than Market Price

The third decision is of little quantitative importance. It is to value the components of the real national product at their base year factor cost (the earnings, including profits, of the suppliers of the resources that contribute to production) rather than at their base year market price.[3] Where a comparison can be made the choice between the two weighting systems appears to affect growth rates observed in the present study by one-tenth of a percentage point or less.

Factor cost valuation is, in principle, a little more convenient for analysis of productivity changes. If the earnings of resources are the same in all activities, a mere shift in the allocation of resources from a lightly taxed to a heavily taxed commodity or industry (or from a subsidized to an unsubsidized one) raises the real product at market prices whereas it leaves product at factor cost unchanged. Anal-

---

1. The necessity of using net product becomes still clearer if one considers the case where consumption is curtailed in order to produce capital goods that turn out not only to yield no net return but to recover only part of their cost. Such an investment reduces total net product but raises total gross product over the life span of the capital goods, including the year they are produced. Clearly this investment should not be made and, if it is made, it should be considered to have subtracted from output, not to have increased it. But only analysis of net product will yield this result.

2. Use of gross product may sometimes derive from the belief that it can be more accurately measured than net product. Even if this belief were correct, it would provide no reason for analyzing an irrelevant series. Actually, any difference between the accuracy of gross and net product growth rates is trivial.

3. Market price equals factor cost plus indirect business taxes minus subsidies. From the standpoint of this study, the decision involves only the selection of the price weights used to combine indexes of the output of each type of end product or of indexes of net production in each industry (depending on the method of estimate).

ysis of the market price measure would necessitate adding a purely statistical "source" of growth to represent the effect upon the market price series of shifts in the composition of output between lightly and heavily taxed or subsidized commodities. The contribution of these shifts, which may be positive or negative, would be the difference between the growth rates of the two measures.[4]

Discussion has so far been confined to the choice of national income from among comprehensive output measures that can be derived from the national accounts. The reader should be aware, however, that all these measures share certain characteristics or limitations that have been exhaustively and repeatedly discussed in a voluminous literature on national income measurement.[5] Perhaps best known is the restriction of the scope of measurement to marketable goods and services, so that work done by a family for itself is not counted except for such marketable items as food produced on farms. Chapter 3 describes four characteristics of national income measures that are especially important in the present study because they dictate that certain procedures be used to analyze the sources of measured growth. These refer to the deflation of the net output of government and households, the effect of changes in channels of retail distribution, the treatment of quality change, and the deflation of exports and imports. Certain other characteristics are touched upon later. But this is not a book about national income measurement as such and I consider only those topics that are essential to explain why national income, as it is actually measured, grew and differed among countries. No attempt is made to measure the changes in growth rates that would

result if any of the myriad of alternative ways of defining and measuring national income were to be substituted for those adopted in the official estimates. This would be an impossible task, and it is not necessary for the present study. The questions this book sets out to answer were raised by a comparison of the official estimates, and it is to these estimates that attention will be confined.

Geographic Definitions

In this book United States data cover the fifty states and the District of Columbia. German data cover the Federal Republic, including the Saar, plus West Berlin. The United Kingdom includes England, Scotland, Wales, and Northern Ireland. (Supplementary data are sometimes presented for Great Britain, the same area minus Northern Ireland.) Data for the remaining countries refer to their territory on the continent of Europe. The term "Northwest Europe," as explained below, refers to the following countries: Belgium, Denmark, France, Germany, the Netherlands, Norway, and the United Kingdom. In accordance with American practice, "Holland" is occasionally used as a synonym for the Netherlands.

The preceding paragraph refers to comparisons of levels of output, inputs, and so on, and to changes within each country beginning with 1960. However, prior to 1960 basic data used for the United States usually exclude Alaska and Hawaii (which represented less than 0.2 percent of national income in 1960) and those for Germany exclude the Saar and West Berlin (which accounted for about 5.8 percent of national income in 1960). In the computation of growth rates and in the analysis of sources of growth, the effect of these changes in geographic coverage is eliminated by linking at 1960.

Growth Rates

The time series used to compute growth rates of national income and GNP are, in general, official estimates of the countries concerned adjusted when necessary to common definitions: those followed by the Organisation for Economic Co-operation and

---

4. Estimates of changes in national income are presumably a little less accurate at factor cost than at market prices because in most countries reweighting to a factor cost basis is not performed in full detail, and in the United States, France, and the Netherlands is practically nonexistent (see Appendix A). On the other hand, the international comparisons of the levels of output are based on factor cost weights in the first instance and would have to be adjusted to arrive at market price comparisons. In both intertemporal and international comparisons any difference between the two measures in accuracy is insignificant compared to the errors likely to be shared by both.

5. The reader is referred particularly to the publications of the Conference on Research in Income and Wealth and the International Association for Research in Income and Wealth. Most of the issues are stated and debated in National Bureau of Economic Research, *A Critique of the United States Income and Product Accounts* [B81].

Development (OECD) and other international organizations. Either unofficial or my own estimates
have been used to fill minor gaps. Each country's
output is measured in its own base year prices.
Growth rates from 1955 to 1962 and 1964 are
computed from series measured in 1958 prices, rates
from 1950 to 1955 in prices of various years. The
choice of base years is largely dictated by the availability of data but is as appropriate as any other.[6]

All the data are subject to estimating errors. The
greatest uncertainty concerning accuracy relates to
the price series used to derive constant price output
measures from series in current prices. If there are
any gross incomparabilities among countries they
are most likely to arise from defects in the data
used for such deflation. Moreover, use of different
base years in deflation would sometimes change
growth rates a little. Differences in estimating procedure affect the comparability of estimates in some
degree despite the efforts toward uniformity exerted
by the international agencies; some of these differences must be considered in appraising particular
sources of growth. Obviously, no precision attaches
to the estimates. But I do not believe any large part
of the big differences among countries in growth
rates is likely to be ascribable to estimating errors,
procedural differences, or choice of base years. The
flow of basic data, though nowhere fully adequate,
appears sufficient to prevent great errors from appearing in the estimates of changes over the time
periods considered.[7]

Comparisons of Total National Income

Growth rates of total national income from 1950
to 1955, from 1955 to 1962, and over the whole
period from 1950 to 1962 are shown in Table 2–1.
These are the periods to which the analysis of the
sources of growth will be devoted. These periods
have, of course, no unique merit and the use of different years would yield different rates. The rates
that result if the periods are extended to 1964 are
shown in Table 2–3. The countries are shown below

6. Data and computations are described in Appendix A.
7. This paragraph does not refer to the effect on output
measures of actual differences *among countries* in the relative prices of different types of goods and services. In Section
II, Chapter 17, I estimate that this effect is substantial.

TABLE 2–1

*Growth Rates of Real National Income and
Real Gross National Product,
Valued at Factor Cost, 1950–62*

(*In percentages*)

Area	National income			Gross national product		
	1950 –62	1950 –55	1955 –62	1950 –62	1950 –55	1955 –62
U. S.	3.3	4.2	2.7	3.4	4.3	2.7
N. W. Europe	4.8	5.7	4.1	4.8	5.5	4.3
Belgium	3.2	3.3	3.2	3.2	3.3	3.1
Denmark	3.5	1.6	4.9	3.8	2.1	5.1
France	4.9	4.8	5.0	4.8	4.5	5.1
Germany	7.3	9.9	5.4	7.2	9.2	5.7
Netherlands	4.7	6.0	3.8	4.7	5.7	4.0
Norway	3.5	3.7	3.3	3.8	3.9	3.6
U. K.	2.3	2.3	2.3	2.4	2.4	2.4
Italy	6.0	6.3	5.7	6.1	6.3	6.0

Sources: See text and Appendix A for derivation.

arranged according to their growth rates from 1955
to 1962 and from 1950 to 1962. In each case, extension of the period to 1964 introduces only one
change in the order of the countries. It does, however, raise the growth rates of the last five countries
in each period and somewhat diminish the spread
among countries.

	Order based on 1955–62			Order based on 1950–62	
	1955–62 rate	1955–64 rate		1950–62 rate	1950–64 rate
Italy	5.7	5.4	Germany	7.3	7.1
Germany	5.4	5.6	Italy	6.0	5.6
France	5.0	5.0	France	4.9	4.9
Denmark	4.9	4.8	Netherlands	4.7	4.9
Netherlands	3.8	4.3	Denmark	3.5	3.6
Norway	3.3	3.9	Norway	3.5	3.8
Belgium	3.2	3.5	U.S.	3.3	3.5
U.S.	2.7	3.1	Belgium	3.2	3.4
U.K.	2.3	2.8	U.K.	2.3	2.6

The range of growth rates is large. How large
may be better appreciated if it is realized that the
5.7 percent growth rate in Italy from 1955 to 1962
meant a 48 percent increase in real national income
in only seven years, the 3.8 percent rate in the
Netherlands an increase of 30 percent, and the 2.3
percent rate in the United Kingdom an increase of
only 17 percent. The United States position is close
to the bottom whatever period is compared and the

TABLE 2–2

Growth Rates of Real National Income per Person Employed and per Capita, 1950–62

(*In percentages*)

Area	National income per person employed			National income per capita		
	1950 –62	1950 –55	1955 –62	1950 –62	1950 –55	1955 –62
U. S.	2.1	2.7	1.7	1.6	2.5	1.0
N. W. Europe	3.8	4.5	3.3	3.9	5.0	3.1
Belgium	2.6	2.6	2.7	2.6	2.7	2.6
Denmark	2.6	1.1	3.6	2.8	0.8	4.2
France	4.8	4.7	4.9	3.9	4.0	3.8
Germany	5.2	7.1	3.8	6.1	8.9	4.1
Netherlands	3.6	4.9	2.8	3.4	4.7	2.5
Norway	3.3	3.5	3.1	2.5	2.7	2.4
U. K.	1.6	1.4	1.8	1.8	2.1	1.7
Italy	5.4	5.3	5.4	5.3	5.7	5.1

Sources: Derived from Tables 2–1, 5–3; total population data: OECD, *Manpower Statistics, 1950–1962* and *1954–1964* [I32].

difference between the United States rate and the rates of the large continental countries is big.

The years 1950, 1955, and 1962 were not necessarily comparable with respect to the intensity with which resources were used so the growth of actual output may not accurately measure the growth in potential output. In the United States productive potential was used more fully in 1955 than in 1950 or 1962, and a little more fully in 1950 than in 1962, so that the growth rate of actual output was larger than that of potential output from 1950 to 1955, smaller from 1955 to 1962, and slightly smaller from 1950 to 1962.[8] From 1962 to 1964 the American economy moved toward fuller utilization of resources and increases in actual output were especially large. This movement continued in 1965 and into 1966. There appears also to have been some acceleration in the growth rate of potential output after 1962. The President's Council of Economic Advisers has estimated that the growth rate of potential GNP in the United States was 3½ percent from 1955 to 1962 and 3¾ percent after 1962.[9] National income growth rates were about the same.

8. The unemployed comprised 5.3 percent of the United States civilian labor force in 1950, 4.4 percent in 1955, and 5.6 percent in 1962.

9. Annual Report of the Council of Economic Advisers, printed with *Economic Report of the President,* January 1966, p. 40 [G52].

Growth rates of national income from 1950 to 1955 differed substantially from those of 1955–62 (Table 2–1). In Germany and the Netherlands the rate was much higher, and in Denmark much lower, in the earlier period. Over the entire 1950–62 period the spread among countries is even greater than in 1955–62. But if one were to group the countries as fast, medium, and slow growing, only the classification of Denmark and the Netherlands would depend on whether the longer or shorter period were used. In this study growth rates in both the earlier and later periods, and in the period as a whole will be examined.

National Income per Person Employed

Also explored are growth rates of national income per person employed, given in Table 2–2 for the period from 1950–62 and the two subperiods. (The rates extended to 1964 are given in Table 2–3.) National income per person employed provides a convenient and natural framework within which to analyze changes and differences in productivity, and for this reason will be stressed in this study.

An additional reason to consider national in-

TABLE 2–3

Growth Rates of Real National Income (Total, per Person Employed, and per Capita), 1950–64

(*In percentages*)

Area	National income		National income per person employed		National income per capita	
	1950 –64	1955 –64	1950 –64	1955 –64	1950 –64	1955 –64
U. S.	3.5	3.1	2.2	2.0	1.8	1.4
N. W. Europe	4.8	4.4	3.9	3.6	3.9	3.3
Belgium	3.4	3.5	2.8	3.0	2.8	2.9
Denmark	3.6	4.8	2.7	3.5	2.9	4.1
France	4.9	5.0	4.7	4.7	3.8	3.7
Germany	7.1	5.6	5.3	4.3	5.9	4.3
Netherlands	4.9	4.3	3.7	3.1	3.5	2.9
Norway	3.8	3.9	3.6	3.7	2.9	3.0
U. K.	2.6	2.8	2.0	2.3	2.2	2.1
Italy	5.6	5.4	5.2	5.4	4.9	4.7

Sources: Same as Tables 2–1 and 2–2.

come per person employed an interesting measure is its relationship to per capita national income, for which growth rates are also given in Table 2–2. Per capita national income is equal to the product of income per person employed and the percentage of the population that is employed. It is noteworthy that because the fraction of the population employed changed so much, and so differently, among countries, there is only a remote relationship between growth rates of national income per person employed and national income per capita. The two measures are by no means interchangeable.

The countries are rearranged below in the order of growth rates of income per person employed. The effect of extending the periods to 1964 is again shown.

	Order based on 1955–62			Order based on 1950–62	
	1955–62 rate	1955–64 rate		1950–62 rate	1950–64 rate
Italy	5.4	5.4	Italy	5.4	5.2
France	4.9	4.7	Germany	5.2	5.3
Germany	3.8	4.3	France	4.8	4.7
Denmark	3.6	3.5	Netherlands	3.6	3.7
Norway	3.1	3.7	Norway	3.3	3.6
Netherlands	2.8	3.1	Belgium	2.6	2.8
Belgium	2.7	3.0	Denmark	2.6	2.7
U.K.	1.8	2.3	U.S.	2.1	2.2
U.S.	1.7	2.0	U.K.	1.6	2.0

Italy, France, and Germany enjoyed the highest rates of growth in all periods distinguished, although in 1955–62 the German rate is much below the other two. The United States and United Kingdom experienced the lowest rates in all periods—much below the large continental countries. All four of the smaller countries are in an intermediate position.[10]

National income per person employed is less affected by differences in cyclical position than total national income but some distortion remains. In the United States the growth rate of potential output per person employed was lower from 1950 to 1955 and higher from 1955 to 1962 than the growth rate

of actual output, but an adjustment of the rates on this account would not change the ranking of the United States in any period distinguished in the text table.

In addition to information for individual countries, the tables give growth rates of national income, total and per person employed, for "Northwest Europe," consisting of the European countries covered in this study except Italy. These rates are not computed from simple aggregates of the countries but instead are based on the use of constant country weights. The index of Northwest European national income per person employed is obtained by weighting the corresponding indexes for the individual countries (1960 equals 100) by 1960 employment (Table 5–2).[11] The results are the same if the national incomes of the countries in 1960 measured in United States prices (Table 2–4) are used as weights. The use of fixed weights eliminates the effect on income per person employed in Northwest Europe of changes in the relative importance of each country in their combined employment total. The rates given for Northwest Europe as a whole are therefore the rates that would be explained by an explanation of income changes in the individual countries.

From 1955 to 1962 the growth rate of income per person employed was 3.3 percent in Northwest Europe as a whole as against 1.7 in the United States and over the whole 1950–62 period it was 3.8 as against 2.1.

Levels of National Income

Levels of real national income in the United States and the European countries in 1960 are compared in Table 2–4. The comparisons are in index form with the United States taken as 100.

Such comparisons are possible only because of the invaluable basic investigation conducted by Milton Gilbert, Irving B. Kravis, and others for the Organisation for European Economic Co-operation

10. The records of Belgium and the Netherlands are appreciably better than earlier studies indicated. Recent revisions in the Belgian national accounts yield a much larger increase in national income than the earlier estimates (but see p. 27 below). Recent revisions in Dutch employment show a much smaller increase in employment than earlier estimates.

11. The index of total national income in Northwest Europe was obtained by multiplying the index of total employment in Northwest Europe by the index of national income per person employed. This index was divided by an index of population to obtain an index of per capita national income.

(OEEC).[12] Their detailed investigation was for the year 1950. The nine countries that are examined in the present study were selected because the OEEC investigation provided an essential starting point for their analysis that was lacking for other countries.

Derivation of the Gilbert Estimates for 1950

The Gilbert group first made some minor adjustments to available estimates of total gross national product to improve comparability among the countries. They then divided the GNP estimates in national currencies among about 250 uniform expenditure categories. For each category they established the ratio of the quantity of expenditures in each European country to that in the United States, and the ratio of the European price to the United States price.[13] The quantity data for the 250 components were then aggregated in various ways, two of which will be used in the present study.

First, the components of the national product of all the countries were valued in United States prices at factor cost, in dollars, and summed to obtain a comparison of United States and European national products with components weighted by United States relative prices. Second, the process was reversed and the components of United States national product were valued in the prices of each European country. This provided a comparison of the national product of each European country with that of the United States with components weighted by relative prices in the European country (termed "national European price weights").[14] The ratio of the national product of each of the European coun-

tries to the national product of the United States was found to be much higher when the comparison was based upon United States relative prices than when it was based upon European relative prices.

Estimates for 1960

Gilbert and Associates brought their 1950 estimates in United States prices forward to 1955 by a quite summary procedure. The 1950 national product in United States prices of each of the European countries was divided into twelve broad product categories including a five-way breakdown of consumption. For each category they assumed the percentage change from 1950 to 1955 to be the same in constant United States prices as in the constant prices of the country concerned.[15] I have used their methodology in this study to obtain estimates for 1960 for components other than consumption. Instead of reweighting consumption on a five-way basis, I used an indirect procedure to approximate the difference between the 1950–60 movement of consumption valued in United States and in national prices. This procedure is described in Section II, Chapter 17.[16]

The Gilbert estimates, carried forward to 1960, refer to GNP at factor cost rather than to national income. The GNP estimates in United States prices were multiplied by the ratio of national income to GNP in national prices in 1960 to obtain approximations of national income in United States prices. National income is a little higher than GNP, compared to the United States, in all the European countries except Norway, where it is lower.[17]

12. Gilbert and Kravis, *An International Comparison of National Products and the Purchasing Power of Currencies* (hereinafter referred to as OEEC, 1954 [I18]); and Gilbert and Associates (Wilfred Beckerman, John Edelman, Stephen Marris, Gerhard Stuvel, Manfred Teichert), *Comparative National Products and Price Levels* (hereinafter referred to as OEEC, 1958 [I17]). A companion study comparing the United States and the United Kingdom provides useful data by industry: Paige and Bombach, *A Comparison of National Output and Productivity of the United Kingdom and the United States* [I22].

13. Knowledge of either the price ratio or the quantity ratio permitted the other to be computed. In practice, both techniques were used. For some components prices were obtained for similar commodities in the different countries, while for other components physical quantities were compared directly. The choice depended upon the availability of data.

14. Gilbert and Associates give per capita data on these two bases in OEEC, 1958, Table 2, p. 23 [I17].

15. *Ibid.*, pp. 157–58.

16. The indexes of national income per person employed in 1960 in United States prices given in Table 2–4 are 1 point higher than five-way reweighting of consumption would yield in Denmark, the Netherlands, and Norway; they are the same in the United Kingdom, 1 point lower in Belgium and Italy, 2 points lower in France, and perhaps 3 points lower in Germany (where the five-way procedure cannot actually be used for 1955–60). The five-way reweighting procedure tends to overstate increases in United States prices in countries experiencing a rapid rise in per capita consumption but in certain countries it also seems to introduce some erratic differences between changes in United States and in national prices.

17. Ratios of national income to GNP at factor cost in 1960, based on each country's own price weights and depreciation practices (but with United States depreciation placed on a replacement cost basis and given OECD scope, like those of the European countries) are estimated as follows: Nor-

The 1960 comparisons are given in Table 2–4 for total national income and for national income per capita, per person in the labor force, and per person employed.

In addition to comparisons based on the use of United States price weights, similar indexes based on the use of national European price weights are shown. These are also based on a rough extrapolation of the Gilbert data and application of 1960 ratios of national income to GNP.

The original study by Gilbert and Associates for 1950 was an excellent one, despite the inherent difficulties. The extrapolations to 1960 add an element of error of unknown size. Repetition for a recent year of the 1950 study would contribute greatly, and in many ways, to comparative studies of growth but it has not been undertaken and is not in prospect. Indirect estimation cannot, therefore, be avoided. The estimates for 1960 are adequate, in my opinion, to give a correct general impression of relative national income levels in the United States and Europe in each set of price weights. However, small differences among the European countries cannot be taken seriously. The European-weighted indexes, moreover, rest on different weights for each country and strictly speaking are not appropriate for comparisons of the European countries with one another.

National Income Comparisons, 1960

The comparisons of total national income, shown in Table 2–4, emphasize the small size of the economies of four of the countries. A single year's incre-

ment to national income in the United States is about as large as the total national income of Belgium or Holland, or of Denmark and Norway combined. Germany, the United Kingdom, and France dominate the Northwest European totals and averages. The national incomes of even the large European countries are small in comparison with the United States. They ranged in 1960 from 12 percent of the United States figure in Italy to 22 percent in Germany when measured in United States prices, and much less in European prices.

The estimates of national income per person employed are of primary interest in this study. Based on United States price weights, national income per person employed in Northwest Europe as a whole was 59 percent of the United States figure. The range for six of the seven individual countries was only from 58 to 61, the exception being the Netherlands for which the percentage is 65. When the comparison is based on price weights of the European countries, European incomes compare much less favorably with the United States. National income per person employed in Northwest Europe was only 46 percent of the United States level. The order of the countries is also different, but there is, again, a close grouping in levels of output. Income per person employed is 45 to 48 percent of United States income in six countries. On this basis it is Belgium, with an index of 53, that stands out as particularly high. It is not useful to attempt an unqualified ranking of the Northwest European countries by level of income per person employed in 1960 because the two sets of weights yield different rankings and use of average European weights (a third alternative provided by the Gilbert data) would yield still another ranking. I have not utilized this last set of weights because my primary interest lies in comparisons with the United States.

The indexes of output per person employed in the Northwest European countries are sufficiently similar to indicate about the same level of development in 1960; the range is, for example, less than that among the broad regions of the United States even if the Southern regions are excluded. National income per person employed in Italy was at a much lower level. Based on United States price weights, it was only 40 percent of the United States figure in 1960; based on Italian price weights, it was only 24

---

way 0.849; United States 0.875; Belgium 0.891; Italy 0.893; Germany 0.898; France 0.899; Netherlands 0.900; Denmark 0.913; United Kingdom 0.915.

European depreciation estimates usually assume longer service lives than American estimates. Use of these ratios overstates slightly European national incomes relative to United States national income in uniform prices if the difference in assumed service lives exceeds the true difference. On the other hand, European incomes are understated insofar as the prices of the capital goods depreciated are higher, relative to average GNP prices, in Europe than in the United States. (In general, prices of producers' durable equipment are higher, relative to all prices, in Europe than in the United States, those of residences are lower, and those of other structures vary; producers' durables receive a heavy weight in depreciation.)

The low ratio of national income to GNP in Norway (the counterpart of a high ratio of depreciation to GNP) is consistent with the very high ratio of depreciable capital stock to GNP implied by estimates presented in Chapter 12.

TABLE 2–4

Indexes of Real National Income, International Comparison, 1960

(*United States = 100*)

Area	Indexes based on United States price weights				Indexes based on national European price weights			
	Total	Per capita	Per person in the labor force	Per person employed	Total	Per capita	Per person in the labor force	Per person employed
United States	100.0	100	100	100	100.0	100	100	100
Northwest Europe	70.1	69	62	59	54.6	54	48	46
Belgium	3.1	61	63	61	2.7	53	54	53
Denmark	1.8	71	60	58	1.4	55	47	45
France	16.7	66	62	59	13.0	51	48	46
Germany	22.3	73	62	59	17.2	56	47	45
Netherlands	3.9	61	67	65	2.9	45	50	48
Norway	1.3	64	62	59	1.0	48	47	45
United Kingdom	21.0	72	61	59	16.5	57	48	46
Italy	11.9	43	41	40	7.1	26	25	24

Sources: Total national income: see text for derivation; population, labor force, and employment data: Table 5–2.

percent.[18] Unlike the other countries Italy cannot be considered part of a reasonably homogeneous area with respect to level of productivity in the economy as a whole.[19]

In 1960, to repeat the summary finding, national income per person employed in Northwest Europe was 59 percent as large as in the United States when the output of both areas is valued in United States prices of 1960, and 46 percent as large when output of both areas is valued at Northwest European prices. Put the other way around, income per person employed in the United States was 69 percent larger than in Northwest Europe based on United States price weights and 117 percent larger based on Northwest European price weights. Such differences are enormous and long familiarity with them should not be permitted to blunt their impact.

18. It should be pointed out that use of national European weights is particularly adverse to Italy. In 1955 substitution of average European weights for national European weights hardly changes the index for Northwest Europe as a whole but raises the Italian index by about one-fifth. It also raises the Norwegian index substantially.

19. It is often suggested that Northern Italy is at about the Northwest European level while Central and Southern Italy are not. Approximately this result is obtained by combining the indexes in Table 2–4 with an estimate by Francesco Forte and Francesco Indovina that per capita income in Northern Italy was 62 percent above the national average in 1961 (in Forte and Lombardini [eds.], *Saggi di Economia*, pp. 273, 287 [B35]).

Use of either set of price weights is equally valid, but it is the difference in United States price weights that I shall explore in this study. This is primarily because (given the availability of data) the uniform use of United States price weights greatly simplifies the analysis of the sources of differences in output levels by permitting comparison of inputs in 1960 also to be based on the use of United States weights.

Indexes of national income per capita are also of interest. Because the percentage of the population employed was much larger in Northwest Europe than in the United States, Northwest European indexes of per capita income in 1960 are much higher than indexes of income per person employed: 69 as against 59, based on United States weights; and 54 as against 46, based on European weights. The spread in per capita income among the Northwest European countries is also much larger. In United States prices, the indexes range from 61 in Belgium and the Netherlands to between 64 and 66 in Norway and France and 71 and 73 in Denmark, the United Kingdom, and Germany. The differences among these countries in per capita income are due mainly to differences in the proportion of the population at work. Among these countries Belgium and the Netherlands had the highest income per person employed and the lowest income per capita, based on either set of price weights.[20] As was noted in the discussion of growth rates, income per person employed and income per capita measure quite different things and cannot be substituted for one another.

The indexes of national income per person in the labor force require only bare mention; they differ from those based on employment only insofar as unemployment rates varied among countries in 1960. Since the United States had the highest unemployment rate, all the European indexes are above those based on employment.

Analysis of the sources of differences in levels of national income per person employed will be confined to the year 1960. Nevertheless, it is of interest to compare 1960 with other years. The changes that occurred are suggested by Table 2–5. This table refers to GNP rather than to national income. The same price weights (those of the United States in 1955) are used for all years.[21]

In Part A, Table 2–5, GNP per person employed

in Europe is compared with United States GNP per person employed in the same year. With the single exception of the United Kingdom, every European country reduced the *percentage* differential between its own GNP per person employed and that of the United States between 1950 and 1960 and again from 1960 to 1964.[22] GNP per person employed in Northwest Europe as a whole rose from 51 percent of the United States in 1950 to 57 percent in 1960 and 59 percent in 1964. The fact that in most countries the largest relative gain occurred between 1955 and 1960 is more a reflection of the time pattern of United States changes in output per man than the time pattern of European changes. The size of the gains varied greatly among the European countries. Over the whole period there was a decided tendency toward reduction of differentials among them.

In Part B, Table 2–5, GNP per person employed in each country in each year is expressed as a percentage of GNP per man in the United States in 1960. One index point therefore always represents the same absolute amount of product per person employed—1 percent of that in the United States in 1960. This panel permits *absolute* differences and changes in GNP per person employed to be com-

20. This inverse relationship is not altogether coincidental. Insofar as differences in the percentage of the population employed reflect differences in labor force participation rates for women, children, and older people rather than differences in age distributions, they affect the average quality of labor. This subject is explored in Chapter 7.

21. The 1960 GNP indexes in Table 2–5 differ from the 1960 indexes for national income per person employed in United States price weights given in Table 2–4 mainly because one refers to GNP and the other to national income rather than because of the difference between 1955 and 1960 price weights. However, GNP indexes computed in 1960 United States prices and consistent with national income estimates in Table 2–4 do differ from those given in Table 2–5 by 1 point, either way, in several countries.

22. This implies, of course, that growth rates of output per person employed measured in United States prices were greater in these countries than in the United States. (They were generally smaller, however, than when measured in European prices.) It may be noted that the 1960–64 gain in the Netherlands disappears in Table 2–5, Part A, because of rounding.

TABLE 2–5

Indexes of Gross National Product per Person Employed,
Based on United States 1955 Price Weights

Area	Part A (United States = 100)				Part B (United States in 1960 = 100)			
	1950	1955	1960	1964	1950	1955	1960	1964
United States	100	100	100	100	82	94	100	112
Northwest Europe	51	52	57	59	41	49	57	66
Belgium	59	59	61	62	48	56	61	70
Denmark	53	50	55	57	44	47	55	64
France	47	50	57	61	39	47	57	69
Germany	44	50	56	58	36	47	56	65
Netherlands	56	58	63	63	46	55	63	71
Norway	55	56	61	65	45	53	61	73
United Kingdom	56	54	56	56	46	51	56	63
Italy	29	33	39	44	24	31	39	49

Sources: GNP: see text for derivation; employment: Table 5–1.

pared. The estimates are rough and the table should not be read too closely, but broad patterns are fairly clear.

The absolute gap between GNP per person employed in Northwest Europe as a whole and the United States in 1964 was about the same as in 1955, and larger than in 1950 or 1960. This implies, as shown below, that the absolute increase in GNP per person employed, measured in United States prices, was about the same in the two areas from 1955 to 1964 and was larger in the United States from 1950 to 1964.

	Absolute increases in GNP per person employed[a]	
	1955–64	1950–64
United States	18	30
Northwest Europe	17	25
Belgium	14	22
Denmark	17	20
France	22	30
Germany	18	29
Netherlands	16	25
Norway	20	28
United Kingdom	12	17
Italy	18	25

a. One point equals 1 percent of GNP per person employed in the United States in 1960.

From 1955 to 1964 absolute increases in GNP per person employed were about the same in the United States, Denmark, Germany, and Italy, and in Northwest Europe as a whole. France achieved a substantially larger increase and Norway a moderately larger one. Increases in the Netherlands, Belgium, and especially the United Kingdom were smaller. Over the whole period from 1950 to 1964, France, Germany, and Norway matched or nearly matched the United States increase; no other country did so.

Although these comparisons of absolute changes in output per man are not utilized in the analyses attempted in subsequent chapters, they do add to

an appreciation of the significance of differences in growth rates. That countries at the productivity levels of France, Germany, and especially (after 1955) Italy were able to achieve absolute gains in output per man as large as the United States is truly remarkable. On the other hand, the comparisons make clear that except for France and Norway after 1955, the higher European growth rates do not imply larger absolute increases in output per person employed than occurred in the United States; nor do they imply a narrowing of absolute differentials between the United States and Europe.

Northwest Europe in 1960 and the United States in 1925

Measured in 1955 United States prices, Northwest Europe's GNP per person employed was 57 percent as large as that of the United States in 1960. Put the other way around, the United States figure was higher by 75 percent. It can be readily calculated that the United States had reached the same 57 percent level by 1924 or 1925.[23] It thus appears —since a national income comparison could not be very different—that output per person employed in Northwest Europe in 1960 was about the same as in the United States some thirty-five years earlier. If this is so, it should be instructive to compare the changes that raised United States GNP per person employed by three-fourths from 1925 to 1960 with those that would be required to bring the conditions that determine the level of output from their position in Northwest Europe in 1960 to their position in the United States in 1960. In the concluding chapter of this volume such comparisons are attempted.

23. This calculation is based on real GNP measured in 1954 rather than 1955 United States prices, but this can hardly impair the comparison.

Characteristics of Output Measures Governing Their Analysis

Procedures used to analyze the reasons that national income as measured differs between dates and places must be consistent with the statistical procedures that underlie the income comparisons themselves. As will become apparent in later chapters, four general characteristics of the income measures particularly affect the analysis of income differences and the interpretation of results. This chapter discusses these characteristics; it is an unavoidable detour in the development of the general theme of the book.

Since this study provides both intertemporal and interspatial comparisons of income, it is also necessary to ask whether the procedures used to derive the two types of measure are sufficiently comparable to permit intermixing them; they were intermixed in Chapter 2 to obtain the finding that the United States in 1925 and Northwest Europe in 1960 were at about equal levels of national income per person employed, and they will be intermixed in comparing sources of international difference in income level in 1960 with sources of growth.

To provide a focus for the discussion it is centered upon the question whether, and in what sense, it is valid to say that national income per person employed was about the same in the United States

in 1925 and in Northwest Europe in 1960. Because this question requires both interspatial and intertemporal comparisons it raises all the points that need to be considered except those that arise if European countries use procedures to adjust for price changes that differ from those followed in the United States. Descriptions of such variations are introduced as digressions.

I conclude from this examination that measurement differences do not seriously impair comparisons of productivity over time and space.[1] However, Belgium and France use deflation procedures for certain sectors that differ from those of other countries and affect growth rates by amounts that are large enough to require special attention.

Sectors Measured by the Equal Productivity Assumption

The techniques used for deflation of United States and European (except Belgian) time series assume

1. I except from the following discussion differences arising because relative prices differ among countries. These do not, of course, affect the comparison of 1960 Europe and 1925 United States in United States prices of 1954 or 1955.

TABLE 3–1

Percentage of Expenditures for GNP at Factor Cost for Which Output Comparisons Are Based on Employment or the Equivalent, 1950

Area	GNP based on United States price weights	GNP based on national European price weights
United States	12	9[a]
Northwest Europe	19	16
Belgium	19	16
Denmark	17	13
France	20	18
Germany	18	15
Netherlands	19	15
Norway	18	16
United Kingdom	19	14
Italy	23	16

Sources: Estimated from detailed data and descriptions given in Gilbert and Kravis, OEEC, 1954 [I18], and Gilbert and Associates, OEEC, 1958 [I17].
a. This figure varies somewhat depending on the individual country whose weights are applied. It is estimated at 8.7 for weights based on Northwest Europe as a whole and 8.5 when Italy is included in the weighting structure.

or imply that real national product per person employed (or sometimes per man-hour worked) is the same in all years in general government, domestic service, nonprofit organizations such as churches, and certain other sectors of the economy for which direct output measures are not available. Gilbert's study assumes or implies that in much the same activities real output per person employed is the same in all countries.[2] In consequence output per man in Europe in 1960 and in the United States in 1925 are both higher relative to the 1960 United States in the economy as a whole than in the portion of the economy for which this assumption is not made.

The weight in Gilbert's 1950 estimates of expenditure categories for which this assumption was made will be needed later in analyzing international differences in output per person employed. Approximations to these weights are given by country in

2. Either real output is equated directly by the number of persons engaged in the activity or, what comes to the same thing, the ratio of prices in European countries to prices in the United States is taken to be the same as the corresponding ratio for average earnings of persons employed in the activity. In some cases indirect procedures involving approximately the same assumption are used. The assumption of equal output per man is applied a little more widely in the international comparisons than in United States time series.

Table 3–1 and, in United States prices only, by type of expenditure in Table 3–2.[3]

If in 1950 Northwest Europe had devoted the same proportion of total employment as the United States to an activity measured on the equal productivity assumption, that activity would have accounted for about twice as large a proportion of GNP in Northwest Europe as in the United States when United States price weights are applied. Each category of expenditure for which the equal productivity assumption was used except "miscellaneous consumption" actually was a larger fraction of Northwest European product than of United States national product, though usually not twice as large.

Exclusion of activities in which output per man is measured as equal by assumption would lower the ratio of Northwest European to United States GNP per person employed in 1950 by about 5 percent (that is, 5 index points with the United States taken as 100). To a smaller extent it would worsen the position of Europe in 1950, and almost certainly in 1960, in comparison with the United States in 1925 because these activities were more important in Europe.[4]

3. Only for 1950 is the detail available sufficient to permit such calculations. Country weights used for the Northwest European aggregate in these tables are also as of 1950.
4. They accounted for 12 or 13 percent of United States product in 1925 (measured in United States 1954 prices) as against 19 percent of Northwest European product and 23 percent of Italian product in 1950 (measured in United States 1950 prices).

TABLE 3–2

Percentage of GNP at Factor Cost, Measured in U.S. Prices, for Which Output Comparisons Are Based on Employment or the Equivalent, by Type of Expenditure, 1950

Type of expenditure	United States	North-west Europe	Italy
Domestic service	.9	1.7	3.0
Health personnel	1.8	2.6	.6
Education personnel	1.6	2.0	3.7
Hotels, restaurants, and cafes[a]	1.7	2.6	2.2
Miscellaneous private consumption[a]	2.1	.5	.8
General administration personnel	2.5	6.1	9.2
Defense personnel	1.7	3.1	3.7
Total	12.4	18.8	23.2

Sources: Same as Table 3–1.
a. Percentages refer to the portion of the group measured by employment or the equivalent.

If productivity in government and similar activities were really the same throughout the comparisons, 1960 European and 1925 American output per man are comparable. If productivity in these activities varied like productivity in other activities, then the estimates yield too favorable a comparison of 1960 European output per man with American output per man in 1925, but the overstatement is only 1 or 2 index points.

A rise in output per person (or per man-hour) in these activities does not contribute to measured growth in either America or Europe, nor would elimination of any present productivity differential in these activities reduce the measured international differential in product per man. These measurement characteristics must be allowed for in analyzing the source of differences in national income between dates and places.

Belgium is an exception to the statements made in this section with respect to time series. In the 1965 revision of the Belgian national accounts, a novel procedure was introduced to measure the compensation of government and school employees valued in constant prices. The constant productivity assumption was replaced by a method that adjusts employee compensation in current prices only to eliminate pay changes made in response to changes in the cost of living. The new procedure affects the series used here beginning with 1953 but not from 1950 to 1953. To approximate the effect of this change on the Belgian growth rate, the new Belgian national income series in constant prices was compared with a series in which the new constant price estimates for three components—public administration, education, and the armed forces—were replaced by series obtained by dividing the new current price estimates by the old deflators. The comparison indicated that the new procedure raised the Belgian growth rate by 0.09 percentage points from 1950 to 1955 (when only a two-year period is affected), by 0.23 points from 1955 to 1962, and by 0.17 points from 1950 to 1962, and that the rate is higher by these amounts than it would be if procedures generally followed by other countries had been retained. These amounts will be treated, in effect, as a special "source" of growth in explaining Belgian growth rates; the growth rates presented in Chapter 2 have not themselves been adjusted. The

German deflation procedures also depart from the usual practice but the amount involved is too small to warrant special treatment.[5]

The treatment of the construction industry must also be mentioned. In the United States time series, defective price data lead to the result that output per man-hour in most on-site construction work is measured as not changing over time. This assumption does not appear to enter into the international comparisons of construction. I am not certain of the practice followed by all European countries in time series deflation but I believe that the general practice is similar to that in the United States.

France, however, builds into its series an estimate of productivity increase. French data imply a growth rate of net output per man-hour in the "buildings, public works" industry of 2.1 percent in 1949–56 and 3.8 percent in 1956–63.[6] I assume these rates can be used for the 1950–55 and 1955–62 periods. Given the weight of this industry in the total, this implies the French growth rate was higher than it would have been if no increase in output per man-hour were estimated in this industry by about 0.15 percentage points in 1950–55, 0.28 in 1955–62, and 0.23 in 1950–62. I use these amounts as an approximation of the amounts by which the French growth rates would be lowered if American practices were followed. I shall classify this as a special source of growth in France. No criticism of the French procedure is intended.

Treatment of Differences in the Quality of Products

In their international comparisons Gilbert and Associates deliberately made their treatment of differences in the quality of products the same in prin-

5. In addition to allowing for changes in occupational mix, which is also done in some other countries, the German estimates assume a productivity increase of 0.4 percent a year in government. If this assumption were not made, the growth rate of German national income would be 0.05 percentage points lower in each period. It is impossible to discover and allow for all international differences in deflation procedures and I give special attention only to two situations where the amounts are big; the Belgian exception and a French departure from usual practice in deflating construction that is described in the text.

6. Vincent, *Etudes et Conjoncture*, February 1966, pp. 75, 81 [G14].

ciple, and insofar as possible in practice, as that followed in intertemporal comparisons. The result is that the two kinds of comparison can, with only moderate reservations, be validly intermixed when interest centers on productivity. The same cannot be said when emphasis is on welfare comparisons.

Gilbert and Kravis distinguish "economic" from "noneconomic" quality differences. They describe the two as follows:

> As between two periods of time or between two countries, a product may be of a higher quality in the sense of being more attractive to the purchaser for one of two reasons. The one is that there is a more advanced state of the arts or state of technical knowledge which enables a better product to be made without requiring the use of more resources. [That is, more resources if both were produced at the same time in the same country.] The other is . . . that the purchasers in one of the markets are either willing, because of their taste preferences, or able, because of their level of income, to pay for a product that requires more resources to produce it. The first type of higher quality is cost free, and hence is non-economic. The second type requires higher cost, and hence is economic. The first cannot be reflected in an economic measure of relative production; the second must be. It does not matter that the ultimate benefits to the consumer from the non-economic differences in quality may be greater in some sense than those from the economic differences . . . a quantitative measure of relative production cannot be constructed in terms of ultimate satisfactions of the users of the goods, but must be limited to the relative quantities of the goods and services they command. The economic differences are quantitative in this sense. The non-economic quality differences are not, because there is no economic unit of quantity by which to measure them.[7]

The distinction is the same as that drawn in my American study between "measured" quality changes that are reflected in temporal changes in the measured national product and those that are not. Where two products existing simultaneously, such as an expensive car and an inexpensive one, sell at different prices, they are counted as different quantities of product, the quantities differing in the ratio of their selling prices. Where different commodities do not in fact exist simultaneously, they are counted as different products in the ratio of

what their cost (used as a substitute for price) would be if both were known and produced at the same time.[8] No account is or can be taken of the fact that some or even all consumers may have a subjective evaluation of the relative merits of products that differs from the ratio of their prices or costs. The quality differences measured by this procedure are "measured" or "economic" quality differences.[9] The procedure is the same in intertemporal comparisons in all countries considered here and in Gilbert's intercountry comparisons.

In my study of American economic growth I tried to make clear the implication of quality change (and of the introduction of "new" products, which is simply an extreme case of quality change) for interpretation of intertemporal comparisons in the following words:

> When we say on the basis of the official estimates that total real consumption increased by 112 percent from 1929 to 1957, we are comparing actual consumer purchases in 1929 with the sum of (1) products purchased in 1957 that were identical with those bought in 1929 and (2) the sum of products *not* available in 1929 valued in terms of the products that the resources used in their production *could* have provided in 1957 if used to produce the products that did exist in 1929. This is only a crude description of the estimates (which rest on a variety of sources that do not follow wholly consistent procedures) but it is approximately correct. Clearly, the estimates do *not* take into account either the improvements made in a great range of products without a corresponding change in their production costs or the vastly greater range of choice open to today's consumer. He can, if he wishes, choose to buy antibiotics that will cure his illness rather than spend the same amount on remedies that will not; to buy a television set rather than spend the same amount for radios; or to cross the continent by plane in hours rather than by train in days.[10]

The position is much the same in comparing Northwest Europe in 1960 and the United States in

7. Gilbert and Kravis, OEEC, 1954, p. 80 [I18]. Comment in brackets added.

8. This is a general and somewhat idealized statement of the results produced by use in deflation of the available price indexes. These indexes, in practice, have many defects and inconsistencies; but I believe the statement to be essentially correct.

9. Actually, it is not necessary to consider the difference between products requiring different quantities of resources as quality differences at all because in principle all differentiated products can be handled simply as different products. The "quality change problem" as the term is used by many national accountants and price index analysts refers only to "noneconomic" or "unmeasured" quality change.

10. *Sources of Economic Growth*, pp. 156–57 [B25].

1925. One may say with approximate accuracy that in 1960 Northwest Europe could have produced, per man, the goods and services that the United States did produce, per man, in 1925. In this sense, output per man in 1925 America and 1960 Northwest Europe can be equated. But the European of 1960 had available nearly all the choices open to the American of 1960 (or at least of 1955) and to that extent was better able to satisfy his wants than the American with the same real income in 1925.[11]

Differences in Channels of Retail Distribution

In the international comparisons, prices of final products used in computing volume indexes for each commodity represent average prices in each country as a whole. The average price of a product in all stores throughout the country is also used (with occasional exceptions for certain product lines) in the compilation of time series for real output in all the European countries except the United

Kingdom for which I have been able to obtain information, and even in the United Kingdom this is the case with respect to food.[12] In United States and, except for food, United Kingdom time series, in contrast, the comparison is not based on average prices throughout the country at two dates but on the average change in the prices that are charged by identical outlets. This difference is important in output measurement if the distribution of sales among different types of retail outlets charging different prices differs between dates or countries.

Physically identical commodities often sell at different prices in different types of stores. Each type of store is considered to sell a different commodity in the United States time series. Thus, a dozen oranges sold by a small fruit store for 60 cents is counted as $1\frac{1}{5}$ times as much product as a dozen identical oranges sold by a self-service supermarket for 50 cents. Consequently, if the total number of such oranges sold were the same in 1925 and in 1960 and the ratio of the price in the one store to that in the other was also the same in both years, but a larger proportion were sold in the low-priced outlet in 1960 than in 1925, the volume (deflated value) of oranges sold would decline. The general result of this procedure is that the widespread displacement of old-style retail outlets by outlets selling with a smaller unit margin did not raise national product per man in retail trade, as measured; a statistical increase could be achieved only by increased efficiency *within* one, or more, type of outlet.[13]

Both European time series and the international comparisons, in contrast, consider a dozen identical oranges to be the same amount of product wherever they are sold; by this treatment, in the example above, the total volume of oranges sold would be the same in 1925 and 1960.

The pattern of retail distribution in 1960 Europe, especially with respect to the prevalence of self-service, home delivery, and large outlets, ap-

11. Mention may also be made of cases where products actually exist in two situations to be compared but are very rare and expensive in one situation (A) and are therefore utilized only for special purposes or by a few wealthy individuals, and are common and relatively cheap in the other (B). Inclusion of such a product may cause the ratio of national product in situation B to national product in situation A to be "unrealistically" high when measured in the prices prevailing in situation A.

In time series comparisons, newly introduced products sometimes provide such extreme cases. The date they are first introduced corresponds to situation A and a later date, when they have gained acceptance and entered volume production, to situation B. In practice, new products are almost never introduced into price indexes until they have reached volume production, and the effect on volume measures is to link them in with something approaching situation B weights regardless of the ostensible weight base. In the international comparisons very closely similar commodities were combined. Once this was done, all European products apparently had important counterparts in the United States so, with United States price weights, the problem did not arise. A few cases did appear of United States products that were present but extremely expensive and little used in European countries in 1950 (most important were the fuels, including natural gas in some countries and fuel oil in France). In such cases, comparisons in European price weights were based on a different product requiring similar factors of production and processing (see Gilbert and Kravis, OEEC, 1954, pp. 85–87 and methodological notes [B18]).

Gilbert and his associates in both studies appear to have been trying to apply to the international comparisons procedures broadly comparable to those used in deflating national series over time and the results appear generally comparable, though a uniform standard for stating how extreme a situation must be to receive such special treatment is absent.

12. In both international and intertemporal comparisons the result is the same whether quantities for the country as a whole are compared directly or the average price ratio is obtained by dividing total value by number of units or the equivalent.

13. The fact that samples and weights are changed periodically in no way modifies this statement; changes based on identical weights for each time period are simply linked together.

pears to have been more similar to the pattern in the United States of the twenties than to the present United States pattern; certainly, the difference is in the same direction. In consequence, European national products measured in United States prices are lower than they would be if each class of store were considered to be selling a different product, and hence are biased downward relative to the United States real national product of 1925.

Because of the difference between American and European deflation procedures, there is also an incomparability in the measurement of growth rates. The replacement of existing outlets by large stores and self-service stores releases resources for other production. This contributes to growth rates as measured in Europe but not as measured in the United States.

Suppose the 1960 European pattern of retail outlets required half again as many resources as the 1960 American pattern to distribute the same quantity of merchandise. With around one-tenth of GNP originating in retail trade, this would imply GNP per man in 1960 Europe is understated relative to United States GNP in 1925 by about 3 percent (or 2 percentage points in the index where 1960 United States output equals 100).[14] This calculation is not intended as an estimate but only as an indication of the possible order of magnitude of the bias.[15]

A discrepancy between intertemporal and international comparisons may also arise because of price differentials between types of establishment providing similar consumer services, but its quantitative importance appears small and even the direction of bias as between international and intertemporal comparisons is uncertain. Geographic price differentials within a country may also introduce an inconsistency of unknown direction.[16] Neither seems a serious limitation on comparisons.

Foreign Trade

The treatment of exports and imports in time series differs from that in the international comparisons but this does not cause an incomparability, at least in a formal sense.

In the time series used here exports are deflated by export prices and added to domestic use of product while imports are deflated by import prices and deducted from domestic use of product. Hence, the movement of the real national product is not directly affected by changes in the terms of trade with the rest of the world, and productivity changes reflect only changes in the productivity of domestically owned resources. This means that we need not be concerned with the terms of trade in seeking direct causes of changes in measured national product over time.[17]

This method may be contrasted with an alternative procedure, sometimes used in other parts of the world, that simply ignores exports and imports except for any difference in their value in current prices. The deflated national product is simply (1) the deflated value of domestic use of product plus (2) a small item representing the difference between the current price values of exports and imports, deflated by import prices. This provides a measure of the quantity of goods and services a nation can command for its own use as a result of its production. National product rises or falls if its terms of trade

---

14. Some economies *external* to retail trade are also involved, but presumably are relatively small.

15. I know of only two calculations, both referring to the United States, that provide any indication of the magnitude of the effect of alternative procedures on growth rates. One refers to food prices in the United States from December 1955 to December 1961. If the shift of food sales from chains to independents were considered to reduce prices, the average annual increase in food prices would be 0.12 percent lower and the growth rate of the quantity of food purchased for home consumption 0.12 percent higher. The period is not necessarily typical (see Hoover and Stotz in *Monthly Labor Review*, January 1964, pp. 58–64 [G67]).

The second calculation refers to the change in net output in wholesaling and retailing foods of farm origin from 1929 to 1958. Based on 1929 margin weights, net output increased 52.3 percent if clerk and self-service stores are separated, and thereby considered to provide different products, and 78.9 percent if they are combined, and thereby assumed to provide the same product. More than all of the difference arose after 1939 (see Waldorf in *Review of Economics and Statistics*, February 1966, p. 90 [P37]).

16. To make the intertemporal comparison in the United States comparable to the international comparisons would require deflation by the average price throughout the country, implying use of shifting geographic weights rather than the constant weights actually used.

It is not obvious just what procedure in international comparisons would be comparable to the United States intertemporal procedure but it might involve comparing prices in cities of different population sizes, and in rural areas.

17. The terms of trade can, of course, indirectly affect measured growth by affecting real resources available for domestic use and hence perhaps the amount of investment or other variables.

improve or worsen, and a productivity measure reflects changes in productivity in other countries as well as at home.

The Gilbert methodology for international comparison is close to this alternative procedure for time series analysis. The quantities of output used in a country (consumption, investment, and government purchases) are compared, and exports and imports are ignored except for the amount by which their values in national prices differ. The residual net exports in national prices are converted to dollars by exchange rates rather than export prices, but this is a detail since the amounts involved are small. By this method, the quantity of a nation's output obviously depends on the terms of trade; if France's exports sold at a higher price she could import and consume more and her national product would be higher, relative to other countries, than it is in fact shown to be by the Gilbert procedure.

However, there is no apparent alternative to this procedure in international comparisons. Indeed, on one fairly reasonable assumption all methods are equivalent in international comparisons. The assumption is that for every internationally traded commodity or service there is only one price, which is applicable to exports and imports of that commodity by all countries. (I assume, of course, that transportation between countries is classified as a separate service and that the prices for commodities are adjusted for transportation cost.)[18] On this assumption, there is no difference between the United States price and the European price for an internationally traded commodity or service, nor is there any difference between the import price and the export price of a commodity for any country. Exchange rates are then appropriate for converting import and export values in any currency into another in order to arrive at the same uniform price. The national product estimate is then the same whether (1) exports and imports of European countries are converted into dollars on a gross basis (as in the OECD method of deflating time series) and imports valued in dollars are deducted from exports valued in dollars, or (2) exports are deducted from imports in national currencies and the residual is converted to dollars. On the assumption stated, consequently, the method used to handle foreign trade in the international comparisons is formally comparable to either of the methods available for the time series comparison.[19]

It is nonetheless comforting that in fact, though only by chance, the size of the United States real national product in 1925 relative to 1960 probably would be almost unchanged if the alternative method had been used to deflate the United States time series; at least this is true of a comparison of 1929 and 1960. Application of the alternative method would raise real GNP in 1929 relative to 1960 by 0.3 percent.[20]

I conclude that international transactions cause no serious incomparability between the estimates of United States product in 1925 and European product in 1960.

There remains, however, this situation: If the ratio of export prices to import prices should rise (or fall) in Europe but not in America, this would not directly contribute to (or detract from) European growth rates either absolutely or relative to the United States growth rate. It would, however, narrow (or widen) the gap between European and United States output per man if a study of the Gilbert type were to be repeated.

Summary of Biases

This examination turned up nothing that invalidates a comparison of output per man in Europe in 1960 and the United States in 1925 if emphasis is on productivity. Two biases were noted, but neither is really large and they are in opposite directions. The imputation of 1960 American output per man in general government and certain other activities to both 1960 Europe and 1925 America appears to be somewhat more favorable to 1960 European than to 1925 American productivity if the assumption

18. Tariffs and taxes cause no trouble in principle because Gilbert's comparisons are based on factor cost rather than market price weights.

19. The conclusion applies literally only to international comparisons based on the current year's prices.

20. The Department of Commerce presents GNP data for exports and imports in current and constant prices, which are required to make the conversion, only from 1929. However, net exports in current prices were about the same small percentage of GNP in 1925 and 1929, and the ratio of export to import unit values was also about the same.

on which it is based is erroneous. The procedures used for retail distribution are biased against 1960 Europe in comparison with 1925 America. In neither case are the amounts really large. The treatment of quality change and that of international trade do not appear to bias productivity comparisons. However, the former clearly introduces an important bias against 1960 Europe for welfare comparisons.[21]

The measuring stick is not exact, but there is sufficient basis for equating output per man in the United States in 1925 and in Northwest Europe in 1960, measured in 1954 or 1955 United States prices, to warrant carrying the comparison further. Such comparisons will only occasionally be introduced in chapters dealing with individual topics but a comprehensive comparison of the determinants of income will be attempted in the final chapter.

21. It ought to be noted, of course, that a welfare comparison would also encounter a great many other complications that are not considered here at all. I also recognize that some analysts consider a distinction between productivity and welfare comparisons meaningless, but I know of no better words to describe the two types of measures.

Income Shares and Their Use in Growth Analysis

Chapters 4 to 15 are concerned with that portion of national income growth which is due to an increase in the labor, capital, and land used in production. The quantities of each of these factors of production, or "inputs," that were used at different dates in each country, and the quantities used in the different countries in 1960, will be measured and compared. However, these measures by themselves would not permit very much to be said about the sources of growth, or why growth rates or income levels differ. It is necessary to estimate the effect upon national income of a change or difference in the quantity of labor, of capital, or of land. To do this, I rely upon marginal productivity analysis. Its application requires a division of national income among earnings of these three factors of production.

This chapter explains why this is so and how income share estimates are used; estimates of the actual income distribution are also given for each country. These estimates are used in subsequent chapters to arrive at the contribution of labor, capital, and land to growth. In Chapter 15 I arrive at the contribution that is made by all inputs combined and this, in turn, permits the contribution made by changes in output per unit of input to be calculated.

The Reason for Using Income Shares

To estimate the total effect of a change in each type of input upon the size of national income would require answers to two questions. One is the subject of Chapter 17 and is mentioned here only to distinguish it from the subject of the present chapter. The question to be discussed in Chapter 17 is: If the quantity of all factors of production were to rise by the same percentage, say 1 percent, with no change in knowledge relevant to production or in other conditions affecting efficiency, how much would the real national income increase? I anticipate the later discussion by noting that my estimate is not 1 percent; rather, the economies under review are presumed to operate under increasing returns to scale so that a 1 percent increase in all inputs yields more than a 1 percent increase in output. This extra gain, however, will be classified as a contribution of economies of scale to the growth of output per unit of input. In estimating the contribution to growth of changes in factor inputs I proceed *as if* the answer to this question were 1 percent.

The second question relates directly to the subject of this chapter: What fraction of the increase in real national income that would result from a 1 percent increase in all factors of production is obtained from a 1 percent increase in only one factor or group of factors? The question refers to conditions in which available resources are utilized at the same rate and rather fully. It does not refer to short-term "cyclical" changes in the position of the economy caused by fluctuations in aggregate demand.

Given the complexities of economies and the limitations of data, this question cannot be answered with absolute precision, but an approximation that is sufficiently accurate for the purposes of this study can be obtained: The fraction is the same as the fraction of total national income that is earned by the factor or group of factors that increases. Suppose, for example, that the factor is labor and that labor earns 80 percent of the national income (my estimate for the United States in the 1960–62 period). A 1 percent increase in the quantity of every type of labor in use will then be equivalent to an increase of 0.80 percent in all types of input. If a 1 percent increase in the quantity of all the factors would yield an increase in total product of 1 percent, as would be the case in an economy operating under constant returns to scale, then a 1 percent increase in labor input will yield a 0.80 percent increase in output. (If the former amount were 1.10 percent, the latter would be 0.88 percent, and so on.) If the increase in the quantity of a factor and its share of national income are known, the resulting increase in national income under constant returns to scale can be readily calculated. Additional gains from scale must be estimated in some other way.

This factor share approach, which has been widely used in economic literature, derives from marginal productivity analysis. It provides an accurate estimate if the earnings (prices) of the various factors of production are proportional to the value of their marginal products. In that case, a finding that labor earns 80 percent of the national income means that the number of units of labor times the marginal product per unit of labor equals 80 percent of the sum of similar aggregates (number of units times marginal products) of all the factors of production. A 1 percent increase in the quantity of labor will then raise total product by

0.80 percent as much as a 1 percent increase in all inputs.

The proportionality of earnings and marginal products must be present *if economic units combine factors in such a way as to minimize costs*. Production at minimum cost to an enterprise implies that, given the price at which each factor can be obtained, factors are combined in that proportion which makes the marginal product of each factor proportional to the marginal cost of obtaining it. Enterprises can always reduce costs by changing factor proportions unless the marginal costs of obtaining various types of labor, capital, and land are proportional to their marginal products. This is so even if the price of a factor is set monopolistically, or by law, or in some other fashion, above the "competitive" price at which its entire potential supply can be utilized. The result of such price setting will not be to destroy this proportionality but to prevent use of the full potential supply of the factor.[1] Hence a tendency toward proportionality must be present provided only that economic units seek to minimize costs and are free to select the combination of resources that best achieves this purpose.

Of course, the tendency toward proportionality is only a tendency toward an equilibrium position that is itself constantly changing. The most efficient combination of factors in any process may be altered by the discovery or dissemination of new techniques of production and distribution or by changes in the relative prices of the factors resulting from changes in their supply, in the pattern of final demand, or other causes.[2] Moreover, proprietors and

1. If a single economic unit holds a monopsonistic position in a factor market the price of the factor is *below* its marginal cost to that enterprise. I do not believe this can be sufficiently important in an economy as a whole to have much effect on the distribution of earnings by the broad classification of factors used in this study; it presumably tends slightly to reduce the labor share.
2. If one factor becomes more abundant relative to the others, and the state of knowledge and consumer preferences is unchanged, either the relative price of the increasing factor must decline or else the additional supply will not be absorbed into production and the increase in its use will not, in fact, occur. In the latter case there would be no increase in input, hence no problem of appraising its contribution.
The primary reason a lower relative price enables the additional supply to be employed is that entrepreneurs or managers using the factor will find it advantageous to use a larger proportion of it, relative to other factors, in their operations wherever this is technically possible. In addition —and itself sufficient to bring a required readjustment— the prices of products from whose production the increasing

managers do not have exact knowledge of least-cost combinations, and competitive pressure may not suffice to eliminate promptly enterprises that do not arrive at the best combination. Furthermore, managers (particularly in some of the European countries) may not be wholly free to arrive at the best factor combinations because of legal and institutional restrictions, the most important of which are those controlling new investment and those imposing special costs for dismissing labor.

Despite all such qualifications, the reasons for believing that, in periods of fairly full utilization of available resources, relative marginal value products fairly closely approximate proportionality to relative earnings are compelling. The incentive (and in most situations the pressure) for enterprises or other producing units to combine factors in a way that will minimize costs is pervasive and strong, and in the long run the opportunity to do so is generally present. One chief task of any entrepreneur or manager in a private, free enterprise sector of an economy is to maximize profit by finding the combination that yields the desired result at the lowest cost. His enterprise will be at a competitive disadvantage if he is less successful than his competitors in doing so. Although ignorance, poor foresight, and time lags cause departures from proportionality in particular situations, these may in general be expected to be random, rather than biased in such a way as to raise or lower the relative returns to labor, capital, and land, and to particular types of these factors, in economies as a whole.

The working hypothesis of this study is that, on the average for all producing units, the tendency toward proportionality of factor prices and marginal products under conditions of reasonably high employment is sufficiently strong in the United States and, though perhaps weaker, in Western Europe for distributive shares to provide an adequate basis for analysis of the relative contributions of the various factors to growth. The general similarity of income distributions for different time periods and for the various countries that are derived in this chapter somewhat strengthens its acceptability.

___

factor receives a greater than average share of total earnings should tend to decline relative to prices of other products, and the production of these products to increase relative to total production. This leads to additional use of the factor that has become more abundant.

It is important to note that nowhere in this study do I assume that the allocation of employed resources among alternative uses, or among industries and firms, is optimal. In stating that a 1 percent increase in labor input would raise the national income by 0.80 percent under the conditions described earlier, I mean that this will be the effect if the allocation of labor and other resources is equally near to the optimum distribution before and after the increase. If there are also changes during the time period that would improve or worsen the allocation of resources, these are developments to be explored separately (in Chapters 16 and 18) but their effects should not be confused with those of changing the quantity of labor.

The preceding statements concerning proportionality require that the term "factor price" (or factor earnings) be restricted to labor, capital, and land, and that it does not include "pure profit" as the return to a productive resource.[3] This introduces a difficulty in actual estimation. Inability to isolate "pure" profits and losses, which include monopoly and monopsony profits, forces me to include them with the return to capital and land.[4] This probably

3. In a competitive situation we could, of course, consider "pure" profit other than monopoly profit a return for a factor of risk taking, or some broader concept of entrepreneurship; indeed, one would like to do so in a study such as this if it were possible to isolate this return and to measure the quantity of entrepreneurship at different times and in different places. I have not found this possible, however.

4. In the absence of price controls, and considering only periods of fairly high employment characteristic of the postwar period, pure profit can be presumed to be positive in the countries studied here. (One indication of this, if evidence is needed, is the spread between average realized profit rates on business investment and interest rates.) Inclusion of pure profit with the earnings of capital and land therefore results in an overestimate of the earnings and marginal products of capital and land and of the amount by which the national product is raised by an increase in their supply, and a corresponding understatement for labor. An opposite bias over the whole of a modern economy seems almost inconceivable in the absence of price controls.

In the presence of price controls, understatement of the capital share arising from negative "pure" profits is, to be sure, at least possible, and particularly if wages are not equally subject to control. It is unlikely that this actually occurred. Although price controls have, in fact, been intermittently in effect in some of the countries, in every case there have been lapses allowing at least a periodic return to something like free market pricing. Moreover, if price controls, when in effect, have significantly affected behavior of the annual relative distributive shares since 1950, this is not apparent from the data. Rent controls have been more persistent, and their effects noticeable, but fortunately it is possible, in analyzing the sources of growth, to estimate the effect of changes in the stock of dwellings by a special procedure that avoids use of the earnings of residential property in the way the other shares are used.

leads to an underestimate of the effect on output of a change in labor input, and an overestimate of the effect of a change in land or capital input.[5]

The treatment of taxes in the measurement of income probably introduces a bias in the same direction. In national income accounting, corporate income taxes are classified as direct taxes and therefore included as part of property income. I regard this as a substantially correct treatment, but any "short run" shifting of corporate income taxes (and there must be some if only in the case of the regulated utilities) leads to understatement of the labor share and overstatement of the property shares. Income shares are also, of course, influenced by national accounting decisions with respect to other taxes, especially the classification of payroll taxes as direct taxes and (usually) of property taxes as indirect taxes.

The use of income shares to assess the contribution to growth of increases in factor inputs assumes unit elasticity of substitution between the factors within limited ranges. The bias resulting from errors in this assumption is slight for any likely amount of departure from unity. It is minimized, first, by breaking up long periods into shorter ones to reduce the size of shifts in factor proportions during each period in which the same share distribution is used; and second, by using income share weights within each shorter period that reflect the average income distribution during that period.[6] An analogous tech-

Estimates of Income Shares

nique will be applied in the international comparisons of output levels.

Statistical estimates of income shares will now be described and presented. These shares will be used in later chapters to calculate the contribution of increases in labor, capital, and land, to growth. The types of income to be distinguished are the earnings of labor, nonresidential land, nonresidential structures and equipment, business inventories, and residential property (including residential land); and, also, the excess of property income received from abroad over property income paid to abroad.[7] The residential and international income components are needed only to isolate them from the other shares since the contribution to growth of housing and of income from international investment is derived in Chapter 11 without reference to the income shares considered as weights. For each country income shares are derived for the average of the pe-

---

5. It may be noted in passing that the presence of some degree of imperfection in product markets, and therefore monopoly profits, is implied insofar as increasing returns to scale in national economies as a whole arise because of economies of scale that are internal to firms in certain industries; increasing returns to scale internal to firms are incompatible with pure competition.

For any reader who may be puzzled by my combination of assumptions that (1) there are returns to scale, some of which may be internal to the firm, and (2) income shares can be used to measure relative marginal products, let me make clear that I do *not* assume pure competition in product markets. Its absence does not alter the combination of labor, capital, and land that produces a given amount of output at least cost, or factor prices at that level of output, and would cause no difficulty in the use of income shares as weights, which derives from the cost minimization principle, if returns to labor, capital, and land could actually be isolated. Because profits arising from imperfect competition in product markets are counted statistically as returns to capital and land, I admit some probable overweighting of these factors, and corresponding underweighting of labor.

6. The procedure followed thus assumes unit elasticity of substitution within the range of factor proportions observed during each time period distinguished (five years or less). If this assumption is not correct, the error in an estimate of

the effect of a change in inputs upon output is greater (1) the more the growth rates of different factor inputs differ (if they do not differ, there is no error); (2) the larger the income shares of the more rapidly growing factors; and (3) the more elasticities of substitution in fact differ from unity. Richard R. Nelson has shown that the use of different constant elasticities of substitution will yield results that are not much different over a wide range, so that use of elasticities of substitution of 1 is not likely to cause much error. In a two-factor model, with a labor share of 70 percent and a capital share of 30 percent, he finds that a 45 percent increase in capital input with no change in labor input (a huge divergence in input growth rates) would increase output by 12.6 percent with an elasticity of substitution of 2, by 11.8 percent with an elasticity of 1, by 10.3 percent with an elasticity of 0.5, and by 7.8 percent with an elasticity of 0.25. Empirical studies, though not definitive, have tended to yield elasticities of substitution between 0.5 and 1.0. The income share estimates derived in this chapter tend to suggest an elasticity between labor and property resources within this range. (In general, the labor share tends to be a little higher when the capital-to-labor ratio is higher.) If the true elasticity in fact lies within, or even close to, the 0.5 to 1.0 range the error resulting from the assumption of unit elasticity of substitution cannot be large in the present study. See Nelson, *Aggregate Production Functions and Medium-Range Growth Projections*, pp. 49–55 [B82], and especially in *Review of Economics and Statistics*, August 1965, pp. 326–28 [P37].

7. This classification differs slightly from that followed in my United States study, where earnings of residential land were classified with other land, and those of farmhouses with nonresidential structures and equipment. To this extent estimates shown in the two studies are not comparable. They also differ because in the earlier study most depreciation was valued at original cost whereas in the present study it is valued at replacement cost.

riods 1950–54, 1955–59, and 1960–62. United States estimates for 1924–28 are also given.

The estimates of total national income valued at factor cost used for the European countries are those provided by the Organisation for Economic Co-operation and Development (OECD) and by the European Economic Community (EEC).[8] For the United States, Department of Commerce data were used but an adjustment was introduced to convert depreciation from an original cost basis to a current replacement cost basis in accordance with international definitions and practice. The income aggregates used appear to be generally comparable from the standpoint of income share analysis. Some of the European countries, to be sure, include an imputed return on property owned by general government, which lowers the labor share, but where this estimate is available separately it is usually only a small fraction of 1 percent of the national income, and in no case more than about 1 percent. Also, European estimates imply longer service lives for depreciable assets than the American estimates. Insofar as this does not correspond to actual differences in the economies, it leads to relative understatement of the American labor share; again, the amount cannot be large.[9]

National income is typically divided in the national accounts among employee compensation, proprietors' income, the rental income of persons, corporate profits, and net interest. This classification refers to the form in which income accrues and these data must be adapted to obtain approximations of returns to the various factors of production. For some countries absence of detail in the official

estimates is a handicap. Errors in the national accounts remain, of course, in my estimates.

The Labor Share

The most important division of income is between earnings of labor, on the one hand, and earnings of property, including "pure" profit, on the other. There can be little error in classifying as labor earnings the entire compensation of employees, and as property earnings the total of corporate profits, interest, and the rental income of persons. This leaves the net income of unincorporated enterprises ("proprietors' income"). This is a mixed income share comprising the return obtained by proprietors from both their investment and the work performed by themselves and unpaid members of their families. How is it to be allocated?

The United States national accounts provide separate estimates of the national income originating in nonfinancial corporations and the national income originating in proprietorships and partnerships. Each income aggregate is divided among types of income. The labor share of income originating in nonfinancial corporations can be readily computed since it consists entirely of employee compensation. For the United States, the allocation of proprietors' income is made by assuming that the percentage of national income that is allocable to labor is the same for proprietorships and partnerships as for nonfinancial corporations. On this assumption the labor share of total national income includes all compensation of employees plus an allocation from proprietors' income that is equal to (1) the product of (a) national income originating in proprietorships and partnerships and (b) the ratio of employee compensation to national income originating in nonfinancial corporations *less* (2) actual compensation of paid employees of proprietorships and partnerships. On the average, this technique allocated 63 percent of proprietors' income in proprietorships and partnerships to the labor share during the fifties, and rather more in the early sixties.[10]

8. It was also necessary to turn to the publications of the individual countries for additional detail.

9. Reference should also be made to consumer interest payments (other than mortgage interest). These are deducted (or omitted) from the national income in all countries, so their treatment is formally comparable. However, consumer interest is much more important in the United States than elsewhere. Its deduction cancels an equal amount of property earnings of enterprises. In my view this is appropriate insofar as consumer interest paid to consumer lenders really is "interest," matched by interest paid to secondary lenders or returns to stockholders, but not to the extent that it represents a service charge that covers salaries, rent, and other expenses of the lender. Insofar as consumer interest contains such a service charge, property earnings are understated and the labor share is overstated. However, if (say) half of consumer interest were counted as a service charge the labor share even in the United States would be lowered by only 0.5 percentage points in the 1950–62 period as a whole.

10. The technique for allocation of proprietors' income used here is, of course, only one of several possible alternatives. In general, it yields an allocation to labor that is a little larger than would be obtained by assuming the rate of return on investment to be the same in noncorporate as in

TABLE 4-1

Percentage Distributions of Total National Income by Type of Income and Time Period[a]

Time period and type of income	United States	North-west Europe	Bel-gium	Den-mark	France	Ger-many	Nether-lands	Nor-way	United King-dom	Italy
1950–54										
National income	100.0	100.0	100.0	100.0	100.0	100.0	100.0	100.0	100.0	100.0
Labor income	77.3	75.4	72.8	75.1	76.4	73.7	73.5	70.8	77.3	72.0
Income from housing	2.9	1.3	5.8	3.8	.1	1.0	1.6	.8	1.7	1.6
Net property income from abroad	.5	.8	.3	−.3	.3	−.1	1.5	−.5	2.3	−.1
Other property income	19.3	22.5	21.1	21.4	23.2	25.4	23.4	28.9	18.7	26.5
Nonresidential land	3.2	4.2	3.7	5.3	4.6	4.9	4.7	5.2	3.0	7.3
Nonresidential structures and equipment	12.2	14.2	13.5	12.2	14.4	16.0	14.4	18.4	12.3	14.4
Inventories	3.9	4.1	3.9	3.9	4.2	4.7	4.3	5.3	3.4	4.8
1955–59										
National income	100.0	100.0	100.0	100.0	100.0	100.0	100.0	100.0	100.0	100.0
Labor income	79.2	75.8	72.4	75.3	77.2	73.3	74.1	74.7	78.0	72.0
Income from housing	3.7	1.9	6.6	4.3	1.0	1.3	1.6	1.3	2.3	3.6
Net property income from abroad	.6	.5	.6	−.1	.3	−.4	1.6	−.9	1.5	−.1
Other property income	16.5	21.8	20.4	20.5	21.5	25.8	22.7	24.9	18.2	24.5
Nonresidential land	2.7	3.8	3.5	4.8	4.0	4.5	4.3	4.4	2.8	6.1
Nonresidential structures and equipment	10.9	14.0	13.1	12.0	13.6	16.6	14.2	15.9	12.0	13.9
Inventories	2.9	4.0	3.8	3.7	3.9	4.7	4.2	4.6	3.4	4.5
1960–62										
National income	100.0	100.0[b]	100.0	100.0	100.0	100.0	100.0	100.0	100.0	100.0
Labor income	79.9	76.5	73.9	75.5	77.7	74.2	74.8	78.5	78.6	72.0
Income from housing	4.2	2.4	5.6	4.4	1.5	2.0	2.2	1.0	3.0	4.9
Net property income from abroad	.7	.4	.3	.1	.2	−.5	1.2	−1.1	1.5	−.2
Other property income	15.2	20.7	20.2	20.0	20.6	24.3	21.8	21.6	16.9	23.3
Nonresidential land	2.5	3.5	3.4	4.3	3.7	4.0	4.1	3.6	2.6	5.4
Nonresidential structures and equipment	10.2	13.4	13.0	12.0	13.1	15.8	13.7	14.0	11.2	13.6
Inventories	2.5	3.8	3.8	3.7	3.8	4.5	4.0	4.0	3.1	4.3
1950–62										
National income	100.0	100.0	100.0	100.0	100.0	100.0	100.0	100.0	100.0	100.0
Labor income	78.6	75.8	72.9	75.2	77.0	73.7	74.0	74.1	77.8	72.0
Income from housing	3.5	1.7	6.1	4.1	.8	1.3	1.7	1.0	2.2	3.1
Net property income from abroad	.6	.6	.4	−.2	.2	−.3	1.4	−.8	1.8	−.1
Other property income	17.3	21.9	20.5	20.9	22.0	25.3	22.9	25.7	18.2	25.0
Nonresidential land	2.9	3.9	3.6	4.9	4.2	4.5	4.5	4.6	2.9	6.4
Nonresidential structures and equipment	11.2	14.0	13.2	12.2	13.8	16.2	14.2	16.4	11.9	14.1
Inventories	3.2	4.0	3.8	3.8	4.0	4.6	4.2	4.7	3.4	4.5

Sources: See text and Appendix B for derivation.

a. Averages of annual percentage distributions during periods shown.

b. A comparison of United States distribution, 1924–28, with that of Northwest Europe, 1960–62, is as follows:

	United States 1924-28	Northwest Europe 1960-62
National income	100.0%	100.0%
Labor income	69.7	76.5
Income from housing	6.0	2.4
Net property income from abroad	.7	.4
Other property income	23.6	20.7
Nonresidential land	5.1	3.5
Nonresidential structures and equipment	14.2	13.4
Inventories	4.3	3.8

The national accounts of the European countries do not show national income originating in corporations and in proprietorships and partnerships.[11] This method therefore could not be applied and, instead, calculations were made on the assumption that 63 percent of proprietors' income represented a return to labor in each European country in all years. This is the average United States percentage in the fifties. This assumption is sufficient to yield an estimate of the labor share, provided that both employee compensation and proprietors' income are given in the national accounts. Employee compensation is available in all countries. Official estimates for Belgium, France, and the United Kingdom provide directly usable data for proprietors' income. Proprietors' income in the Netherlands and Norway had to be partially estimated and in Denmark and Germany it had to be extracted by estimation from broader share aggregates. For Italy it was impossible to derive an estimate of proprietors' income, and a guess was made that the labor share was 72.0 percent in each period.

The estimates of proprietors' income are described in Appendix B. So also is the extent to which the labor share estimates would be altered by different assumptions concerning the allocation of proprietors' income. If 80 percent instead of 63 percent of proprietors' income were allocated to labor, the simple average of the labor shares in the nine countries in 1960 would be raised by 3.7 points, from 75.2 to 78.9. The increases would range from 1.4 percentage points in the United Kingdom, where proprietors' income is least important, to 4.9 in France and 5.4 in Italy. Use of 46 percent instead of 63 percent would lower the labor share by the same amounts.

Average labor shares are shown in Table 4–1 for the 1950–54, 1955–59, and 1960–62 periods, and for 1950–62 as a whole. In the early sixties the

range was from 79.9 percent in the United States down to 72.0, the figure assumed for Italy. Among the Northwestern European countries the range is only from 78.6 percent to 73.9. These percentages are affected by the amounts of property income received from abroad and income from housing, both of which are rather special types of income. The labor shares will be compared again after eliminating these types of income.

Changes in the labor share from the fifties to the sixties were moderate except in Norway.[12] The estimates for Norway show a sharp rise, from 70.8 percent in 1950–54, the lowest of any of the countries in that period, to 74.7 in 1955–59 and 78.5 in the early 1960's, among the highest percentages.[13] The estimating procedure used may have slightly exaggerated the change,[14] but the basic Norwegian data, as well as known changes in profits, can only lead to the conclusion that a pronounced rise in the labor share did take place.[15] (This rise may have been at the expense of pure profit rather than the earnings of capital.)

Table 4–1 shows a general similarity both among countries and between time periods. Every percentage for the labor share falls within a 10-point range. Except for Italy throughout the period and Norway

12. Two possible time biases in the European estimates resulting from the assignment of a constant 63 percent of proprietors' income to labor earnings may be noted. First, use of a higher (lower) constant percentage would have caused the labor share to have risen less (more) over time because the importance of proprietors' income in national income was declining everywhere. Second, the percentage allocation of proprietors' income to labor was rising in the United States, and a similar estimating procedure in Europe, had it been possible, might also have yielded an increase. If so, this biases the labor shares downward slightly over time.

13. These periods do not show the timing of changes well; the major shift in level was between 1957 and 1958. From 1950 to 1957 the computed annual share ranged from 70.1 to 73.3 percent except in 1951, when it was 66.9. From 1958 to 1962 it was 77.4 to 79.3.

14. I refer to the use of a constant 9 percent of national income to estimate the unsegregated portion of proprietors' income (see Appendix B). If the percentage was declining this would slightly dampen the calculated rise in the labor share.

15. Odd Aukrust, Central Bureau of Statistics of Norway, comments (in letter to author, July 1964): "Your table shows a very marked decreasing trend for 'other property income' of Norway from 1950–54 to 1960–62. This, I firmly believe, reflects reality. There is absolutely no doubt that shipping, pulp and paper, basic metals, etc. secured extremely high profit in 1950–54 due to devaluation and the Korean war. Nor is there any doubt—witness the shipping crisis—that things have changed radically for these industries since 1958."

corporate enterprises, and appreciably lower than would be obtained by assuming the average labor earnings of proprietors and unpaid family workers (or even of proprietors alone, with no allowance for unpaid family workers) to be the same as the average earnings of paid employees (with or without industry weighting). Proprietors' income in the United States is not large enough to accommodate both the assumption that the rate of return on capital and land is the same as in corporations and the assumption that the average earnings of proprietors and unpaid family workers are the same as those of employees.

11. The United Kingdom is an exception; see Appendix B.

in 1950–54 (and for the United States in 1924–28), the percentages lie within an 8-point range.

Net Property Income from Abroad

The excess of receipts of property income from abroad over payments abroad must be isolated from earnings of capital and land located within the country. The desired estimates are, of course, those included in the national income. Such data are available from detailed published or unpublished national income tables. Only in the Netherlands, the United Kingdom, and Norway in 1960–62 does net property income from abroad fall outside the range of −1.0 to +1.0 percent of national income.

Earnings of Residential Capital and Land

Residential structures comprise a large fraction of the capital stock in all countries, and the land on which they are situated represents a considerable part of total land values. Because residental property is treated separately, this study requires estimates of the percentage of national income represented by its earnings. In general, these earnings are equal to mortgage interest plus net rent or profit, including imputed rent, earned by the owner. They are also equal to net national product at factor cost originating in the "ownership of dwellings" industry minus, in some countries, a small amount of employee compensation. Such data or a close approximation to them were directly available from either published or unpublished national sources with the exception of Denmark, where they were available only for 1946, and Belgium, where 1950–52 data were missing.[16] Series gross of depreciation, which

were available for all years, were used to extrapolate the 1953 Belgian estimate to 1950–52, and the 1946 Danish estimate to 1950–62.[17]

The estimated share of income from housing, shown in Table 4–1, is much higher over the 1950–62 period as a whole in the United States, Belgium, Denmark, and Italy than in the other countries.[18] The percentage has risen during the postwar period in all countries except Belgium and Norway,[19] presumably because of large increases in the housing stock and because, with relaxation of rent controls (including upward adjustment of controlled rents and absence of controls on new units), rental rates have tended to catch up with other prices. By 1960–62 net property income from housing varied widely among countries. It ranged from 1.0 percent of national income in Norway to 5.6 percent in Belgium.

The fact that national policy with respect to rent control strongly influences earnings from housing in no way handicaps investigation of the sources of growth of national income as measured, but it does affect the weight given to the increase in the housing stock in the measurement of the growth of national income.[20]

---

16. The French national income series has a break, with an overlap provided, at 1959. The "new" series estimates for 1959 for GNP at market prices originating in "buildings," taxes upon them, and depreciation were each extrapolated by the corresponding "old" series, and net product at factor cost originating in buildings prior to 1959 was obtained by subtraction. The level of the series thus derived was adjusted to the 1959 level of "other income" (excluding employee compensation) originating in the dwellings industry as reported in the French input-output tables published by OSCE, *Tableaux "Entrées-Sorties" pour les Pays de la Communauté Economique Européenne,* December 1965 [I48].

For the United States, housing depreciation series at both original cost and reproduction cost were available for the estimates as they stood prior to the August 1965 revision of the national accounts, but only at original cost for the revised series. The percentage revision at reproduction cost was assumed to be the same as at original cost.

For other countries, the only gap was employee compensation which in some cases was available for only one year (usually from input-output tables).

17. The ratio of net income to gross income at factor cost was unusually high for the dwellings industry in Denmark (only partly because property taxes are counted like direct taxes, unlike the general practice). For this reason the experience of other countries seemed inapplicable for use in varying the Danish net-gross ratio. (Employee compensation was known to be about 3 percent of gross income originating in the industry throughout the period.)

18. Both the United States and Belgium were largely free from rent controls. The Belgian and Danish ratios indicate the effect of the inclusion of property taxes, and the Italian ratios reflect what appears to be a very low estimate of depreciation on houses.

19. In Norway, at least, the housing share has been far lower in the postwar than in the prewar period. The Norwegian Central Bureau of Statistics gives the percentages as 7.0 in 1930–34, 5.2 in 1935–39, 1.1 in 1946–49, 0.8 in 1950–54, 1.3 in 1955–59, and 1.0 in 1960–62 (*Norges Økonomi etter Krigen,* p. 212 [G34]).

20. The use of shares in total national income to analyze the contributions of factors other than dwellings and international assets is equivalent to using their shares in national income excluding property income from international assets and dwellings (as in Table 4–2) to compute their contribution to the growth of national income other than these special types, and multiplying the result by the ratio of this incomplete income aggregate to total national income. In other words, the results are the same as would be obtained if the economy were divided into three sectors—international, dwellings, and "all other"—and within the "all other" sector share weights referring to that sector alone were used.

Domestic Property Income, Excluding Earnings from Dwellings

The remaining income represents earnings on investment in structures and equipment, inventories, and land used in domestic production (other than in the provision of housing services), together with the pure profit, including monopoly profit, of enterprises.[21] The entire amount is treated as earnings of capital and land because it was not considered possible to isolate the pure profit ingredient.

The total earnings of domestic nonresidential capital and land were further divided, on a very rough basis, among three components: earnings of land, of structures and equipment, and of inventories. This breakdown is necessary in order to treat each of these types of input separately at a later stage of the investigation. For the United States the division was made in two steps. Aggregate earnings were first divided between earnings in agriculture and earnings in the rest of the economy. Income in each sector was then allocated among land, structures and equipment, and inventories in proportion to the value of these assets in the private net capital stock of the sector, as estimated by Raymond W. Goldsmith.[22] This procedure was followed in order to implement (as nearly as could be done statistically) the assumption that within each of the two sectors the rate of return was the same on investment in the three types of assets—a requirement that would be satisfied under equilibrium conditions.[23]

It was necessary to treat the farm and nonfarm sectors separately because both the rate of return and the relative values of land and capital differ greatly. Failure to follow this procedure would result in an overestimate of the earnings of land and an underestimate of the earnings of structures and equipment.

For the European countries, total nonresidential property income was divided between farm and nonfarm activities in proportion to the shares of the two sectors in total domestic national income, exclusive of national income originating in general government and in the services of dwellings industry.[24] Applied in the United States, this procedure would yield estimates reasonably close to those obtained more directly.

Although scattered data exist for asset values in Europe, a systematic attempt to value the national wealth components for each European country in order to duplicate the procedure followed for the United States appeared impossible in the present investigation. In the absence of such data, separate estimates of property income in the farm and nonfarm sectors were allocated in each period among the three types of assets in proportion to the average allocation in the United States from 1950 to 1962. The farm and nonfarm components were then combined. The results appear in Table 4–1.

21. It presumably also includes any difference between (1) the current net return from past expenditures on such intangibles as research and development, advertising, and training, and (2) "net investment" included in current expenditures of these types.

22. Goldsmith's postwar estimates of the value of non-farm, nonresidential private land were reduced by the ratio of his 1945 estimate comparable to earlier years to his 1945 estimate comparable to later years. Direct use of his postwar estimates would yield a larger land share and smaller capital shares. The adjustment was made partly to maintain comparability with my estimates for earlier periods and partly to avoid any possibility of understating the earnings of capital. Goldsmith's 1958 estimates, the latest available, were used for subsequent years. See Goldsmith, *The National Wealth of the United States in the Postwar Period*, pp. 117, 118, 122, 184, 206, 303 [B41].

23. Paul F. McGouldrick has asserted that inventory investment can be carried to the point where marginal earnings are smaller than "average or marginal earnings on fixed capital assets" because inventory investment carries less risk than fixed investment (in U.S. Congress, Joint Economic Committee, *Inventory Fluctuations and Economic Stabiliza-*

tion, Pt. II, p. 97 [G46]). If inventory investment were less risky and there were a positive charge for risk aversion, it would mean that I have overweighted inventories at the expense of fixed capital. McGouldrick's view would imply that industries with a high ratio of inventories to fixed assets earn low rates of return and industries with a low ratio high rates of return—a proposition that could be, but insofar as I know has not been, tested. Neither the assumption that average realized earnings are positively correlated with risk nor the proposition that investment in inventories is on the average less risky than investment in fixed capital seems obviously correct. With respect to the latter, it should be noted that the bulk of inventories consists of finished goods (held by manufacturers, wholesalers, and retailers) and work in process. Unlike buildings and most equipment, which have alternative uses, such inventories are frozen in form and highly subject to risk related to miscalculation and the short run vagaries of the market. A large proportion of inventories consists of commodities that must be turned over quickly or sold at a sacrifice; much of the remainder consists of raw materials and agricultural commodities subject to wide, quick price fluctuations.

24. Gross national product at factor cost (Belgium, Denmark, and United Kingdom) or at market prices (France) was substituted where national income by industry was not available; the choice has only a minor effect on the final estimates.

TABLE 4–2

Labor, Land, and Capital Shares of National Income[a] *by Time Period*

(*In percentages*)

Time period and type of income	United States	North-west Europe	Bel-gium	Den-mark	France	Ger-many	Nether-lands	Nor-way	United King-dom	Italy
1950–54										
Labor	80.0	77.0	77.5	77.8	76.7	74.4	75.9	71.0	80.5	73.1
Land	3.3	4.3	3.9	5.5	4.6	4.8	4.9	5.2	3.1	7.4
Reproducible capital assets	16.7	18.7	18.6	16.7	18.7	20.8	19.2	23.8	16.4	19.5
1955–59										
Labor	82.8	77.7	78.0	78.6	78.2	74.0	76.5	75.0	81.1	74.6
Land	2.8	3.9	3.8	5.0	4.1	4.5	4.4	4.4	2.9	6.3
Reproducible capital assets	14.4	18.5	18.2	16.4	17.7	21.5	19.1	20.6	16.0	19.1
1960–62										
Labor	84.0	78.7[b]	78.5	79.1	79.0	75.3	78.2	78.4	82.3	75.6
Land	2.6	3.6	3.6	4.5	3.8	4.1	4.3	3.7	2.7	5.7
Reproducible capital assets	13.4	17.7	17.9	16.4	17.2	20.6	17.5	17.9	15.0	18.7
1950–62										
Labor	82.0	77.6	78.0	78.3	77.8	74.4	76.4	74.2	81.1	74.2
Land	3.0	4.0	3.8	5.1	4.2	4.5	4.6	4.5	2.9	6.6
Reproducible capital assets	15.0	18.4	18.2	16.6	18.0	21.1	19.0	21.3	16.0	19.2

Source: Derived from Table 4–1.

a. Excluding income from housing and net property income from abroad.

b. A comparison of United States, 1924–28, and Northwest Europe, 1960–62, is as follows:

	United States 1924–28	Northwest Europe 1960–62
Labor	74.7%	78.7%
Land	5.5	3.6
Reproducible capital assets	19.8	17.7

Differences among countries and time periods in the shares of total national income assigned to non-residential land, nonresidential structures and equipment, and inventories result primarily from differences in their combined share of national income. The proportionate division within their combined share varies only because of differences in the importance of agriculture.

Distributive Shares Excluding Housing and Property Income from Abroad

Table 4–1 provides the weights needed in this study but comparisons of income shares as such in the different countries are somewhat more interesting if, as in Table 4–2, property income from dwellings and net property income from abroad are omitted from the totals. This yields the division of income in the domestic economy, exclusive of dwellings. The aggregate still includes income originating in general government, consisting entirely, or almost entirely, of employee compensation. However, the influence of differences in its weight on international comparisons is not so great as may be supposed; it may be illustrated by the change over a long period in the labor share in the United States. Compensation of general government employees amounted to 5.0 percent of the United States national income (excluding income from dwellings and abroad) in 1924–28 and 12.6 percent in 1960–62. With this type of income omitted, the increase in the labor share from 1924–28 to 1960–62 in the remainder of the economy would be 8.2 percentage points, only 1.1 points smaller than the change indicated in Table 4–2. Intercountry and intertemporal comparisons for recent years are much less affected by differences in compensation of general government employees than is this intertemporal comparison for the United States. The importance of the compensation of general government employees in 1960–62 was about the same in Northwest Europe as a whole, in Italy, and in the United States.[25]

There are, of course, other institutional and structural differences between the countries that may affect income shares; for example, differences in the extent to which governments operate business enterprises and in the pricing and investment policies of such government enterprises. The non-labor shares include net income of government enterprises as well as private firms,[26] and the former are more likely than the latter to sacrifice profit maximization and cost minimization to other considerations. On the other hand, they are often in a position to exploit a monopoly position.

With these caveats in mind, we may examine the shares obtained after elimination of property income from abroad and earnings from residences. The dominant position of labor earnings everywhere and the fairly narrow range within which the labor share lies remain the outstanding characteristic of the distributions. The earnings of labor in all nine countries fell within a 9-point range in 1960–62, from 75.3 to 84.0 percent. Labor earned about 75.5 percent of the total in Germany and Italy, 78 or 79 in Belgium, Denmark, France, the Netherlands, and Norway, 82 in the United Kingdom, and 84 in the United States.

I do not, of course, imply that the differences are trivial; that they are not becomes obvious when the other shares are examined. In 1960–62, the share of reproducible capital in Germany, where it was highest, was 54 percent larger than in the United States, where it was lowest; and in the 1950–62 period as a whole, it was 41 percent larger. This means that, on the average over the period, each 1 percent increase in domestic nonresidential capital input contributed about 41 percent more to the growth rate of national income (other than property income from dwellings and abroad) in Germany than it did in the United States—0.211 percentage points as against 0.150. In Northwest Europe as a whole reproducible capital contributed

23 percent more than in the United States. Among the Northwest European countries the shares of reproducible capital in domestic nonresidential national income ranged from 15.0 to 20.6 in 1960–62; those of land from 2.7 to 4.5. It must be remembered, of course, that variations in the division between land and capital reflect only the importance of agriculture and are very rough.

The labor share was higher in 1960–62 than it was in the fifties in every country, and in all but Germany it was higher in 1955–59 than in 1950–54. Except in the United States and Norway, the changes were small and would scarcely be worth mentioning were it not for the consistency of this pattern of a rising labor share. Subsequent data indicate a further rise in most continental countries in 1963–64.

Estimates for Northwest Europe as a whole are likely to be better than those for most of the individual countries because of the probability of offsetting errors. In 1960–62 Northwest Europe as a whole compared with the United States as follows:

	Northwest Europe	United States
Labor	78.7%	84.0%
Nonresidential land	3.6	2.6
Nonresidential structures and equipment	13.8	10.8
Inventories	3.9	2.6

The approximate character of the calculations prohibits close reading of these results, but the conclusion that the labor share is larger and the property shares smaller in the United States than in Europe, once housing and property income from abroad are eliminated, can be considered fairly well established.[27] It will be seen later (in Chapter 15) that, in real terms, the ratio of capital input to labor input is considerably lower in Northwest Europe than in the United States and land is also less plentiful. Under these circumstances, the finding that the labor share in the United States is higher than in

25. Omission of general government would, of course, reduce the level of the labor share. In the United States, for example, the share would be reduced from 80 percent to 78 in 1950–54 and from 84 to 82 in 1960–62.

26. Net income of government enterprises is omitted from the United States estimates, but would in any case be quantitatively unimportant.

27. Although the 1960–62 period was one of underemployment in the United States and the division of income ordinarily moves in favor of labor in such periods, the differences between the two areas cannot be explained on these grounds. The labor share of total income other than income from dwellings and abroad was nearly as high in the United States (82.9 percent) in 1956–57, the last preceding period of high employment, and the same in the 1963–64 recovery period, as it was in 1960–62.

Northwest Europe or any of the European countries suggests that the elasticity of substitution between the factors is somewhat less than unity. The tendency for labor shares to rise in this period gives some faint support to this conclusion (although in most of the countries an elasticity not much below unity is implied). However, comparisons of shares in the individual European countries suggest no clear pattern so that little weight can be given to this implication. Differences in the share distributions are obviously affected by other determinants in addition to the relative quantities of the factors.

The estimates of the sources of growth presented in this study do not, in fact, rest heavily upon *differences* among areas in the share distributions. No major conclusion would be altered if the average of the distributions in all the countries were used for each country. What *is* important is to establish the approximate size of the shares of each of the inputs in all the countries. In the 1950–62 period as a whole, the extreme ranges among *all* the nine countries, with property income from dwellings and abroad excluded, were 74.2 to 82.0 percent for labor, 11.7 to 16.4 for structures and equipment, 3.3 to 4.7 for inventories, and 2.9 to 6.6 for land.[28] The approximate weight to be assigned to each of these factors, and particularly the dominant importance of labor, is not in question.

These percentages do not, of course, mean that labor is in any sense more productive than capital or land. They do mean that labor represents several times as large a quantity of resources as capital when, in each country, quantities are measured, as they should be, by marginal products. In 1960–62 an increase of 1 percent in the quantity of labor meant an increase of 0.74 to 0.82 percent (depending on the country) in total domestic productive resources, excluding housing. With housing still excluded, an increase of 1 percent in all land and capital resources together meant an increase of 0.18 to 0.26 percent in total resources and an increase of 1 percent in structures and equipment alone meant an increase of 0.12 to 0.16 percent in total resources. Bias in these estimates is likely (for reasons already given) to be in the direction of understating the fraction of resources that labor represents and overstating the fractions represented by capital and land.

These percentages also indicate the approximate percentage increase in national income, excluding earnings from dwellings and net investment abroad, that could be expected from a 1 percent increase in each type of resource if the economy as a whole were operating under constant returns to scale in the periods distinguished. This statement assumes that any changes in the structure of the economy required to use additional resources as efficiently as those previously in use were made. This assumption is appropriate in dealing with continuing expansion of a nation's productive potential.

The income share data for each country reflect the relative values of marginal products of the factors in that country, and the relative values differ from country to country. Income shares therefore tell nothing about the relative quantities of labor and capital in different countries.

28. Separate percentages for structures and equipment and for inventories, not shown in Table 4–2, can be readily computed from data in Table 4–1.

⇛ CHAPTER FIVE ⇚

Labor Input: General Features and Numbers Employed

People are the largest economic resource of any advanced nation. Evidence that labor earns 70 to 80 percent of the national income in all countries studied is hardly needed to make the point. If asked why the French national income is larger than the Norwegian national income, most people reply instinctively that it is because there are more French than Norwegians. For many purposes, in fact, comparisons are uninteresting unless they are made on some sort of a per person basis. It rightly is the first instinct, too, to seek an explanation for really big differences even in income per person by examining the characteristics of the people involved. No one is greatly surprised to find, for example, that the per capita income of Europeans in Africa is comparable to that of Europeans in Europe and larger, by far, than the income of native Africans. No one should be amazed to learn that Germany, with its people's skills intact in 1945, could surpass its prewar output within a few years despite the loss of territory and a devastated capital stock.

In world perspective the similarities among the peoples of Northwest Europe and the United States with respect to physical characteristics, economic motivation, cultural background, education, and attitudes toward work are much more striking than the differences. These similarities stem from their common ancestry and cultural heritage, their common institutions and systems of incentives, and the continual interchange of their peoples, ideas, and commodities. Most of the men and women in these countries have standards of nutrition, housing, sanitation, and medicine adequate for health. Thus, there are no great disparities in energy due to malnutrition or chronic disease. Nor does life expectancy vary enough to create vast differences in the age distribution, and hence the experience, of their working populations. Only because the peoples of Western Europe and the United States are so similar is it worthwhile and possible to attempt to measure in some detail differences in the characteristics that influence the volume of production. For when contrasts become so great that they amount to differences in kind rather than in degree, quantitative comparison becomes impractical.

Because, as stated in Chapter 1, it is not feasible to cross-classify workers simultaneously by all characteristics affecting output, a sequential approach is adopted to measure labor input in Chapters 5 through 9. The number of people at work is first estimated and compared by country and at

TABLE 5-1A

Estimated Labor Force and Employment, 1950

(*Estimates in thousands*)

Labor force category	United States[a]	North-west Europe[b]	Bel-gium	Den-mark	France	Ger-many[b]	Nether-lands	Nor-way	United King-dom[c]	Italy
Total labor force	**64,749**	**75,617**	**3,545**	**2,060**	**19,519***	**21,580**	**3,865**	**1,477**	**23,571***	**20,417***
Male	46,069	50,797	2,555	1,367	12,803*	13,995*	2,943*	1,036	16,098*	13,745*
Female	18,680	24,820	990	693	6,716*	7,585*	922*	441	7,473*	6,672*
Unemployment	3,351	2,498	174	82	271	1,580	80	9	302*	1,549*
Total employment	61,398	73,119	3,371	1,978	19,248*	20,000	3,785	1,468	23,269*	18,868*
Armed forces	1,650	1,420	65	29*	496*	—	108	32	690	235*
Civilian employment	59,748	71,699	3,306	1,949*	18,752*	20,000	3,677	1,436	22,579*	18,633*
Male	42,164	47,598	2,358	1,275*	12,125*	12,870*	2,761*	998	15,211*	12,493*
Female	17,584	24,101	948	674	6,627*	7,130*	916*	438	7,368*	6,140*
Agriculture, forestry, hunting, and fishing[d]	7,497	13,653	368	545	5,631*	4,965	533	352	1,259*	8,069*
Wage and salary workers	1,724	3,599	40	236*	1,314*	995	134	56	824*	1,770*
Employers and own-account workers	4,346	4,431	206*	211*	1,934*	1,270	236*	139	435*	2,691*
Unpaid family workers	1,427	5,623	122*	98*	2,383*	2,700	163*	157	—	3,608*
Male	661	1,568	85*	—	794*	538*	96*	55	—	1,877*
Female	766	4,055	37*	98*	1,589*	2,162*	67*	102	—	1,731*
Nonagricultural activities	52,251	58,046	2,938	1,404*	13,121*	15,035	3,144	1,084	21,320*	10,564*
Wage and salary workers	45,778	49,901	2,324	1,135*	10,316*	12,680	2,543	899	20,004*	7,260*
Employers and own-account workers	6,069	6,960	514*	230*	2,301*	1,930	484*	185	1,316*	2,583*
Unpaid family workers	404	1,185	100*	39*	504*	425	117*	—	—	721*
Male	74	317	42*	—	108*	105*	62*	—	—	363*
Female	330	868	58*	39*	396*	320*	55*	—	—	358*

Sources: OECD, *Manpower Statistics, 1950–1962* [I32]; or national statistics consistent with those given in *Manpower Statistics, 1954–1964* [I32]; see Appendix C for derivation of data for the Netherlands and Denmark and for more details.

a. Excludes Alaska and Hawaii.
b. Excludes the Saar and West Berlin.
c. Excludes persons on release from armed forces not yet in civilian employment.
d. Agriculture only in the United States and Norway.
* Derived from other sources or author's estimate. See Appendix C.

different dates. Next, characteristics of the working population that influence productivity are examined. Quality indexes have been computed to measure the effect upon output of differences in each of these characteristics. If a quality index for some characteristic is 5 percent higher in country A in one year than in another—or if it is 5 percent higher in country A than in country B—this means that the effect on labor input (and hence on total output) is estimated to be the same as that of a 5 percent difference in employment. Such quality indexes for evaluation of a year's work are computed, among countries and over time, for three sets of characteristics. One measures the impact of the distribution of employed persons between full-time and part-time workers, and of the number of hours a year that each group works. A second measures the effect of differences in the distribution of total

hours worked among seven categories of workers classified by sex, age, and civilian or military status. A third measures the effect of differences in the education of the working population. Duration of work, sex, age, and education are all important determinants of an individual's earnings within a country, and clearly must also be explored in a study like this. They do not exhaust the variables that may affect the quality of labor, and Chapter 9 comments upon some others. It also provides summary indexes of labor input.

The quality indexes refer to all employed persons. This is desirable for the assessment of labor quality as such. However, as explained in Chapter 3, national income estimates assume that there is no difference between dates or places in output per person in certain activities so that, no matter how the quality of labor may change or differ in

TABLE 5–1B

Estimated Labor Force and Employment, 1955

(*Estimates in thousands*)

Labor force category	United States[a]	North-west Europe[b]	Bel-gium	Den-mark	France	Ger-many[b]	Nether-lands	Nor-way	United King-dom[c]	Italy
Total labor force	68,896	79,232	3,628*	2,120	19,638	23,760	4,049	1,496	24,541	21,133*
Male	48,054	52,732	2,583	1,400	12,878	15,176*	3,102*	1,057	16,536	14,669*
Female	20,842	26,500	1,045*	720	6,760	8,584*	947*	439	8,005	6,464*
Unemployment	2,904	1,724	139	95	283	930	53	13	211	1,324*
Total employment	65,992	77,508	3,489	2,025	19,355	22,830	3,996	1,483	24,330	19,809*
Armed forces	3,049	1,815	141	43*	628	20	136	44	803	386*
Civilian employment	62,943	75,693	3,348	1,982*	18,727	22,810	3,860	1,439	23,527	19,423*
Male	43,153	49,851	2,344	1,282*	12,103	14,585*	2,918*	1,005	15,614	13,353*
Female	19,790	25,842	1,004	700	6,624	8,225*	942*	434	7,913	6,070*
Agriculture, forestry, hunting, and fishing[d]	6,718	12,013	310	505	5,014	4,250	489	295	1,150	7,560*
Wage and salary workers	1,688	3,021	33	196	1,170	740	123	38	721	1,757*
Employers and own-account workers	3,731	4,326	176*	209	1,912*	1,230	242*	128	429	2,646*
Unpaid family workers	1,299	4,693	101*	100	1,959*	2,280	124*	129	—	3,157*
Male	489	1,311	69*	—	645*	476*	83*	38*	—	1,512*
Female	810	3,392	32*	100	1,314*	1,804*	51*	91*	—	1,645*
Nonagricultural activities	56,225	63,653	3,038	1,477*	13,686	18,560	3,371	1,144	22,377	11,863*
Wage and salary workers	49,815	55,718	2,455	1,221*	11,113	16,080	2,816	972	21,071	8,419*
Employers and own-account workers	5,886	6,702	476*	212	2,144*	1,938	454*	172	1,306	2,696*
Unpaid family workers	524	1,223	107*	44	429*	542	101*	—	—	748*
Male	60	287	40*	—	89*	107*	51*	—	—	356*
Female	465	936	67*	44	340*	435*	50*	—	—	392*

Sources: OECD, *Manpower Statistics, 1954–1964* [I32]; or national statistics consistent with that source; see Appendix C for derivation of data for the Netherlands and Denmark and for more details.
a. Excludes Alaska and Hawaii.
b. Excludes the Saar and West Berlin.
c. Excludes persons on release from armed forces not yet in civilian employment.
d. Agriculture only in the United States and Norway.
* Derived from other sources or author's estimate. See Appendix C.

these activities, national income is not affected. To assess the contribution of changes in labor quality to measured growth rates and to international differences in levels of measured national income, it is therefore necessary to pretend that the quality of labor in these activities is always the same. In the original indexes presented in Chapters 6 through 9 this is done only for the armed forces. An allowance for other groups covered by the equal productivity assumption is deferred to Chapter 15 and estimates of the contributions of labor quality presented in earlier chapters are therefore preliminary.

All indexes, both for international comparisons and for time series, are computed with 1960 weights. However, time series indexes in the tables are expressed with 1950 equal to 100, simply to make it easier to compare changes from 1950 to 1962.

Labor Force and Employment Estimates

The measurement of labor input begins with employment. Table 5–1 provides aggregate employment data as well as breakdowns for subsequent analyses. It is divided into five parts, A–E, to cover 1950, 1955, 1960, 1962, and 1964 estimates. The latter, in Part E, are included although they are not discussed.

Most of the data are official estimates of the countries, taken from the compilations of the Organisation for Economic Co-operation and Develop-

TABLE 5-1C

Estimated Labor Force and Employment, 1960

(*Estimates in thousands*)

Labor force category	United States	North-west Europe	Bel-gium	Den-mark	France	Ger-many	Nether-lands	Nor-way	United King-dom	Italy
Total labor force	73,126	82,769	3,616	2,200	19,723	26,518	4,193	1,493	25,026	21,210
Male	49,507	54,561	2,527	1,435	13,014	16,620	3,231*	1,054	16,680	14,952
Female	23,619	28,208	1,089	765	6,709	9,898	962*	439	8,346	6,258
Unemployment	3,931	1,073	120	50	240	271	49	17	326	836
Total employment	69,195	81,696	3,496	2,150	19,483	26,247	4,144	1,476	24,700	20,374
Armed forces	2,514	1,987	111	49*	841	293	130	45	518	372
Civilian employment	66,681	79,709	3,385	2,101*	18,642	25,954	4,014	1,431	24,182	20,002
Male	44,484	51,848	2,324	1,346*	12,032	16,149	3,058*	998	15,941	13,976
Female	22,197	27,861	1,061	755	6,610	9,805	956*	433	8,241	6,026
Agriculture, forestry, hunting, and fishing[a]	5,723	10,262	257	455	4,185	3,623	429	260	1,053	6,567
Wage and salary workers	1,866	2,424	29	149	949	533	107	22	635	1,733
Employers and own-account workers	2,802	4,035	155*	203	1,748*	1,159	236*	116	418	2,419
Unpaid family workers	1,055	3,803	73*	103	1,488*	1,931	86*	122	—	2,415
Male	433	999	49*	—	461*	383	65*	41	—	1,033
Female	621	2,804	24*	103	1,027*	1,548	21*	81	—	1,382
Nonagricultural activities	60,958	69,448	3,128	1,646*	14,458	22,331	3,585	1,171	23,129	13,435
Wage and salary workers	53,976	61,443	2,565	1,392*	12,051	19,505	3,082	1,015	21,833	9,953
Employers and own-account workers	6,367	6,699	461*	206	2,037*	2,125	418*	156	1,296	2,767
Unpaid family workers	615	1,306	102*	48	370*	701	85*	—	—	715
Male	91	234	34*	—	65*	93	42*	—	—	316
Female	524	1,072	68*	48	305*	608	43*	—	—	399

Sources: OECD, *Manpower Statistics, 1954–1964* [I32]; or national statistics consistent with that source; see Appendix C for derivation of data for the Netherlands and Denmark.
a. Agriculture only in the United States and Norway.
* Derived from other sources or author's estimate. See Appendix C.

ment (OECD), *Manpower Statistics, 1950–1962* and *1954–1964,* and from national sources consistent with the OECD series.[1] The principal omissions in these sources are French data for 1950 and Italian data for 1950 and 1955.[2] For the Netherlands, a revised series was provided by the Central Planning Bureau, comparable in definition to that contained in the 1950–62 OECD compilation. To point up the omissions of certain categories of unpaid family workers in particular countries, Table 5–1 shows a classification, by sex, of unpaid family workers in farm and nonfarm activities. This classification is frequently missing from OECD data. Where official sources did not provide all the information required to complete Table 5–1, I have

1. OECD, *Manpower Statistics, 1950–1962* and *1954–1964* [I32].
2. Italian data for 1955 are given in *Manpower Statistics* but were not used in this study.

included my own estimates. Appendix C further describes the sources of data.

That there are inconsistencies among countries in the definition and measurement of employment is abundantly clear, but it is impossible to say just how much these affect aggregate employment. My own impression is that such inconsistencies may commonly create errors of 2 or 3 percent in comparisons of aggregate employment in the various countries in 1960; that differences larger than, say, 5 percent are unlikely in comparisons involving the United States and the major countries of Northwest Europe; but that the possibility of even larger differences cannot be wholly dismissed in comparisons involving the small countries.

Differences between countries in the proportion of the population employed, and hence the divergence between rankings of countries by income per capita and by income per person employed, are

TABLE 5–1D

Estimated Labor Force and Employment, 1962

(Estimates in thousands)

Labor force category	United States	North-west Europe	Bel-gium	Den-mark	France	Ger-many	Nether-lands	Nor-way	United King-dom	Italy
Total labor force	74,681	83,989	3,675	2,249	19,737	26,937	4,323	1,514	25,554	20,800
Male	50,175	55,550	2,555	1,461	13,212	16,998	3,331	1,064	16,929	14,650
Female	24,507	28,439	1,120	788	6,525	9,939	992	450	8,625	6,140
Unemployment	4,007	954	77	39	230	154	33	15	406	611
Total employment	70,673	83,035	3,598	2,210	19,507	26,783	4,290	1,499	25,148	20,189
Armed forces	2,827	1,975	107	52*	792	401	136	45	442	399
Civilian employment	67,846	81,060	3,491	2,158*	18,715	26,382	4,154	1,454	24,706	19,790
Male	44,892	52,922	2,391	1,381*	12,277	16,495	3,167*	1,009	16,202	13,851
Female	22,954	28,138	1,100	777*	6,438	9,887	987*	445	8,504	5,939
Agriculture, forestry, hunting, and fishing[a]	5,190	9,575	240	424	3,889	3,383	398	248	993	5,810
Wage and salary workers	1,666	2,171	26	121*	873	460	93	18	580	1,752
Employers and own-account workers	2,619	3,856	148*	202*	1,685	1,066	232*	110	413	2,126
Unpaid family workers	905	3,548	66*	101*	1,331	1,857	73*	120	—	1,932
Male	388	883	45*	—	392*	347	58*	41*	—	778
Female	517	2,666	21*	102*	939*	1,510	15*	79*	—	1,154
Nonagricultural activities	62,656	71,485	3,251	1,734*	14,826	22,999	3,756	1,206	23,713	13,980
Wage and salary workers	55,762	63,601	2,686	1,484*	12,503	20,192	3,265	1,053	22,416	10,538
Employers and own-account workers	6,271	6,643	463*	205*	1,978	2,137	410*	153	1,297	2,749
Unpaid family workers	623	1,243	102*	45*	345	670	81*	—	—	693
Male	90	200	32*	—	56*	73	39*	—	—	295
Female	532	1,043	70*	45*	289*	597	42*	—	—	398

Sources: OECD, *Manpower Statistics, 1954–1964* [I32]; or national statistics consistent with that source; see Appendix C for derivation of data for the Netherlands and Denmark.

a. Agriculture only in the United States and Norway.

* Derived from other sources or author's estimate. See Appendix C.

much larger than any likely error in the employment comparisons. It is much better, therefore, to use employment data in productivity comparisons than to adopt the practice, occasionally followed as a statistical expedient, of substituting total or adult population figures or estimates based on some standard set of labor force participation rates applied to all countries. Even a 5 percent error in the employment estimate would cause only about a 2 percentage point error in the ratio of employment to population.

Errors in measurement of employment changes over the period are not likely to be large enough to seriously affect the analysis of the sources of growth. Neither is the analysis highly sensitive to the exact definition of employment except in the case of Italy. In Italy there are large numbers in categories whose employment status is marginal or ambiguous and whose numbers have declined sharply over time. The series used here is a com-

prehensive estimate of employed persons in Italy, including "casual" workers when employed and child workers under 14 years of age. If these categories were omitted as they are in some Italian employment series the employment increase shown for Italy would be raised sharply. A fuller evaluation of the employment estimates is given in Appendix C.

International Comparison of Employment in 1960

With a population only 2 million larger than the United States, the seven countries of Northwest Europe employed 12.5 million more people in 1960. Of the 82 million employed, Germany had 26 million, the United Kingdom 25 million, France 19 million, and the four small countries together 11 million (Table 5–2). In Northwest Europe, 44.8 percent of the population was employed as against

TABLE 5–1E

Estimated Labor Force and Employment, 1964

(*Estimates in thousands*)

Labor force category	United States	North-west Europe	Bel-gium	Den-mark	France	Ger-many	Nether-lands	Nor-way	United King-dom	Italy
Total labor force	76,971	84,997	3,726	2,282	20,080	27,148	4,450	1,531	25,780	20,348
Male	51,118	56,344	2,576	1,481	13,629	17,269	3,429*	1,073	16,987	14,707
Female	25,854	28,553	1,150	801	6,451	9,879	1,021*	458	8,793	5,641
Unemployment	3,876	864	56	30	214	169	30	16	349	549
Total employment	73,095	84,133	3,670	2,252	19,866	26,979	4,420	1,515	25,431	19,799
Armed forces	2,738	1,824	104	52*	615	456	125	48	424	410
Civilian employment	70,357	82,310	3,566	2,200*	19,251	26,523	4,295	1,467	25,007	19,389
Male	46,139	54,036	2,430	1,406*	12,891	16,698	3,279*	1,016	16,316	13,921
Female	24,218	28,273	1,136	794	6,360	9,825	1,016*	451	8,691	5,468
Agriculture, forestry, hunting, and fishing[a]	4,761	8,901	216	397	3,653	3,084	366	237	948	4,967
Wage and salary workers	1,582	1,939	22	98*	793	391	81	15	539	1,535
Employers and own-account workers	2,366	3,725	136*	201*	1,651*	1,001	223*	104	409	1,930
Unpaid family workers	813	3,237	58*	98*	1,209*	1,692	62*	118	—	1,502
Male	333	803	39*	—	345*	328	50*	41	—	589
Female	480	2,434	19*	98*	864*	1,364	12*	77	—	913
Nonagricultural activities	65,596	73,408	3,350	1,803*	15,598	23,439	3,929	1,230	24,059	14,422
Wage and salary workers	58,736	65,696	2,797	1,557*	13,358	20,700	3,447	1,076	22,761	10,893
Employers and own-account workers	6,266	6,517	452*	201*	1,919*	2,088	405*	154	1,298	2,865
Unpaid family workers	594	1,195	101*	45*	321*	651	77*	—	—	664
Male	77	182	31*	—	48*	66	37*	—	—	292
Female	516	1,013	70*	45*	273*	585	40*	—	—	372

Sources: OECD, *Manpower Statistics, 1954–1964* [I32]; or national statistics consistent with that source; see Appendix C for derivation of data fo the Netherlands and Denmark.

a. Agriculture only in the United States and Norway.

* Derived from other sources or author's estimate. See Appendix C.

only 38.3 percent in the United States. Greater unemployment in the United States accounted for one-fourth (1.6 points) of this difference of 6.5 percentage points. A lower ratio of labor force to population was responsible for the remainder (4.9 points), in part due to greater concentration of the European population in the working age groups, and in part to the latter's higher labor force participation rates. If the labor force is compared with the population aged 15 to 64 years, rather than with total population, the difference in participation rates between Europe and the United States drops from 4.9 percentage points to 2.4, suggesting that the two factors may be of about equal importance.[3] The female participation rate was 3.3 points higher

in Northwest Europe as a whole than in the United States.

The proportion of the population employed varied hugely among the individual Northwest European countries. In the Netherlands it was 36 percent and in Belgium 38, the same as in the United States. In Denmark, Germany, and the United Kingdom it was about 47 percent, almost one-fourth higher. Norway, at 41 percent, and France, at 43, were in an intermediate position. Differences in age distribution and in male labor force participation, especially among the young and the elderly, contributed to these differences between European countries, and so did unemployment rates. But the decisive factor was the prevalence of females in the labor force. They equaled about half the female population aged 15 to 64 in Denmark and Germany, and only moderately less in France and the United Kingdom. The ratio in all these countries

3. A more precise result cannot be obtained by standardization by detailed age-sex groups. The detailed labor force participation rates differ so much from country to country that the results are sensitive to the choice of weights.

is above the United States figure of 43 percent. In the Netherlands, Belgium, and Norway, in contrast, the number of females in the labor force equaled only 27 to 39 percent of the female population, substantially less than in the United States.

Employment in Italy amounted to 20 million in 1960. The ratio of employment to population was three points higher than in the United States. Many more Italians were of working age, but female employment was much less common.

Changes in Employment, 1950–62

Between 1950 and 1962 total employment increased by 14.6 percent in the United States and 11.6 percent in Northwest Europe (Table 5–3). In the United States the employment increase was about the same as that in the labor force, but in Northwest Europe, where unemployment was reduced by seven-tenths, growth in employment exceeded the 9.2 percent increase in the labor force.

Individual Northwest European countries diverged sharply from each other. The West German position is unique. Immigration—mainly from East Germany, but also from Italy, Spain, and other countries—combined with a drop of 1.5 million in unemployment to produce a remarkable 27 per-

cent employment increase in twelve years. In absolute terms, Germany accounted for 5.5 million, or 63 percent, of the total increase of 8.5 million in Northwest European employment. Germany also accounted for over four-fifths of the total decline in unemployment.[4] No other country matched the United States employment expansion. The Netherlands and Denmark came fairly close, but in the other countries employment increases were much smaller, ranging from only 1 or 2 percent in France and Norway to 7 or 8 percent in Belgium and the United Kingdom. Reduced unemployment was a significant factor in employment gains in Belgium, Holland, and Denmark, as well as Germany, but this was not the case in France, Norway, or the United Kingdom.

Employment in Italy increased 7 percent from 1950 to 1962. Seven-tenths of this was due to a reduction in unemployment and three-tenths to the expansion of the labor force. The employment increase was held back by a reduction in child labor. It must be remembered, too, that the data exclude large numbers of Italians working abroad, and that the increase in total employment includes a sharp decline in the numbers classified as "casually employed" in Italian statistics.

4. Absolute changes cited in this paragraph exclude the Saar and West Berlin until 1960.

TABLE 5–2
Population, Employment, and Selected Labor Force Ratios, 1960

Area	Population (thousands)	Labor force (thousands)	Employment (thousands)	Labor force as percentage of population	Employment as percentage of population	Labor force as percentage of population aged 15 to 64 years	Female labor force as percentage of female population aged 15 to 64 years
United States	180,684	73,126	69,195	40.5	38.3	67.8	43.2
Northwest Europe	182,462	82,769	81,696	45.4	44.8	70.2	46.5
Belgium	9,154	3,616	3,496	39.5	38.2	61.2	36.6
Denmark	4,581	2,200	2,150	48.0	46.9	74.8	51.5
France	45,684	19,723	19,483	43.2	42.6	69.6	47.0
Germany	55,433	26,518	26,247	47.8	47.3	71.2	49.8
Netherlands	11,486	4,193	4,144	36.5	36.1	59.8	27.2
Norway	3,585	1,493	1,476	41.6	41.2	65.9	38.8
United Kingdom	52,539	25,026	24,700	47.6	47.0	73.2	48.0
Italy	49,642	21,210	20,374	42.7	41.0	62.9	36.1

Sources: OECD, *Manpower Statistics, 1954–1964* [I32]; Dutch labor force and employment data: Table 5–1C; West Berlin population aged 15 to 64 years: estimated on the assumption that it was the same proportion of the total West Berlin population in 1960 as in 1961.

The growth of employment was faster from 1950 to 1955 than from 1955 to 1962 in both the United States and Northwest Europe. The United States advantage in the annual growth rate of employment was 0.3 percentage points before 1955 and 0.1 in the later period. For the most part, the classification of countries as fast-, medium-, or slow-growing with respect to employment is the same for the two subperiods as for the period as a whole, but in Denmark employment expansion was slow before 1955 and among the most rapid thereafter.

The growth rates of total employment and the estimated contributions of the employment increases to the growth rates of national income are given in Table 5-3 for the entire 1950–62 period and for the two subperiods. The estimated contributions are calculated as the product of the growth rate of employment and the labor share of national income, as explained in Chapter 4.[5] They include no allowance for gains from economies of scale. Since labor generally earns about three-fourths or four-fifths of the national income, the contribution of employment to the growth of national income is generally about three-fourths or four-fifths the size of the employment growth rate over the whole twelve-year period; the contribution of the increase

5. Estimates given in Table 5-3 are approximations that do not include interaction effects but they happen to agree fully with final estimates given in Chapter 15 when rounded to one decimal point.

in employment ranged all the way from 0.1 percentage points in France to 1.5 percentage points in Germany. Except in Denmark, France, the Netherlands, and Norway, employment contributed appreciably more to growth in 1950–55 than in 1955–62.

These estimates do not distinguish among categories of employed persons. The estimated contribution to growth from an increase in employment represents the contribution that would have been made if there had been no change in employment composition.

In the United States, in fact, there was a substantial change in composition. The increase in employment was smallest among adult males, the group contributing most to the value of output, and largest among females and part-time workers. The inference from the aggregate data that the increase in employment was more favorable to growth of total national income in the United States than in Northwest Europe must therefore be strongly qualified, as is indicated by the following comparisons:[6]

1. Employment of males actually increased less (8.5 percent) in the United States than in Northwest Europe (10.4 percent) from 1950 to 1962. From 1955 to 1962 the increases were 2.9 percent in the United States and 4.7 in Northwest Europe.

6. All comparisons are adjusted, when necessary, to eliminate the effect of changes in geographic coverage.

TABLE 5-3

Total Employment Indexes, Growth Rates, and Contribution to Growth of National Income

Area	Employment indexes (1950 = 100)					Employment growth rates (percentages)			Contribution to growth rate of national income (percentage points)		
	1950	1955	1960	1962	1964	1950–62	1950–55	1955–62	1950–62	1950–55	1955–62
United States[a]	100.0	107.5	112.2	114.6	119.1	1.1	1.5	.9	.9	1.1	.7
Northwest Europe[a]	100.0	106.0	109.8	111.6	113.1	.9	1.2	.7	.7	.9	.6
Belgium	100.0	103.5	103.7	106.7	108.9	.5	.7	.4	.4	.5	.3
Denmark	100.0	102.4	108.7	111.7	113.9	.9	.5	1.3	.7	.4	.9
France	100.0	100.6	101.2	101.3	103.2	.1	.1	.1	.1	.1	.1
Germany[a]	100.0	114.2	124.3	126.9	127.8	2.0	2.7	1.5	1.5	2.0	1.1
Netherlands	100.0	105.6	109.5	113.3	116.8	1.0	1.1	1.0	.8	.8	.8
Norway	100.0	101.0	100.5	102.1	103.2	.2	.2	.2	.1	.1	.1
United Kingdom	100.0	104.5	106.1	108.1	109.3	.7	.9	.5	.5	.7	.4
Italy	100.0	105.0	108.0	107.0	104.9	.6	1.0	.3	.4	.7	.2

Sources: Computed from Table 5–1, except that the last three columns are the product of employment growth rates and labor shares given in Table 4–1.
a. Indexes adjusted to eliminate the effects of changes in geographic coverage.

2. Over the 1950–62 period the armed forces absorbed more of the male employment increase in the United States. Civilian male employment increased only 6.0 percent in the United States as against 9.5 in Northwest Europe.

3. Female employment, in contrast, increased 29.9 percent in the United States, more than double the 14.3 percent figure for Northwest Europe. Even if the huge relative increase in female employment had not meant more part-time employment, it would imply a dilution of the average quality of United States labor. Actually, however, it was due in large part to the many married women in the middle and older age groups who voluntarily sought part-time jobs. There was also a growing number of teenagers in after-school and Saturday jobs as school enrollment rose.[7] These teenagers contributed to both the male and the female employment increases. From May 1950 to May 1962, the number of persons working part-time rose by 58 percent, and accounted for more than one-third of the total increase in persons at work. The bulk of the increase in part-time employment, moreover, was in the categories working very few hours: Half was in the category working 1 to 14 hours, and 73 percent in categories working 21 hours or less. According to the Commissioner of Labor Statistics, the increase in part-time work was in the nonfarm

sector, mostly in the trade and service industries, and overwhelmingly among individuals who did not wish to work full-time.[8]

Of course, even full-time civilian male employment increased more in the United States than it did in several of the European countries. But the shift in the composition of United States employment contrasts with experience throughout Europe. Growth in part-time employment was absent or slight in most countries and nowhere comparable to the increase in the United States.[9] Neither was the rise in female employment nearly as large in Europe as in the United States. From 1950 to 1962 the number of females rose from 29.6 to 34.1 percent of the civilian labor force in the United States, or by 4.5 percentage points. The increase in Northwest Europe as a whole was only 1.0 percentage points, and, in regard to individual countries, it exceeded 2.1 only in Belgium (where it was 3.0).

Thus, much of the employment increase in the United States did not add proportionately to labor input as it did in Europe. Subsequent chapters dealing with hours of work and labor force composition attempt to measure the effect of these changes and others (some of which were relatively favorable in the United States) upon labor input.

7. The number of persons aged 14 to 24 who were both employed and in school increased from 1,821,000 in October 1953 to 3,562,000 in October 1962. Almost two-thirds of this group were males, and they averaged only 16 hours of work a week in October 1962 (U.S. Congress, Senate Subcommittee on Employment and Manpower of the Committee on Labor and Public Welfare, *Selected Readings in Employment and Manpower*, Vol. 3, pp. 1345–46 [G48]).

8. See statement of Ewan Clague as Commissioner of the Bureau of Labor Statistics in *Hours of Work*, Hearings before the House Select Subcommittee on Labor of the Committee on Education and Labor, Pt. 1, pp. 34–38 [G49]. Full-time workers are measured as those working 35 hours or more. The division at 35 hours, conventional in United States government statistics, provides a rather clean break between full-time and part-time employment in the absence of holidays during the survey week.

9. See note 25, p. 65.

⇛ C H A P T E R S I X ⇚

Length of the Work Year

This chapter examines international differences in working hours in 1960 and the changes that took place in each country from 1950 to 1962. For each comparison the analysis is in two stages. The number of hours actually worked is first established. Then the effect of differences in the average number of hours worked upon effective labor input is estimated.

In 1960 part-time employment was much less prevalent in Northwest Europe than in the United States and both full-time and part-time workers, considered separately, worked longer hours than their American counterparts. My estimates show that, for these reasons, the effective labor input represented by an average year of employment was 8 percent greater in Northwest Europe than in the United States. The percentages for the individual European countries ranged only from 6.5 to 8.5 except for the Netherlands and Italy, where they were 12 or 13.

I also estimate that because of changes in the proportions of part-time workers and reductions in working hours of full-time workers the effective labor input represented by a year of employment was 3 percent less in 1962 than in 1950 in the United States, in Northwest Europe as a whole,

and in Belgium, Denmark, the Netherlands, Norway, and the United Kingdom. Consequently, this was not a factor making for growth rate differentials among these areas. Changes were much more favorable to growth in France and Italy and much less favorable to growth in Germany than they were in the other countries. Most of the changes measured occurred after 1955.

International Comparison of Hours Worked in 1960

Table 6–1 provides estimates of the average *weekly* hours worked by civilians actually on the job during a week in October 1960 or another early autumn period. Persons employed but not at work are excluded. The data refer to full weeks that did not include holidays. Estimates are given for various categories of workers, classified by sex and by full- or part-time status. Table 6–2 gives the same information in the form of indexes with the United States equal to 100. The indexes are later adjusted to an annual basis (Table 6–3) but first it is useful to examine the actual data for a full workweek.

Only the existence of special household surveys

TABLE 6–1

Average Weekly Hours of Work of Civilians at Work, by Employment Category, Early Autumn 1960[a]

Employment category	United States	North-west Europe	Bel-gium	Den-mark[b]	France	Ger-many	Nether-lands	Nor-way	United King-dom	Italy
All civilian	**41.3**	**46.4**	**46.4**	**44.8**	**47.5**	**46.8**	**48.2**	**45.4**	**44.9**	**45.6**
Male	43.9	48.9	48.2	47.2	50.5	48.5	50.1	47.2	48.2	47.4
Female	36.1	41.6	42.0	40.4	42.6	43.8	42.3	40.7	38.5	41.3
Full-time only[c]	46.0	49.2	50.4	47.9	51.7	49.2	50.0	48.3	47.2	50.1
Male	47.4	50.3	50.4	49.2	52.8	49.4	51.1	49.3	49.5	50.5
Female	42.6	46.6	50.4	45.1	49.3	48.9	46.4	45.3	42.1	48.9
Part-time only[c]	20.5	24.5	24.2	21.6	25.5	25.9	24.4	20.1	21.2	26.7
Male	21.2	25.4	26.5	20.7	28.5	28.2	25.6	17.7	22.1	29.6
Female	19.9	23.6	22.4	22.1	23.7	25.1	23.7	22.1	19.3	24.3
All agricultural	47.4	52.4	54.5	48.0	52.6	53.1	57.2	51.1	48.3	44.4
Male	50.9	57.2	61.6	50.5	58.1	61.1	59.9	53.7	48.7	47.8
Female	35.5	44.8	41.5	42.2	44.3	46.0	38.6	43.4	44.5	37.7
All nonagricultural	40.6	45.4	45.3	43.9	45.9	45.7	47.1	44.2	44.7	46.1
Male	43.0	47.6	46.6	46.2	48.1	47.1	48.6	45.7	48.1	47.2
Female	36.1	41.2	42.1	40.0	42.0	43.2	42.7	40.3	38.4	43.4
All nonagricultural wage and salary	39.7	44.5	43.5	42.8	44.6	44.8	46.3	43.3	44.3	45.5
Male	41.9	46.9	44.5	45.2	47.4	46.0	47.4	45.2	47.9	46.3
Female	35.7	40.1	40.6	39.0	40.4	42.7	42.0	39.0	37.9	42.9
Full-time only[c]	43.7	46.6	45.9	44.9	47.6	46.4	47.5	45.2	46.4	48.4
Male	44.7	47.9	46.2	46.0	49.0	46.6	48.2	46.0	48.8	48.8
Female	41.5	43.8	44.7	42.8	45.0	45.9	45.3	42.8	41.4	47.4

Sources: See text and Appendix D for derivation. Appendix D gives exact dates to which estimates for each country refer; it also describes the estimates and their limitations, which are greater for Denmark, Norway, and the United Kingdom than for the other countries.
a. Persons with a job but not at work are excluded. Periods including holidays are, with trivial exceptions, excluded.
b. Estimates for Denmark by assumption.
c. Both persons who ordinarily work part-time and persons who ordinarily work full-time but worked only part-time during the survey week are classified as part-time workers in this table.

conducted under the auspices of the Statistical Office of the European Communities (Office Statistique des Communautés Européennes—OSCE) made the construction of these tables feasible. These surveys provide estimates for Belgium, France, Germany, the Netherlands, and Italy that appear to be reasonably comparable with one another and with United States data obtained from the monthly household survey. Household survey data are not available for the other three countries. Estimates for the United Kingdom were derived from establishment data, but adjusted to improve comparability with the other countries. The Norwegian estimates are similar but the underlying data are less comprehensive. Data available for Denmark were judged too fragmentary to form the basis of a comprehensive estimate; the Danish estimates assume that hours worked by comparable

classes of workers were the same as in Norway, where hours legislation is similar.

The estimates are believed sufficiently comparable to warrant analysis, but significance cannot be attached to small differences. A special caution should be given concerning the inherent difficulties of measuring hours worked in agriculture and by the self-employed and family workers in nonagricultural industries.

In Northwest Europe as a whole, average weekly hours of all persons at work in a full workweek were 12.3 percent longer than in the United States in 1960: 46.4 hours as compared with 41.3. The differentials for males and females were 11.4 percent and 15.2 percent, respectively. These comparisons are not representative of full-time workers because the United States had far more part-time workers than Northwest Europe and, in addition,

TABLE 6-2

Indexes of Average Weekly Hours of Work of Civilians at Work,
by Employment Category, Early Autumn 1960

(*United States = 100*)

Employment category	United States	North-west Europe	Bel-gium	Den-mark	France	Ger-many	Nether-lands	Nor-way	United King-dom	Italy
All civilian	**100.0**	**112.3**	**112.3**	**108.5**	**115.0**	**113.3**	**116.7**	**109.9**	**108.7**	**110.4**
Male	100.0	111.4	109.8	107.5	115.0	110.5	114.1	107.5	109.8	108.0
Female	100.0	115.2	116.3	111.9	118.0	121.3	117.2	112.7	106.6	114.4
Full-time only	100.0	107.0	109.6	104.1	112.4	107.0	108.7	105.0	102.6	108.9
Male	100.0	106.1	106.3	103.8	111.4	104.2	107.8	104.0	104.4	106.5
Female	100.0	109.4	118.3	105.9	115.7	114.8	108.9	106.3	98.8	114.8
Part-time only	100.0	119.5	118.0	105.4	124.4	126.3	119.0	98.0	103.4	130.2
Male	100.0	119.8	125.0	97.6	134.4	133.0	120.8	83.5	104.2	136.8
Female	100.0	118.6	112.6	111.1	119.1	126.1	119.1	111.1	97.0	122.1
All agricultural	100.0	110.5	115.0	101.3	111.0	112.0	120.7	107.8	101.9	93.7
Male	100.0	112.4	121.0	99.2	114.1	120.0	117.7	105.5	95.7	93.9
Female	100.0	126.2	116.9	118.9	124.8	129.6	108.7	122.3	125.4	106.2
All nonagricultural	100.0	111.8	111.6	108.1	113.1	112.6	116.0	108.9	110.1	113.5
Male	100.0	110.7	108.4	107.4	111.9	109.5	113.0	106.3	111.9	109.8
Female	100.0	114.1	116.6	110.8	116.3	119.7	118.3	111.6	106.4	120.2
All nonagricultural wage and salary	100.0	112.1	109.6	107.8	112.3	112.8	116.6	109.1	111.6	114.6
Male	100.0	111.9	106.2	107.9	113.1	109.8	113.1	107.9	114.3	110.5
Female	100.0	112.3	113.7	109.2	113.2	119.6	117.6	109.2	106.2	120.2
Full-time only	100.0	106.6	105.0	102.7	108.9	106.2	108.7	103.4	106.2	110.8
Male	100.0	107.2	103.4	102.9	109.6	104.3	107.7	102.9	109.2	109.2
Female	100.0	105.5	107.7	103.1	108.4	110.6	109.2	103.1	99.8	114.2

Source: Computed from Table 6-1.

American part-time workers worked fewer hours. The result is that weekly hours differentials between the two areas for full-time and part-time workers combined were nearly double those for full-time workers alone.

The length of the average workweek of full-time workers in the United States (covering all who worked 35 hours or more) may surprise many Americans who are accustomed to the idea of a standard 40-hour week. Full-time workers averaged 46.0 hours in September 1960 (the month to which the United States data refer). The average is raised substantially by farm workers and the nonfarm self-employed, but even nonagricultural wage and salary workers averaged 43.7 hours. Full-time males worked even longer. In September 1960 all full-time males averaged 47.4 hours and male nonagricultural wage and salary workers 44.7. These figures are not out of line with data for other avail-

able months. For example, full-time male nonagricultural wage and salary workers averaged 44.4 hours in May 1955 and May 1960 and 44.9 in May 1962.

Average hours of all full-time workers were only 7.0 percent longer in Northwest Europe than in the United States. The differential was 6.1 percent for males and 9.4 percent for females. Among persons employed full-time as wage and salary workers in nonagricultural industries, Northwest European hours exceeded those in the United States by 6.6 percent, with the differential 7.2 percent for males and 5.5 percent for females.

Hours are generally long in agriculture and self-employment, and short for women, so the large differences from country to country in the importance of these groups complicate comparisons of individual countries. Perhaps the most interesting comparison is in the different number of hours worked by full-time male nonagricultural wage and salary workers in each country. For this category, the European countries fell into two groups in 1960. Average hours in Holland, France, the United Kingdom, and Italy were 48.2 to 49.0 a week. In Denmark, Norway, Belgium, and Germany they were 46.0 to 46.6. The main point to be observed, however, is not the difference between countries but the similarity. The range in Europe was only 3 hours or 6.5 percent; even the addition of the United States only increases the range to 4.3 hours, or 9.6 percent.

Were it not for France, the range for all full-time male workers combined would be even smaller. The other European countries all lie within a range of only 1.9 hours, and even the inclusion of the United States raises it only to 3.7. The French figure is high because an exceptionally large proportion of French males were self-employed or engaged in agriculture, not because these groups worked longer hours than they did elsewhere.

Male-female hours differentials for full-time workers varied greatly among countries. In the United Kingdom full-time females in the nonfarm wage and salary worker category averaged 7 fewer hours per week than males. The difference was about 4 hours in France, 3 in the United States, Denmark, and Norway, and 1.5 or less in Germany, Italy, and Belgium. As a result, hours of full-time female workers differed more between countries than those of males, and the countries are in a different order. The intercountry range of average hours for full-time females in the nonfarm wage and salary group was from about 41.5 hours in the United Kingdom and the United States to 45.9 in Germany and 47.4 in Italy. For all full-time female workers the range was from 42.1 in the United Kingdom and 42.6 in the United States to between 48.9 and 50.4 hours in Germany, Italy, France, and Belgium.[1]

The hours data discussed so far refer to persons actually at work during a full workweek in early autumn. The indexes require adjustment so that they can be used with annual employment estimates

1. The particularly long hours shown for all full-time females in Belgium may be a reflection of the seasonal impact of sugar beet harvesting or some other peculiarity of the data. Hours of female nonfarm wage and salary workers in Belgium are not especially long.

to measure annual labor input. They must be adjusted to refer to all persons counted as employed (including those not actually at work) and to be representative of the year as a whole. The adjusted indexes are given in Table 6–3.[2] For lack of data, it was necessary to assume that most seasonal and other special influences have a similar effect in all countries. Three adjustments have been introduced, however. An allowance for holidays and vacations reduces hours in Europe, except in the United Kingdom and the Netherlands, relative to the United States. An adjustment for sickness also reduces European hours relative to the United States, except in Germany and the Netherlands. The third adjustment was required to eliminate the effect of differences in time lost as a result of bad weather during the particular week surveyed. In this instance, the assumption is made that, over the whole year, time lost by employed persons because of bad weather is the same in all countries. All three adjustments affect the indexes for full-time and part-time workers combined; only the first two affect the separate indexes for full-time workers. These adjustments change none of the indexes by more than 2 percent except in France, where all are lowered by 3.1 percent (see Appendix Table D–4).

The relationships discussed in terms of hours during the sample week are only slightly affected by the adjustments. The similarity of hours of full-time male nonagricultural wage and salary workers in 1960 remains; it is even slightly greater on an annual than on a full-week basis. By 1962, this similarity had increased. Comparative indexes of the average annual hours of full-time male nonagricultural wage and salary workers have been computed from Tables 6–3 and 6–5 as follows (United States equals 100):

	1960	1962
United States	100.0	100.0
Belgium	102.1	100.6
Denmark	100.9	98.3
France	106.2	105.4
Germany	102.9	98.1
Netherlands	108.7	102.0
Norway	100.9	98.6
United Kingdom	109.5	107.0
Italy	107.0	102.2

2. See Appendix D for details of the estimates.

TABLE 6-3

Indexes of Average Annual Hours of All Workers by Employment Category, 1960

(*United States = 100*)

Employment category	United States	North-west Europe	Bel-gium	Den-mark	France	Ger-many	Nether-lands	Nor-way	United King-dom	Italy
All civilian	**100.0**	**110.8**	**110.6**	**106.4**	**111.4**	**111.5**	**117.3**	**107.8**	**109.0**	**110.2**
Male	100.0	110.0	109.7	105.5	111.4	108.7	114.7	105.5	110.1	107.8
Female	100.0	112.9	114.6	109.8	114.3	116.9	117.8	110.6	106.9	114.2
Full-time only	100.0	105.7	108.2	102.1	108.9	105.6	109.6	103.0	102.9	106.7
Male	100.0	104.9	106.9	101.8	107.9	102.8	108.7	102.0	104.7	104.4
Female	100.0	108.1	116.8	103.9	112.1	113.3	109.8	104.3	99.1	112.5
All agricultural	100.0	108.4	113.3	99.4	107.6	110.2	121.3	105.8	102.2	93.5
Male	100.0	110.3	119.2	97.3	110.6	118.1	118.3	103.5	96.0	93.7
Female	100.0	123.4	115.1	116.6	120.9	127.5	109.2	120.0	125.8	106.0
All nonagricultural	100.0	110.5	109.9	106.0	109.6	110.8	116.6	106.8	110.4	113.3
Male	100.0	109.9	106.8	105.4	109.6	107.7	113.6	104.3	112.2	109.6
Female	100.0	112.3	114.9	108.7	112.7	117.8	118.9	109.5	106.7	120.0
All nonagricultural wage and salary	100.0	110.9	108.0	105.8	108.8	110.5	117.2	107.0	111.9	114.4
Male	100.0	110.7	104.6	105.8	109.6	108.4	113.7	105.8	114.6	110.3
Female	100.0	111.1	112.0	107.1	109.7	118.0	118.2	104.2	106.5	120.0
Full-time only	100.0	105.6	103.6	100.7	105.5	104.8	109.6	101.4	106.5	108.6
Male	100.0	106.1	102.1	100.9	106.2	102.9	108.7	100.9	109.5	107.0
Female	100.0	104.4	106.3	101.1	105.0	109.2	110.1	101.1	100.1	111.9
Full-time other than nonagricultural wage and salary										
Male	100.0	100.9	106.0	95.6	100.2	102.8	103.8	100.3	96.5	90.4
Female	100.0	109.5	122.0	100.0	108.3	110.7	101.0	103.0	111.1	98.6
All employed (civilian and military)	100.0	110.4	110.2	106.1	110.9	111.1	116.7	107.5	108.7	109.8

Sources: Computed from Table 6-1 and Appendix Table D-4.

Hours in the United States rose slightly from 1960 to 1962, while in the Netherlands and Italy they dropped, and small reductions occurred in other countries. By 1962 hours in the United States were no longer the shortest, and only in the United Kingdom and France were hours for this group much above the United States level. It is possible, as the British *Ministry of Labour Gazette* has argued in discussing other comparisons, that British hours are overstated relative to those on the continent because allowance is not made for the coffee (or tea) break, which is more common in the United Kingdom.

From 1962 to 1966 annual hours in all of the European countries were further reduced by longer vacations, a shorter workweek, or both. There was no reduction in the United States.

Table 6-3 omits some of the detail shown in

Table 6-2 but adds another grouping: all full-time workers except nonfarm wage and salary workers. Indexes for this group are needed at the next stage of the analysis. The group includes all farm workers and nonfarm proprietors and family workers. Their hours are characteristically very long, and also difficult to define or measure precisely.[3] Some of the

3. The actual hours for "persons at work" in these categories in the United States during the week for which data are given in Table 6-1 were as follows:

All full-time workers except nonfarm wage and salary workers:

Males	57.0
Farm workers	58.5
Nonfarm proprietors and family workers	55.3
Females	50.4
Farm workers	48.4
Nonfarm proprietors and family workers	52.4

They are calculated from unpublished data for September 1960 provided by the U.S. Bureau of Labor Statistics.

international differences indicated for this group are inexplicable unless there are either statistical incomparabilities or special seasonal factors for which no allowance has been made.

The concept of working hours has little meaning for military personnel, but this group must nonetheless be taken into account. The output comparison assigned the same value of output per man to military personnel in all countries. To prevent distortion of the international productivity indexes, it must be assumed that the average hours of military personnel is the same in all countries; I have used the average hours of civilian males 20 to 64 years of age in the United States. The last row of Table 6–3 shows the indexes of average hours of all full-time and part-time workers combined. With the armed forces included, one man-year of measured employment is found to represent in 1960 10.4 percent more hours of work in Northwest Europe than in the United States. The range is from 6.1 percent in Denmark to 16.7 percent in the Netherlands.[4] All the European indexes are very slightly below those for civilians alone.

If one could assume that the amount of work done in an hour is independent of the number of hours worked, these indexes would measure (insofar as hours are concerned) the amount of work represented by one man-year of employment. One man-year of employment in Northwest Europe in 1960 would then have represented 10.4 percent more labor input than it did in the United States. But this assumption is not tenable.

Effect of the Length of Hours on the Quality of Work

The following discussion is concerned with differences and changes in hours ordinarily worked. It is not concerned with fluctuations in actual working hours associated with intensity of demand or other short-term influences.

The quantity and quality of work done in an hour is affected by the length of the workweek or work year. As hours are shortened—within the range encountered in these comparisons of full-time workers—the product turned out in an hour typically increases as a direct consequence of the change in hours, so that the loss of output is less than proportional to the reduction in hours. This is partly because of the effect upon the individuals employed. Shorter hours result in less fatigue, greater intensity of work, fewer mistakes, better quality of output, less wastage, and less absenteeism. This personal effect is greatly reinforced by an institutional factor. Many jobs require an individual's presence so long as an establishment is open, but do not fully occupy him throughout this time so that he can readily compress the same amount of work into fewer hours. This is the case with many auxiliary jobs, such as those involving dealing directly with the public. Shortening the hours that establishments are open will, within limits, usually concentrate the work of salespeople, receptionists, switchboard operators, and the like within fewer hours and reduce the year's performance little if at all. This is especially applicable to establishments (such as barber shops) that usually provide services outside their customers' normal working hours and which can shorten their own day if the customers' workday is also shortened. Just how much a change in hours at any particular level of hours affects output in particular kinds of situations or on the average unfortunately cannot be stated with assurance, even within a wide range.

The available case studies refer mainly to manufacturing. They show rather convincingly that working persistently more than a 6-day, 48-hour, week does not typically increase total output; the famous conclusion of Webb and Cox that "in the arithmetic of labour, as in that of the Customs, two from ten is likely to produce, not eight, but even eleven," has stood up in later studies.[5] That persistently working longer than 48 hours a week cannot raise total output is also the position taken by the United States government during the Korean

---

4. It will be recalled, however, that the Danish estimates were developed wholly by assumption of similarity with Norway.

5. The quotation is from Webb and Cox, *The Eight Hours Day*, p. 4 [B108]. For summaries of American studies, see Brinberg and Northrup, *Economics of the Work Week* [B14]; and Brown in Dankert, Mann, and Northrup (eds.), *Hours of Work*, pp. 147–60 [B15].

hostilities. The position was stated to be based on experience during World War II.[6]

The available information also suggests that output per week is likely to be greater in a 48-hour week than in a 40-hour week but output per hour smaller. A report of the International Labour Organisation reviews evidence from various countries and concludes:

> ... the balance of evidence available appears to point to the conclusion that the reductions in hours already achieved in the more highly industrialized countries have brought the normal hours of work in most jobs in these countries within a range (40 to 48 hours per week) where further reductions, though they might and frequently would lead to higher output per hour, would tend to slow down, or temporarily to reverse, the tendency for output per man-week to increase, especially if they took the form of sharp and sudden reductions in hours. There may still be cases where shorter hours would lead to a larger weekly output. Such cases may indeed be more common than is generally believed. But it is difficult to suppose that they can be frequent.[7]

However, the available studies do not seem to lead to firm generalizations concerning either the amount of the productivity offset or the reasons for it under particular circumstances.[8] The results in particular case studies appear to depend in part upon the way in which hours are changed, and on whether they are increased or decreased. If hours are shortened substantially without a reduction in

weekly or annual pay, and especially if the reduction is not general throughout an industry, there is likely to be an immediate "shock effect" leading to a special effort by management to increase efficiency to keep costs from rising. Over a longer period increased investment may be induced.

Some assumption concerning the relationship between hours and output is unavoidable in a study such as this. Until the last few years most statistical studies of productivity implicitly accepted one of two extreme assumptions. Some measured labor input by man-hours worked, assuming the quality of an hour's work to be unaffected by the length of the workweek. Others measured labor input by man-years worked, implying that hours reduction is wholly offset by higher output per hour. Within the range of hours relevant here, it is much more probable that a reduction in hours is partly offset by higher output per hour, and that the amount of the offset declines as hours are shortened.[9]

In my study of economic growth in the United States I assumed a particular relationship of this type. Specifically, I assumed that at the level of normal hours prevailing in 1929 (an average of 2,529 hours a year for all workers combined, or an average of 48.6 hours a week for 52 weeks) a slight reduction in hours was fully offset by a rise in output per man-hour, whereas at the level prevailing in 1957 (2,069 hours a year or 39.8 a week for 52 weeks), a slight change in hours is offset to the extent of 40 percent by an opposite change in output per man-hour. A curve based on proportional interpolation was drawn for the estimation of intermediate points. If extended, the curve implied that changes in output become fully proportionate to changes in hours at 1,762 hours a year (33.9 hours a week based on 52 weeks, but higher if allowance is made for vacations). P. J. Verdoorn

---

6. Executive Office of the President, Office of Defense Mobilization, "Statement on Hours of Work for Maximum Production," ODM Doc. 8, July 8, 1951.

7. International Labour Organisation, *Hours of Work*, p. 122 [I10].

8. Neither is there any consensus of opinion. One interesting view is that of Jean Fourastié, who thinks the productivity offset is greatest in intellectual work (including that of industrial executives) where thinking is the crucial task and "in those industrial occupations in which the work itself is very hard and exhausting," and least for those in "tertiary occupations" such as "office messengers, museum guards, lawyers, and clerks in which the conditions of work have not changed in 150 years." This view of "tertiary occupations," based on the character of the work, does not take account of the institutional factors mentioned above (*The Causes of Wealth*, pp. 171–73 [B36]). Fourastié's observations about intellectual workers (including business managers) may be set against the fact that this group accounts for a high proportion of both the absolute number and the postwar increase in the number of nonfarm wage and salary workers working over 48 hours a week in the United States. (See testimony of Ewan Clague in House Hearings on *Hours of Work* [G49].)

9. I have no information that would enable me to differentiate the effects of the various forms of hours reduction; the subsequent discussion assumes that a reduction in the annual hours of full-time workers has the same impact on productivity whether it takes the form of shorter daily hours, elimination of Saturday work, more holidays, or longer vacations, and whether vacations are highly concentrated (as they are in France, in August) or spread over a longer period. My procedure differs in this respect from the working hypothesis of the fifth French plan, which supposes that this productivity offset is negligible when vacations are lengthened but amounts to 40 percent when the workweek is shortened.

and Lloyd Reynolds have each suggested curves that are similar to mine in shape but each of the three is pitched at a different level.[10] My curve implied a larger productivity effect than that of Verdoorn and a smaller offset than that of Reynolds. Its use resulted in a calculation that during the 1929–57 period two-thirds of the reduction in hours was offset by higher output per man-hour directly attributable to the shortening of hours.[11]

A similar approach to evaluation of the effect of hours reduction has been increasingly used in Europe, but usually with smaller values for the assumed productivity offsets. The experts who prepared the methodology for projections by the European Economic Community (EEC) recommended use for nonagricultural industries of a curve, similar to my own, in which a partial productivity offset is assumed with the amount declining as hours are shortened.[12] They left the exact specification of the curve to those preparing the individual country projections, but clearly envisaged a smaller productivity offset at any given level of hours than I employed. In the actual projections the productivity offsets used were 30 percent for France, 15 percent for Germany (with weekly hours projected to drop from 44 hours to 39.8), and 25 percent for Holland (with projected weekly hours dropping

from 48 hours to 45). For the other countries the assumption is not made explicit.[13]

The French Planning Commission, which may have been the first to adopt this approach, assumed a 30 percent productivity offset in its earlier plans, 20 percent in the fourth plan, and 40 percent (for reductions in weekly hours) in the fifth plan. The Dutch Planning Bureau assumes that in manufacturing there is a one-third productivity offset so that an hours reduction of 1 percent reduces production by $2/3$ percent.[14] The same assumption has been applied to the United Kingdom economy as a whole by the National Institute of Economic and Social Research.[15]

A study by the Norwegian government suggests a much larger offset. When hours were cut in March 1959 output per man-hour immediately jumped enough, even after allowing for trend and a cyclical upswing, to offset most of the reduction in hours.[16]

One of the few recent studies that have explicitly rejected the assumption of a partial productivity offset was made by the German research institutes at the request of the German government. They analyzed the probable effects of a contemplated reduction in hours of work in Germany and concluded that there would be *no* significant adverse effect upon output per man—that is, that the productivity offset would be complete. This conclusion was based partly upon the effects of shorter hours on the individual worker observed in enterprises, but more on the expectation that the "shock effect" of shorter hours would produce greater efficiency in the long run and prevent a rise in costs (which could be construed as an induced improvement in the quality of management) and mainly on the expectation that shorter hours would cause the substitution of capital for labor and a shift of resources toward capital-intensive industries where the value

10. Verdoorn's curve, as described by Hartog in *Zeitschrift für die gesamte Staatswissenschaft*, p. 675 [P53], places the point of maximum output per man at 60 hours a week and assumes no significant hourly productivity gains below 40 hours. The productivity offset is put at 60 to 80 percent between 48 and 56 hours, and at 25 to 35 percent between 40 and 48 hours. Reynolds' curve, in contrast, puts the point of maximum output per man between 40 and 50 hours a week, and assumes a 60 percent productivity offset in going from 40 hours to 30 (Reynolds, *Labor Economics and Labor Relations*, pp. 255–56 [B92]).

Max Lehmann has suggested that, for work of average laboriousness, a cut in *daily* hours from 10 to 9 is offset 65 percent, from 9 to 8 by 45 percent, and from 8 to 7 by 36 percent (reported in *Revue Française du Travail*, January–March 1966, p. 381 [G12]).

11. Denison, *Sources of Economic Growth*, p. 40 [B25]. Note that the hours levels to which this curve was related were reduced by inclusion of part-time workers, although I did not make a point of this in my American study. The assumption was intended to allow for the effect of shortening labor hours upon the hours that capital is used, so that no adjustment to measures of capital input was required on this account. I follow the latter procedure in the present study.

12. The procedure for agriculture implied either that changes in hours would not occur, so the problem would not arise, or that the productivity offset to hours changes would be complete.

13. Estimates from EEC, *The Economic Development Prospects in the EEC from 1960 to 1970*, pp. 30 and 38 [I56]. (French assumption obtained orally.) The methodology was described in OSCE, *Statistical Information*, No. 6, 1960, pp. 64–65 [I49].

14. *Centraal Economisch Plan, 1964*, p. 91 [G29]. The assumption probably stems from the Verdoorn curve described in note 10.

15. Godley and Shepherd in *National Institute Economic Review*, August 1964, p. 35 [P30].

16. Kommunal- og arbeidsdepartementet, *Virkninger av arbeidstidsforkortelsen fra 48 til 45 timer* [G30].

of output per man is high.[17] Since the contribution of capital is considered separately in the present study, it is not appropriate to take account here of the effect of hours reduction upon the size of the capital stock.[18]

The calculations in this chapter are based on an assumption roughly similar to that adopted in my United States study with regard to the relationship between hours of work and output. However, all workers are not treated as a single group. This modification is needed, especially for international comparisons, because the patterns of hours worked by different labor force groups, and the importance of the groups, differ greatly. Clearly, full-time workers and part-time workers should be considered separately. The fact that the distribution of the labor force by sex, class of worker, and industry varies greatly among countries must also be taken into account. After considering both the economics of the situation and the available statistics, I adopted the following procedure.

Total hours worked by civilians in each country were divided among (1) hours worked by part-time workers; (2) hours worked by full-time agricultural workers and nonfarm proprietors and family workers; and (3) hours worked by full-time nonfarm wage and salary workers. Each component was further subdivided by sex so that, in all, civilian hours were divided into six categories. I then made the following assumptions, applied separately to each sex:

The output per hour of part-time workers of either sex is assumed not to be affected by the number of hours worked. Therefore no quality adjustment was introduced for an *hour* worked by part-time workers and the quality of a year's work is proportional to the number of hours.

The output per man-year of full-time agricultural workers and nonfarm proprietors and family workers of either sex is assumed not to be affected by the number of hours worked. On this assumption the quality of a year's work is not affected by differences in hours. The appropriate quality adjustment indexes to apply to man-hours worked are simply the reciprocals of the annual hours indexes for males and females in this category given in Table 6–3. The reasons for this assumption are both economic and statistical. Hours of both farm workers and nonfarm proprietors and family workers are very long in both Europe and America so the case for a large or complete efficiency offset is inherently strong. The hours of nonfarm proprietors and unpaid family workers are likely in large degree to reflect local custom with respect to how long establishments are open and to have a high productivity offset on this account. On the statistical side, the possibility that the estimated international differences in hours are affected by reporting differences or (in the case of agriculture) seasonal differences is especially great for these groups. The desirability of using comparable procedures in cross-sectional and time series estimates provides still another reason for this assumption. Time series for hours worked by proprietors and own-account workers and hired farm workers that would be needed for any alternative procedure are generally lacking in Europe. The effect of the assumption stated here upon my measure of labor input is that for these groups international differences in the level of hours worked are ignored. The same procedure will be followed in the time series.

Differences in hours worked by full-time nonfarm wage and salary workers are assumed to be partially offset by differences in productivity. I assume, for males and females separately, that at the level of hours worked by full-time nonfarm wage

17. "Arbeitzeit und Produktivität," Vol. 4 of *Untersuchungsergebnisse wissenshaftlicher Forschungsinstitut* [B65]. Krengel, who wrote this section of the study, has generally taken the position that there is a strong tendency toward constancy of capital-output ratios in individual industries, so that a change in man-hours would not be expected to affect total output much in the long run unless it discouraged capital formation. This line of thought clearly dominates the analysis.

Time series data suggest, though they of course cannot prove, that in the short run reduction of hours did affect output per man adversely. My own inspection of data (starting with 1950) assembled by the Deutsches Institut für Wirtshaftsforschung (DIW) for manufacturing and mining in Germany, where the greatest hours reduction among all the countries studied occurred, indicates a pronounced tendency for year-to-year increases in output per man to have been below average when reductions in annual average hours worked were above average. A similar tendency in the Netherlands was noted by the Dutch Planning Bureau when hours were reduced in 1960–62 (*Centraal Economisch Plan, 1963*, p. 38 [G29]) but similar retardation earlier without hours changes must be noted.

18. Views of some additional European authors and studies are summarized by Berger in *Bulletin* SEDEIS, July 1965, Supplement, pp. 3–13 [P6].

TABLE 6–4

Indexes of Effect of Differences in the Length of Hours Worked
on the Quality of Labor per Hour and per Year, 1960

(United States = 100)

Area	Actual annual hours worked			Quality index for an hour's work			Quality index for a year's work		
	All employment (1)	All civilian employment (2)	Full-time nonfarm wage and salary workers (3)	All employment (4)	All civilian employment (5)	Full-time nonfarm wage and salary workers (6)	All employment (7)	All civilian employment (8)	Full-time nonfarm wage and salary workers (9)
United States	100.0	100.0	100.0	100.0	100.0	100.0	100.0	100.0	100.0
Northwest Europe	110.4	110.8	105.6	97.8	97.7	97.8	108.0	108.2	103.3
Belgium	110.2	110.6	103.6	96.8	96.5	99.0	106.6	106.7	102.6
Denmark	106.1	106.4	100.7	101.2	101.2	99.7	107.3	107.4	100.4
France	110.9	111.4	105.5	98.0	97.9	97.9	108.6	109.0	103.3
Germany	111.1	111.5	104.8	97.5	97.4	98.3	108.3	108.6	103.0
Netherlands	116.7	117.3	109.6	96.8	96.7	96.5	113.0	113.4	105.8
Norway	107.5	107.8	101.4	99.6	99.5	99.7	107.0	107.3	100.9
United Kingdom	108.7	109.0	106.5	98.0	97.8	97.2	106.5	106.6	104.1
Italy	109.8	110.2	108.6	102.2	102.2	96.8	112.3	112.7	105.1

Sources: Columns (1)-(3): Table 6–3; Columns (4)-(6): estimates derived as described in text; Columns (7)-(9): products of Columns (1)-(3) and (4)-(6).

and salary workers in the United States in 1960 a small change in average hours worked has a 30 percent offset in output per man-hour, and that the point at which a small change in average hours worked is fully offset in output per man-hour is higher by 520 hours a year (10 hours per week throughout the year).[19] Intermediate points are set by proportional interpolation. This permits curves for males and females to be constructed that relate the hours indexes of Table 6–3 to indexes measuring the quality of an hour's work.

The range of hours of full-time male nonfarm wage and salary workers in 1960 is limited to 9.5 percent at the extreme (between the United States and the United Kingdom) and only 6.1 percent between the United States and Northwest Europe as a whole. This fact fortunately limits the extent to which the results can be thrown off by an erroneous assumption. For females the range between the United States and certain of the European coun-

tries is greater, but the weight of female hours in the total measure of labor input is not nearly so large as for males.

Average hours of full-time wage and salary workers (males and females combined) were 5.6 percent longer in Northwest Europe as a whole than in the United States. The assumed curves yield the result that for this category of workers 5.6 percent longer hours meant 3.3 percent more effective labor input per person employed and 2.2 percent less labor input per hour worked. The quality adjustment index for a year's work, with the United States equal to 100, is therefore 103.3 for this group, and for an hour's work 97.8 (Columns 6 and 9, Table 6–4).[20]

When the three civilian groups are combined and the hours of military personnel (which do not differ among countries and therefore require no quality adjustment) are included, indexes to adjust for differences in the quality of the average *hour's* work of all workers in the various countries are

19. This is, appropriately, a somewhat smaller offset than was applied in my United States study to all employment including the self-employed and agricultural workers (40 percent at the 1957 hours level).

20. The Northwest European figures mentioned here are weighted averages of the results for the individual countries.

obtained.[21] These indexes are shown in Column 4 of Table 6–4. The index for Northwest Europe is by chance the same as that for full-time nonfarm wage and salary workers. In some of the individual countries, however, the indexes are quite different. The indexes for all employment in Denmark and Italy may seem paradoxical at first sight since they exceed 100 even though average hours are longer than in the United States. The explanation is that hours of full-time workers other than nonfarm wage and salary workers, as estimated in Table 6–3, are shorter than in the United States, and the quality adjustment index offsets this difference.

Estimates of the effect of differences in hours upon the quantity of labor input per *man-year* of employment are shown in Column 7, Table 6–4. I estimate that, because of differences in average hours worked, a year's employment in Northwest Europe in 1960 represented 8.0 percent more labor input than it did in the United States. The main reason for this difference should not be overlooked: It is that so much of United States employment represents part-time work. Part-time work is responsible for more than half of the 8 percent differential between the two areas in effective labor input per person employed. The percentages for all the Northwestern European countries are close to the 8 percent average except that for the Netherlands, which is 13.0 percent. The Italian figure, 12.3, is also high.

Labor input represented 75 or 80 percent of total input around 1960. We may therefore judge that if there were no other differences between the countries, differences in hours worked would put Northwestern European output per person employed about 6 percent *above* that in the United States, with a range from about 5 percent in Denmark to 10 in the Netherlands. Estimates are given in Chapter 15 that take account of the facts that there are other differences between countries and that the international income comparisons assume output per person is the same in all countries for

---

21. The procedure followed in combining groups was to calculate total hours worked by each component labor force group; convert each to quality adjusted United States-equivalent hours by use of the assumptions described in the text; and divide the sum of the quality adjusted hours by the sum of the actual hours to obtain the combined quality adjustment index for the combined groups.

TABLE 6–5

Indexes of Average Annual Hours Worked by Employed Nonagricultural Wage and Salary Workers

(*1950 = 100*)

Area	Category of workers[a]	1950	1955	1960	1962
U. S.					
	All males	100.0	100.0	98.5	98.7
	Full-time males	100.0	99.8	99.5	100.0
	All females	100.0	96.8	94.2	92.7
	Full-time females	100.0	98.7	98.4	97.4
N. W. Europe					
Belgium	All workers	100.0	99.0	94.1	93.2
Denmark	All workers	100.0	100.9	94.1	92.2
France	All workers	100.0	100.9	99.5	99.2
Germany	All males	100.0	99.6	90.4	86.6
	All females	100.0	100.0	90.3	86.4
Netherlands	All workers	100.0	100.6	99.8	94.1
Norway	All males	100.0	101.3	96.3	94.6
	All females	100.0	101.8	92.3	90.5
U. K.	Full-time males	100.0	102.5	100.2	98.4
	All females	100.0	99.5	96.0	92.5
	Full-time females	100.0	99.3	96.8	94.0
Italy	All workers	100.0	102.2	102.6	98.7
	Full-time workers	100.0	101.0	96.9	93.0

Sources: See text and Appendix D for derivation.
a. "All" in this table means simply that data for full-time and part-time nonfarm wage and salary workers are combined. Indexes for "all workers" are given for every country in Table 6–6.

---

certain categories of civilian workers, as well as for military personnel.

Changes in Hours of Work, 1950–62

Changes in working hours were estimated only for nonagricultural wage and salary workers. The original information on which estimates for the United States, France, Germany, and the United Kingdom are based has a broad industrial scope. Except for the United Kingdom, it covers salaried employees as well as wage earners. For Italy and most of the smaller countries reliance is placed upon data for industrial wage earners only.[22]

22. Although Danish data were regarded as insufficient for the estimation of the level of hours, they were used for changes over time.

The estimates, shown in index form in Table 6–5, represent average actual hours worked by employed nonfarm wage and salary workers (that is, they have been adjusted where necessary for changes in vacations, and the like).[23] They are comparable in definition to the cross-sectional indexes for annual hours of nonfarm wage and salary workers given in Table 6–3, although in most cases they are based on different sources. Their derivation is described in Appendix D.

For the United States, Germany, Norway, and the United Kingdom separate indexes are shown for males and females. Only indexes for the two sexes combined are available elsewhere, and in measuring changes in labor input it will be necessary to assume the index for each sex is the same.[24] But any resulting errors are largely offsetting.

Indexes of the hours both of full-time workers and of full-time and part-time workers combined are needed for analysis. These indexes diverge significantly only if there is an important change in the proportion of part-time workers in total employment. Such a change did not occur in Northwest European countries and the same indexes are used for both, except in the case of females in the United Kingdom.[25] In the United States and Italy the proportion of part-time workers changed greatly, though in opposite directions, and separate estimates were prepared for full-time workers. Large and persistent increases in voluntary part-time employment in the United States caused indexes of the average hours of all workers to drop below those of full-time workers, especially for females. In Italy, in contrast, a sharp decline in involuntary part-time employment as more job opportunities opened up caused the index for hours of full-time workers to drop below that of all workers combined. From 1955 to 1960 the difference in movement was pronounced.

The indexes indicate that from 1950 to 1955 there was no major change in working hours anywhere, if we confine attention in the United States and Italy to hours of full-time workers. The fluctuations that appear are moderate. They are mainly upward and reflect chiefly tightening of labor markets. After 1955 sharp divergences appear between countries. Changes result mainly from legislation and collective bargaining agreements governing normal weekly hours and vacations.

The countries fall into three groups with respect to changes in annual full-time hours over the entire period from 1950 to 1962. Reductions were smallest in France, the United States, and the United Kingdom. In 1962 annual hours in France and

23. The indexes are sensitive and should not be read too closely; even original data are ordinarily given only to the nearest one-tenth of an hour per week, which usually translates into two-tenths of an index point.

24. Separate data for adult males, for adult females, and for adults and boys and girls combined are available for Dutch manufacturing in October 1960 and October 1962. This spans the period when most of the 1950–62 change in Dutch hours occurred. Changes in the three series are much the same: –4.5, –5.0, and –4.7 percent (Central Bureau of Statistics, *Sociale Maandstatistiek*, April 1964, p. 159 [G26]).

25. If part-time workers average half as many hours as full-time workers, the percentage working part-time must change about two points (as from 8 to 10 percent) to cause the indexes to diverge by 1 percentage point. The problem mainly concerns females. Among females in the United States, the part-time percentage rose by 7.5 points, from 20.5 percent in May 1950 to 28.0 in May 1962, and I estimate very roughly that it rose by 4 points in the United Kingdom over this period. In most of the Northwest European countries part-time employment was too rare for any change that might have occurred to be great enough to substantially affect average hours indexes. Part-time proportions that are low in comparison with the United States have already been noted in the discussion of Table 5–1, and the proportions tend to be even lower in the data used for time series. For example, in April 1960 only 1.6 percent of the French wage and salary earners (both sexes) covered by the data worked less than 40 hours, and only 0.7 percent less than 20 hours. The proportions were virtually the same as in April 1950 (*Revue Française du Travail*, September-October 1950, pp. 452–53, and April-June 1960, p. 116

[G12]). An international survey of part-time employment (*International Labour Review*, October 1963, pp. 380–407 [I9]) makes (or implies) the following statements about nonfarm workers: Few Belgian women work part-time. In Germany in 1961 only 5 percent of all workers (the Federal Statistical Office has subsequently published 4.8 percent for March 1961), and 9 percent of females, worked part-time; young workers normally do not work part-time. In the Netherlands (it can be inferred) 10 to 12.5 percent of women workers work part-time, and women represent a small fraction of employment. In Denmark and Norway part-time employment of women is less prevalent than in Sweden (but in Sweden it is widespread and growing). In the United Kingdom (it can be inferred from data given) only about 25,000 males (a negligible percentage) worked part-time in 1961.

Two facts provide additional, though indirect, evidence that the percentage of part-time workers did not increase greatly in these countries: First, actual average hours of work generally dropped less than normal hours of full-time workers, whereas a large increase in part-time employment would have tended to cause them to fall more; and second, the proportion of women workers in European employment did not increase nearly so much as in the United States. In Norway, one of the countries for which direct information on part-time work is not available, there has been no increase in female participation rates, which strongly suggests there was no appreciable increase in part-time employment.

TABLE 6–6

Derivation of Quality Indexes of a Man-Year's Work
as Affected by Changes in Annual Hours of Work

(*1950 = 100*)

	Nonagricultural wage and salary workers: full-time and part-time combined									All employment		
	Average hours per person employed			Quality of an hour's work			Quality of a year's work			Quality of a year's work		
Area	1955 (1)	1960 (2)	1962 (3)	1955 (4)	1960 (5)	1962 (6)	1955 (7)	1960 (8)	1962 (9)	1955 (10)	1960 (11)	1962 (12)
United States	98.7	96.3	96.0	100.2	100.2	100.2	98.9	96.5	96.2	99.1	97.2	97.0
Northwest Europe	100.7	96.0	93.4	99.6	102.0	102.8	100.3	97.8	96.1	100.2	98.4	97.0
Belgium	99.0	94.1	93.2	100.5	102.6	102.9	99.5	96.5	95.9	99.6	97.5	96.9
Denmark	100.9	94.1	92.2	99.6	102.4	102.9	100.5	96.4	94.9	100.3	97.6	96.7
France	100.9	99.5	99.2	99.6	100.2	100.3	100.5	99.7	99.5	100.3	99.8	99.7
Germany	99.6	90.7	86.9	100.2	105.5	107.1	99.8	95.7	93.2	99.9	96.7	94.8
Netherlands	100.6	99.8	94.1	99.7	100.2	101.9	100.3	100.0	95.9	100.2	100.0	97.0
Norway	101.4	95.2	93.5	99.3	101.8	102.3	100.7	96.9	95.7	100.5	97.9	97.0
United Kingdom	101.5	98.6	96.2	98.9	100.1	100.8	100.4	98.7	97.0	100.4	98.9	97.3
Italy	102.2	102.6	98.7	99.4	101.6	103.5	101.6	104.2	102.2	100.7	102.0	101.0

Source: See text for derivation.

those of full-time males in the Anglo-Saxon countries were still within 2 percent of the 1950 level.[26] Hours of full-time females dropped slightly more than this in the United States and decidedly more (9 percent) in the United Kingdom.

Annual hours dropped 6 to 8 percent from 1950 to 1962 in Belgium, Denmark, the Netherlands, Norway (averaging males and females), and Italy (for full-time workers only).

In Germany annual hours dropped 13.5 percent from 1950 to 1962, much more than in any other country. Tables 6–3 and 6–5 together imply that in 1950 annual hours of full-time male wage and salary workers in Germany were exceeded only in Italy, while in 1962 they were the shortest among all the countries examined (though the difference from Norway and Denmark is insignificant).

Indexes of the average annual hours worked by employed nonfarm wage and salary workers when both sexes and full- and part-time workers are com-

bined are shown in Columns 1 to 3, Table 6–6. These indexes reflect changes in the proportions of workers in each group as well as changes in hours worked by each group separately. To appraise the effect of changes in average hours upon effective labor input the same assumptions concerning the relationship between hours and productivity were made as in the comparison of countries in 1960.[27] The resulting indexes, given in Columns 4 to 6, are estimates of the change in the amount of work done in one hour by nonfarm wage and salary workers as the result of changes in working hours.[28] These indexes are determined mainly by levels of and

26. However, in the United Kingdom this statement cancels a 1950–55 increase against a subsequent decline. From *1955* to 1962 average annual hours of full-time males dropped nearly 4 percent (and those of females 5 percent) in the United Kingdom. *Normal* hours of each sex were practically unchanged from 1950 to 1956, then dropped 4.9 percent from 1956 to 1962 according to the series published in the *Ministry of Labour Gazette* [G42]. (From 1962 to 1964 actual hours increased despite a further drop in normal hours. In 1965 and 1966 both declined.)

27. The indexes of Table 6–3 were first multiplied by those of Table 6–5 to obtain, separately for male and for female full-time nonfarm wage and salary workers, indexes of annual hours in each country in each year expressed as a percentage of United States hours in 1960. The corresponding quality adjustment index per hour of work was then obtained from the curves previously described. The male and female indexes and indexes held constant at 100 for part-time workers were next combined by use of 1960 manhour weights. The index for each country was then recomputed with its own index for 1950 taken as 100.

28. It is likely that no quality adjustment ought to be made for short-term variations in hours due to fluctuations in the intensity of demand for labor. Consideration was given to the use of smoothed hours data in the calculation of quality indexes, but the procedure was rejected when it became apparent that the smoothing procedure would become quite arbitrary and have but little effect on the end results.

changes in hours of full-time workers, and bear no necessary relationship to changes in the average hours of full- and part-time workers combined (the indexes given in Columns 1 to 3). The products of Columns 1 to 3, indexes of average hours, and Columns 4 to 6, indexes of the quality of an hour's work, yield indexes of the amount of work done per man-year of employment of nonfarm wage and salary workers (insofar as this depends upon working hours). These are shown in Columns 7 to 9.

Nonfarm wage and salary workers represent only part of the employed labor force. Changes in hours of the other groups were not estimated but are not needed if, as in the cross-sectional estimates, it is assumed that changes in the average full-time hours of persons employed in agriculture, of the nonfarm self-employed and family workers, and of the armed forces have no effect upon output. For these groups indexes of the effect of hours changes upon labor input per man-year are 100 throughout the period.[29]

The mere increase over time in the number of nonfarm wage and salary workers relative to the other groups, whose hours are longer, tended to reduce the average hours of all employed persons combined. This occurred to a greater or lesser extent in all the countries included in the study. In Chapter 16 I shall consider the effect upon growth of these shifts in labor force composition. To allow changes in the proportions of the different groups to influence the evaluation of the effect of hours changes on labor input would complicate, without adding to, the analysis. I therefore estimate the effect of hours changes upon effective labor input per man-year of employment in the economy as a whole by combining the indexes for nonfarm wage and salary workers given in Columns 7 to 9, Table 6–6, and those for the other groups, taken as 100 in all years, by use of fixed 1960 employment weights.[30] The resulting indexes are given in Columns 10 to 12.

These indexes represent my final estimates of the effect of hours changes upon the amount of work

29. It is also assumed that the proportions of full-time workers and part-time workers and the average hours of part-time workers were unchanged within these groups.
30. The calculations were made from indexes expressed with 1960 = 100, and reconverted to a 1950 base.

done per person employed. It is instructive to discuss them in terms of growth rates.

Effect of Hours Changes on Labor Input

In the United States, changes in average hours worked reduced the annual growth rate of labor input per person employed by about 0.2 percent a year in the 1950–55 period, and by 0.3 percent in 1955–62. Unlike the great changes in worktime that occurred between the 1880's and the late 1940's, hardly any of this reflects a true reduction in hours of work that could be interpreted as the sacrifice of income for leisure. Instead, it reflects the addition to the labor force of women and minors who found part-time jobs for only a few hours a week. Expanded opportunity for part-time employment was in all respects a welcome development. It added, though only slightly, to the amount of work done and to total and per capita real income, while increasing the range of choice open to women and children. Since these part-time workers were not distinguished from full-time workers in the computation of national income per person employed, their increase did reduce the growth rate of that statistical measure.

In Northwest Europe changes in average hours worked had little effect on labor input from 1950 to 1955; in individual countries the effect on the growth rate of labor input was either zero or an addition of 0.1 percentage points. In this period, consequently, changes in average hours were more favorable to growth in Europe than in America. In contrast, from 1955 to 1962 hours changes cut the growth rate of labor input by 0.5 percentage points in Northwest Europe as a whole, and were adverse to output in all countries. The amount was as much as 0.7 in Germany. In the United Kingdom it was 0.4, and it was also 0.4 or 0.5 in all the small countries. In France, in contrast, hours reduction curtailed the 1955–62 growth rate of labor input by only 0.1 percentage points.

This drag upon Northwest European growth after 1955 was caused almost entirely by conscious decisions to reduce the amount of work done, decisions that impaired the growth rates of total labor input and total and per capita income as well as of labor input per person employed. The reduction in the duration of work made a substantial contribution to welfare that is additional to the rise that took place in real income.

Changes in average hours after 1955 were more favorable to growth of effective labor input in the United States than in any of the Northwest European countries except France. In the case of Germany the difference was as much as 0.4 points in the growth rate.

Over the 1950–62 period as a whole the effect of changes in working hours (including the changing proportions of part-time workers) upon the growth of labor input, and national income, was about the same in the United States, Northwest Europe, and all of the component countries except France and Germany. The reduction in labor input per person employed was about 3 percent in all these areas. Hours changes in France were much more favorable to growth and in Germany much less favorable than in the United States or the other Northwest European countries.

In Italy alone changes in average hours had a slightly positive effect upon labor input in both the 1950–55 and 1955–62 periods. This was the net result of two developments, both conducive to economic welfare but offsetting in their influence upon labor input per person employed. Hours of full-time nonfarm wage and salary workers fell as much in Italy as in most Northwestern European countries. But, in addition, full-time work became available to many who had previously been able to find only part-time employment. This latter development was not a cyclical phenomenon resulting from comparison of noncomparable years; it resulted from a sustained expansion of employment opportunities. By 1960 part-time work had dwindled to a small proportion of nonfarm wage and salary employment and Italy could no longer tap this source to increase labor input.

The estimates of the effects of international differences in the level of, and changes in, working hours that I have just reviewed depend, of course, upon my specific assumptions as to the size of productivity offsets. They may be too large or too small, and I have given my estimates in detail to permit any reader to apply alternative assumptions. But it is not very likely that the assumptions

result in a misrepresentation of the general pattern of international differences.

For example, I estimate that from 1955 to 1962 changes in hours reduced the growth rate of labor input in Germany by 0.7 percentage points more than in France, meaning that the effect on output was the same as that of a similar difference in the growth rate of employment.[31] The growth rate of employment was in fact 1.4 percentage points greater in Germany than in France, so I imply about half the difference in employment growth was offset by changes in hours. I think it safe to say there was such an offset and that it was substantial, but readily concede that it may have been greater or less than half.

Hours of full-time workers in Northwest Europe in 1960 were much closer to what full-time hours were in the United States in 1960 than to United States hours in the mid-twenties, when output per man was at the 1960 European level. By 1962 the gap had been further narrowed. If it could be assumed that European working hours will be at the 1960 United States level when European income reaches the 1960 United States level, it would be concluded that future hours reduction will be small, and that this would help Europe to achieve the same gain in output per man in a shorter period than the United States required. The assumption, though plausible, may be questioned on two counts. First, United States hours may again be reduced, and the current tendency is to narrow and eliminate hours differentials among Western nations regardless of income differences. Second, European labor appears to be seeking to match a supposed 40-hour week in the United States. Forty hours is, of course, the duration of work beyond which overtime rates must be paid in most activities, and it is also not far below the average that emerges for actual hours when all full- and part-time workers of both sexes are thrown together. But 40 hours is much below the average for hours actually worked by full-time workers in full weeks. In addition, vacation policy in a number of European countries is more liberal than in the United States, especially

31. When account is taken, in Chapter 15, of industries where output is measured by employment, the difference relevant to the growth of measured national income is narrowed to 0.53 percentage points.

for those who have not served a single employer for a long time.[32] Misconceptions about the number of hours that Americans actually work could very easily result in the average duration of work in some of the European countries becoming appreciably shorter than the average in the United States.

The other great development that has affected labor input per person employed in the United States is the huge postwar increase in voluntary part-time employment. A similar development may well lie ahead for Europe. It would be beneficial in all respects, but would appreciably restrain the growth of output per person employed.

32. Unlike most European countries the United States has no legislation requiring vacations. Legislation limiting daily or weekly hours is confined to state laws restricting the hours of females and, sometimes, minors in selected activities; the weekly limits set by these laws are usually in the range of 48 to 60 hours.

At the time of writing (1966) strong pressure is being exerted for repeal of even this legislation, one state (Delaware) has already repealed its law, another (Virginia) has dropped enforcement in interstate activities, and a federal government agency (the Equal Employment Opportunities Commission) is questioning the validity of all the state hours laws for women on the grounds that they conflict with federal law prohibiting discrimination in employment based on sex. Thus the United States is in peril of losing even the limited protection against hours deemed long enough to be hazardous to the health of women and children (and, incidentally, inefficient as well) that was adopted during the reform movement before World War I.

Hours Worked by Men, Women, and Young People

The proportions of total hours worked that are performed by men in the prime working ages, by women of the same ages, by teenagers, by older persons, and by members of the armed forces differ appreciably among the nine countries. For example, the proportion of hours worked in 1960 by civilian males aged 20 to 64 years ranged all the way from 58 percent of the total in Denmark and Germany to 69 percent in the Netherlands. Such differences must affect average output per hour worked.

In this chapter the effect of differences in the composition of hours worked upon the average quality of labor is estimated by the use of earnings weights. This effect turns out to be appreciable. A quality index computed for Northwest Europe as a whole is 2.5 percent below that for the United States. Estimates for individual countries show that, compared with the United States, the quality of labor with respect to age-sex composition and civilian or military status is 2 percent higher in the Netherlands; about the same in Belgium and Norway; 1.5 to 2.5 percent lower in the United Kingdom, Italy, and France; and 4.5 percent lower in Denmark and Germany.

The age-sex composition of hours worked also affected the quality of labor over time. A quality index for the United States drops by 2 percent from 1950 to 1962 while a similar index for Northwest Europe rises by 0.5 percent; the difference in growth rates is about 0.2 percentage points.

Computation of Quality Indexes

To compute quality indexes, two types of information are needed: distributions of total man-hours worked among the categories of workers distinguished, and earnings weights to apply to each category. Data for 1960 will be considered for each in turn.

Distributions of Employment and Total Hours Worked

Percentage distributions of 1960 employment are provided in Table 7–1. Total male civilian employment, total female civilian employment, and military employment were taken from Table 5–1C. Civilian males and females were then further divided among workers in the following age groups: under 20, 20 to 64, and 65 and over. For the United States the source of employment data

TABLE 7-1

*Percentage Distributions of Employment Among Civilian Age–Sex Groups,
and Military Personnel, 1960*

Area	Total employment	Civilians by age group						Military personnel
		Males			Females			
		Under 20 years	20 to 64 years	65 years and over	Under 20 years	20 to 64 years	65 years and over	
United States	100.0	4.2	56.9	3.2	3.0	27.8	1.3	3.6
Northwest Europe	100.0	5.4	55.6	2.5	5.1	27.8	1.2	2.4
Belgium	100.0	4.4	60.5	1.5	4.3	25.2	.8	3.2
Denmark	100.0	6.9	52.8	2.9	6.8	27.5	.9	2.3
France	100.0	4.4	54.5	2.9	3.3	28.6	2.0	4.3
Germany	100.0	6.3	53.2	2.0	6.0	30.3	1.1	1.1
Netherlands	100.0	6.2	65.0	2.6	6.5	16.0	.5	3.1
Norway	100.0	4.5	58.8	4.3	5.0	22.8	1.5	3.0
United Kingdom	100.0	5.3	56.6	2.6	5.3	27.2	.9	2.1
Italy	100.0	7.7	58.7	2.2	5.9	22.9	.8	1.8

Source: See text for derivation. Details may not add to totals because of rounding.

also provided statistics for these age groups. For other countries percentage distributions of each sex by age were assumed to be the same for employment as for the labor force.[1]

Table 7–2 shows a similar distribution of total man-hours worked. Appendix E describes the way these estimates were derived by the combination of employment and hours data. Since males 20 to 64 years of age work the longest hours, they contribute more proportionately to total man-hours than to employment in all countries. The distributions of man-hours are not highly accurate, but the main differences between countries are clearly established.

Hours worked by male civilians in the prime working ages—taken here to be 20 to 64—comprise a much higher proportion of total man-hours in the Netherlands than in the United States and a moderately higher proportion in Belgium. The proportion was comparable to the United States in Norway, the United Kingdom, and Italy, and much smaller in Denmark, France, and Germany. The offsets were mainly in the proportion of hours

1. Unemployment was too small a proportion of the labor force for errors in this assumption (made for other years as well) to have any perceptible effect upon the estimates except possibly in Germany in 1950 and Italy in 1950 and 1955. It must be noted, however, that age distributions of the labor force usually could not be obtained directly from sources that provided the total labor force estimates given in Table 5–1.

worked by females in the same age group, but variations in the other age-sex groups were not negligible. Hours worked by persons under 20 were more significant in all European countries than in the United States whereas those worked by older workers were less significant except in France and Norway. Military hours were more important in 1960 in France and the United States than in the other countries, and they were least important in Germany.

Earnings Weights

To obtain international comparability in the measures of labor input, these differences make it necessary to weight hours worked by the various labor force groups. Average hourly earnings provide the appropriate weights.

Table 7–3 provides estimates of differentials in average hourly and weekly earnings in the United States in 1960.[2] They refer to all industries and classes of workers combined. The estimates are approximate, especially for the younger and older workers, but adequate for use as weights. Females 20 to 64 years of age earned, on the average, only 59 percent as much per hour as males in the same age group; younger males and, to a lesser extent, younger females, earned considerably less. Males

2. See Appendix E for a description of these estimates.

TABLE 7-2

Percentage Distributions of Man-Hours Worked Among Civilian Age–Sex Groups,
and Military Personnel, 1960

Area	Total man-hours worked	Civilians by age group						Military personnel
		Males			Females			
		Under 20 years	20 to 64 years	65 years and over	Under 20 years	20 to 64 years	65 years and over	
United States	100.0	2.9	62.5	2.8	1.9	24.9	1.0	4.0
Northwest Europe	100.0	4.8	60.4	2.1	3.4	25.3	1.0	2.4
Belgium	100.0	3.9	64.7	1.3	3.4	22.9	.7	3.1
Denmark	100.0	6.0	57.6	2.5	5.4	25.4	.7	2.4
France	100.0	3.9	59.2	2.5	2.6	26.0	1.6	4.2
Germany	100.0	5.5	57.3	1.7	4.9	28.6	.9	1.1
Netherlands	100.0	5.4	69.6	2.2	5.1	14.4	.4	2.9
Norway	100.0	3.9	63.2	3.6	3.9	20.9	1.2	3.1
United Kingdom	100.0	4.9	62.3	2.5	4.0	23.5	.7	2.1
Italy	100.0	6.7	63.1	1.9	4.7	21.3	.6	1.8

Source: See text for derivation. Details may not add to totals because of rounding.

65 and over averaged 82 percent as much per hour as males 20 to 64, and females aged 65 and over only 34 percent. Differentials in weekly earnings between males 20 to 64 and the other age-sex groups are much larger than those in hourly earnings.

If hourly earnings differentials came about because men, women, and children doing identical work equally well received different rates of pay they could not, of course, be used to measure differences among the age-sex groups in the average quality of labor. Discrimination in pay for the same work would affect the distribution but not the size of total national income and product.[3] Discrimination in pay for identical work does occur but it appears to account for only a small part of observed earnings differences.[4] The earnings differentials

mainly reflect different distributions of the age-sex groups among jobs involving different degrees of skill, strength, experience, and responsibility, and differences in performance on similar jobs.

Differences in occupational distributions presumably result mainly from actual differences among the groups in aptitude, training, necessary experience, strength, and, particularly in the case of married women and older men, willingness to accept heavy responsibility. Discrimination against women, youngsters, and older persons is also pres-

3. It may be noted that in the United States discrimination against women was already prohibited by law in a number of states by 1960; these states accounted for a high proportion of total U.S. employment. Subsequently, discrimination has been forbidden by two federal laws. It also has been, or is becoming, illegal in European countries, and is being eliminated under Article 119 of the Treaty of Rome. Reviews of progress in the Common Market countries appear in Fitzgerald, *The Common Market's Labor Programs*, pp. 66–67 [B33] and in Information Service of the European Community, *Labor in the European Community*, November 1965, pp. 2–6 [I47].
4. A careful analysis of the causes of earnings differentials between men and women in the United States will be found in Sanborn, *Industrial and Labor Relations Review*, July 1964, pp. 534–50 [P23].

TABLE 7-3

United States: Estimated Earnings Differentials
of Civilians by Sex and Age, and of
Military Personnel, 1960

(*Average earnings of civilian males 20 to 64 = 100*)

Status, sex, and age group (in years)	Average hourly earnings	Average weekly earnings
Civilians		
Males		
Under 20	31	19
20–64	100	100
65 and over	82	65
Females		
Under 20	40	24
20–64	59	48
65 and over	47	34
Military personnel	69	69

Source: Appendix Table E-1.

ent in hiring and promotion. United States employers and unions have had more difficulty in adapting to laws prohibiting employment discrimination by sex than they have had in adapting to equal pay laws; this suggests that, as is commonly believed, job discrimination is more common than pay discrimination. For the present purpose, however, it makes no difference whether the groups with lower earnings are actually lacking in ability to fill better paying jobs or are denied the opportunity to obtain them. Unutilized potential ability adds nothing to national product and does not affect relative marginal value products in different occupations. An 18-year-old newsboy might make an excellent newspaper editor, but if he is denied the opportunity to use this talent his contribution is no greater than that of his companion who lacks it. Nor does this unrecognized skill add to the supply of editors and subtract from the supply of news-

boys, and thus affect marginal value products in the two occupations. Given employment practices as they actually exist, observed differentials in average earnings may be used as approximate measures of differentials in the actual average marginal products of the different types of labor.

Weekly compensation (including income in kind) of military personnel is estimated at 69 percent of the earnings of adult male civilians. Hours of the two groups are the same by assumption so that the same percentage applies to hourly earnings.

Use of United States earnings weights to equate the various groups in the labor force is appropriate for analysis of changes over time in the United States and for international comparisons of the quality of labor. (The latter is consistent with use of United States price weights in the output comparisons.) For time series analysis in Europe it is necessary to examine some European data.

TABLE 7-4

Comparison of Earnings Differentials in the United States and Great Britain (1960), Germany and France (1963), by Sex and Age

Sex and age group (in years)	United States, 1960[a] (Males 20–64 = 100)		Great Britain, 1960[b] (Males 21 and over = 100)		Germany, 1963[b] (Males except apprentices = 100)		France, 1963[b] (Males 21–64 = 100)	
	Weekly earnings	Hourly earnings	Weekly earnings	Hourly earnings	Weekly earnings	Hourly earnings	Annual earnings (A)[c]	Annual earnings (B)[c]
Males								
20–64	100	100						
21 and over			100	100				
Total except apprentices								
21–64					100	100	100	100
Females								
20–64	48	59						
18 and over			47	59				
Total except apprentices								
21–64					64	70	67	71
Males								
Under 20	19	31						
Under 21			43	45			38	32
Apprentices					17	n. a.		
Females								
Under 20	24	40						
Under 18			32	37				
Under 21							40	43
Apprentices					17	n. a.		

Sources: United States: Table 7–3; Great Britain, Germany, and France: see text for derivation.
a. Estimates refer to earnings of all employed civilians, including proprietors and family workers.
b. Estimates refer to earnings of wage and salary workers only. The armed forces and household employees are included in Germany but not in Great Britain and France. Farm and general government workers are excluded in France.
c. Column (A) refers to full-time workers. Column (B) refers to full-time workers employed throughout the year by a single employer.
n.a. Not available.

For Great Britain rough estimates of differentials in October 1960 hourly and weekly earnings of wage and salary workers (who comprised about 93 percent of total civilian employment in 1960) are given in Table 7–4. They are based on a combination of hourly and weekly earnings of wage earners covered in the semiannual British survey, and of weekly earnings of administrative, technical, and clerical employees, coal miners, and hired agricultural workers.

The estimates indicate that the most important differential—between hourly earnings of adult males and females—is about the same in the United States and Great Britain (although older workers could not be isolated in Great Britain). The differentials between adults and young workers are difficult to compare with the American figures because of the different age breaks. (The British differentials by age, as adjusted, are in any case considerably less reliable than the adult male-female differential.) The figures suggest that if the age break were the same in both countries, hourly earnings of young workers, relative to adult males, probably would be moderately higher in the United Kingdom. Weekly earnings appear to be much higher, presumably because the American figures are greatly depressed by students with after-school and Saturday jobs. The same factors may underlie the apparent difference in hourly earnings, although these would be much less affected by this factor.

In any case, substitution of British for American weights for hourly earnings would scarcely affect the calculations to be made.

Data are available for male and female wage and salary workers in West Germany. These include the armed forces (unlike the British and American data) and (unlike the British figures) also domestic servants. A classification by age is not available, but apprentices are isolated.[5] The esti-

mates show hourly earnings of females (other than apprentices) to be 30 percent below those of males, about three-fourths as large a differential as the 41 percent indicated by the most similar comparison for the United States and Great Britain. However, the German differential is greatly affected by the exclusion of proprietors and unpaid family workers, who are numerous in Germany. If they were included it is likely that the German differential would be as great as those in the Anglo-Saxon countries.[6] The data for apprentices cannot be compared directly with the American data for workers under 20 years of age but they confirm that in Germany, too, earnings of young workers are only a small fraction of those of adult males.

Data for France also refer to wage and salary workers, in this case excluding domestics, farm workers, and general government employees.[7] Column A refers to annual earnings of full-time workers, Column B to annual earnings of full-time workers employed by one employer throughout the year. The male-female differentials for adults are generally similar to those in weekly earnings in Germany, to which the coverage of the data most nearly corresponds. As shown, the differential is actually a little narrower than in Germany but this may be due to the omission of domestics and farm workers. Self-employed and unpaid family workers are even more numerous in France than in Germany.

On the whole, the British, German, and French data suggest that patterns of earnings differentials

---

5. Data refer to the fourth quarter of 1963. The data for weekly earnings differentials are derived from data for gross wages and salaries, employment, and average monthly wage rates reported in DIW, *Economic Bulletin,* April 1964, p. 3 [P15]. Conversion to an hourly basis is based on the ratio of hours worked by female wage and salary workers to those worked by males in October 1960 computed from OSCE, *Statistical Information,* 1963, No. 2 bis, Tables 57 and 71 [I49]. Weekly earnings indexes are available for 1950, 1955, and 1960, as well as for 1963. For adult females the indexes in these four years are 61, 62, 66, and 64, respectively.

6. The proper treatment of unpaid family workers in these comparisons is debatable. The United States estimates ascribe the whole income of unincorporated enterprises to the proprietors and none to unpaid family workers. Since females are a larger proportion of unpaid family workers than of proprietors, this tends to depress the ratio of female to male earnings. In the United States this tendency is slight because there are few unpaid family workers. No unpaid family workers are included in the United Kingdom employment estimates so the problem does not arise. In Germany, however, unpaid family workers represent 22 percent of female civilian employment and only 3 percent of male civilian employment (1960). If the practice of assigning no income to unpaid family workers is followed, and if it were assumed for illustration that the average income of proprietors is the same as that of wage and salary workers of the same sex, the ratio of female to male earnings for all classes of workers combined would be only 0.56, less than in the Anglo-Saxon countries.

7. The French indexes, which are for 1963, are derived from INSEE, *Etudes et Conjoncture,* November 1965, Tables XIXB, XIXC, and XX [G14].

among the various civilian age-sex groups in Europe are not very different from those in the United States.[8] I have not been able to develop data for the European countries that are clearly more representative of their earnings structures than are the United States differentials when a uniform classification is utilized for all countries. For this reason the United States differentials in hourly earnings will be used for time series analysis in all the countries as well as for international comparisons.

International Comparison for 1960

Quality indexes to adjust man-hours worked in the European countries in 1960 to equivalence with American man-hours, insofar as the distribution among age-sex groups and between civilian and military personnel are concerned, are given in Table 7–5. The indexes are constructed by weighting man-hours worked by each of the seven groups in each country, given in rounded percentage form in Table 7–2, by the hourly earnings indexes for the United States given in Table 7–3, and converting the results to index form. In Table 7–5 the resulting quality adjustment indexes are given for all employed persons (including the armed forces) and for civilians alone. Hourly earnings of the armed forces are below average. The armed forces represent a lower percentage of the total in all the European countries except France than they do in the United States, and their inclusion therefore raises the European indexes, but only slightly.

The composite index for Northwest Europe is 97.5. This means that if hourly earnings in each of the separate age-sex civilian groups and of military personnel were the same in Northwest Europe as in the United States, average hourly earnings for all workers would be 97.5 percent as large as in the United States. Since I accept hourly earnings differentials as measures of differentials of the average quality of an hour's work, I conclude that, on

TABLE 7–5

International Comparison of the Quality of a Man-Hour's Work as Affected by the Distribution of Man-Hours Among Civilian Age-Sex Groups, and Military Personnel, 1960

(*Indexes, United States = 100*)

Area	Total (including armed forces)	Civilians only
United States	100.0	100.0
Northwest Europe	97.5	97.2
Belgium	99.8	99.8
Denmark	95.5	95.2
France	97.8	97.8
Germany	95.4	94.8
Netherlands	101.8	101.6
Norway	99.7	99.5
United Kingdom	98.6	98.2
Italy	98.1	97.6

Source: See text for derivation.

this account, the average quality of an hour's work in Northwest Europe is 97.5 percent of the average quality in the United States. This means that if there were no other differences between the two areas we should expect output per man-hour to be about 2 percent lower in Northwest Europe than in the United States, based on United States weights. With differences in hours of work taken into account separately, the same percentage applies to national income per person employed.

Among the Northwest European countries the indexes (including the armed forces) range all the way from 95.4 in Germany, where man-hours worked by male civilians in the prime working ages accounted for only 57.3 percent of total man-hours, to 101.8 in the Netherlands, where the same group accounted for 69.7 percent of total man-hours.[9]

8. An exception may be noted for the over 65 groups in France, whose relative earnings are higher than in the United States. Corresponding to Column A, Table 7–4, I obtain indexes of 122 for males 65 and over and 66 for females 65 and over. Corresponding to Column B, I obtain indexes of 125 and 74 for these groups. The restricted coverage of the data—both the exclusion of part-time workers and exclusion of agricultural workers and the self-employed—should be borne in mind.

9. It is of interest at this point to comment upon an article by Brakel in *Review of Economics and Statistics*, May 1962, pp. 123–33 [P37]. Brakel noted that 1956 data for GNP per capita placed the Netherlands last by a considerable margin among the Northwest European countries, and that it remained last, though by a much reduced margin, if only the population of the working ages (15-64) were counted in the calculation. This contradicted ideas of the Dutch statisticians and economists as to the true position of productivity in the Netherlands. Brakel therefore, quite properly, substituted calculations of GNP per person in the labor force and obtained the remarkable result that, by this measure, productivity in the Netherlands was exceeded in Europe only by Belgium. (Compare Table 2–4 above for

TABLE 7-6

United States and Northwest Europe: Percentage Distributions of Employment, Man-Hours,
and Labor Input Among Civilian Age-Sex Groups, and Military Personnel, 1960

Status, sex, and age group (in years)	Total employment		Man-hours worked		Labor input (as measured by earnings)	
	United States	Northwest Europe	United States	Northwest Europe	United States	Northwest Europe
Total	100.0	100.0	100.0	100.0	100.0	100.0
Male civilians						
Under 20	4.2	5.5	2.9	4.8	1.1	1.8
20–64	56.9	55.4	62.5	60.4	74.1	73.4
65 and over	3.2	2.6	2.8	2.1	2.7	2.1
Female civilians						
Under 20	3.0	5.1	1.9	4.0	.9	1.9
20–64	27.8	27.8	24.9	25.3	17.4	18.1
65 and over	1.3	1.2	1.0	1.0	.6	.6
Military personnel	3.6	2.4	4.0	2.4	3.3	2.0

Source: See text for derivation. Details may not add to totals because of rounding.

The Dutch quality index is 6.7 percent above that for Germany. When multiplied by the labor share, this difference indicates that the composition of hours worked would of itself put output per man-hour in the Netherlands 5 percent above that in Germany. The composition of man-hours was about as favorable in Belgium and Norway as in the United States while in the other European countries (except the Netherlands) it was less favorable. The Italian index is below the United States despite a lower female component because of the much larger proportion of young workers.

An interesting by-product of the calculations is given in Table 7–6, which compares the shares of the different labor force groups in employment, man-hours, and labor input (as measured by earnings). In the United States all groups except male civilians 20–64 were together responsible for 43 percent of employment, 37.5 percent of man-hours

worked, and only 26 percent of labor input. The proportions in Northwest Europe as a whole were fairly similar: 45, 40, and 27, respectively. Employment and even man-hours data can be quite misleading as measures of the economic importance of the various groups.

In view of these pronounced differences, and of large differences among countries in labor force composition, perhaps the most interesting result of the computation of the quality indexes for the various countries is that the indexes do not differ by more than 7 percent.

Changes Over the 1950–62 Period

An identical method may be used to measure changes over time in the individual countries. Percentage distributions of man-hours worked by each of the seven labor force groups in each year in each country were computed, and the components were weighted by hourly earnings differentials for the United States in 1960. The resulting quality adjustment indexes are given in Table 7–7.

Changes in the composition of man-hours by age, sex, and military status reduced the average quality of labor in the United States by 1.8 percent from 1950 to 1962 while raising it by 0.5 percent in Northwest Europe. The difference is equivalent

1960 national income data.) The reason for this remarkable change in the Dutch position lies in the very low Dutch labor force participation rate for women. But it is just this low female participation rate that helps to create a high Dutch output per person in the labor force. By counting all members of the labor force as equal, Brakel has raised the true productivity position of the Netherlands too much. If his indexes of the GNP per economically active person are divided by my indexes of the quality of labor as affected by labor force composition, the position of Holland drops relative to all the other countries he shows. Despite the overcorrection, his major point—that use of total rather than working population gives too adverse a picture of Dutch productivity—is, of course, correct.

TABLE 7-7

Quality Indexes of a Man-Hour's Work as
Affected by the Distribution of Man-Hours,
Among Civilian Age-Sex Groups
and Military Personnel

(1950 = 100)

Area	1950	1955	1960	1962
United States	100.0	99.1	98.4	98.2
Northwest Europe	100.0	99.7	100.1	100.5
Belgium	100.0	101.1	101.2	101.6
Denmark	100.0	99.5	98.8	98.7
France	100.0	100.7	101.3	102.0
Germany	100.0	99.0	99.7	100.7
Netherlands	100.0	100.5	100.4	100.2
Norway	100.0	99.7	99.3	98.7
United Kingdom	100.0	99.5	99.6	99.3
Italy	100.0	101.3	101.1	101.9

Source: See text for derivation.

to almost 0.2 percentage points in the growth rate of labor input. Changes in age-sex composition raised the quality of labor in five of the eight European countries and in none did the index decline as much as in the United States. In the 1955–62 period this factor accounted for a difference of nearly 0.4 points in the growth rates of labor input in the United States and Germany and accounts for an appreciable fraction of the difference in their growth rates.

In most European countries the movement of the index was controlled by changes in the relationship between hours worked by males and by females, but a general drop in total hours worked by teenagers was also of some importance. The drop in the United States index is almost entirely due to the increased proportion of female workers. Over the longer periods covered in my American study, it may be noted, the reduction in employment of children had offset the rise in employment of adult females.[10] By 1950 this offset had run out.

10. Denison, *Sources of Economic Growth,* p. 82 [B25].

CHAPTER EIGHT

Education of the Labor Force

Educational background is a crucial determinant of the quality of labor. It conditions both the types of work an individual is able to do and his efficiency in doing them.[1] In all the countries considered here there has been a gradual upward movement of the distribution of the labor force by amount of formal education. The measurement of this movement and its effect on the quality of labor is the principal subject of this chapter.

In the United States, the educational level of the labor force has been rising at a remarkable rate for several decades. My previous study found that this made a very large contribution to economic growth from 1929 to 1957—much larger than education's contribution in the 1909–29 period.[2]

The education of the American labor force also increased rapidly during the postwar period. From 1950 to 1962, I estimate, education raised the average quality of American labor by 9 percent (or 0.7 percent a year) and contributed one-half a percentage point to the growth rate of national income. Improvement in the educational quality of the labor

force was only half as great in Northwest Europe as in the United States, and the increase in actual amount of education was proportionately even less. Only in Belgium and Italy was the increase in the quality of labor, measured in terms of education, comparable to that in the United States. In France, the Netherlands, Norway, and the United Kingdom it was a little above the Northwest European average. In Denmark and Germany the increase was very small. Education does not help to explain why growth rates in Europe were higher than in the United States but, on the contrary, adds to the difference that must be explained by other sources.

On the other hand, education does help to explain the differences between Europe and the United States in the 1960 levels of national income per person employed. The American labor force had received more education than the Northwest European labor force and much more than the Italian labor force.

Education as a Source of Growth Defined

This chapter attempts to measure the improvement in the quality of labor in the 1950–62 period that

---

1. A somewhat more extended discussion is given in my article in OECD, *The Residual Factor and Economic Growth,* pp. 36–38 [I43].
2. See Denison, *Sources of Economic Growth,* Chapter 7 and p. 266 [B25].

resulted from increased education of the labor force. Comparisons of the quality of labor, as affected by education, are also attempted between countries, but are much less satisfactory than the intertemporal comparisons. They are affected to a much greater extent by limitations of information and technique and also encounter the inherent difficulties of comparing different educational systems.

This chapter is concerned only with the quality of labor. It is not concerned with all the direct and indirect effects of education upon output. Thus, it is necessary to clarify at the outset the relationship between education and the classification of growth sources adopted in this study:

1. The value of the work an individual can perform is greatly affected by his educational background. To count a high school or college graduate as only the same amount of labor, on the average, as an elementary school graduate of the same age and sex would be altogether unsatisfactory. The more educated groups earn more and contribute more to the national product. If workers with one level of education earn 50 percent more, on the average, than *otherwise similar* individuals with less education, they will be counted in this chapter as 50 percent more labor. The reason is by now familiar: Average earnings of large groups of individuals are taken to be proportional to the average values of their marginal products.

The upward trend in education apparent in both Europe and the United States has meant that the skills and versatility of labor have been upgraded. There has been a shift in occupational composition toward occupations in which workers typically have higher levels of education and, more importantly, there has been an increase in the skills of individuals within what is conventionally termed an occupation, often with considerable changes in the work actually performed. This increase in the quality of labor has been a source of increase in national income. Quality indexes are developed in this chapter to measure the increase in the ability of workers to contribute to production as a result of additional education.

2. It is essential to distinguish between: (a) society's stock of knowledge relevant to production, which (along with other conditions) governs the output obtained with given inputs; and (b) the quantity and quality of inputs (including the education of the labor force) that govern the output obtained with a given stock of knowledge. This chapter is concerned only with the latter.

Increases in output resulting from advances in society's stock of knowledge are credited in my classification to the growth source, "advances of knowledge." This does not, of course, deny that the education of the labor force as a whole, and particularly the number of highly educated individuals, may be among the factors that influence the pace of inventions, new ways of organizing production, and new business practices that reduce unit costs and increase the output *that can be obtained with given inputs* (including labor of constant skills).

3. A better educated work force—from top management down—will be better able to learn about and to utilize the most efficient production practices known. The effect of education on this ability is one aspect of the quality of labor measured here, insofar as it is reflected in earnings differentials. Consequently, the growth source, "changes in the lag in the application of knowledge" (discussed in Chapter 20), does not include changes brought about as an incidental result of changes in the amount of education of the labor force; it is confined to the effects of other changes, such as improvement in channels of information, opportunities to observe the practices of other firms or countries, and changes in the age of the capital stock. I would not pretend this distinction is precise, but it is clear enough for general understanding.

4. While education may affect the pace of advances in knowledge, it is also true that advances of knowledge change the content of education; what is taught in a physics or economics course today is not what was taught a generation ago, and this is one of the main ways in which new knowledge is disseminated. If what is taught in schools and colleges lags further behind or more closely approaches the current state of the arts, this can influence changes in the lag of actual practice behind the best known. It is not reflected in my quality indexes for the education of the labor force, which take no account of the content of courses.

5. Most individuals in school do not work and those who do usually work part time. Hence, ex-

tending schooling for young people immediately influences at least three measures of labor input that have already been examined: Employment is reduced, average hours of work may be lowered, and (since the proportion of young people in the labor force is reduced) the age composition is improved. The net effect of these three changes is to reduce total labor input while raising the average quality of labor. Cross-sectional data suggest that the reduction in employment is later offset by a tendency for more education to raise labor force participation rates.[3] I do not trace these effects back to education, but leave them classified as effects of employment, hours, or the age-sex composition of employment.[4] It should be noted that the timing of these effects bears no close relationship to changes in the education of the labor force.

6. The more years an individual spends in school the higher is the age at which he enters the labor force. This means that the more educated individuals in any age group have had less work experience than the less educated. In measuring the effect of education on the quality of labor by quality indexes, I measure the excess of the benefit from longer education over the associated loss from curtailed work experience.[5]

7. Additional education, especially general education, presumably increases versatility, mobility, and awareness of employment opportunities. For this reason individuals with more education are more likely than those with less education to find employment where, given their abilities, their marginal value products are greatest. This is one of the subsidiary reasons they earn more. If they lose their positions because of shifts in the demand for labor, they are likely to be able to shift to alternative jobs with less (if any) reduction of earnings and less loss of time in unemployment. These advantages of education are reflected in the education quality indexes.

3. This effect is best known and most pronounced for women and older men but in the United States is evidently also present to a small degree among men in the prime working ages (see Bowen and Finegan, *American Economic Review*, Papers and Proceedings, May 1966, pp. 567–82 [P1]).
4. Any effect of education upon the hours worked by employed persons who have completed their education *is* classified as an effect of education (see p. 85 below).
5. As will be seen below, this is accomplished by basing the weights for individuals with different amounts of education on earnings differentials based on age groups rather than length-of-experience groups.

The Shape of Educational Distributions

Distributions of the labor force by amount of education differ radically in the United States and Northwest Europe, and the Italian distribution is very different from both. Knowledge of the shape of the distributions is necessary background for the ensuing discussion.

Distributions of males by years of education for four countries are given in Table 8–1. (Distributions

TABLE 8–1

Percentage Distributions of the Male Labor Force by Years of School Completed, Four Countries, Selected Dates

Years of school completed	United States 1957	France 1954	United Kingdom 1951	Italy 1961
0	1.4	.3	.2	13.7[b]
1–4	5.7	2.4	.2	26.1[b]
5–6	6.3	19.2[a]	.8	38.0[c]
7	5.8	21.1	4.0	4.2
8	17.2	27.8	27.2	8.1
9	6.3	4.6	45.1	.7
10	7.3	4.1	8.4	.7
11	6.0	6.5	7.3	.6
12	26.2	5.4	2.5	1.8
13–15	8.3	5.4	2.2	3.0
16 or more	9.5	3.2	2.1	3.1

Source: See Appendix F, Section II, for derivation.
a. Largely at 6 years.
b. As indicated subsequently in the text, the percentage with 0 years probably is overstated and the percentage with 1–4 years correspondingly understated.
c. Consists of 33.8 percent at 5 years and 4.2 percent at 6 years.

for some other countries, and for females, are given in Appendix F, Section II.) Table 8–1 does not compare identical dates but this has little effect on a comparison of the shape of the distributions.

The dominant feature of most Northwest European distributions, as illustrated by the United Kingdom and France, is extreme concentration at a level governed by past legal school attendance requirements. In the United Kingdom fully 72 percent of the 1951 labor force had either 8 or 9 years of education. This corresponds to the legal requirement for school attendance from age 5 to 13 years at the time the older age groups had attended school, and 5 to 14 when the younger groups attended school. (The 1947 change to 15 years affected only the very youngest age group by 1951.) Few escaped the legal requirement; only 5 percent had less than 8 years of school, and most of these had 7 years. On the other hand, only the exceptional worker had remained in school after the age at which the law allowed him to leave (unlike most countries, it did not require him to complete the school year), and very few continued after the extra year readily available to all. Of the male British labor force only 16 percent had 10 or 11 years of education, and a scant 7 percent 12 years or more. Even now most British children leave school as soon as legally allowed, although the percentage is dropping rapidly. Of British boys and girls 15 years old, only 40 percent in 1957–58 and 47 percent in 1962–63 were receiving full-time education. At age 16 the percentages were 22 and 28.5, respectively.

Extreme concentration also characterizes the French distribution. There were, however, the following differences. First, because the French student started a year later than the British student and (at most dates) left at the same age, the concentration is at 7 and 8 years of education rather than at 8 and 9. Second, more of the French labor force fell below the level that the legal school-leaving age would seem to yield. Even so, about two-thirds of the French labor force had 6 to 8 years of education. Third, in both countries just under one-fourth had 10 or more years of education, but in contrast to the 7 percent with 12 or more years of education and the 16 percent with 10 or 11 in the United Kingdom, France had about twice as large a percentage at the level that includes graduates of high schools, universities, teachers colleges, and technical institutes (12 years or more) and 11 percent with only 10 or 11 years.[6]

The extreme concentration of the labor force shown for the United Kingdom and France is typical of the Northwest European countries but the Netherlands, with a large secondary concentra-

tion at 10 and 11 years, is an exception and Belgium also probably has less concentration than the other countries.

The tendency to leave school as soon as allowed may never have been quite as strong in some of the continental countries as it was in the United Kingdom, and clearly is breaking down more rapidly in some of them. Voluntary continuation of education is most common in Belgium. Even by the immediate postwar years, 68 to 70 percent of the 14- and 15-year-olds in Belgium (where 14 has been the school-leaving age since the 1920's) were in school and the percentage has been rising about 1 point a year. Voluntary continuation is also quite prevalent in the Netherlands. In France, only 5 percent of the children continued after compulsory schooling (then completed at age 13) in 1914 but by 1950, 42 percent, and by 1962, 70 percent, were continuing after compulsory schooling (then completed at age 14).[7] In Germany, in contrast, voluntary continuation of education is even less common than in the United Kingdom. Only 39 percent in 1960 and 37 percent in 1963 were continuing full-time education after the 8 or 9 years required (the latter was the minimum in Länder having one-ninth the total German population).[8] Voluntary continuation was also low in Denmark until very recently when a great change occurred: By 1964 the percentage leaving after the compulsory 7 years had fallen to 27 percent.[9]

The Italian distribution is also highly concentrated, but the concentration occurs at the bottom of the distribution, corresponding to compulsory education of only 3 years when the older age groups were in school, and 5 or 6 when the younger age groups (except the very youngest) were in school. Lax enforcement and inadequate school facilities

---

6. France had half again as many as Britain with 16 or more years of education. From tables in Great Britain, Committee on Higher Education, *Higher Education*, App. Four, Pt. V [G40], one can derive an estimate that, in 1961, 1.6 percent of the British male labor force had obtained the equivalent of *some* higher education through part-time courses or private study. If all of these were transferred from the 13–15 to the 16-plus group (which could hardly be justified) and no adjustment were made for France, the British percentage at the 16-plus level would equal the French but the comparison in the text would be unaffected.

7. The figures cited in this paragraph are mainly from EEC, "Formation professionnelle des travailleurs qualifiés dans les pays de la C.E.E.," Brussels: Communauté Economique Européenne, 1963 (mimeo.), and from Le Thanh Khoi, *Revue Economique*, January 1966, p. 5 [P40].

8. Council of Europe, Council for Cultural Co-operation, *School Systems: A Guide*, pp. 93, 95 [161]. The percentages given are those for children who did not continue their studies in general education minus the percentages of 15-year-olds enrolled in full-time vocational schools (Berufsfachschule).

9. *Ibid.*, p. 79. (See also ILO, *European Apprenticeship: Effects of Educational, Social and Technical Development on Apprenticeship Training in Eight Countries*, p. 202 [18].)

accompanied the low school-leaving age. Nearly three-fourths of the whole male labor force in 1961 had 5 years or less of education. In Italy alone among the countries considered in this study illiteracy was still important in the period examined. The Italian distribution has a small secondary concentration at 8 years (corresponding to the "Licenza di scuola media inferiore"); a nearly complete gap in the 9- to 11-year range (which includes only the estimated number starting but not completing work for a diploma); and, perhaps surprisingly, numbers with 13 or more years of education that lie between the French and British figures.

To an American, the most extraordinary feature of the European distributions is the paucity of people who have completed secondary education without continuing to advanced education. In some countries, in fact, hardly anyone who did not plan to go to the university entered an advanced secondary course. Even in recent years the proportion of secondary school graduates (itself a very small fraction of the appropriate age group) who do not actually enter higher education has typically ranged downward from around one-third; it is about one-fifth in France and Germany.[10] The proportion is almost one-half (of a vastly larger number completing secondary education) in the United States. The European distributions are remarkably lacking in individuals corresponding to American high school graduates.

The distribution of the United States labor force bears no resemblance to the European distributions. Educational background is diverse. There is but little concentration at any one point or in any narrow range. Whereas a 3-year span can cover two-thirds of the distribution in France and three-fourths in the United Kingdom, only 40 percent of the American male labor force can be covered in any 3-year span (at 10 to 12 years). Large numbers appear at the lower and upper ranges of the distribution as well as in the middle. In 1957 nearly one-fifth had 7 or fewer years of schooling, many of them much less. Almost as large a fraction had 13 or more years, representing at least one year of college completed; almost one-tenth had graduated from college, and nearly half of these had one or

more years of graduate work. In the middle, 17 percent had 8 years of school, 20 percent were about equally divided among the 9-, 10-, and 11-year levels, and 26 percent had 12 years of schooling.

The great dispersion in the United States reflects in part (especially at the bottom) past differences among states and changes over time in the provisions and enforcement of school attendance and child labor laws. Far more important in determining the distribution as a whole, however, is the fact that compulsory school attendance laws have not been, and are not now, decisive in governing the time at which most Americans leave school; if they were, most Americans would now end their education on their sixteenth birthday after 9 or 10 years of schooling. Such concentrations as occur in the distribution correspond to completion of some type of school. These fall at 16 years for college, 14 for junior college, 12 for high school, 9 for junior high school, 8 (formerly 7 in the South) for the older type of elementary school, and 6 for the newer type.

Extremely important on the American scene has been the availability of free public education far beyond the requirements of school attendance laws. But this would have accomplished little unless the opportunities were freely grasped. To a great extent they have been, because of the widespread faith of American parents that education is the key to future advancement; the child should and could rise above the station of the parent, and the way to do so was to obtain more education. The process was, of course, cumulative. Faith in education led to the demand for free public schools and colleges available to all; availability facilitated the rise in educational achievement; and this led to a rise in the level considered normal or necessary. But this process created not uniformity but great dispersion of the length of education in each age group and, of course, great differences among age groups.

Quality Indexes Over Time

The calculation of indexes of the effect of education on the quality of labor requires two types of information. First, it requires a set of weights to

10. See OECD, *Resources of Scientific and Technical Personnel in the* OECD *Area*, pp. 70–74, 82–83 [I38].

combine individuals with different amounts of education. (Is a college graduate to be counted as the equivalent of 1½, 2, or 3 elementary school graduates?) Second, distributions are needed of the labor force by amount of schooling at different dates, to which these weights may be applied.

Weights for the United States

Suppose the United States labor force is divided among groups consisting of college graduates, those with 1 to 3 years of college, high school graduates, and so on, according to a classification similar to the one adopted in Table 8-2. The selection of weights for each group would be simple if the members of each group differed only in education and were similar in all other respects that affect earnings—that is, if they were divided in the same proportions by age, sex, native ability and energy, family background, and so on. In that case the average earnings of members of each group, taken as measuring their marginal value product, would provide the appropriate weights. If the average earnings of college graduates were double those of high school graduates, one college graduate would be counted as the equivalent of two high school graduates. But the different education groups do differ substantially in other respects, and the necessity of eliminating the effects of these differences makes the selection of weights more difficult.

The effect of differences in sex and, approximately, age was first eliminated. The 1949 average income of males cross-classified by highest school grade completed and age, and the 1959 average earnings of males in the labor force, similarly cross-classified, were known. For each age group the average income (1949) or earnings (1959) of males in each education group was expressed as a percentage of the average income or earnings of those with 8 years of education.[11] The percentages for the several age groups were then averaged. The resulting differentials for 1949 are shown in Column 1, Table 8-2. Appendix Table F-2 compares

11. Data were used for age classes 25-34, 35-44, 45-54, and 55-64. Since the 1949 data include persons not in the labor force, and even the 1959 data include persons working part time, age groups which include substantial numbers not in the labor force or working part time and occasionally could not be used. Differentials for the separate age groups in 1959 are shown in Appendix Table F-1.

TABLE 8-2

United States Income Differentials by Years of School Completed, 1949: Average of Selected Age Classes of Males

Highest level of school completed	Usual number of years of education required	Mean income as a percentage of mean income of eighth grade graduates	
		Actual (1)	Used for education weights (2)
None	0	50	70
Elementary School			
1 to 4 years	1–4	65	79
5 to 7 years	5–7	80	88
8 years	8	100	100
High School			
1 to 3 years	9–11	115	109
4 years	12	140	124
College			
1 to 3 years	13–15	165	139
4 years or more	16 or more	235	181

Source: Denison, *Sources of Economic Growth*, p. 68 [B25].

them with 1959 earnings indexes. Use of the 1959 earnings indexes, which became available after the computations were made, would be more appropriate, but they are so similar that their substitution would not alter the education quality indexes.

Differences in amount of education and the loss of work experience due to additional education clearly are not the only remaining elements that distinguish the education groups. Hence average earnings cannot be used without adjustment to measure earnings differences that are *due to* differences in education and associated loss of experience. The higher the education group, the higher is the proportion of individuals who had obtained high marks in earlier schooling, who had scored well on standardized intelligence tests, who had attended the better schools at lower educational levels, and who also had parents who were themselves well educated and had substantial incomes. After examining the available information, I decided in my United States study to assume that three-fifths of the reported income differential between each of the other groups and the group with 8 years of education represented differences in earnings *due to* differences in education as distinguished from other associated characteristics. This assumption yielded the adjusted differentials shown in Column 2, Table 8-2. These were used for weights in my study of American economic growth and I use them again in the present study. Taking the labor of a person with 8 years of education as 1 unit, I count the labor of a person with no education as 0.70 units, of a person with 12 years of education as 1.24 units, of a college graduate as 1.81 units, and so on.

The three-fifths assumption on which these weights rest was originally based on no statistical procedure but only a general impression derived from examining the characteristics of different education groups. Subsequently, support for the differentials used in the upper range of the distribution was obtained from an analysis of data collected by Dael Wolfle and Joseph P. Smith.[12] Their survey provided the 1953 earnings of male high school graduates of the mid-1930's for whom high school records and respondents' answers provided a great deal of collateral information. The survey made possible an effort to isolate the effects of differences in education on income from the effects of the more important measurable associated variables: rank in high-school class, intelligence test scores, father's occupation (taken as an indication of family background), and geographic area (which to a considerable extent removes the effect of quality of high school and of race). After removal of the influence of these associated variables, the analysis indicated that in comparison with high school graduates without college education (but including those with other types of further education), 1 to 3 years of college added 13 percent and 4 or more years of college 45 percent to average earnings. The corresponding percentages calculated from Column 2, Table 8-2, are 12 and 45, respectively. The analysis of the survey results is not definitive or precise. It does, however, give fairly strong support to the general size of the differentials used in the range above high school.

The survey analysis suggested that two-thirds of the salary differential of college graduates over the high school group is "due to" education.[13] Table

8-2, which is based on the assumption that three-fifths of the differential between every other group and the 8th grade group is "due to" education, also happens to imply that two-thirds of the differential between high school and college graduates is "due to" education. The experiment was made of using the survey analysis for differentials above the high school level, and assuming that up to the high school level two-thirds of the differential of earnings at each educational level distinguished (as given in Column 1, Table 8-2) above earnings at the next lower level was "due to" education. The resulting differentials are almost identical with those given in Column 2, Table 8-2, except that the weight for the "no education" group, which is applied to very few people, would be lowered from 70 to 65.[14]

There has been no general tendency for earnings differentials to narrow since 1949 despite the increase in education. In particular the differential between high school and college graduates has not narrowed—the data even suggest some widening— even though the percentage increase in the number of male college graduates has much exceeded that of male high school graduates since 1949 (Appendix Table F-9).[15] Apparently the pattern of demand for persons with different amounts of education has been shifting toward the most educated group at least as rapidly as the supply or else the elasticity of substitution among education groups is very high.[16]

The education weights derived for males are also

12. The analysis is given in OECD, *The Residual Factor and Economic Growth*, pp. 86-100 [143].

13. It may be noted that the results cited here refer to what I considered the best way to analyze the Wolfle-Smith survey results [143]; an alternative procedure that I also explored allocated higher fractions of the crude differential to education as distinguished from associated variables.

14. Gary S. Becker has also explored the fraction of observed income differentials that is "due to" education. His published results are difficult to compare with mine but he appears to imply a moderately higher fraction above the high school level. One of two studies he cites (the J. Morgan-M. H. David study) may suggest a lower fraction of the elementary-high school differential than I have used but this is not very clear because some of the variables that were used to eliminate the influence of other factors were themselves affected by education. The second study (by Donald E. Gorseline) yields a fraction about the same as I have used. See Becker, *Human Capital*, Chapters V and VI [B10].

15. See Miller, *American Economic Review*, December 1960, pp. 962-86 [P1]; Denison in OECD, *The Residual Factor and Economic Growth*, pp. 13-55 [143]; and Morgan and Lininger, *Quarterly Journal of Economics*, May 1964, pp. 346-47 [P34].

16. In the OECD paper just cited I note the possibility that, in the *lower* part of the distribution, differentials between education groups in natural ability and other associated variables may be widening.

used for females in the absence of separate information for women in the labor force. Since females receive only about one-fifth of the weight in the calculations (see below), this assumption is unlikely to introduce serious error.[17] Use of the same percentage differentials implies that *absolute* differentials are much smaller for females since their average earnings are much lower.

In the United States employed persons with more education work more hours per year than those with less education. Because my education weights are derived from annual earnings, the quality adjustment indexes derived from them reflect, and my estimates of the contribution of education to growth therefore include, the effect of changes in education upon hours worked. In other words, insofar as an increase in the education of the labor force raises hours worked above what they would be otherwise, this is classified as an effect of increased education.[18]

17. Victor Fuchs has compiled estimates based on the 1960 U.S. population census returns that suggest differentials between education groups in female annual earnings in 1959 were not systematically wider or narrower than differentials in male earnings (except for those with 0–4 years of schooling) but did differ irregularly. His data, which are not yet published, refer to *nonagricultural* employed persons with earnings. Ratios of female to male average earnings in each of the four 10-year age groups within the 25–64 range were calculated. The averages of these ratios were as follows for various years-of-education classes:

0–4	.50	12	.46
5–8	.44	13–15	.44
9–11	.45	16 or more	.44

These data became available after the calculations for this study had been completed.

As indicated below I also use male differentials for females in the European countries. No direct check is available. Data for the nonfarm labor force of Canada, which like that of Europe has less education than that of the United States, show that in Canada percentage differentials are a little larger for females than for males. For the four 10-year age groups, 25–64, the average ratio of female to male earnings for the Canadian nonfarm labor force for the year ending May 31, 1961, was 0.46 for those with elementary schooling, 0.47 for high school graduates, and 0.48 for those with a university degree (Podoluk, *Earnings and Education,* p. 21 [G76]).

18. This is not troublesome in itself but it points up an inconsistency with my procedure to measure the effect of changes in hours worked in the United States. The indexes of hours worked by nonagricultural wage and salary workers (Table 6–5) are based on the average hours worked by all education groups combined. For consistency with the education estimates they should be based upon weighted averages of separate indexes for each educational level. Such indexes would presumably decline from 1950 to 1962 relative to the indexes shown and result in a larger negative contribution to growth from changes in hours worked than the —0.16 percentage points at which I arrive. Consequently,

TABLE 8–3

Earnings Weights Used for Different Education Groups in the United States, Northwest Europe, and Italy

Years of school completed	United States	Northwest Europe	Italy
0	70	70	50
1–4	79	79	65
5–7	88	88	80
8	100	100	100
9–11	109	122	122
12	124	139	139
13–15	139	152	152
16 or more	181	194	194
Supplementary Detailed Weights			
5–6	86	86	—
7	95	95	—
9	104	107	—
10–11	111	129	—
16	170	180	—
17 or more	195	210	—

Sources: See text and Appendix F, Section I, for derivation.

The Weights for Europe

It is impossible to derive separate sets of weights for the education groups in each of the individual Northwest European countries from information now available and I use the same weights for all these countries.[19] They are given in Table 8–3. Those shown in the upper panel of the table for the 8-year and higher education levels are adjustments of data for France, the country for which the most adequate European data on earnings differentials by amount of education are available. As in the United States I assumed that three-fifths of earnings differentials from the 8-year level are due to education. The differential between the 8-year and 16-plus levels is larger in the European than in the United States set of weights, but the main difference is that indexes at the intermediate levels are much higher.

Information concerning earnings differentials in the United States and France is reviewed and compared with information available for other coun-

when my estimates for the effect of changes in hours and changes in education are combined, the rise in the quality of labor is slightly overstated.

19. This has the incidental advantage of facilitating comparisons of quality indexes among the Northwest European countries.

tries in Appendix F, Section I. Comparisons of earnings differentials in different countries are difficult because the educational classifications utilized, the summary measures available, and the "industrial" and "class of worker" coverage are not uniform. Those attempted in Appendix F tend to confirm the conclusion from French data that differentials between those with about 8 years of education and those with 16 or more years are larger but not much larger in Northwest Europe than in the United States, and that earnings of those with around 10 to 15 years of education are much higher relative to both higher and lower groups than in the United States. (Dutch data did not support the latter finding.)

None of the European data distinguish among individuals with different amounts of elementary education. For those with less than 8 years I have used United States indexes. Very few Northwest Europeans have less than 5 years of schooling so the weights assigned to the two least educated groups have a negligible effect.

Because a major part of the increase in European education has resulted from discrete one-year-at-a-time increases in the legal school leaving age, it is necessary to assign separate weights to each individual years-of-education class at the affected levels. Unless this is done, an increase in the school-leaving age will have no effect if the change falls within an education class (as from 6 to 7 years, or 9 to 10) and an exaggerated effect if it moves individuals between groups (as from 7 to 8, or 8 to 9). I have therefore assigned separate weights for individual years-of-education classes, largely by interpolation of the United States indexes, and used them wherever the data are affected by changes or differences in the legal school leaving age or are highly concentrated within a broader group.[20] For some calculations a distinction between 16 and 17-plus years is also useful. The detailed weights are shown in the lower half of Table 8–3.

20. There are no actual data that yield usable earnings differentials by one-year education classes just below or above the school leaving age in Europe. Such information would be difficult to obtain because in any age group the concentration at exactly the school leaving age is so great. In the French survey, data were collected and classified by age of leaving school. The few who left one year beyond the legal age were mainly those who required an extra year to complete the same school grade as those who left at the compulsory age.

The finding that the earnings of individuals with a secondary education are higher in Europe than in the United States relative to those with less or more education was not surprising in view of the great scarcity of such persons in Europe.[21] I had anticipated that the European earnings differentials between those with an elementary education and those with higher education would exceed those in the United States by more than the bulk of the evidence indicates to be the case.

The educational levels and distributions in the Northwest European countries are sufficiently similar to one another to make use of the same weights for all these countries plausible. The Italian distribution, on the other hand, is very different. Adults with even 7 or 8 years of education comprise a select group in Italy since the bulk of the labor force is below this level. Much larger earnings differentials therefore seem probable at the lower end of the distribution.[22] Weights assigned these groups have a far greater effect on the calculations for Italy than for other countries. For Italy, I shall use the Northwest European differentials above the 8-year level and below that level—quite arbitrarily—the United States earnings differentials *before* adjustment for correlation with other variables. The differentials below the 8-year level are thus five-thirds as large as those used for the United States and Northwest Europe.

The male percentage differentials are used for

21. Errors in the allowances for ability and other elements could provide a partial alternative explanation of higher relative earnings at this level. M. Blaug (in *Manchester School of Economic and Social Studies,* September 1965, p. 216 [P28]) suggests that secondary school graduates in the United Kingdom differ more in these respects from those with less education, but less from university graduates, than they do in the United States. He believes that the British selection process is largely completed when students enter the "advanced sixth forms." Division of my unadjusted by my adjusted indexes shows that implied earnings differentials *not* due to education are 13 percent in the United States and 19 percent in Europe between the 8-year and 12-year levels, and are 15 percent in the United States and 12 percent in Europe between the 12-year and the 16-plus levels. The difference between the two areas in my allowances is thus in the direction suggested by Blaug but may not go far enough.

22. Very large differentials appear in Latin American countries (Colombia and Mexico) that also have low-pitched educational distributions according to data by Camacho in *Rendimiento de la Inversión en Educación en Colombia* [B16], and data collected by Martin Carnoy, "The Cost and Return to Schooling in Mexico" (unpublished Ph.D. dissertation, University of Chicago, September 1964).

females in the European countries as well as in the United States.

It is apparent that the larger the differentials in the weighting system adopted, the more a quality adjustment index will rise over time as the education of the labor force increases. If the differentials are too large, the index will rise too much; if too little, not enough. Also, the size of the error in a quality adjustment index resulting from weighting errors is related directly to the change in the quality index. For example, if the differentials in the weights used were *uniformly* only two-thirds as large as they should be, and if for two countries the quality of labor is estimated to increase 2 percent and 4 percent, respectively, as a result of increased education, then the "true" changes would be 3 percent and 6 percent. However, if the error is in an intermediate index there is usually a substantial offset; the effect on the quality index as individuals move up to that group will be overstated while the effect of moving up to a still higher group will be understated.

Labor Force Distributions by Amount of Education; Computation of Quality Indexes

Calculation of quality indexes for education requires distributions of the labor force by amount of education in the years to be compared, to which these weights can be applied. These distributions are needed separately for males and females, so that separate quality indexes can be computed for each.

If distributions of the labor force of each sex, classified in terms of an unchanging measure of educational attainment, were available for each of the key years used in this study (1950, 1955, 1960, and 1962), computation of education quality indexes for males and females would be simple. The average quality of each sex in each year could be calculated by weighting the proportion in each education group by the weight for that group in Table 8–3. The estimates for males and females would then be converted to indexes, with 1960 equal to 100. For most countries more complex procedures were actually required to approximate the indexes for males and females that would be obtained by

this procedure, and there is inevitably some question as to whether the measures of education used are actually unchanging.[23]

The quality index for the labor force as a whole is a weighted average of the separate indexes for male and female civilians and an index for the armed forces (taken always as 100 since the output measures do not allow for differences in the quality of labor). The weights used, shown in Table 8–4, are

TABLE 8-4

Percentage Distributions of Labor Input Among Male and Female Civilians and Military Personnel, 1960

Area	Male civilians	Female civilians	Military personnel
United States	77.9	18.9	3.2
Northwest Europe	77.4	20.6	2.0
Belgium	79.4	18.0	2.6
Denmark	76.3	22.1	1.6
France	75.7	20.8	3.5
Germany	75.1	23.9	1.0
Netherlands	85.2	12.4	2.4
Norway	80.2	17.3	2.5
United Kingdom	79.1	19.1	1.8
Italy	80.7	17.8	1.5

Sources: United States and Northwest Europe: Table 7–6; similar computations for the individual European countries.

the labor input (earnings) weights for 1960 derived in Chapter 7. They are similar to those that were given for the United States and Northwest Europe in Table 7–6.[24] Females, of course, receive a weight much smaller than their share in the labor force, and the movement of the quality indexes is dominated by the indexes for male civilians.

UNITED STATES ESTIMATES. Distributions of the United States labor force by highest school grade completed are available from labor force surveys for one month in each of the years 1948, 1952, 1957, 1959, 1962, 1964, and 1965 (Appendix Table F–9). Quality indexes were computed for

23. In this chapter I give only a broad picture of the approach and the quality of the data. The estimates for each country are described in Appendix F, Section II.

24. Full consistency with Chapter 7 would have required separate educational quality indexes for three age groups within each sex. This further refinement was not practical. More refined indexes would presumably tend to lag slightly behind those computed here because the youngest age group has the lowest earnings. In the unlikely event of a sudden sharp break in the growth rates of the education quality indexes, this could disturb the timing of changes.

these dates and interpolated to obtain estimates as of the middle of the desired years. These are shown, for males, females, and all civilians, in Columns 1 to 3, Table 8–5.

TABLE 8–5

United States: Estimation of Education Quality Indexes

(1960 = 100)

| | Preliminary indexes based on years of school completed | | | Final indexes allowing for changes in days of education per year of school completed | |
| | Male civilians (1) | Female civilians (2) | Civilian labor force (3) | Civilian labor force (4) | Total labor force (5) |
Year					
1950	94.8	96.5	95.1	92.9	93.1
1955	97.0	98.2	97.2	96.1	96.2
1960	100.0	100.0	100.0	100.0	100.0
1962	101.2	101.2	101.2	101.6	101.5

Sources: See text and Appendix F, Section II, for derivation.

These calculations, however, would imply that a person who had attended school for any given number of years around the year 1900, and was still working in 1950, had an education equivalent to that of a person who attended school for the same number of years in the 1920's or 1950's. Taking the United States as a whole this assumption is not tenable, and an adjustment is required to allow for the fact that the amount of education represented by a year has increased over time.

From 1900 to 1956, according to the United States Office of Education, the average number of days attended per pupil enrolled in public elementary and secondary schools increased from 99 to 158 days per year, the increase being continuous until 1950.[25] This came about in the following way. First, in the large city school systems there was no increase, but actually a small decline, in the average length of the school term.[26] Second, in the smaller cities and towns, in rural schools, and in the South, much shorter school terms were gradually brought

close to the standards of big cities in the North, and in addition enrollment shifted toward the urban areas. In consequence the reported average length of the school term in the country as a whole (with schools in effect weighted by enrollment) rose from 144 days in 1900 to 178 days in 1956.[27] Third, the reported ratio of days of school attended to the product of enrollment and the average number of days in the school term rose from 0.686 percent in 1900 to 0.890 percent in 1956. These ratios suggest more absenteeism than actually existed because enrollment statistics exceed average class membership.[28] Also, the rise in the ratio may overstate the decline in absenteeism if there was a reduction in the gap between enrollment and membership. In any case, the bulk of the rise in this ratio clearly is genuine. It accounts for a greater proportion of the increase in days of school attended per year than does the extension of the school term outside the cities.

I base an allowance for these changes on the assumption that the same number of years of education represents the same amount of education throughout the period for persons attending school regularly in large city school systems, or in college (the emphasis is on *regularly*). The individual who regularly attended for 8 years a rural school system operating (say) 135 days a year is considered to have had only the same education as one who for 6 years regularly attended a city school system operating 180 days. And a pupil who, in either school system, missed (say) one-quarter of his scheduled classes (usually because he was work-

25. The figure increased after 1958; it reached 163 in 1964 (U.S. Bureau of the Census, *Long-Term Economic Growth, 1860–1965,* pp. 196–97 [G58]).
26. The simple average for New York, Philadelphia, Chicago, Los Angeles, and Washington was 188 days in 1900 and 182 in 1960.

27. The situation in recent years has been that almost all state laws require at least 180 days, the exceptions permitting 160 days in rural areas. Large urban school systems are still likely to go somewhat above 180 days and it is a bit surprising that the computed average was not larger than 178 in 1948–60 and 179 in 1962–64. The actual number may vary a little from year to year due to such uncertainties as weather and epidemics, etc. For example, in my own home county—Montgomery County, Maryland—the schedule is set on the assumption that schools will be closed a certain number of scheduled days because of snow. If the actual number of "snow days" falls short of the number anticipated, the school term will be longer than planned, but if it exceeds the planned number the difference is made up by curtailing vacations. In some other jurisdictions this may not be required.
28. In 1957–58 average daily attendance equaled 92.5 percent of average membership, implying true absenteeism, as distinguished from dropouts, duplication of enrollment due to transferring among schools, and the like, was 7.5 percent. These data are not available for early years.

TABLE 8-6
Education Quality Indexes, Alternative Weights, 1950–62
(1950 = 100)

Area	Part A Each area based on its own weights				Part B Each area based on United States weights			
	1950	1955	1960	1962	1950	1955	1960	1962
United States	100.0	103.3	107.4	109.0	100.0	103.3	107.4	109.0
Northwest Europe	100.0	101.8	103.6	104.5	100.0	101.4	102.8	103.5
Belgium	100.0	103.6	107.2	109.1	100.0	103.0	106.0	107.6
Denmark	100.0	101.1	102.2	102.7	100.0	100.9	101.7	102.1
France	100.0	102.2	104.6	105.7	100.0	101.8	103.8	104.6
Germany	100.0	100.9	101.8	102.2	100.0	100.6	101.3	101.7
Netherlands	100.0	102.1	104.2	105.0	100.0	101.5	103.0	103.6
Norway	100.0	102.1	104.2	105.1	100.0	101.7	103.4	104.2
United Kingdom	100.0	102.1	104.4	105.5	100.0	101.7	103.2	104.0
Italy	100.0	103.4	106.9	108.6	100.0	101.9	103.7	104.6

Sources: See text, Table 8–3, and Appendix F, Section II, for derivation.

ing) is treated as having received only three-quarters as much education as a pupil who was present every day for the same number of years.

As older individuals in the labor force are replaced by those educated under more recent conditions, the same number of years of education comes to mean more education. I estimate that the increase in the average quality of the civilian labor force from 1950 to 1962, put at 6.4 percent (as implied by Column 3, Table 8–5) when only changes in years of schooling were considered, should be raised to 9.4 percent (Column 4) to allow for this major development.[29]

EUROPEAN ESTIMATES. When the present study was started data on the education of the labor force were almost wholly lacking for Europe. The gap has now been partially filled thanks to other recent research studies, the cooperation of OECD, and census enumerations. Although information remains much less complete than for the United States, estimates of either the distribution of the labor force by level of education or of the average number of years of education (from which changes in the quality index can be approximated with the

aid of collateral information) could be obtained or derived for certain years for all countries.[30] Appendix F, Section II, describes these data and my use of them to derive quality indexes. The indexes are, of course, offered as approximations rather than as precise measures, but the patterns that emerge are consistent with relevant collateral information.

Table 8–6 provides two sets of quality adjustment indexes for each country. Part A presents indexes based on application of the education weights referring to each area; these are the indexes appropriate for the analysis of growth rates. Part B, which permits a better comparison of countries with respect to changes in the education of the labor force as such, presents similar indexes computed by the uniform application of United States education weights to all areas.

Two general comments are in order. First, the

29. The reader is cautioned that translation of the treatment described in the text to the adjustment of the quality index required some statistical assumptions. These are detailed in Appendix F, Section II. As pointed out there, the allowance made for changes in the number of days in the school year is much smaller than that I used in the *Sources of Economic Growth* [B25].

30. Some of the studies used are unpublished (in some cases because the investigators hope to incorporate still-unavailable results of the censuses for 1960 or 1961) and I am indebted to the authors for making them available to me. I particularly acknowledge the aid, in either furnishing data or helping me to interpret available education statistics, of the following: E. Raymaekers and M. Frank in Belgium; Henning Friis and colleagues at the National Institute of Social Research and Einar Kallsberg, in Denmark; Michel Debeauvais and colleagues at the Research Institute of Economic and Social Development in France; Hermann Schubnell and Friedrich Edding in Germany; P. J. Verdoorn in the Netherlands; Anne-Marie Arnesen in Norway; and Rose Knight in the United Kingdom. Giovanni Ruffo reviewed the estimates for Italy and George A. Male the chapter as a whole.

computations usually were not based on data referring to the specific years shown; the indexes are interpolations between available years, sometimes only one year near the beginning and one near the end of the period. This is not a serious limitation on the estimated change over the 1950–62 period as a whole, but does mean that the subdivision between the 1950–55 and 1955–62 periods has no claim to accuracy in the European estimates. The second comment concerns changes in the number of days of school attended per school year in Europe.

In France and Denmark, as in large American cities, the scheduled length of the school year has declined a little since the turn of the century due to an increase in the length of vacations.[31] Data for other countries, most of which also operate national school systems, were not available but such a change is likely to have been rather general. No evidence was found of any lengthening of the school year such as occurred in the United States outside the large cities. I agree with Michel Debeauvais and his colleagues, from whose study the French data were taken, that it is sensible to ignore this change, particularly since the number of school years required to attain particular certificates or degrees was not changed on this account. The more important question concerns absenteeism.

In the United Kingdom there has been a substantial reduction in absenteeism and an adjustment to allow for this, similar to that made for the United States, was introduced in the quality adjustment indexes. From 1950 to 1962 past reductions in absenteeism are estimated to have raised the quality index for civilians by 0.8 percent; without this adjustment, the United Kingdom indexes for 1962 in Table 8–6 would be lower by approximately this amount (based on either Northwest European or United States weights). This is less than one-third the size of the similar adjustment of 2.8 percent in the United States (including the effect of lengthening the school year outside large cities).

Data for the continental countries of Northwest Europe were secured only for France and the Netherlands. In France there apparently has been no reduction in absenteeism since 1900, as indicated by a ratio of the number of pupils present to enrolled students that has been almost constant at around 90 percent. The reported ratios before that were 75 percent in 1851, 77 percent in 1876, and 78.6 percent in 1891.[32] Apparently France, where the national government assumed extensive control under a law of 1886, was several decades ahead of the United States in reaching a stable ratio. According to this evidence, no upward adjustment of the movement of the quality adjustment index for the increase in the number of days attended per school year, such as was made for the United States, is needed for France.[33] Dutch data provide the number of absences from elementary schools per 10,000 class periods, divided between excused absences (such as those for sickness) and unexcused absences. Data are available for a large number of years scattered over the period from 1902 to 1950.[34] They show no trend at all (though some irregular fluctuation) in excused absences. Unexcused absences dropped from 1.33 percent in 1902 to a negligible figure of 0.05 percent in 1950. The percentage of students present averaged 93.4 percent in three years from 1902 to 1905, 94.8 in three years from 1921 through 1927, 95.0 in five years from 1930 through 1935, and 95.1 in three years from 1948 through 1950. The change was too small to have any noticeable effect on quality indexes and no adjustment was made.

In the absence of information covering a long period for the other continental countries of Northwest Europe I assume that the situation was similar and introduce no adjustment for changes in the length of the school year or in absenteeism. The opinion expressed by nearly all informed persons

31. French data are from Michel Debeauvais, Jacqueline Pillet, Pierre Maes, and Nicolas Panayotakis, "L'Education de la Population française et son Evolution de 1850 à 1980," Paris: Institut d'Etude de Développement Economique et Social, August 1963 (mimeo.). Danish data back to 1911 consistent with those given in the Statistical Department, *Børneskolen, 1957–61* [G6] were obtained by correspondence, April 1965.

32. Data are from Debeauvais, Pillet, Maes, and Panayotakis, "L'Education . . . 1850 à 1980" (note 31). The authors believe the true rise was less than this because of numerous duplicate enrollments in the earlier data.

33. The French estimate for 1946 (which I averaged with a 1954 estimate to obtain 1950) does incorporate an adjustment, referring to members of the 1946 labor force who were educated before 1900, but it is so negligible that its effect on my 1950 estimate can be ignored. See Appendix F, Section II.

34. Data are published in various issues of *Jaarcijfers voor Nederland* [G23].

queried is that there has been little or no increase in the number of days attended per year of school during this century. I confess some skepticism concerning this evidence, in view of the large rural populations in most countries, the improvement of transportation, and the advances in medicine.[35] But it does seem that any downward bias over time on this account in the Northwest European indexes, absolutely and relatively to the United States index, is not large. To add 0.1 percentage points to the growth rate of the education quality indexes in Northwest European price weights (1.2 points to the 1962 index) the change would have to have been half again as large as in the United Kingdom. A change as large as this seems unlikely.

In Italy school attendance is still irregular in some areas, especially but not only in the South, and actual school terms vary. I think it must be assumed that the average number of days attended per year has been rising. As indicated in Appendix F, Section II, I have tried to make rough allowance for this in the distributions of the labor force by years of education rather than to attempt a specific adjustment for changes in days of education per year. Except at the bottom, my educational distributions for Italy were obtained by translating degrees or certificates into years of education. I have supposed that the same degree or certificate obtained at different times represented equivalent education, so that if more years were required to obtain it in the past than now, because of absenteeism, this is automatically allowed for. An adjustment at the bottom of the distribution involves the division between those with no education and those with 1 to 4 years of school.

Inter-Country Quality Indexes

The procedure used for time series can also be applied to obtain an international comparison of the quality of labor if it is assumed that—subject to examination and modification—individuals with the

35. Indirect evidence mentioned in Appendix F, Section II, and comments by Jean Debiesse (in *Compulsory Education in France*, pp. 33–36 [I4]) even raise doubts that there has been no decline in absenteeism in France.

TABLE 8–7

Education Quality Indexes, Based on United States Weights, 1960

(*United States* = 100)

Area	Based on years of school completed (1)	Based on age of leaving school (2)	Average (final estimates) (3)
United States	100.0	100.0	100.0
Northwest Europe	93.3	92.2	92.7
Belgium	93.9	90.3	92.1
Denmark	88.3	95.5	91.9
France	92.5	91.9	92.2
Germany	90.9	92.7	91.8
Netherlands	94.8	96.6	95.7
Norway	90.7	97.9	94.3
United Kingdom	96.9	90.9	93.9
Italy	79.7	82.1	80.9

Sources: See text and Appendix F, Section II, for derivation.

same number of years of education in the various countries have an equivalent education. Indexes so computed, with the United States level taken as 100, are given in Column 1, Table 8–7. United States weights are used in this comparison.

The specific assumption underlying this column is that, for persons receiving their education in very recent years, the same number of years of education represents equivalent education. For comparisons involving the United States this is quite different from an alternative assumption that, for all persons in the labor force, the same number of years of education represents equivalent education. Its importance may be indicated by describing the calculation of the index for France given in Column 1, Table 8–7.

When the United States education weights are applied to distributions of the labor force in 1960, and the quality of those with 8 years of education is taken as 100, computed quality indexes for the civilian labor force (weighted averages of indexes for males and females) of 118.9 for the United States and 103.6 for France are obtained. But the adjustment made for changes in days per school year in the United States implies that the quality of civilian labor in the United States in 1960 was only 94.5 percent of what it would have been if all age groups had attended school for as many days per year as recent students. For comparison with other countries, the United States index is therefore multiplied by 94.5 percent, which reduces the United States index to 112.4. Thus it is calculated that the average educational quality of the French civilian labor force is 103.6 ÷ 112.4, or 92.2 percent, of the American quality. When the quality of the armed forces is taken as equal in the two countries for familiar reasons, the percentage for the entire labor force becomes 92.5, the figure given in Column 1, Table 8–7. All the Northwest European indexes except that for the United Kingdom are about 5.5 percent higher than they would be if the "days adjustment" had not been made in the United States. They are too high if some similar (though much smaller) adjustment should have been made in Europe. The United Kingdom index is 4.5 percent higher than if no adjustment had been made for either country.

The comparison given in the first column of Table 8–7 is not my final estimate of the comparative educational quality of the labor forces. A further adjustment, described below, will be introduced.

Use of Years of Education: Alternatives and Limitations

The quality adjustment indexes just described assume that individuals obtaining the same number of years of full-time schooling in different countries at the present time receive, on the average, equivalent educations. In the comparison of different dates in one country, it was assumed the same number of years represented equivalent education except for the special adjustments for days of education introduced explicitly for the United States and United Kingdom and implicitly for Italy.

It is instructive to consider limitations of this procedure, and some possible alternatives and modifications. Most of these alternatives would hardly affect time series within a particular country, but some would affect the comparison of countries. One (the second considered) leads me to modify the international comparison based on years of education.

Hours in School

Without departing from the use of time spent in school, total hours or total days rather than total years might have been used as a common denominator to compare countries. It was not possible to make direct comparisons of hours or days spent in school by the labor force; however, estimates given for the recent school population in Table 8–8 permit the effects of these alternatives to be evaluated. Even comparisons for recent students are extraordinarily difficult but the results should portray the general situation.

Columns 1 to 3 show, respectively, the average number of scheduled days per year, hours per day, and hours per year spent in classes. Only the last of these, hours per year, provides a reasonably valid comparison. The first two columns, taken separately, are almost meaningless because of differences in schedules. American schools operate 5 days, of equal length, a week. European schools operate, variously, 5 full days, 6 full days, 4 full days and 2 half days (perhaps the most common arrangement), 5 full days and 1 half day, or 3 full days and 3 half days. Although Column 1 counts half days as one-half, this goes only part way toward obtaining comparability; German and Italian elementary schools, for example, operate 6 days of equal length, but the children do not return after lunch and the schedule (9 a.m. to 1:10 p.m. in Italy) approximates half days in some other countries. However, in Column 1 all 6 days are counted as full days.

The division of weekly hours among the days of the week in Europe is a matter of convenience and is not considered to affect the quality or content of education. Similar schools in the same system often operate with the same weekly hours but different daily schedules, and changeovers are made from one schedule to another (recently, for example, in parts of Holland from 4 full and 2 half days to 5 full days) without change in curriculum.

This particular difficulty is not encountered in comparisons of the number of scheduled hours per year, given in Column 3. Although equal to the product of Columns 1 and 2, scheduled hours per year are better thought of as the product of weekly hours and number of school weeks, reduced on a

TABLE 8-8

Time Spent in School by Recent Students[a] and Possible Alternative
Adjustments to 1960 Education Quality Indexes

Area	Time per year of schooling			Time spent in school during school career					Possible adjustment (in percentage points) to education quality adjustment indexes, based on hours per year (9)
	Number of scheduled days per year[b] (1)	Number of scheduled hours per day[b] (2)	Number of scheduled hours per year (3)	Number			Indexes (United States = 100)		
				Years (4)	Scheduled hours (5)	United States equivalent years based on annual hours[c] (6)	Years (7)	Scheduled hours (8)	
United States	180	5.69	1,024	12.90	13,210	12.90	100	100	—
Northwest Europe	200	5.32	1,069	10.26	10,968	10.71	80	83	2.7
Belgium	198	5.39[d]	1,071	11.39	12,199	11.91	88	92	3.1
Denmark	212	5.08	1,079	8.84	9,539	9.32	69	72	2.9
France	184	5.54	1,019	10.74	10,944	10.69	83	83	−.3
Germany	229	4.83	1,110	9.13	10,134	9.90	71	77	4.6
Netherlands	202	5.41	1,092	10.43	11,390	11.12	81	86	4.1
Norway	193[e]	5.62	1,086	9.99	10,849	10.59	77	82	3.6
United Kingdom	189	5.64[f]	1,069	10.96	11,716	11.44	85	89	2.9
Italy	202	4.47	902	8.86	7,992	7.80	69	60	−6.4

Source: See Appendix F, Section III, for derivation.
a. Students in school in 1957–58.
b. Part days are counted as half a day.
c. Calculated by multiplying the United States figure from Column (4) by Column (8) (before rounding).
d. Assumed to be the same as in the Netherlands in each age group.
e. Assumed to be the same as in Sweden in each school grade.
f. Assumed to be the same as in the United States in each school grade.

proportional basis to allow for holidays. Except for Italy, yearly school hours are rather similar in all the countries. The shortest hours, in France, are only 8 percent below the longest, in Germany. Annual hours in the United States are 4 percent below the Northwest European average, mainly because the longer American summer vacation is not wholly offset by the longer vacations at other times and the more numerous holidays prevailing in Europe. In comparison with most Northwest Europeans, American students attend school more hours per day but fewer days a year.

Columns 4 to 8 compare the total time spent in school by American and European students as of 1957–58. Northwest European children were, on the average, receiving 80 percent as many years of education, and spending 83 percent as many hours in school, as American students. There is substantial variation among the Northwest European countries, and it is about equally large whether years or hours are used (although the order is not the same).

It is possible to approximate the changes in the international quality indexes for the labor force, given in Column 1, Table 8–7, that would result from the assumption that the same number of hours of school attendance rather than the same number of years represents equivalent education at the present time. Column 6, Table 8–8, shows years of education of recent students adjusted to equivalence with the United States on this assumption. Substitution of this assumption would raise the United States-equivalent number of years of education of the labor force in the various countries by the difference between Columns 6 and 4. Given the pattern of Northwest European educational distributions, a difference of 1 year in the average education of the labor force would change the quality index based on United States weights (United States equal to 100) by something like 6 index points. As indicated in Column 9, Table 8–8, the alternative assumption would therefore raise the quality index for Northwest Europe, as given in Column 1,

Table 8–7, by about 2.7 index points. All the Northwest European indexes based on years of education except that for France would be raised 3 to 5 points relative to the United States and France.[36]

Although it is impossible to be sure, I doubt this change would be an improvement. Modest differences in class time are unlikely to measure anything relevant to the quality or intensity of education. Work at home may be as relevant as time in class and the various school systems presumably try to adapt their annual schedules of both classwork and homework together to take best advantage of the absorptive capacities of the children they teach. Differences in the institutional environment (including the workweek and vacation habits of adults) and differences in climatic conditions must affect the pattern selected. My preference for the assumption that a year of schooling is equivalent in all countries is reinforced by the inherent difficulties of the statistical comparisons attempted in Table 8–8, as well as by the absurdity of downgrading the highly regarded French schools on the basis of such calculations.

These comments are less relevant to the case of Italy. Annual hours are much shorter there than elsewhere. They are 12 percent below the United States and 16 percent below the Northwest European average according to Column 3, Table 8–8. It is doubtful that Italians would justify short hours entirely on the grounds that an educational loss is not entailed. Rather, it appears that resources available for education are a limiting factor (Italy has been straining to provide facilities to meet her obligations under the compulsory education laws); also the multiplicity of national and religious holidays is a contributing influence. A case could be made for reducing the Italian labor force quality index by about 6 points, as calculated in Column 9, or at least by some substantial fraction of this amount.

Age at Leaving School: The Malinvaud Proposal

Edmond Malinvaud has urged a second alternative. Malinvaud would agree—indeed, he stresses

36. The effect on my "final indexes," which are described in the following section, would be only half this large.

this point more strongly than I do—that differences in the scheduled length of the school year should be ignored in the calculation of quality indexes. However, he believes the age at which full-time education ceases provides a better indication of educational achievement than the number of school years. Thus he would consider labor force members who left school at, say, 15 years of age to have an equivalent education regardless of whether they started school at age 5, 6, or 7, and hence had had 10, 9, or 8 years of education.[37]

I believe this view would receive support from American educators, at least if no major change in the primary school curriculum is envisaged. They consider that only the exceptional child is capable of successful first grade work at age 5, and that considerable numbers, particularly among boys, still lack sufficient maturity to make it worthwhile to enter first grade at age 6. Most would argue that to reduce the normal age for starting first grade, as presently constituted, from 6 to 5 would add little or nothing to educational achievement at a later age, and might entail a net loss as a consequence of frustration and discouragement unless the content of the course was radically downgraded.[38] Raising the age to 7, it seems to be implied, would not involve a loss nearly equivalent to a whole year's work, since progress in reading and other elementary subjects would be more rapid.

On the other hand, English children have started school at age 5 for generations without creating any general belief that this is a wasteful practice. None of the numerous British commissions on education has suggested that a substantial net gain could be achieved without lengthening compulsory education by raising the age at which it commences

37. OECD, *The Residual Factor and Economic Growth*, p. 63 [143].
38. This section is not considering, it should be clear, the value of kindergarten and other pre-first-grade training, which is briefly discussed later in the chapter. It *is* argued that children from culturally deprived homes who, by age 6, are already at a distinct disadvantage would benefit from earlier exposure to school but the recommended prescription is not to enter first grade earlier but to extend kindergarten (which is not now available in all geographic areas in the United States) and to provide nursery school training.

A recent report of the NEA Educational Policies Commission (*Universal Opportunity for Early Childhood Education* [B79]) recommends universal education for 4- and 5-year-olds with an accompanying revision, which is not spelled out, of the first grade program.

TABLE 8-9

Calculation of School Leaving Age; Effect of Basing International Education Quality Adjustment Indexes on School Leaving Age Instead of on Years of Education

| | Recent students[a] | | | | | Labor force | |
Area	Computed average starting age (years) (1)	Adjusted average starting age (years) (2)	Average years of education (years) (3)	Implied average age of leaving school[b] (years) (4)	Difference from United States in starting age (years) (5)	Estimated adjustment in quality index (percentage points) (6)	Adjusted quality index 1960 (United States = 100) (7)
United States	6.0	6.1	12.9	19.0	—	—	100.0
Northwest Europe	6.1	5.9	10.3	16.2	−.2	−1.1	92.2
Belgium	5.5	5.5	11.4	16.9	−.6	−3.6	90.3
Denmark	7.4	7.3	8.8	16.1	1.2	7.2	95.5
France	6.0	6.0	10.7	16.7	−.1	−.6	91.9
Germany	7.0	6.4	9.1	15.5	.3	1.8	92.7
Netherlands	6.4	6.4	10.4	16.8	.3	1.8	96.6
Norway	7.3	7.3	10.0	17.3	1.2	7.2	97.9
United Kingdom	5.1	5.1	11.0	16.1	−1.0	−6.0	90.9
Italy	7.1	6.5	8.9	15.4	.4	2.4	82.1

Source: See text for derivation.
a. Students in school in 1957–58.
b. Columns (2) + (3).

to 6 years.[39] Adherence to this early starting age is the more impressive since implementation of a desired increase to 16 years in the compulsory school leaving age has been delayed by lack of educational resources. Against this, Svenillson and his associates state that "reforms to extend [compulsory education in all the OECD countries] below the present entrance age do not seem to be envisaged, not even in countries where school starts at as late an age as seven."[40]

The school starting age is ordinarily said to be 5 years in the United Kingdom, 6 in the United States, Belgium, France, Germany, Italy, and the Netherlands, and 7 in Denmark and Norway. However, these nominal starting ages are interpreted differently in each country. Also, the age at which a child *may* be admitted to school and the age at which he *must* attend school often differ. For example, in the Netherlands a child cannot start

school until the September following his sixth birthday, whereas in Belgium he may enter public school at 5½ and in the private schools, with roughly half the enrollment, he may often start at an even earlier age. The average starting age can easily vary as much as one-half year in either direction from the nominal age. Calculated estimates of the starting age are given in Column 1, Table 8–9. These were computed from enrollment ratios by a uniform, but approximate, statistical procedure.[41] The results, for the most part, appear generally consistent with school laws and practice but in some cases the calculated numbers appear to be outside the likely range suggested by other information and modifications appear appropriate; the major adjustments are for Germany and Italy. These modified estimates, given in Column 2, provide a more accurate picture of differences than the nominal

39. Raising the compulsory starting age has been suggested on other grounds: to meet a teacher shortage anticipated by 1971 because of a sudden rise in the birth rate. According to *The Economist* (September 12, 1964, p. 996 [P19]), this would have little effect on enrollment of 5-year-olds unless the permissible age were also raised, which is considered unthinkable.

40. Svenilson with Edding and Elvin, *Policy Conference on Economic Growth and Investment in Education*, p. 84 [146].

41. The 1957 or 1958 ratio of enrollment to population in the 10-year age span, 5 to 14, was obtained from *ibid.,* p. 108. The average starting age given in Column 1, Table 8–9, equals 15 years minus ten times this ratio. The estimates will be too high to the extent that the older children within the age bracket are not in school. They are subject to slight variation from unbalanced age distributions, and rather more from the time of year to which the data refer as well as from errors in the data. The source is the same as was used to compute average years of school in Column 3, Table 8–9 (which is transferred from Table 8–8).

starting age, but the estimates for some of the countries may be off a few tenths of a year relative to others.

The sum of the average age of starting school and the average years of education gives the approximate average (arithmetic mean) age at leaving school. This is given, for recent students, in Column 4. The average age at leaving school as of 1957–58 varies less among Northwest European countries than the years of schooling. The order of countries is also different: The United Kingdom had among the longest average spans of education but the youngest average school leaving ages.

As far as I can determine, differences among countries in the average age of entering school were about the same at the time when the labor force was being educated as they have been in the postwar period. The age of leaving school is the starting age plus the number of years of education (unless education is interrupted).[42]

These considerations make it possible to approximate the change that would be introduced in the quality adjustment indexes if the Malinvaud proposal to base comparisons on age of leaving school were substituted for comparisons based on years of education. The difference between the average school beginning age in each European country and the United States (Column 5) is simply multiplied by six. This relies on the rule of thumb that, in Europe, a difference of 1 year in average years of education is equivalent to about 6 points in the quality adjustment index (United States equal to 100) in United States weights. Columns 6 and 7, Table 8–9, show the changes that would be introduced in the quality adjustment indexes given in Column 1 of Table 8–7, and the indexes so adjusted. Shifting from school years to school leaving age would sharply raise the Scandinavian indexes and sharply lower the British index. It would eliminate the difference between the French and British indexes. However, it would only slightly affect the comparison of the United States and Northwest Europe as a whole.[43]

I find Malinvaud's suggestion persuasive but believe its full acceptance would go too far. I adopt the compromise of averaging the results of basing international comparisons on years of school and on school leaving age. This assumes that half the disadvantage of a later start is made up by the time of leaving school. The averages, which represent my final estimates of education quality indexes among countries, are given in Column 3, Table 8–7.

No significant adjustment of the time series for individual countries is implied by this decision because important changes in the age of starting school seem not to have occurred.[44]

Omitted Types of Education

With minor exceptions, the education data used in this study cover all types of full-time education except kindergarten, whether obtained in public schools, in church-affiliated schools, or in other private schools.

Types of education that have been excluded are examined briefly below:

YEARS IN KINDERGARTEN AND NURSERY SCHOOL. The time spent in these programs is omitted, even when they form part of the regular elementary school programs.

In 1962 the number enrolled in kindergarten in the United States equaled 56 percent of the number of 5-year-olds. The proportion had risen sharply since World War II. From 1920 to 1940 it seems to have been increasing only slowly, with the proportion somewhere around one-fourth. Since 18-year-olds in 1962 would have been 5 in 1949, the recent great expansion in kindergarten attendance can have had but little effect on the labor force by 1962, and it is unlikely that as many as one-fourth of 1962 labor force members attended kindergarten. The proportion could hardly have risen more

---

42. Wars interrupted education to a greater or lesser extent in all countries covered, either by causing the temporary disruption and closing of schools or by delaying the education of servicemen. The procedure followed here treats the individuals affected as if they had obtained their education at the usual age. Interruption of education for other reasons should not seriously distort comparisons of countries or dates.

43. It should be noted that in Table 8–9 no close relationship exists or should be expected between the school leaving age of *recent students* given in Column 4 and quality indexes for the *labor force* based on school leaving age given in Column 7.

44. By changing the weights attached to different education groups in a country, as estimated here, the shift from years of school to age at leaving school could change the time series indexes, but only slightly.

than 5 percentage points from 1950 to 1962, which would have meant an increase over a 12-year period of 0.05 years in average time spent in kindergarten by labor force members. Even if this were counted as equivalent to a similar increase in regular school years—which would be far too much—it would have only a small effect on the United States education quality index. Nursery schools have been expanding but had touched only a small percentage of persons in the labor force by 1962.

Patterns of preschool enrollment vary widely among the Northwest European countries. Belgium, the Netherlands, and France have very large attendance, not only during the year immediately preceding the first grade but also at ages three and four. In Belgium four-fifths of the 3-year-olds and over nine-tenths of 4- and 5-year-olds were receiving pre-primary education in 1960. It is estimated that 40 percent of French children between the ages of 2 and 6 are enrolled in some kind of kindergarten or nursery school. Preschool attendance has been less prevalent in the other countries and it is very low in the United Kingdom. Raymond Poignant gives the average number of years of preschool education about 1962–63 as 2.7 in Belgium, 1.9 in France, 1.3 in Italy, 0.9 in Germany, and 0.32 in the United Kingdom. In 1961, 3- to 6-year-olds in the Netherlands spent an average of 1.8 years (compared to 1.3 years in 1940) in "Kleuteronderwijs," which is translated as "nursery schools" in Dutch sources.[45]

Preschool training is thought to facilitate learning in subsequent years but I have found no way to quantify its impact on the quality of the labor force.

ADULT SELF-EDUCATION PROGRAMS. In all countries, a considerable proportion of the labor force has participated in home study programs, evening extension courses, and other forms of adult education. This defies measurement on any comparable basis, but its omission is unlikely to impair seriously

international or intertemporal comparisons of the quality of labor.

COMMERCIAL AND TRADE SCHOOLS. Courses offered on a fee basis in proprietary commercial and trade schools are generally omitted even if study is full time during the day (though often for only a matter of months). Also omitted are correspondence courses and courses taken in the armed forces.[46]

In the United States, regular schools and colleges employ over one hundred times as many persons as proprietary commercial, trade, and correspondence schools, which gives some idea of the relative resources used in such schools. On the other hand, a large proportion of the labor force has had some formal education, usually of short duration, in these forms. For example, a 1954 survey showed that, of a sample of 1,028 males who graduated from high school in the thirties but did not attend college, 55 percent had attended trade, technical, or business schools after high school, an additional 8 percent had received some training in the armed forces or company schools, and only 37 percent had had no education beyond high school. Average earnings of the first group were around 4 percent above those of the other two groups combined, after standardization for rank in high school class.[47]

Data are not available to allow for these types of education in the quality adjustment indexes but, if the earnings differential typically is not much over 4 percent, differences between 1950 and 1962 in the amount of such education held by the labor force could hardly have been great enough to have affected the United States quality index appreciably.[48] I believe this also to be true of the European

45. Calculations for Belgium, France, and the Netherlands were based on data contained in their statistical yearbooks except that the statement concerning France is a quotation from George A. Male, *Education in France*, p. 40 [G64]. Poignant's data are given in *L'Enseignement dans les Pays du Marché Commun*, p. 71 [B87]. Comparisons with the other countries are based on data in UNESCO, *Pre-school Education* [16].

46. However, individuals obtaining in these ways academic certificates or diplomas, such as a high school diploma, ordinarily obtained by full-time study will usually be credited in the data with the same number of years of education as persons obtaining the certificate in the usual way. Where data are derived entirely from the age at leaving school this is not the case.

47. See my analysis of the Wolfle-Smith survey in *The Residual Factor and Economic Growth*, pp. 87–89 [143].

48. My procedure automatically includes the effects of increases in this type of training that are associated with an increase in general education. Thus, if high school graduates are more likely than elementary school graduates to receive such training, the increase in the total amount of such training resulting from an increasing proportion of high school graduates will be automatically reflected in my quality indexes.

indexes, and probably of intercountry comparisons. In a comparison of the United States and Europe these types of education probably offset the greater use of released time in Europe, mentioned below.

PART-TIME PROGRAMS. Many young European workers attend school, usually one day a week, on released time. Most of them are enrolled in what is intended to be a coordinated work-study program for learning an occupation, and they usually receive a certificate, upon examination, if the program is completed. Young people in Germany and Denmark, and certain groups elsewhere, are legally required to attend part-time day classes after leaving full-time schools until they reach age 18, whether they are employed or not.

Countries have different systems of on-the-job training, varying greatly in their formality and degree of government supervision. In America reliance is overwhelmingly on informal on-the-job training and experience. Most workers become qualified in this way even in those few occupations for which registered apprenticeship programs exist.[49] In most occupations qualification is judged mainly by ability to do the work required after a brief learning period. In Europe government supervised programs and certificates play a much greater role both in training and in obtaining a job. This extends in some countries to nearly all occupations. To measure the efficacy of on-the-job training in different countries or at different dates appears impossible and I make no effort to do so in this study.

Time spent in day schools on a part-time basis, whether as part of a work-study program or not, could be converted to full-time equivalence and counted in the education measures if sufficient data were available and the magnitudes warranted it. Available data are not altogether satisfactory but

are sufficient to show that amounts involved are small. From information summarized in Appendix F, Section IV, it seems clear that inclusion of part-time day education on a full-time equivalent basis could have only a small effect upon our labor quality indexes. Inclusion of such education could hardly change a comparison of average years of education of the labor force between any two countries covered by more than 0.2 years, or more likely 0.1, or the international quality indexes (United States equals 100) by more than one point. It is unlikely that in any country it would raise the increase in average years of schooling from 1950 to 1962 by more than 0.1 years, or the 1962 quality index for any country by as much as one point. Most comparisons would scarcely be affected.

Type and Quality of Education

Measures of education used in this study are unavoidably in quantitative terms. Certain assumptions and implications of this procedure must be specified.

1. No distinction has been made with respect to subject matter. The procedure followed implies that, on the average, the education that had been received at one date by members of the labor force in a country was as relevant to participation in economic life as that received at other dates. The international comparison assumes education is equally relevant in different countries. The assumption is not, it must be stressed, that all subjects or curricula have equal economic value. It is that differences between times and countries in subjects studied are not correlated with differences in economic value, a much less restrictive assumption.

To test this assumption is not possible. It would require, first, that distributions of the labor force at different times and places by years of schooling be also divided by type of education throughout the years spent in school; and, second, that corresponding data on earnings, adjusted for differences in natural ability and other correlated factors, be obtained for individuals with each type of educational background. Comprehensive information of this type is not available for any country. I have no preconception as to the relative economic value of

---

49. The National Manpower Council estimated that replacement needs for skilled workers in trades having apprentices are met as follows: proportion not receiving formal training, 58–64 percent; registered apprentices completing training, 12–16 percent; registered apprentices leaving without completing training, 6–8 percent; apprentices, not registered, 14 percent; vocational school graduates, 4–10 percent; immigrants trained abroad, 4 percent (Wason in U.S. Congress, Senate Subcommittee on Employment and Manpower of the Committee on Labor and Public Welfare, *Selected Readings in Employment and Manpower,* Vol. 3, p. 1337 [G48]).

TABLE 8–10

The Netherlands: Median Yearly Earnings of Male Employees[a] by Type of Education and by Age Group, 1962

(In Dutch guilders)

Level of school and type[b]	Age group (in years)					
	25–29	30–34	35–39	40–44	45–49	50–64
Upper lower						
Technical	6,923	8,304	9,171	9,861	10,111	10,253
Other	6,489	7,605	9,068	9,657	10,034	10,410
Middle						
Technical	7,823	9,855	11,321	12,382	13,667	12,917
Other	7,393	9,316	10,804	11,875	13,225	13,596
Semi-higher						
Technical	8,932	11,134	13,404	14,859	16,344	16,957
Total[c]	8,944	11,066	13,452	14,930	16,368	17,333

Source: *Maandschrift van het Centraal Bureau voor de Statistiek*, June 1964, p. 554 [G24].
a. Data cover manufacturing, coal mining, construction, banking, and insurance.
b. For classification by level of education, see Appendix Table F–5.
c. Data for "other" not given separately.

different types of education (except for a great distrust of judgments often expressed) and, consequently, no guess as to the direction of any biases that may be involved.[50]

There are some scattered data, by no means meeting the tests just prescribed, that suggest earnings differentials between persons with technical and academic training are not so very great nor consistent in direction. In the Netherlands five broad levels of education are recognized, the lowest of which includes nearly two-thirds of the labor force. For the three middle groups, median annual earnings by type of education and age are available (Table 8–10). The data cover employees of manufacturing, coal mining, construction, banking, and insurance firms. They suggest that the technical graduates earn more than the others up to age 34, a little more from 35 to 49, and less thereafter, ex-

cept at the "semi-higher" level where the technical graduates are a bit below average in all age groups except 30 to 34. A very large change in the distribution of the labor force between technical and other graduates would be required for earnings differences of the size indicated in this table to affect quality indexes significantly.

Table 8–11 shows the average hourly earnings of vocational and academic high school graduates with no college education obtained in a small national sample in the United States. The data refer

50. It should be recognized, of course, that the relative value of different types of study varies from time to time and place to place. One aspect of this deserves special mention. The great subdivision of work in American industry is often regarded as an important reason for high American productivity. It has the effect of reducing the need for craftsmen with comprehensive skills while increasing the need for flexibility and adaptability to change. It seems likely that the extensive and rapidly growing vocational training programs in Europe may be appropriate so long as continuation of European production practices is presupposed, but that they would not be appropriate in America, and that in Europe they may discourage reorganization of production along American lines.

TABLE 8–11

United States: Comparison of Mean Hourly Earnings of Male Vocational and Academic High School Graduates with No College Education

Year of high school graduation	Type of high school training	Initial earnings per hour	Earnings in 1964 per hour
1953	Vocational	$1.31	$3.00
	Academic	1.44	3.22
1958	Vocational	1.46	2.40
	Academic	1.48	2.40
1962	Vocational	1.46	1.94
	Academic	1.44	1.73
Combined	Vocational	1.43	2.36
	Academic	1.46	2.50

Source: Max U. Eninger, "The Process and Product of T and I High School Level Vocational Education in the United States," Pittsburgh: American Institutes for Research, 1965, Tables 148 and 153 (mimeo.).

to males who finished high school in 1953, 1958, and 1962. Both initial earnings after high school graduation and earnings in 1964 are given. Differences are in general moderate and not systematic in direction. None are statistically significant according to the report from which they are taken.

A study of Pittsburgh high school graduates of June 1959 who entered full-time employment found that choice of high school curriculum among academic, business, or general programs had no significant bearing on earnings two years after graduation.[51]

2. The comparisons ignore differences in educational requirements imposed by differences among nations. They thus assume that differences in the difficulties of the native language are insufficient to affect greatly the time required to learn to read and write, which is basic to most school subjects. This would be quite unacceptable in a comparison of France and China, or of Turkey before and after 1924. Differences among the languages relevant to the present study do not appear drastic, but it is true that the English language requires much more attention to spelling than the continental languages, in which spelling and pronunciation usually coincide. The complexity, relative to the metric system, of Anglo-Saxon weights and measures (or the British currency) may also be noted.

Against this, and probably more important, may be set the size and contiguity of the continental countries which have forced them, and especially the smaller countries, to devote a large proportion of school time to the learning of a second and third modern language. English itself is becoming more and more important. The more limited attention the United States has devoted to the study of foreign languages handicaps few Americans in their economic life.

3. Comparisons based on years of schooling assume equivalence, in some difficult-to-define sense, of the quality of a year of education. Individuals in the labor force with the same number of years of schooling, obtained at the same age, are considered to have received an equivalent educa-

tion no matter when, or in what country, it was received (aside from the "days" adjustment, where made). Even to discuss similarities and differences among countries would require extended space and be wholly inconclusive.[52] Adequate comparisons of achievement are simply not available.[53]

Over time, it is likely that the quality of education in the United States has improved; at least, all objective measures of inputs into the educational system (such as teachers' qualifications, class size, school facilities, and expenditures per pupil) have shown marked improvement. Quality in Europe presumably has also improved; at least the same type of input measures show this to be the case. There is, therefore, some presumption that the quality indexes are biased downward over time.

It is, of course, the net impact of education upon participation in economic life, rather than the valid-

52. An interesting short discussion of some of the difficulties of comparison (but itself, I think, not wholly free of errors) is contained in Kaulfers, *Educational Record*, July 1963, pp. 275–81 [P20].

53. Often enough to require comment, the frequent admission to American colleges, with third-year standing, of European-trained students who are ready to enter European universities is adduced as "evidence" that American schools achieve in 14 years what European schools achieve in 12. If the comparison were valid at all, it would suggest equivalence of 14 years of American education with 13 in Europe. The European student usually has had not 12 years of preparation but 13, and is typically at least one year older than the American college entrant. In addition, much of the advanced credit granted is for knowledge of the language of the country in which he was trained.

But this comparison has almost no pertinence for the comparisons made here. The main point is that a very small percentage of the European labor force ever attained an education sufficient to qualify for university admission. This group typically had attended different schools from the mass of students, sometimes from as early as age 12, and its education was not representative. Often entrance to such schools required excelling in examinations. The group who attained the qualifications for admission to universities was small and select.

The assumption of the international quality index computations is not that individuals with the same amount of education represent the same quality of labor. If it were, United States earnings differentials would not have been reduced by two-fifths for use as weights in the computation of earnings differentials, and the American edge in the international quality indexes would be much larger than has been computed here. The assumption is rather that individuals of the same natural ability with the same amount of education represent the same quality of labor. To have any relevance, even for comparison of the small numbers who reach this level, the achievement of Europeans qualified to enter university would have to be compared with a similarly small and select group of American students with the same length of education and age; for most comparisons this level appears to be entrance into the second year of college, and at least age 19.

51. S. P. Marland, Jr., "A Follow-up Study of High School Graduates—Class of June 1959," Pittsburgh: Pittsburgh Public Schools, 1963, p. 22 (mimeo.).

ity of each of these assumptions separately, that is relevant to the comparisons here. Thus it could be true, as Graham Hutton asserts, that average intellectual standards (as the term "standard" is understood by Europeans) are lower for public education at all ages in the United States than in Europe; but that education itself serves economic purposes better in the United States than in Europe (except in Scandinavia and Switzerland).[54]

Conclusions

The following conclusions appear warranted from the data presented in this chapter and from the additional detail and description provided in Appendix F. I deal first with changes over time, and then with levels in 1960.

Educational Quality of the Labor Force: Intertemporal Comparisons

1. *From 1950 to 1962 the amount of full-time education of the labor force increased in all the countries examined.* This is shown by any possible weighting scheme, including a simple count of the average years of education of the labor force (Table 8–12).[55]

2. *The amount of education of the labor force increased more in the United States than in Northwest Europe or in any of the individual European countries.* The exact comparisons depend on the weights assigned to different levels of education, but uniform application of any sensible weighting scheme to all countries would yield this conclusion.

Series based on use of United States weights were given in Part B of Table 8–6. By this measure the education of the labor force increased 9 percent in the United States compared to 3.5 percent in Northwest Europe. In no European country except Belgium was the increase much more than half as

large as in the United States; in Belgium the increase came much closer to, but was still below, that in the United States. Even if (quite unjustifiably) no allowance had been made for the great increase in the number of school days represented by a year of education in the United States, the American index would have risen appreciably more than those for any of the European countries except Belgium (compare Tables 8–5 and 8–6). If a fraction other than three-fifths had been applied to United States earnings differentials to obtain earnings weights, the relative position of the American and European indexes would be unchanged.

The United States would also show the largest increase if European rather than American weights were uniformly applied. The upward shift in the American educational distribution has, in fact, been so general throughout the distribution that no reasonable set of weights, uniformly applied, could produce a different result.

An alternative measure of educational stock sometimes used is the average number of years of schooling of the labor force. This counts all years of education, from the first grade up, as of equal value—an unsatisfactory though simple procedure. Table 8–12 provides estimates for 1950 and 1962. When the education received in the past in the United States is reduced to equivalence with recent education on the basis of days attended per year, the 1950–62 increase in the average education of male members of the labor force increased by 1⅔ years. Even without this necessary adjustment it is a full year. This exceeds the increase in any of the European countries. As with the weighted indexes, the difference between the United States and the major Northwest European countries is large.

The finding, which I consider unambiguous and firmly based—that the education of the labor force has increased less, not more, in Europe than in the United States—is a major one. The increase in education has been a principal source of growth in the United States and it is important to know that European countries have not been achieving more rapid growth by raising the education of the labor force more rapidly. This finding in itself does not indicate whether or not increased education of the labor force has contributed more to European than to American growth rates. It does indicate that if

54. *We Too Can Prosper,* p. 44 [B52].
55. Germany (in which the increase was smallest and the data were least satisfactory) is the only country where there could be any doubt at all whether education increased and, even in this instance, the possibility that there has been no rise is remote.

education *has* contributed more in Europe, this can only be because European conditions are different, not because Europe has succeeded in obtaining a greater increase in education of the labor force.[56]

3. *In general, an equivalent increase in education raises the average quality of labor more in Europe than in America, and contributes more to the growth rate.*

The same addition to the number of individuals with a given amount of education that is appreciably above the average amount raises the average quality of labor by a greater percentage in Europe than in the United States, provided that the earnings weights assigned are correct in showing larger earnings differentials in Europe above the 8-year level. That a similar increment to the percentages in the upper education groups raises the average quality of labor more in Europe than in the United States shows up in larger increases in quality indexes when European weights are used than when United States weights are used.

The increase in educational levels in most European countries, however, has not been due mainly to larger numbers at the upper levels, but rather to past advances in the compulsory school leaving age. These raised, one year at a time, the number of years of education received by the mass of the population. In several countries the labor force includes persons educated when the school leaving age was at three different levels. Changes in compulsory education were important in all the European countries except Denmark, Germany, and Norway. As younger age groups replace older groups in the labor force, the average educational level gradually advances. An increase in average years of education obtained in this way—by raising the level at which the bulk of the population is concentrated—has, properly, less effect on the quality indexes than one of equal size obtained by raising the proportions in the scarce higher educational levels.

56. The increase that occurred in the education of the labor force from 1950 to 1962 (and the contribution of this increase to growth) depends very little upon changes in the education of the young that took place during this period, and no international comparison of these changes has been made or is implied. What affects the figures is the difference between the education of those who entered and those who left the labor force from 1950 to 1962 and this depends upon changes in the education of the young that took place over more than half a century.

Extension of education beyond the compulsory school leaving age contributed in widely varying degree to the rise in the average level of education of European labor forces. Until the postwar period, the United Kingdom did little to encourage, or even to permit, an increase in the number of students who extend education much beyond the compulsory level and, although this situation is now changed, the bulk of students still leave school as soon as possible. The proportion in Germany who have voluntarily continued is even smaller. In France the number of students remaining in school has been rising for many years and the legal school leaving age is no longer decisive in determining the time at which most students complete their full-time education.

The weighting structure used to compute European quality indexes implies that a given increase in the number of years of education per member of the labor force is associated with a larger increase in the quality index if it results from a general upward movement of the distribution than if it stems from a rise in the point of concentration due to extending compulsory education. This is a correct reflection of what I believe to be a fact: that expansion of the numbers of persons with higher education and, especially, advanced secondary education, can do more for the European economies than any feasible rise in the general school leaving age.

The United States has not had a heavy concentration of the labor force in any one narrow range, and changes take the form of a general rise in the distribution as a whole, with percentages rising sharply at all upper levels and falling sharply at all lower levels.[57]

In practice, the ratio of the increase in the quality index (when each area is based on its own weights) to the increase in average years of education of the labor force (adjusted to recent attendance levels in the Anglo-Saxon countries) was much higher in all the European countries than in

57. The dividing line between "upper" and "lower," of course, changes in the long run, but throughout the postwar period it has remained at the 9- to 11-year level. Percentages in each education group below that level have persistently fallen, in each group above that level have persistently risen, and in the 9- to 11-year group itself have shown only small and irregular fluctuations (see Appendix Table F-9).

the United States, but in no case as much as twice as high.

4. *It is almost certain that, from 1950 to 1962, the increase in education nevertheless raised the quality of labor more in the United States than in Northwest Europe and contributed more to the American growth rate.*

Estimates appropriate for this comparison are given in Part A of Table 8–6, where quality indexes in each area are computed by the use of weights appropriate to that area. I estimate that in the United States the increase in education raised the average quality of labor by 9.0 percent, or at an average annual rate of over 0.7 percent. The comparable estimates for Northwest Europe are just half as large. Among the European countries, only the Belgian and Italian indexes match or even closely approach the United States index.

It is true that the European indexes would rise more than they do if larger earnings differentials had been adopted. But to raise the indexes for Northwest Europe as a whole (or any of the large Northwest European countries) up to or near the United States level in 1962 (1950 equal to 100) by changing the weights above the 8-year level would require the adoption of impossibly large differentials.

With the labor share 75 or 80 percent of the national income, the indexes imply that increases in the quality of the labor force related to additional education contributed about half a percentage point to the growth rate of real national income per person employed in the United States and about a quarter of a point in Northwest Europe. This is, as usual, without allowance for economies of scale.[58]

5. *There are substantial differences among the European countries in the amounts by which the quality of labor was raised by additional education.*

The Northwest European countries fall into three groups when the percentage increases in quality indexes from 1950 to 1962 are considered. Belgium is alone at the top, Denmark and Germany are at the bottom, and the other countries are in the middle. This pattern, given below, is readily explained.

	Northwest European weights	United States weights
Belgium	9.1	7.5
France	5.7	4.6
United Kingdom	5.5	4.0
Norway	5.1	4.2
Netherlands	5.0	3.6
Denmark	2.7	2.1
Germany	2.2	1.7

The amount of schooling of the European labor force has risen for two main reasons. Compulsory education was extended and the proportions continuing education beyond the compulsory stage increased between the time those leaving the labor force in the 1950–62 period and the time those entering the labor force in this period were educated. In all the countries the proportion continuing beyond the compulsory level when most of the departing group was educated was so small that the increase in voluntary education can be inferred from the proportions continuing beyond the compulsory stage in the postwar period.

The postwar proportion continuing beyond the compulsory level was higher in Belgium than in any of the other countries. In addition, compulsory education was raised by two years (from age 12 to 14) in the 1920's, so that those entering the labor force in 1950–62 were educated in a period when compulsory education was two years longer than it had been when those retiring had been educated.

The situation in Denmark and Germany was at the other extreme. During the 1950's the proportion continuing full-time education beyond the compulsory age was lower than in any of the other countries. And neither country had changed its compulsory education period recently enough for many of those retiring to have been educated under a law less stringent than that under which those entering the labor force were educated.[59]

France, the United Kingdom, Norway, and the Netherlands are in an intermediate position. All except Norway introduced one or two one-year

58. Estimates of this type given in this chapter are preliminary. More precise computations will be given in Chapter 15.

59. It must be remembered that these two countries do have compulsory part-time education to age 18.

changes in the period of compulsory education over the relevant time span. All have had postwar proportions continuing education beyond the compulsory level that lie between Germany and Denmark, at the one extreme, and Belgium at the other. The extent to which the rise in the quality indexes reflects changes in compulsory education and changes in voluntarily continued education varies considerably among these four countries.

The change in Italy was about the same as in the intermediate group of countries when United States weights are uniformly applied but approached that in the United States and Belgium in its own weights, which allow for broader differentials at the lower education levels.

The reader will note that there is no correspondence between a ranking of the countries by increases in education quality indexes and a ranking by growth rates of national income per person employed, so the education of the labor force is not a factor that *systematically* helps to explain differences in growth rates.

Educational Quality of the Labor Force: International Comparisons

Comparisons of the levels of education in the different areas are much more tenuous than those of changes over time, but some statements appear to be warranted.

1. *The education of the labor force in Northwest Europe may fairly safely be put below that in the United States.* My education quality indexes, given in Column 3, Table 8–7, put the Northwest European labor force at 93 percent of the United States level; the individual countries range from 92 to 96 percent. Almost any quantitative appraisal of the data places the education of the United States labor force above that of the Northwest European area as a whole and above the individual countries except the United Kingdom.

My quality indexes also place the education of British labor below that of the United States, but not every possible quantitative measure yields this result. Thus, if the education of older labor force members in both countries is reduced to equivalence with that of recent students, as in the adjusted

figures of Table 8–12, the average number of years of education in the United States in 1962 falls slightly below that in the United Kingdom for males. Also, if no adjustment had been made for the difference in the age at which school is attended, the quality index using United States weights would be only 3 percent higher in the United States than in the United Kingdom (Column 1, Table 8–7), and this could be offset by incorporating the possible adjustment for a longer school year computed in Table 8–8.

As measured by adjusted years of education, even the United States advantage over most of the other Northwest European countries is recent; in 1950 the adjusted United States figure was below them (Table 8–12). However, this is not a good measure of educational quality since it counts all levels of education equally. Even in 1950 the United States quality index was higher in the United States than in these countries, though only slightly.

2. *If United States education weights are used, as is most nearly appropriate for an effort to explain differences in real national income valued in United States prices, the difference in educational quality between the United States and Northwest Europe is moderate.* My estimates, given in Table 8–7, show the quality of labor as affected by education in the Northwest European countries to have been 4 to 8 percent below the United States in 1960 and 7.3 percent lower in Northwest Europe as a whole. Based on United States weights, they imply that if the education of the labor force were the only difference between the areas, real national income per person employed would be about 6 percent lower in Northwest Europe, with the amount ranging from 4 percent in the Netherlands to between 6 and 6.5 percent in Germany, Denmark, Belgium, and France.

My final estimate was a compromise between two others, one of which assumed equivalence between individuals receiving the same number of years of education, the other between individuals leaving school at the same age. All three measures yield much the same comparison between the United States and Northwest Europe, but the choice makes a considerable difference for some of the individual countries, particularly Denmark, Norway, and the United Kingdom.

If allowance for the current difference in annual class hours in the school year between Northwest Europe and the United States were deemed appropriate, this would eliminate about one-fourth the estimated gap between Northwest Europe and the United States. On the other hand, the gap would be about doubled if allowances had not been made in the United States estimates for poor attendance and a shorter school year outside the cities when most of the labor force was being educated.

I know of no way to assess possible biases due to differences in subject matter or quality of education.

3. *The gap between the educational quality of labor in the United States and Northwest Europe would be greater if Northwest European education weights were used.* This would be appropriate if we were trying to explain the difference between United States and European national income per person employed based on European prices (which is much larger than the difference based on United States prices).

For the comparisons of Northwest Europe and the United States based on years of education, quality indexes using Northwest European weights, as well as the indexes using United States weights that were given in Column 1, Table 8–7, were computed. The two sets of quality indexes are as follows:

	United States weights	Northwest European weights
United States	100.0	100.0
Northwest Europe	92.7	88.6
Belgium	93.9	92.5
Denmark	88.3	85.3
France	92.5	88.3
Germany	90.9	84.7
Netherlands	94.8	94.6
Norway	90.7	88.9
United Kingdom	96.9	91.5

The extent to which the shift to Northwest European weights would lower the European indexes depends mainly on the proportions of the labor force in the upper middle education range. This group represents an especially large fraction of the American labor force and it is weighted more heavily in Northwest European than in American

weights. The index for the Netherlands, which like the United States has large numbers in this range, is reduced scarcely at all while the index for Germany is cut a full 6 points.

I have not made a detailed computation based on age of leaving school, and cannot therefore compute accurately a European weighted index comparable to my "final" United States weighted index.

The final estimates given in Table 8–7 are the most appropriate I can devise for the purposes of this study. However, the difference between Columns 1 and 2 of that table, together with the changes that would be introduced by a shift to Northwest European weights, make it clear that the differences among the Northwest European countries are not great enough to allow an unambiguous ranking of them in any absolute sense. Moreover, the calculations in this section should not obscure the fact that by any method of measurement differences among the United States and the Northwest European countries in educational background are almost trifling in comparison with the differences between any of them and most of the rest of the world. For example, in Turkey in 1960 some 96.7 percent of the labor force 15 years of age and over had 0 to 5 years of education (including 61.5 percent with no education) and the average number of years of education of the labor force was 1.94.[60] The percentage of males 25 years of age and over with 0 to 3 years of education was 62 in Costa Rica, 85 in El Salvador, 87 in Guatemala, 88 in Honduras, and 84 in Nicaragua.[61] Per capita incomes in all countries studied are higher than those of countries with most of the world's population, and the same is probably true of educational attainment.

4. *The quality indexes based on United States weights may not take the American advantage in dispersion sufficiently into account, and their use may lead to some understatement of the difference between United States and European national incomes that is attributable to the education of the labor force.* The diversity of educational back-

60. Estimated by James Blum in an unpublished memorandum prepared for OECD, based on the Turkish census of population for 1960.
61. Committee for Economic Development, *Economic Development of Central America*, p. 35 [B20].

grounds among Americans must be an advantage in that it provides broad opportunity to match the education of workers with educational requirements for specific types of work. The uniformity in education level of the great bulk of European workers may imply that individuals in the occupations least in need of educational background have more education than contributes much to job performance. It almost surely implies that in the more demanding occupations the European countries must often make do with workers having much less education than would be advantageous, or else they must be content with fewer workers in these occupations. As between two distributions of the labor force by amount of education that yield the same quality index, there is reason to think that, within limits, the distribution with the greater dispersion is the more conducive to a large national income.

If the British compulsory school leaving age had, in the past, been about one year higher than it actually was, the "final" British educational quality index, in United States weights, would probably now be about equal to the present United States index. The point of concentration in the British distribution would be higher than it is, but the numbers with advanced secondary and higher education would not be larger. For the reasons just given I doubt that this would have made the British labor force as well adapted to high production (measured in United States prices) as the American labor force, despite the equality of the index.

5. *The educational quality of the labor force in Italy is far below that in the United States, and this accounts for a sizable fraction of the difference in output per man.* My finally adjusted education index for Italy, in United States weights, is only 81 percent of the American index in 1960.[62] Based on United States weights this implies by the usual calculation that, if the education of the labor force were the only difference between the two countries, real national product per person employed would be 15 percent lower in Italy.

If any allowance were made for the unusually short duration of the Italian school year, the gap between the United States and Italian education indexes would be even larger.

A comparison of the United States and Italy based on Italian weights has not been made, but it is evident that use of Italian weights would yield a gap between the United States and Italy far greater than does use of United States weights.

Relationship Between Levels and Changes in Education: Future Trends

Education of the labor force had an unusual characteristic as an income determinant in that the gap between the United States and Europe was widening in favor of the United States from 1950 to 1962. Another unusual feature was that, based on United States weights, the educational quality of Northwest European labor in 1960 was almost the same as in the United States as recently as 1950; it was much above the quality index of the United States in 1925 when real national income per person employed approximated the 1960 Northwest European level. A rough estimate would put the 1925 United States index at about 80 (United States in 1960 equal to 100) which is much below the 1960 indexes of 92 to 96 for the Northwest European countries and only equal to the 1960 Italian index.[63]

Available information suggests that, in the United States, the educational quality of labor will rise during the sixties about as much as it did in the fifties while, in the Northwest European countries, the rise will be more rapid in the sixties. Projections indicate the average rate of increase in the education quality indexes (in Northwest European weights) will be higher in the sixties than the fifties by something like 0.15 percentage points in Belgium, France, and the United Kingdom, and 0.05 points in Norway.[64] Only Belgium and Italy seem

62. It is perhaps worth noting that the minimum possible value for this index, given the United States education weights and the computed quality of United States labor, is 63. This is the figure that would be calculated if no one in Italy had any education.

63. The extrapolation from 1950 to 1925 is based on my earlier study, but after sharply reducing the adjustment for days of schooling in accordance with changes introduced in the present study.

64. The statement with respect to the United States is based on previous projections by the author. (A new projection of the labor force by amount of education, made by the U.S. Department of Labor, is contained in the *Manpower Report of the President, March 1966*, p. 218 [G51].

TABLE 8-12

Mean Years of Education of the Labor Force, by Sex, 1950 and 1962

Area	Males			Females		
	1950	1962	Increase 1950–62	1950	1962	Increase 1950–62
United States	9.68	10.68	1.00	10.01	11.08	1.07
Adjusted for attendance[a]	7.59	9.25	1.66	7.87	9.62	1.75
Northwest Europe						
Belgium	7.98	8.93	.95	7.95	8.81	.86
Denmark	7.46	7.82	.36	7.55	7.83	.28
France	8.09	8.65	.56	7.89	8.51	.62
Germany	7.93	8.24	.31	7.95	8.19	.24
Netherlands	8.43	9.11	.68	8.35	9.02	.67
Norway	7.90	8.40	.50	7.70	8.28	.58
United Kingdom	9.16	9.71	.55	9.43	9.86	.43
Adjusted for attendance[a]	8.56	9.36	.80	8.96	9.54	.57
Italy	4.23	5.10	.87	3.89	4.88	.99

Sources: See text and Appendix F, Section II, for derivation.

a. Years of education of labor force members reduced to equivalence with years of education of postwar students by allowing for absenteeism and, in the United States, extension of the school year outside large cities.

likely to match the United States increase. Education is therefore likely to remain a factor operating towards widening the gap in income levels between the United States and Northwest Europe.

A final calculation gives an indication of the longer run outlook. This is the amount by which the average years of schooling being provided about the middle of the postwar period, in 1957–58 (Table 8–8), exceeds the average years of education of the 1962 labor force (Table 8–12). For the latter calculation I use a simple average of the figures for males and females. The differences are given in the first column below. The second column

Differences in years of full-time schooling

	1957–58 students minus 1962 labor force	1962 male labor force minus 1950 male labor force
Italy	3.9	0.9
United States	3.5 (2.0)	1.7 (1.0)
Belgium	2.5	1.0
France	2.2	0.6
Norway	1.6	0.5
United Kingdom	1.5 (1.2)	0.8 (0.6)
Netherlands	1.4	0.7
Denmark	1.0	0.4
Germany	0.9	0.3

However, it excludes persons who will be under 25 years of age and the education classes are somewhat condensed.) Estimates for the European countries are all deduced from projected changes in the average number of years of education; data are described in Appendix F, Section II.

shows the increase that took place from 1950 to 1962 in average years of schooling of male members of the labor force (Table 8–12). Figures in parentheses exclude adjustments for changes in days attended per year.

The first column suggests that Italy, the United States, and Belgium can anticipate the largest increases in the education of the labor force in the future; France, Norway, the United Kingdom, and the Netherlands are in an intermediate position; and Denmark and Germany can expect the smallest increases. This broad grouping is the same as that observed in the second column for actual changes from 1950 to 1962. The difference between the education recently being provided the younger generation in Italy and the education of the labor force in Italy is particularly noteworthy. It is a very favorable factor for future growth. Among the large countries of Northwest Europe, the future increase in education suggested for France is bigger than that for the United Kingdom, and that for Germany is especially small.[65] Indeed, one can infer directly from Column 4 of Table 8–8 that, in the absence of a major change in education provided young people, Germany is heading to-

65. Attention is also called to Appendix F, Section II, in which it is shown that the younger age groups in Germany have but little more education than the older age groups soon to leave the labor force.

ward a position in which its labor force will have the least full-time education of any of the countries covered except Italy, and eventually little, if any, more than Italy.[66] One would have to attach great weight to the part-time education provided by the part-time Berufsschule to avoid the conclusion that the future position of Germany with respect to the education of the labor force will become decidedly inferior to that of its neighbors. There appears to be substance to the comment that Germany has

been "living off the educational capital it built up before and during the war."[67]

Use of enrollment ratios for a year later than 1957–58 in the comparisons would yield somewhat different results, of course, and educational changes still to be made will affect the more distant future. But the course of changes in the education of the labor force for a long time to come will be largely determined by changes that have already occurred and that can be observed in a classification of the adult population by amount of education. The education of most of the labor force for decades ahead has already been determined.

66. The figure in Table 8–8 for average years of education in Denmark in 1957–58 is below that for Germany, but allowance should be made for the higher age at which education is being received in Denmark; in addition Danish enrollment ratios are now rising.

67. Unidentified "independent expert" quoted by Olsen in *New York Times*, January 13, 1965 [P32].

Labor Input: Unmeasured Elements and Summary

Preceding chapters have measured four aspects of the quantity and quality of labor. These were the numbers employed, the hours they work, their age and sex, and their education. In this chapter these results will be combined to obtain summary measures of labor input. These measures do not, of course, take into account all of the characteristics of employed persons that may affect the quality of labor. Insofar as omitted characteristics differ among countries or change over time, the comparisons of labor input are incomplete. Before the summary measures are presented, therefore, I shall call attention to some of these characteristics and try to indicate their potential significance.

Remaining Characteristics of the Labor Force

Some characteristics influence relative earnings of different individuals within a country but can be quickly dismissed as irrelevant to comparisons of entire populations at different dates, and to comparisons of the nine countries. Thus there is no reason to suppose that the distribution of "native intelligence," viewed as aptitude at birth, varied

significantly among these countries in 1960, or between the 1950 and 1962 populations of one particular country. Family position and the element of chance may greatly affect an individual's career but do not reflect differences in the quality of labor and, in any case, these factors may be expected to average out in comparisons of whole populations. Experience, effort, and health, on the other hand, require more extensive comment.

Experience

Experience greatly influences the earnings and productivity of individuals.[1] In comparing labor quality I have taken only partial account of differ-

1. That experience *may* also be an attribute of *increasing* importance is suggested by the facts that (1) earnings differentials by age are greater for more educated than for less educated groups, and (2) educational distributions are shifting upward. However, the former may reflect mainly the concentration of more educated workers in *occupations* in which earnings rise most with age. To infer from such data that the importance of experience *is* rising, it would be necessary to isolate the effects of occupation from those of education on earnings differentials by age, and then to examine separately changes in the occupational structure and in the educational distribution within occupations.

Denis F. Johnston has shown that from 1946 to 1958 earnings differentials by amount of education among males of the same age rose relative to earnings differentials by age among males with the same education. He interprets this fact

ences in this important attribute. Insofar as the value of experience is related to length of experience, the omission does not appear to be important, however.

Loss of experience that accompanies longer formal schooling has already been allowed for by measuring the benefits of additional education net of the disadvantage of associated loss of experience. Differences between the extreme ranges of the age distribution in experience and vigor have also been taken care of by dividing the man-hours worked by the employed population of each sex among hours worked by each of three age groups—19 years and under, 20 to 64 years, and 65 years and over. The man-hours worked by each group have then been weighted by average hourly earnings. Length of experience is closely associated with age if allowance is made for differences in time spent in school, and the rise of earnings with age reflects, in part, the effect on ability of experience, or "on-the-job training," as some prefer to term it. The decline in earnings in the oldest age groups reflects loss of vigor, a preference by some older workers for easier work, and discrimination in hiring, which affects those who must change jobs.

The possibility remains that differences between countries and dates in the distribution among detailed age groups of man-hours worked by employed persons 20 to 64 years old could significantly affect the average quality of labor. It is possible to test whether or not this can be of much importance by applying earnings weights to hours worked by the detailed age groups. Very rough estimates of annual income differentials by age for United States males, standardized by amount of education, are given below. These are averages of

Age (in years)	Average income as a percentage of income of males aged 45 to 54 years[a]
20–24	47
25–29	64
30–34	79
35–44	86
45–54	100
55–64	93

a. Data are derived from Houthakker, *Review of Economics and Statistics*, February 1959, p. 25 [P37].

as an indication that the importance of experience declined *relative to that of education* as a determinant of income differentials (in *Monthly Labor Review*, May 1963, p. 514 [G67]).

differentials for all men with 8 years and 12 years of education, weighted one each, and with 1 to 4 years and 16 years of education, weighted one-half each. The only adjustment made for differences in labor force participation was a minimal upward income adjustment for college graduates in the 20 to 24 age bracket. The higher the education group considered, the more income rises with age.

Differentials in hourly earnings, which would be appropriate for use in this test, would be smaller so use of annual earnings to represent them probably overstates the effect of differences in age distributions. Percentage differentials in hourly earnings among females must be smaller than among males, and I arbitrarily assume them to be two-thirds as large as the differentials in annual income of males, after standardization for education.

Table 9–1 gives the results of two calculations. The first column shows that if earnings (adjusted for education) of members of each detailed age-sex group within the 20 to 64 age bracket were the same in other countries as in the United States in 1960, then the difference in age distribution within the 20 to 64 age bracket would cause earnings of all employed persons to be 0.2 percent higher in Belgium than in the United States, 0.4 percent higher in Denmark, and so on. The difference from the United States would be as much as 1 percent only in Germany and the Netherlands, where it would be lower by 2 percent. The calculation shows rather conclusively that differences in length of experience within the 20 to 64 age bracket cannot cause great variation in the quality of labor input.[2]

These results have not been used as quality adjustment indexes because I suspect differences calculated in this way are considerable overstatements. The method assumes that age can be used to measure useful experience. In aggregate comparisons this assumption needs qualification, especially for males. It is probable that many people remain in the same jobs longer than is necessary to gain about as much benefit as experience can offer toward obtaining either maximum performance in that job

2. These calculations were made before certain revisions incorporated in the estimates presented in Chapter 7 became available. Since they are illustrative and it did not appear that they could be appreciably changed by the additional data it seemed unnecessary to recompute these indexes.

TABLE 9-1

Illustrative Quality Adjustment Indexes for Differences in Experience Within the Labor Force Aged 20 to 64 Years, 1960

(*United States = 100*)

Country	Adjustment made for both sexes	Adjustment made for females only
United States	100.0	100.0
Belgium	100.2	99.5
Denmark	100.4	99.8
France	99.6	100.0
Germany	98.0	99.2
Netherlands	98.2	99.0
Norway	100.5	99.0
United Kingdom	100.8	99.8
Italy	100.9	99.4

Source: See text for derivation.

or training useful for a better job. Learning curves indicate that the period in which output rises appreciably with experience is quite short in many kinds of work. A *moderately* younger age distribution within the prime working ages is likely to mean more rapid advancement without much loss of really useful experience.

This comment applies less forcefully to calculations for females. The big contrasts in age distributions of female workers do not result from different age distributions of the female population. They are between countries where women frequently work for many years, though often after a lapse when they are raising young children, and countries such as the Netherlands and Norway where women workers 20 to 64 years of age are heavily concentrated in the youngest age bracket because women typically leave the labor force on marriage or birth of children. The second column of Table 9-1 shows the results of calculations which allow only for international differences in the age distribution of female workers 20 to 64 years of age. The average quality of all labor differs no more than 1 percent between any two countries because of this factor.[3] The largest differences probably reflect a genuine difference in the quality of female labor resulting from the experience of (and hence the kinds of work done by) female workers. Use of this column might improve slightly the esti-

mates of labor input. However, the computed differences are so small (between the United States and Northwest Europe less than 0.5 percent) both absolutely and relative to the likely margin of error that it has seemed better to omit this adjustment. This decision is reinforced by the fact that for a majority of countries quality differences calculated for females alone happen to be in the opposite direction from those calculated for both sexes together.

It is apparent from the age distributions that, over the period considered here, changes over time in individual countries must be much smaller than differences between countries.[4]

The calculations in this section, it must be pointed out, have dealt with only one aspect of experience: the years that individuals have spent at work. As noted in the discussion of education, I have found no way to judge whether more useful experience is obtained in the same time span in some countries than others because of differences in deliberate efforts to provide on-the-job training, in the nature of work done, or in the way work is performed and supervised. This applies also to comparisons of the same country at different dates.[5]

3. For females in the 20–64 age bracket alone the differences are several times as large as this, of course.

4. In *Sources of Economic Growth* [B25] I estimated that in the United States increased experience and better utilization of women workers raised the average quality of all labor by about 4 percent over the twenty-eight years from 1929 to 1957, and I indicated that increased experience must have been the main factor. This estimate now appears to me too large; the method used here yields a gain from increased experience of women workers of only 1.2 percent from 1930 to 1960. One reason for the previous overestimate is that males and females were weighted by numbers rather than earnings so females were overweighted in total labor input. In addition, the earlier estimate was based on a less direct method; it relied on changes in the ratio of female to male earnings. The difficulty was not with the method, which had some specific advantages in that study, but with the data used. Derived ultimately from information referring to wage earners in manufacturing, they showed the ratio of adult female to adult male hourly earnings to have risen from 0.58 in 1939 to 0.67 in 1949, and this rise was assumed to have continued in the fifties. I am now persuaded that in the economy as a whole there has not, in fact, been an increase of any such magnitude in the male-female earnings ratio since 1939.

5. For the United States an interesting effort to appraise changes over time in the value of "experience" has been made by Jacob Mincer. He has tried to estimate investment in training on the job, valued by the cost of income foregone by the recipient. He used a highly sophisticated but also highly indirect approach. Mincer's calculations imply that, from 1949 to 1958, changes in the expected value of per capita lifetime investment of males in "on-the-job training," in 1954 dollars were + 5 percent for those with a college education, − 22 percent for those with a high school

Effort

It is likely that people simply work harder in some countries than in others. A common, though not uncontroverted, opinion is that at all levels of responsibility Americans work harder than their counterparts in at least several of the European countries.

J. Frederic Dewhurst has reviewed the evidence and finds, with respect to industrial workers, that this is in fact the case:

> European observers with industrial experience on both sides of the Atlantic agree that the typical working pace in Canada and the United States is markedly faster than in Western Europe. That this is not due to inherent differences of strength or skill is obvious from the fact that although immigrants from Europe to North America first work at the tempo to which they have been accustomed, they soon adjust to the higher working speed of their fellow workers. Nor are these differences in working pace due to the quality of machines and equipment, for they exist where facilities and operating procedures are identical.[6]

Much of the difference seems to relate to the maintenance of a rapid and uninterrupted pace of work

throughout the day, which requires efficient management as well as effort and initiative by the industrial worker.

Unfortunately for our purposes, Dewhurst does not try to quantify differences. He states, "The extent to which these differences in attitude and working habits affect labor productivity is difficult to measure and in any event varies widely from industry to industry and from country to country."[7]

Differences in the pace of work (insofar as they are not an indirect reflection of differences in education or working hours) could be, and to some extent probably are, due to national differences in attitudes toward the trade-off between work and income. But they are likely to result much more from a different evaluation of the effect of work upon income and through income upon social status. In America the belief that individual earnings and advancement depend on individual performance is much more prevalent. Indeed, one can hardly doubt that Americans have long believed in the possibility of economic advancement through individual effort much more strongly than Europeans, and that much of this difference in attitude remains. With decreasing certainty, and yet some conviction, one may assert, first, that this belief was justified in the past, and, second, that it is still justified. European societies seem to be becoming increasingly fluid but appear rigid by comparison with the United States.

This line of thought, it should be noted, necessarily stresses advancement to a better job rather than international differences in the extent to which individual earnings in a particular job depend upon individual performance. The latter probably does not vary greatly in whole economies, nor is the interconnection obviously greater in the United States. For the self-employed the relationship is automatic everywhere. Efforts to tie earnings to performance in other labor force groups below the top management level, when made at all, usually depend upon the commission system for salesmen, individual salary determination for salaried employees, and some form of "payment by results"— usually individual piecework or relating the pay of a small group to its output—for wage earners. In

---

education, and + 13 percent for those with an elementary school education. Of the total "investment" in 1949, 48 percent was ascribed to the college group, 42 percent to the high school group, and 10 percent to the elementary group, so the fixed weight change from 1949 to 1958 can be calculated as − 6 percent. (From 1939 to 1949 a 36 percent *increase*, based on 1939 weights, is implied by his calculations.) Our quality adjustment indexes for education already allow for differences between formal education groups in the amount of informal education they receive. Consequently, such a fixed weight index could, in principle, perhaps be used as a quality adjustment index for labor if it could be made to refer to the "stock" of on-the-job training rather than to annual investment. (Theodore W. Schultz has attempted a conversion of Mincer's data to a stock basis for the years 1929 and 1957, though he does not give the detail required for a fixed weight index.) However, the statistical foundation of the estimates seems to me too weak, the results for annual investment are too erratic, and the changes too large to be believable. I do not myself see how changes could be other than minor if, as would be necessary for this study, the constant price value attached to any given type and amount of experience were the same at all dates (Mincer in *Journal of Political Economy*, Supplement, October 1962, Tables 1 and 2 [P25]; and Schultz in *Journal of Political Economy*, Supplement, October 1962, Table 1 [P25]).

6. Dewhurst in *Europe's Needs and Resources*, p. 105 [B31]. Dewhurst cites reports of the Anglo-American Council on Productivity that document the difference in the pace of work "at great length insofar as British and American workers are concerned," and studies by Graham Hutton, Lewis C. Ord, and Robert W. Smuts.

7. *Ibid.*, p. 106.

United States manufacturing only 27 percent of wage earners were paid "by results" in 1958 and the 1945–46 figure was apparently similar.[8] The percentages for certain countries were: United Kingdom, 32 or 33 in the 1950's; Germany, 38 or 39 in 1957 and 1962; Denmark, 38 to 40 throughout the 1954-63 period; France, 42 in 1960; and the Netherlands, 50 to 55 from 1953 through 1960 (perhaps an overstatement because data refer to larger establishments).[9] It also appears high for Norway.[10] Comparisons of United States and European productivity differentials in industries where piecework is and is not used are not available.

One may speculate not only that one reason productivity is higher in America than Europe is that Americans work harder, but also that one reason growth rates on the continent are higher than in the United States may be that the differential is declining as belief in opportunities for advancement through individual effort is strengthened in Europe.

One may also suppose—and a large and growing group of British observers do suppose—that productivity has increased less in the United Kingdom than on the continent because attitudes concerning the relationship between individual performance and rewards, and the environment that validates individuals' attitudes, have changed less since the war in Britain.[11] It is even said that the trend is

"back to status."[12] Not only do British workers feel individual effort and reward are unrelated but, it is said, they are also convinced that the gains from rising productivity in a firm accrue to the bosses. Reinforced by an exaggerated fear of redundancy, these attitudes lead British manual and white collar workers to oppose letting output standards rise as much as technical progress and investment would permit them to do without changing the intensity of work. They succeed in doing so to a greater extent than elsewhere, it is said, because employers are unprogressive, lack vigor and determination to force changes, and in any case are themselves loath to disturb an employee's status or established routine. If this is really so, then insofar as innovation and investment are not halted, the effect after a time is that British workers simply work less hard than others and by an increasing margin.[13] They take much of their wages "in leisure, mostly enjoyed at the place of employment."[14] The assertion that in most branches of the British economy a great gap has developed between actual and necessary employment is a recurrent theme of British economic journals. The hope and intent of reducing this gap is a major ingredient of British economic policy.

It seems to me probable that differences in effort are partially responsible for a higher level of output in the United States than in Europe, and not implausible that changes in effort contribute to a slower growth rate in the United States than on the continent and for a still lower growth rate in the

8. Lewis, in *Monthly Labor Review*, May 1960, pp. 460–63 [G67].

9. Data: United Kingdom, *Ministry of Labour Gazette*, September 1961, p. 369 [G42]; Germany, (for "Industrie"), Federal Statistical Office, *Gewerbliche Wirtschaft und Dienstleistungsbereich, Arbeitverdienste, 1962* [G17], and *Verdienste der Arbeiter in der Industrie im Oktober 1957* [G15]; Denmark, *Statistisk Årbog*, various issues [G8]; France, *Revue Française du Travail*, April–June 1961 [G12]; and the Netherlands, *Jaarcijfers voor de Nederland*, various issues [G23].

10. The ratio of total hours worked at piece rates to all hours worked in industry in 1949 is given as 57 in Norway, 41 in Denmark, 38 in the United Kingdom, and 37 in Germany (see ILO, *Payment by Results*, p. 55 [I11]).

11. It has also been suggested that British income differentials are too small to provide proper incentives to get ahead, but the distribution of income does not seem, in fact, to be more equal in the United Kingdom than in other countries. Irving Kravis reviewed the evidence (in *The Structure of Income*, pp. 237–39 [B63]) and concluded that the United Kingdom distribution is about the same as—or possibly a little more unequal than—that of the United States, and "hazards the guess" that the Netherlands distribution is a little more equal and the Danish still more equal. The general impression created by Kravis's data is that differences among all these countries are slight. R. J. Nicholson indicates that, over time, the British distribution

did become less unequal between 1949 and 1957, but not between 1957 and 1962 or 1963 (in *Lloyds Bank Review*, January 1967, pp. 11–21 [P27]).

Another common suggestion, heard less often today than in former years, is that too much social welfare interferes with workers' initiative and willingness to give a good day's work. This view seems difficult to support, in comparison with other countries, and is dismissed out of hand by Webb in *Britain Faces the Sixties*, pp. 22–30 [B107].

12. Hennessy, in *Rebirth of Britain*, p. 243 [B49].

13. For a sampling of views on the British situation see various articles in *Rebirth of Britain*; and articles by Koestler, Shanks, Crawley, and Cole in Koestler (ed.), *Suicide of a Nation?* [B61]. Browaldh (in *The Three Banks Review*, June 1963, pp. 3–16 [P46] and Beckerman and Associates (*The British Economy in 1975*, pp. 26 and 65–66 [B11]) are among those who are skeptical that worker attitudes as such offer a greater block to growth than elsewhere.

14. Hennessy, *Rebirth of Britain*, p. 246 [B49]. (Here he is endorsing views of William W. Allen, an American management consultant who is widely quoted on the extent of overmanning in the United Kingdom.)

United Kingdom. But the quantitative importance of differences in the intensity of work I find impossible to judge, much less to measure by any direct approach.[15] Inability to answer the simple question—How hard do people work?—and to compare different places and dates, is probably the most serious gap in my measure of labor input.

Health

Sickness and injury have four main consequences that reduce labor input. Two of these, death and inability to hold a job, are already reflected in employment estimates and cause no difficulty in measuring labor input. A third, time lost by employed persons, is similarly reflected in average hours worked.[16] The fourth, impairment of an individual's performance while he is at work, should also be, but is not, taken into account in my measurement of labor input.

Omission of an allowance for debility from disease and malnutrition would be of great importance in comparing labor input in low income countries with advanced nations.[17] It clearly is not in comparing the United States and the countries of Northwest Europe over the time period covered here. I do not intend to suggest that no one in any of these countries goes hungry (though most who do are not among the employed), that there are no cases of chronic disease, nor that the common cold is no problem. Neither do I suggest that inefficiency due to alcoholism is equally prevalent at all times and places, nor that public health programs are ineffectual. But it seems apparent that these factors

could not importantly affect international or intertemporal comparisons of labor input among these countries in the period since 1950.

With respect to the prevalence of disease and the availability of medical care, differences among these countries appear to be moderate.[18] With respect to nutrition, P. Lamartine Yates, a former official of the Food and Agriculture Organization (FAO), points out that in what I call Northwest Europe, per capita calorie consumption is well above per capita requirements, the distribution of food among income classes and other subdivisions of the population is such that national per capita data do not conceal significant groups who are undernourished, and that the types of food eaten are satisfactory. "In each of the central and northern countries [of Europe]," he concludes, "the national average is so well provided with calories, proteins, vitamins and minerals that no sizable segment of the population can be malnourished." And, further, "if any malnutrition still exists it must now indeed be due to ignorance or fecklessness." Diets have improved since 1950 but they seem to have been adequate for health throughout the period.[19]

It is true that the statistical results of a study by Hector Correa that tried to estimate the effect of nutrition upon labor efficiency in a large number of countries show appreciable differences among the Northwest European countries and the United States but, as explained in Appendix G, Correa's procedures appear inappropriate for comparisons among high income countries.

It *is* probable that inadequate food has significantly impaired the capacity of Italian workers in the postwar period, and that the substantial increase in calorie consumption during the period since 1950 has enlarged their working capacity. Yates, who notes that the nutritional status of the Mediterranean countries is much below Northern and Central

---

15. Some comments based on indirect evidence are offered in Chapter 20.

16. The allowance made for this factor may be inaccurate, but no gross error can be involved. Hector Correa (*The Economics of Human Resources* [B22]) estimates that, in the countries that concern us, time lost ranges only between 2 and 4 percent of total work time—that is, the maximum difference is 2 percent. Not much greater are the ranges suggested by Philip E. Enterline (if some allowance is made for the difference between American and European reporting) and by Common Market statistics (see Appendix D, p. 364). Time lost is certainly not greater in America than in Northwest Europe as a whole, and is probably less. Beyond this, little can be said about the direction of the differences because the ranking of individual countries in the various sources is quite dissimilar.

17. The problem of measuring such differences is considered, and some citations are given, by Mushkin in *Journal of Political Economy*, Supplement, October 1962, pp. 142–43 [P25].

18. See, for example, Fuchs in *Milbank Memorial Fund Quarterly*, October 1966, pp. 65–102 [P9]; and Houssiaux in *Analyse et Prévisions*, February 1966, pp. 83–102 [P3].

19. Yates, *Food, Land and Manpower in Western Europe*, pp. 42, 57–58, 75 [B111]. An FAO analysis of per capita protein consumption of families classified by the amount of their total expenditures, which refers to the early and mid-fifties and also covers the United States, supports the conclusions reached by Yates (in FAO, *The State of Food and Agriculture, 1964*, Chapter 3 [I7]). Additional data given in FAO, *The State of Food and Agriculture, 1965*, Chapter 5 [I17].

Europe, says that Italy "has a foot in both camps: the north Italians eat more like central Europeans while those of the centre and south eat more like Spaniards."[20] Correa finds a large difference between Italy and the other countries (Appendix G). It is likely that improvements in nutrition raised the quality of Italian labor and contributed to growth during the period under review, and inadequate nutrition of some workers may have contributed to the gap that existed between Italy and the other countries in national income per person employed even in 1960.

Summary Measures of Labor Input

Summaries of labor input based on the characteristics I have measured are given in Tables 9–2 and 9–3. They take account of (1) employment, (2) hours worked, (3) the division of man-hours worked among broad age-sex groups and between civilians and military personnel, and (4) the education of the labor force. The procedure is simply to multiply together the separate indexes for these four aspects of labor input.

In the international comparisons for 1960, given in Table 9–2, United States weights are used. In the time series for each country, given in Table 9–3, 1960 weights appropriate to that country are used. The indexes for Northwest Europe as a whole were

20. Yates, *Food, Land and Manpower in Western Europe*, p. 69 [B111].

TABLE 9–2

Indexes of Labor Input: International Comparison, 1960[a]

(United States = 100)

Area	Total labor input	Labor input per person employed	Labor input per capita
United States	100.0	100.0	100.0
Northwest Europe	115.3	97.7	114.2
Belgium	4.9	97.9	97.6
Denmark	2.9	94.2	115.4
France	27.6	97.9	109.1
Germany	36.0	94.8	117.2
Netherlands	6.6	110.0	103.6
Norway	2.1	100.6	108.1
United Kingdom	35.2	98.6	121.0
Italy	26.2	89.1	95.5

Sources: Derived from Tables 5–2, 6–4, 7–5, and 8–7.
a. Based on United States weights.

calculated by use of fixed 1960 employment weights for the seven component countries; they do not, therefore, reflect changes in the shares of the seven countries in total Northwest European employment.

International comparisons and time series are provided for total labor input, labor input per person employed, and labor input per capita.[21] The last two measures differ, sometimes widely, because of differences or changes in the ratio of employment to total population.

21. In the case of the time series, the multiplications were based on series with 1960 = 100, and reconverted to a 1950 base; this was also done at each step of the underlying calculations.

TABLE 9–3

Indexes of Labor Input: Time Series, 1950–62

(1950 = 100)

Area	Total labor input				Labor input per person employed				Labor input per capita			
	1950	1955	1960	1962	1950	1955	1960	1962	1950	1955	1960	1962
United States	100.0	109.0	115.3	118.9	100.0	101.4	102.8	103.8	100.0	100.0	97.6	97.1
Northwest Europe	100.0	107.9	112.3	114.0	100.0	101.7	102.0	101.9	100.0	104.3	103.8	102.9
Belgium	100.0	106.9	109.6	114.7	100.0	103.3	105.7	107.5	100.0	104.1	103.5	107.5
Denmark	100.0	103.3	107.1	109.4	100.0	100.9	98.6	97.9	100.0	99.4	99.9	100.4
France	100.0	103.8	107.0	108.8	100.0	103.2	105.7	107.4	100.0	100.0	98.0	96.9
Germany	100.0	113.9	122.1	123.8	100.0	99.8	98.2	97.6	100.0	108.6	109.5	108.1
Netherlands	100.0	108.6	114.5	115.6	100.0	102.8	104.6	101.9	100.0	102.1	100.8	99.0
Norway	100.0	103.4	101.8	102.7	100.0	102.4	101.2	100.6	100.0	98.5	92.7	92.1
United Kingdom	100.0	106.7	109.1	110.0	100.0	102.0	102.8	101.8	100.0	105.4	105.1	104.2
Italy	100.0	110.7	119.0	119.6	100.0	105.5	110.2	111.8	100.0	107.4	112.1	111.4

Sources: Derived from Tables 5–3, 6–6, 7–7, and 8–6.

Three specific points warrant repetition here:

1. These estimates of the quantity and quality of labor input are not intended to take account of the efficiency with which labor is allocated among uses, or used. This will be the subject of later analysis.

2. The estimates of 1960 level, relative to the United States, would be lower in all the European countries if European rather than United States education weights were used.

3. The estimate of the 1960 level for Italy, given in Table 9–2, would be lower if plausible adjustments in the education estimate or an allowance for deficient nutrition had been introduced.

There is no need to describe in the text what the tables show, since similarities and differences stand out clearly enough and both the factors determining them and qualifications concerning their accuracy have been discussed in preceding chapters. Calculation of the contribution of changes in labor input to growth rates and to differences in the levels of national income in 1960 will be deferred to Chapter 15, where all inputs are considered simultaneously.

Although the United States increase in total labor input was exceeded by two European countries, the analysis of preceding chapters suggests that, within the limits set by the demographic position of each country and its initial situation, the United States has done more than any of the European countries to stimulate growth by increasing labor input. First, more additional women have been drawn into the labor force, relative to population, in the United States than in any of the European countries— far more than in any but Belgium.[22] Second, the European countries, except France, have reduced working hours of full-time wage and salary workers since 1955, while the United States has not. Third, the educational qualifications of the labor force have been upgraded more in America than in Europe—much more than in any of the large Northwest European countries.

Germany, to be sure, obtained a large employment increase by immigration, which the United States could also have done, but the German experience reflects mainly the special circumstance of a divided country. Germany also gained, as did Italy, by eliminating large amounts of structural unemployment existing in 1950, which the United States did not have. The United States could, of course, have done more than it did before 1962 to eliminate unemployment due to deficient demand. By the beginning of 1966 this had been accomplished.

22. For examination of the reasons that measured growth rates differ it is not germane that entry of women into the labor force entailed some loss of household production; this loss would partially offset the gain in production for the market if a more comprehensive concept of income were used.

CHAPTER TEN

Capital Input and Gross Investment

The capital of a nation, as I use the term, consists of the structures, equipment, and inventories available for use in domestic production, together with the nation's net claims upon other countries. In the nine countries under consideration, capital of all types represented less than one-third as large a fraction of total productive resources as labor, according to the estimates presented in Chapter 4; typically the fraction was nearer one-quarter. For this reason, about four times as large a percentage increase in capital as in labor is typically required to raise total input, and hence national income, by any given percentage. However, during 1950–62, percentage changes in capital input did exceed those in labor input. In five of the nine countries, it turns out, the difference was so large that the increase in capital input contributed more than the increase in labor input to the 1950–62 growth rate. The amount of capital per person employed also varied greatly among countries. Changes and differences in capital input, in fact, are so large that capital requires quite as much consideration as labor in this study.

The three chapters to follow examine and estimate the contribution of capital to growth. The remainder of this chapter is devoted to a preliminary topic: the presentation of the percentages of national product that the nine countries have devoted to gross investment. Inclusion of these data is, in part, merely a bow to a recent tradition dictating that no study of growth can be considered complete without them. Although such gross investment ratios have often been used directly in attempts to analyze the relationship between capital and growth, I shall argue that they have, in fact, little value for this purpose.

There are, however, two other reasons for presenting these ratios at this time. First, they are of interest as an indication of the resources devoted to one source of growth and therefore bear upon one of the questions under investigation: Were other countries doing more than the United States to promote growth? Second, gross investment data underlying the ratios also enter into the construction of series measuring the capital stock that are used in subsequent chapters. It is therefore necessary to examine the definition and scope of these investment data, and to explore their comparability among countries, before time series for the components of capital stock and international comparisons of the levels of the stock in different countries are derived and presented.

TABLE 10–1

Gross Investment as a Percentage of Gross National Product at Market Prices,
by Type of Investment and Time Period[a]

(*Averages of percentages of individual years*)

Type of investment and time period	United States	Bel- gium	Den- mark	France	Ger- many	Nether- lands	Nor- way	United King- dom	Italy
1950–54									
Total gross investment	18.7	18.4	17.9	19.1	23.9	23.9	29.0	14.8	19.2
Nonresidential fixed investment	11.8	12.9	13.5	13.2	14.7	16.0	22.6	10.3	15.2
Construction	5.6	5.3	5.1	5.5	4.3	6.5	8.6	3.5	5.9
Machinery and equipment	6.2	7.6	8.4	7.6	10.4	9.6	14.0	6.8	9.3
Residential construction	5.6	4.7	3.2	3.3	4.8	4.0	5.2	3.1	3.5
Inventories	1.6	.7	1.6	1.9	2.7	2.6	1.9	.7	.8
Net foreign lending	−.3	.1	−.4	.8	1.6	1.4	−.7	.8	−.4
1955–62									
Total gross investment	18.5	19.6	19.4	19.7	27.2	27.3	28.1	16.9	23.4
Nonresidential fixed investment	12.5	13.4	15.1	14.1	18.1	19.4	25.1	12.6	15.8
Construction	6.3	5.5	5.4	5.6	6.2	7.3	9.2	4.5	6.6
Machinery and equipment	6.2	7.8	9.7	8.5	12.0	12.1	15.8	8.0	9.1
Residential construction	5.0	4.7	3.1	4.7	5.2	4.4	4.5	2.9	5.7
Inventories	.8	.5	1.6	1.6	2.1	1.9	.7	1.1	1.0
Net foreign lending	.2	1.1	−.4	−.7	1.8	1.6	−2.2	.3	.9
1950–62									
Total gross investment	18.4	19.2	18.8	19.5	25.9	26.0	28.4	16.1	21.8
Nonresidential fixed investment	12.1	13.2	14.5	13.7	16.8	18.1	24.1	11.7	15.5
Construction	6.0	5.5	5.3	5.6	5.5	7.0	9.0	4.1	6.4
Machinery and equipment	6.1	7.7	9.2	8.2	11.4	11.1	15.1	7.6	9.2
Residential construction	5.2	4.7	3.1	4.1	5.0	4.2	4.8	3.0	4.9
Inventories	1.1	.6	1.6	1.7	2.4	2.2	1.1	1.0	.9
Net foreign lending	.0	.7	−.4	−.1	1.7	1.5	−1.6	.5	.4

Sources: OECD, *National Accounts Statistics, 1955–1964* [I35], OSCE, *General Statistical Bulletin*, No. 11, 1965 [I48], and other sources cited in Appendix A. For the United States an addition was made for state and local government purchases of machinery and equipment based on data given in the *Survey of Current Business*, March 1961 [G63]. For Germany, the Saar and West Berlin are included beginning with 1960. For France new series beginning 1959, old series for earlier years; net foreign lending differs greatly in the two series. Nonresidential fixed investment in Belgium in 1950–52 was not divided between construction and machinery and equipment in the source used; in this table it was allocated in the same proportion as in 1953.
a. Details may not add to totals because of rounding. Percentages are based on data in current prices.

Investment Data: Definition and Appraisal

Table 10–1 shows the percentage of gross national product at market prices that each country invested in physical assets in the 1950–62 period and two subperiods. Investment is measured gross of capital consumption. It is defined as gross domestic investment plus net investment abroad. In accordance with OECD definitions, investment in this table includes government acquisitions of structures and equipment except military facilities and equipment. Investment in "human capital" through expenditures for education and training, or through any other channel, is not included, nor are expenditures for research and development.

Investment so measured is equal to "gross national saving" as defined by the international agencies plus net gifts from abroad (or minus net gifts to other countries). Gross national saving is, by definition, equal to gross private saving plus the surplus of governments on current account.

Investment data published by the international agencies for the several countries are formally comparable in definition.[1] This does not guarantee that they are statistically comparable, although con-

1. T. P. Hill, formerly of the OECD staff, states (in *Economic Journal*, June 1964, p. 296 [P17]) that the omission from United States data of government expenditure on machinery and equipment is the only known conceptual discrepancy in OECD figures for gross fixed investment. In Table 10–1, I have included an estimate for state and local government purchases (0.2 percent of GNP in 1950–54 and 0.3 percent in 1955–62) but federal purchases, believed small, are still omitted.

sistency has certainly been improved in recent years.[2]

Data to estimate investment are less than satisfactory in all countries. Business fixed investment is usually estimated either by the commodity flow approach or from reports on capital expenditures by business firms, or by some combination of the two approaches. In the United States, at least, the two types of estimates are difficult to reconcile. Inventory estimation is often based on inadequate samples and usually encounters difficult problems of converting book values to a usable measure. Differences of a point or two in investment percentages clearly cannot be relied upon or even confidently be expected to survive future statistical revisions.[3]

But it is not likely that the larger differences among countries in investment ratios are due to incomparabilities or errors in measurement. For one particularly interesting comparison—that between the United Kingdom and Norway, the countries with the lowest and highest investment ratios—an independent investigation by Geoffrey Dean confirmed that the difference is real.[4] Reported investment ratios in these two countries differ greatly and so do estimating methods for construction and producers' durable equipment. The United Kingdom uses mainly the "expenditure" method and Norway the "commodity flow" method. For 1958 the United Nations (which reports the same data as OECD) reported that gross fixed investment was 15.0 percent of GNP at market prices in the United Kingdom and 32.2 percent in Norway (where 1958 was a year of exceptionally large investment). Dean's independent investigation, which was specifically directed at obtaining comparability, arrived at 16.7 percent for the United Kingdom and 32.4 percent for Norway. The unadjusted difference between the countries of 17.2 percentage points was reduced only 1.5 points by Dean.[5] Norwegian gross fixed investment has been so large in comparison with other countries that it is particularly useful to have confirmation that this is not the result of inconsistent statistical procedures.

Table 10–1 classifies total investment among several types. There is some question about the comparability of the division of nonresidential fixed investment between nonresidential construction and machinery and equipment.[6] The distinction is not a natural one in important types of producing enterprises, and firms have difficulty in providing this breakdown of capital outlays in capital expenditure surveys. The Conference of European Statisticians has, to be sure, recommended a classification by type of asset and urged combination of the expenditure and commodity flow approaches in implementing it. In an analysis of the actual data for OECD members countries, however, T. P. Hill found "absolutely no correlation whatsoever" between the share of GNP devoted to machinery and equipment and the share devoted to nonresidential (or total) construction.[7] This is, as Hill says, "a remarkable feature of these statistics." Conceivably it could be accounted for by differences in the industrial composition of investment, in the proportion of investment that represents replacement, and in the price of construction relative to machinery and equipment prices.[8] Hill himself did not consider it an

---

2. Hill (*ibid.,* p. 288) points to the division of passenger cars between consumption and investment as one example of probable incomparability in investment statistics.

In the United States, total purchases of passenger cars by consumers and business amounted to 4.5 percent of gross national product in 1962. Only 18 percent of these purchases —equal to 0.8 percent of GNP—were classified as for business use and thus appear in the gross investment data. In recent years the United States allocated 18 percent of passenger car purchases to business, the United Kingdom less than 30 percent, Belgium about 36, France about 40, Norway 50, Italy 60, and the Netherlands still more. These differences appear improbably large even though the percentages do tend to go down with greater use of passenger cars. (The United States has never used a business allocation above 30 percent, except in wartime.)

3. Actual inspection of the data reveals some estimates that may be regarded with suspicion. For example, the low percentages for Belgian inventory investment imply an improbably low growth rate of the stock of inventories. See Chapter 13.

4. *Journal of the Royal Statistical Society,* Series A, 1964, pp. 89–107 [P26].

5. Dean also estimated fixed investment in both countries on the Scandinavian "gross-gross" basis used in Norway's own national accounts. In these figures, investment is measured not only gross of depreciation but also inclusive of repairs. The large difference between the two countries remained. Dean found "gross-gross" investment to be 22.2 percent of "gross-gross" national product in the United Kingdom and 39.3 percent in Norway.

6. Throughout this book the terms "machinery and equipment," "equipment," and "producers' durables" are used as synonyms.

7. Hill, *Economic Journal,* June 1964, p. 296 [P17].

8. Measurement in common prices and elimination of government investment helps to bring the proportions in several countries together, but some large differences remain. See Chapter 12.

obstacle to separate comparison of machinery and equipment expenditures. But it seems to me to cast doubt on the comparability of this breakdown.

Investment Ratios and Resource Costs

Investment ratios provide a limited guide to the resource cost of investment. Thus Table 10–1 furnishes a rough indication of the proportion of each nation's production that was devoted to saving, and hence to the increase of future output as against current consumption. It is relevant to one of the questions to be investigated: Is Europe doing more than the United States to stimulate growth?

It is, of course, rather artificial to identify differences in saving rates with differences in the proportion of income that represented consumption foregone if inadequacy of aggregate demand prevented full use of the labor and capital available to an economy (or would have done so if investment were smaller). Under these circumstances more investment would have meant more rather than less consumption. This was the situation in the United States from 1958 through 1964, for example, and at times in other countries.

Even aside from this consideration, Table 10–1 is not entirely appropriate for the measurement of consumption that was foregone because resources were devoted to saving in physical assets. For this purpose the appropriate ratio is that of *net* investment to *net* national product with product and investment in each country valued at that country's own current factor cost prices. Ratios in Table 10–1 are based on each country's own current prices but they are market prices. More serious, investment and product are gross rather than net of depreciation.

The following listing ranks the countries by their ratios of total gross investment to GNP in the 1950–62 and 1955–62 periods, and gives the ratios for these periods and for 1964:

	1950–62	1955–62	1964
Norway	28.4	28.1	27.8
Netherlands	26.0	27.3	27.1
Germany	25.9	27.2	28.0
Italy	21.8	23.4	22.9
France	19.5	19.7	21.3
Belgium	19.2	19.6	20.6
Denmark	18.8	19.4	21.1
United States	18.4	18.5	18.7
United Kingdom	16.1	16.9	18.0

The countries divide into three fairly well defined groups in the 1950–62 and 1955–62 periods. Norway, the Netherlands, and Germany had much the highest ratios. Italy was in an intermediate position. France, Belgium, Denmark, the United States, and the United Kingdom had much lower ratios than the first group. Differences between these groups of countries seem large enough to be significant. Differences among countries in the same group are smaller and may not be significant in view of conceptual and statistical limitations. Apparently four of the European countries, at least, were in fact saving much more of their current output in the form of physical investment than the United States.[9]

Depreciation in 1960 was put earlier at about 15 percent of GNP at factor cost in Norway, 12.5 percent in the United States, 11 in Belgium and Italy, and 9 or 10 percent in the other countries.[10] If these rough estimates for 1960 are at all representative of the period, the main effect of shifting from gross to net saving on the *percentage point* spreads between countries would be to lower appreciably, but still leave very high, the position of Norway. The position of the United States would also be lowered, perhaps enough to permit a cautious suggestion that the United States may have had the lowest net saving rate among the nine countries. The common generalization that the European countries as a whole have saved a larger proportion of their income in the form of physical and international assets than has the United States is clearly correct. *Relative* differences among countries in net saving rates are greater than those in gross saving rates since depreciation ratios clearly differ much less than gross saving rates. If the ratio of gross saving to GNP is half again as high in one country as in another, the ratio of net saving to net product is much more than half again as high.

The gross investment ratios for the single year 1964, also shown in the text table, indicate that the pattern of international differences was still much the same as in 1955–62. However, investment ratios for the five countries in the lowest group were all a little higher in 1964 than in 1955–62 while those for

9. This would be the case in 1950–62 even if the contribution of American saving to European investment through the Marshall Plan during the early fifties were transferred from European to American saving.

10. See Chapter 2, note 17.

countries with the higher ratios, except Germany, were a little lower.

What Investment Ratios Do *Not* Mean

Investment ratios provide no information concerning the relative quantities of capital goods that the various countries obtained in return for their saving. GNP's are, of course, not the same in any two countries; and, even if they were, differences among the countries in price relationships could easily create the result that a country devoting a larger percentage of GNP to a particular type of investment than another country obtained less capital goods for its expenditure. Subsequent chapters present estimates of the relative quantities of durable capital goods that the nine countries under review obtained by their investment expenditures.

No inferences can be drawn directly from the percentages in Table 10–1 about either the rate of increase of the capital stock or the contribution of capital to growth. Various investigators have, to be sure, expended a good deal of effort on comparisons of and correlations between investment ratios and growth rates in an effort to test the effect of investment on growth. One difficulty with this approach is that the main reason for expecting a correlation would have the causation running the other way—that is, from growth rates to investment ratios. Investment demand is likely to be strong in a booming, fast-growing economy and weak in a slow-growing economy. This relationship is apparent in time series for individual countries, and it may be expected to emerge in some degree in international comparisons of investment percentages.

Although there is also some reason to expect a correlation to emerge with causation running from investment ratios to growth rates, this expectation is tenuous. The increase in physical capital is only one of many sources of growth so that its effects could easily be either magnified or obscured by positive or negative correlation between it and other growth sources. Moreover, the rate of increase in the stock of physical capital is not measured by investment ratios. There is not even any general theoretical reason to expect correlation between investment ratios and capital stock growth

rates. Indeed, it is well known that the long-term growth rate of the capital stock (and, consequently, the growth rate of national income that would emerge if capital *were* the only source of growth and if there were unit elasticity of substitution of capital for labor) would be the same regardless of the *permanent* level of the investment or saving ratio; only the *level* of capital stock and output is affected by differences in the permanent investment rate. Any expectation of a correlation between investment ratios and growth rates, with causation running in that direction, must therefore rely on a correlation between present investment percentages and the difference between present and past investment percentages (adjusted for war damage). Data presented in Chapter 12 indicate that, for nonresidential structures and equipment, the association between postwar investment ratios and growth rates of the capital stock actually is very imperfect indeed. The extent to which such a correlation exists can be tested only by referring to capital stock series and, if these are available for testing, they are more appropriately used directly.[11]

Rates of increase in capital stock and the contributions of capital to growth are explored in the following three chapters, but with only incidental

11. The extent to which investment ratios are correlated with growth rates of *national income* or GNP—regardless of the direction of causation—is a matter of dispute. Since any investigator is free to select from among a large range of alternatives the scope of investment, the countries, and the time periods to compare, it is not surprising that high correlations between one investment ratio or another and growth rates sometimes appear for a particular group of countries. These have had a remarkable tendency to vanish with the addition of other countries. Possibly the best known example is Colin Clark's addition of other countries to an original selection published by Governor Nelson D. Rockefeller (*Growthmanship*, pp. 46–50 [B18]).

The article by T. P. Hill mentioned above is among the most thorough and frankest explorations by a writer believing in the value of this approach, although it is confined to one time period and to OECD countries. Hill obtained a high correlation between 1955–62 growth rates of GNP and the 1954–61 percentage of GNP spent on machinery and equipment when he examined the five large OECD countries; but the correlation worsened if carried out on a per person employed basis, and some of the smaller countries did not fit the pattern at all. The direction of causation is hardly examined. Hill's general conclusion was that a high investment percentage for machinery and equipment was a necessary but not sufficient condition for rapid growth. An alternative conclusion from Hill's analysis might be that a high growth rate is likely to create a strong demand for investment but investment demand may also be strong in the absence of a high growth rate.

European investigators have often computed so-called

reference to investment ratios. The three chapters also examine the levels of the stock in different countries and their effects upon output levels. For this analysis, capital is divided among four compo-

nents: Chapter 11 deals with two of these, dwellings and international assets; Chapter 12 with nonresidential structures and equipment; and Chapter 13 with inventories.

---

incremental capital-output ratios (ICOR's): the ratios of investment percentages to growth rates (total or per person employed). These have sometimes been used as if they provided information on the rate of return on investment and meant that doubling the percentage of GNP invested would double the growth rate. The central, but by no means the only, objection to this use of ICOR's is, of course, that it assumes investment is the only source of growth. As is to be expected, ICOR's show stability neither among countries nor over time in the same country. Harvey Leibenstein has shown that ICOR's ought to be and usually are *inversely* related to growth rates (in *Review of Economics and Statistics,* February 1966, pp. 20–27 [P37]). Use of ICOR's to measure rates of return is declining but has not disappeared.

An article in *The Economist* (January 16, 1965, pp. 233–34, [P19]) provides an amusing example of the continuing influence of this "tool" on language. The article properly

stresses the importance of growth sources other than aggregate investment, and in a happy departure from custom even plots growth rates as the independent variable in a chart showing the relationship between growth rates and investment ratios. But, in noting that ICOR's were higher almost everywhere in 1957–63 than in 1950–56, it says: "Almost without exception, these ratios suggest a lower payoff on fixed investment for the period 1957–63 than for the period 1950–56. Germany, for example, was having to put in nearly twice as high a proportion of investment for each unit of growth in the second period as it had in the first (Sweden, alone, was getting a slightly better return on its money)." One can only ask: If investment is not the dominant source of growth, and causation runs from growth rates to investment ratios, how can ICOR's tell anything about the proportion of investment Germany had to put in, or the return Sweden obtained on its money?

CHAPTER ELEVEN

Dwellings and International Assets

Dwellings and international assets are two important types of capital that, though otherwise dissimilar, share the convenient characteristic that their contributions to changes in the national income are easily measured. Disentangling their contributions to growth from those of labor and other growth sources poses almost no problems except that of assembling data.

Both these types of capital contributed more to American than to European growth. During 1950–62, dwellings are estimated to have contributed 0.25 percentage points to the United States growth rate —about one-thirteenth of the total—and international assets 0.05 points. These are larger than the contributions in any European country except for international assets in the Netherlands. In both the United Kingdom and the Netherlands, income from abroad importantly affects comparisons of growth before and after 1955.

These two sources also contributed more to national income per person employed in the United States than in any of the European countries in 1960. They would have placed national income per person employed in Northwest Europe 3 percent below the United States if there had been no other differences between the two areas.

Dwellings

Dwellings represent a very large fraction of the capital stock of all countries. In the United States the value of residential structures at the end of 1961 was 72 percent as large as the total value of all the fixed nonresidential capital of enterprises.[1] The contribution made to growth rates by this component of capital is estimated below.

Contribution to Growth

An increase in the housing stock contributes to growth by enlarging the services provided to occupants of dwellings in future years. The change in the net value in constant prices that is placed on these services in national income measures can be isolated, so that its direct contribution to the increase in national income can be readily calculated;

1. The estimate cited is based on use of service lives given in "Bulletin F," a guide to depreciation allowable for tax purposes that was published by the Bureau of Internal Revenue in 1942. The percentage is the same whether the calculation is based on values before deducting accumulated depreciation or after deducting accumulated depreciation computed by the straight line formula. Estimates used are in 1958 prices.

this is facilitated by the fact that "ownership of dwellings" is regarded as a separate "industry" in the standardized system of national accounts.[2] Changes in net output (national income originating) in this industry are due almost entirely to changes in the quantity of capital and land used in the industry; labor input is almost negligible and productivity change is of little importance as output is measured.[3] I have not attempted to separate the contribution of residential structures from that of the sites on which they stand; the estimates to be presented include the contribution of both structures and sites.

National income or product originating in the "services of dwellings" industry does include a very small amount of employee compensation—for managers, janitors, and other employees of apartment houses—in addition to property income. To obtain the contribution of residential capital and land to the constant price national income I have therefore reduced national income originating in housing by the ratio of employee compensation to

2. For details of the estimates, see Appendix I.
3. Of course, changes in the actual series for net output included in national income aggregates also reflect estimating errors. In addition, the procedure of deducting maintenance and repairs as current expenses rather than capitalizing and depreciating them may cause irregular movements in the net output series.

national income. This is, however, a trifling adjustment.[4]

Suppose that between two dates the absolute increase in the net value at factor cost of the services of dwellings was equal to 5 percent of the absolute increase in total constant price national income. Suppose, also, that the growth rate of national income between those dates was 4 percent. Then 5 percent of the growth rate of national income of 4.00 percent, or 0.20 percentage points, can be attributed to the services of dwellings.[5] The contribution of the increase in housing services to the growth rate of total national income in each country computed by this method is shown in the first three columns of Table 11–1.[6] Except that they in-

4. Several countries actually include no employee compensation at all in this industry, apparently classifying it elsewhere.
   It may be noted in passing that insofar as owner occupants personally do more maintenance around their homes than tenants, and gross rental values of owner-occupied homes are estimated by reference to rents paid for tenant-occupied dwellings, the value of some of the work performed by owner occupants is credited as a return to capital and land; this return would be smaller if the owner occupant contracted out all maintenance work. To this extent the contribution of residential capital and land to national income is overstated, but the point is not important.
5. Appendix I gives an illustration of actual calculations.
6. The method of estimating the contribution of housing to growth differs from that adopted in my American study in two respects. First (as mentioned in Chapter 4 of this study), the scope of housing is larger; the present estimates

TABLE 11–1

Contribution of Dwellings to Growth Rates of Total National Income, Total GNP, and National Income per Person Employed

(*In percentage points*)

Area	Contribution to total national income			Contribution to total GNP			Contribution to national income per person employed		
	1950–62	1950–55	1955–62	1950–62	1950–55	1955–62	1950–62	1950–55	1955–62
United States	.25	.26	.25	.32	.35	.30	.21	.22	.21
Northwest Europe	.07	.05	.08	.13	.09	.15	.04	.04	.05
Belgium	.02	.04	.01	.10	.15	.06	−.01	.00	−.02
Denmark	.13	.14	.12	.18	.17	.19	.10	.12	.09
France	.02	.00	.03	.10	.04	.13	.02	.00	.03
Germany	.14	.12	.16	.19	.17	.20	.12	.10	.14
Netherlands	.06	.04	.07	.11	.11	.11	.04	.02	.06
Norway	.04	.05	.04	.08	.10	.07	.04	.05	.04
United Kingdom	.04	.02	.06	.09	.04	.12	.02	.00	.04
Italy	.07	.02	.11	.10	.05	.13	.05	.02	.09

Sources: See text and Appendix I for method of derivation of income data; employment from Table 5–1.

clude a slight interaction factor, the estimates show what the growth rate of national income or product would have been if nothing had changed except the services of dwellings. For example, in 1958 prices the national income of the United Kingdom was £ 18,022 million in 1955. From 1955 to 1962 the net value of housing services in 1958 prices increased by £ 83 million. This change alone would have raised the United Kingdom national income by 0.46 percent in 7 years, or approximately the 0.06 percent a year given in Table 11–1 for the 1955–62 period.

The contribution of housing to the growth rate of United States national income was about 0.25 percentage points in each subperiod. In Northwest Europe it was only 0.05 in 1950–55 and 0.08 in 1955–62. Among the European countries it ranged from 0.01 to 0.16 points in 1955–62, and from 0.02 to 0.14 in the 1950–62 period as a whole. In all periods distinguished in the table the contribution of housing to growth was larger in the United States than in any European country and much larger than in most of them.

Contributions of dwellings to growth rates of GNP, also shown in Table 11–1, are larger because of the importance of depreciation on dwellings, but even on this gross basis they do not exceed 0.2 percentage points in Europe or 0.35 in the United States.[7]

The right side of Table 11–1 shows the contribution of changes in the value of housing services to growth rates of national income per person employed. The method of calculation is similar to that followed to obtain the contribution to the growth of total income, except that national income and income from housing were divided by employment before making the computations. A zero contribution, such as appears for Belgium, France, and the United Kingdom in the 1950–55 period, means that employment and the net value of dwellings services increased by the same percentage from 1950 to 1955 so that housing income per person employed did not change.

Two facts stand out from Table 11–1. First, the biggest contribution of housing services to any European growth rate of total national income was 0.16 percentage points, and to national income per person employed 0.14. This is an important finding in itself. It means that nowhere in Europe was housing a major factor in growth, and that the large differences among the countries in the share of national product devoted to increasing the housing stock can be dismissed as a really big direct source of differences in growth rates. In part this is a reflection of the low rate of return on residential capital.[8] The return was below the average return to other capital even in the United States and, because of rent control, it was still lower in most of the European countries.

Second, housing contributed more to growth in the United States than it did to growth in any of the European countries both before and after 1955. It

---

include farm residences and residential land, while the earlier estimates were confined to nonfarm structures. Second, the technique of estimation differs. In the former study the contribution of housing was measured as the product of the growth rate of the gross housing stock and the share of property income from housing in the current price national income. If all national income and capital stock data were consistent the two procedures would yield almost identical results. (The difference between current and constant price share weights could cause a discrepancy.) But the present method is superior in its ability to reproduce the contribution of housing to changes in the national income as it is actually measured for each country. It also eliminates the need to compile and rely upon series for the deflated value of the gross stock of dwellings; these are not available in all countries.

7. I have included in Table 11–1 contributions to the growth rate of GNP at factor cost—which, as is to be expected when depreciation is increasing, are higher but not greatly higher than contributions to national income—to show that the rather small size of the figures for the contribution of housing to national income is not heavily dependent upon the accuracy of the depreciation estimates. The objective in deriving Table 11–1 was to determine the contribution of the services of dwellings to the national income or gross product as it is actually measured for each country. Some approximations were required and the per-

centage errors in certain of the smaller figures may be substantial; it is not inconceivable that a figure of, say, 0.04 should be 0.08, an error of 100 percent. But I should be surprised if any figure was in error by as much as 0.1 percentage points. There is no question about the orders of magnitude. Table 11–1, like other similar tables, is shown to hundredths of a percentage point because the numbers are so small, not because of its accuracy.

8. Only returns in the base years used in the deflation of the national product are relevant to these calculations in principle. However, it may be noted that, under rent control, earnings of new dwellings in *current* prices often are higher than those of old dwellings because new units are exempted from rent controls. Whether or not this is reflected in increases in constant price series for value added in dwellings depends on the characteristics of the price series used to deflate gross rents in the various countries. (If rents charged on an identical sample of units are priced it will be.) In either case the correct estimate of the contributions of housing to growth of national income as measured is automatically obtained by the procedure followed.

contributed at least 0.1 percentage points more in the United States than in any European country to the growth rates of both total national income and income per person employed with the sole exception of Germany in 1955–62. Housing, consequently, does not help to explain why European growth rates were higher. Even among the European countries the size of the contribution made by housing was not systematically related to differences in growth rates.

These estimates fill the requirements for analysis of the sources of growth of national income as measured. However, it is of interest to analyze further the record of the various countries in the field of housing.

Changes in Housing Services

Differences among countries in the contributions of housing reflect differences in the importance of income from housing as well as differences in the growth rate of housing services. The larger contribution of housing to United States than to European growth is partly due to the greater weight in national income of property income from housing. (Table 4–1 gives period averages.) However, the percentage increase in the deflated net value of the services of dwellings was itself larger in the United States than in any other country except Germany. This is the case in 1950–55, 1955–62, and 1950–62. Even if the services of dwellings received the same weight in the national income of all countries, therefore, only in Germany would their increase, as measured in each country, have contributed as much to growth as in the United States. The increase in the net value of housing services in Germany was much greater than in the United States.[9]

Several sets of collateral data are of further as-

sistance in appraising performance in the housing field. Series measuring consumer expenditures for rent in constant prices, for which indexes are given in the following table, tell much the same story as the net value data:

	1962÷1950	1955÷1950	1962÷1955
United States	182	133	137
Belgium	115	109	105
Denmark	150	118	127
France	158	112	141
Germany	227	135	169
Netherlands	144	118	121
Norway	143	120	119
United Kingdom	123	107	114
Italy	138	113	122

They indicate that only Germany, and in the 1955–62 period, France, achieved larger percentage increases in the constant price value of rent, and by implication in the housing stock, than the United States.[10] Aside from the slight French advantage over the United States in 1955–62, this is the same conclusion that was reached from net income data.

Volume of Residential Construction

We may also inquire as to the amount of residential construction during the 1950–62 period. One indicator is the number of dwelling units built, although data may not be entirely comparable and the units built in the United States were presumably more costly (and much more concentrated in single family units) than those built in Europe. Over the whole period from 1950 through 1962 about 19.4 million new dwelling units were built in the United States. The seven Northwest European countries, with about the same population and a larger labor force, built about 15.5 million units.[11] Germany alone (here including the Saar but not West Berlin) accounted for 6.8 million of these; the United Kingdom built 3.8 million and France 2.8 million.[12] If the total number of units built from 1950 through 1962, and then from 1955 through

9. Over the 1950–62 period the indexes of real property income from housing (1962 ÷ 1950) at which I arrive are 427 in Germany, 244 in the United States, 152 in Denmark and the Netherlands, 141 in France, 132 in Norway, and less in the other countries. These indexes (like those given in the text table for consumer expenditure for rent) are computed by linking series computed in 1958 prices from 1955 to 1962 and in the same prices used to compute growth rates in each country (see Appendix A) from 1950 to 1955. These indexes obviously are greatly affected by differences in estimating procedures.

10. The necessity of linking French data at 1959, when the "new" series replaces the "old," makes the French indexes both for rent and for national income originating in housing (the latter increased 45 percent from 1955 to 1962 as against a 58 percent increase in the United States) somewhat questionable.

11. European data are from OECD, Industrial Statistics, 1900–1962 [129]; United States data are revised estimates by the U.S. Bureau of the Census.

12. For the 1955–62 period alone the figures, in millions of units, are: United States 11.4; Northwest Europe 10.6; Germany 4.4; United Kingdom 2.4; France 2.3.

1962, is divided by 1962 employment the following results are obtained:

	1950–62	1955–62
United States	.28	.16
Germany	.26	.17
Norway	.25	.15
Netherlands	.22	.15
Northwest Europe	.19	.13
Belgium	.16	.11
Italy	.15	.11
United Kingdom	.15	.10
Denmark	.14	.10
France	.14	.12

In the United States 0.28 new dwelling units were built from 1950 through 1962 for each person employed in 1962, and 0.16 of these were built from 1955 to 1962. On this basis, which counts all units equally, new construction was greatest, per person employed in 1962, in the United States and Germany. Norway followed rather closely, as did the Netherlands in the 1955–62 period. The five other countries were much behind.

The amount of residential construction can also be compared in another way. Gilbert and Associates provide estimates of the value of residential construction in 1950 measured in United States prices. I have adjusted their data for 1950 to incorporate a large revision in the United States estimate, but could not incorporate any subsequent revisions for the other countries. From the national estimates in constant prices, the ratio of total residential construction in the whole 1950–62 period (or any other period) to 1950 construction can be computed. The product of Gilbert's dollar estimates in 1950 and these ratios provide estimates of construction in the 1950–62 period in common prices (United States prices of 1950, but the results would be the same, except for the Northwest Europe aggregate, in any prices). These, like the dwelling unit data, have been divided by 1962 employment and converted to index form with the United States equal to 100. The results, and corresponding data for the 1955–62 period, are given in Table 11–2.[13]

These data allow, in principle, for international differences in the size and quality of units. In the 1950–62 period as a whole the ranking of countries

TABLE 11–2

Indexes of Cumulated Expenditures for Residential Construction in United States Prices per Person Employed in 1962

(*United States = 100*)

Area	Expenditures 1950–62	Expenditures 1955–62
United States	100	100
Norway	89	89
Germany	85	93
Belgium	65	66
Netherlands	65	66
Northwest Europe	64	69
Denmark	57	57
United Kingdom	53	54
France	49	57
Italy	42	52

Sources: Appendix H and Table 5–1.

based on value is similar to that obtained from the number of dwelling units built, with one exception —Italy drops to the lowest position. That Italy should rank lower by value than by number of units is entirely plausible. In two cases adjacent countries change places (Norway with Germany and the United Kingdom with Denmark) and in one (Belgium and the Netherlands) they are equal but no larger differences appear. Comparisons are also similar in the 1955–62 period but on a value basis the United States stands just above, rather than just below, Germany.

The two preceding comparisons refer to absolute amounts of residential construction. It may also be of interest to compare the proportions of GNP, measured uniformly in United States prices, that were devoted to residential construction. GNP in United States prices was not estimated for all years so an exact calculation cannot be made. However, comparison of the construction indexes for the 1955–62 period, given in Table 11–2, with GNP indexes for selected years, given in Table 2–5, suggests that in 1955–62 the proportion was fairly similar in the United States, the United Kingdom, and France; a little higher in Denmark, the Netherlands, and Belgium; and decidedly higher in Norway, Germany, and Italy.[14]

It should be noted that Gilbert and Associates found the ratio of the cost of new dwellings to aver-

13. The data are described in full in Appendix H. The reason that indexes are the same in any price weights is that Gilbert and Associates treat residential construction as a single commodity.

14. European ratios of residental construction to GNP would be even higher, relative to the United States, if GNP comparisons were based on European prices.

age GNP prices to be much lower in the European countries than in the United States. For this reason European ratios of residential construction to GNP are much higher when European output is valued in United States prices than when it is valued in European prices (as in Table 10–1).

In order to present all the evidence, I should mention that estimates of the number of dwelling units in the stock show the following percentage increases from 1950 to 1962: Germany 68; Netherlands 35; Northwest Europe 32; United States and Italy 30; the United Kingdom, Belgium, and Norway, each 19 to 21; Denmark 16; and France 12. But these estimates convey little information. Aside from the fact that the data are neither very good nor entirely comparable, they bear little relationship to the quantity of housing available. Since everyone lives some place, they are crude reflections of changes in the number of families less the numbers sharing accommodation with others. (They are also affected by changes in the number of seasonal and vacant dwellings, which are not, however, uniformly treated in these estimates.)

I have stated unequivocally, on the basis of the statistics that enter into the calculation of national income for each country, that housing contributed more to the growth of national income, as actually measured, in the United States than in any European country. Even if net income from housing had had the same weight in all countries, this result would have been changed only in the case of Germany. The collateral data show the increase in rent in constant prices and the volume of homebuilding to have been very great in the United States compared to Europe, suggesting that this conclusion is not a mere reflection of bad or inconsistent national income statistics. The United States appears to have done more to obtain growth through residential investment than the European countries except Germany.[15]

It may also be asked whether the European countries have sacrificed more than the United States in terms of alternative uses of resources to obtain growth through an increase in the stock of housing. Table 10–1 showed investment ratios when each country's ratio is based on its own prices, as is appropriate for measuring resource cost. The United States devoted an average of 5.2 percent of GNP to residential construction in the 1950–62 period. This was the highest percentage of any country. It was fairly closely approached by Germany, Italy, Norway, and Belgium. Percentages were much lower for Denmark and the United Kingdom and, to a lesser degree, for the Netherlands and France. Evidently no country covered devoted a greater proportion of its output to housing than the United States over the period as a whole. It may be noted, however, that in the 1955–62 period alone, Germany and especially Italy exceeded the United States percentage of 5.0; all countries except Denmark and the United Kingdom reached at least 4.4 percent.

All countries entered the fifties with a backlog of demand for housing, but the shortage was particularly acute in Germany. Subsequently Germany was faced with the need to provide housing space for a large influx of refugees and foreign workers. The policy of the German government has been to support and subsidize residential construction at almost any price, and despite sharply mounting construction costs, in a successful effort to alleviate the shortage. By mid-1965 the housing deficit had been eliminated and rents decontrolled in about nine-tenths of the districts of Germany.[16]

In this chapter only the direct effects of changes in the housing stock on the growth of national income have been considered. Availability of housing has also indirect effects on productivity, mainly by affecting the geographic allocation of labor. This subject will be briefly discussed in Chapter 18.

Contribution of Housing to Differences in Output Levels

Table 11–3 presents estimates of the difference between the United States and European countries

15. The position of Norway is ambiguous. Gross investment in housing was about as large per person employed in Norway as in Germany, but even though Norway was not exceptionally well housed in 1950 this did not result in large increases in consumer expenditures for rent, in property income from housing, or in the number of dwelling units. The explanation apparently lies in part in the shift of population from the countryside to Oslo and other cities, accompanied by abandonment of rural dwellings; I do not know whether this is a sufficient explanation.

16. See OECD *Observer*, February 1966, p. 27 [136].

in national income per person employed that is due to differences in housing stock.

The aggregate amounts of national income created by this source are compared in the first column. The derivation of these estimates started with the international indexes of consumer expenditures for housing in 1950 prepared by Gilbert and Associates. These are actually indexes of the value of the gross stock of occupied dwellings, with allowance for the condition of dwellings. Gilbert and Associates extrapolated the 1950 estimates to 1955 by deflated consumer expenditures for rent, and I have carried their 1955 estimates to 1960 by the same procedure.[17] The 1960 indexes are used to measure international differences in the value of the net contribution of the housing stock to national income. This use assumes that the ratio of the net services of dwellings to the stock and gross rental value of dwellings is the same in all countries when measured in the same prices. Paige and Bombach made a similar assumption in comparing gross national product of the United States and the United Kingdom.[18]

The derivation of the remainder of Table 11–3 can most easily be explained by illustration, and I describe the estimates for France. The contribution of net income from dwellings to the national income in 1960 is estimated to have been 13.4 percent as large in France as in the United States (Column 1). This implies it was 48 percent as large per person employed (Column 2). Income from dwellings contributed $16.6 billion or $240 per person employed to the United States national income, and therefore contributed $117 per person employed (48 percent as much) to French national income per person employed when French national income is measured in United States prices. The

TABLE 11–3

Dwellings: International Comparison of Levels and Contribution to Differences in National Income per Person Employed, 1960

Area	Indexes of national income originating in dwellings (United States = 100)		Contribution to difference from United States in national income per person employed (in index points) (3)	Percentage of difference in national income per person employed explained by income from dwellings (4)
	Total (1)	Per person employed (2)		
U. S.	100.0	100	—	—
N. W. Europe	63.8	54	1.9	4.6
Belgium	2.4	48	2.1	5.5
Denmark	1.8	57	1.8	4.2
France	13.4	48	2.1	5.1
Germany	20.1	53	1.9	4.8
Netherlands	3.2	53	1.9	5.6
Norway	1.0	48	2.1	5.2
U. K.	21.9	61	1.6	3.9
Italy	6.5	22	3.2	5.3

Sources: See text and Appendix I for method of derivation; employment from Table 5–2.

difference of $126 is equal to 2.1 percent (Column 3) of total United States national income per person employed of $5,898. French national income per person employed, measured in United States prices, was estimated in Table 2–4 to have been 59 percent as large as, or 41 percent less than, the United States figure. Of this total difference of 41 percentage points, I thus estimate that the difference in the stock of dwellings alone is responsible for 2.1 points, or 5.1 percent. The results for the other Northwest European countries are not very different.

International Assets

Residents of each country own, and receive income from, assets abroad. Each country also remits income to other countries that own assets within its borders. It is convenient to treat net ownership of international assets as a separate component of capital.

17. Gilbert handles housing as a single commodity so the international indexes are the same in any price weights. Gilbert's data for 1955 are rounded to such a degree that the estimates for the small countries present difficulties. (The Norwegian estimate is given as $0.3 billion.) I therefore extrapolated his 1950 data (which can be accurately calculated) to 1955 by deflated consumer expenditures for rent and used the 1955 figure so calculated if it was within the range of his rounded estimates or, if it was not, the figure closest to it that was consistent with Gilbert's rounded estimates.

18. The Paige-Bombach assumption refers to income gross of depreciation, mine to income net of depreciation (*A Comparison of National Output and Productivity of the United Kingdom and the United States*, p. 222 [122]).

Contribution to Growth

The net flow of property income from abroad that is included in the constant price national income series of each country is known (exactly or approximately). The contribution that changes in this income flow made to the growth rate of national income can therefore readily be calculated; the procedure is similar to that used for housing.[19] The contributions to growth rates of total and per person national income are given in Table 11–4.

These contributions reflect all influences on net property income from abroad, measured in constant prices. International asset holdings are changed both by net investment and by confiscations and other types of capital gains and losses. The amount of property income received from and paid to abroad changes not only because of changes in the balance sheet but also, and sometimes sharply, because of changes in the return from existing asset holdings and in the proportion of earnings remitted.[20] Finally, in a few cases changes

19. See Appendix I for details.
20. Undistributed profits of corporations (including corporate income taxes) are counted in the national income of the country where they are earned, not the country of the owners, except in the case of foreign branches. In extreme cases this can make the measured national income a poor indicator of the output attributable to the resources owned by a nation.

in the constant price value of income from abroad that is included in national income bear little resemblance to changes in current prices.[21]

Over the 1950–62 period as a whole changes in the flow of international property income contributed 0.05 percentage points to the growth rate of national income in the United States and subtracted 0.03 points in Northwest Europe. In individual countries the range was from 0.10 in the Netherlands to −0.08 in Germany.

Net income from abroad had a much greater influence on growth rates in the subperiods, particularly in the United Kingdom and the Netherlands. Indeed, its influence on a comparison of the United Kingdom's 1950–55 growth rate of national income per person employed with its 1955–62 rate is remarkable. The growth rate was 1.4 in 1950–55 and 1.8 in 1955–62 (Table 2–2). The

21. In my United States study I approximated the contribution to growth of changes in international asset holdings by multiplying the growth rates of the constant dollar values of private assets owned abroad and of U.S. private assets owned by foreigners by their shares in the national income. For the United States that procedure yields results close to those obtained here. It is obvious that this would not be the case for some of the European countries. Although it would be possible, in principle, to duplicate for the European countries the procedure followed in my United States study in order to isolate the contribution of net investment from that of other changes affecting net property income from abroad, the difficulties of obtaining constant price stock series and of interpreting the results of varied deflation procedures on net income from abroad made the project appear unpromising.

TABLE 11–4

Contribution of Net Property Income from Abroad to Growth Rates of Total National Income and National Income per Person Employed

(In percentage points)

Area	Contribution to growth rate of total national income			Contribution to growth rate of national income per person employed		
	1950–62	1950–55	1955–62	1950–62	1950–55	1955–62
United States	.05	.03	.06	.04	.02	.05
Northwest Europe	−.03	−.12	.03	−.04	−.13	.03
Belgium	−.06	−.03	−.08	−.06	−.03	−.08
Denmark	.02	.01	.03	.02	.01	.03
France	.02	.02	.02	.02	.02	.02
Germany	−.08	−.13	−.05	−.08	−.12	−.05
Netherlands	.10	.39	−.10	.09	.37	−.11
Norway	−.07	−.04	−.09	−.07	−.04	−.09
United Kingdom	−.05	−.36	.17	−.06	−.37	.17
Italy	−.03	.00	−.05	−.03	.00	−.05

Sources: See text and Appendix I for method of derivation; employment from Table 5–1.

contribution of net income from abroad is −0.4 and +0.2, so that it can be seen that this source more than accounts for the difference in growth rates in the two subperiods. All other sources contributed 1.8 points to the growth rate in 1950–55 and 1.6 points in 1955–62. The change in net property income from abroad was equal to − 15 percent of the total absolute change in United Kingdom national income in 1958 prices from 1950 to 1955 and to +7 percent of the total change from 1955 to 1962. There is no question that changes in net income from abroad did have this effect on the United Kingdom growth rates being analyzed, and that the remaining amounts therefore are in fact the amounts that must be explained by other growth sources.

The reasons for the large drop and subsequent recovery in the deflated flow of net property income from abroad cannot be fully isolated but the following observations aid in an interpretation of the data.

Net lending abroad by the United Kingdom actually was positive in both periods but was smaller from 1950 to 1955, when it aggregated £ 265 million in current prices (if half the annual figures for each of the terminal years is counted) than from 1955 to 1962, when it aggregated £ 568 million (by a similar calculation). Annual net property income from abroad in current prices dropped by £ 227 million a year from 1950 to 1955 despite the fact that intervening investment had been positive. It then increased by £ 227 million from 1955 to 1962.[22] Income received from abroad and income paid to abroad both rose in each period, but the rise in payments was particularly sharp from 1950 to 1955 and this contributed heavily to the rather drastic contrast between the two periods. Two factors that can be identified contributed strongly to this result. From 1950 to 1955, interest paid on sterling balances increased from £ 33 million to £97 million, or by £64 million, and interest on North American loans rose from zero to £38 mil-

lion.[23] Both series were at approximately the 1955 level in 1962.[24]

The only other country in which changes in income from abroad substantially affected growth rates of national income was the Netherlands, where this flow increased sizably from 1950 to 1955 and declined from 1955 to 1962. The decline from 1955 to 1962 reflected the fact that income from abroad was erratically high in 1955 and low in 1962, rather than any persistent downward trend. The 1961–63 average exceeded the 1954–56 average. Except for the United Kingdom and the Netherlands, income from abroad did not affect growth rates of either total national income or national income per person employed by much more than 0.1 percentage points in either subperiod.

The persistent negative contribution in Germany and Norway may be noted. Both are examples of an increasing net outflow of property income. Curiously, while Norway had the largest negative percentage of GNP devoted to net foreign lending, Germany had the largest positive percentage (Table 10–1). There is, in fact, hardly any relationship among the countries between net investment abroad (including changes in non-income yielding monetary reserves) and changes in net property income from abroad.

The estimates accurately measure the effect of changes in the international flow of property income upon the growth rate of national income, as national income is actually measured for each country, but to try to explain *why* these changes occurred would be a study in itself that cannot be undertaken here. It should be noted that this type of income is often erratic and the use of different years to bound the periods studied would change some results substantially.

The resource cost of increasing income from abroad by net investment abroad as indicated by the percentage of GNP devoted to this purpose is shown in Table 10–1. The United States percentage averaged approximately zero over the whole 1950–62 period; it was −0.3 from 1950 to 1954 and

22. These figures are based on OECD definitions. Data based on the United Kingdom's own definitions are given in Appendix A.
On both the OECD and United Kingdom definitions the series for net income from abroad reached a peak in 1950, dropped steadily to a trough in 1955, and then increased almost steadily through 1964.

23. Gilbert in *National Institute Economic Review*, November 1960, pp. 50–52 [P30].
24. R. L. Major of the National Institute of Economic and Social Research provided by letter, October 1966, estimates of about £ 100 million and £ 38–39 million, respectively.

TABLE 11-5

*Net Property Income from Abroad:
International Comparison of Levels and
Contribution to Differences in
National Income per Person Employed, 1960*

Area	Indexes of net property income from abroad (United States = 100)		Contribution to difference from United States in national income per person employed (in index points)	Percentage of difference in national income per person employed explained by property income from abroad
	Total (1)	Per person employed (2)	(3)	(4)
U. S.	100.0	100	—	—
N. W. Europe	31.5	27	.4	1.0
Belgium	2.0	39	.3	.9
Denmark	.2	7	.5	1.3
France	2.7	10	.5	1.3
Germany	−9.2	−24	.7	1.7
Netherlands	4.2	69	.2	.5
Norway	−1.6	−76	1.0	2.5
U. K.	33.2	93	.0	.0
Italy	−1.2	−4	.6	1.0

Sources: See text and Appendix I for method of derivation; employment from Table 5-1.

+0.2 in 1955–62. (After 1959 it rose almost steadily and reached 0.8 in 1964.) Over the period as a whole Germany and the Netherlands devoted an average of 1.7 and 1.5 percent of GNP, respectively, to this purpose, and Belgium, the United Kingdom, and Italy smaller positive amounts. Norway and Denmark were net borrowers, on the average.[25] This measure is not a very satisfactory indicator of sacrifice because it ignores military costs of protecting investments as well as grants from one country to another, including those from the United States to Europe in the early part of the period.

Contribution of International Assets to Differences in Levels of National Income

Table 11–5 compares, by country and area, the amounts of net property income received from

25. The percentage for France averaged −0.1 in 1950–62, +0.8 in 1950–54, and −0.7 in 1955–62. The figures are consistent with the national income figures used but the contrast has little meaning because of a change in the treatment of North Africa with the introduction of the "new" series starting in 1959.

abroad in 1960. The net income from abroad received by each country, measured in its own currency, was converted to United States dollars by use of exchange rates. This method is consistent with, and required by, Gilbert's procedure for measuring net exports of goods and services in the comparison of national incomes.[26]

The calculations of the contribution of net property income from abroad to differences in national income per person employed are similar to those for housing, and may again be illustrated by France. This income flow amounted in 1960 to $34 per person employed in the United States ($2.33 billion in the aggregate) and to 10 percent as much (Column 2) or $3 in France. The difference of $31 is equal to 0.5 percent (Column 3) of total national income per person employed in the United States, or to 1.3 percent of the entire difference between the two countries.

Summary

A comparison of Northwest Europe as a whole with the United States indicates that, if there were no other reasons for a difference, national income per man would be lower in Northwest Europe by 1.9 percent because of the difference in the housing stock and by 0.4 percent because of the difference in net property income from abroad. Together, these two sources account for almost 6 percent of the actual difference between the two areas in national income per person employed.

What would have been required to eliminate this source of difference? To bring the Northwest European net stock of dwellings and international assets up to the American level, per man, would have required net saving equal to about 7 months of Northwest European GNP (in United States prices) as of 1960. However, given the long service lives and high value of existing dwellings it would probably be uneconomic and impractical to bring European housing up to the American standard in less than two or three generations. Destruction of sound dwellings and their replacement by new ones, or even complete renovation and remodeling, are not often profitable even if existing dwellings are ill adapted to modern living.

26. See pp. 30–31.

CHAPTER TWELVE

Nonresidential Structures and Equipment

This chapter considers the contribution of increases in the stock of nonresidential structures and equipment to growth rates of national income, and the effect of international differences in the size of the stock upon levels of national income.

The increase in this type of capital is estimated to have contributed 0.4 percentage points to the growth rate of the United States and 0.6 percentage points to the growth rate of Northwest Europe in 1950–62; the difference was somewhat greater after 1955. The contribution varied considerably among the individual countries; it was as high as 1.1 percentage points in Germany in the 1955–62 period. Several topics that concern changes in output per unit of input (discussed in Chapters 16 to 20) but are closely related to capital are also discussed in this chapter. Among these, the balancing of the capital stock is found to have contributed importantly to German growth in 1950–55, and a reduction in the average age of capital is estimated to have made a small contribution to 1950–55 growth rates in three countries.

Northwest Europe is estimated to have had in 1960 less than half as much capital in the form of enterprise structures and equipment as the United States, per person employed. It is calculated that

this alone would have caused national income per person employed to have been nearly 6 percent lower. The amount varies widely among the individual European countries.

Estimates in this chapter refer to the contribution made by capital to the growth rate of *potential* national income rather than to actual national income. This is because adjustments are not introduced for cyclical differences in the intensity of utilization of the capital stock in the selected years used in the computation of growth rates.[1]

Because this is a long chapter, an advance indication of its organization may be helpful. First comes a discussion of certain characteristics of the capital stock series to be used and their implications for the estimates derived from them. Estimates of the changes that took place in the stock of nonresidential structures and equipment are then presented by country, and the effect of these changes upon growth rates of national income is computed. To complete the discussion of capital and growth, several conditions or changes closely related to capital or investment that had or may be supposed to have had a

---

1. Chapter 19 introduces adjustments for the effect of differences in the intensity of resource utilization upon output per unit of input.

special effect on productivity are examined. I turn next to a comparison of levels of investment and capital stock. First, the amounts that the various countries invested during the postwar period are measured in common prices and compared. This leads to an attempt to compare the size of the capital stock of the various countries and to calculate the effect of differences in the stock upon differences in output per man in 1960.

Data pertaining to the stock of depreciable assets are only approximations due to the inherent difficulties of estimation. This is so even where the basic data are most adequate and thorough and systematic investigations have been made; where these conditions are not met the data are, of course, subject to greater error. Nonetheless, I believe that approximations of the growth rates of the stock of structures and equipment in the countries covered in this study that are sufficiently accurate to permit useful approximations of the contributions of this type of capital to the growth of national income can be obtained despite statistical problems. Comparisons of levels of the stock in the various countries are cruder but attempted nonetheless.

General Characteristics of Capital Stock Series

The capital stock series used in this study have two characteristics that require explanation before data for the various countries are presented. The first relates to the treatment of quality change in capital and the second to the treatment of capital owned by general government and households.

The Treatment of Quality Change in Capital[2]

All statistical series that are available to measure changes over time in the services of capital assets share one important characteristic. Just like measures of real national product, they reflect what I referred to earlier as economic or measured quality change but not noneconomic or unmeasured qual-

ity change. This characteristic is common to series measuring the real (constant dollar) gross capital stock, the real net capital stock, and real capital consumption.[3]

The form that capital goods take is constantly changing. Largely because of technological progress (but also for several other reasons), machines and buildings made today are not the same as those that were built a decade or two ago. How are these capital goods, built at different times, at different costs, and with different performance characteristics, equated in the construction of time series for the value of the capital stock measured in constant prices? The answer, as nearly as I can formulate it, is given in the following quotation from a previous article:

> The value, in base period prices, of the stock of durable capital goods (before allowance for capital consumption) measures the amount it would have cost in the base period to produce the actual stock of capital goods existing in the given year (*not* its equivalent in ability to contribute to production). Similarly, gross additions to the capital stock and capital consumption are valued in terms of base year costs for the *particular* types of capital goods added or consumed. This must be modified immediately, in the case of durable capital goods not actually produced in the base year, to substitute the amount it would have cost to produce them if they had been known and actually produced. But a similar modification is required in all deflation or index number problems.[4]

The available series provide usable measures once this characteristic of their definition is accepted. However, it must be understood that they match this definition only crudely; there is, in fact, good reason to believe that in the case of structures they are biased, possibly seriously, in the direction of understating the growth of capital stock and capital consumption.[5]

2. This section is reproduced with little change from *Sources of Economic Growth*, pp. 94–96 [B25], by permission of the Committee for Economic Development. Although the description refers to United States data, it is applicable also to data for the other countries.

3. The value of the gross stock exceeds that of the net stock at a point in time by the value of accumulated depreciation on assets in the stock.

4. Denison, in *Problems of Capital Formation: Concepts, Measurement, and Controlling Factors*, pp. 222–23 [B26]. (The same article greatly amplifies this and other points that are considered in this section.) It may be noted here that the principle stated handles changes in the "mix" of the capital stock resulting from changes in demand patterns or relative factor prices as well as changes resulting from technological progress.

5. This is because of the way "construction cost" indexes used in converting current dollar to constant dollar con-

This method of measurement must be sharply distinguished from an alternative that is conceivable though impossible to implement. This alternative would equate capital goods produced at different times by their ability to contribute to production, taking full account of their capacity, operating costs (including the amount of labor required for their utilization), quality of product, and other aspects of performance. The difference may be illustrated by the case of steam and diesel locomotives. The last steam locomotive was retired from line-haul service in the United States early in 1960. Even if new steam locomotives were available free, the railroads today evidently would not use them in preference to buying diesels because their operating costs are excessive and their performance inferior. Suppose that a certain model steam locomotive that was produced in 1930 would cost half as much to produce in 1962 as a certain model diesel. How does one compare the capital stock, valued in 1962 prices, in years when the steam locomotive was still in use with the capital stock in later years when such a locomotive would be useless? Available estimates of the capital stock for years when the 1930 locomotive was in use, when expressed in 1962 prices, will tend to count the steam locomotive produced in 1930 as half as much capital as (or as capital of half the quality of) the diesel locomotive. An alternative measure of the capital stock in 1962 prices in years when the 1930 locomotive was in use would value such a locomotive at zero (disregarding scrap value) in a comparison of the capital stock in earlier years with that in (say) 1962, since it could contribute nothing to production in 1962. If a series for the capital stock based on this alternative could be constructed

it would rise more sharply than the series that are available. However, there is no basis whatsoever for the development of comprehensive series of this type.

Fortunately, in this respect the series for capital goods that are available are the type needed for an orderly analysis of the sources of economic growth. They enable the contribution of the growth of inputs into the productive process to be distinguished from that of technological progress and other advances in knowledge.[6]

In this respect the treatment of quality change for capital goods is, as nearly as possible, comparable to that for labor and land. The main point is that in no case is an increase in the ability of a resource to produce resulting from an advance in the society's stock of knowledge considered to be an increase in the quantity or quality of the resource. None of the quality adjustments for labor were of this character.[7]

Omission of the Capital of General Government and Households

The capital stock indexes to be presented are comprehensive measures of the nonresidential structures and producers' durable goods owned by all business enterprises, including government enterprises. General government capital and household capital are omitted. The capital stock of nonprofit organizations should also be omitted; it was not possible to do so uniformly but such capital is too small for its inclusion to have much effect on any of the indexes. Omission of these types of capital is dictated by the necessity for consistency with the net product measures and with earnings data. The earnings of nonresidential structures and equipment that are included in national income, and that will be used as weights to calculate the contribution of capital to growth, are confined to

---

struction expenditure figures are computed. For the most part these indexes price labor and materials inputs used in the construction industry rather than the output of the industry, and thus fail to reflect changes (presumably increases) in productivity in on-site construction work. The result is to bias the price indexes upward over time, and consequently to bias deflated construction outlays downward over time. By the "perpetual inventory" method of estimating the capital stock, which adds new additions in each year and deducts capital consumption, this also biases downward series measuring the deflated value of the stock of structures and depreciation on them. For the United States, alternative capital stock estimates based on the assumption that construction prices moved like prices of the GNP as a whole have been published, but I see no reason to adopt this assumption, which is hardly plausible.

6. This method of measuring capital also leads to a convenient classification of means of influencing the growth rate. To do so by altering capital input requires changing the rate of saving and investment. This is clearly distinguishable from steps to affect the rate at which knowledge advances; such steps are considered to affect the productivity, rather than the amount, of capital and other inputs.

7. It will be recalled that in measuring the effect of increased education upon the quality of labor no account was taken of the ability to impart better information in school because of advances in society's stock of knowledge.

the earnings of enterprise capital.[8] This contrasts with the treatment of the compensation of government and household employees, which is included in national product and the labor share and requires that government and household employees be included in labor input.

The consequences of including government capital in the capital stock estimates is not always appreciated. Its inclusion would reduce the growth rate of the capital stock in most countries. This would lead to understatement of the contribution of enterprise capital to growth, since this is estimated as the product of the growth rate of capital and its share of the national income.

To point out that no return to general government capital is included in the national income is not, to be sure, the same as to say that changes in government capital have no effect on the growth rate of national income. Changes in the adequacy and efficiency of certain types of government services may cause changes in productivity in the business sector.[9] This observation has no special relevance to capital, however. The adequacy and honesty of police services and the judicial system, for example, are neither measured by nor mainly dependent upon the value of police stations, patrol cars, and courthouses.

I do not attempt to measure the effect of changes in government services on private productivity because I have not been able to devise a procedure to do so.[10] It may be observed, however, that the two biggest categories of government expenditure for goods and services are defense and education. Defense expenditures are largely irrelevant to the present discussion. Education expenditures, including the construction of school buildings and other capital outlays, do not affect output per unit of input if the quality adjustment indexes for labor input presented in Chapter 8 are correct.

Streets, highways, and other public transportation facilities are by far the largest component of public capital that may affect output per unit of input in the business sector. The road network has been extended and improved much more in the United States than in Europe so this is presumably

8. This statement must be qualified by noting again that some of the European countries do apply a low interest rate to government capital to compute a small imputed return that is included in the national income. It would in principle be simple to calculate the contribution of this imputed property income to growth (using a procedure similar to that followed for housing and income from abroad), but the necessary detailed data are not easily available for all countries and the amounts involved are too small to make their pursuit worthwhile. No significant error results from proceeding as if these small amounts were omitted from national income and product in all countries.

9. It can be argued that, strictly speaking, this is because of errors in the deflation of business output. See Jaszi in *A Critique of the United States Income and Product Accounts*, pp. 72, 127, and 144 [B54].

10. Services performed by households may also affect private productivity. In Chapter 17, I consider the effect on business productivity of changes in the ownership and use of automobiles by households.

TABLE 12-1

Indexes of Gross and Net Stock of Enterprise Structures and Equipment[a]

(1950 = 100)

Area	Gross stock				Net stock			
	1950	1955	1960	1962	1950	1955	1960	1962
United States	100.0	122.5	148.7	155.0	100.0	124.8	147.4	155.6
Northwest Europe	100.0	118.7	146.2	160.6	100.0	123.2	161.1	180.7
Belgium	100.0	114.7	133.2	141.4	100.0	114.8	132.9	141.2
Denmark	100.0	125.8*	157.3*	175.3*	100.0	132.8	174.3	200.6
France	100.0	117.8	141.2	153.5	100.0	120.0	150.3	166.5
Germany	100.0	124.4	167.8	189.5	100.0	133.2	191.6	221.9
Netherlands	100.0	118.3*	148.8*	163.9*	100.0	119.8	158.9	179.5
Norway	100.0	124.6*	153.1*	164.6*	100.0	130.7	166.7	181.0
United Kingdom	100.0	114.5	132.1	142.6	100.0	118.4	147.9	163.0
Italy	100.0	116.9*	138.8*	152.8*	100.0	117.5	141.6	159.6

Source: Appendix J.
a. Excluding dwellings.
* Series inferred from the movement of the net stock series.

a factor favorable to a higher growth rate in the United States. Only business use of such facilities affects business output per unit of input. If the rate of return were assumed to be the same on public transportation facilities as it is on business capital, a calculation of the effect on growth rates would yield only a small contribution.

Changes in Stock

Indexes of the value in constant prices of the gross and net stock of nonresidential structures and equipment, excluding general government, are presented in Table 12–1.[11] The indexes were computed from averages of the value of the stock at the beginning and end of the year. Table 12–2 presents growth rates based upon these indexes. It was possible to derive the net stock series for all countries from national sources, although adjustments of certain of the national series were required to approximate the desired scope of the stock. Only for the United States, Belgium, France, Germany, and the United Kingdom could gross

11. The base years of the deflated series are 1953 for Belgium and the Netherlands, 1954 for Italy and (with some use of 1958 weights) Germany, 1955 for Denmark and Norway, 1956 for France, and 1958 for the United States and the United Kingdom.

stock series be obtained from national sources. Gross stock indexes for Denmark, the Netherlands, Norway, and Italy were inferred from the movement of the net stock, and these inferred series are so designated in the tables. The sources of the direct estimates and the method of inferring gross stock indexes from net stock indexes are fully described in Appendix J. The basis for inferring the missing gross stock indexes is regrettably weak, but errors in this step would have to be very large to affect appreciably the conclusions I shall reach. Appendix J also discusses the methods, including depreciation patterns and assumed service lives, that are used to derive the estimates in various countries. It notes that shorter service lives are used in the United States than in Europe in compiling the estimates; that although capital goods almost surely are actually used longer in Europe the differences assumed in the estimates may exceed the true differences; but that the use of much longer service lives would not, in any case, change the *indexes* of the American capital stock very much.

Comparisons of Growth Rates

The following listing arranges the countries in the order of the growth rates of the stock of structures and equipment over the 1950–62 period as a whole. The order differs somewhat as between

TABLE 12-2

Growth Rates of Gross and Net Stock of Enterprise Structures and Equipment[a]

(In percentages)

Area	Gross stock			Net stock		
	1950–62	1950–55	1955–62	1950–62	1950–55	1955–62
United States	3.7	4.1	3.4	3.8	4.5	3.2
Northwest Europe	4.0	3.5	4.4	5.1	4.3	5.6
Belgium	2.9	2.8	3.0	2.9	2.8	3.0
Denmark	4.8*	4.7*	4.8*	6.0	5.8	6.1
France	3.6	3.3	3.9	4.3	3.7	4.8
Germany	5.5	4.5	6.2	6.9	5.9	7.6
Netherlands	4.2*	3.4*	4.8*	5.0	3.7	5.9
Norway	4.2*	4.5*	4.1*	5.1	5.5	4.8
United Kingdom	3.0	2.7	3.2	4.2	3.4	4.7
Italy	3.6*	3.2*	3.9*	4.0	3.3	4.5

Source: Computed from Table 12–1.
a. Excluding dwellings.
* Series inferred from the movement of the net stock series.

gross stock and net stock, and that used is based on an average of the two sets of growth rates.

	Growth rates of nonresidential structures and equipment, 1950–62 (In percentage points)		Average percentage of GNP devoted to nonresidential structures and equipment, 1950–62[a]
	Gross stock	Net stock	
Germany	5.5	6.9	16.8
Denmark	4.8	6.0	14.5
Norway	4.2	5.1	24.1
Netherlands	4.2	5.0	18.1
France	3.6	4.3	13.7
Italy	3.6	4.0	15.5
United States	3.7	3.8	12.1
United Kingdom	3.0	4.2	11.7
Belgium	2.9	2.9	13.2

a. From Table 10–1; includes expenditures by general government.

The nine countries fall into three broad groups. Germany and Denmark had much the largest increases in capital stock (with Germany well above Denmark). Next come Norway and the Netherlands, with about the same rates. France, Italy, the United States, the United Kingdom, and Belgium comprise a third group with much lower rates. Within this group, the Belgian rates are well below the first three countries. The United Kingdom is about even with Belgium with respect to gross stock but with the other three countries with respect to net stock.

Also shown above are the average percentages of GNP devoted to gross investment in nonresidential structures and equipment (including government investment) in the 1950–62 period; these investment ratios have often been used as a substitute for capital stock growth rates. The comparison shows that in fact there is hardly any correspondence between the two measures. Thus, Norway has a far higher investment ratio but the same capital stock growth rates as the Netherlands. Both have higher investment ratios and much lower capital stock growth rates than Germany and Denmark. Neither is any particular relationship apparent in the other countries. The only faint suggestion of correspondence is that three of the four countries with the highest investment ratios were among the four with the highest capital stock growth rates.

It appears, therefore, that the gross investment ratio is a very poor substitute indeed for the growth rate of the capital stock.[12] While the use of the gross investment ratio has sometimes been justified on the grounds that capital stock indexes are inaccurate—and indeed they are—it is not possible to believe that errors are such that their elimination would bring capital stock indexes in line with the investment ratios.

The three-way grouping of countries set out above was based on growth rates over the period 1950–62 as a whole. In all European countries except Norway growth rates of the stock of nonresidential structures and equipment were higher from 1955 to 1962 than from 1950 to 1955; the acceleration was pronounced in France, Germany, the Netherlands, the United Kingdom, and Italy and small in Belgium and Denmark. In contrast, the growth rate of the stock was much lower in 1955–62 than in 1950–55 in the United States and it was also lower in Norway. Consequently, comparisons based on the period since 1955 are somewhat different:

	Growth rates of nonresidential structures and equipment, 1955–62 (in percentage points)		Average percentage of GNP devoted to nonresidential structures and equipment, 1955–62[a]
	Gross stock	Net stock	
Germany	6.2	7.6	18.1
Denmark	4.8	6.1	15.1
Netherlands	4.8	5.9	19.4
Norway	4.1	4.8	25.1
France	3.9	4.8	14.1
Italy	3.9	4.5	15.8
United Kingdom	3.2	4.7	12.6
United States	3.4	3.2	12.5
Belgium	3.0	3.0	13.4

a. From Table 10–1; includes expenditures by general government.

Gaps in the distribution of the rates suggest that in the 1955–62 period it would be appropriate to distinguish four groups of countries: Germany alone in the highest group; a second group consisting of Denmark and the Netherlands; a third of Norway, France, and Italy; and a fourth of the United States and Belgium. The United Kingdom falls with the third group based on net stock and with the fourth based on gross stock.

12. Comparison with Column 1, Table 12–11, shows that the elimination of government investment from the investment ratios would do little to eliminate the differences between growth rates of capital and investment ratios.

TABLE 12-3

Growth Rates of Gross and Net Stock of Enterprise Structures and Equipment per Person Employed[a]

(*In percentages*)

Area	Gross stock			Net stock		
	1950–62	1950–55	1955–62	1950–62	1950–55	1955–62
United States	2.5	2.6	2.5	2.6	3.0	2.3
Northwest Europe	3.1	2.3	3.6	4.1	3.1	4.8
Belgium	2.4	2.1	2.6	2.4	2.1	2.5
Denmark	3.8	4.2	3.5	5.0	5.3	4.7
France	3.5	3.2	3.7	4.2	3.6	4.7
Germany	3.4	1.7	4.6	4.8	3.1	6.0
Netherlands	3.1	2.3	3.7	3.9	2.6	4.9
Norway	4.1	4.3	3.9	4.9	5.3	4.6
United Kingdom	2.3	1.8	2.7	3.5	2.5	4.2
Italy	3.0	2.2	3.6	3.4	2.3	4.2

Sources: Computed from Tables 12–1 and 5–3.
a. Excluding dwellings.

Again, there is little correspondence between growth rates and investment ratios. There also is only a very poor positive relationship between changes in capital stock growth rates from 1950–55 to 1955–62 and changes in investment ratios. (Investment ratios for 1950–54 are shown in Table 10–1.)

Growth Rates per Person Employed

Growth rates of the stock of enterprise nonresidential structures and equipment per person employed are shown in Table 12–3. Comparisons of countries based on changes in the amount of this type of capital per worker differ appreciably from those based on aggregate amounts. The following listing arranges the countries from highest to lowest growth rate, again based on an average of gross stock and net stock growth rates, in the 1950–62 and 1955–62 periods. The growth rates, expressed in percentage points, are:

	1950–62			1955–62	
	Gross	Net		Gross	Net
Norway	4.1	4.9	Germany	4.6	6.0
Denmark	3.8	5.0	Norway	3.9	4.6
Germany	3.4	4.8	Netherlands	3.7	4.9
France	3.5	4.2	France	3.7	4.7
Netherlands	3.1	3.9	Denmark	3.5	4.7
Italy	3.0	3.4	Italy	3.6	4.2
United Kingdom	2.3	3.5	United Kingdom	2.7	4.2
United States	2.5	2.6	Belgium	2.6	2.5
Belgium	2.4	2.4	United States	2.5	2.3

The shift to a per person basis lowers the relative position of Germany, reduces the position of the United States in comparison with the other large countries except Germany, and improves the relative position of France. Over the 1950–62 period as a whole the increase in structures and equipment per worker in Germany was below that in Norway and Denmark.

In the 1955–62 period Germany retains first position but by a reduced margin. Next come Norway, the Netherlands, France, and Denmark with very similar rates. The exact positions of Italy and the United Kingdom, which follow next, depend on the choice between gross and net stock. Belgium and the United States had the smallest increases in this type of capital per worker.

Contribution to Growth Rate of Total National Income

To arrive at the contribution of the increase in capital to growth rates of national income it is necessary to decide whether gross stock, net stock, or some compromise, best measures changes in capital services. Most analysts, I believe, favor gross stock over net stock for this purpose but some hold the contrary view. It will be useful to know how much difference the choice makes in practice.

Table 12–4 gives the estimated contributions of increases in the stock of nonresidential structures and equipment to the growth rates of national income that result from use of each of the two measures of capital input, and also a simple average of the two estimates.

The arithmetic, by now familiar, may be illustrated by the calculations for the United Kingdom based on use of gross stock. The growth rate of gross stock from 1955 to 1960 was 2.90. Nonresidential structures and equipment earned an estimated 12.0 percent of the national income in 1955–59 (Table 4–1). Based on use of the gross stock index, nonresidential structures and equipment therefore contributed 0.35 percentage points (2.90 × 0.120) to the growth rate of national income in 1955–60. Similar calculations were made for the 1950–55 and 1960–62 periods. Estimated contributions for the longer periods are simply weighted averages of those in the subperiods.

Selection of Capital Input Measure

In principle, the selection of a capital input measure should depend on the changes that occur in the ability of a capital good to contribute to net production as the good grows older (within the span of its economic service life). Use of net stock,

with depreciation computed by the straight line formula, would imply that this ability drops very rapidly—that it is reduced by one-fourth when one-fourth of the service life has passed, and by nine-tenths when nine-tenths of the service life has passed. Use of gross stock would imply that this ability is constant throughout the service life of a capital good.

I believe that net value typically declines much more rapidly than does the ability of a capital good to contribute to production. This is inevitable if the net stock measures what it is intended to measure— the discounted value of the future services of capital goods—because the change in the net value of each capital good reflects the reduction in remaining service life as well as deterioration of current services. On the other hand, the gross stock assumption of constant services throughout the life of an asset is extreme. For at least some types of capital goods, maintenance and repair costs must be increased as a good grows older or else performance deteriorates; it may deteriorate in any case.[13] Also, newer capital is more likely to be in the place and use where it is most advantageous to production. A

13. An investigation by Tibor Barna found capital goods in United Kingdom manufacturing to be maintained in good condition until a decision is made to scrap them (in Lutz and Hague [eds.], *The Theory of Capital*, pp. 75–94 [B7]).

TABLE 12–4

Contribution of Enterprise Structures and Equipment[a] to Growth Rates of Total National Income

(*In percentage points*)

Time period and basis	United States	North-west Europe	Bel-gium	Den-mark	France	Ger-many	Nether-lands	Nor-way	United King-dom	Italy
1950–62										
Gross stock	.43	.57	.39	.58	.50	.89	.60	.71	.36	.50
Net stock	.43	.71	.39	.72	.60	1.11	.71	.85	.50	.56
Average	.43	.64	.39	.65	.55	1.00	.65	.78	.43	.53
1950–55										
Gross stock	.51	.50	.37	.57	.48	.72	.49	.83	.34	.46
Net stock	.55	.61	.38	.71	.53	.94	.53	1.01	.42	.47
Average	.53	.55	.37	.64	.50	.83	.51	.92	.38	.46
1955–62										
Gross stock	.37	.61	.40	.58	.52	1.01	.67	.63	.38	.53
Net stock	.34	.78	.39	.73	.65	1.24	.84	.73	.55	.62
Average	.35	.69	.39	.66	.58	1.13	.76	.68	.46	.57

Sources: Computed from Tables 12–2 and 3–1.
a. Excluding dwellings.

correct index of capital services would fall somewhere between indexes of the gross and net stock but I believe it would lie much closer to a gross stock index. For this reason, I relied in my United States study of the sources of growth upon the gross stock (although when estimating the addition to output that would be made by an increase in investment, a special allowance was made for the fact that capital does deteriorate).[14] Perhaps a better procedure would have been to use a weighted average of gross and net stock with, say, three-fourths of the weight assigned to the gross stock index, but in that study this procedure would not have changed my results.

In the present study there are two statistical points to consider in addition to matters of principle. One is that gross stock indexes may be more sensitive than net stock indexes to errors in assumed service lives unless, as is usually not the case, the estimator either divides capital goods among a great many categories of goods with different service lives or uses a procedure of dispersing retirements around the average service life.[15] The second statistical consideration is the fact that in the present study gross stock series for four of the countries are not independent estimates but were inferred from the movement of the net stock.

The alternative estimates of the contributions

of nonresidential structures and equipment to growth rates of national income given in Table 12–4 may now be compared in light of these considerations. The comparison shows that the contributions calculated from gross and net stock series separately differ from their average by no more than 0.12 percentage points in any country in any time period. The typical difference is much smaller.[16] The difference from a series that would assign three-quarters of the weight to the gross stock (as I suggested might be warranted on theoretical grounds) is only half as big. To minimize possible error and incomparability among countries it has seemed best to adopt the compromise of using the simple average even though I believe greater weight should attach to the gross stock if possible errors in the data are ignored. By adopting this compromise procedure my estimates are nowhere very far from those that the use of either gross or net stock would yield.

Comparisons of Contributions

Estimated contributions in percentage points (rearranged from Table 12–4) are as follows:

	1950–62	1950–55	1955–62
Germany	1.00	.83	1.13
Norway	.78	.92	.68
Netherlands	.65	.51	.76
Denmark	.65	.64	.66
France	.55	.50	.58
Italy	.53	.46	.57
United States	.43	.53	.35
United Kingdom	.43	.38	.46
Belgium	.39	.37	.39

The order of countries and comparisons of the periods differ somewhat from those for the growth rates of the stock because these results depend, in addition, on the weight of the earnings of this type of capital in national income.

Changes in the stock of nonresidential structures and equipment made an important contribution to growth in all countries. Over the 1950–62 period as a whole this contribution ranged from 0.39 percentage points in Belgium to 1.00 in Germany. Differences in the size of the contributions help to explain differences in the growth rates of national

14. See Denison, *Sources of Economic Growth* [B25], especially pp. 112–13 and Appendix D.

15. Appendix Table J–10 tests the sensitivity of United States estimates by showing for the 1950–61 period the gross and net series that result from using five different sets of assumed service lives. In general, the table is reassuring on this point. Although the longest assumed lives are 2-1/3 times as long as the shortest, all five of the net stock indexes and four of the five gross stock indexes are fairly close to one another. In a similar comparison of changes from 1929 to 1957, the period analyzed in my American study, all ten indexes showed about the same change. However, on rare occasions gross stock indexes computed without great detail or dispersion may respond erratically to even a moderate change in estimated service lives. One of the United States gross stock indexes (that based on assumed service lives 20 percent shorter than Bulletin F) illustrates the danger. From 1955 to 1961 this series rises much less than the others because, in the nonfarm nonmanufacturing sector, equipment and structures installed during years of exceptionally heavy investment happen to drop out of the stock during this period when these particular service lives are used. Indexes of the net stock, from which values are eliminated gradually, are less sensitive to moderate differences in estimates of service lives. (Gross stock series are not inherently inferior in this respect since undue sensitivity can be avoided by the use of considerable detail, and of dispersion, in their construction.)

16. Differences between the estimates based on gross and net stock themselves are, of course, twice as large.

income. This source contributed 0.21 points more to Northwest European than to United States growth in 1950–62 and 0.34 points more in the 1955–62 subperiod. The largest difference in contributions—that between Germany and the United States in 1955–62—is 0.78 percentage points. All the European countries obtained more growth from this source than the United States in 1955–62 and all except Belgium and the United Kingdom did so in the 1950–62 period as a whole.

Rates of Return

The estimates just presented indicate that the increase in the stock of nonresidential structures and equipment made an important contribution to postwar growth rates. But they do not assign a dominant role to this growth source as some other studies of growth have done. The present section further explains the meaning of my estimates by indicating an alternative approach that would yield much the same results.

As actually calculated, the estimates imply that if nonresidential structures and equipment earned (say) 15 percent of the national income in a particular period and increased (say) 5 percent a year, then they would be raising national income by 0.75 percent a year (plus a trifling interaction factor and an allowance for economies of scale, both of which are considered in subsequent chapters). Aside from some intricate short-run complications related to the effect of investment on the net-gross ratio, the same result could be obtained by multiplying the absolute increase in the capital stock by the rate of return on capital and dividing by national income. The method actually used does not require that the rate of return be known, but it is useful to have in mind a notion of approximate levels of rates of return.

The rate of return on a capital good may be defined as that rate of discount that equates the income stream the good produces with the cost of the asset, when each year's gross earnings are discounted to the acquisition date. (For present purposes all figures would have to be placed in constant prices.) True rates of return, unfortunately, cannot be calculated from available information. However, it is possible to calculate approximate ratios of the

earnings of nonresidential stuctures and equipment (measured after deduction of depreciation but not of income taxes) to net and gross stock when both income and net stock are based on straight line depreciation. This requires use of the income share estimates, and of capital stock data described in Appendix J. To obtain an appreciation of the general level of such ratios I have ventured to make such computations for four of the large countries in the 1955–59 period. The data used are rough approximations. Moreover, unlike the *indexes* of the stock that underlie calculations of the contribution of capital to growth, the *levels* of both the gross and net stock that underlie these ratios are highly sensitive to errors in assumed service lives. Consequently, if United States service lives are not really so much shorter than European lives as the estimates imply, the error leads to overstatement of the United States ratios relative to those for the European countries. This point should be recalled in interpreting the data to be presented. The levels of net stock ratios could also be changed considerably by use of a different depreciation pattern.

The calculated ratios of earnings to net stock in 1955–59 are 0.109 in the United States, 0.102 in France, 0.104 in Germany, and 0.086 in the United Kingdom. Such ratios are sometimes used as measures of rates of return. Even if the ratios were entirely accurate, however, only by chance would they accurately measure rates of return or even provide an accurate comparison of countries.[17]

International comparability probably is somewhat improved by substituting the gross for the net stock in the denominator of the ratio. The calculated ratios of earnings to gross stock in 1955–59 are 0.059 in the United States, 0.055 in France, 0.065 in Germany, and 0.048 in the United Kingdom.[18] If gross stock ratios are doubled (which does not alter the relationship among countries but

17. It seems to me a curious fact that writings on physical capital often use such ratios as if they were rates of return, while writings on "human capital," particularly education, seem never to do so but instead attempt computations that actually equate costs with the discounted value of the flow of future earnings.

18. The preceding ratios are based on the following rough estimates of average values in the 1955–59 period. United States in billions of 1954 dollars: gross stock $617.1; net stock $334.4; national income $333.8; earnings of nonresidential structures and equipment 10.9 percent of national income. France in billions of 1956 francs: gross stock Fr.

allows some subsequent statements to be made) the figures obtained are 0.118 for the United States, 0.110 for France, 0.131 for Germany, and 0.095 for the United Kingdom. These figures indicate what the ratios of net earnings to net stock would have been if (1) the net-gross ratio had been 50 percent in all four countries and (2) the earnings of capital goods actually do not change during their service lives. If the latter condition were met, the use of the gross stock would have the advantage over the net stock that the distorting effect of differences in the net-gross ratio, which is particularly high in Germany, would be eliminated. Insofar as the services of capital goods do decline with age, this calculation overstates the relative rate-of-return position of Germany. Presumably something in between ratios based on gross stock and those based on net stock gives the "best" comparison.

No great reliance can be placed on the *differences* in these ratios in view of the possibilities for error in and incomparability of the data. However, since the lowest ratio (the British) is 73 percent of the highest (the German) based on the gross stock, and 83 percent based on the net stock, the comparisons probably do warrant the conclusion that rates of return do not vary among these countries by really enormous amounts. This is in general accord with the results obtained by Bagicha Singh Minhas and others in comparing advanced countries, but any such comparison encounters the difficulty that only earnings-stock ratios can really be estimated.[19]

The *levels* of the ratios of earnings to half the value of the gross stock—0.095 to 0.131 in 1955–59—are considerably above true rates of return if the service lives are not overestimated, if my estimates of the share of national income earned by this type of capital are not too low (in Chapter 4 I argued they were probably too high), and if the annual services yielded by capital goods do not decline much with age.[20] There is no guarantee that all these conditions are fully met but it is highly probable that true rates of return fall short of these ratios by appreciable amounts.

Suppose the true rate of return in a country is 10 percent and that the ratio of the net value of enterprise nonresidential structures and equipment to national income is between 1.0 and 1.6, the range implied by the estimates for the four countries in 1955–59.[21] To raise the national income by 1 percent then requires net investment in enterprise non-

---

372.0; net stock Fr. 199.2; national income Fr. 150.0; earnings percentage 13.6. Germany in billions of 1954 marks: gross stock DM. 386.9; net stock DM. 244.1; national income DM. 152.4; earnings percentage 16.6. United Kingdom in billions of 1958 pounds: gross stock £ 46.45; net stock £ 25.70; national income £ 18.47; earnings percentage 12.0. The capital stock estimates are described in Appendix J. The Kirner estimates for Germany in 1954 prices and the Office of Business Economics estimates for the United States in 1954 prices were used without adjustment in these calculations.

19. Minhas estimated that in manufacturing the "rate of return" before income tax (by which he evidently means the ratio of business earnings to net stock, including fixed capital, inventories, and other assets) averaged 15.98 percent in the United States and 15.79 percent in the United Kingdom in 1954–58, and 14.30 percent in Canada and 17.92 percent in Japan in 1953–57. Except for Japan, the level of these ratios is overstated because the book values of fixed assets he used for the most part were not revalued to allow for price increases (*An International Comparison of Factor Costs and Factor Use*, p. 88 [B77]).

Angus Maddison, it is true, has shown what he calls the "real annual return on capital" to vary greatly among countries. However, this is a measure of the average yield on stock market shares plus the average annual increase in share prices, deflated by the cost of living. This measure may have relevance to the *incentive* to purchase stocks or even to make equity investments in general, but it is not relevant to the contribution of investment to national income (in OECD, *Productivity Measurement Review*, May 1963, pp. 3, 8 [I23]).

20. Given estimates based on straight line depreciation, the ratio of annual net earnings to half the gross stock value (or to the net stock value when half the service life is exhausted) will always exceed the true rate of return that is earned on the asset throughout its service life if gross earnings are constant throughout the life of an asset. The amount by which it exceeds the true rate of return will be greater, the higher the rate of return and the longer the total service life of the asset. With fairly long service lives and high rates of return the difference becomes large. For example, for a capital good with a true rate of return of 12 percent and a thirty-year service life, the ratio of net income to net stock is 0.168 when the net-gross ratio is 50 percent (and the ratio of net income to net stock is equal to the true 12 percent rate of return when the net-gross ratio is 70 percent rather than 50). With low rates of return and short service lives the figures tend to converge. For example, with a 6 percent true rate of return the ratio of net annual earnings to half the value of the gross stock is 0.064 for an asset with a ten-year life and 0.061 for an asset with a five-year life. On this point see *Sources of Economic Growth*, p. 28, note 16, p. 33, pp. 112–13, and Appendix D [B25].

21. These ratios are derived from the numbers given in note 18; however, under no circumstances should they be used to compare capital-output ratios among the individual countries. They are much too sensitive to differences in estimated service lives to permit such comparison—much more so than ratios of earnings to net stock, where an offset to incomparability of stock estimates is obtained in net earnings via the effect on depreciation.

residential structures and equipment equal to 10 to 16 percent of the national income. To obtain a contribution of one percentage point to the long-term growth rate from this source, *continuous net investment* in nonresidential structures and equipment equal to 10 to 16 percent of the national income would be required; such rates are rarely obtained. One would have to assume net rates of return of an altogether different order of magnitude than 10 percent to secure estimates of the contribution to growth of the increase in structures and equipment large enough to warrant assigning this source the central position in growth analysis. There is no factual basis at all to support such high rates of return.

Further Discussion of the Relationship of Capital to Growth

Proper interpretation of my estimates of the contribution of nonresidential structures and equipment to growth requires a precise understanding of my classification of growth sources. The distinction between the contribution of capital and sources classified under "output per unit of input" is of greatest importance. Five topics bearing upon this distinction will now be considered. They are quality change, changes in age distribution, filling gaps in the capital stock, the hours per year that structures and equipment are used, and the allocation of capital among industries. In addition to explaining my classification, I shall examine the substantive importance of these topics where possible. This will avoid the need to return to them later in this study (when changes in ouput per unit of input are explored) and permit the reader to judge how adoption of some alternatives to my classification would affect the estimates of capital's contribution to growth.

Quality Change and the Contribution of Capital

I indicated earlier in this chapter that some analysts would like to measure changes in the capital stock by use of a different definition than that adopted in this study. By that definition, capital goods in the stock at different dates would be equated by their ability to contribute to production at a common date, the capital stock would grow faster, and a larger contribution of capital to growth would be computed. This procedure would classify gains in production resulting from advances in the ability to design capital goods as contributions of capital. In my classification, these gains are counted as part of the contribution of "advances of knowledge." Since it is impossible to construct a capital stock series of the alternative type, I do not attempt to isolate gains from advances in the ability to design capital goods from the gains provided by other advances in knowledge that permit more output to be obtained with the same use of resources. My classification seems to me not only unavoidable but also desirable because it permits the contribution of capital to be identified with the process of saving, and the contribution of advances of knowledge to be identified with determinants, such as research, of changes in the "state of the arts." But in any case, no matter of principle, only one of classification, is involved.

Changes in Age Distribution

"Embodiment" models developed by Robert M. Solow and others raise issues both of classification and of substance. If the average age of capital is shortened the ratio of the average quality (ability to contribute to production) of existing capital goods to the quality of new capital goods is raised, according to the postulates of these models, while if the average age is lengthened the ratio declines. (This statement assumes a constant rate of improvement in new capital goods.) In my United States study, I classified gains or losses in production associated with the change in age distribution in the growth source, "changes in the lag in the application of knowledge."[22] I do so again in the present study. Alternatively, they could be classified as an addition to or subtraction from the contribution of capital.[23] This classification question is unimportant, but the size of the gains or losses

22. Denison, *Sources of Economic Growth,* pp. 234–37 [B25].

23. This classification, it must be understood, would be very different from that described in the previous paragraph. It would not count all gains from noneconomic quality improvement of capital goods as a contribution of capital formation but only the difference (positive or negative) between the gains actually realized and those that would have

associated with changes in the age distribution of capital goods needs to be considered.

PROBLEM OF APPRAISING EFFECTS. The gains or losses associated with a change in age distribution cannot be measured directly, and analysts concerned with the subject have been forced to resort to very indirect and controversial methods of estimation. The debate has revolved upon efforts to judge the size of four magnitudes. These are: (1) the size of the total contribution of advances in knowledge to growth; (2) the fraction of this amount that is introduced into the production process by "embodiment" (noneconomic quality change) in capital goods; (3) the effect of a change in average age upon the average quality of the capital stock; and (4) the size of changes in average age that actually have occurred or are likely to occur.[24] The first two of these magnitudes enter the discussion only because, if they were known, their product would provide an indirect estimate of the average rate of noneconomic quality change in structures and equipment, a rate that cannot be estimated directly.

As will be explained shortly, my estimate of (1), the total contribution of advances in knowledge to growth, is about three-fourths of a percentage point in the United States. Numerous attempts have been made to estimate (2), the fraction of advances in knowledge that are "embodied" as quality improvements in capital goods, but they have been altogether inconclusive. In "The Unimportance of the Embodied Question" I argued that under reasonably normal circumstances, and specifically at the present time in the United States, it was not necessary for analysis to know this fraction. This is because the magnitudes of the other items are too small to allow changes in average age to have more than a negligible effect on output even if the maximum (and absurd) assumption that all advances of knowledge are embodied is made. This, in turn, is partly because a reduction of (say) one year in average age does not, under normal circumstances, mean adding one year's average quality improvement to the stock of capital goods (the usual assumption of embodiment models) but very much less than that. It is also because the changes in average age that have occurred or are likely to occur are small.[25] These two points will now be examined.

The reason that a change in the age distribution does not under normal circumstances have the effect that embodiment models suppose, may be outlined as follows. During any span of time, different types of capital goods undergo very different amounts of quality improvement. The greater is quality improvement in new goods, the greater is obsolescence on existing capital for which the new goods are a substitute. Other things being equal, rates of return on replacement investment will be highest for types of capital goods that have experienced the most quality improvement (hence obsolescence). Any substantial amount of gross investment—certainly less than would be needed to hold the capital stock constant—permits investment opportunities that are created by sizable quality improvements in new capital goods to be grasped. Variations in the amount of gross investment, upon which changes in average age depend, determine only whether the less profitable opportunities involving the replacement of types of capital goods for which quality change has been small, are taken up. Even for the same type of good the advantage of improvements will be greater in some uses than others, and new acquisitions will be used first where the gains are greatest. Consequently, differences in the level of gross investment, and resulting differences in average age, will not have nearly so large an effect on the average quality of the capital stock

---

been realized if the age distribution of capital goods were unchanged.

24. I cannot review here the extensive literature that has developed upon this subject, nor do more than summarize even the views I have myself published. The latter were expressed mainly in the *Sources of Economic Growth*, pp. 235–37 [B25]; in *American Economic Review*, March 1964, pp. 90–94 [P1]; and in "Capital Theory and the Rate of Return" (a review of Robert M. Solow's book of the same title), *American Economic Review*, September 1964, pp. 721–25 [P1].

25. There is a procedural question, discussed below, that must be mentioned here. If the average age of both structures and equipment, separately, is unchanged, a mere shift in the composition of the stock as between structures and equipment will cause their combined average age to change. Similar shifts may occur within the structures and equipment components. I have not considered such changes in the composition of the stock to represent a change in average age that is relevant to the question at issue. A few other writers have done so, most have not. In recent writings Solow has treated structures and equipment separately, which is broadly consistent with my procedure.

as embodiment models suppose. The gain in the average quality of the capital stock that is supposed to derive from additional new investment is not realized because the change in average age is automatically largely offset by a reduction in the average amount of quality improvement incorporated in new capital.[26]

In "The Unimportance of the Embodied Question" I added, however, that:

... there is an important reservation to universal application of the conclusion that it makes little difference to analysis whether or not one takes account of embodiment effects. It need not hold in countries where (or times when) capital goods are used much longer than in the present day United States (hence have more room for variation) or their age distribution is greatly distorted and where (or when) tendencies toward equalizing rates of return are (or recently have been) extremely weak because of lack of competition or because of controls on investment. These conditions existed to a degree in the United States in the immediate postwar years, their effects on short term productivity changes perhaps being important until around 1950. Because specific investment controls during the war and wartime demand patterns prevented the introduction of new capital in the industries serving postwar markets, at war's end there presumably was a significant backlog of high yielding investment opportunities deriving from improvement in capital goods. This was reflected [in the United States] in a catching-up of productivity, particularly from 1948 to 1950. Opportunities deriving from previous improvement in capital goods are therefore significant in examination of the early postwar period. A one-year change in the true average age of equipment had a different effect then than in normal times.[27]

The immediate postwar period in Europe falls within this exception so that it is necessary to ask what changes actually have occurred in the average age of capital, the fourth item in our original listing.

ESTIMATES OF CHANGE IN AVERAGE AGE. To be of use in the present study, estimates of average age must be at least approximately consistent, statistically, with the capital stock estimates used. Such estimates are available in the form required only for the United States and Germany.[28] However,

the United States and Germany represent extremes with respect to the growth rate of the capital stock, and presumptively therefore with respect to changes in average age.[29] They are consequently of particular interest. It may be noted that both the estimates of the stock and those of average age are based on the assumption of constant service lives for particular types of capital goods. If service lives were in fact declining, any reduction in average age would be understated but this would be offset by an overstatement of the increase in the stock itself.

The best way to measure changes in the average age of the gross capital stock is not settled but fortunately calculations based on all plausible alternatives can be provided. Averages for Germany in 1950 and 1960 and the United States in 1950 and 1961 are given in Table 12–5.[30]

The average age of a single group of assets with a uniform service life is unambiguous, but the

represents only a small fraction of the total capital stock. In addition, these data cannot be related to capital stock values even within their coverage.

The average age of machine tools alone was typically rather high immediately after the war. In the Netherlands, for example, it was 16 years in 1948 from which it dropped to no more than 10 in 1965, according to the Planning Bureau (*Centraal Economisch Plan, 1966*, p. 44 [G29]).

Two attempts at international comparisons may be mentioned. In order to test whether slow Belgian growth was related to old equipment, Jean Paelinck assembled information on the age distribution of industrial equipment, excluding vehicles, in Belgium, the United States, France, Germany, the Netherlands, and Italy. He concluded that only in the Netherlands was the percentage of the equipment stock over ten years of age sharply lower than in Belgium (in *Recherches Economiques de Louvain*, March 1962, pp. 43–74 [P35]). Harry Ward cites a Swedish compilation that showed the percentages of machine tools, by number, that were under 10 years old ranged only from 38 to 41 in the United States (1958), France (1955), Germany (1953), the United Kingdom (1961), Italy (1958), and Sweden (1959) (in *Journal of the Royal Statistical Society*, Series A, 1964, p. 356 [P26]). However, comparisons of the average age of machine tools cannot be inferred from such percentages because age distributions are very irregular. For example, in France the percentage of machine tools under 10 years of age dropped from 42.6 in 1955 to 37.8 in 1960 but the average age of machine tools also dropped, from 18.4 years to 16.2 (Ministère de l'Industrie, *Le Parc de Machines-Outils dans les Industries Mécaniques et Electriques*, Table 7 [G11]).

29. The average age of the British stock may possibly have declined more than that of Germany after 1955; see note 39.

30. The German estimates refer to the original Kirner capital stock series in 1954 prices, and the United States estimates to the original Office of Business Economics estimates in 1954 prices, both of which were somewhat modified for use in Table 12–1 (see Appendix J). The modifications should not seriously affect the consistency of the estimates of average age and capital stock.

26. Arnold C. Harberger presents a similar argument in *The Role of Direct and Indirect Taxes in the Federal Revenue System*, pp. 69–70 [B47].

27. *American Economic Review*, March 1964, p. 93 [P1].

28. Most information available on age of capital covers only machine tools or, at most, industrial equipment and

weights appropriate to combine asset groups in order to obtain a combined average are not self-evident. George Jaszi, Robert D. Wasson, and Lawrence Grose used gross stock values as weights in preparing their United States estimates whereas Wolfgang Kirner used depreciation weights in compiling his estimates for Germany.[31] Kirner presumably believes that annual depreciation, as a measure of capital used up each year, provides the better indication of the relative importance of different types of capital in annual production. In Table 12–5 I give the data for each country based on both alternatives since the two sets of weights are quite different.

The use of depreciation gives much more weight to equipment and much less to structures than the use of gross stock weights.[32] There are also differences in industry weights.

Whether gross stock or depreciation weights are preferred, simple changes in the average age of the whole stock combined have, I believe, no signifi-

cance for the present discussion, although for completeness I show them in Table 12–5 in the rows labeled "current year" weights. They are dominated by changes in the composition of assets classified by length of service life. Such changes have no apparent relevance to the subject being investigated. In both the United States and Germany, as in other countries covered in this study, the declining importance of structures has reduced the average age (and the average total service life) of structures and equipment combined when shifting weights are used.

The effect of shifts in weights can be eliminated by applying 1950 weights to both the 1950 and 1960 or 1961 data for the average age of each type of capital to which a separate service life was assigned.[33] Changes in average age so calculated are shown in the rows labeled "1950 weights" in Table 12–5.

With weights held constant, the decline in average age in Germany over a ten-year period was 3.2 years if gross stock weights are used and 2.7 years if depreciation weights are used. The decline was mainly in the average age of structures rather than

31. Citations to the published estimates of these authors are given in Appendix J. The data given in Table 12–5 are calculated from unpublished data they generously provided.

32. In Germany in 1950 equipment receives the same weight as structures if gross stock weights are used but three times as much weight if depreciation is used. In the United States in 1950 equipment receives only two-thirds the weight of structures by gross stock weighting but 88 percent more weight than structures by depreciation weighting, based on Bulletin F lives.

33. The calculation required distinguishing as many components of the stock as were distinguished in the original estimates. These components numbered six in the United States and thirty in Germany.

TABLE 12–5

Average Age of Gross Capital Stock of Enterprise Structures and Equipment[a] *in the United States, 1950 and 1961, and in Germany, 1950 and 1960: Alternative Calculations*

(*In years*)

Weights	Germany			United States[b]			United States, alternate based on service lives 40 percent longer		
	1950	1960	Change 1950–60	1950	1961	Change 1950–61	1950	1961	Change 1950–61
Gross stock weights									
Current year weights	25.0	17.5	−7.5	15.6	13.6	−2.0	20.9	18.3	−2.6
1950 weights	25.0	21.8	−3.2	15.6	14.7	− .9	20.9	19.8	−1.1
Depreciation weights									
Current year weights	17.2	13.6	−3.6	10.6	10.3	− .3	14.2	13.9	− .3
1950 weights	17.2	14.5	−2.7	10.6	10.9	.3	14.2	14.4	.2

Sources: Computed from German data provided by Wolfgang Kirner and United States data provided by the Office of Business Economics; see text for method of derivation.
a. Excluding dwellings.
b. Based on the use of Bulletin F service lives as interpreted by the Office of Business Economics in constructing the capital stock series shown in Part A of Appendix Table J–1.

of equipment.[34] Use of a decline of three years, or 0.3 years per annum, will approximate either estimate. The annual change was probably about the same as this in both the 1950–55 and 1955–60 periods although the data to check this statement directly are not available.[35] Since Germany had the fastest growth rate of capital stock of any of the countries considered, it is unlikely that a much greater reduction in average age occurred in any other country when weights are held constant.[36]

In the United States the average age of structures and equipment changed very little. From 1950 to 1961 it declined 0.9 years (0.08 years per annum) if gross stock weights are used and increased 0.3 years (0.03 years per annum) if depreciation weights are used. From 1950 to the average of 1953 and 1957 (data for 1955 were not obtained), the average age based on 1950 gross stock weights declined 0.6 years and there was no change based on 1950 depreciation weights. These results are based on the use of Bulletin F service lives and are consistent with the Office of Business Economics capital stock series based on these lives. As shown in Table 12–5, the results would scarcely be altered if the calculations were based on service lives 40 percent longer; such lives would be closer to those used for Germany. None of the four alternatives based on fixed weights yields an annual change in average age for the United States of more than about one-tenth of a year from 1950 to either 1953–57 or 1961.

The change in average age that occurred in Germany took place under conditions of about as rapid capital expansion as one is likely to find in a modern Western nation. The difference between the United States and Germany in capital stock

34. Use of 1950 gross stock weights yields declines in average age of 5.1 years for structures and 1.0 years for equipment. Use of 1950 depreciation weights yields declines of 5.6 years for structures and 1.7 years for equipment. Since the importance of equipment increased from 1950 to 1960, the change in the combined average age is smaller if 1960 weights rather than 1950 weights are used to combine structures and equipment.

35. It is inferred from the fact that the difference between the growth rates of gross stock and net stock was about the same in 1950–55 and 1955–60.

36. If weights are not held constant, other countries may have had a larger reduction than Germany. In Denmark, for example, there was apparently an extreme shift from structures to equipment in the composition of the stock; this must have brought a very large reduction in their combined average age.

growth rates was extreme. Thus, one is unlikely in real cases to encounter changes, or "differences in the change," in average age of more than 0.3 or 0.4 years per annum.

EFFECTS OF CHANGE IN AVERAGE AGE. What is the significance of an annual decline of 0.3 years in the average age of structures and equipment such as occurred in Germany? The usual assumption of "embodiment" models would have it mean that instead of picking up the gains from one year's average quality improvement in capital goods each year, Germany was picking up the gains from 1.3 years of average improvement. For reasons indicated earlier, I would accept this assumption as reasonable in the early part of the period—say from 1950 to 1955—but not in the later period, after the composition of the stock had become more normal. For the earlier period, this assumption can be used to try to assess the importance to the growth rate of this additional quality improvement of capital achieved by the reduction in average age.

The index of the quality of nonresidential structures and equipment may be defined as the quotient that would be obtained by dividing (1) an index of the capital stock in constant prices that uses ability to contribute to production to equate different types of capital goods by (2) an index of the capital stock that uses cost at a common date to equate different types of capital goods. Put the other way round, it is simply the amount by which we would need to adjust a capital stock index of the type we have in order to convert it to an index that would measure changes in the ability of nonresidential structures and equipment to contribute to production. By this definition, the effects on output of a 1 percent increase in quantity and a 1 percent increase in quality are identical. Consequently, a change of one year in average age in Germany in the 1950–55 period would have raised output by 16.0 percent (the share of nonresidential structures and equipment in the national income in 1950–54) of the annual rate of quality improvement. The actual annual reduction of 0.3 years in average age would therefore have contributed 0.05 percentage points to the growth rate of national income if the quality of new capital goods increased 1 percent a year, and proportionately more if the rate of quality improvement were greater. If the rate of quality improvement were 5 percent a year, the highest figure that Solow has used for the United States, this factor would have contributed 0.25 percentage points to the 1950–55 German growth rate. How much *does* the quality of capital improve in a year? No one knows, but two considerations suggest some upper limits.

There is no obvious reason for the rate of quality improvement in new capital goods in Germany to differ greatly from that in the United States. In my United States study I estimated that all advances in knowledge, whether or not they operated by improving the quality of capital, contributed about 0.6 percentage points a year to the United States growth rate from 1929 to 1957. In Chapter 20 of the present study I arrive at 0.75 points from 1950 to 1962.[37] Assume, quite unreasonably, that to raise output *all* advances of knowledge had to be "embodied" as quality improvements in nonresidential structures and equipment. With these types of capital earning about 15 percent of national income, contributions of 0.60 or 0.75 from advances of knowledge would then imply that the quality of nonresidential structures and equipment was rising 4 or 5 percent a year. This is far too high because all advances of knowledge need not be embodied in capital goods.

There is another more limiting, and perhaps more persuasive, consideration. The rate of quality improvement in new capital goods determines the rate of obsolescence of existing capital goods. The higher the rate of obsolescence, the shorter the period it pays to retain capital goods. Kirner estimated that service lives in Germany average about 76 years for structures and 25 for equipment (as of 1960), or 46 years for the two together.[38] It would be uneconomic to use capital goods anywhere near this long if the average rate of obsolescence on the whole stock were as high as 4 or 5 percent of the

gross stock value per year. Given any reasonable allowance for the facts that important components of the stock, such as motor vehicles, are known to have a physical life very much shorter than the average service life of the whole stock, and that physical wearing out is a general phenomenon, it is hard to see how a rate of quality improvement above 2 percent a year could be consistent with these service lives. A 2 percent average rate of quality improvement would imply, under the usual embodiment assumption, that the reduction in average age of 0.3 years annually contributed about 0.1 percentage points to the growth rate of national income in Germany from 1950 to 1955 (equal to $2 \times 0.3 \times 0.160$).

Some analysts have identified quality improvement mainly with equipment as distinct from structures. This is not unreasonable, although a counter-case can be made that building of new structures permits new arrangements and techniques to be introduced that would not be possible by replacing equipment alone. It would be consistent with the data to suppose a higher rate of quality improvement in equipment if a lower rate were supposed for structures. This would yield a smaller effect of the change in average age on the growth rate because the change in average age of equipment was much smaller than that of structures or of the two together (when combined with constant weights).

The calculations I have given suggest the change in the average age of capital could not have been a very important factor in German growth even in 1950–55. My guess—it can be no more than that—is that 0.1 percentage points on this account would be generous and I shall use this estimate. A similar allowance is probably justified in the cases of Denmark and Norway, where the stock was growing at about the same rate as in Germany from 1950 to 1955 and the change in average age may, therefore, have been similar.

In all the European countries except Germany, Denmark, and Norway the capital stock was increasing less rapidly than in the United States from 1950 to 1955, and in the United States the average age was constant (depreciation weights) or declining only 0.1 years per annum (gross stock weights). This probably implies that, with weights held constant, the average age of the stock was not changing

---

37. The difference results mainly from a change in estimating techniques rather than from the difference in time period.

38. This is with the use of gross stock weights to combine structures and equipment, which is consistent with the gross stock indexes and the procedures of the "embodiment" models. Net stock weights yield 45 years. The depreciation weights used by Kirner yield 34 years. In 1950, when structures were more important, the average service life with any set of weights was even longer than in 1960.

much in the other European countries. If so, no appreciable allowance for this factor would seem to be required and none has been made. Since actual data on average age consistent with capital stock estimates and with weights held constant are not available, this may involve an omission for one or more countries.

By 1955, a decade after the end of the war, the composition of the stock in all countries had become much better attuned to the requirements of postwar peacetime production. Perhaps the compelling reasons for giving special attention to changes in average age had not altogether vanished. The French Social Science Research Council group studying growth finds that investment in France up to 1955 was concentrated in the basic industries and public utilities, and only thereafter did it become large in most manufacturing industries. But it seems unlikely that after 1955 a further special allowance of significant size is required in any of the countries. Even if this judgment were not accepted and the assumptions of the "embodiment" models were deemed appropriate, there probably would be no cases where the change in average age was large enough to provide a contribution larger than about one-tenth of a point to the growth rate of national income.[39] Indeed, the data for the United States and Germany strongly suggest that changes in average age are unlikely ever to be large enough to contribute much more than this to the growth of an economy as a whole even if the basic assumption of the "embodiment" models—that a one-year

change in average age means a one-year gain in the quality of the capital stock—were acceptable.[40]

Filling Gaps in the Capital Stock

At the end of World War II, Germany was left with a capital stock that was not only greatly depleted but also greatly unbalanced by wartime destruction and postwar dismantling. The division of Germany into occupation zones, and the fact that during the war consumer goods industries had received but little investment, intensified the imbalance. Repair and replacement of facilities that had been destroyed, damaged, or removed, and small amounts of new investment, made it possible to bring back into use other complementary facilities that previously were not utilized or fully utilized. Changes in the stock of structures and equipment that were in use therefore diverged sharply from changes in the stock that was in existence.

For German industry, Rolf Krengel has provided a series for the value of capital utilized as well as for the value of the capital stock. His procedure was to compute the trend in the capital-output ratio in each detailed industrial component in the period 1953–62, and extend the trend values back to 1950. Deviations of the actual capital-output ratios from the trend values (summed from detailed components) reflect, according to this analysis, changes in the rate of utilization and permit construction of a series for capital utilized. After 1955, differences between the indexes of capital stock and capital utilization were irregular and fairly moderate; they presumably reflected primarily fluctuations in the pressure of demand on output. In contrast, from 1950 to 1955 (but especially from 1950 to 1953), capital utilization rose much more sharply than capital stock. Rolf Krengel, Willi Lamberts, and Karlheinz Oppenländer have

39. It is often suggested that the capital stock of Germany has been growing younger in the postwar period while that of the United Kingdom has not and that this helps explain the difference in growth rates. The preceding discussion argues that the point would be unimportant even if true. It may be noted, in addition, that since 1955 the divergence between growth rates of gross and net stock has been even greater in the United Kingdom than in Germany. (The British capital stock growth rate, though lower than most of the other countries, is much higher in postwar days than it was prewar.) This suggests the possibility that the average age of the stock may have been declining as much, or more, in Britain as in Germany, although the difference between changes in gross and net stock is not an infallible guide to changes in average age. Geoffrey Dean has published estimates of the average age of components of the British stock at the end of 1961 but calculations of the average age at different dates, based on the same coverage as my enterprise stock estimates and with constant weights for components, have not been made (see Dean in *Journal of the Royal Statistical Society*, Series A, 1964, pp. 89–107 [P26]).

40. Some embodiment models assume that not only all advances in knowledge but also all other sources of change in output per man-hour and unit of capital must be embodied as quality change in structures and equipment in order to affect output. This, of course, yields larger estimates than those I have calculated for the effect of a change in average age. The logic of this assumption eludes me completely but, in any case, it should be noted that it implies far higher rates of quality improvement than I have considered and that such rates are altogether inconsistent with observed service lives.

attributed this to just the factor under exploration—that is, to the balancing of the stock—and the explanation is reasonable.[41]

From 1950 to 1955 the gross capital stock in industry increased by 39.6 percent while capital utilization increased by 72.0 percent, according to the Krengel estimates in 1958 prices.[42] The difference in growth rates is 4.56 percentage points. If this amount was the same throughout the economy —I have no basis for a different assumption—there is an effect from the balancing out of the stock equivalent to an increase of 4.56 percent a year in the growth of the stock from 1950 to 1955.[43] This would account for a contribution to the growth rate of national income of 16.0 percent of this amount, or of 0.73 percentage points, and represent an important aspect of German growth in that period. This method would, however, pick up the 0.1 points already allowed for changes in the average age of capital, and should therefore be cut to 0.63 percentage points. I shall use this estimate.[44]

Something similar may have occurred on a smaller scale in other countries in the early fifties. In the absence of any basis for doing so, I make no allowance for this possibility. The omission may be of more than marginal importance in some of the continental countries, but I do not think its contribution after 1950 could be at all comparable in magnitude to that in Germany. War damage to the stock of nonresidential structures and equipment was far greater in Germany than in other countries and reconstruction was considerably slower.[45] Ger-

many was the only country in this study that had not surpassed prewar output levels by 1950. Even in Germany the gains had been exhausted by 1955, and largely so by 1953. Elsewhere the process must have been almost completed by 1950.

The contributions estimated in this and the preceding section are shown in tabular form in Table 12–6. These will be classified as contributions to growth rates of output per unit of input rather than as contributions of capital since they refer to the productivity rather than to the amount of inputs.

TABLE 12–6

Contribution of Special Factors Related to Capital to Growth Rates of Total National Income

(*In percentage points*)

Special factor	1950–55	1955–62	1950–62
Reduction in the average age of capital			
Denmark	.10	.00	.04
Germany	.10	.00	.04
Norway	.10	.00	.04
Balancing of the capital stock			
Germany	.63	.00	.26

Source: See text for derivation.

Differences in the Hours Capital Is Used

Changes in the number of hours per year that structures and equipment are used do not affect my estimates of capital input or of the contribution of such capital to growth but may affect output per unit of input.[46] In the short run the use of capital varies with fluctuations in demand. These fluctuations will be considered in Chapter 19; the present discussion is concerned only with differences in capital utilization between dates when demand pressures are similar—that is, with long-term changes. One reason that capital hours may decline in the long run, a reduction in the working hours of labor,

41. "Der Einfluss von Substitution und technischen Fortschritt auf den Kapitalkoeffizienten verschiedener Industriezweige im Gebiet der Bundesrepublik Deutschland," Berlin, n.d., p. 4 (unpublished memorandum). See also Krengel in *Banca Nazionale del Lavoro Quarterly Review*, March 1963, pp. 121–44 [P4].

42. Krengel describes these estimates in *Vierteljahrshefte zur Wirtschaftsforschung*, Vol. 4, 1964 [B65]. Data are from Deutsches Institut für Wirtschaftsforschung, *Produktionsvolumen und Produktionsfaktoren der Industrie im Gebiet der Bundesrepublik Deutschland, Statistische Kennziffern 1950 bis 1960* [B30]. In his *Banca Nazionale del Lavoro* article cited in note 41 Krengel states that the utilization rate in 1955 was the highest attained and not sustainable, so use of this year may slightly overstate the estimate derived in this paragraph for the contribution to growth from eliminating imbalance.

43. For a comment on agriculture, see pp. 277–78.

44. In a sense this factor was even more important than this estimate suggests since the balancing of the stock facilitated the reemployment of labor, but this, of course, is counted in our measure of labor input.

45. In the opinion of Angus Maddison (in *Productivity*

Measurement Review, May 1963, p. 4 [I23]) "opportunities ... of reactivating war damaged capital stock by small complementary investment or repairs" were present only in Germany and Japan.

Tibor Barna compares his estimate that war damage in United Kingdom industry was "on the order of only 5 per cent of the 1938 stock of assets" with an estimate by Krengel that it was nearly one-third of the 1938 stock in Germany (in *The Banker*, April 1957, p. 227 [P5]).

46. Some writers would prefer to say that they affect the quantity of capital input rather than its productivity. Because such a classification would divorce the contribution of

need not be considered here; the assumption under-lying the estimates of the costs of hours reduction presented in Chapter 5 was intended to include, without isolating, the cost of any associated reduction in capital utilization. But there are additional possible reasons for long-term changes in intensity of use. Multiple shifts may become more or less common. Improved management, or newly devised management techniques, may bring about more continuous use of machinery and equipment through better scheduling of work. Use of equipment may become more or less subject to interruptions due to breakdowns and for maintenance. Changes in the composition of the stock by industry and type of capital good may result in changes in the average hours that all capital is used.

PREVALENCE OF SHIFT WORK. Changes in the prevalence of shift work do not appear to be an important factor in the 1950–62 period. Simple observation suggests that the bulk of the capital stock is devoted to activities in which capital either is used almost exclusively by first shift workers at all dates, or else is almost always used for multiple shifts. Only a very small percentage of office workers, for example, is employed on other than the usual day shift. This is the case even in activities like banking where a night shift is customary. The use of office buildings and their furnishings is therefore unlikely to vary appreciably because of changes in shift work. The same is true of most capital in agriculture, retail trade, and consumer service establishments (although some variation occurs in store hours, involving the use of part-time workers during the evening). Certain other forms of capital—hotels, hospitals, and many transportation facilities, for example—are used around the clock, the intensity of use at different hours of the day or on different days varying, if at all, with the pattern of customer habits.[47] In the so-called con-

tinuous-process manufacturing industries, around-the-clock operations are dictated by technical considerations.

Situations in which management has much effective choice as to whether, and to what extent, multiple shifts should be used are concentrated in the manufacturing and mining industries other than the continuous-process industries and it is here that important changes are most likely to occur.[48] These industries account for less than one-fourth of the capital stock (excluding dwellings and government) in the United States and probably not much more in any of the countries under consideration. For the United States there are some data concerning the importance of shift work in manufacturing and mining but the continuous-process workers are not excluded.[49] In 1959–60, 22.8 percent of plant workers in manufacturing establishments located in metropolitan areas were working on the second (16.4 percent) or third (6.4 percent) shift.[50] The figure was only slightly higher, 23.3 percent, in 1963–64, a period of more active business.[51] In mining (excluding crude petroleum and

pairers, distributors, garages and filling stations," and "repair of boots and shoes" in both April 1954 and October 1964. In October 1964 they accounted for 2 percent of workers in central government public administration and 3 percent in local government service. The percentage in gas, electricity, and water was 16 in April 1954 and 15 in October 1964 (19 in gas, 14 in electricity, and 11 in water). Percentages working on *other* than the first shift were probably less than half of the percentages quoted in all cases. Data are from the *Ministry of Labour Gazette*, April 1965 [G42]. In Holland, the percentage in 1960 working on other than the first shift was below 9 percent in gas, electricity, and water (based on calculations from the de Jong compilation discussed below).

48. The technical possibilities for change are great. For example, an increase in shift work was a principal ingredient of the first Russian five-year plan. According to M. Kabaj, it was expected to contribute almost as much as new investment to the increase in industrial output in 1931. The percentage of workers in industry employed on other than the first shift was raised from 32 in 1927 to 42 in 1932. In the clothing industry it was raised from 12 percent to 48 percent (Kabaj in *International Labour Review*, January 1965, p. 57 [I9]).

49. The only country providing separate data for continuous-process workers is (so far as I know) Norway. In 1960 shift workers on continuous-process operations, including the first shift, were 5.5 percent of all plant workers in industry and 28 percent of all the shift workers, including those on the first shift. (Central Bureau of Statistics, *Lønnsstatistikk, 1960*, p. 26 [G32]).

50. *Monthly Labor Review*, April 1961, p. 382 [G67].

51. Bureau of Labor Statistics, *Wages and Related Benefits*, No. 1385–82, June 1965, Pt. II, p. 80 [G66]. In 1964–65 the percentage reached 24.3 (*Wages and Related Benefits*, No. 1430–83, May 1966, Pt. II, p. 88 [G66]).

capital from the saving-investment process, it would, in my view, confuse a classification of growth sources and be inconvenient for analysis of long-term changes. But no question of principle is involved.

47. Actual statistics on the prevalence of shift work in industries outside manufacturing and mining are scarce but some are available. In the United Kingdom shift workers (*including* workers on the first shift where, in a given establishment, a second shift is worked on the same process) accounted for only 1 percent of workers in "laundries," "dry cleaning, job dyeing, carpet beating, etc.," "motor re-

natural gas) 20.3 percent of employment was on second (16.9 percent) and third (3.4 percent) shifts in 1939.[52]

Information on changes in the use of shift work in the United States is scanty. Moses Abramovitz found no basis for guessing whether shift work has grown or declined over the period since 1870.[53] Murray F. Foss suggests that shift work was probably more important after World War II than before but believes it probably didn't change much during the postwar period, the period that is under review.[54] The metropolitan area data show little change from 1959–60 to 1963–64.

Use of multiple shifts is much less prevalent in Europe than in the United States. In the Northwest European countries so few workers are employed on other than the first shift in manufacturing that *changes* in their numbers could hardly have affected utilization of the stock as a whole; moreover, the evidence is against changes of any size. Among the European countries Italy appears to make most use of multiple shifts. Thus the countries with the most and the least capital per worker (as we shall see) are, curiously, those that economize on capital most through this device.

European data generally report the number of workers engaged in shift work inclusive of the number on the first shift where, in a given establishment, a second shift is worked on the same process. Those on the first shift must be eliminated (sometimes by estimation) for comparability with American statistics. Compared to 23 percent of American plant workers in metropolitan areas on the second and third shifts in 1959–64, estimates by Robin Marris and the Ministry of Labour imply that in Great Britain only perhaps 9 percent of operatives in 1951 and 10 percent in 1964 were on other than the first shift in manufacturing establishments employing ten persons or more. (There was an intermediate, evidently "cyclical," dip to 6 percent in 1954.)[55] In mining and quarrying, ex-

cept coal, the percentage working other than the first shift was at most 3.0 percent in 1954 and 2.5 percent in 1961.[56]

If, as Marris suggests, capital per person employed is the same in manufacturing industries working shifts as in other industries, then in 1964 the capital used by manufacturing operatives was, in effect, "stretched" by 11 percent in the United Kingdom and by 30 percent in the United States in comparison with what its use would have been if only a single shift were worked. Unless there is also a difference in other industries, however, the gap of 19 points would be cut to perhaps 5 in the business sector as a whole. Marris considers stringent legislation prohibiting night work for women (only three American states have comparable prohibitions in manufacturing) and the small size of most establishments to be important restraints on greater use of shift work in the United Kingdom.[57]

Percentages of manufacturing workers on other than the first shift appear to be close to the British level of 9 or 10 percent in Norway, the Netherlands, and France, perhaps a little lower in Belgium, and higher (but well below the American figures) in Italy.

Norwegian data are available for five years in the 1950–60 period. Approximately 10 percent of adult

52. Foss in *Survey of Current Business,* June 1963, p. 16 [G63].

53. Abramovitz, *Resource and Output Trends in the United States since 1870,* p. 10 [B1].

54. Foss in *Survey of Current Business,* June 1963, p. 8 [G63].

55. Marris estimates the "average shift-work ratio" at 16 percent in 1951 (based on census data) and possibly 5 points lower (due almost entirely to the engineering industries for

which demand had fallen) in 1954 (based on adjustment of Ministry of Labour data). The shift-work ratio is the proportion of operatives reported as engaged on shifts. It includes workers on the first shift. On the assumption that capital per man is the same where shift work is used as where it is not, Marris estimates that capital used in shift work is used 2¼ times as intensively as other capital. This would seem to imply that, on the average, employment when shift work is used is 2¼ times employment with the same capital when shift work is not used so that the first shift accounts for 44 percent (1 divided by 2.25) of all shift workers. A simpler assumption suggested by Marris in correspondence would be that half of shift workers are on the first shift. This would be the case if workers on third and fourth shifts offset the tendency for the first shift to be larger than the second. This assumption would yield slightly lower percentages than those given in the text (Marris assisted by MacLean and Bernau, *The Economics of Capital Utilisation,* pp. 120, 136, 138, 155 [B74]).

56. These percentages assume one-third of workers on three-shift systems and half of the workers on two-shift systems worked on the first shift, and yields a maximum figure for other shifts since the first shift in fact is usually larger than the others. Data from *Ministry of Labour Gazette,* April 1965, p. 149 [G42].

57. Marris found that only large establishments use multiple shifts to any extent. This is an aspect of "internal" economies of scale that had received little attention until the Marris study appeared.

Norwegian plant workers in manufacturing establishments worked on other than the first shift in 1960, and the percentage had displayed no particular trend since 1950.[58] The Norwegian data provide a breakdown between shift workers on continuous-process operations and those on other shift work. The former represented 28 percent of shift workers in 1960.

J. R. de Jong has assembled information concerning the extent of shift work in the Netherlands, France, Belgium, and Italy.[59] The percentage of wage earners working on other than the first shift in manufacturing was *at most* 11 percent in Holland in 1960.[60] The official survey for 1957 yielded a percentage very similar to that for 1960. De Jong states the percentage had been very stable since 1950. In France, the corresponding figure was at most 8 percent in 1957, 9 in 1959, and 11 in 1963.[61]

A May 1960 survey of *all* compulsorily insured wage earners in Belgium, cited by de Jong, showed 7 percent on shift work schedules, implying that 3 or 4 percent were employed on other than the first shift. Because of its broad coverage this figure is especially interesting; it suggests the extent to which shift work is used in the economy as a whole.

It implies a percentage for manufacturing (which is not isolated) that is at least not higher than in the other Northwest European countries.

De Jong, citing an Italian report, puts the percentage of shift workers among wage earners in Italian industry at 25 to 30 percent, a high figure for Europe. This probably implies that something between 13 and 18 percent were on other than the first shift; it almost certainly puts the Italian percentages between the American and Northwest European percentages.

The data cited show that, even for industrial workers, percentages on other than the first shift are small and, where information is available, that they have changed little since 1950.[62] It seems very unlikely that changes in shift work could have caused utilization of structures and equipment in the business economy as a whole to have changed significantly during the time period that concerns us. Neither, to anticipate a later section, does it appear likely (when the limited weight of manufacturing is considered) that differences among countries in the proportion of workers on other than the first shift can exceed a few percentage points; the United States is clearly in the lead in using shift work.[63]

RISE IN MACHINERY HOURS. Shift work is, however, only one factor that could cause capital utilization to change secularly. An important study by Murray F. Foss indicates that a remarkable increase in the number of hours per year that machinery is worked took place in the United States between the 1920's and the mid-1950's. He estimated that for the bulk of equipment in manufacturing—that run by electric motors—there was an

58. Percentages of males and females employed on shift work are given in Central Bureau of Statistics, *Lønnsstatistikk 1960*, p. 27 [G32]. In 1960 22.1 percent of adult males and 8.6 percent of females, or 19.5 percent of the two sexes combined, were engaged in shift work. Statisticians of the Central Bureau of Statistics calculate that 7.7 percent worked on the second and 2.3 percent on the third shift. On the assumption that the percentage of shift workers who worked on other than the first shift was the same (51.3) in other years, the following time series is obtained: 1950, 9.4 percent; 1952, 9.1 percent; 1955, 8.0 percent; 1957, 9.2 percent; 1960, 10.0 percent. An increase in Norwegian shift work after 1959 is reported in *Revue Française du Travail*, January–March 1966, p. 376 [G12].

59. J. R. de Jong, "De Toepassing van Ploegenarbeid," Amsterdam: Raadgevend Bureau Ir. B. W. Berenschot N.V. (management consultants), August 1964, Chapter IV (unpublished memorandum).

60. The computations for the Netherlands and that for France given just below count half of the workers on two-shift systems, two-thirds of those on three-shift systems, and three-fourths of those on four-shift systems as working on other than the first shift. As noted earlier, the first shift is larger than the others, so such calculations are overstatements. The corresponding figure for mining in the Netherlands is 52 percent, but this may be vastly overstated for the reason just given. The 1957 figure for manufacturing given in the following sentence is derived from Central Bureau of Statistics, *Sociale Maandstatistiek*, August 1958 and February 1962 [G26].

61. The 1957 figure is derived from de Jong. The 1959 and 1963 estimates are derived from *Revue Française du Travail*, April–June 1965, pp. 87–93 [G12].

62. This is not to deny large fluctuations in individual industries. The textile industry is almost everywhere unique in the extent to which adjustment to changing demand conditions is accomplished by varying shift work. In Norway there was a swing from 43 percent in 1950 to 6 percent in 1952, and back to 26 percent in 1960 among males, and from 29 to 6 to 19 among females. For the swing in the United Kingdom engineering industries, see note 55.

63. No specific information for Denmark or Germany was located except for an OECD tabulation (in *Modern Cotton Industry*, p. 93 [I34]) that shows shift work in the textile industry in Denmark and Germany about the same as (or in Germany a bit lower than) in the other European countries covered in this study in 1959–63. All the European countries shown in this comparison had much less shift work than the United States. I shall assume shift work is about as prevalent in Denmark and Germany as in the other Northwest European countries.

increase on the order of one-third to one-half in the utilization rate over this period. The calculation is based on a careful study of the relationship between electricity consumption and the horsepower of motors installed. In mining (except petroleum and gas) the increase was about one-fifth. In electric utilities an average unit of generating equipment worked about 60 percent more hours per year in 1955–57 than in 1929. There was no increase in freight car utilization on the railroads, but freight locomotives worked about 20 percent more and passenger locomotives two-thirds more. These estimates do not include structures, and the machinery and equipment Foss considers is much narrower in scope than producers' durables, so the figures cited cannot be used as typical of changes in utilization of the stock of fixed business capital as a whole, which must have been much less. Even so, the results are very striking and seem to offer a partial explanation for the pronounced drop that occurred between the 1920's and the 1950's in the capital-output ratio.

Foss offers an increase in multiple shift operation as one reason for the increased utilization of machinery and equipment from the 1920's to the 1950's, but shift work was much too rare even in the fifties for this to have been the principal reason. Foss writes:

> Also of importance over the long run has been the advance in knowledge acquired by management in making more efficient use of machines. One example of this has been the efforts by many firms to smooth out within the year the production peaks which come from seasonal or other short-lived peak loads and which frequently entail the use of standby equipment with relatively low annual utilization. The success of the electric utilities in making more intensive use of capacity needed for peak loads . . . has been outstanding. Moreover, it is probably safe to say that over the long run, there has been a relative reduction in "downtime" for equipment repairs. The diesel locomotive is an excellent example of an innovation that has been successful in no small measure because it has required relatively less time-out for repairs and has thus increased the available working time for locomotives.

Within particular industries there have undoubtedly been efforts to introduce continuous, automatic operations in which machines tend to be used with a high degree of intensity. Moreover, there has probably been a change in product mix toward industries in which continuous operations are important—aluminum, refined petroleum, chemicals, and electric power are important examples that may be cited.[64]

Foss indicates that but little of the change he describes may have occurred after 1950, so it may not have been an important factor in United States growth between 1950 and 1962. But his showing that utilization of important types of equipment did change so much from the twenties to the fifties suggests that this has been an important aspect of the longer run growth of output per unit of input.[65]

This development was not confined to the United States. A study of the relationship between electricity consumption and the horsepower of motors installed in manufacturing in the United Kingdom indicates that a very sharp rise in capital utilization also occurred in that country from 1924 and 1930 to 1951.[66] If the British experience was typical of Northwest Europe, as seems likely although it cannot be proven in the absence of direct data, then Europe was not falling behind the United States in the utilization of capital from the 1920's to the 1950's. Thus the British data, insofar as they can be generalized, count strongly against what would in their absence be a tempting supposition: that Europe had fallen behind the United States in use of machinery and equipment between the 1920's and 1950; that increasing use of machinery and equipment has been one aspect of the postwar catching-up of European technique to American practice; and that remaining differences in equipment utilization provide part of the explanation for differences in the level of output per man in 1960.

The Allocation of Investment

Some writers believe the contribution of investment to growth is greatly affected by its industrial allocation. Much of the discussion has been

64. Foss, in *Survey of Current Business*, June 1963, p. 8 [G63].

65. It is of interest to note that, of the several explanations Foss gives for the increased use of capital, only the reduction of "downtime" would qualify as "embodied" technical progress, and that only insofar as the reduction in downtime was achieved without raising the cost of capital goods.

66. The results are given in the forthcoming Social Science Research Council study of British economic growth by R. C. O. Matthews, C. H. Feinstein, and J. Odling-Smee.

concerned with allocation among dwellings, general government, and the business sector as a whole and this aspect is clearly of importance. However, only the allocation of investment in structures and equipment *within* the business sector is relevant here.[67] Is there reason to think that this needs to be given special consideration?

In the framework of the present study, it may first be noted, the question must be reformulated to refer not to investment but to capital stock. My procedure for estimating the contribution of increases in the capital stock to the growth rate may appear to assume that the allocation of capital in the stock among different uses is as appropriate for current needs in one year as in the preceding year.[68] Actually, this is not so much an assumption as a

matter of classification. If decision-making improves secularly, leading to an improving allocation of the capital stock, the gains ought not to be regarded as the result of an increase in factor input but as deriving from better management, management technique, the organization of society, or the like.

It is difficult even to consider the allocation of capital apart from the allocation of resources as a whole, a subject that is discussed in Chapters 16 and 18.[69] Nonetheless a few specific situations relating particularly to investment and capital stock will be examined here. The question is whether there is something about the industrial allocation of additions to the capital stock that causes the stock as such to become significantly better or worse allocated with the passage of time.[70]

The importance of the allocation of investment has most often been raised specifically in connection with the United Kingdom, Italy, Norway, and France, the suggestion being that allocation has been especially unfavorable to growth in the first three countries and particularly favorable in France. What grounds are there for holding this belief?

INVESTMENT IN GOVERNMENT ENTERPRISES. One reason for misinvestment may be the direction of capital into government-owned enterprises, despite a low or negative rate of return, in order to pursue objectives other than a maximum national

---

67. The separate treatment given to dwellings prevents the lower rate of return to housing from distorting the estimates. It is likely that every country considered would have obtained a higher growth rate of measured national income (though not necessarily of economic welfare) by diverting investment from housing to nonresidential business investment if it could have done so. In Europe this generally was politically impossible while in the United States the demand for nonresidential investment was insufficient in much of the period to have taken up any slack that would have been created by reducing residential construction.

68. It does not, of course, imply that allocation is as good in one country as another since allocation affects the marginal products, income shares, and rates of return in each country that underlie the estimated contributions of capital. For the same reason it does not imply that allocation is as good in one time period (of the three distinguished in Table 4-1) as another. Only the effects of *shifting* toward a better or worse allocation of the stock are under discussion.

This leads me to comment on the relevance to the present study of a point advanced by Alexandre Lamfalusy. He has argued (in *Investment and Growth in Mature Economies: The Case of Belgium* [B66]; and in *The United Kingdom and the Six* [B67]) that the United Kingdom and Belgium, because they are the countries that have been industrialized longest, have the oldest capital stocks. The Paelinck survey cited earlier (note 28, p. 146) was undertaken to test, and can be interpreted as tending to refute, this assertion with respect to Belgium. However, Lamfalusy's emphasis is not so much on individual capital goods as on the age of industrial complexes as a whole. His principal argument is that capital in industrial complexes is replaced piecemeal, the complex as a whole hardly ever being replaced. The return on new investment, he concludes, is less in Belgium and the United Kingdom than in countries where industrial complexes developed more recently. The result of the situation described by Lamfalusy would be a less efficient allocation of capital than exists in other countries. However, this would be a continuing situation that would not affect my analysis of the sources of growth. It would not bias the estimates of the contribution of capital to Belgian and British growth presented in Table 12–4, either absolutely or relative to other countries, because any effect upon the marginal productivity of capital would be reflected in the income share of capital in these countries. It would not

affect changes in output per unit of input unless the cost of misallocation were changing. It *would* affect the analysis of the sources of differences in the *level* of output per person employed. In the framework of my estimates it would provide a reason for output per unit of input to be lower in Belgium and the United Kingdom than in other countries. I do not try to quantify this effect.

69. It is evident that those who stress the composition of investment often really have in mind the whole industrial structure of countries. Tibor Barna, for example, has suggested (in *The Banker*, January 1958, pp. 21–22 [P5]) that in the 1950's British manufacturing investment was less well adapted to changing patterns of export trade than was German investment. The suggestion is repeated with respect to a more recent period by David Williams (in *Banca Nazionale del Lavoro Quarterly Review*, March 1963, pp. 108–20 [P4]). Whatever the merit of their position, their discussions indicate that both authors really have in mind the composition of British production, not merely of investment of capital.

70. I am not concerned with the question whether the allocation of new investment is optimal. It never is, of course. Whether it is better in some countries than others is, however, of some interest.

income. Since government ownership has increased, this could lead to worsening, from the standpoint of output, of the allocation of capital.

It has been suggested, for example, that the United Kingdom has obtained less growth than others from new investment because too much has been invested in the nationalized industries, especially coal and the railroads. Both these industries have been declining and relatively unprofitable sectors of the economy.[71] It cannot, of course, be simply assumed from this fact that there was misinvestment; for a time some of the coal mining investment was evidently related to an overestimate of future demand, but in the railroads, and in recent years in coal mining, emphasis has been on cost reduction.[72] In any case, a look at the data shows that over the 1950–62 period as a whole coal mining accounted for only 3.6 percent and the railroads 5.1 percent of total gross fixed investment (excluding dwellings and general government).[73] Even if much of this investment was misdirected, the amounts are not large enough to have had a great effect. Moreover, whereas these industries held nearly one-fifth of the total gross stock of enterprise nonresidential structures and equipment in 1950, the increase in the gross stock of these industries accounted for only 3 percent of the total increase in the gross stock from 1950 to 1962.

Among the countries under consideration, government-owned enterprises are most important in Italy where they operate in a wide range of industries. Many of these enterprises are efficient and profitable. However, the desire to maintain employment in unprofitable enterprises and other considerations of "public policy" appear, according to Vera Lutz, to have been responsible for a good deal of unprofitable investment in Italy, although no quantification is available.[74] Her criticism is properly applicable chiefly to investment made during the early 1950's.

John Sheahan reports that in France, where government enterprise is also important, "the consensus of the best studies of the question is that government firms have largely escaped direction by other agencies of the government and have acted very much as private enterprise might have done in the same markets."[75]

GOVERNMENT INFLUENCE ON GEOGRAPHIC DISTRIBUTION. Several countries have used government subsidies or controls to try to influence the geographic location of new private and public enterprise investment. Italy has tried to develop the South, the United Kingdom and France to divert the location of new factories from the London and Paris areas, the United States to encourage investment in depressed metropolitan areas, Belgium to boost declining coal mining areas, and Norway to check the movement of population from the North. To whatever extent these efforts have actually been successful in diverting investment, they have presumably required some sacrifice of a maximum rate of return, and growth, to other considerations. Except perhaps in Italy the cost can hardly have been very large, however, because the efforts were not very successful. There was apparently a good deal of wasteful investment in, or related to, agriculture in Southern Italy.

GOVERNMENT CONTROLS ON PRIVATE INVESTMENT. This brings me to the more general matter of government participation in the allocation of investment within the private enterprise sector, although this topic merges into the still more general

71. See H. M. Treasury, *The Financial and Economic Obligations of the Nationalised Industries*, p. 12 [G44], for a comparison of earnings-net stock ratios in these and other industries. Returns in such nationalized industries as electric power and communications are lower than in the private sector; this is also the case where these industries are not government owned and is not usually considered evidence that there has been overinvestment in these industries.

72. See Political and Economic Planning (PEP), *Growth in the British Economy* [B88], for a discussion of this question and of the allocation of British investment generally.
William G. Shepherd, who examined coal, gas, and electricity, summarized his conclusions as follows: "By and large, misallocation in the public fuel and power corporations has been less than has been commonly thought. Similar patterns and problems have emerged in corresponding industries in other countries, including the United States. Also, the causes of misallocation have mostly been specific, rather than general and institutional. Accordingly, much of the British discussion—which has dwelt on misallocation in public firms—has been beside the point and has misemphasized the need for future policy" (in *Yale Economic Essays*, Spring 1964, p. 219 [P51]).

73. Data are cumulated from Central Statistical Office, *National Income and Expenditure, 1963*, Table 58, and *National Income and Expenditure, 1964*, Table 63 [G38]. Industries included in the total are those listed in these tables through the line "Other transport and services."

74. Lutz, *Italy: A Study in Economic Development*, pp. 276–84 [B69].

75. Sheahan, *Promotion and Control of Industry in Postwar France*, p. 190 [B100].

one of the allocation of resources as a whole. In the United States, investment decisions within the non-residential business sector have been left very largely to private enterprise in the belief that in a reasonably competitive economy the pursuit of profit would lead to the most efficient allocation of resources, including capital, that is obtainable. This approach has also been characteristic of Germany, though perhaps with less ideological conviction. In most other European countries the allocation of investment among private firms has been more subject to government guidance and influence.

From the standpoint of growth, government guidance has the same danger as government ownership, namely that considerations other than efficiency may enter more strongly into investment policy.[76] In fact, it is clear that not only geographic distribution and the desire to maintain employment in declining activities but also concern with the balance of payments, leading to the favoring of export- or import-substituting industries, and various other objectives have at times been paramount. Since the precise purpose of most direct investment controls has been to divert the flow of capital from the points where profit opportunities were beckoning, it is hard to conceive that they did not reduce rates of return. However, controls were usually intermittent and often not very effective, so the amount may not have been important.[77]

Where pursuit of efficiency is not diluted by other considerations it is an open question, usually resolved by faith rather than analysis, whether extensive government participation in investment planning and decisions is helpful or harmful to growth.[78] The answer need not be the same in all countries; it may depend on the competitiveness and initiative of private business and the relative competence of businessmen and government officials. In contrast to the dominant American viewpoint, the prevailing opinion in France is clearly that the French planning process, involving participation by both government and enterprise (as well as labor and other groups) has improved investment decisions and enabled France to obtain more growth from the volume of investment undertaken than would otherwise have occurred. Sheahan notes two reasons that this may be so. First, "planning interventions on the supply side may help considerably to improve efficiency in so far as they aid in offsetting defects in the price system," particularly in the presence of price controls and monetary disequilibrium. Second,

> ... planning may help to locate discrepancies between private and social gains and to counteract their continuously changing causes. Even given completely competitive markets ... and with forceful entrepreneurs seeking to maximize profits in a well conceived, long run sense, interdependence beyond the horizon of the firm and discontinuities associated with major investment decisions make it likely that unguided separate decisions will be collectively suboptimal. If all these conditions are fulfilled, the scope for further gain may be small. If they are met only to the unsatisfactory degree observable in France immediately before and for some time after the war, the scope for gain may be large.[79]

It may well be true that allocation in France has been better than it would have been in the absence of planning. It may also be better than in the past, resulting in a better allocation of capital in 1962 than in 1950 or 1955. If so, this is a factor contributing to the rise in productivity. There is no pre-

76. I do not, of course, imply that there is anything improper about this; growth is not the only objective to which policy should be directed. Failure to deal with other types of issues, moreover, could have ultimate consequences more adverse to growth than inefficient allocation.

77. For a discussion of British experience through 1955, covering intermittent periods when a wide range of controls were in effect, see Rozen in *Canadian Journal of Economics and Political Science*, May 1963, pp. 185–202 [P11].

78. Pierre Massé, Commissaire Général du Plan, France, summarized the position as follows: "All Western nations have recognized that no government can afford to neglect investment, the necessary condition of prosperity and progress. But though they agree on the principle they differ as to how it should be applied. Some think the State should confine itself to investment in the traditional public sector, and merely encourage the productive activity of free enterprise by creating favourable conditions, supplemented if need be by financial or fiscal incentives. Others take a more active line favouring nationalisation or government participation in basic industries, selected for their booster effect. Others again consider that the Government should co-operate with the employers and trade unions in drawing up target plans pointing the way to economic growth, without imposing them on the private sector.

"Experience over the last 15 years has been too short, and too many disturbing factors have been at work, for it to be possible to say that any one of these policies is the best" (in OEEC, *Problems of Development: Series of Lectures on Economic Growth*, p. 87 [I21]).

79. Sheahan, *Promotion and Control of Industry in Postwar France*, pp. 187–88 [B100]. In Sheahan's view, it may be noted, "the system has not been one of government control, but decentralized enterprise decision plus a promotional push" (p. 189).

sumption that it has or has not been better or worse than in the United States or other countries.

HEAVY INVESTMENT CONCENTRATION IN SPE-
CIFIC INDUSTRIES. Some attempts to explain why the high Norwegian investment ratio has not produced a higher growth rate have pointed to the heavy industrial concentration of investment but I have not seen a developed argument as to why such concentration should be unfavorable. The only really striking aspect of the composition of Norwegian investment is that over the 1950–62 period the shipping industry accounted for 32 percent of total fixed investment (excluding dwellings and general government).[80] This concentration cannot have depressed the Norwegian growth rate. Shipping was an unusually *profitable* activity, with a high rate of return, through 1957. Shipping rates and earnings subsequently declined, but even if the current price rate of return dropped below an average rate, as appears likely, this could not have affected the Norwegian growth rate adversely.[81] This is because Norwegian national product data are based on 1955 price weights, and the method of deriving a deflated output series for shipping is simply to extrapolate the base year value by the volume of freight transported, so that subsequent shipping rates do not enter the calculation.[82]

80. Reference sometimes is also made to electric power which earns a relatively low rate of return in most countries, but this industry actually received under 9 percent of the investment total, not an extraordinary figure. Data cited for Norway are from Central Bureau of Statistics, *Nasjonalregnskap, 1949–1962*, Table 23 [G33]. They are in 1955 prices and reported on the Scandinavian "gross-gross" basis. Separate data for industries that are heavy users of electric power, which have also been mentioned, are not available.

81. I have no direct data to evaluate the recent rate of return on shipping in comparison with the average rate of return. However, after 1957 there was a radical drop in nonwage earnings in the shipping industry. Even after a substantial recovery in 1964 these earnings were little more than half what they had been in 1957. Shipping investment has nevertheless remained high (at least through 1962, the latest year for which complete data are available from the national accounts). A large part of this investment has been financed by American loans (two-thirds of Norwegian capital imports in 1962–65 went for this purpose according to *The Economist*, May 29, 1965, p. 1064 [P19]). This continued high investment does not appear to represent misallocation, but rather the consequence of the technological revolution in shipping resulting in Norwegian shipowners losing money on the operation of older ships (when their value is not reduced for rapid obsolescence) but earning a return on new ships.

82. The OECD data I have used are, it is true, nominally expressed in 1958 prices. However, the shift of base has

EFFECT OF FAST GROWTH ON MISALLOCATION.
It is often pointed out that rapid growth of an economy as a whole probably has a tendency to minimize the number of unprofitable and altogether wasteful investments by reducing the number of sectors in which absolute declines in production are taking place. At the point that a sharp upward change in the growth rate is occurring this might mean that new investment yields a higher return than it formerly did. But it does not provide reason to expect the yield on new investment to exceed the current yield on existing capital, and hence gives no reason to expect the results of the procedures followed to obtain the contribution of capital to be biased downward in fast-growing economies.

This examination, though sketchy and in some respects inconclusive, does not suggest any specific allowance for specially favorable or unfavorable allocation of investment within the enterprise sector, nor does it seem to me likely that they should be given much emphasis. A presumption may exist that in the early part of the period allocation was less favorable in Italy than elsewhere because Italian policy gave so much attention to objectives other than efficiency in production, but this was also the case in Italy before World War II. It would be surprising to learn that the allocation of the Italian capital stock deteriorated after 1950. Specific suggestions relating to United Kingdom investment in coal mining and the railroads and Norwegian investment in shipping do not seem to survive quantitative analysis.

Absolute Levels of Postwar Gross Investment

Having completed my discussion of the relationship of structures and equipment to growth, I shall devote the remainder of this chapter to an examination of international differences in the *levels* of investment in, and the stock of, nonresidential

little effect on the Norwegian growth rate. Either reweighting was not done in sufficient detail to imply a true shift to 1958 weights for shipping prices, or else the shift had little effect. In either case the concentration of investment in shipping must be dismissed as an adverse factor.

structures and equipment and their relationship to levels of output.

In this section the quantities of nonresidential structures and equipment that the various countries obtained from their investment during the postwar period are compared. Comparisons are also made of the proportions of GNP that each country invested in structures and equipment when the output of all countries is measured in uniform prices.

Although these estimates are of considerable interest in themselves, they have a more important purpose in this study because they provide the starting point for comparisons of the levels of capital stock in the various countries offered in the following section. The latter are essential for analysis of the differences in 1960 levels of output per person.

The investment comparisons presented here are hinged on the estimates of expenditures for nonresidential construction and for equipment, valued uniformly in United States and in European prices, that Gilbert and Associates prepared for 1950. To obtain estimates for periods other than 1950, percentage changes in the volume of construction and in equipment expenditures, separately, in each country were assumed to be the same in constant United States prices as in the country's own constant prices. The derivation of the estimates is fully described in Appendix H.[83] Estimates were prepared on three sets of price weights: United States prices in 1950, average European prices in 1950, and (for comparisons with the United States) each European country's own prices in 1950.

Comparison of Investment per Person Employed in 1950 and 1962

Table 12–7 compares gross investment in nonresidential construction and equipment in the single years 1950 and 1962. The investment data used in this table include both enterprise investment and nondefense structures and equipment acquired by general government. The estimates are presented in the form of indexes of expenditures per civilian

83. The accuracy of the estimates depends on (1) the accuracy of the estimates for 1950 prepared by Gilbert and Associates (OEEC, 1958 [I17]); (2) the accuracy of the movement of deflated expenditures for each of these two types of gross investment as reported in each country's time series; and (3) the amount of error involved in assuming that, if expenditures for nonresidential construction or equipment (treated separately) in some other period are x times as large as expenditures in 1950 when measured in constant prices of that country, they were also x times as large when measured in the prices used in these comparisons. As is so often the case there is no good basis for appraising margins of error.

TABLE 12–7

International Comparison of Gross Investment in Nonresidential Construction and Equipment, per Civilian Employed, Alternative Price Weights, 1950 and 1962[a]

(Indexes, United States = 100)

Area	1950			1962		
	United States price weights	Average European price weights	National European price weights	United States price weights	Average European price weights	National European price weights
United States	100	100	100	100	100	100
Northwest Europe	35	32	—	56	52	—
Belgium	55	52	48	68	66	62
Denmark	44	39	35	74	68	61
France	38	33	30	58	52	48
Germany	28	27	26	61	59	56
Netherlands	47	43	38	70	68	60
Norway	65	54	49	84	72	66
United Kingdom	31	28	28	41	38	38
Italy	20	17	15	39	35	32

Sources: Computed from gross investment, given for 1950 in Table H–1 and described for 1962 in Appendix H, and civilian employment given in Table 5–1.
a. Investment by general government is included.

employed. In both 1950 and 1962 the United States invested more than any of the European countries per civilian worker and far more than any of the large European countries. Northwest Europe as a whole invested, per civilian employed, only 35 percent as much as the United States in 1950 and 56 percent as much in 1962 when investment expenditures in all countries are valued in United States prices. If average European prices or national European prices are used in the comparison the gap between the European countries and the United States is still larger.

Comparison of Investment Ratios in Uniform Prices

Measurement of investment expenditures in United States prices permits a calculation that yields a surprising result. If, as in the first two columns of Table 12–8, both investment expenditures and national products are valued in United States prices, it turns out that even in 1962 the United States was spending as large a percentage of GNP for nonresidential structures and equipment as France, Italy, or Northwest Europe as a whole; more than the United Kingdom; and not greatly less than Germany. It had been investing a much larger percentage than any of these areas in 1950.[84] This is a major difference from the results obtained when investment ratios for each country were based on its own prices. The principal reason the uniform use of United States prices changes the result is that the prices of investment goods were much higher in Europe, relative to the prices of other goods and services, than in the United States.

84. To obtain these ratios for each European country the following procedure was adopted. United States GNP in 1950 and 1962 in current market prices was multiplied by the ratio of European to United States GNP measured in 1955 United States prices to obtain total GNP in United States prices. (For 1962 the average of 1960 and 1964 GNP's in 1955 United States prices was used to obtain the ratios because 1962 itself had not been estimated.) United States gross investment in nonresidential construction and equipment in 1950 and 1962 in current prices (as reported in or, for 1950, consistent with OECD, *National Accounts Statistics, 1955–1964* [I35], plus an allowance for state and local government purchases of equipment) was multiplied by the ratios in these years of European to United States gross investment in United States prices of 1950 to obtain European investment in United States prices. The investment ratios are obtained by dividing investment in United States prices by GNP in United States prices.

TABLE 12–8

Expenditures for Nonresidential Structures and Equipment as a Percentage of Gross National Product at Market Prices, in United States and National Prices, 1950 and 1962[a]

Area	United States prices		National prices	
	1950	1962	1950	1962
United States	12.0	12.1	12.0	12.1
Northwest Europe	9.6	11.9	12.8[b]	16.6[b]
Belgium	11.3	13.5	12.3	15.1
Denmark	10.1	16.4	12.7	16.7
France	9.7	11.8	13.6	14.9
Germany	7.9	13.4	14.2	20.1
Netherlands	10.0	13.7	16.1	20.1
Norway	14.4	16.6	23.0	25.1
United Kingdom	6.6	9.1	10.3	13.2
Italy	8.4	11.9	14.8	17.4

Source: See text for explanation of derivation.
a. Differences between the percentages shown in United States and European prices reflect not only differences in price ratios but also measurement differences. See text for explanation and sources.
b. Total investment computed by multiplying GNP in United States prices in each country by the ratio of investment to GNP in national prices and summing the results for the individual countries. The change from 1950 to 1962 is strongly affected by the change in country weights.

Although Table 12–8 also gives the investment ratios in national prices for these years that are comparable to those shown for longer periods in Table 10–1, the two sets of ratios do not differ solely because of international differences in relative prices since they were developed independently. Only the estimates in United States prices incorporate classification adjustments introduced by Gilbert and Associates to improve international comparability. Only the ratios in national prices incorporate revisions in United States and European estimates for 1950 that have been made since the Gilbert study was completed. There are also some additional minor differences in weighting. Consequently, price ratios as such cannot be derived from this table.[85]

The contrast between the comparisons obtained when United States prices are used and those

85. *Changes* from 1950 to 1962 in the relationship between ratios in United States and European prices reflect mainly (though not exactly) differential price movements. For example, ratios for Denmark in United States and Danish prices converge because capital goods prices rose more than GNP prices in the United States and less than GNP prices in Denmark. Shifts in the composition of investment between construction and equipment influence changes in the price ratios strongly.

TABLE 12–9

Ratios of Prices of Producers' Durables and Nonresidential Construction to Average GNP Prices, 1950 and 1955

(*United States ratio = 1.00*)

Area	Based on national European quantity weights, 1950		Based on United States quantity weights			
			Producers' durables		Nonresidential construction	
	Producers' durables	Nonresidential construction	1950	1955	1950	1955
United States	1.00	1.00	1.00	1.00	1.00	1.00
Northwest Europe						
Belgium	1.33	.74	1.27	1.33	.79	.81
Denmark	1.44	.95	1.35	1.41	1.01	1.05
France	1.50	1.05	1.35	1.35	.67	.75
Germany	1.73	1.03	1.27	1.45	.94	.81
Netherlands	1.74	1.04	1.44	1.31	.72	.86
Norway	1.72	.91	1.46	1.63	.71	.82
United Kingdom	1.38	1.39	1.16	1.22	.73	.92
Italy	2.47	1.06	1.59	1.54	.67	.75

Source: Computed from Gilbert and Associates, OEEC, 1958, pp. 31, 56, 79, 80 [I17].

obtained when each country's own prices are used do nevertheless *mainly* reflect the fact that the price of these types of investment goods was far higher in Europe, relative to the average price of all GNP components, than in America. The first two columns of Table 12–9 give Gilbert's price ratios based on national European quantity weights. These are the weights that correspond to the use of United States price weights in the volume comparisons, and that explain why European investment ratios drop so much when output is measured in United States prices. The ratio of producers' durables prices to GNP prices in 1950 was anywhere from 33 percent to 74 percent higher in the Northwest European countries than in the United States, and 147 percent higher in Italy. Nonresidential construction prices were not consistently higher in Europe, but this is the smaller investment component in most countries.

In the absence of comparable data for other years, I show in Table 12–9 price ratios based on United States quantity weights to give an indication of changes from 1950 to 1955.[86] There were

some irregular movements but it is evident that price differentials generally persisted to 1955. Volume comparisons suggest that this was the case throughout the 1950–62 period. It may be noted that Gilbert's data show that in 1950 and 1955 producers' durables prices not only were higher in the European countries than in the United States relative to GNP prices, but also in absolute terms. The lone exception is the United Kingdom in 1950.

Tables 12–7 and 12–8 together show that in United States prices the investment ratio in 1962 was as high in the United States as in Northwest Europe, and that substitution of European for United States price weights lowers the ratio of European to United States investment. A shift to European weights worsens the European GNP position even more than the investment position, however, so that on the basis of European weights the large continental countries were devoting a larger fraction of GNP to investment in 1962 than was the United States. Elimination of government investment would also raise Europe's investment ratio relative to the United States (see pages 165–66). How-

86. These ratios run much lower, primarily because the ratios of European to American GNP prices are higher. This is the price counterpart of the difference in volume relationships indicated, on a net product basis, in Table 2–4. However, the relative price of nonresidential structures and equipment combined in Europe was well above that in the

United States even if United States price weights are used. Gilbert and Associates (OEEC, 1958, pp. 41, 54 [I17]) found little difference in the relative price of *all* investment goods in 1955 only because residential construction was much cheaper in Europe (see pp. 127–28).

ever, the difference between the two areas would still be much smaller than when the percentage for each country is based on its own prices.

These results place a different perspective on the investment ratios examined in Chapter 10. It has already been shown that investment ratios are not a guide to growth rates of the capital stock, and it now becomes clear that they even fail to provide information about the amounts of investment the different countries were making currently. A country can increase its real national income by increasing its stock of actual capital goods—buildings, machines, and the like—but it cannot do so merely by raising the price of capital goods relative to the price of end product. Similarly, if one country spends more than another on capital goods, absolutely or relative to GNP, because the absolute or relative price of capital goods is higher, this does not imply that its higher investment expenditure makes a greater contribution to future output. Several writers have noticed the important differences in relative prices brought out by Gilbert and Kravis and by Gilbert and Associates, but few seem to have fully grasped their significance. One who has is John Sheahan.

In his analysis of French experience in the 1950's Sheahan notes that the ratio of fixed investment to national product in France compared favorably with ratios in the United States and other Western European countries, and that this indicates "a major sacrifice of alternative uses of the national product in order to increase and modernize productive capacity. But the gain achieved by the loss of alternative consumption has been undermined by the fact that prices of capital goods in France are higher relative to other domestic prices than is true in the United States or other major West European countries."

This price ratio "remained throughout the decade one of the most important restraints on the French growth rate. This relationship means that a given ratio of investment expenditure to national income results in an unusually low real gain in productive equipment."[87]

Similarly, the smaller United States percentage (Table 10–1) of GNP devoted to nonresidential fixed investment may indicate that less consumption was sacrificed than in Europe (except the United Kingdom) relative to national product. But it does not indicate that the United States was getting less capital goods relative to its output.

Comparison of Gross Investment Over the Postwar Period

So far, discussion has centered on data for individual years. Now investment in the postwar period as a whole will be considered. This provides the basis for comparisons of capital stock attempted in the following section but investment is itself not without interest.

Expenditures for nonresidential construction and equipment have been cumulated over the whole period from 1948 to 1963 and the aggregate divided by 1964 civilian employment. This provides a comparison of the total amount of capital goods of these types installed during the previous sixteen years that was available per civilian worker in 1964. The results based on three sets of prices are given in index form, with the United States equal to 100, in the upper portion of Table 12–10. For the United States and the large European countries they are as follows:

	United States price weights	Average European price weights	National European price weights
United States	100	100	100
France	48	43	39
Germany	44	42	40
United Kingdom	37	34	33
Italy	31	27	24

The exact results depend upon the particular price weights used but the general position is clear. By the comparison least favorable to the United States (use of United States weights), the United States had invested 2.1 times as much during the previous sixteen years as France for each civilian employed in 1964, 2.3 times as much as Germany,

87. Sheahan, *Promotion and Control of Industry in Postwar France*, pp. 18–19 [B100]. Sheahan's comparisons are between France and the United States, the United Kingdom, and Germany. With respect to Germany his statement appears to need qualification. Although the relative price of

producers' durables was higher in France than in Germany in 1950, based on United States quantity weights (the calculation on which Sheahan bases his statement—see p. 96 of his book), this was no longer true by 1955, and the relative price of nonresidential construction was lower in France at both dates (though the latter result seems to be heavily influenced by road construction).

TABLE 12–10

International Comparison of Cumulated Gross Expenditures for Nonresidential Construction and Equipment, per Civilian Employed, Various Periods and Price Weights[a]

(*Indexes, United States = 100*)

Period covered by investment	Year used for employment	Price weights[b]	Type of investment	United States	Northwest Europe	Belgium[c]	Denmark	France	Germany	Netherlands	Norway	United Kingdom[c]	Italy
1948–63	1964	U.S.	Total	100	45	59	56	48	44	58	81	37	31
			Construction	100	37	37	45	45	36	53	92	25	39
			Equipment	100	52	76	64	51	50	61	73	47	25
1948–63	1964	A.E.	Total	100	42	57	50	43	42	54	69	34	27
			Construction	100	35	31	37	45	35	46	76	24	36
			Equipment	100	45	71	57	42	46	58	65	39	22
1948–63	1964	N.E.	Total	100	—	54	45	39	40	48	63	33	24
			Construction	100	—	29	32	45	31	39	67	25	32
			Equipment	100	—	66	53	37	44	53	61	39	21
1955–63	1964	U.S.	Total	100	51	62	63	52	54	65	85	41	35
			Construction	100	40	38	48	45	44	55	91	27	42
			Equipment	100	60	82	75	58	62	74	80	51	30
1948–59	1960	U.S.	Total	100	39	55	48	43	35	52	76	34	24
			Construction	100	32	35	40	41	29	49	86	21	31
			Equipment	100	45	71	54	44	40	55	67	43	19
1955–59	1960	U.S.	Total	100	44	56	51	45	44	60	78	36	27
			Construction	100	34	33	39	38	36	49	80	23	33
			Equipment	100	53	75	62	51	51	68	76	48	22

Sources: See text and Appendix H for derivation.
a. Expenditures by general government are included.
b. Symbols stand for United States, Average European, and National European price weights of 1950.
c. Differences in classification cause Belgian and perhaps British indexes for nonresidential construction to be understated and indexes for equipment to be overstated.

2.7 times as much as the United Kingdom, and 3.2 times as much as Italy. If the prices of each of the European countries are adopted for bilateral comparisons with the United States, the United States had invested two and one-half times as much as France or Germany, three times as much as the United Kingdom, and four times as much as Italy. France and Germany invested much more than the United Kingdom per civilian employed in 1964.[88]

The indexes for the small countries are:

	United States price weights	Average European price weights	National European price weights
Norway	81	69	63
Belgium	59	57	54
Netherlands	58	54	48
Denmark	56	50	45

88. Indexes based on their own price weights are lower for all the European countries than indexes based on average European price weights, and this is usually true also of the separate indexes for construction and for machinery and equipment. This pattern presumably results from the

Each of these small European countries had invested much more than any of the large countries. The Norwegian figures are much above the others, though well below those of the United States.[89]

The data make it very clear that the sharp differences among countries in the growth rates of the stock of structures and equipment from 1950 to

elimination of extreme price relationships when European weights are averaged.

89. I know of no statistical reason (other than the general possibility of error that pervades all these estimates) for suspecting the Norwegian indexes of being too high. On the other hand, there is reason to wonder whether they may not be too low. Ships were not among the items that Gilbert and Associates (OEEC, 1958 [I17]) priced, insofar as their published descriptions indicate. The price of ships at factor cost must have been lower in Norway, where they are mostly purchased from foreign sources, than in America, where in 1950 many were produced in high-cost American shipyards. Other producers' durables, in contrast, were more expensive in Norway. If Gilbert and Associates applied the average Norwegian-American price ratio for other producers' durables to ships, this would have led to appreciable understatement of the ratio of Norwegian investment to American investment, since ships (including fishing boats)

1962 bear no simple relationship to the amounts invested during the postwar period. The United States and Belgium were among the three countries with the lowest growth rates and also among the three with the largest absolute amounts of postwar investment per civilian employed in 1964. Germany had the highest growth rate of the stock but her postwar investment per civilian employed in 1964 exceeded only the United Kingdom and Italy. The main reasons for such differences lie in the capital stock position at the beginning of the period and the investment price ratios, although it should be noted that these particular sets of data are not comparable with respect to coverage of general government and that employment changes *during* the period complicate the comparison.

Within the 1948–63 period, gross investment in nonresidential construction and equipment was increasing more, in percentage terms, in Europe than in the United States. In consequence, ratios of European to American investment made in the 1955–63 period are higher than those covering investment made during the entire period from 1948 to 1963.[90] The difference is particularly large for Germany, the Netherlands, and Denmark. Based on United States price weights, the indexes of cumulated investment during the preceding nine and sixteen years, per civilian employed in 1964, compare as follows:

	1955–63	*1948–63*
United States	100	100
Northwest Europe	51	45
Norway	85	81
Netherlands	65	58
Denmark	63	56
Belgium	62	59
Germany	54	44
France	52	48
United Kingdom	41	37
Italy	35	31

Gross Investment Excluding
General Government

Comparisons of investment levels presented thus far include capital expenditures by general govern-

ment for roads, schools, hospitals, office buildings, and other nondefense purposes. The percentage of total investment in nonresidential structures and equipment that was made by general government can be computed when each country's investment is measured in its own prices; the ratios are given in Columns 1 and 2 of Table 12–11. General government investment represented a much larger proportion of total gross investment in the United States than it did in Northwest Europe. The proportion varied only moderately among the individual European countries except Holland, where it was raised by substantial expenditures for marine construction and land reclamation. These ratios are used in Columns 3 and 4, Table 12–11, to adjust the investment indexes in United States prices to exclude investment by general government and thus arrive at indexes that include only enterprise investment (private and public). A bias leading to overstatement of the European indexes for enterprise investment probably results from the fact that the government percentages are based on expenditures valued in each country's own prices rather than in United States prices.[91]

Investment by enterprises was 49 percent as large in Northwest Europe as in the United States from 1948 through 1963 per civilian employed in 1964, and 56 percent as large from 1955 through 1963, when investment is valued at United States prices. These results compare with percentages of 45 and 51 when government investment is included.

Differences in Levels of Stock and Their Effects on National Income Levels

To analyze the reasons that levels of national income per person employed differ among countries, comparisons are required of the levels of the stock of nonresidential structures and equipment of enterprises. Postwar investment provides the best

account for about one-third of total Norwegian investment in nonresidential structures and equipment (in Norwegian prices).

90. Comparison with Table 12–7 also shows that even the 1955–63 ratios are well below those for the year 1962 alone.

91. The bias arises from the fact that government investment is largely construction. Since construction is more expensive, compared to producers' durables, in the United States than in Europe, government investment in Europe is presumably a higher proportion of total investment in United States prices than in European prices. I used 1950–63 government percentages to adjust 1948–63 investment. This cannot introduce any appreciable error.

TABLE 12-11

Adjustment of Cumulated Investment in Nonresidential Construction and Equipment, per Civilian Employed in 1964, To Obtain Indexes of Enterprise Investment

	Ratio of general government investment to total investment		Indexes of enterprise investment				
			In United States prices		Average of 1948–63 and 1955–63 indexes in:		
					United States prices	Average European prices	National European prices
Area	1950–63 (1)	1955–63 (2)	1948–63 investment (3)	1955–63 investment (4)	(5)	(6)	(7)
United States	.220	.228	100	100	100	100	100
Northwest Europe	.159	.163	49	56	53	50	—
Belgium	.143[a]	.143	65	69	67	65	61
Denmark	.140	.145	62	70	66	59	53
France	.159	.163	52	57	54	48	45
Germany	.177	.183	46	58	52	50	48
Netherlands	.216	.215	58	66	62	59	52
Norway	.135	.140	90	94	92	78	72
United Kingdom	.130	.131	41	46	44	40	38
Italy	.160	.158	33	38	36	31	28

Sources: Columns (1) and (2): Common Market countries (except Belgium), 1953–63: OSCE, *General Statistical Bulletin*, No. 11, 1964 [148]; Belgium, 1955–63: *ibid.*, No. 11, 1965; other European countries, 1955–63: OECD, *General Statistics*, January 1965 [128]; United States: OECD, *National Accounts Statistics, 1955–1964* [135], adjusted to allow for state and local government purchases of machinery and equipment based on data in *Survey of Current Business*, March 1961 [G63]. All countries, data for 1950–52 or 1950–54: national or OECD sources consistent with later data were used. Note that Germany includes the Saar and West Berlin beginning in 1960, and that the French "new" series begins in 1959, the "old" series being used for earlier years.
  Columns (3) and (4): Products of one minus Columns (1) or (2), and the corresponding indexes based on data including government investment from Table 12–10, readjusted to the base, United States = 100.
  Column (5): Average of Columns (3) and (4).
  Columns (6) and (7): The ratios of the 1948–63 indexes in corresponding price weights to the indexes in United States weights, as given in Table 12–10, were applied to Column (5).
  a. 1953–63.

guide I can devise to the relative size of the stock of structures and equipment in the different countries, valued in United States prices. Although less than satisfactory it is better than the only alternative available: to try to convert available capital stock estimates to common prices and scope and to allow for differences in assumed service lives.

Comparison of Net Stock at the Beginning of 1964

I shall use simple averages of the indexes of 1948–63 and 1955–63 gross enterprise investment per civilian worker (the United States equal to 100) as indexes of the net stock per civilian worker at the beginning of 1964.[92] This procedure counts investment made from 1948 to 1954 in only one of the indexes that are averaged and investment made

92. This estimate is subsequently used as a starting point to derive the relative net stock position at other dates, and for gross stock comparisons in 1960.

from 1955 through 1963 in both indexes, while investment made before 1948 is not counted at all. The assumptions and defects of this procedure will be considered at length but first the results, given in Column 5 of Table 12–11, will be quickly examined. They indicate that, at the beginning of 1964, the net stock of enterprise nonresidential structures and equipment available per employed civilian worker, when valued in United States prices, was 52 to 54 percent as large in France, Germany, and Northwest Europe as a whole as in the United States. It was 62 to 67 percent as large in Holland, Denmark, and Belgium; 92 percent in Norway; and only 44 percent in the United Kingdom and 36 percent in Italy. As a reminder that comparisons are more favorable to the United States if European price weights are used (and also that the relative position of the European countries is somewhat modified), Columns 6 and 7, Table 12–11, give approximations to similar indexes based on average and national European prices.

This use of cumulated investment to infer levels of the net stock at the beginning of 1964 requires justification. The international comparisons obtained are admittedly approximations but I shall try to show that the qualifications are less serious than might be supposed at first sight.

The net stock of structures and equipment at the beginning of 1964 differs from gross investment in the 1948–63 period in two ways. First, it includes the remaining value of assets acquired before 1948 and still in service in 1964. Second, it excludes assets acquired in the 1948–63 period but no longer in service in 1964 as well as accumulated depreciation on the assets that do remain in service.

OMISSION OF ASSETS ACQUIRED BEFORE 1948. Assets acquired before 1948 are omitted from the gross investment figures. How serious is this omission? Such assets would have been at least seventeen years old in 1964. Except for the year 1947 in the United States and a few other countries, 1948 was preceded by a long period in which investment was rather low because of the Great Depression and World War II. The depression affected America more than Europe, the war affected Europe more than America. Europe, in addition, suffered wartime destruction of buildings and equipment. Prior to the depression, the gross national product of all the countries was small by recent standards, and in Europe the percentage of GNP invested was also much smaller than in recent years.[93] Under these conditions a very high proportion of the value of the 1964 net stock of nonresidential structures and equipment must have consisted of assets less than seventeen years old.

United States data confirm this expectation. Commerce Department estimates (based on straight line depreciation and Bulletin F lives) suggest that only about 15 percent of the value of the net stock of private nonresidential structures and equipment (and less than one-fourth even of the value of the gross stock) pertained to assets over sixteen years old. Machinery and Allied Products

Institute data yield similar estimates.[94] Thus capital installed in the 1948–63 period represented around 85 percent of the total net stock in 1964.

The percentage is also high in the United Kingdom even though the service lives used by the Central Statistical Office are longer than those used in the United States. Even by the end of 1961, two years earlier, some 53.5 percent of the *gross* stock had been installed after 1947.[95] Rough calculations indicate that by the end of 1963 this percentage was around 65. This suggests that something like 80 percent of the value of the *net* stock had been installed after 1947. If pre-1948 investment represented a larger percentage of the British than of the American stock at the beginning of 1964 this is due only to the assumption of longer service lives, which I shall argue below is at least partially irrelevant to the present comparison. In any case, the "tail" of assets acquired before 1948 is too small a proportion of total assets for its omission to affect international comparisons of the nonresidential enterprise stock very much. If uniform service lives were used this tail would probably be larger in the United States than in almost any of the other countries so a small bias against the United States stock position may be introduced by its omission.[96]

ASSETS ACQUIRED BETWEEN 1948 AND 1963 NO LONGER IN USE. The proportions of the capital goods installed during the 1948–54 and 1955–63 periods remaining in the net stock at the start of 1964 could have varied among countries for several reasons. These relate to (a) the distribution of investment among assets with different service lives; (b) differences among countries in the service

93. Maddison (in *Productivity Measurement Review,* May 1963, p. 3 [123]) states that "in almost all the countries under consideration, except the United States, the rate of investment in the 1950's was half as high again as it had ever been before." His examination included all the countries covered in the present study.

94. Numbers given in this paragraph are necessarily approximations since neither the U.S. Department of Commerce nor the Institute has compiled estimates in exactly the form required here.

95. Computed from Dean in *Journal of the Royal Statistical Society,* Series A, 1964, Table 9, p. 343 [P26]. Industrial components were selected to obtain approximately the same components as are used to measure the value of the enterprise stock.

96. Rolf Krengel estimated that even at the start of *1957* 70 percent of the *gross* stock in German *industry* was less than *sixteen* years old (*Anlagevermögen, Produktion und Beschäftigung der Industrie im Gebiet der Bundesrepublik von 1924 bis 1956,* p. 63 [B64]).

This cannot be directly compared with the American and British data but does suggest that the percentage of the *total* enterprise *net* stock that was less than seventeen years old at the beginning of *1964* must have been rather small.

lives of similar assets; and (c) the time pattern of investment within the 1948–63 period.

(a) Since the service life of construction exceeds that of equipment, more of the value of postwar construction investment than of equipment investment remained in the stock at the end of 1963. Consequently, use of cumulated investment to measure the stock would distort the stock position if there were large differences in the division of investment between construction and equipment. Data to check this possibility are inadequate but it does not appear likely to be a substantial source of bias except that it may result in understatement of the capital stock position of Norway and Italy.

The first column of Table 12–12 shows the percentage of construction in the 1948–63 investment total in United States prices as calculated from the

TABLE 12–12

Calculated Percentage of Construction in Nonresidential Construction and Equipment Expenditures, 1948–63

(*In United States prices*)

Area	Including government	Excluding government[a]
United States	43.5	27.6
Northwest Europe	35.6	23.4
Belgium[b]	27.5	15.4
Denmark	35.2	24.6
France	40.7	29.5
Germany	36.0	22.3
Netherlands	39.8	23.2
Norway	49.3	41.4
United Kingdom[b]	28.9	18.2
Italy	54.5	45.8

Source: See text for derivation.
a. Computed on the assumption that all general government investment included in the total consists of construction.
b. As indicated in the text, the percentages for Belgium and perhaps the United Kingdom are not comparable to those for other countries.

components entering into the investment aggregate; they are, therefore, tied to Gilbert's 1950 classification. Government investment is included. In the second column general government investment is excluded on the assumption that it consists entirely of construction. Since over 90 percent of government investment typically does consist of construction, any distortion of the comparisons introduced by this assumption probably is not serious.

With general government eliminated, construc-

tion percentages for Northwest Europe as a whole, Denmark, France, Germany, and the Netherlands are all within about 5 points of the United States percentage, a difference that could hardly affect by more than 2 index points the indexes for these countries in Column 5, Table 12–11, used to measure capital stock.

The Belgian and United Kingdom construction percentages appear low in the table but in the case of Belgium this is surely due to incomparability with other countries in the division of investment between structures and equipment—and in the case of the United Kingdom this is likely to be at least part of the explanation.[97]

The construction percentages for Norway and Italy are high. If the differences from the other countries are genuine, use of postwar investment to measure the capital stock probably leads to understatement of the 1964 capital stock position of Norway and Italy.[98] The resulting understatement of the indexes given in Column 5, Table 12–11, might be as much as 2 or 3 index points for Italy and 4 or 5 (out of a much larger figure) for Norway, when these indexes are used to compare net stock.

(b) The use of investment cumulated over the same time periods for all countries implies that the same service lives are used to measure their capital stocks. I have already noted that service lives used

97. The division for Belgium used here stems from the estimates used by Gilbert and Associates (OEEC, 1958 [I17]) for 1950 based on information available at the time they made their estimates. These show a radically lower construction percentage than is derived by carrying back to 1950 current official Belgian estimates that are available beginning with 1953. In the case of the United Kingdom, both OECD and Gilbert and Associates classify in machinery and equipment all of the category that appears in United Kingdom statistics as expenditures for "plant and machinery." Some of these expenditures would be classified as construction in United States estimates and I suspect also in those of other countries (see Appendix H, Section II, paragraphs referring to Belgium and the United Kingdom).

98. It may be observed that in Norwegian prices the Norwegian construction percentage is not so extraordinary. The high percentage in United States prices results (statistically speaking) from an extraordinarily high ratio of producers' durables prices to construction prices (see Table 12–9). As noted earlier in connection with shipping this could reflect an overestimate of producers' durables prices. If so, the Norwegian capital stock position is understated not because of the high construction percentage but because investment in producers' durables has been underestimated. There is, in other words, really one reason, rather than two, for suspecting understatement of the estimate of the Norwegian stock.

by European estimators in compiling capital stock estimates exceed those used by American estimators for similar capital goods. Insofar as this is due to different appraisals of the same real situation, it does not concern us here since these service lives do not enter into the investment comparisons. If there are genuine differences in service lives—and observations by qualified observers indicate that there are differences—a larger fraction of 1948–63 investment remained in the European stock valued in European prices at the end of 1963 than remained in the United States stock valued in United States prices. But how is a comparison in United States prices affected?

If the reason for a difference in service lives were simply that European capital was used less intensively or better maintained (or even that it was discarded less often as a result of less rapid shifts in the composition of output or less rapid geographic shifts), the same difference would arise when both stocks are valued in United States prices. The principal reasons, however, are almost surely associated with improvements in capital goods. A higher ratio of unit labor costs to unit capital costs makes it profitable to replace more quickly in the United States than in Europe. In addition, and I suspect more important, American firms apparently give greater weight to obsolescence in making investment decisions than European firms and would replace more rapidly even if conditions were the same. For these reasons, American firms consider some capital goods still in use in Europe to be wholly obsolete. In the United States such goods have only scrap value and no value at all as instruments of production. I know of no value in United States prices other than zero that could appropriately be applied to such capital. It of course makes no difference to an evaluation of the stock of European countries in United States prices whether such capital is considered to be in the stock with a zero valuation (the European case) or simply omitted from the stock entirely (as in the United States).[99] This means that, insofar as the difference in service lives is due to obsolescence rather than to physical exhaustion, it is necessary to use

United States service lives to depreciate European capital goods in order to value the net stock of European countries in United States prices. I therefore conclude that differences in service lives for similar capital goods do not greatly bias the comparison of capital stocks.[100]

(c) The time pattern of investment within the postwar period remains to be considered. Other things being equal, the more recently investment was made the larger is the fraction that remained in the net stock at the beginning of 1964. Although more complicated and detailed calculations were considered, the simple expedient of averaging indexes based on cumulative investment over the preceding sixteen years and over the preceding nine years seemed as satisfactory as any other, given the uncertainties about the comparability of the

---

99. It should be noted that the United States could have a (useless) counterpart to this capital at little cost simply by retaining obsolete capital goods in the stock.

100. This conclusion supposes, as noted, that any real differences in service lives not due to differences in the composition of the stock are largely associated with obsolescence. As Barna (in Lutz and Hague [eds.] *The Theory of Capital*, p. 85 [B7]) says of depreciable assets "it is obsolescence rather than wear-and-tear which is the dominant cause of mortality—homicide to make room for a new favorite, rather than natural death."

There may be differences in the rate of physical exhaustion if capital goods are originally built more sturdily, better maintained, or used less intensively in one country than another. If differences in original sturdiness or in maintenance exist, however, they must be largely a reflection of differences in the expectation of the duration of the period that capital goods are to be used, and serve mainly to prolong European service lives beyond the point at which capital goods would anyhow be discarded, and have no value, in the United States. Still relevant today is the fascinating discussion of the early nineteenth century by H. J. Habakkuk (in *American and British Technology in the Nineteenth Century*, pp. 86–90 [B45]). Habakkuk describes how British machinery was more heavily and durably built than was American machinery because American firms always expected to replace their machinery quickly with something better and were consequently unwilling to pay for durability. My strong impression is that European firms, in the continental countries as well as in the United Kingdom, still demand machinery and equipment that is, or at least gives the appearance of being, more solidly built than that sold in the United States. Firms selling in both markets often must offer different, and more expensive, models in Europe.

The ratio of maintenance costs to original equipment prices may be lower in Europe than in America. This provides a possible reason unrelated to obsolescence to expect greater maintenance and longer physical service lives but it seems unlikely that sizable errors in the capital stock comparisons for the countries considered here could result from this factor. There is little actual information on intensity of use; the relationship of capital costs to labor costs would be expected to yield greater intensity in Europe but, as noted earlier, the shift work comparison actually showed more shift work in the United States than in Europe. Better management and greater specialization may also lead to greater intensity of use in the United States.

detail of the annual investment data.[101] Other things being equal, failure to treat each year's investment separately tends to understate the relative net stock position at the beginning of 1964 of countries that had a rapid growth rate of the stock after 1955. It should tend to offset any bias introduced by omission of the remaining value of pre-1948 investment.

This review has pointed out various possible biases, both in the estimates of cumulated enterprise investment and in its use to measure the stock at the beginning of 1964 and there are, of course, unknown errors in the basic data used. Consequently no precision can be attached to the results. But unless the guardian angel of the national income estimator—the usual tendency for errors to be offsetting—has completely abandoned us, we should have at least reasonable approximations of the position of Northwest Europe as against the United States, and of the major differences among the European countries.[102]

101. The procedure followed yields European indexes just a little higher than would be obtained from a single index based on adding half of 1948–54 investment to 1955–63 investment. This weighting appears reasonable. For example, if investment each year is divided between structures and equipment as it was in the United States over the whole 1948–63 period, if average service lives of fifteen years for equipment and forty years for structures are assumed (approximately Bulletin F averages), if investment in 1948–54 and 1955–63 were centered at the middle of each period, and if straight line depreciation is used, then 31 percent of 1948–54 investment and 75 percent of 1955–63 investment remained in the stock at the end of 1963. On these assumptions, which are not necessarily accurate, a dollar of 1948–54 investment should be given a weight of 0.41 if a dollar of 1955–63 investment is given a weight of 1.00.

102. The one result that is really startling—the high position of Norway—is relatively well supported. There is the Dean comparison between Britain and Norway to indicate the Norwegian investment estimates in Norwegian prices are not significantly overstated, at least compared with United Kingdom estimates. (Gilbert's 1950 data in national currencies for both countries, to which the expenditure estimates are tied, are approximately consistent with the series analyzed by Dean.) In addition, reasons have been given in this chapter for suspecting that the procedures followed by Gilbert in converting to United States prices, and/or the procedures used in the present investigation, may understate rather than overstate the Norwegian position.

It should also be noted that some 20 percent of the Norwegian enterprise stock but only 5 percent of civilian employment is accounted for by Norwegian shipping. Exclusion of shipping would therefore lower enterprise structures and equipment per person employed by 16 percent in Norway. A similar adjustment would hardly affect the United States figure. Exclusion of shipping would therefore lower the Norwegian index (Column 5, Table 12–11) from

Net Capital Stock Comparisons, 1950–64

The comparisons of the net stock of nonresidential structures and equipment derived in Table 12–11 refer to the beginning of 1964. Table 12–13 carries these estimates back to earlier years by

TABLE 12–13

International Comparison of Net Stock of Enterprise Structures and Equipment[a]
per Civilian Employed, 1950, 1955, 1960, and 1964

(*Indexes, United States = 100*)

Area	1950[b]	1955[b]	1960[b]	1964[a]
United States	100	100	100	100
Northwest Europe	42	42	47	53
Belgium	68	65	67	67
Denmark	47	52	57	66
France	43	44	49	54
Germany	37	36	43	52
Netherlands	52	50	57	62
Norway	68	75	86	92
United Kingdom	39	37	40	44
Italy	30	28	29	36

Source: See text for derivation.
a. Excluding dwellings; comparisons are based on use of 1950 United States prices.
b. Annual averages used for both stock and employment.
c. Stock at the beginning of 1964 divided by 1964 employment.

the use of indexes of net stock in national prices (given for 1950–62 in Table 12–1 and extended to the beginning of 1964 by estimates provided in Appendix J). This procedure assumes that the indexes would be the same in United States prices, and with the use of United States service lives, as they are in national prices and with national service lives.[103] Also, for some countries stock indexes for the beginning of 1964 are tentative.

92 to 77. The importance of shipping in Norway as compared with other countries is suggested by the fact that the ratio of gross registered tonnage of merchant shipping to total employment in all activities is 8½ to 9 times as large in Norway as in Holland or Denmark, 11 times as high as in the United Kingdom, and at least 34 times as high as in any other country covered in this study.

103. Two opposite biases in this procedure should be noted. Since stocks of equipment were growing more rapidly than stocks of structures, and the ratio of equipment prices to structures prices is higher in Europe than in the United States, European stocks probably grew less in United States prices than in European prices. If so, this change in composition would cause European indexes for the earlier years to be progressively understated as they are carried back in time, and the improvement in the European position to be overstated. Substitution of the shorter United States service

Table 12–13 compares the net value of enterprise nonresidential structures and equipment per civilian employed at four dates.[104] It brings out the very substantial changes that have taken place since 1950 in the position of the countries. The position of Northwest Europe as a whole was unchanged relative to the United States from 1950 to 1955 but by 1964 had risen enough to cut the 1955 gap between the two areas by nearly one-fifth. All European countries except Belgium reduced the relative gap in stock position between themselves and the United States. Norway and Germany made the largest *absolute* gains, Germany and Denmark the largest relative gains. The German net stock, per civilian employed, was slightly below the British in 1955 and 18 percent below the French. By 1964 it was 18 percent above the British stock and only 4 percent below the French.[105] Each of the four small countries had a larger stock per civilian employed than any of the three large Northwest European countries at all dates, and all except Belgium greatly reduced the gap between themselves and the United States.[106] Italy by 1964 had reached about the same position relative to the United States that the United Kingdom and Germany had occupied in 1950 and 1955.[107]

Changes shown in Table 12–13 result, of course, from changes in employment as well as from changes in capital stock. The sudden improvement in the relative position of Italy from 1960 to 1964 resulted in part from a decline in Italian employment while employment in the United States was increasing.

No matter how crude the estimates may be, there can be no doubt that changes in the net stock of capital per person employed have been so disparate as to create very pronounced changes in the relative position of the countries and to make most general statements concerning such comparisons almost meaningless unless they are related to a particular year.[108] The table also makes clear that the European countries were able to cut significantly into the United States advantage in capital stock position in a period as short as a decade.

Contribution to Differences in Levels of National Income per Person Employed

This brings me to estimation of the part of the difference in the levels of national income per person employed in 1960 ascribable to differences

---

lives would probably have an opposite effect. Compared to the large changes that appear in Table 12–13, however, these counterbalancing biases are surely minor.

104. The indexes for 1960, which will be used in the analysis of international differences in income levels, can be compared with indexes given at the bottom of Table 12–10, representing cumulative gross investment during the 1948–59 and 1955–59 periods divided by 1960 civilian employment. Most of the European indexes for 1960 in Table 12–13 are higher than could be obtained by weighting the Table 12–10 indexes of pre-1960 postwar investment. However, I do not think the 1948–59 period was long enough for cumulated investment to provide an adequate indication of the 1960 capital stock position. Nevertheless, I provide and call attention to the comparison to enable the reader to evaluate it for himself.

105. As will be noted below, the British *gross* stock position compares much more favorably than the net stock position with that of Germany (but not of France).

106. The first bias, which is discussed in note 103, applies with special strength to Denmark, where the equipment stock increased particularly rapidly; if adjustment could be made for this factor it might appreciably raise the Danish estimate for 1950, the lowest of the small-country indexes.

107. The reader is again reminded that if European weights were used, comparisons of the levels of the indexes would be more favorable to the United States and would show somewhat different relationships among the European countries. He is also cautioned again that the estimates are crude.

108. However, the statement by the PEP research group, published in 1960 but related to no particular year, that "it is commonly estimated that the amount of capital per worker in manufacturing industry in the United States, whether measured directly, or indirectly in terms of horsepower used per worker, is about two-and-a-half times as great as in the United Kingdom" is in approximate agreement with the estimate given in Table 12–13 for the civilian economy as a whole throughout the 1950–60 decade (PEP, *Growth in the British Economy*, p. 33 [B88]).

My estimates are consistent, except for the small countries separately, with Rolf Krengel's statement that "the present average capital provision per person employed in West European industrial countries is not even half as much as in the United States" if he refers to 1960, the last year for which time series data are given in the article quoted (in *Banca Nazionale del Lavoro Quarterly Review*, March 1963, p. 18 [P4]).

Maurice Allais (in *Econometrica*, October 1962, p. 721 [P14]) is precise in his dating. He states that in 1955 the real volume of equipment (in which he evidently includes structures) per worker in the United States economy was 2.4 times higher than (i.e., as high as) in the French economy. This is very close to the 1955 ratio (2.3) implied by Table 12–13. By 1964 the ratio had dropped below 1.9.

The Economist statement (August 28, 1965, p. 759 [P19]) that the British labor force is "working on just about the biggest accumulation of capital equipment per head" in Europe is at sharp variance with my net stock estimates for 1964, which show the United Kingdom last except for Italy.

in the quantity of nonresidential structures and equipment of enterprises.

Columns 1 and 3 of Table 12–14 provide indexes of the total net stock of this type of capital and the stock per person employed. The latter indexes differ slightly from those for 1960 in Table 12–13 because military personnel are included in the denominator.

Columns 2 and 4 provide corresponding indexes, which are even more approximate, for the gross stock. Gross stock estimates for five of the countries were obtained by dividing net stock in United States prices by the ratio of the net stock to the gross stock in 1960 as shown by the estimates for each country in its own prices. These net-gross ratios (computed from data given in Appendix J) are: United States 0.54; Belgium and France 0.56; United Kingdom 0.58; Germany 0.65. In the absence of net-gross ratios for the remaining countries the following guesses, based on the growth rates of the stock and the time pattern of postwar investment, were used: Italy 0.56; Netherlands and Norway 0.57; Denmark 0.59.

Although this procedure for arriving at gross stock indexes is not very satisfactory it is introduced

in the belief that the principal differences in the net-gross ratios would persist if estimates uniformly based on United States prices and service lives could be obtained.

The gross stock position of all the European countries is lower in comparison with the United States than the net stock position. The gross stock indexes for Germany are much lower than the net stock indexes in comparison with all the other countries; the German gross stock index per person employed was a little lower than that for the United Kingdom in 1960 although the German net stock index was already appreciably higher.

In Columns 5 and 6 of Table 12–14 the effect of differences in the stock of nonresidential structures and equipment on levels of national income per person employed in 1960 are computed by use, first, of the net stock and, second, of the gross stock indexes. As in the analysis of growth rates (and for similar reasons), I shall use an average of the results of using the two procedures (Column 7). As was the case for growth rates, the difference between the two measures is largest for Germany. Even for Germany, however, the average estimate differs from that which the use of either gross or

TABLE 12–14

Enterprise Nonresidential Structures and Equipment: International Comparison of Levels and Contribution to Differences in National Income per Person Employed, 1960

(*United States price weights*)

	Indexes (United States = 100)				Contribution to difference from United States in national income per person employed if enterprise nonresidential structures and equipment were the only source of difference (in index points), based on:		
	Total stock		Stock per person employed				
Area	Net (1)	Gross (2)	Net (3)	Gross (4)	Net stock (5)	Gross stock (6)	Average (7)
United States	100.0	100.0	100	100	—	—	—
Northwest Europe	55.7	50.2	47	42	5.4	5.9	5.6
Belgium	3.4	3.2	67	64	3.4	3.7	3.5
Denmark	1.8	1.6	58	52	4.3	4.9	4.6
France	13.7	13.0	49	46	5.2	5.5	5.4
Germany	16.9	13.8	45	36	5.6	6.5	6.1
Netherlands	3.4	3.2	57	53	4.3	4.7	4.6
Norway	1.8	1.7	86	80	1.4	2.1	1.7
United Kingdom	14.7	13.5	41	38	6.0	6.3	6.2
Italy	8.8	8.4	30	29	7.1	7.3	7.2

Source: See text for derivation.

net stock would yield by only one-half percentage point.

The calculations may be illustrated by the Belgian estimates based on the net stock. Belgium had 66.9 percent as much capital in the form of nonresidential structures and equipment, per person employed, as the United States, or 33.1 percent less than the United States. This type of capital earned 10.2 percent of the national income in the United States in 1960–62 (Table 4–1). By use of the net stock indexes, I therefore calculate that national income per person employed would have been lower in Belgium than in the United States by 3.4 percent (33.1 × 0.102) if the two countries were similar in all respects except the stock of nonresidential structures and equipment per person. A similar calculation based on the gross stock yields 3.7 percent.

The smaller stock of nonresidential structures and equipment, according to the average estimates in Column 7, would in itself have caused the 1960 value of national income per person employed in Northwest Europe as a whole, and in France, Germany, and the United Kingdom, to be 5.4 to 6.2 percent lower than in the United States in 1960. The percentage is less than this in all the small countries and larger in Italy.

The extent to which these results are sensitive to errors in the 1960 capital stock indexes can be readily indicated. A change of almost 10 points in the average of the gross and net stock indexes given in Columns 3 and 4, Table 12–14, would be required to change Column 7 by 1 percentage point.

These calculations are based on United States weights. Use of European weights would ascribe a larger difference in national income per person employed to structures and equipment. Not only are the differences between the United States and the European countries in the quantities of structures and equipment per person employed larger if European weights are used, but also the shares of nonresidential structures and equipment in the national income are generally larger in Europe than in the United States. However, the total difference in national income per person employed is also larger if European weights are used.

The 1960 gap between the net stock of structures and equipment per person employed in Northwest Europe and the United States, when multiplied by Northwest European employment, was equal to about eight and one-half months of 1960 Northwest European GNP when both stock and GNP are valued at national European prices, or about seven and one-half months when both are valued at United States prices. Thus, Northwest Europe would need a much higher saving rate than the United States for a long period of time to eliminate the gap.

Factors Closely Related to Capital That Affect Productivity

In discussing the relationship of capital to growth rates I found it convenient to discuss several possible reasons that the productivity of capital might change over time. Many of these topics also have relevance to international comparisons of the levels of national income. Discussion of these topics again in the context of levels of output would be repetitious and, with one exception, permit no specific estimates, and I confine myself to this reminder of their possible relevance.

The exception refers to shift work. Data offered in the earlier discussion indicate that in 1960 the percentage of manufacturing production workers employed on other than the first shift was around 23 in the United States, 10 in each of the countries of Northwest Europe, and 16 in Italy.[109] This means that in Northwest Europe structures and equipment were used by manufacturing production workers 11 percent less than in the United States (13 ÷ 123) and 6 percent less in Italy than in the United States because of shift work.[110] Suppose there is no difference in the prevalence of shift work outside manufacturing, and capital used by manufacturing production workers is one-fifth of total enterprise capital.[111] This implies that enterprise

109. The variations noted earlier among the Northwest European countries are too small to affect the calculations to be made in this paragraph.

110. As before, capital per worker is assumed to be the same in manufacturing establishments where shift work is used as where it is not.

111. In the United States manufacturing capital represented 24 percent of the total enterprise stock (on both a gross and net basis) in 1960, according to the detail of the estimates given in Part A, Appendix Table J–1. I use one-fifth to allow for capital not used by production workers. The manufacturing share of the stock varies among countries, but probably not enough to affect the estimates derived in this paragraph.

capital as a whole is used about 2.2 percent less in Northwest Europe and 1.2 percent less in Italy than in the United States. The difference may be treated as equivalent to a similar difference in the quantity of capital. Multiplication by the share of structures and equipment in the United States national in-come (10.2 percent) yields an estimate that in the Northwest European countries national income per person employed is lower than in the United States by 0.2 percent, and in Italy by 0.1 percent, for this reason. These estimates will be classified as a source of difference in levels of output per unit of input.

⫸ CHAPTER THIRTEEN ⫷

Inventories

Enterprise inventories are the final type of reproducible capital to be examined. Inventories typically represent one-third or one-fourth as much capital as nonresidential structures and equipment. Inventories are quite as necessary for production as structures and equipment and compete with them for a nation's saving and a firm's funds.[1]

The increase in the capital stock in the form of inventories is estimated to have contributed about 0.1 percentage points to the 1950–62 growth rates of national income in the United States, Belgium, Norway, the United Kingdom, and Italy, 0.2 points in Denmark, France, and the Netherlands, and 0.3

1. It is difficult to understand why a number of attempts (by no means all) to relate inputs and output in different countries have ignored inventories. Perhaps the most plausible explanation is that some of these studies are based on correlation analysis in which quarterly or annual data are used. Very short-run fluctuations in inventories are often the undesired result of poor sales forecasts rather than adjustments desired to support production and sales. Involuntary accumulation results in excess capacity in the same sense that the term is applied to structures and equipment. This is undoubtedly an obstacle to attempts to apply correlation analysis to quarterly or annual data. However, the difficulty is equally present for fixed capital. For analysis of changes over a period of several years, such as is attempted in the present study, changes in excess capacity create less difficulty for inventories than for fixed capital because inventories can be more quickly adjusted to desired levels.

points in Germany. The difference in the quantity of this type of capital is estimated to be the source of 2 percent of the difference between the United States and Northwest Europe in the 1960 level of national income per person employed.

The Estimates

Although fluctuations in inventories have been studied exhaustively in investigations of trade cycles, less attention has been devoted to longer term changes. International comparisons are almost entirely absent, so there is no precedent for the estimates attempted in this chapter. I shall present and describe all the estimates before considering their accuracy or discussing the results.

Table 13–1 provides indexes of the stock of inventories, valued in constant prices. They are calculated from data representing the average of stocks at the beginning and end of the year. Raw materials, work in process, finished goods, and livestock are all included. The data represent inventories held in the enterprise sector. However, strategic materials and surplus commodities held by government agencies are omitted even if these agencies are classified as government enterprises.[2] Omission of strategic and surplus stocks, which are important only in the United States and the United Kingdom, was considered desirable since these are not generally needed or available to support current production.[3]

The series used for the value of inventories in constant prices are, in general, those from which the statistical offices of the various countries derive the "change in inventories," a component of constant price GNP. The change in inventories in constant prices is published annually by every country. If the level of inventories is known for any one date, the entire series for the value of inventories can be reconstructed by cumulating the annual changes.[4] The official series for the level of inventories either was directly available for all years or could be reconstructed in this way for the United States, Denmark, Germany, Netherlands, Norway, and the United Kingdom, except that the base year level of farm inventories in Germany had to be estimated. The cumulation procedure was also followed for France but the starting level was an unofficial estimate. Unofficial series for the value of inventories were used for Belgium and Italy; these imply changes in inventories that are close to, but not identical with, those shown in the national accounts. The derivation of Table 13–1 is described in detail in Appendix K. Growth rates of inventories, based on these indexes, are given in Table 13–2.

Table 13–3 provides estimates of the contribution of the increase in inventories to the growth rates of national income. For each subperiod, the contribution is the product of (1) the growth rate

of inventories; and (2) the percentage of national income that was estimated to represent the earnings of inventories.

Comparisons of the levels of inventories in 1960 are given in the first two columns of Table 13–4. Appendix K describes their derivation. In brief, it consisted of compiling estimates of the value of inventories in each country in 1960 measured in its own 1955 prices, and converting these estimates to United States dollars by use of purchasing power parities. The estimates necessarily are crude approximations.

Estimates of the difference in national income per person that would have been present if inventories were the only source of difference in national income per person employed are given in Column 3, Table 13–4. For each European country the contribution is simply the product of (1) the percentage by which its inventory holdings per person employed fell short of the United States in 1960;

TABLE 13–1

Indexes of the Quantity of Enterprise Inventories
(1950 = 100)

Area	1950	1955	1960	1962	1964
United States	100.0	121.0	135.6	142.5	153.7
N. W. Europe	100.0	121.6	153.2	160.0	180.4
Belgium	100.0	106.2	114.0	120.5	125.1
Denmark	100.0	116.5	139.7	161.0	172.2
France	100.0	122.2	158.5	174.9	193.9
Germany	100.0	143.4	200.5	226.4	239.8
Netherlands	100.0	129.3	159.3	181.6	200.6
Norway	100.0	120.5	128.4	138.3	141.1
U. K.	100.0	108.4	126.1	135.4	141.2
Italy	100.0	108.2	128.6	137.0	143.4

Source: See Appendix K for derivation.

TABLE 13–2

Growth Rates of the Quantity of Enterprise Inventories
(In percentages)

Area	1950–62	1950–55	1955–62
United States	3.0	3.9	2.4
Northwest Europe	4.5	4.0	4.8
Belgium	1.6	1.2	1.8
Denmark	4.0	3.1	4.7
France	4.8	4.1	5.3
Germany	7.0	7.5	6.7
Netherlands	5.1	5.3	5.0
Norway	2.7	3.8	2.0
United Kingdom	2.6	1.6	3.2
Italy	2.7	1.6	3.4

Source: Derived from Table 13–1.

2. There are some departures from this definition but none appear important. Government enterprises are excluded from United States data but their inventories are very small (except for strategic materials and surplus farm products). On the other hand, civilian-type inventories held by general government, including strategic stocks where they exist on the continent, are sometimes included but the amounts are also small.

3. However, strategic stocks have on occasion been released to supplement the supply of commodities when shortages have developed.

4. In some countries the statistical offices obtain inventory changes for certain commodities, particularly livestock and crops, by multiplying the change in physical units by the unit price in the base year instead of by differencing the constant price value of stocks at the beginning and end of the year. The value of stocks of such commodities has, of course, been included in the base year level.

TABLE 13-3

Contribution of Enterprise Inventories to
Growth Rates of Total National Income

(*In percentage points*)

Area	1950–62	1950–55	1955–62
United States	.10	.15	.07
Northwest Europe	.18	.16	.19
Belgium	.06	.05	.07
Denmark	.15	.12	.18
France	.19	.17	.20
Germany	.33	.35	.32
Netherlands	.22	.23	.21
Norway	.13	.20	.09
United Kingdom	.09	.06	.10
Italy	.12	.08	.15

Sources: Derived from Tables 13–2 and 4–1.

and (2) the ratio (0.025) of the earnings of inventories to national income in the United States in 1960–62.

Examination and Evaluation of the Estimates

It is customary to appraise inventory estimates as among the least satisfactory of economic time series. This is a correct appraisal where emphasis is on short-term changes in GNP, since it is the change—the first difference—in the value of inventories that is a component of GNP, whereas other GNP components are not of this character. But in analyzing growth rates we are concerned with changes over a period of several years in the inventory series themselves, as distinct from first differences in them. In most countries these series do not appear to be much weaker estimates than, for example, most components of deflated GNP. This general statement refers to countries like the United States, the United Kingdom, and Germany that have fairly comprehensive reporting systems designed to obtain inventory data. This is not the case in all countries. Published descriptions indicate available information to have been particularly fragmentary until recently in Belgium; Italian data appear also to be weak.

Increases in inventory holdings from 1950 to 1962 varied widely among the countries. As shown in Table 13–2, the growth rate was only 1.6 percent in Belgium (though this may be an underestimate), 2.6 or 2.7 in the United Kingdom, Italy,

TABLE 13-4

Enterprise Inventories: International Comparison of
Levels, and Contribution to Differences in
National Income per Person Employed, 1960

Area	Indexes (United States = 100)		Contribution to difference from United States in national income per person employed if inventories were the only source of difference (in index points)
	Total inventories valued in United States prices (1)	Inventories per person employed in United States prices (2)	(3)
U. S.	100.0	100	—
N. W. Europe	78.4	66	.8
Belgium	3.0	60	1.0
Denmark	2.3	73	.7
France	18.1	64	.9
Germany	23.1	61	1.0
Netherlands	5.6	93	.2
Norway	1.6	77	.6
U. K.	24.6	69	.8
Italy	13.7	46	1.3

Sources: See text and Appendix K for derivation.

and Norway, and 3.0 in the United States. In contrast, it was 4.0 to 5.1 percent in Denmark, France, and the Netherlands, and 7.0 in Germany.

The *level* of inventories per person employed in 1960, shown in Table 13–4, also varied widely. In the Northwest European countries it ranged from 60 to 93 percent of the United States level, although the three large countries varied only from 61 to 69 percent of this level.

When these estimates are compared with national income per person employed (Table 2–4), a rather interesting pattern emerges. If Belgium is excluded (for a reason to be explained shortly), the European ratios of inventories to national income, measured in United States prices, all exceeded the ratio in the United States. In ascending order, the European inventory-national income ratios exceeded the United States ratio by 3 percent in Germany, 8 in France, 15 in Italy, 17 in the United Kingdom, 26 in Denmark, 30 in Norway, and 43 in the Netherlands. The European ratios would be still higher, compared to the United

States, if the comparison were based on European prices. The fact that the ratio of inventories to national income (and also to labor input) is much higher in the three small European countries (other than Belgium) than in the four large ones, and higher in the large European countries than in the much larger American economy, suggests that inventories may be an area in which economies of scale are important. Such a conclusion seems highly plausible insofar as national boundaries delay deliveries and add to uncertainty about delivery dates, and insofar as there is an association between size of country and size of firm or establishment. But there are, of course, reasons other than size that inventory ratios might vary widely among countries, the most obvious being industrial structure.[5] In addition, the inventory comparisons are subject to the possibility of substantial error.

Despite the extraordinarily large increase in German inventories from 1950 to 1960, the level of the stock in 1960, per person employed, was still below that in other Northwest European countries.

The Belgian estimates, which imply an inventory-national income ratio much lower than that obtained for other small countries, were omitted from the preceding discussion of inventory levels because they are not based on independent evidence. Belgian inventory data are fragmentary. I have relied for both level and change in Belgium on the series constructed by G. Labeau. Labeau was forced to establish the level of his series by assumption—namely, that in 1953 total inventories were equal to the value of livestock inventories plus 25 percent of the annual value of gross output of manufacturing, wholesale trade, retail trade, and agriculture, except livestock. The Belgian estimates yield not only a low level but also much the smallest rate of increase in inventories, so small indeed

as to be almost implausible; if a higher level and the same absolute change in inventories were used, the percentage increase would be even smaller. A much higher absolute increase cannot be reconciled with the Belgian national accounts.[6]

The estimates given in Table 13–3 indicate that both over the whole 1950–62 period and in the 1955–62 subperiod, the increase in inventories contributed about 0.1 percentage points to the growth rates of the United States, Belgium, Norway, the United Kingdom, and Italy; 0.2 to those of Denmark, France, and the Netherlands, and 0.3 to that of Germany. It contributed 0.1 points less to the American than to the Northwest European growth rate. The differences in contributions tend to correspond to differences in national income growth rates, and hence help to explain differences in the latter rates, but the amounts are only moderate.[7] The weight of inventories in total input is so small that sizable errors in the series used would have little effect on the analysis of growth sources.

During the 1950–62 period the United States devoted an average of 1.1 percent of GNP to net investment in inventories (Table 10–1); Belgium, Norway, the United Kingdom, and Italy devoted the same or a smaller percentage; and the remaining countries devoted larger percentages: Denmark 1.6 percent, France 1.7, the Netherlands 2.2, and Germany 2.4. These percentages of GNP devoted to inventory accumulation are computed from data measured in each country's own current prices and,

---

5. One might suppose this could be explored, but even where data are available for inventory holdings by industry such an effort seems doomed to be defeated by other differences. For example, at the end of 1963 the value of inventories held by wholesale and retail trade firms in the United States was about as large as that held by manufacturers. In the United Kingdom inventories held by wholesale and retail firms had only one-third, and in Germany less than one-half, as large a value as those held by manufacturers. These differences are much too big to be explained by the differences between these countries in the relative importance of manufacturing and trade. Various possible explanations are easy to suggest but cannot be tested from available data.

6. It is possible, by tying the official estimates of inventory change from 1953–62 and the revised DULBEA estimates for 1950–52 to Labeau's 1953 level, to construct an alternative series that yields a larger inventory increase from 1950 to 1955. The total increase from 1950 to 1962 would then become 25 percent instead of 20.5, but this is still below the other countries. If Labeau's level for the series is too low, moreover, this would overstate the rise. (The Belgian estimates of inventory change are compiled without establishing a level for stocks in all branches of the economy so a comparison with national accounts data cannot be made.) No reasonable alternative that could fit available estimates of inventory change would raise the growth rate of inventories in Belgium materially. The inventory series used are discussed at length in Appendix K.

7. Inventories in Germany may have been to some extent unbalanced in 1950 although there had been time since the currency reform for adjustments to take place. It is possible that in the 1950–55 period some allowance should be made for the elimination of imbalance, similar to that introduced for structures and equipment. In Germany, national income grew faster than inventories in 1950–55 and slower in 1955–62.

subject to the reservations expressed in Chapter 10, are appropriate for measuring the sacrifice of consumption for this purpose.

Table 13–4 indicates that the difference in inventory holdings in itself would account for a difference between Northwest Europe and the United States of less than 1 percent in output per man, or 2 percent of the total difference. It is not likely that better inventory data could change these estimates much. The latter figure varies, by countries, from 0.5 to 2.6 percent; some of the individual country comparisons are much more subject to error. These estimates are without allowance for economies of scale.

The estimated quantity of inventories per person employed was less in Northwest Europe than in the United States in 1960 by amounts ranging from 7 percent in Holland and 23 in Norway to 39 in Germany and 40 in Belgium (if the assumption on which the Belgian estimates are based is correct). Except perhaps for Belgium, the European countries came closer to matching the United States in inventory holdings than they did in national income. If inventories per man in Northwest Europe as a whole were 34 percent below the United States in 1960, as estimated in Table 13–4, the total gap in inventories was equal in value to only about two months' GNP in Northwest Europe (at the 1960 level). The inventory deficiency would not appear to be one that would impose a serious long-term barrier to closing the income gap.

In the United States, improved management techniques for controlling inventories and faster transportation have reduced the quantity of inventories per unit of output or sales that is required to operate at a given level of efficiency; at least there is much descriptive evidence that this type of capital-saving innovation has occurred. United States data, in fact, show a pronounced long-term decline in the ratio of inventories to output in manufacturing and in wholesale and retail trade since 1919, 1929, or 1934–41. During the postwar period these trends have not continued. The ratio of *total* inventories to *total* national income in constant prices, which has also dropped since the 1920's, continued to decline in the postwar period but only slightly. The behavior of the capital-output ratio for inventories in the United States somewhat

resembles that for structures and equipment over the past four decades. The reason the decline has been interrupted is not clear but it is apparent that changes in industrial composition of output and sales, increased product diversification requiring larger stocks, and other changes affecting aggregate inventory requirements have been taking place. These may or may not have obscured continuing advances in the efficiency with which inventory capital is used.[8] Some experts in inventory management believe the opportunities for further gains through inventory control are nearly exhausted.

Procedures for inventory control and management in Europe probably are behind those in the United States. If so, this would explain why inventories are larger, relative to output, in Europe than in America. However, there are plausible alternative explanations. In addition to the smaller scale of operations of individual firms in Europe and greater dependence on foreign suppliers, these include the lesser importance of service industries and perhaps other aspects of industrial composition.

A comparison of the *growth rates* of inventories and national income in the European countries suggests no strong general pattern. Over the 1950–62 period as a whole the growth rate of inventories (Table 13–2) was less than that of national income (Table 2–1) in Belgium, Norway, and Italy; about the same in France, Germany, the United Kingdom, and Northwest Europe as a whole; and moderately higher in Denmark and the Netherlands.[9]

8. See U.S. Congress, Joint Economic Committee, *Inventory Fluctuations and Economic Stabilization,* articles by Terleckyj in Pt. II, 1961, pp. 161–94, and by Smith in Pt. I, 1961, pp. 153–54 [G46]. Terleckyj calculated that from 1939 to 1957 the combined inventory-sales ratio in manufacturing and trade dropped 12 percent and would have dropped 17–18 percent in the absence of a change in industry mix. From 1948 to 1957 the overall ratio increased 8.8 percent and would have increased 5.4 percent in the absence of changes in industry mix. His calculations were based on only a fifteen-way breakdown of industries, and cannot handle changes in industry-mix and product-mix within industries very accurately. Inventory-output ratios in the United Kingdom are analyzed in Central Statistical Office, *Economic Trends,* November 1964, pp. ii–xxii [G37]. The period examined, which begins at 1956, is too short for trend analysis.

9. Something might be made of the similarity of growth rates of national income and inventories from 1950 to 1962 in all the large countries except Italy (that is, the United States, France, Germany, and the United Kingdom) were it not for the fact that in Germany and the United Kingdom it does not hold up in the subperiods.

⤳ CHAPTER FOURTEEN ⬳

Land and Natural Resources

Land, the third of the classical "factors of production," comprises a much smaller quantity of economic resources than labor or capital. Residential land was treated with dwellings so this chapter is concerned only with nonresidential land and natural resources. According to the estimates presented in Table 4–1, in the 1950–62 period the economic rent of nonresidential land averaged about 3 percent of national income in the United States, 4 percent in Northwest Europe, and 6 percent in Italy.

In most of the countries the bulk of nonresidential land earnings is a return for the use of sites desired for commercial, industrial, transportation, and similar purposes. The details of the income share estimates imply that, in 1960–62, agricultural land earned only 17 percent of the total earnings of nonresidential land in the United States and that only in Denmark and Italy did it earn more than 36 percent. Earnings of mineral land, including depletion, were much smaller than those of agricultural land in the United States, and probably even less important in Europe.[1]

Contribution of Land to Growth

An ideal index of land input would take each parcel of land available to a country in the base period, use an input index for each parcel that would always remain 100 unless there was some change in its quality, and weight the indexes for the separate parcels by their base period economic rent. In the absence of a change in land area or quality the total land input index would necessarily be 100.[2] In the present study I use a constant index

2. See *ibid.*, pp. 89–91, for my reasons for (1) preferring to measure available land, rather than land in use, for analysis of growth, and (2) believing that with proper weighting the choice makes little difference.

My procedure contrasts with one sometimes adopted that causes the total value of land in constant prices to rise if land is transferred from one use to another use in which the average value per acre is greater. That method, if followed here, would confuse the consequences of growth with its causes. As Solomon Fabricant has said, if we look back over the past 10,000 years or so to the end of the last ice age "it's fair to say that nature has been a passive factor over this period in the great changes that have occurred in the number and condition of men. . . . Only if we were to deal with periods of a hundred thousand years would we have to worry about [changes in the physical environment]" (in U.S. Department of Labor, *Seminar on Manpower Policy and Program,* July 1965, p. 4 [G71]).

One amendment to this statement is, however, necessary in dealing with changes over short periods of time. The weather in individual years compared may differ and, by

1. See Denison, *Sources of Economic Growth,* p. 88 [B25], for information concerning the United States.

TABLE 14-1
Indexes of Agricultural Land Utilized, 1950–64

(1950 = 100)

Area	1950	1955	1960	1962	1964
United States[a]	100.0	99.7	96.7	—	95.6
N. W. Europe	100.0	100.1	99.9	99.5	98.7
Belgium	100.0	96.2	95.4	94.2	92.9
Denmark	100.0	98.4	98.4	98.9	96.6
France[b]	100.0	100.4	100.6	100.4	99.2
Germany[c]	100.0	101.0	99.9	99.7	99.0
Netherlands	100.0	98.7	99.1	98.9	97.3
Norway	100.0	99.1	98.9	98.2	97.3
U. K.	100.0	99.9	99.1	98.5	98.6
Italy	100.0	101.6	102.1	100.9	100.2

Sources: United States: U.S. Bureau of the Census, *Statistical Abstract of the United States,* selected issues [G60] and *Census of Agriculture, 1964* [G53]; Common Market countries: OSCE, *Statistique Agricole,* No. 8, 1964 and No. 1, 1966 [I50]; United Kingdom: Central Statistical Office, *Annual Abstract of Statistics,* 1958 and 1964 [G36]; Denmark: Statistical Department, *Statistisk Årbog,* selected issues to 1965 [G8]; Norway: Central Bureau of Statistics, *Jordbrukstatistikk,* selected issues, 1951–65 [G31].
a. United States indexes refer to 1954 instead of 1955 and to 1959 instead of 1960.
b. French indexes for 1950–55 and 1956–62 are linked on the assumption there was no change from 1955 to 1956. (There was a change in the basis of reporting between 1955 and 1956.)
c. German data include the Saar but not West Berlin throughout the period.

of 100 in each country to measure the quantity of land available for uses other than for residences or by general government. This cannot be substantially in error.

There were no significant changes in total land area.[3] Some land was diverted to residential use and there may have been changes in land used by general government but the effect on land available for other purposes could only have been a minor percentage of the total. This is confirmed by series for the area of agricultural land, by far the largest component of usable land in terms of area. This changed but little in any country during the 1950–62 period (Table 14–1), and the changes that did occur probably were due mainly to shifts of land into or out of use rather than to or from use for dwellings and by general government.

affecting agricultural output, influence growth rates calculated between those years. This might be handled by adjusting indexes of land input. I prefer to deal with differences in weather in the years between which growth rates were computed as an influence affecting changes in output per unit of input and do so in Chapter 19.
3. The addition in 1960 of Alaska and Hawaii to United States national income statistics, and of the Saar and West Berlin to German national income statistics was handled by a linking procedure in the computation of growth rates.

Some adjustment for changes in the quality of land would be desirable but I have not found this feasible nor does it seem likely that such changes are important. Except in Italy most economic rent is earned by urban land and other sites whose value is almost entirely the result of location. For this dominant component, changes in physical properties are of no consequence and questions of quality change hardly arise. Any changes in quality would refer only to agricultural land, timberland, and mineral resources.

New discoveries of mineral resources since 1950 might be considered equivalent to an increase in the quantity of land. The main discoveries were of oil and natural gas in Italy, the Netherlands, and France. Their contribution to the increase in national income is approximately the difference between the cost of the labor, capital, and materials required to produce the oil and gas that was obtained from these fields and the cost of importing or producing the fuels for which they were substitutes. Illustrative calculations do not suggest these discoveries can have had a large effect on 1950–62 growth rates. The total increase from 1950 to 1962 in annual crude petroleum and natural gas production in these countries, not all of which can be ascribed to new discoveries, was equal in hard coal equivalents to 16 percent of apparent consumption of energy in 1962 in Italy, 9 percent in Holland, and 8 percent in France.[4] If these increases are ascribed entirely to new discoveries, if fuel costs (valued at the point of production or import) were equal to 4 percent of the national income (the United States percentage), and if the saving in costs on the new fuels were half, the saving in Italy would be equal to 0.6 percent of the 1962 Italian national income, equivalent to 0.05 percentage points in the growth rate in the 1950–62 period, and half that much in Holland and France.[5]

4. All 1962 data are from OSCE, *Basic Statistics of the Community: Comparison with Some European Countries, Canada, the United States of America and the Union of Soviet Socialist Republics,* 1964, pp. 60–61 [I51]. Production data for 1950 were based on changes given in OSCE, *Statistical Information,* No. 1 bis, 1965, Tables III/26 and IV/34 [I49].
5. These numbers are not introduced as actual estimates but only as indications of the possible order of magnitude. It should be stressed that these discoveries have had and

The use of constant indexes for land means, of course, that changes in land input make no contribution to the growth rate of total national income. The constancy of land availability does, however, exert a slight drag on the growth rate of output per person employed. Quantitatively, the size of this negative contribution works out to about 3 to 6 percent of the growth rate of employment, the amount depending on the importance of land in each country's national income. In no case is this drag as much as one-tenth of a percentage point. The estimates are given in the following chapter (Table 15–5).

The weight of land in the national income is too small for any possible error in the use of unchanging indexes for land input to have any real effect on the analysis of the sources of growth.

International Differences in Land Availability

Whereas changes in land input in a country over a dozen years can clearly be judged as slight because changes in relevant characteristics usually occur only very slowly if at all, differences among countries are extraordinarily difficult to appraise. An adequate evaluation would deal with the whole natural environment of a nation. This includes not only its building sites, agricultural and forest lands, mineral resources, and hydroelectric power sites but also its geographic location relative to potential trading partners and to fisheries, the suitability for transportation of its rivers, lakes, and harbors, distances and terrain between internal population and supply centers, various aspects of the climate, and a host of other factors.

Even the comparison that is appropriate depends

on the institutional environment assumed. In a world of free trade and complete international specialization in conformity with the principle of comparative advantage, differences in natural resource endowment would create international differences in national income per person employed primarily because of transportation costs. With modern transportation these would not be expected to create large differences among the countries with which the study is concerned. At the other extreme, in a world of nearly complete autarchy where each nation produced nearly all the products it used, the difference would be very great. In such a world the abundance and variety of its farmlands and mineral resources and its diversity of climates would give the United States an enormous advantage over any of the individual European countries. The actual position is, of course, much closer to the first situation than the second, even though the world is a long way from having a perfect international division of labor. Restrictions on international specialization are usually limited to products for which cost differentials are not extreme, and their effects are further dissipated by the influence of relative prices on consumption patterns. Norway does not try to grow its own oranges and few would be consumed if it did.

In principle, one could measure the effect on average income levels that differences in land input exert either in the presence or in the absence of existing trade barriers.[6] The difference between the two measures could be classified as due either to the presence of trade barriers or to differences in land input. I shall attempt no such refined measures, but in considering these questions I think it more useful to adopt the former classification so as to distinguish natural from institutional restraints on output. This means that output differences that are imposed by natural factors are classified as resulting from differences in input, and those im-

---

will have other important economic effects, particularly on the balance of payments and on the location and structure of industry. Also, the impact of the discovery of gas in the Groningen field in 1959 had barely begun to be felt by 1962. Even by 1964, according to the *Wall Street Journal* (June 24, 1965 [P48]), Groningen was supplying only 3 percent of Dutch energy requirements whereas it was expected to supply one-third by the mid-1970's (a Common Market report says 25 to 30 percent in 1975) and to allow substantial exports to Belgium and Germany.

6. For example, with respect to farmland one can ask how much higher German national income would be, given its present reliance on domestic farm production, if its farmlands were equal (per person) to those of the United States. Or one can first ask how much higher German national income would be with complete international division of labor, and then how much *additional* gain in national income it would achieve if its farmlands were equal to those of the United States.

posed by institutional factors as differences in output per unit of input.

If the matter is looked at in this way, some initial limits can be placed on the importance of land input with respect to those aspects that give rise to economic rent, because of land scarcity, in the United States. It seems self-evident that, by almost any evaluation, the United States has a greater endowment of land and natural resources, per worker, than any of the European countries covered in this study. Indexes of land input per person employed in the European countries can, almost without investigation and by almost any approach, be assumed to lie somewhere between, say, 10 and 90 when the United States is taken as 100. Nonresidential land earned 2.5 percent of total national income in the United States in 1960–62. My usual procedure must then yield the result that the difference between the United States and each of the European countries in national income per person employed, in United States price weights, that can be accounted for by differences in land input lies between 0.25 and 2.25 percent of United States national income per person employed. However, this calculation cannot fully take account of some differences between countries, such as the relative location of whole countries in relation to other countries and differences in the costs imposed by distance and terrain in providing equivalent internal transportation.

Comparison of Nonresidential Land

I know of no attempt to make a comprehensive quantitative comparison of the countries being examined with respect to input of land and natural resources. An adequate effort to do so is quite beyond the capabilities of the present study, but some estimate is unavoidable. What is required is an index of land input, per person employed, in each of the European countries, based on the use of United States weights for the earnings of different types of land. To construct such an index I divide total nonresidential land into three parts. I assign 73 percent of the weight to business sites, 17 percent to farmland, and 10 percent to mineral lands. These weights are intended to represent the division of the total earnings of land in the United States among the three types.[7] The procedure is equivalent to treating total land input as three separate types of input.

BUSINESS SITES. Sites for structures and other uses except dwellings, agriculture, and mining are assumed to be the same, per person employed, in all the countries, and therefore not to be responsible for any difference between these countries in national income per person employed. This implies that if a European country has 15 percent as much employment as the United States, it can find 15 percent as many equally desirable sites as the United States is using. My reasoning—other than observation—is simply that sites require only a very small fraction of total land area; are generally a use superior to agriculture, the principal alternative use; and for the most part require no special physical characteristics of land that are not available in large quantity in all the countries. Since land is generally scarcer in Europe than in the United States there may be a greater tendency to economize land even for sites, but it can hardly be strong. If significant differences exist, they must be mainly associated with the extent to which population is concentrated in large cities.

It must be admitted that this assumption takes no account of several factors of possible importance that were mentioned earlier. For example, climatic differences may need to be offset by the use of labor and capital for heating and air conditioning of business structures, and if not offset they may affect labor productivity. No account is taken of differences in geographical and climatic features that affect access to transportation facilities, or the need for and cost of providing internal transportation. A point considered important by some observers, that Italy, or much of it, is less conveniently situated in relation to other principal industrial nations than the other European countries, is ignored. For a comparison of Northwest Europe as a whole with the United States the assumption of equality in site land is probably not seriously in error, but it is conceivable that for individual countries the error is appreciable.

7. This division ignores forest lands and implicitly assigns their very small weight to business sites. The weights used are, of course, very rough.

TABLE 14-2

International Comparison of Arable Land and Agricultural Land Areas and of Minerals Production, 1960

(Indexes, United States = 100)

Area	Total land area				Land area per person employed				Value of selected minerals production	
	All land (1)	Agricultural area (2)	Arable land (3)	Adjusted arable land[a] (4)	All land (5)	Agricultural area (6)	Arable land (7)	Adjusted arable land[a] (8)	Total (9)	Per person employed (10)
United States[b]	100.0	100.0	100.0	100.0	100	100	100	100	100.0	100
Northwest Europe	15.7	15.6	23.1	19.1	13	13	20	16	30.5	26
Belgium	.3	.4	.5	.4	6	8	10	9	1.1	21
Denmark	.5	.7	1.5	1.1	15	23	49	35	.1	2
France	5.9	7.8	11.5	9.5	21	28	41	34	7.7	27
Germany	2.7	3.2	4.6	3.9	7	8	12	10	11.5	30
Netherlands	.4	.5	.6	.5	6	9	10	9	.9	14
Norway	3.5	.2	.5	.3	162	11	22	16	.2	10
United Kingdom	2.6	2.8	3.9	3.3	7	8	11	9	9.2	26
Italy	3.2	4.5	8.1	6.1	11	15	27	21	1.4	5

Sources: Columns (1)–(4): same as Table 14–1 and OSCE, *Basic Statistics for Fifteen European Countries: Comparison with the United States and the Union of Soviet Socialist Republics*, 1961 [I51]; Columns (5)–(8): computed from Columns (1)–(4) and Table 5–2; Columns (9) and (10): see text for derivation.
a. Arable land plus one-third of permanent meadows and pastures.
b. Total land area in the United States is (in thousands of square miles) for Columns (1) to (4), respectively, 3,615, 1,704, 716, and 1,044.

FARMLAND. Table 14–2 compares the arable land area and the agricultural land area of the nine countries.[8] Arable land is cropland, including land under permanent cultivation in orchards, vineyards, and the like. The agricultural area includes both arable land and permanent meadows and pastures. In 1960 Northwest Europe as a whole had 13 percent as much agricultural land and 20 percent as much arable land as the United States per person employed in all activities. The proportion of total agricultural land that is classified as arable is greater, by varying amounts, in all eight European countries than it is in the United States. Arable land is, on the average, of much greater value than permanent meadows and pastures. To take account of this in a rough way, I give indexes in Columns 4 and 8 that are computed by adding to the arable land area one-third of the area in permanent mead-

ows and pastures.[9] I shall use this index to measure input of agricultural land. This calculation ignores differences in the average quality of farmland except that the weight attached to permanent meadows and pastures is reduced. Despite this deficiency, the indexes do seem to provide a ranking that corresponds to general impressions of the availability of agricultural lands except that the Italian index is rather high.

It will be noted that the indexes per person employed in Column 8 are based on total, not agricultural, employment. Agricultural land input per worker in agriculture works out to the following percentages of the United States figure: United Kingdom, 18; Denmark and France, 13; Belgium, 10; Norway, Netherlands, and Germany, 6 to 8; Italy, 5.

8. Total land area is also given for general background, but no use is made of the data.

9. Land used for grazing that is not in farms, which is extensive in the United States, is completely omitted from the computation.

MINERAL LANDS. An approximate comparison of minerals production in 1960, valued in United States prices, is given in Columns 9 and 10, Table 14–2.[10] Products measured were bituminous coal, lignite, anthracite, peat, natural gas, crude petroleum, iron ore, copper, uranium, zinc, lead, gold, silver, china clays, lime, phosphate rock, salt, sulphur, pyrites, and potassium salts.[11] I use this minerals production index to measure land input for this sector. The measure is defective in that it takes no account of international differences in the quality of the resources being exploited that affect production costs. Also, weighting of products is by value of product whereas it would be more appropriate to weight by value added less labor and capital costs. These defects probably cause the ratio of Europe to the United States in coal to be overstated and also assign too much weight to coal in the total index. In consequence, the Belgian, British, and German indexes, particularly, are probably somewhat too high. Nevertheless, the measure does provide a rough guide to international differences in minerals resources and seems to provide a reasonable differentiation of countries.[12] Northwest Europe as a whole is credited with only 26 percent as much input from minerals resources as the United States, per person employed. It is likely that even this small figure is biased upward.

TOTAL NONRESIDENTIAL LAND INPUT. Table 14–3 assembles the three indexes and provides the weighted average used to compare total nonresidential land input per person employed. Since site land is given 73 percent of the weight, and an index of 100 is used in all the countries for this component, the procedure cannot yield an index below 73 for any country. All the European countries are far below the United States in both agricultural

TABLE 14–3

Indexes of Land Input per Person Employed and Contribution to Differences in National Income per Person Employed, 1960

| Area | Indexes of land input per person employed measured in United States price weights (United States = 100) | | | | Contribution to difference from U.S. in national income per person employed if land were the only source of difference (in index points) |
	Non-residential sites (1)	Agricultural land (2)	Mineral resources (3)	Weighted total (4)	(5)
United States	100	100	100	100	—
N. W. Europe	100	16	26	78	.5
Belgium	100	9	21	77	.6
Denmark	100	35	2	79	.5
France	100	34	27	81	.5
Germany	100	10	30	78	.6
Netherlands	100	9	14	76	.6
Norway	100	16	10	77	.6
U. K.	100	9	26	77	.6
Italy	100	21	5	77	.6

Sources: Columns (2) and (3): Table 14–2; other columns: see text for derivation.

lands and mineral lands, and only France is high in both even by European standards. The European indexes consequently fall within the narrow band from 76 in the Netherlands to 81 in France.

Contribution to Differences in Output Levels

In Column 5, the contribution of differences in land input to the differences in national income per person employed in United States prices are calculated. The procedure parallels that used for other types of input. It shows that the difference in land input alone would cause national income in United States prices per person employed in each of the European countries to be 0.5 or 0.6 percent below the United States if all other income determinants were the same.[13]

10. The table was constructed as follows. For each product considered, the value of United States production in 1960 was multiplied by the ratio of the quantity of production in each European country to United States production in 1960 to obtain the corresponding value in the European country. The values for the individual products were then added. Data were obtained from the U.S. Bureau of Mines, *Minerals Yearbook, 1962* [G65].

11. It may be noted that hydroelectricity power sites are omitted from the calculation.

12. The Groningen gas field, discovered only in 1959, gets little weight in this computation. This seems appropriate for analysis of income differences in 1960, but in the future the Dutch position will be much improved.

13. Use of European price and share weights would assign a larger role to land except in the case of the United Kingdom. For Denmark and Italy it is much larger. If the rent shares and agricultural components as estimated in Chapter 4 are used, and rent in mining is assumed to be

These results reflect an evaluation (1) that, per person employed, differences among countries in land needed for sites are unimportant and (2) that although differences in the availability of farmland and mineral resources are very great, in the absence of man-made barriers to international specialization of production they would create but little difference in national income per person employed under present-day conditions. While the measurement is

very crude, I think the general conclusion is correct. However, both the probable bias with respect to the quality of agricultural land and, more importantly, the inability to take account of locational factors with respect to foreign and domestic transportation may mean that the position of Italy is put in too favorable a light.[14]

___

0.05 percent of the national income of Italy and Denmark (an altogether arbitrary figure), then with national European price and share weights, land input would be responsible for a difference of 2.7 percent of United States national income per person employed between the United States and Denmark and 3.0 percent between the United States and Italy. The total difference in national income per person employed is also greater in European prices, but not proportionately. This calculation is merely to suggest the sensitivity of the results to the weights selected.

14. Aspects that have been ignored are also particularly important in Norway, but for Norway they seem to be both favorable (for example, nearness to fishing grounds, great hydroelectricity potential, an above-average supply of softwood) and unfavorable (particularly the long winter, and the difficulties of road and rail building and maintenance imposed by heavy snowfall and by the long distances and rugged terrain between the principal centers). International comparisons of forest and hydroelectric resources and a useful map of the main fisheries are provided in Dewhurst, Coppock, Yates, and Associates, *Europe's Needs and Resources,* Chapters 16, 17, and 18 [B31].

CHAPTER FIFTEEN

Contributions of Total Factor Input and Output per Unit of Input

The review of individual components of factor input was completed with the examination of land. Now estimates of the contributions of labor, capital, and land to growth rates of and international differences in national income can be refined and summarized. This, in turn, permits changes and differences in output per unit of total input to be computed. The reasons that output per unit of total input changes over time and varies among countries are analyzed in the five chapters that follow. Thus, this chapter serves as a bridge between the two major divisions of the study.

The Contribution of Inputs to Growth Rates

Growth rates of inputs and the contributions of inputs to growth rates of national income were computed for the time periods 1950–55, 1955–60, and 1960–62. These were averaged (using weights of 5, 5, and 2) to obtain estimates for the longer periods shown in the tables. The intent of this procedure is to change the marginal product weights assigned the factors of production often enough to catch persistent changes but not so often that cycli-

cal fluctuations in income shares will cause the results to be sensitive to the particular year in which the quantity of a factor increases.

Adjustment of Labor Quality Indexes for the Equal Productivity Assumption

The three quality indexes for labor, developed in Chapters 6, 7, and 8, must be adjusted before they can be used to measure contributions to the growth of national income as measured. Deflated national product estimates, as noted in Chapter 3, imply that output per person employed does not change in industry segments falling within the general government, nonprofit organization, and private household sectors, and certain other industry components.[1] No matter what happens to the quality of

---

1. Sometimes the alternate assumption is made that output per man-hour does not change, and occasionally the assumption that output per man does not change within occupational components but may change in an industry if the occupational mix changes. I am unable to give quantitative recognition to such variants. Belgium, which it was noted in Chapter 3 is a special case, is treated in this chapter like the other countries. The lift given the measured Belgian growth rate by the unusual deflation procedure adopted will be treated as a special component of output per unit of input.

labor in such industry segments, or how much output per person employed may in fact change within them, this does not affect the real national income or product as measured. Hence, changes in the quality of a year's work in such activities do not affect the growth rates under investigation and, for analysis of the sources of measured growth, labor quality indexes should not be affected by changes in the quality of labor in these activities. Recognition has already been given to this fact in the case of military personnel; quality indexes of 100 were used for the armed forces at all dates. Ideally the same treatment would be given to civilian personnel in this category. The results that this procedure would yield must now be approximated.

To do so, I assume that growth rates of quality indexes for civilians employed in activities *other* than those given this special treatment are the same as those for all employed persons. On this assumption the growth rates previously calculated need simply be reduced by the percentage of labor income that arises in civilian activities given this special treatment in deflation. These percentages can only be approximated. I start with the percentages of GNP at factor cost that Gilbert and Associates measured on the "equal output per man" assumption in their international comparisons for 1950. Column 1, Table 15–1, shows these percentages after eliminating the services of defense personnel.[2] GNP originating in these activities consists almost entirely of labor income. The percentage of total labor earnings originating in these activities is typically two-fifths higher than the percentage of GNP at factor cost originating in these activities, and I have therefore used percentages two-fifths higher (Column 3). These percentages are used throughout the period.[3] The estimates given in Column 3 do not take account of minor

2. They are a bit low because civilian as well as military defense personnel are omitted. On the other hand, I believe Gilbert used the "equal output per man" assumption a little more widely than is customary in deflation of time series.

3. For Germany and Italy the percentages were adjusted downward on the grounds that the 1950 percentages were exceptionally high in these countries because private production was still very low (by the standard of later years) in 1950. I assumed that the German percentage in United States prices is the same as the highest among the other Northwest European countries, and reduced the German percentage in German prices proportionately. The same percentage reduction was then applied to the Italian figures.

TABLE 15–1

Percentages of GNP (1950) and Labor Input (1950–62) Originating in Nondefense Activities in Which Output Comparisons Are Based on Employment or the Equivalent

Area	Percentage of GNP at factor cost, based on 1950 international comparisons		Estimated percentage of labor input, 1950–62	
	National price weights (1)	United States price weights (2)	National price weights (3)	United States price weights (4)
U. S.	10.7	10.7	15	15
N. W. Europe	—	—	19	21
Belgium	14.8	15.9	21	22
Denmark	12.3	15.0	17	21
France	14.1	14.7	20	21
Germany	15.3	17.7	19	22
Netherlands	13.3	15.6	19	22
Norway	14.3	15.0	20	21
U. K.	11.9	15.0	17	21
Italy	14.1	19.5	20	24

Sources: Columns (1) and (2): Table 3–1 except that defense personnel have been excluded; Columns (3) and (4): see text for derivation.

variations among countries in the scope of activities to which the equal productivity assumption is applied.

Computation of Growth Rates and Contributions to Growth

This section describes the procedures followed to obtain the contribution of each of the inputs and of total input to the growth rate of total national income in each subperiod. I shall illustrate the computations with United States data for the 1950–55 period.[4]

Growth rates of labor quality indexes in the United States from 1950 to 1955 for annual hours of work, age-sex composition, and education were −0.19, −0.19, and 0.66, respectively, when computed from indexes presented in Chapters 6 to 8. After they are reduced by 15 percent (Column 3,

4. Computations in this and other chapters were greatly facilitated by use of the "Growth Rate Conversion Table" prepared and kindly made available by the Economic Research and Analysis Division of the U.S. Bureau of the Census.

Table 15–1) they become −0.16, −0.16, and 0.56. Table 15–2 shows these growth rates and those of all the other individual factor inputs except dwellings and international assets. They were combined by use of income share weights to obtain the growth rates of total capital input and factor input, both exclusive of dwellings and international assets.[5]

Table 15–2 brings out the very considerable differences among countries in the rate at which total input and the various components of input grew. The same table shows the implied growth rates of output per unit of input (excluding dwellings and international assets).

Table 15–3 divides the growth rate of total national income among the contributions made by changes in each of the inputs and the contribution of increased output per unit of input. Derivation of the estimates is again illustrated by the estimates for the United States in 1950–55. The growth rate of total national income was 4.23. I retain the estimates that dwellings contributed 0.26 and international assets 0.03 percentage points, respectively (Tables 11–1 and 11–4), leaving 3.94 as the contribution of all other sources.[6] The contribution of each other input or aspect of labor quality was initially calculated as the product of its growth rate (Table 15–2) and its share of national income (Table 4–1). The labor share was, of course, applied to each aspect of labor input. The total contribution to the 1950–55 United States growth rate of increased inputs except dwellings and international assets is initially estimated at 1.99. (It is equal to their 2.06 growth rate shown in Table 15–2 times the sum of their shares of national income, 0.966.) This is the growth rate that would have resulted if there had been no change in output per unit of input or in income from dwellings and international assets. The growth rate of output per unit of input (excluding dwellings and international assets) was 1.91 (103.94 ÷ 101.99 = 101.91), as shown in Table 15–2.

The sum of the separate contributions of increased input (excluding dwellings and international assets) and of output per unit of input is 3.90, which falls short of their combined contribution of 3.94 because of the "interaction" between them. The combined contribution of 3.94 is allocated between the increase in output per unit of input and the increase in inputs (and the estimate for the latter is divided among the several inputs) in proportion to the initial estimate of the contribution of each component. This is merely a matter of convenience; the interaction term is trifling in all cases, so its allocation scarcely changes the original estimates. Two advantages of basing these calculations upon growth rates rather than directly upon indexes, as is sometimes done, are that interaction terms are negligible and that the results are not affected by the length of the time period covered if growth rates are constant.[7]

The estimate of the contribution to the growth rate made by each source of growth measures the difference between the actual percentage increase in national income in an average year of the period covered and the increase that would have occurred if that factor had not changed while all other factors had changed as they actually did. For example, the average United States growth rate in 1950–55 would have been 1.13 points lower if employment had not changed, or 0.13 higher if hours of work (including the division of employment between full-time and part-time workers) had not changed, or 1.93 lower if output per unit of input had not changed.

5. The weights used to combine inputs are, of course, different in each country and time period.

6. Income from dwellings and international assets is viewed as purely a contribution of capital so that no "interaction" factor is involved.

7. Assume, for example, that from 1950 to 1962 total input in a country had a growth rate of 1 percent a year, output per unit of input 3 percent a year, and national income therefore 4.03 percent a year. The interaction term of 0.03 (4.03 − 1.00 − 3.00) is equal to 0.7 percent of the growth rate of national income. If growth rates continue unchanged, the allocation procedure will ascribe 25.0 percent of the growth rate (1.01 points) to inputs and 75.0 percent (3.03 points) to output per unit of input regardless of the length of the time period.

These growth rates would yield indexes in 1962 (1950 = 100) of 112.7 for total input, 142.6 for output per unit of input, and 160.7 for national income. The interaction term is 5.4 index points (60.7 − 12.7 − 42.6) or 8.7 percent of the increase in national income. Allocation of the change in national income among the two sources in proportion to their "direct" contributions would ascribe 23.0 percent to inputs and 77.0 percent to output per unit of input. If growth rates continue unchanged, the proportion of growth ascribed to the less important factor (in this case, inputs) will decline indefinitely as the length of the time period considered increases. With the growth rates in this example, the proportion would decline from 25.0 percent after 1 year to 23.0 percent after 12 years and to 17.8 percent after 40 years.

TABLE 15-2

Growth Rates of Factor Inputs and Output per Unit of Input[a]

(*In percentages*)

Factor input and total factor productivity	United States	North-west Europe	Bel-gium	Den-mark	France	Ger-many	Nether-lands	Nor-way	United King-dom	Italy
1950–55										
Total factor input[b]	2.06	1.86	1.40	1.27	1.14	3.15	1.93	1.53	1.44	1.91
Labor[c]	1.69	1.46	1.22	.62	.60	2.65	1.55	.57	1.22	1.86
Employment	1.45	1.19	.69	.47	.11	2.68	1.09	.20	.89	.98
Hours of work[c]	−.16	.03	−.06	.05	.03	−.02	.04	.09	.06	.12
Age-sex composition[c]	−.16	−.05	.02	−.08	.10	−.16	.08	−.05	−.08	.21
Education[c]	.56	.29	.57	.18	.36	.15	.33	.33	.35	.54
Capital[b]	4.22	3.90	2.43	4.75	3.65	5.70	3.94	4.73	2.76	2.81
Nonresidential structures and equipment[d]	4.34	3.88	2.78	5.27	3.52	5.18	3.54	5.00	3.08	3.22
Inventories	3.88	3.98	1.21	3.10	4.09	7.47	5.28	3.80	1.63	1.58
Land	.00	.00	.00	.00	.00	.00	.00	.00	.00	.00
Output per unit of input[e]	1.91	3.86	1.90	.20	3.57	6.60	3.63	2.12	1.26	4.32
1955–62										
Total factor input[b]	1.46	1.53	1.20	1.57	1.24	2.39	1.69	.74	.96	1.46
Labor[c]	1.22	.80	.90	.89	.56	1.26	.91	−.05	.45	.94
Employment	.92	.74	.44	1.25	.11	1.52	1.02	.16	.47	.27
Hours of work[c]	−.25	−.34	−.30	−.45	−.07	−.60	−.39	−.41	−.38	.04
Age-sex composition[c]	−.10	.10	.17	−.09	.15	.20	−.04	−.12	−.03	.07
Education[c]	.65	.30	.59	.18	.38	.15	.32	.33	.38	.56
Capital[b]	3.12	4.98	2.74	5.29	4.54	6.85	5.27	3.87	3.78	4.00
Nonresidential structures and equipment[d]	3.32	5.02	3.01	5.46	4.33	6.88	5.36	4.41	3.93	4.18
Inventories	2.37	4.82	1.81	4.73	5.25	6.75	4.97	2.00	3.22	3.43
Land	.00	.00	.00	.00	.00	.00	.00	.00	.00	.00
Output per unit of input[e]	.96	2.47	2.10	3.22	3.71	2.85	2.19	2.57	1.11	4.19
1950–62										
Total factor input[b]	1.71	1.67	1.28	1.45	1.20	2.71	1.79	1.07	1.16	1.65
Labor[c]	1.42	1.08	1.03	.78	.58	1.84	1.17	.21	.77	1.32
Employment	1.14	.93	.55	.93	.11	2.00	1.05	.18	.65	.56
Hours of work[c]	−.21	−.18	−.20	−.24	−.03	−.36	−.21	−.20	−.19	.07
Age-sex composition[c]	−.13	.04	.11	−.09	.13	.05	.01	−.09	−.05	.13
Education[c]	.62	.30	.58	.18	.37	.15	.32	.33	.37	.55
Capital[b]	3.58	4.53	2.61	5.06	4.17	6.37	4.72	4.23	3.35	3.50
Nonresidential structures and equipment[d]	3.74	4.55	2.92	5.38	3.99	6.17	4.60	4.65	3.58	3.78
Inventories	3.00	4.47	1.56	4.05	4.77	7.05	5.10	2.75	2.56	2.66
Land	.00	.00	.00	.00	.00	.00	.00	.00	.00	.00
Output per unit of input[e]	1.36	3.04	2.01	1.94	3.65	4.43	2.79	2.39	1.18	4.25

Source: See text for derivation.

a. Growth rates shown here are weighted averages of rates computed for the 1950–55, 1955–60, and 1960–62 periods, as appropriate.

b. Excludes dwellings and international assets in addition to general government capital.

c. Adjusted to exclude quality changes in labor employed in activities where output is measured by employment.

d. Average growth rates of gross stock and net stock.

e. This measure, appropriate for calculating contributions to growth in Table 15–3, is calculated as (100 + growth rate of national income − contribution of dwellings and international assets) ÷ (100 + growth rate of total factor input excluding dwellings and international assets) − 100. It differs only slightly from the growth rate of output per unit of input in the domestic nonresidential sector, which can be approximated by dividing the figures shown by (1 minus the income shares of dwellings and international assets, as given in Table 4–1).

Summary of the Results

In the United States, the growth rate of national income over the whole period from 1950 to 1962 was 3.32 percent. Of this amount 1.95 points, or almost three-fifths, resulted from the increase in labor and capital used in production and 1.37 points from the increase in output per unit of input. The increase in labor contributed 1.12 percentage points and the increase in capital 0.83 percentage points.[8]

In the following listing, the areas are arranged in the order of the contributions of total inputs to the growth rate of total national income from 1950 to 1962. The contributions in the whole period and the subperiods are as follows:

	1950–62	1950–55	1955–62
Germany	2.78	3.19	2.51
United States	1.95	2.30	1.70
Netherlands	1.91	2.33	1.62
Northwest Europe	1.69	1.77	1.62
Italy	1.66	1.92	1.48
Denmark	1.55	1.38	1.67
France	1.24	1.17	1.28
Belgium	1.17	1.33	1.06
United Kingdom	1.11	1.05	1.15
Norway	1.04	1.55	.69

From 1950 to 1962 the United States obtained more growth by increasing inputs than Northwest Europe as a whole. The 1.95 contribution of increased inputs to growth in the United States was exceeded only in Germany and approximately matched only in the Netherlands. As compared with Northwest Europe as a whole, the United States advantage occurred mainly in the 1950–55 subperiod.

These estimates will not be reviewed in detail here. Each of the inputs has been discussed separately in preceding chapters and the detailed components are provided in Table 15–3. A comprehensive discussion of the sources of growth will be deferred until the reasons for changes in output per unit of input have also been explored.[9]

8. As noted in Chapter 2, contributions of capital to the growth of GNP would always be larger (and contributions of total input usually larger and those of labor and output per unit of input usually smaller) than the corresponding contributions to the growth rate of national income.

9. The effects of changes in the average age of capital, and the balancing of the capital stock, which have already

The areas are arranged in the order of the contributions of output per unit of input to the growth rate of total income from 1950 to 1962 in the following listing. The contributions (in percentage points) were:

	Contribution of output per unit of input to growth		
	1950–62	1950–55	1955–62
Germany	4.48	6.74	2.88
Italy	4.30	4.38	4.23
France	3.68	3.60	3.75
Northwest Europe	3.07	3.91	2.49
Netherlands	2.82	3.67	2.21
Norway	2.41	2.14	2.58
Belgium	2.03	1.92	2.12
Denmark	1.96	.20	3.25
United States	1.37	1.93	.97
United Kingdom	1.18	1.27	1.12

The increase in output per unit of input contributed 2.2 times as much to the 1950–62 growth rate of Northwest Europe as to that of the United States. The contribution was much greater in all of the European countries except the United Kingdom than it was in the United States. Differences among the European countries themselves were very large. Succeeding chapters will explore reasons for the increase in output per unit of input in all countries, and for the variations among the countries studied. It may be noted immediately, however, that the great differences between subperiods occurring in some countries are often due, at least in part, to differences between 1950, 1955, and 1962 in either the intensity of resource utilization or the effect of weather upon farm output. Chapter 19 explores these differences, which are most important in the United States, Denmark, the Netherlands, and the United Kingdom. The reader is also reminded that gains from economies of scale are classified as contributions of output per unit of input.

In sharp contrast to the United States, in all the European countries the increase in output per unit of input contributed more than the increase in

been discussed, are classified as components of the change in output per unit of input and are not included in the contribution of changes in capital or total input in the tables of this chapter.

TABLE 15–3

Contributions of Factor Inputs and Output per Unit of Input to Growth Rates of Total National Income

(*In percentage points*)

Source of growth	United States	North-west Europe	Bel-gium	Den-mark	France	Ger-many	Nether-lands	Nor-way	United King-dom	Italy
1950–55										
National income	4.23	5.68	3.25	1.58	4.77	9.93	6.00	3.69	2.32	6.30
Total factor input	2.30	1.77	1.33	1.38	1.17	3.19	2.33	1.55	1.05	1.92
Labor	1.32	1.12	.90	.47	.46	1.99	1.15	.41	.95	1.35
Employment	1.13	.91	.51	.35	.08	2.01	.81	.14	.69	.72
Hours of work	−.13	.03	−.04	.04	.02	−.01	.03	.06	.05	.09
Age-sex composition	−.12	−.04	.01	−.06	.08	−.12	.06	−.03	−.06	.15
Education	.44	.22	.42	.14	.28	.11	.25	.24	.27	.39
Capital	.98	.65	.43	.91	.71	1.20	1.18	1.14	.10	.57
Dwellings	.26	.05	.04	.14	.00	.12	.04	.05	.02	.02
International assets	.03	−.12	−.03	.01	.02	−.13	.39	−.04	−.36	.00
Nonresidential structures and equipment	.54	.56	.37	.64	.52	.85	.52	.93	.38	.47
Inventories	.15	.16	.05	.12	.17	.36	.23	.20	.06	.08
Land	.00	.00	.00	.00	.00	.00	.00	.00	.00	.00
Output per unit of input	1.93	3.91	1.92	.20	3.60	6.74	3.67	2.14	1.27	4.38
1955–62										
National income	2.67	4.11	3.18	4.92	5.03	5.39	3.83	3.27	2.27	5.71
Total factor input	1.70	1.62	1.06	1.67	1.28	2.51	1.62	.69	1.15	1.48
Labor	.97	.62	.66	.68	.44	.94	.68	−.03	.35	.68
Employment	.73	.57	.33	.95	.09	1.13	.76	.13	.37	.20
Hours of work	−.20	−.26	−.22	−.34	−.06	−.45	−.29	−.31	−.30	.03
Age-sex composition	−.08	.08	.12	−.07	.12	.15	−.03	−.10	−.02	.05
Education	.52	.23	.43	.14	.29	.11	.24	.25	.30	.40
Capital	.73	1.00	.40	.99	.84	1.57	.94	.72	.80	.80
Dwellings	.25	.08	.01	.12	.03	.16	.07	.04	.06	.11
International assets	.06	.03	−.08	.03	.02	−.05	−.10	−.09	.17	−.05
Nonresidential structures and equipment	.35	.70	.40	.66	.59	1.14	.76	.68	.46	.59
Inventories	.07	.19	.07	.18	.20	.32	.21	.09	.11	.15
Land	.00	.00	.00	.00	.00	.00	.00	.00	.00	.00
Output per unit of input	.97	2.49	2.12	3.25	3.75	2.88	2.21	2.58	1.12	4.23
1950–62										
National income	3.32	4.76	3.20	3.51	4.92	7.26	4.73	3.45	2.29	5.96
Total factor input	1.95	1.69	1.17	1.55	1.24	2.78	1.91	1.04	1.11	1.66
Labor	1.12	.83	.76	.59	.45	1.37	.87	.15	.60	.96
Employment	.90	.71	.40	.70	.08	1.49	.78	.13	.50	.42
Hours of work	−.17	−.14	−.15	−.18	−.02	−.27	−.16	−.15	−.15	.05
Age-sex composition	−.10	.03	.08	−.07	.10	.04	.01	−.07	−.04	.09
Education	.49	.23	.43	.14	.29	.11	.24	.24	.29	.40
Capital	.83	.86	.41	.96	.79	1.41	1.04	.89	.51	.70
Dwellings	.25	.07	.02	.13	.02	.14	.06	.04	.04	.07
International assets	.05	−.03	−.06	.02	.02	−.08	.10	−.07	−.05	−.03
Nonresidential structures and equipment	.43	.64	.39	.66	.56	1.02	.66	.79	.43	.54
Inventories	.10	.18	.06	.15	.19	.33	.22	.13	.09	.12
Land	.00	.00	.00	.00	.00	.00	.00	.00	.00	.00
Output per unit of input	1.37	3.07	2.03	1.96	3.68	4.48	2.82	2.41	1.18	4.30

Source: See text for derivation.

inputs to the increase in national income over the 1950–62 period as a whole, and in most countries in both subperiods.

Changes in the Capital-Labor Ratio

The preceding calculations permit changes in the ratio of capital (excluding dwellings and international assets) to labor to be computed. Table 15–4 shows the growth rates of capital per person employed and capital input per unit of labor input. The latter provides the most accurate measure I can derive of changes in factor proportions.[10] Capital input rose more than labor input everywhere, but differences among countries in the amounts were large. Over the whole period from 1950–62 the capital-labor ratio in the domestic nonresidential sector rose at an annual rate of 3.41 percent in Northwest Europe as against 2.13 percent in the United States. From 1955 to 1962 the gap was much greater.[11] All the European countries except Belgium were becoming more capital intensive at a

10. It should be recalled that the labor measure counts only employed labor while the capital measure counts all capital in the stock. However, adjustment of labor input to a "high employment" basis could not greatly affect these comparisons.

11. The difference between the two areas would be reduced in all periods if dwellings and international assets were included.

much more rapid pace than the United States in the 1955–62 period.

National Income per Person Employed

Table 15–5 provides breakdowns of the sources of growth of national income per person employed similar to those provided for total national income in Table 15–3. Employment, of course, disappears from this table. The growth rate of output per unit of input is the same for national income per person employed as for total national income but its contribution to the growth rate of national income per person employed is usually a trifle lower because its interaction with employment disappears. In principle a similar difference arises with respect to the contribution of the three aspects of labor quality, but in practice the difference is almost always within the range to which the estimates are rounded and the same contributions are used in Tables 15–3 and 15–5. The contributions of nonresidential structures and equipment, inventories, and land are computed as the product of the growth rate of the amount of each input per person employed and the share of that input in the national income, except for the usual trifling differences due to interaction effects. The contributions of dwellings and property income from abroad are taken directly from Tables 11–1 and 11–4.

TABLE 15–4

Growth Rates of Capital Input per Person Employed and per Unit of Labor Input[a]

(*In percentages*)

Area	Capital input per person employed			Capital input per unit of labor input		
	1950–55	1955–62	1950–62	1950–55	1955–62	1950–62
United States	2.73	2.18	2.41	2.49	1.88	2.13
Northwest Europe	2.68	4.20	3.57	2.40	4.14	3.41
Belgium	1.72	2.29	2.05	1.19	1.83	1.56
Denmark	4.26	3.99	4.10	4.10	4.36	4.25
France	3.54	4.42	4.05	3.03	3.95	3.57
Germany	2.94	5.25	4.28	2.97	5.52	4.45
Netherlands	2.82	4.21	3.63	2.36	4.32	3.50
Norway	4.52	3.70	4.04	4.14	3.92	4.01
United Kingdom	1.86	3.29	2.69	1.52	3.31	2.56
Italy	1.81	3.72	2.92	.93	3.03	2.15

Source: See text for derivation.

a. In this table capital includes only nonresidential structures, equipment, and inventories of enterprises. It excludes dwellings and international assets as well as general government capital.

TABLE 15–5

Contributions of Factor Inputs and Output per Unit of Input to
Growth Rates of National Income per Person Employed

(*In percentage points*)

Source of growth	United States	North-west Europe	Bel-gium	Den-mark	France	Ger-many	Nether-lands	Nor-way	United King-dom	Italy
1950–55										
National income per person employed	2.74	4.46	2.55	1.11	4.65	7.06	4.86	3.48	1.41	5.28
Total factor input per person employed	.82	.57	.64	.91	1.06	.44	1.23	1.35	.15	.93
Labor	.19	.21	.39	.12	.38	−.02	.34	.27	.26	.63
Hours of work	−.13	.03	−.04	.04	.02	−.01	.03	.06	.05	.09
Age-sex composition	−.12	−.04	.01	−.06	.08	−.12	.06	−.03	−.06	.15
Education	.44	.22	.42	.14	.28	.11	.25	.24	.27	.39
Capital	.67	.41	.27	.81	.68	.59	.90	1.09	−.08	.37
Dwellings	.22	.04	.00	.12	.00	.10	.02	.05	.00	.02
International assets	.02	−.13	−.03	.01	.02	−.12	.37	−.04	−.37	.00
Nonresidential structures and equipment	.34	.38	.28	.58	.49	.39	.34	.89	.27	.32
Inventories	.09	.12	.02	.10	.17	.22	.17	.19	.02	.03
Land	−.04	−.05	−.02	−.02	.00	−.13	−.01	−.01	−.03	−.07
Output per unit of input	1.92	3.89	1.91	.20	3.59	6.62	3.63	2.13	1.26	4.35
1955–62										
National income per person employed	1.73	3.34	2.70	3.62	4.91	3.81	2.78	3.11	1.79	5.42
Total factor input per person employed	.77	.85	.60	.40	1.17	.94	.59	.53	.68	1.19
Labor	.24	.05	.33	−.27	.35	−.19	−.08	−.16	−.02	.48
Hours of work	−.20	−.26	−.22	−.34	−.06	−.45	−.29	−.31	−.30	.03
Age-sex composition	−.08	.08	.12	−.07	.12	.15	−.03	−.10	−.02	.05
Education	.52	.23	.43	.14	.29	.11	.24	.25	.30	.40
Capital	.55	.83	.28	.73	.82	1.20	.68	.69	.71	.73
Dwellings	.21	.05	−.02	.09	.03	.14	.06	.04	.04	.09
International assets	.05	.03	−.08	.03	.02	−.05	−.11	−.09	.17	−.05
Nonresidential structures and equipment	.25	.59	.33	.49	.57	.87	.58	.67	.41	.55
Inventories	.04	.16	.05	.12	.20	.24	.15	.07	.09	.14
Land	−.02	−.03	−.01	−.06	.00	−.07	−.01	.00	−.01	−.02
Output per unit of input	.96	2.49	2.10	3.22	3.74	2.87	2.19	2.58	1.11	4.23
1950–62										
National income per person employed	2.15	3.80	2.64	2.56	4.80	5.15	3.65	3.27	1.63	5.36
Total factor input per person employed	.79	.73	.62	.62	1.13	.72	.86	.86	.45	1.07
Labor	.22	.12	.36	−.11	.37	−.12	.09	.02	.10	.54
Hours of work	−.17	−.14	−.15	−.18	−.02	−.27	−.16	−.15	−.15	.05
Age-sex composition	−.10	.03	.08	−.07	.10	.04	.01	−.07	−.04	.09
Education	.49	.23	.43	.14	.29	.11	.24	.24	.29	.40
Capital	.60	.65	.28	.77	.76	.93	.78	.85	.37	.57
Dwellings	.21	.04	−.01	.10	.02	.12	.04	.04	.02	.05
International assets	.04	−.04	−.06	.02	.02	−.08	.09	−.07	−.06	−.03
Nonresidential structures and equipment	.29	.51	.31	.53	.53	.66	.49	.76	.35	.45
Inventories	.06	.14	.04	.12	.19	.23	.16	.12	.06	.10
Land	−.03	−.04	−.02	−.04	.00	−.09	−.01	−.01	−.02	−.04
Output per unit of input	1.36	3.07	2.02	1.94	3.67	4.43	2.79	2.41	1.18	4.29

Source: See text for derivation.

Contributions of changes in the amounts of labor and capital per worker differ considerably among the countries. But output per unit of input is far more important than total input in creating differences in growth rates of national income per person employed. This is partly because the contribution of total input is a net figure in which positive and negative contributions are offset. In most countries hours reduction appreciably curtailed growth after 1955. The dominance of output per unit of input is greater than in the analysis of total national income because employment itself is responsible for much of the variation in growth of *total* factor inputs.

Over the 1950–62 period as a whole the contribution of increased inputs to the growth rate of national income per person employed was 0.79 percentage points in the United States and 0.73 percentage points in Northwest Europe. The contributions of labor, capital, and land were all fairly similar in the two areas, labor contributing 0.10 percentage points more in the United States, capital 0.05 percentage points less, and land 0.01 percentage points more. Within the capital total, a larger contribution from dwellings and international assets in the United States largely offset smaller contributions from nonresidential structures and equipment and inventories. The American figures are considerably affected by the increase in part-time employment. If the calculations were made on a full-time equivalent basis, the United States growth rate of national income per person employed would be higher; so would the contributions of capital and, especially, hours of work. On that basis, the contribution of hours would be approximately zero instead of −0.17, and the total contribution of labor quality would be raised accordingly.

The contribution of total input to the growth of income per person employed in Northwest Europe was greater (0.85) after 1955 than before (0.57) despite the sharp reduction in working hours after 1955. Enterprise capital per worker was growing much more rapidly, and the swing in property income from abroad in the United Kingdom was also important. In the United States, in contrast, capital contributed less (0.55) after 1955 than before (0.82).

Differences in Level of National Income per Person Employed

The procedure for analyzing differences in the level of national income per person employed in 1960 is essentially similar to that utilized for growth rates.

The labor quality indexes must first be adjusted to allow for the assumption, made in the international output comparisons, that output per person employed in certain civilian activities is the same in all countries. Column 2 of Table 15–1 shows the percentage of GNP at factor cost in United States prices that Gilbert and Associates estimated in this way. Column 4 gives corresponding estimates for labor input, obtained by a procedure similar to that used to obtain estimates at national prices. The percentages in 1960 are assumed to be the same as in 1950.[12] Their use to adjust the labor quality indexes may be illustrated by Norway. The Norwegian labor quality indexes for hours, age-sex composition, and education, initially estimated to be, respectively, 7.00 percent above, 0.34 percent below, and 5.70 percent below those for the United States, were reduced by 21 percent, becoming 5.53 percent above, 0.27 percent below, and 4.50 percent below those for the United States.

Comparisons of Inputs and Output per Unit of Input

International indexes for each of the factor inputs, with this adjustment incorporated, are given in Table 15–6. United States income share weights are used to combine separate inputs to obtain total factor input. (In this and subsequent calculations average shares in 1960–62 rather than shares for the single year 1960 are used to avoid reliance on data for a single year.) This table gives indexes including as well as excluding dwellings and international assets, but the inclusive figure uses property income from abroad directly to measure the input of international assets (which receive 0.7 percent of the total weight).

The quality of a year's labor and the amount of

12. Except that a downward adjustment paralleling that described in note 3, p. 188, was introduced for Germany and Italy.

capital and land per person employed differ substantially between the United States and the Northwest European countries. But the main impression created by Table 15–6 is that differences between the United States and Europe in output per unit of input are very much larger than the differences in total input per person employed; they are responsible for the bulk of the difference between the two areas in national income per person employed.[13] Total input per person employed in Northwest Europe as a whole was 11 percent below the United States while output per unit of input was 34 percent lower.

Indexes of national income per unit of input (which is the same on an aggregate or per-person-employed basis) compared as follows with indexes of national income per person employed in 1960:

	Indexes of national income[a]	
	Per unit of input	Per person employed
United States	100	100
Germany	68	59
Belgium	67	61
Northwest Europe	66	59
France	66	59
Denmark	66	58
Netherlands	66	65
United Kingdom	66	59
Norway	63	59
Italy	50	40

a. Both measures are based on the use of United States weights.

The similarity of output per unit of total input in all the Northwest European countries in 1960 is striking. The indexes for the area as a whole, France, Denmark, the Netherlands, and the United Kingdom are all 66; those for Germany and Belgium a little higher; and that for Norway 3 points lower. This is not altogether surprising since the similarity of the indexes for national income per person employed in these countries, except the Netherlands, has already been noted. The decided advantage of the Netherlands in national income per person employed in 1960 is found to be associated entirely with more inputs, especially labor

13. It goes without saying, of course, that the difference in inputs is the overwhelmingly more important reason that *total* national income varies among countries.

input. Among the Northwest European countries, the Netherlands had the highest input indexes for all three aspects of labor quality. In addition, it was second only to Norway in total capital input per person employed.

The estimates permit further computations that throw additional light on factor proportions in Europe and America. Table 15–6 shows capital input per person employed. Table 15–7 shows estimates of the amount of capital input in the form of enterprise structures and equipment and inventories per unit of labor input. It indicates that in 1960 Northwest Europe as a whole had only 50 percent as much of such capital per unit of labor input as the United States, and only 46 percent as much in the form of structures and equipment alone (based on an average of gross and net stock). Thus it remains true that capital was much scarcer relative to labor in Europe than in America even if labor input is adjusted for quality. Among the individual European countries the differences in factor proportions were large. Norway had a capital-labor ratio (excluding dwellings and international assets) 86 percent higher than the United Kingdom and 131 percent higher than Italy.

Handling of Two Computation Problems

The next step is to allocate the difference between national income per person employed in the United States and Europe among the contributions made by inputs and by output per unit of input. My method of dealing with two minor complications will first be described.

THE STATISTICAL INTERACTION AMONG INCOME DETERMINANTS. In discussing sources of growth, I noted that the sum of the contributions of the individual sources as initially calculated differs from the actual growth rate of national income because of the "interaction," but that when all calculations are based on growth rates rather than indexes the difference is small. As noted earlier, the actual growth rate was allocated among the sources in proportion to their contributions exclusive of the interaction term.

There is a similar interaction among the sources in comparisons of levels. Earlier chapters presented

TABLE 15-6

Factor Input per Person Employed and Output per Unit of Input,
Based on United States Income Share Weights, 1960

(*Indexes, United States = 100*)

Source of growth	United States	North-west Europe	Bel-gium	Den-mark	France	Ger-many	Nether-lands	Nor-way	United King-dom	Italy
National income per person employed	100.0	59.0	61.0	58.0	59.0	59.0	65.0	59.0	59.0	40.0
Total input per person employed[a]	100.0	89.2	91.1	88.2	89.2	86.4	98.8	94.1	90.0	80.6
Labor quality, total[a]	100.0	98.3	98.5	95.5	98.5	96.1	107.9	100.5	99.0	92.1
Hours[a]	100.0	106.3	105.2	105.8	106.8	106.5	110.1	105.5	105.1	109.4
Age-sex composition[a]	100.0	98.1	99.8	96.5	98.3	96.4	101.4	99.7	98.9	98.5
Education[a]	100.0	94.3	93.8	93.6	93.8	93.6	96.6	95.5	95.2	85.5
Capital, total	100.0	49.4	59.5	56.2	48.4	43.9	60.7	67.5	51.0	28.6
Dwellings	100.0	54.0	48.2	56.8	47.7	53.0	52.8	48.5	61.4	22.0
International assets[b]	100.0	26.7	39.0	6.9	9.6	−24.2	69.4	−76.3	93.2	−4.4
Other	100.0	49.1	64.4	58.7	50.7	44.6	62.8	81.7	45.3	32.7
Structures and equipment[c]	100.0	44.9	65.5	55.1	47.5	40.6	55.3	82.9	39.5	29.3
Inventories	100.0	66.3	59.7	73.2	64.1	60.7	93.4	76.6	68.7	46.2
Land	100.0	78.3	76.6	79.1	81.4	77.8	76.0	76.7	77.2	77.0
Output per unit of input[d]	100.0	66.2	67.0	65.8	66.1	68.3	65.8	62.7	65.6	49.7
Addendum: Total input excluding dwellings and international assets	100.0	91.2	93.4	90.2	91.7	88.7	101.1	97.4	91.2	83.8

Source: See text for derivation.
a. Labor indexes are adjusted to eliminate quality differences for labor employed in activities where output is measured by employment.
b. Input index measures net property income from abroad.
c. Average of indexes of gross stock and net stock.
d. National income per person employed divided by total input per person employed.

estimates of the differences in levels of national income per person employed that would be present if the countries differed in only *one* respect while all other income determinants were the same. The sum of such estimates would not coincide with actual differences in national income per person employed because *all* income determinants differ among countries. As with changes in one country over a period of years, the discrepancy would be appreciable if calculations were based on indexes. Because my principal purpose in estimating sources of difference in level of national income per person employed is to compare them with the sources of growth, the procedure for allocation among sources should be as comparable as possible. This consideration led me to adopt a procedure that might be described as based on the use of pseudo growth rates.[14] For the purpose of this calculation, I sup-

14. There is no uniquely correct method of dealing with the interaction and my procedure, as indicated, is related to the purpose of the study. Adoption of any other reasonable procedure would yield different numbers in the tables but would scarcely alter my broad conclusions.

posed that at some imaginary future date—assumed to be 1980—each European country would be at the 1960 position of the United States with respect to the level of national income per person employed, the level of each of the input factors per person employed, and the level of output per unit of input.

The contribution that each source would make to the growth rate from 1960 to 1980 if this were to happen was then computed in the same way as was done for actual periods in analyzing the sources of past growth. This meant that an artificial growth rate over a twenty-year time span was computed for each of the input factors (except dwellings and international assets) and multiplied by its income share weight. An artificial growth rate was also computed for output per unit of input. The percentage distribution of the contributions that the individual sources would make to 1960–80 growth rates under the conditions supposed was then applied to the difference between European and United States national income per man in 1960. If, for example, total input in a European

TABLE 15-7

*Indexes of Capital Input
per Unit of Labor Input, 1960*

(United States = 100)

Area	Total[a]	Type of capital Structures and equipment[b]	Inventories
United States	100	100	100
Northwest Europe	50	46	67
Belgium	65	67	61
Denmark	61	58	77
France	51	48	65
Germany	46	42	63
Netherlands	58	51	87
Norway	81	83	76
United Kingdom	46	40	69
Italy	35	32	50

Source: See text for derivation.
a. Excluding dwellings and international assets as well as general government capital.
b. Average of indexes of gross stock and net stock.

country would have to grow 1 percent a year and output per unit of input 3 percent a year to reach the 1960 United States level in 1980, then one-fourth of the difference between output per person employed in the United States and that country in 1960 is ascribed to the difference in inputs and three-fourths to the difference in output per unit of input. If the increase in education of the labor force would contribute one-fifth of the total contribution of inputs to the hypothetical growth rate, it is considered the source of one-twentieth (one-fifth of one-fourth) of the 1960 difference in output per person employed. The use of a twenty-year period is arbitrary but the results are not sensitive to the length of the period, provided it is long enough to reduce interaction terms to negligible size.[15]

As in the computation of sources of growth, an exception to the procedure described was made for the contribution of dwellings and income from abroad; for these sources the original estimates were used because no difference in "output per unit of input" or in other inputs enters into the results so there should be no interaction.

15. Neither is it very sensitive to use of the assumption that the European countries move to the United States levels rather than that the United States moves to European levels.

THE CHOICE OF WEIGHTS. The second complication concerns the income share weights. If income shares were the same in all countries despite differences in factor proportions, which would imply unit elasticity of substitution among the factors and no differences in shares for reasons other than factor proportions, the procedure followed to eliminate the interaction problem would also take care of the weighting problem. Use of these shares to weight the pseudo growth rates of the factors would be clearly indicated, and comparable to the procedures used to obtain the sources of growth. In fact, the estimated shares in the United States and Europe are not identical, and it is necessary to decide what share weights should be used in this calculation. The choice lies between the use of 1960–62 United States shares and an average of the 1960–62 shares of the United States and the European country. United States shares were adopted as probably the better for the purpose at hand (and as certainly yielding more comparable estimates for the several countries) but the choice admittedly is not clear.[16] In practice, the decision has but little effect on comparisons of the United States and most of the Northwest European countries. The greatest difference appears for Germany because German shares differ most from those in the United States. The allocation of the 41-point

16. The issues are complicated. Although the reasons for differences among shares in the several countries, after eliminating housing and income from abroad, are unknown and influences other than factor proportions probably are important, it would perhaps be better to use as weights the average of the income shares of the United States and the European country if it were not for the consideration introduced below. This procedure would assume if everything else gradually became the same as in the United States in 1960, as supposed in the calculation, income shares would also gradually become the same.

Use of an average of United States and national European shares would, however, seem to be equally appropriate whether output comparisons were based on United States or national European price weights and it has been seen that the choice of price weights greatly affects output comparisons. The use of average share weights would imply that there is no connection between (1) differences among countries in input proportions and relative earnings of the factors and (2) differences between output comparisons that are obtained when United States and European price weights were used. That is to say, it would imply that the difference in factor inputs contributes the same amount to the difference in national income whether income is measured in United States or European prices, so that the difference between the two income comparisons is entirely related to output per unit of input. I think that the difference, in fact, *is* largely related to output per unit of input

TABLE 15-8

*Differences from the United States in National Income per Person Employed and
Contributions Made by Factor Inputs and Output per Unit of Input, 1960*

(*Percentage of United States national income per person employed*)

Sources of difference	United States	North-west Europe	Bel-gium	Den-mark	France	Ger-many	Nether-lands	Nor-way	United King-dom	Italy
National income per person employed	100.0	59.0	61.0	58.0	59.0	59.0	65.0	59.0	59.0	40.0
Difference from United States	—	41.0	39.0	42.0	41.0	41.0	35.0	41.0	41.0	60.0
Due to										
Total factor input per person employed	—	11.3	8.5	11.0	11.0	14.0	2.8	5.3	11.0	18.7
Labor	—	1.1	1.0	2.8	1.0	2.5	-4.7	-.4	.6	4.4
Hours of work	—	-3.9	-3.2	-3.5	-4.1	-3.9	-5.9	-3.4	-3.1	-4.9
Age-sex composition	—	1.2	.1	2.2	1.1	2.3	-.9	.1	.7	.8
Education	—	3.8	4.1	4.1	4.0	4.1	2.1	2.9	3.0	8.5
Capital	—	9.7	6.9	7.7	9.6	11.0	7.0	5.2	9.9	13.8
Dwellings	—	1.9	2.1	1.8	2.1	1.9	1.9	2.1	1.6	3.2
International assets	—	.4	.3	.5	.5	.7	.2	1.0	.0	.6
Nonresidential structures and equipment	—	6.6	3.5	4.8	6.1	7.4	4.8	1.5	7.5	8.7
Inventories	—	.8	1.0	.6	.9	1.0	.1	.6	.8	1.3
Land	—	.5	.6	.5	.4	.5	.5	.5	.5	.5
Output per unit of input	—	29.7	30.5	31.0	30.0	27.0	32.2	35.7	30.0	41.3

Source: See text for derivation.

difference between Germany and the United States in income per person employed that results from using an average of German and United States weights differs from that obtained by using United States weights as follows:[17]

	United States income share weights	Average United States and German income share weights
Total input per person employed	14.0	16.3
Labor quality	2.5	2.4
Capital	11.0	13.3
Land	.5	.6
Output per unit of input	27.0	24.7

Even for Germany the results are not grossly different.

Estimates by Area and Country

Table 15-8 provides the estimates of the sources of difference in level of national income per person employed, with output per unit shown as a single

component. They show that national income per person employed in Northwest Europe as a whole was 41 percent below the United States; that of this difference 29.7 percentage points (or 72 percent) were due to the difference in output per unit of input and 11.3 points (or 28 percent) to the difference in input per person employed. Of the latter amount 9.7 points were due to the difference in capital per person employed, 1.1 points to the difference in the average quality of a year's work, and 0.5 points to the difference in land and natural resources. The difference in the average quality of a year's work is the net result of offsetting factors. Education contributed 3.8 points and age-sex composition of the labor force 1.2 points to the difference in income levels, but this was offset to the extent of 3.9 points by longer hours in Europe—mainly a reflection of the prevalence of part-time employment in the United States. The estimate for capital is divided among four components in Table 15-8.

National income per person employed in Italy was below Northwest Europe by 19 percent of the United States level. Of this additional difference from the United States 11.6 points were due to output per unit of input, 4.7 points to education,

(economies of scale being the primary cause—see Chapter 17, Section II). But inputs play some role, and it seems to me the lesser of evils to use United States weights for income shares to analyze output measured in United States prices.

17. The same estimates are used for dwellings and property income from abroad.

and 4.1 points to capital, with offsets of 1.0 points from longer hours and 0.4 points from a more favorable age-sex composition.

The estimates presented in this chapter indicate that inputs contributed importantly to growth in all countries and to differences in growth rates and income levels. However, output per unit of input is responsible to a much greater extent for differences in growth rates and income levels. The five chapters that follow explore the reasons that output per unit of input has changed, that it has changed by different amounts in different countries, and that it is much higher in the United States than it is in Europe.

Excessive Allocation of Labor to Farming and Self-Employment

Chapters 16 through 20 of this study examine determinants of output per unit of input. Among these determinants, gains achieved by improving the allocation of resources have been particularly important in establishing international differences in postwar growth. This chapter examines the most important of these changes in resource allocation.[1] Some others will be considered in Chapter 18.

In each country a large fraction of the agricultural workers in the 1950 labor force could have been eliminated with little loss of national product. The situation among the nonfarm self-employed and their family helpers was much the same. Transfer of workers out of these groups to activities in which they are more productive, specifically to nonfarm wage and salary employment, has helped to raise the national product in all the countries considered in this study.[2] The amounts by which it has done so vary greatly among countries. They have depended mainly on the numbers in agriculture and self-employment at the start of the period.

This chapter examines these particular changes in employment composition and attempts to quantify the relationship between them and the growth of national income per person employed. It concludes that the United States has curtailed excessive employment in agriculture about as much as any European country and has also curtailed unproductive labor in nonfarm family businesses. However, the large continental countries started in 1950 from a position where the waste from misallocation was much greater, and reduction of this waste contributed much more to the 1950–62 growth rate of output per man in continental Europe than in the United States. The estimated contribution to the 1950–62 growth rate of national income per person employed is 0.29 percentage points in the United States. It is not much larger, 0.35 percentage points,

1. The first part of this chapter has drawn upon an earlier essay in Brennan (ed.), *Patterns of Market Behavior: Essays in Honor of Philip Taft*, pp. 65–88 [B24]. However, revisions of data and modifications of procedures have been incorporated and the estimates have been shifted from a GNP to a national income basis. Use of a different agricultural employment series for Italy considerably raises both the growth rate of national income per man and the estimated contribution to that growth rate made by the shift of labor from agriculture. (See the "Note on Statistics" in the earlier essay.)

2. For simplicity of presentation, in this chapter I shall often write as if the labor force shifts discussed entailed the actual movement of individuals from one activity to another although this is only partly the case. The shifts result from a lower ratio of new entrants to total departures in the declining activities than in the labor force as a whole.

in Belgium and it is smaller, 0.10 percentage points, in the United Kingdom. The contribution to growth in the large and fast-growing continental countries was far bigger—0.88 points in France, 0.90 in Germany, and 1.26 in Italy. The contributions in the remaining small countries were intermediate—0.47 in the Netherlands, 0.58 in Denmark, and 0.77 in Norway. The ranking of countries by the size of gains from reducing the waste of resources in this way is the same as a ranking by growth rates of national income per person employed, except for some differences within the intermediate group of small countries. This source consequently explains much of the difference in growth rates between the United States and Northwest Europe as a whole and among the individual countries.

This type of misallocation also contributes to the differences between the United States and the European countries, except the United Kingdom, in the levels of national income per person employed and output per unit of input. The United Kingdom wastes much less of its resources in this way than the other Northwest European countries. It is only this circumstance that keeps national income per person employed in the United Kingdom from being much lower than in the rest of Northwest Europe. Overallocation to agriculture and self-employment explains most of the difference between Italy and Northwest Europe in output per unit of total input—that is to say, of the difference in national income per person employed that remains after taking account of lower inputs in Italy.

Changes Over Time

I shall first examine the relationship between the allocation of labor and growth rates, and then turn to the comparison of income levels.

Too Many Farmers and Nonfarm Self-Employed

The nine countries examined here have had too many agricultural workers. Many farms have been too small or their soil too poor to yield an output from full-time work that would provide an income at all comparable to that obtained in nonfarm ac-

tivities.[3] Large fractions of the farms produced so little that if they and the workers employed on them had simply disappeared, nearly as much output would have been obtained in each country with many fewer workers. If the workers were eliminated but the land given up had been transferred to the remaining farms, increasing their size, the loss of output could have been held to even smaller proportions. On the other hand, the labor used so ineffectively in agriculture could have contributed importantly to nonfarm output. At any given time, the values of the total national product and national product per person employed in the economy as a whole were smaller than they could have been had a smaller proportion of the labor force been allocated to agriculture and a larger proportion to nonfarm activities—provided, of course, that other changes necessary to adapt to a reallocation of labor had also been made. During the brief period from 1950 to 1962, the percentage of employment devoted to agriculture was actually reduced enormously in all the countries and a net gain in national income was realized.

Many proprietors, own-account workers, and unpaid family workers in nonagricultural industries also are engaged in work that could be foregone without much loss of national income. Large numbers in this group operate very small businesses and have very low earnings. Of course, low earnings per person do not automatically indicate misallocation.[4] They may indicate labor of low quality; where earnings of groups of wage and salary workers are low, this is likely to be the case. But there is an impor-

3. In addition, overallocation of resources to farming has tended to depress farm prices and, hence, the incomes of even those farmers whose returns from their labor and investment would match what could be obtained in nonfarm activities if the total allocation of resources to agriculture were optimal; however, this has often been offset by price support programs, government subsidies to farmers, or both.

4. The reader should be aware that for brevity I use (or misuse) the word "misallocation" in this chapter to denote an allocation that yields a lower measured national income than an alternative allocation, because it has other advantages, this use is appropriate only because this study focuses on measured national income. As noted in Chapter 1, if workers prefer one activity to another despite lower income, because it has other advantages, this means less national income but not misallocation in the general sense that total welfare is curtailed (see p. 9). The same observation applies if farm income is understated relative to nonfarm income in a welfare sense because products produced and consumed on farms are valued at lower prices than those paid by urban consumers, or if living costs generally are lower.

tant difference between the two categories. Wages and salaries are an actual out-of-pocket expense to employers, who are likely to pay out good money only if it contributes to their profits. Wage or salary workers, on their part, are less likely than the self-employed to weigh heavily considerations other than present and future income in selecting employment. They are more inclined to change jobs to increase their earnings or to avoid a decrease. Over-allocation of paid labor to an activity is unlikely to persist on a large scale for a long time. When persistent earnings differentials prevail among wage and salary workers, there is some justification for supposing that they correspond in a rough and ready way to differences in the quality of labor employed. It certainly cannot be presumed that the existence of differentials is evidence of misallocation, nor that the mere transfer of nonfarm paid employees from occupations or industries where average earnings are low to categories where they are higher would raise the national product.[5]

The situation is different when employer and employee are one and the same, or the employee is an unpaid member of the family. Large numbers of proprietors and own-account workers tend to stress independence, position, and nonmonetary aspects of their work at the expense of income. They do not contract for any predetermined income, and vast numbers of new entrants into business are ignorantly or irrationally optimistic about their future prospects. In the United States a large proportion of nonfarm proprietors at any time are in their first year or two of operation, continuing only until they have lost their capital. Nowhere do the self-employed who once obtain a living, however modest, abandon their posts simply because they could earn more in paid employment. They are slow to change when their earnings decline in relation to those in alternative employments or even absolutely.[6] The presence of unpaid family workers enables the proprietor to continue operations when he could not afford hired labor. Their availability often yields extreme income results; if two enterprises each yield a bare subsistence for a family, but one absorbs the work of family helpers in addition to the proprietor, income per person employed is even lower than in the other. Moreover, the real alternative open to family workers is often to leave the labor force altogether rather than to look for a wage or salary job. Since the physical presence of proprietors and family workers is required to maintain the enterprise as a going concern, they usually remain in an "employed" status, often with long nominal working hours, when little work is available.

The consequence of such factors is that in large numbers of trade and service "enterprises" (I use the term broadly to include own-account workers without places of business) the net income per proprietor and family member falls far below the average earnings of wage and salary workers.

The proportion of the nonfarm labor force engaged in such activities has declined everywhere, so this statement is less characteristic of the situation in 1962 than of the situation in 1950. There can be no doubt that large numbers of these enterprises could and did disappear with no other effect than to increase the business (but not employment) of those remaining, or at most to require a disproportionately small increase in paid employment in larger establishments.

The situations described need not imply (although in most countries it appears to be the case) that the average income from labor of all persons engaged in agriculture combined, or all nonfarm self-employed and family workers combined, falls below that of nonfarm wage and salary workers.

Table 16–1 shows the ratio of national income originating in agriculture per person employed in agriculture to national income in nonagricultural industries per person employed (including proprietors and own-account workers). Income from dwellings and net property income from abroad were excluded from the income totals because they have

---

5. An exception might be made for compulsory military service. The arbitrarily determined pay of draftees is not an indication of the quality of labor, and an increase in the armed forces usually depresses national product per man. However, this is an essentially different phenomenon from the labor force shifts considered in this chapter.

6. As *The Economist* says, writing of France: ". . . small shopkeepers have the knack, like the peasants, of subsisting for a time at the margin. One of the awkward reasons why competition does not always have the effects that the text-

books say it should is the uneconomic reluctance of businesses to shut up shop; in practice elimination of the small retailer in France often takes a generation, the son refusing to follow his father's blind alley" (February 1, 1964, p. 429 [P19]).

TABLE 16-1

Ratios of Real National Income per Worker in Agriculture[a] *to Real National Income per Worker in Nonagricultural Industries*[b]

Area	In various prices[c]		In 1958 prices	
	1950	1955	1955	1962
United States[d]	.42	.44	.44	.54
Northwest Europe				
Belgium	.80	.91	.84	1.07
Denmark	.80	.78	.70	.79
France	.35	.37	.42	.49
Germany	.42	.42	.44	.49
Netherlands	1.02	1.04	.98	1.14
Norway	.27	.24	.20	.20
United Kingdom	.85	.93	.93	1.16
Italy	.55	.54	.46	.52

Sources: Employment data: Table 5–1 except for adjustment indicated in note d; national income data: see text for derivation.
a. Includes forestry and fishing except in the United States and Norway.
b. Excludes income from dwellings and international assets.
c. Years used for deflation of prices in 1950–55 period: Belgium, 1953; Norway, 1955; United States and United Kingdom, 1958; other countries, 1954.
d. Nonfarm employment data adjusted; see note 9, p. 205.

no significant employment counterpart. The national income data are expressed in constant prices, and the base years are the same as those used to compute growth rates. The estimates refer to national income rather than to labor earnings and the table is intended only to suggest the relative average earnings position of agriculture in the areas studied. In the large countries where agriculture is important—the United States, France, Germany, and Italy—the ratio never exceeds 0.55. In Belgium, Denmark, the Netherlands, and the United Kingdom it is higher, and in some cases even exceeds 1.0 (although only in Holland in 1950 did it do so at the beginning of either subperiod considered in the study). Differences among countries in these ratios are, of course, greatly affected by relative farm and nonfarm prices, which in turn are heavily influenced by government policy.[7]

Since the farm data are an average of prosperous large farms and the farms with low productivity, a ratio near or above 1 does not indicate the absence of large numbers of farms with little output

per worker. All countries have large fractions of farm employment devoted to such operations.[8]

Examination of available data also indicates that the average earnings of nonfarm self-employed and family workers (even with the return to their capital included) are usually but not invariably below the average labor earnings of wage and salary workers. Even where they are higher, this does not indicate the absence of misallocation. The self-employed can be visualized as consisting of three groups. One is a core of high-income professionals, proprietors of large business establishments, proprietors of successful smaller establishments, and some own-account workers in skilled trades who do well enough operating on their own. Members of this "core" group could not, in general, improve their economic status by shifting to paid employment. Their average income is usually very high. The second is what I shall call the "fringe" group, consisting of the large numbers who could improve their earnings by shifting to paid employment; it is in this group that an addition to national income could be made by reducing their numbers. Counts of the self-employed also pick up certain numbers of the shiftless or incompetent, who are unable to hold a paid job, and of individuals who cannot accept employment away from home and must earn what they can in their homes; these I shall call the "immovable" group. The high income of the "core" group offsets the low earnings of the "fringe" and "immovable" groups when the three are combined.

In all countries the total number of nonfarm self-employed and family workers combined has declined relative to the number of nonfarm wage and salary workers; except in the United States, Germany, and Italy, there was also a decline in their absolute number. Since core group members lack an incentive to move to paid employment (unless their position deteriorates) and the immovable group is unable to do so, the contraction must refer mainly to the large number of individuals in the fringe group who contribute little to output in a nonpaid status but are quite competent to hold wage and salary jobs.

7. Differences in the 1955 figures for certain countries where the base years used for deflation differ for the 1950–55 and 1955–62 periods show that the choice of base year is also important.

8. See, for example, OECD, *Problems of Manpower in Agriculture* [I37], and OECD, *Low Incomes in Agriculture* [I30].

Comparison of Employment Aggregates

The nonagricultural wage and salary worker component of total employment provides a useful though imprecise indicator of the changes in employment that have influenced output the most. Columns 1 to 3, Table 16–2, compare the increases from 1950 to 1962 in total employment, total nonfarm employment, and nonfarm wage and salary employment in the nine countries.[9]

Nonagricultural wage and salary employment increased more than total employment in every country, but the amounts differed greatly. As shown in Column 6, Table 16–2, the index of nonfarm wage and salary employment exceeds that of total employment by only 2 percent in the United Kingdom

and 7 percent in the United States as against 20 in Germany, 21 in France, and 36 in Italy, with the smaller countries ranged between the United States and Germany. It is a thesis of this chapter that it is in the nonfarm wage and salary category that employment changes affect national income most.

In all countries the index of nonfarm wage and salary employment exceeded that in total employment *both* because total nonfarm employment increased more than total employment and because nonfarm wage and salary employment increased more than total nonfarm employment. This is shown by Columns 4 and 5, Table 16–2. Column 6 is the product of these columns so the two developments

9. For use in this chapter two adjustments have been made to the employment data presented in Table 5–1:
(1) In Norwegian and United Kingdom statistics no one is classified as a nonfarm unpaid family worker, principally because legislation makes it advantageous to pay family workers. I have assumed that for every four proprietors and own-account workers in nonagricultural industries in these countries there is one wage and salary worker whose position is not essentially different from that of unpaid family workers in other countries. (This is the approximate ratio of unpaid family workers to proprietors and own-account workers in the other countries of Northwest Europe.) The numbers obtained by this assumption were transferred from the nonfarm wage and salary worker category to the nonfarm unpaid family worker category. This adjustment was made in all the tables of this chapter in which these data are used. Although Denmark counts no *male* unpaid family workers in nonagricultural industries, the ratio of unpaid family workers to proprietors and own-account workers was nevertheless higher than 1 to 4 and no adjustment was made.
(2) Use of an unadjusted employment count would overstate the shift of labor out of agriculture in the United States because of the huge increase in part-time nonfarm wage and salary workers working very few hours. I have therefore reduced the employment *increase* in this category to something like a full-time equivalent basis. The 1950 ratio of part-time to total nonfarm wage and salary workers was multiplied by the total number of nonfarm wage and salary workers in later years to obtain the number of part-time workers who would have been included if the 1950 ratio had not changed. Two-thirds of the difference between the actual number of part-time nonfarm wage and salary workers and this hypothetical number was subtracted from total employment, total nonfarm employment, and nonfarm wage and salary worker employment. This adjustment is made in all tables relevant to time series analysis presented in this chapter (that is, Tables 16–1 through 16–11), but not in Tables 16–12 through 16–14, which refer to comparisons of levels.

TABLE 16–2

Indexes of Employment, Including the Armed Forces, 1962

(1950 = 100)

Area	Total employment (1)	Total nonagricultural employment[a] (2)	Nonagricultural wage and salary worker employment[a] (3)	Indexes of differences		
				Column (2) divided by Column (1) (4)	Column (3) divided by Column (2) (5)	Column (3) divided by Column (1) (6)
United States[b]	112.2	118.2	119.9	105.4	101.4	106.8
Northwest Europe						
Belgium	106.7	111.8	116.9	104.8	104.6	109.5
Denmark	111.7	124.6	132.0	111.5	105.9	118.1
France	101.3	114.7	122.9	113.2	107.2	121.3
Germany	126.9	148.9	152.6	117.4	102.5	120.3
Netherlands	113.3	119.7	128.3	105.6	107.2	113.2
Norway[b]	102.1	112.1	119.8	109.8	106.8	117.3
United Kingdom[b]	108.1	109.7	110.7	101.6	100.8	102.4
Italy	107.0	133.2	145.9	124.4	109.6	136.4

Sources: Computed from Tables 5–1 and C–1 except for adjustments indicated in note b.
a. Forestry and fishing are classified with agriculture except in the United States and Norway.
b. Employment data adjusted; see note 9.

TABLE 16-3

*Indexes of Farm Employment and Nonfarm
Self-Employment, 1962*

(1950 = 100)

Area	Indexes of employment[a]		Indexes of percentage of total employment[a]	
	Farm employment (1)	Nonfarm self-employed and unpaid family workers (2)	Farm employment (3)	Nonfarm self-employed and unpaid family workers (4)
U. S. [b]	69	106	61	95
N. W. Europe				
Belgium	65	92	61	86
Denmark	78	93	70	85
France	69	83	68	82
Germany	67	113	53	89
Netherlands	75	82	66	72
Norway[b]	70	83	69	81
U. K.[b]	79	99	73	91
Italy	72	104	67	97

Sources: Same as Table 16-2.
a. Forestry and fishing are classified with agriculture except in the United States and Norway.
b. Employment data adjusted; see note 9, p. 205.

can be considered separately. The decline in the importance of agriculture had the greater effect in most countries and will be examined first.

Among the large countries, the index for total nonagricultural employment exceeds that for total employment by 2 percent in the United Kingdom and 5 percent in the United States, as against 13 in France, 17 in Germany, and 24 in Italy (Column 4). These are the percentages by which 1962 non-farm employment exceeded what it would have been if agriculture had absorbed the same percentage of total employment as it did in 1950.

These results do not mean that the United States curtailed excessive employment in agriculture less than France, Germany, and Italy—not even if the fraction of total farm employment that was excessive is supposed as large in the United States as in those countries. The agricultural employment decline was 31 percent in both the United States and France, 28 in Italy, and 33 in Germany—a very narrow range (see Column 1, Table 16–3). In addition to Germany, only Belgium, at 35 percent, had a larger percentage decline than the United States.

Moreover, within the farm employment total the United States had the largest percentage decline in proprietors and unpaid family workers, and the next to the smallest (after Italy) in wage and salary workers. This pattern suggests especially great success in eliminating categories where underemployment is greatest.

Use of the percentage decline in the percentage of employment devoted to agriculture, rather than in the absolute number of farm workers, would not greatly change the picture (Column 3, Table 16–3).

The increase in nonfarm employment exceeded that in total employment so much more in France, Germany, and Italy than in the United States and the United Kingdom because of the much greater importance of farm employment at the beginning of the period. By 1950 farm employment was already down to 5 percent of total employment in the United Kingdom and 12 percent in the United States, whereas the percentages were 25 in Germany, 29 in France, and 43 in Italy (Table 16–4). Similar percentage declines in agriculture consequently added far more to nonagricultural employment in the latter countries.

A percentage decline in total farm employment that was as large in the United States as in continental Europe must have meant an even greater percentage decline in excessive employment. It is in-

TABLE 16-4

*Farm Employment[a] as a Percentage of
Total Employment*

Area	1950	1955	1960	1962	1964	Decline, 1950–62
U. S.[b]	12.2	10.2	8.4	7.5	6.7	4.7
N. W. Europe						
Belgium	10.9	8.9	7.4	6.7	5.9	4.2
Denmark	27.6	24.9	21.2	19.2	17.6	8.4
France	29.3	25.9	21.5	19.9	18.4	9.3
Germany[c]	24.8	18.6	13.8	12.6	11.4	11.6
Netherlands	14.1	12.2	10.4	9.3	8.3	4.8
Norway	24.0	19.9	17.6	16.5	15.6	7.4
U. K.	5.4	4.7	4.3	3.9	3.7	1.5
Italy	42.8	38.2	32.2	28.8	25.1	14.0

Source: Computed from Table 5–1 except for adjustment indicated in note b.
a. Forestry and fishing are classified with agriculture except in the United States and Norway.
b. Total employment adjusted; see note 9, p. 205.
c. Percentages shown include the Saar and West Berlin in 1960–64 and exclude them in 1950 and 1955. The 1960 percentage comparable to earlier years is 14.4.

conceivable that with an optimum allocation of labor the difference between the percentage of workers devoted to agriculture in France, Germany, or Italy and the percentage in the United States would be as large as it actually was in 1950 (and as it continues today). The United States advantage in efficiency is surely as great in agriculture as in nonagricultural activities, and probably greater. The relatively low income elasticity of demand for agricultural products would perhaps explain some differential because of transport costs, but not an agricultural proportion twice as high in 1950 in Germany as in the United States, and still higher in France and Italy. The implication is that the distribution of labor was (and is) farther from optimal in these countries than in the United States. It seems probable that this is so even if artificial barriers to international trade are taken into account.

To transfer labor out of agriculture to correct an imbalance, it is in principle necessary to offer nonfarm job opportunities, to overcome the resistance to movement of the agricultural labor force (including potential replacements from among the farm population), and to avoid subsidizing low income farmers so heavily as to impair the incentive to move. To provide nonfarm jobs for the individuals transferred so that the additional labor can be effectively used requires adequate demand for nonfarm products and either the provision of additional nonfarm capital or more labor-intensive use of capital. Provision of adequate demand poses no inherent problem since, given the extra labor available, it implies no addition to inflationary pressure. The pace of change may be limited by the speed with which capital can be provided for balanced nonfarm production, either by adding to capital through saving or foreign borrowing or by reallocation of capital. The expansion of nonfarm jobs may sometimes have been restricted by this limitation in Italy, but not significantly so during most of the period in the other countries.[10] In practice, the decline in farm employment was so general and so similar in all the countries as to appear to be almost inexorable; the pressures for change were so great as to override all differences in government policies and national conditions.

It is quite clear that the differences between continental Europe and America in the growth obtained by reducing the waste of labor in agriculture reflected the amount of waste to be eliminated rather than the degree of success in curtailing it. The United Kingdom had even less opportunity than the United States to expand output in this way.

I turn now to the effect on the employment indexes of the reduction in the importance of nonfarm proprietors and unpaid family workers.[11] Column 5, Table 16–5, repeats the ratios of 1962 indexes (1950 equals 100) of nonagricultural wage and salary employment to indexes of total nonagricultural employment. The index for nonfarm wage and salary employment exceeds that for total nonfarm employment by amounts ranging from 1 percent in the United Kingdom and the United States to 7 in France, the Netherlands, and Norway, and 10 in Italy.

These percentages would be smallest for the Anglo-Saxon countries even if the differential between employment indexes for wage and salary workers and for the self-employed and family workers had been the same in all countries. This is because self-employed and family workers represented the smallest fraction of nonfarm employment in the Anglo-Saxon countries in 1950, as shown in Column 1. There is a general though quite imperfect tendency for Column 5, Table 16–5, to be high when Column 1, Table 16–5, is high; this is a reflection of differences in the 1950 weight of the self-employed.

It is also true, as shown in Column 6, that the total number of self-employed and unpaid family workers contracted least (11 percent) relative to wage and salary workers in the Anglo-Saxon countries. In all the other countries the reduction was 21 to 36 percent. This comparison does not tell whether

10. If the reallocation process in Italy had gone much faster it might also have adversely affected the balance of payments by stimulating imports more than exports and the inflow of capital. The fundamental limitation in Italy in recent years seems, however, to have been the speed with which it is possible to absorb workers straight off the farm, many of whom are illiterate or nearly so, into the nonfarm work force without impairing productivity much.

11. A variety of data referring to this group are provided in Tables 16–3 and 16–5. It may be noted that in Columns 1 to 4, Table 16–5, self-employment is expressed as a percentage of civilian nonfarm employment because data in this form are needed later in this chapter, whereas elsewhere the armed forces are included in total nonfarm employment. Exclusion of the armed forces has too little effect to disturb the analysis in the present discussion.

TABLE 16-5

Self-Employment and Family Workers: Importance and Relative Movement
Within Nonfarm Employment[a]

Area	Self-employed and unpaid family workers as a percentage of civilian nonfarm employment				1962 index (1950 = 100) of nonfarm wage and salary employment divided by index of total nonfarm employment (5)	1962 index (1950 = 100) of nonfarm self-employed and unpaid family workers divided by index of total nonfarm wage and salary employment (6)
	1950 (1)	1955 (2)	1962 (3)	1964 (4)		
United States[b]	12.3	11.5	11.3	10.7	101.4	89
Northwest Europe						
Belgium	20.9	19.2	17.4	16.5	104.6	79
Denmark	19.2	17.3	14.4	13.6	105.9	70
France	21.4	18.8	15.7	14.4	107.2	67
Germany[c]	15.7	13.4	12.2	11.7	102.5	74
Netherlands	19.1	16.5	13.1	12.3	107.2	64
Norway[b]	21.3	18.8	15.8	15.6	106.8	69
United Kingdom[b]	7.7	7.3	6.8	6.7	100.8	89
Italy	31.3	29.0	24.6	24.5	109.6	71

Source: Computed from Table 5–1 except for adjustments for the United States, Norway, and the United Kingdom indicated in note b.
a. Forestry and fishing are classified with agriculture except in the United States and Norway.
b. Employment data adjusted; see note 9, p. 205.
c. Percentages shown include the Saar and West Berlin in 1962 and 1964 and exclude them in 1950 and 1955. In 1960 the percentage comparable to the preceding years was 12.8 and the percentage comparable to following years was 12.7.

or not the United States and United Kingdom were less successful than others in reducing the size of the fringe group—those who could be transferred with gain to wage and salary status—because the fringe group probably accounted for most of the *decline* in all countries but for a much smaller proportion of all the self-employed and family workers present in 1950 in the Anglo-Saxon countries than on the continent.

Table 16–6 provides a breakdown of nonfarm employers and own-account workers in France in 1954 that is typical of countries with large numbers of self-employed. All employers together with professionals without paid employees comprised only slightly more than one-third of the French total.[12] This grouping suggests the size in France of what I have called the core group.[13] Small merchants without employees alone were more numerous. The remainder were largely "artisans" without employees, a group that includes own-account workers in most of the service industries. Unpaid family workers, who are excluded from this table, are even more

heavily concentrated outside the core group than are proprietors.[14]

The fringe group is largely responsible for international differences in the ratio of the self-employed and unpaid family workers to total nonagricultural employment. It also largely determines the amount by which indexes of total nonfarm employment and of self-employed and family worker employment diverge within each country. The dominant size of the fringe group would in itself assure that this is so. But one can add that differences between places and dates are *disproportionately* due to the fringe group.

Data for the Common Market countries, which have been compiled on a consistent basis from a special survey for early autumn 1960, support this statement with respect to international differences. Among these six countries the percentage of employers has a range of only 2.0 percentage points. Independent professionals without employees, who are included with own-account and unpaid family

12. I include with professionals the category, "Professors, literary and . . ."
13. Were it not for the exclusion of family workers from the total, the grouping would probably understate the core's proportions to a moderate degree.

14. A division of unpaid family workers between those who were engaged in establishments whose proprietors were own-account workers and those who were employers is not available but 71 percent of the unpaid family workers were working for small merchants as compared with 48 percent of employers and own-account workers who were small merchants.

TABLE 16-6

*France: Distribution of Employers and
Own-Account Workers, 1954*

(*In thousands*)

Branch of employment	Em-ployers	Own-account workers	Total[a]
Manufacturers	76	0	76
Artisans	198	458	657
Large merchants	93	48	141
Small merchants	190	762	952
Professions	44	68	112
Professors, literary and scientific personnel, teachers, medical and social services	2	23	25
Service workers not earning a wage	1	21	22
Artists	1	16	17
Total	605	1,397	2,003

Source: Marchal, *La Répartition du Revenu National*, Vol. II, p. 26 [B73]. Based on 1954 French population census.
a. Details may not add to totals because of rounding.

workers, are too few and cannot vary enough among countries to account for much of the difference among countries in that category, which has a range of 12.0 points. It seems clear that nonprofessionals without employees together with unpaid family workers account for nearly all of the difference among countries in the proportion of the self-employed in nonfarm employment. The data are:

*Percentage of nonfarm
civilian employment*

	Employers	Own-account workers and unpaid family workers	Total self-employed and family workers
Belgium	3.5	18.2	21.7
France	4.7	13.8	18.5
Germany	4.4	8.7	13.1
Italy	5.1	20.7	25.8
Luxembourg	4.7	13.3	18.1
Netherlands	5.5	9.5	15.0

NOTE. Data are from OSCE, *Statistical Information*, No. 2 bis, 1963, Table 57 [I49]. They are not strictly comparable with those used in the present study.

French and Belgian data indicate that the core group was not shrinking as much *over time* as total self-employment.[15] This was to be expected every-

15. The French censuses for 1954 and 1962 show that between these years the number of employers together with professionals and "Professors, literary and..." dropped 49,000, or 7.0 percent. The number of other own-account workers dropped 123,000, or 9.4 percent, and unpaid family workers 112,000, or 24.6 percent. The last two groups combined dropped 13.3 percent and accounted for 83 percent of

where because members of this group had no incentive to leave self-employment. The immovable group lacked opportunity to do so. Declines were concentrated in the fringe group. Hence, if the fringe group declined by the same percentage in two countries, the percentage decline in the total number of self-employed and family workers would be greater in the country where they are more numerous. This corresponds to the general pattern observed in Table 16-5.

The large size of the fringe group and the evidence that it is in this group that differences and changes in self-employment are concentrated assure that Column 5, Table 16-5, refers very largely to the relative gain in wage and salary employment at the expense of the fringe group whose labor was used very unproductively, rather than at the expense of the core group of skilled professionals and owner-managers of substantial enterprises.

Contributions to Growth

I now attempt to quantify the effect of the developments just discussed upon the growth rates of national income per person employed. All calculations are made separately for the 1950–55 and 1955–62 periods. The general procedure is to estimate the amount by which 1950 national income would have been higher if the 1955 employment pattern had prevailed, and the amount by which

the total decline in proprietors and unpaid family workers.

In Belgium, according to census data adjusted for changes in classification that were kindly provided by the National Statistical Institute, the number of employers in distribution increased by 34,000, or 14 percent, from 1947 to 1961 while the number of merchants without paid employees declined by 57,000, or 14 percent, and the number of unpaid family workers declined by 34,000, or 37 percent. (The total decline in distribution shown in this source does not appear to be consistent with all-industry aggregates used in the present study.)

The situation in retailing in Italy, as described by Richard H. Holton, appears to have been in the same direction but it is rather less clear. In absolute terms, it will be recalled, self-employment in all nonfarm industries combined increased a little in Italy. The increase in retailing was evidently larger. However, while the number of retail stores increased 32 percent from 1951 to 1961, the number of retail units increased only 22 percent because the number of peddlers declined. Holton does report a continued expansion of the absolute number of small stores. He also says: "Common observation would suggest that the typical retail outlet in Italy could sell perhaps twice its present volume without increasing its capital or labor requirements" (in *Banca Nazionale del Lavoro Quarterly Review*, September 1962, pp. 240–57 [P4]).

1955 national income would have been higher if the 1962 employment pattern had prevailed. It is supposed, of course, that time for necessary adjustments was available, as it actually was between these dates. The calculations involve the general assumption, which I believe to be correct, that if the farm percentage of total employment in 1950 had been as low as it was in 1955, and if the percentage of civilian nonfarm employment represented by self-employed and family workers had been as low in 1950 as it was in 1955, there would still have been overallocation of labor to agriculture and to nonfarm self-employment in 1950. Similarly, it is assumed that even with 1962 proportions there would have been overallocation in 1955.

The procedures adopted are intended to yield correct estimates of contributions to growth rates of national income per person employed and per unit of input. Contributions to total national income do not reflect the possibility that total employment itself was affected by shifts in employment composition, as would occur if the movement of farm families from the farm raised paid employment of wives and children more (the probable effect) or less than it reduced the number of unpaid family workers; my classification of growth sources takes the actual change in employment as given. To put the matter another way, the shift of families out of agriculture may have had two effects. It may have influenced labor force participation rates and hence total employment. If so, this influence is counted in my estimates of the contributions of employment changes. It is only the second effect—the effect on output per person employed or per unit of input—that I attempt to measure here.

The calculations require that national income in 1950 and 1955, valued in the prices used to compute growth rates in the 1950–55 and 1955–62 periods, respectively, be divided among three components: income from dwellings and net property income from abroad, which have no significant employment counterpart; national income originating in agriculture; and national income originating in nonagricultural industries. The division between agricultural and nonagricultural industries corresponds to the one used for employment data in that forestry and fisheries are included with farming except in the United States and Norway. The

TABLE 16-7

Percentages of National Income in Constant Prices Originating in Agricultural and Nonagricultural Industries, 1950 and 1955[a]

Area	1950 (in various prices)[b]		1955 (in 1958 prices)	
	Agri-culture	Non-agri-cultural indus-tries	Agri-culture	Non-agri-cultural indus-tries
United States	5.4	91.6	4.6	91.6
Northwest Europe				
Belgium	8.3	84.5	7.1	86.0
Denmark	22.5	74.2	18.0	77.7
France	12.5	86.9	12.7	86.6
Germany	12.0	87.2	9.0	90.4
Netherlands	14.0	83.3	11.6	84.9
Norway	7.7	91.6	4.6	93.2
United Kingdom	4.4	90.0	4.3	92.3
Italy	28.3	69.4	21.3	74.1

Source: See text for derivation.
a. The difference between the sum of the percentages shown and 100 represents income from dwellings and net property income from abroad. Forestry and fisheries are classified with agriculture except in the United States and Norway.
b. Years used for deflation of prices in 1950–55 period: Belgium, 1953; Norway, 1955; United States and United Kingdom, 1958; other countries, 1954.

statistical allocation between agriculture and nonagricultural industries is an approximation since agricultural net product was not directly available from national sources. A breakdown of gross domestic product in constant prices was available but the depreciation estimates in constant prices had to be estimated, except for Norway; in four countries even a division of depreciation in current prices was lacking. The farm and nonfarm percentages are shown in Table 16–7.

Estimates of the gains from improved allocation of resources and reduction of concealed unemployment are derived separately for the shift from agriculture and for the shift from nonfarm self-employment.[16]

16. The calculations for the shift from agriculture assume in effect that those moving to nonfarm industries were divided between nonfarm wage and salary workers and others in the same proportions as existing nonfarm employment. The calculations for the shift from nonfarm self-employment to nonfarm wage and salary employment then handle the entire shift in composition of nonfarm employment. This procedure yields the correct sum for the two estimates but, since it is likely that only a few of those leaving agriculture move into nonfarm self-employment, the procedure may in

CURTAILMENT OF AGRICULTURE. The gain from the shift out of agriculture is calculated as (1) the gain in nonfarm national income from reducing the percentage of resources devoted to agriculture minus (2) the offsetting loss in farm national income resulting from the same cause. Table 16–8 is a "worksheet" to help the reader follow the derivation of this estimate; it is explained below with the use of the French estimates for 1955–62 as an illustration.

1. The decline in the farm percentage of total employment from 1950 to 1955 and from 1955 to 1962 is shown in Line 1, Table 16–8; the latter was

---

a certain sense allocate too small a fraction of the total gain to the shift from agriculture. The point is of most importance in Italy, where nonfarm proprietors and family workers dropped sharply as a percentage of nonfarm employment but insignificantly as a percentage of total employment.

5.97 points in France. The increases in nonfarm percentages are, of course, the same. Line 2 expresses these figures as percentages of the 1950 and 1955 nonfarm percentages of total employment. The figure of 8.06 given for France in Line 2b (5.97 divided by the 1955 percentage of 74.09) means that nonfarm employment in France in 1955 would have been higher than it was by 8.06 percent if the nonfarm percentage of total employment had been what it was in 1962 and total employment had been what it actually was in 1955.

I wish to assume that a given percentage increase in nonfarm input, with inputs comprehensively measured as in the previous chapter, would raise nonfarm output proportionately. But *total* nonfarm input was probably raised less than employment by the shift from agriculture. The percentage of total capital devoted to agriculture probably declined less

TABLE 16–8

Derivation of Estimated Gains in National Income from
Shift of Resources Out of Agriculture

Item	United States	Bel-gium	Den-mark	France	Ger-many	Nether-lands	Nor-way	United King-dom	Italy
1 Decline in farm percentage of employment (points)									
a. 1950 to 1955	1.98	2.03	2.61	3.34	6.21	1.84	4.09	.68	4.61
b. 1955 to 1962	2.73	2.22	5.75	5.97	5.41	2.96	3.35	.78	9.38
2 Decline in farm percentage as percent of nonfarm employment percentage									
a. 1950–55 as percent of 1950 percentage	2.26	2.28	3.60	4.72	8.26	2.14	5.38	.72	8.06
b. 1955–62 as percent of 1955 percentage	3.04	2.44	7.66	8.06	6.65	3.37	4.18	.82	15.17
3 Estimated percentage increase in nonfarm national income due to shift									
a. 1950–55	1.70	1.82	2.88	3.78	6.61	1.71	4.30	.58	6.04
b. 1955–62	2.28	1.95	6.13	6.45	5.32	2.70	3.34	.66	11.38
4 Line 3 times nonfarm percentage of national income									
a. 1950	1.56	1.54	2.14	3.28	5.76	1.43	3.94	.52	4.19
b. 1955	2.09	1.68	4.76	5.58	4.81	2.29	3.11	.61	8.44
5 Decline in farm percentage as percent of farm employment percentage									
a. 1950–55 as percent of 1950 percentage	16.22	18.59	9.47	11.42	25.01	13.07	17.06	12.57	10.78
b. 1955–62 as percent of 1955 percentage	26.69	24.97	23.06	23.04	29.27	24.18	16.84	16.49	24.58
6 Estimated percentage reduction in farm national income due to shift									
a. 1950–55	5.35	4.65	3.13	2.86	6.25	3.27	4.27	4.15	.00
b. 1955–62	8.81	6.24	7.61	5.76	7.32	6.05	4.21	5.44	.00
7 Line 6 times farm percentage of national income									
a. 1950	.29	.39	.70	.36	.75	.46	.33	.18	.00
b. 1955	.41	.44	1.37	.73	.66	.70	.20	.23	.00
8 Percentage increase in national income due to shift of resources from agriculture									
a. 1950–55 (4a − 7a)	1.27	1.15	1.44	2.92	5.01	.97	3.61	.34	4.19
b. 1955–62 (4b − 7b)	1.68	1.24	3.39	4.85	4.15	1.59	2.91	.38	8.44

Source: See text for explanation.

than the percentage of labor. It is even possible that in certain countries there may have been no decline at all (and perhaps no overallocation of capital to agriculture). There was no substantial transfer of land out of agriculture. The quality of labor gained by nonfarm industries as a result of the shift from agriculture may also have been below the average quality of nonfarm labor. Wherever data are available, the farm labor force has had less education than the nonfarm labor force.[17] In Northwest Europe this takes the form of a smaller percentage with education beyond the compulsory requirement, usually 6 to 9 years; in the United States and Italy percentages with very little education are also much higher in the farm labor force. However, agriculture has retained a disproportionate number of older workers, which both moderated the effect on education of the nonfarm labor force and had a slightly favorable effect upon its age distribution. On balance, the quality differential between the nonfarm labor force as it was and as it would have been in the absence of the shift may have been small in Northwest Europe, but it was greater in the United States and Italy because the education differential between those leaving the farm and the nonfarm labor forces was greater. In both countries the drop in farm employment was especially large in the South, where educational standards in rural areas were relatively low.[18] I shall assume the percentage increase in total nonfarm inputs resulting from the shift out of agriculture was four-fifths as large as the percentage increase in nonfarm employment in the Northwest European countries and three-fourths as large in the United States and Italy. These are, of course, rough approximations.

Line 3, Table 16–8, gives the resulting estimates of the percentages by which total inputs, and there-

fore total output, in nonagricultural industries would have been increased in 1950 and 1955 if total inputs had been distributed as they were in 1955 and 1962. For France in 1955 the estimate is 6.45 percent (8.06 × .80). This is an estimate of the percentage by which national income in nonfarm industries would have been above its actual level in 1955 if resources had been allocated in 1955 as they were in 1962 (and time for adjustment were available). Since national income in nonfarm industries was 86.58 percent of total national income (the rounded figure appears in Table 16–7) this was equal to 5.58 percent of total national income. Similar estimates for all countries in each period are shown in Line 4.

2. I next try to estimate the loss of national income in agriculture that resulted from the shift of resources.

Line 5, Table 16–8, shows the percentages by which farm employment in 1950 and 1955 would have been lowered if total employment had been what it actually was in those years but if the farm percentages of total employment had been the same as they were in 1955 and 1962, respectively. For example, 1955 farm employment in France would have been 23.04 percent lower than it was if the farm percentage of total employment had been the same as in 1962.

What is the effect on farm output of a reduction in farm employment? The farms from which farm families drop out without replacement are mostly those with little output. If the farms were simply abandoned, and there were no offset in larger production by the remaining farms, the percentage reduction in total farm output would be only a small proportion of the percentage reduction in farm labor. This is, indeed, the main point. But, in addition, the reduction in the number of farms actually had little effect on the amount of farmland in use in any country and even less on the amount of good land. Rather, it resulted in the enlargement of the remaining farms. Nor, as far as can be judged from available information, was the reduction in the farm share of capital proportional to that in the farm share of labor.

Estimates of the relationship between reductions in farm employment and in farm income would be greatly facilitated by (a) a size distribution of per-

17. See Colin Leicester, "The Manpower Link Between Economic Growth and Education," Paris: OECD, 1966, Table 3 (mimeo.), and OECD, *Manpower Policy and Programmes in the United States*, p. 64 [131].

18. About 58 percent of the actual drop in farm employment in the United States from 1950 to 1962 occurred in the South and 42 percent in other regions. The educational background in the rural South is far below the average for the nonfarm labor force. In 1960 the median number of years of school completed was 7.7 in Southern farm areas as against 11.0 in urban areas in the United States as a whole. For nonwhites in the rural South the median was only 4.7 years; nonwhites were heavily represented among those leaving Southern agriculture. (Data are based on U.S. Bureau of the Census, *Census of Population, 1950* [G54] and *1960* [G55].)

sons employed, classified by amount of national income, per person employed, produced by the farm on which each individual was employed; and (b) information as to the position in this distribution of farm workers who left their farm jobs during the period under review. The United States distribution closest to that desired—and it is not very close—is a distribution, from the monthly labor force survey, of males employed in agriculture classified by money income.[19] Income from property (whether part of the net income of farm proprietors or a cash receipt) is included. The data cover males employed in agriculture in March of the year following that to which the income data refer. Those with no money income are excluded. The numbers covered fall short of average male employment in the prior year by about 15 percent on the average. This is partly because unpaid family workers without money income are omitted, partly because of the secular decline in farm employment, and partly for seasonal reasons. Females, who accounted for 16 percent of total farm employment in 1950, are also omitted.[20] If the data for 1949 and 1950, and for 1959 and 1960, are averaged to reduce random and sampling fluctuations in annual data, the cumulative distributions shown in Table 16–9 are obtained. The percentage change from 1949–50 to 1959–60 in the male employment covered is virtually identical with that in total farm employment.

The data show a pronounced decline in the concentration of income at the top, corresponding to the expectation.[21]

The following experimental calculation was made to judge the effect of reducing employment on national income per person employed in agriculture

19. U.S. Department of Agriculture data are less suitable. The Department has estimated the number of farms and sales for 1949 and 1959 classified by sales-size class in 1959 prices, but has not provided corresponding employment data for these years. In any case, Department of Agriculture employment data bear no close resemblance to employment as counted in the *Monthly Report on the Labor Force* and in the present study.

20. A similar distribution of females employed in agriculture is available, but covers only a small fraction of female employment (presumably because most females are unpaid family workers without money income) and, the numbers in the sample being very small, the data are highly erratic from year to year.

21. That the share of the lowest fifth, which is very small, did not increase may be due to inclusion of unpaid family workers with small amounts of money income from outside sources.

TABLE 16–9

United States: Males Employed in Agriculture Classified by Money Income, Averages for 1949–50 and 1959–60

Portion of income distribution	1949–50		1959–60	
	Number (thousands)	Percentage of total income	Number (thousands)	Percentage of total income
Upper 5 percent	266.8	28.85	199.6	22.76
Upper 20 percent	1067.3	57.65	798.5	52.72
Upper 40 percent	2134.6	79.10	1597.0	76.24
Upper 60 percent	3201.9	91.60	2395.5	90.46
Upper 80 percent	4269.2	97.30	3194.0	97.83
Total	5336.5	100.00	3992.5	100.00

Source: Computed from Miller, U.S. Bureau of the Census, *Trends in the Income of Families and Persons in the United States: 1947 to 1960*, Table 15 [G62].

in the United States. Farm income in 1949–50 was distributed among income size classes like money income. Employment was then reduced from the 1949–50 to the 1959–60 level (a 25.2 percent reduction) on three alternative assumptions. First, the extreme assumption, that the employment decline came from the bottom of the distribution; on this assumption, elimination of 25.2 percent of 1949–50 employment would have cut total farm national income by only 4.2 percent even if it had no favorable effect on the income of the remaining 74.8 percent. Second, that the employment decline came equally from each of the three lower fifths of the distribution; on this assumption it would have reduced farm national income by 8.9 percent. Third, that the employment decline came from each of the fifths in inverse proportion to income (that is, in proportion to the reciprocals of the share of each fifth in total income); on this assumption it would have reduced farm income by 9.1 percent.[22] The second and third assumptions seem plausible and yield almost identical results.

If the third assumption is adopted, the percentage reduction in 1949–50 farm national income that would have been caused by the reduction of farm employment to the 1959–60 level is only 0.36 of the percentage reduction in farm employment (9.1 divided by 25.2). This figure ought to be further reduced on the grounds that the elimination of some

22. In each case, I assume that *within* each fifth the reduction was proportional throughout the distribution.

small farm units released land for others, increasing output per man on the remaining units. I shall take account of this additional point only to the extent of rounding the percentage down from 0.36 to one-third. The assumption of the calculation is somewhat arbitrary, but the result that farm national income was reduced one-third percent for each 1 percent employment decline seems, intuitively, to be generous and therefore conservative from the standpoint of measuring the gains from employment shifts.

Separate calculations for other countries were not attempted but in most of them each 1 percent reduction in farm employment probably involved an even smaller reduction in farm national income than in the United States. In addition to the presumption that agriculture was more overmanned than in the United States, consideration must be given to the fact that reduction of the number of farms and farmers facilitated the consolidation of separated plots—except in the United Kingdom and the Scandinavian countries, where fragmentation is not a serious problem. Wastage of human and machine time traveling between plots and the difficulty of using machinery on small areas are among the drawbacks of fragmentation. I shall use the same ratio, 0.33, for the United Kingdom and Denmark as for the United States; and 0.25 for the other Northwest European countries, the difference representing an allowance for the effects on fragmentation.[23] The view held by Italian experts is that the gains from consolidating farms and plots have been so great in Italy that the reduction in farm labor had no adverse long-run effect on farm output. (Temporary effects in years when the withdrawal was especially large are not necessarily denied.) I accept this view and use a ratio of 0.00 for Italy.

Line 6, Table 16–8 shows the products of these ratios and the percentage reductions in the farm share of employment as given in Line 5. For France, I estimate that farm national income in 1955 would have been 5.76 percent lower (23.04 × 0.25) than it was if agricultural employment had been the same percentage of total employment as in 1962—

23. Farm income in Norway is so small it makes no practical difference which ratio is applied. I use the 0.25 ratio despite the absence of fragmentation because Norway is especially burdened with small and unproductive farms.

assuming, of course, that time had been allowed for necessary readjustments. Line 7 converts these percentages to percentages of total national income; for France in 1955 the calculation is 5.76 percent times the farm share of national income, 0.127, or 0.73 percent.

Finally, in Line 8 the losses from farm output are subtracted from the gains in nonfarm output. For France, I thus estimate that, in comparison with the 1955 distribution of resources between farm and nonfarm activities, the superior 1962 distribution added 4.85 percent (5.58 minus 0.73) to national income.

The gain in national income from reducing over-allocation to agriculture was thus 4.85 percent in 7 years, representing a contribution to the 1955–62 French growth rate of national income per person employed of 0.68 percentage points, or 0.69 when a slight "interaction" effect is allowed for in the same way as it was in Chapter 15 for the contribution of labor and capital inputs. The contribution in all the countries in each subperiod and in the 1950–62 period as a whole, obtained by weighting the subperiods, is shown in Table 16–10.

At two points in the calculations, it will be recalled, different ratios were used for different countries. If the ratios used for the other five countries had been used, the estimated contribution in the 1950–62 period would have been higher by 0.01 in the United Kingdom and by 0.04 in the United States and Denmark, and lower by 0.10 in Italy. Thus, these variations have but little effect on the results.

The contributions in the 1950–62 period are given in order of size in the first column of the following listing (in percentage points):

	Contribution of shift of resources out of agriculture	Growth rate of employment differential	Growth rate of national income per person employed differential
Italy	1.04	1.84	.91
Germany	.76	1.35	.72
France	.65	1.04	.79
Norway	.54	.78	.53
Denmark	.40	.88	.33
United States	.25	.44	.33
Netherlands	.21	.46	.09
Belgium	.20	.39	.27
United Kingdom	.06	.13	.12

The reduction in the overallocation of resources to agriculture emerges as a principal source of growth in several countries and an important source in all except the United Kingdom. Differences in the gains from this source are responsible for much of the difference among countries in growth rates of national income per person employed.

The remaining columns show two related series for comparison. The second column gives the growth rate of the ratio of nonfarm to total employment—that is, the growth rate that would yield the indexes shown in Column 4, Table 16–2. My estimates of the contributions are, of course, smaller than these rates but with minor aberrations the ranking of countries is similar. The third column shows the amount by which the growth rate of national income per person employed in all industries exceeded the growth rate of nonfarm national income per person employed in nonfarm industries. (The rates themselves are given in Table 16–11; property income from dwellings and international assets is excluded from both series.) Such a calculation is sometimes used to judge the contribution of the shift of resources from agriculture to the growth rate.[24] Although the assumptions implied by this use

are different from mine, the results are close to my own estimates of the contribution in most countries, and in none do they differ as much as 0.15 percentage points.[25]

Reference may also be made to a study prepared for OECD which provides two alternative sets of estimates of gains from 1950 to 1960 resulting from the shift of labor out of agriculture. Both assume that the output per man of the additional labor force in the nonagricultural sector in 1960 was equal to the average for that sector. One alternative assumes output in agriculture to have been unaffected by the reduction in numbers. The other alternative assumes that agricultural output in 1960 would have been proportionately higher than it actually was if the 1950 labor force proportion had been maintained. These assumptions are not very different from those underlying the second and third columns, respectively, of the text table above. However, the OECD calculations are based on gross domestic product in current prices, rather than national income in constant prices, and span a shorter

---

24. The principal assumptions in this use are apparently (1) that the growth rate of total input per person employed is the same in nonfarm industries and in all industries, and (2) that any difference between the growth rate of output per unit of input in farm and nonfarm industries is due to the shift of resources from agriculture.

25. In the subperiods, the difference is greater than this only in Denmark and Italy in 1950–55.

TABLE 16–10

Contribution of Shifts of Resources Out of Agriculture and Self-Employment to Growth Rates of National Income per Person Employed

(In percentage points)

Type of shift and time period	United States	North-west Europe	Bel-gium	Den-mark	France	Ger-many	Nether-lands	Nor-way	United King-dom	Italy
1950–62										
Total contribution	.29	.60	.35	.58	.88	.90	.47	.77	.10	1.26
Shift from agriculture	.25	.46	.20	.40	.65	.76	.21	.54	.06	1.04
Shift from nonfarm self-employment	.04	.14	.15	.18	.23	.14	.26	.23	.04	.22
1950–55										
Total contribution	.34	.70	.40	.45	.84	1.22	.44	.96	.12	1.00
Shift from agriculture	.25	.52	.23	.29	.59	.99	.19	.72	.07	.83
Shift from nonfarm self-employment	.09	.18	.17	.16	.25	.23	.25	.24	.05	.17
1955–62										
Total contribution	.25	.54	.31	.67	.91	.66	.50	.64	.09	1.44
Shift from agriculture	.24	.42	.18	.48	.69	.59	.23	.41	.05	1.18
Shift from nonfarm self-employment	.01	.12	.13	.19	.22	.07	.27	.23	.04	.26

Source: See text for derivation.

TABLE 16-11

Growth Rates of National Income per Person Employed:
Nonagricultural Industries[a] *and All Industries*[b]

Area	1950–62		1950–55		1955–62	
	Nonfarm industries	All industries	Nonfarm industries	All industries	Nonfarm industries	All industries
United States[c]	1.83	2.16	2.38	2.68	1.44	1.78
Northwest Europe						
Belgium	2.64	2.91	2.53	2.78	2.72	3.00
Denmark	2.23	2.56	.99	1.01	3.11	3.67
France	4.02	4.81	3.95	4.66	4.07	4.91
Germany	4.46	5.18	6.25	7.13	3.19	3.78
Netherlands	3.43	3.52	4.58	4.61	2.61	2.74
Norway	2.81	3.34	2.88	3.50	2.76	3.22
United Kingdom	1.62	1.74	1.79	1.89	1.50	1.63
Italy	4.58	5.49	4.86	5.39	4.38	5.56

Sources: Derived from income estimates described in text and employment data cited in Table 16–2.
a. Forestry and fishing are classified with agriculture except in the United States and Norway.
b. Excludes income from dwellings and international assets.
c. Employment data adjusted; see note 9, p. 205.

time period. Despite this, in each country my estimate of the gains per year happen to fall within the range of the estimates for OECD.[26]

REDUCTION OF NONFARM SELF-EMPLOYMENT. The gains from reducing the importance of nonfarm proprietors and family workers within the nonfarm employment total must now be estimated. The contraction must have been concentrated among members of the fringe group, and especially those with the lowest earnings. Hence, the increment to wage and salary employment required to make up for the work formerly performed by self-employed and family workers could hardly be large. Not only did those leaving self-employment have a low value of output per person but also the work they formerly did could often be absorbed by those remaining.[27] I shall assume that an increase in wage and salary employment one-fourth as large as the decline in self-employment was required. More pre-

26. *Agriculture and Economic Growth: A Report by a Group of Experts,* pp. 42–43 and 116–18 [I26]. It should be noted that Table 8, p. 43, neglects to note that the estimates for France and Italy measure changes only from 1955 to 1960; this is indicated on p. 118.

27. This is not contradicted by the observation that there are cases, particularly among repair services, where the process has gone far enough to increase delays in obtaining service in some countries. However inconvenient to the consumer, slow service is not a characteristic that price indexes allow for; consequently, delay does not impair the measured national product except to the small extent that the actual work done in the course of a year may be curtailed.

cisely, I shall suppose that the transfer of four workers from the status of nonfarm proprietors and family workers was equivalent to a net addition of three workers to nonfarm employment. This assumption refers only to labor. I make no allowance for any possible saving in the use of capital or land corresponding to this shift.

The following illustration describes one situation in which the one-fourth reduction would be appropriate. Assume that the unincorporated firms that disappeared are drawn from the lower portion of a distribution, by volume of business, of firms without paid employees; that firms of this type could readily handle more volume without increasing employment; and that the volume, per person engaged, of such firms was half that of firms in the same business with paid employees. Let half the business formerly handled by the disappearing firms go to other firms without paid employees which would be able to absorb it without adding to employment. Let the other half go to firms with paid employees, which would need to add only one employee to handle the volume formerly handled by two self-employed and family workers in the discontinued firms. Under these circumstances, the business handled by the discontinued firms would be taken care of by the addition of one paid employee to replace four self-employed and family helpers in the discontinued firms.

The contributions made to the growth rate by the reduction in the importance of nonfarm self-employment can be readily calculated once these assumptions are introduced.[28] They are shown in Table 16-10 and are listed below in order of size for the 1950–62 period (in percentage points):

Netherlands	.26
France	.23
Norway	.23
Italy	.22
Denmark	.18
Belgium	.15
Germany	.14
United States	.04
United Kingdom	.04

The gains from this source were smaller than those from the movement of labor from agriculture, except in the Netherlands, but were nonetheless appreciable in most countries. As in the case of agriculture, the United States and the United Kingdom obtained the smallest contributions because they had the least misallocation to eliminate. The countries obtaining the larger contributions were generally those in which the importance of nonfarm proprietors and own-account workers in the labor force was greatest at the beginning of the period. However, the Netherlands was rather more and Belgium rather less successful than the other continental countries relative to the apparent opportunities for gain.

The *combined* contributions to growth rates of the shifts of resources from agriculture and from nonfarm self-employment are also given in Table 16-10 and in the following listing, which ranks countries in the order of the contribution in the 1950–62 period (in percentage points):

	1950–62	1950–55	1955–62
Italy	1.26	1.00	1.44
Germany	.90	1.22	.66
France	.88	.84	.91
Norway	.77	.96	.64
Denmark	.58	.45	.67
Netherlands	.47	.44	.50
Belgium	.35	.40	.31
United States	.29	.34	.25
United Kingdom	.10	.12	.09

Not only did these sources contribute greatly differing amounts in different countries but in several instances they also contributed very different amounts to the growth rate of the same country in the two subperiods. The contribution was higher in the second subperiod by as much as 0.44 points in Italy, and lower by as much as 0.56 points in Germany.[29]

Relationship to Composition Studies

Investigators in most of the countries covered in this study have divided the growth rate of national income or GNP into two components: the part that reflects increases in output per man or man-hour in each separate industry, when industries are combined with fixed weights, and the part that results from changes in industry composition. The effect of changes in industry composition nearly always turns out to be almost entirely a reflection of the declining importance of agriculture; shifts within the nonfarm sector usually have but little net effect on these calculations.

These studies are not the same as, but do bear a resemblance to, my analysis of the farm-nonfarm shift.[30] They suggest that an attempt to analyze

28. The estimate for France in the 1955–62 period may again be used to illustrate the calculation. French national income in 1955, in 1958 prices, is estimated at 161.77 billion francs including 140.06 billion francs originating in nonfarm industries (excluding property income from dwellings and abroad). Nonfarm wage and salary employment in 1955 would have been higher than it actually was by 428,000 if the percentage division of nonfarm civilian employment between wage and salary workers and proprietors and unpaid family workers had been the same as in 1962. By my assumption, the 428,000 "extra" proprietors and family workers could have been replaced by only one-fourth as many wage and salary workers. Subtracting three-fourths (321,000) of this number from total nonfarm employment (including the armed forces) of 14,314,000 yields an adjusted employment total of 13,993,000, which is viewed as comparable to the 1962 employment figure as a measure of effective labor input. Division of 140.06 billion francs by this adjusted employment yields 10,009 francs as nonfarm national income per adjusted person employed, and multiplication by the 1955–62 labor share (excluding property income from dwellings and abroad) of .785 yields 7,857 francs as adjusted labor earnings. The gain that would have been achieved if the ratio of proprietors and own-account workers had been as low as in 1962 is the product of 321,000 workers and 7,857 francs or 2.52 billion francs. This is 1.56 percent of total national income. Spread over a seven-year period this is equal to a contribution to the growth rate of 0.22; the amount is unchanged after allowing for the "interaction."

29. These estimates do not include gains from economies of scale resulting from the increase in the size of markets to which the reduction in misallocation contributed.

30. The main difference is that they imply that a reduction in farm employment means a proportional reduction in farm output, and an increase in nonfarm employment a proportional increase in nonfarm output (somehow defined).

gains or losses from changes in misallocation by industry within the nonfarm sector would probably yield small estimates. I have not made such an attempt because I am unwilling to assume that differentials among nonfarm industries in the level of national income per person employed are the same as differentials in national income per unit of total input, and because I am unable to conduct an investigation to examine each industry in each country in detail in order to judge whether misallocation is present.[31] The estimates introduced for nonfarm proprietors and own-account workers seem to me likely to catch much of the desired effect, and especially the differential effect on growth rates of the various countries.

Contribution to Differences in Output Levels

Differences in the allocation of resources to agriculture and self-employment also contribute to differences in levels of output per person employed. In this section an attempt is made to estimate the amounts in 1960.

National Income per Person Employed in Nonagricultural Industries

The allocation of resources between agricultural and nonagricultural industries will be examined first. The matter may be approached initially by considering the effect of agriculture upon indexes of national income per person employed. Column 1, Table 16–12, repeats the indexes of total national income per person employed that were given in Table 2–4. Column 2 gives similar indexes computed after eliminating from the income aggregates property income from abroad and income from dwellings, which have no important employment counterpart. Column 3 gives indexes of nonagricultural national income (excluding income from dwellings and abroad) divided by nonagricultural

employment. Column 4 shows the difference between Columns 3 and 2 and thus measures the effect of excluding agriculture.

Preparation of Table 16–12 required estimation of net agricultural product in United States prices so that nonagricultural income could be obtained. Although the farm estimates themselves are subject to substantial percentage errors, the effect of such errors upon the indexes of nonfarm income per person employed is not large.[32]

A large percentage of employment in agriculture pulls down the all-industry index relative to the nonfarm index because, in United States prices, farm national income per person employed was below nonfarm income per person employed in all countries. In the United States itself it was only 44 percent as large. Thus the principal reason that the all-industry index is higher than the nonagricultural index in the United Kingdom, about the same in Belgium and the Netherlands, and lower in Denmark, France, Germany, Norway, and Italy is that the percentage of employment devoted to agriculture is smaller in the United Kingdom than in the United States, not very different from the United States in Belgium and the Netherlands, and much higher in the other countries. However, the difference between the two indexes for Germany, Norway, and especially Italy is much enlarged because the ratio of farm product per person in these countries to farm product per person in the United States is much below the corresponding ratio for nonfarm product per person. The difference in the ratios is smaller in France but this factor is nevertheless of importance because French farm employment is very large and receives a heavy weight in the all-industry index.[33]

The nonagricultural indexes are interesting in their own right. When total national income per person employed was compared, the Northwest European countries were found to be at a roughly similar level and Italy at a much lower level. Exclusion of dwellings and property income from abroad changes the indexes only slightly. When agriculture is also excluded the position of North-

---

31. In countries where coal mining is important, it is often the most important nonfarm industry in which a reduction in overallocation has contributed to growth. This is particularly the case in Belgium and Germany.

32. The estimates are described and appraised in Appendix L.

33. The indexes of farm national income per person employed implied by the estimates used are given in Appendix Table L–1.

TABLE 16–12

National Income per Person Employed, Total and Nonfarm, 1960, and Estimated Cost of Greater Overallocation of Resources to Agriculture in Europe than in the United States

(*In United States prices*)

| Area | Indexes of national income per person employed (United States = 100) | | | | Excess cost of overallocation as a percentage of country's own national income[a] | |
| | All industries (1) | Excluding income from dwellings and international assets | | | | |
		All industries (2)	Nonagricultural industries (3)	Nonagricultural industries minus all industries[b] (4)	Assumption A (5)	Assumption B[c] (6)
United States	100	100	100	—	—	—
Northwest Europe	59	60	62	2.5	4.1	3.3
Belgium	61	62	62	.0	.0	.3
Denmark	58	59	63	4.1	6.5	4.3
France	59	60	67	6.9	10.2	8.0
Germany	59	60	64	4.0	6.3	5.3
Netherlands	65	65	65	.0	.0	−.3
Norway	59	61	67	6.2	9.3	7.8
United Kingdom	59	59	57	−1.4	−2.4	−1.7
Italy	40	41	55	13.3	24.3	19.2

Sources: Column (1): Table 2–4; Columns (2)–(4): Appendix Table L–2; Column (5) = Column (4) ÷ Column (3) (before rounding) except in the case of Northwest Europe, which is a weighted average; it assumes total input per person employed is the same in nonagricultural industries (excluding property income from dwellings and abroad) and in agriculture; Column (6) assumes total input per person employed is 20 percent greater (25 percent in Italy) in nonagricultural industries than in agriculture; see text for explanation.
a. Excluding income from dwellings and international assets.
b. Before rounding.
c. Assumption B is accepted in this study.

west Europe as a whole vis-à-vis the United States is improved by 2.5 index points, and the improvement is 4.4 points outside the United Kingdom. The spread among the Northwest European countries is widened and their relative positions change. France and Norway had the highest national income per person employed in nonagricultural industries in 1960, followed by the Netherlands, Germany, Denmark, and Belgium. Exclusion of agriculture improves the positions of Denmark and Germany considerably, and those of France and Norway to an even greater extent, relative to the United States.

The most striking changes when farming is excluded are the deterioration in the position of the United Kingdom and the improvement in the position of Italy relative to the other European countries. Presentation of actual dollar values for the large countries may help to explain the relationships.

My estimates of national income per person employed in 1960 in United States dollars follow:

| | Total national income | National income excluding income from dwellings and international assets | |
		All industries	Nonfarm industries only
United States	$5,898	$5,624	$5,894
France	3,507	3,387	3,954
Germany	3,472	3,355	3,757
United Kingdom	3,476	3,300	3,378
Italy	2,380	2,330	3,224

Total national income per person employed in France, Germany, and the United Kingdom fell within a 1 percent range in 1960. Elimination of income from dwellings and international assets drops the United Kingdom only slightly below the other two countries. In nonagricultural industries, however, output per person employed in the United Kingdom was 15 percent below France, 10 percent below Germany, and 8 percent below Belgium, the lowest among the remaining Northwest European countries.

The position of nonagricultural industries in Italy, in contrast, was very much better than the overall position of that country. Outside of agriculture output per man in Italy was only 19 percent below France, 14 percent below Germany, and 5 percent below the United Kingdom.[34]

Cost of Overallocation of Resources to Agriculture and Self-Employment

The difference between a European country and the United States in the cost of overallocation of resources to agriculture could be calculated directly from the indexes in Table 16–12 if these measured output per unit of total input instead of output per person employed. (They would do so if input per person employed were the same in farm and nonfarm industries.) Overallocation of resources to farming should not affect output per unit of total input in nonagricultural activities (except through economies of scale). If the cost of overallocation to agriculture were the same percentage of national income in all countries, indexes of total national

income per unit of input would, therefore, be about the same as indexes of nonagricultural national income per unit of input. Consequently, the difference between the two indexes for a European country (Column 4, Table 16–12) would measure the cost in a European country of having greater misallocation than the United States, expressed as a percentage of United States national income per person employed.[35] Column 5, the quotient of Columns 4 and 3, would then given the percentage by which United States national income (excluding income from housing and abroad) would be lower if the misallocation cost were the same percentage of national income as in the European country but every other income determinant were the same as in the United States. It would also represent the percentage by which the national income (excluding income from housing and international assets) of each European country fell short of what it would have been if the misallocation cost were the same percentage of national income as in the United States but everything else were the same as in the European country.[36]

The actual indexes refer to output per person employed rather than to output per unit of input. Indexes of total input, and therefore output per unit of input, could not be constructed separately for nonagricultural industries. The effect of excluding agriculture upon output per unit of input indexes can only be inferred. Use of Column 5 to measure costs of misallocation, which would be correct if total input per person employed in each country

34. The conclusion that in nonagricultural output per man the United Kingdom was closer to Italy than to France and Germany in 1960 is not altogether novel. It has been foreshadowed by certain British writers who have surmised that productivity levels in manufacturing are about the same in Britain and Italy. Recently, Angus Maddison has estimated that output per man-hour is even 4 percent higher in Italy (in *The Economist*, October 22, 1966, p. 410 [P19]). However, it may be pointed out for readers who are skeptical of this finding that, unless the ratio of *total* national income in Italy to that in the United Kingdom is much overstated or the ratio of Italian to British *nonfarm* employment much understated, the conclusion is inescapable that in United States prices the levels of nonfarm national income per person must be fairly close. Impossibly large errors in the estimates of farm product would be required to invalidate the conclusion. Estimates given in Appendix L imply that *in United States prices* nonfarm product accounted for 98 percent of the national product in the United Kingdom and 94 percent in Italy, whereas 96 percent of British but only 68 percent of Italian employment was in nonagricultural activities. Doubts about the comparability of British and Italian employment data refer mainly to farm employment; changing the farm employment estimates would alter the all-industry but not the nonfarm comparison of output per man. This is in no way to deny, of course, that any such comparison is at best very crude and that it is affected by the price weights used. United States prices are not the most appropriate for the comparison of European countries.

35. It should be noted, however, that if technique in a European country is farther behind the United States in agriculture than in nonagricultural industries, this measure would ascribe (as does the measure that I shall actually use) the *extra* lag in agriculture to misallocation rather than to the lag in the application of knowledge. If such a differential does exist, it introduces a slight and unavoidable peculiarity to my classification of sources of difference in level of income per person employed.

36. The meaning of the percentages in Columns 5 and 4, for example the 10.2 and 6.9 percent figures for France, may be clearer if the calculation is based on the absolute numbers given above in the text. If the ratio of the all-industry figure (excluding income from dwellings and abroad) to the nonfarm industry figure had been the same in the United States as in France, the all-industry figure would have been $5,049. This is $575, or 10.2 percent, below the actual figure of $5,624. Also, if the ratio of the all-industry figure to the nonagricultural industry figure had been the same in France as in the United States, the all-industry figure in France would have been $3,773. The actual figure is $386 or 10.2 percent below this hypothetical figure. The 6.9 percent figure given in Column 4 is equal to the ratio of $386 to $5,624.

were the same in agriculture as in nonagricultural industries, is likely in general to overstate differences among countries in the cost of misallocation. In the United States, at least, the quantity of nonlabor input per person employed is larger in agriculture than in nonagriculture (after eliminating dwellings and international assets) but the quantity of labor input per person employed is smaller in agriculture.[37] The situation is probably the same in Northwest Europe.[38] Labor is the most important factor; and on balance it seems probable, though not certain, that total input per person employed is generally less in agriculture than in nonfarm industries. I have reworked the estimates on the assumption that total input (excluding dwellings and international assets) per person employed is 20 percent larger in nonfarm industries than in agriculture, except in Italy, and that in Italy it is 25 percent larger.[39] The reason for distinguishing Italy is the low ratio of capital to employment in Italian agriculture.[40] On the assumption stated, misallocation lowered national income per person employed more in Europe than in the United States by the amounts shown in Column 6, Table 16–12. The 8.0 percent estimate for France, for example, means that if everything else were the same in the two countries,

greater misallocation alone would have caused national income per person employed (excluding income from dwellings and international assets) to be 8.0 percent lower in France than in the United States.

I use Column 6 as my measure of the costs of misallocation. It indicates that the advances in output per man that could be achieved by transferring additional workers into nonfarm production vary greatly among countries. Belgium and the Netherlands had only the same cost and potential in 1960 as the United States, and the United Kingdom had even less.[41] In the remaining countries national income per person employed in United States prices was lower by amounts ranging from 4 to 8 percent in Denmark, France, Germany, and Norway than it would have been if misallocation costs had been the same as in the United States. The corresponding figure in Italy was 19 percent. These are rough estimates but they should rank the countries properly and give approximate orders of magnitude.[42]

In presenting these estimates I do not, of course, suggest that such gains could be secured overnight by reallocation; time is required for structural changes of these magnitudes to take place. It should also be noted that these estimates refer to national income per person employed. They can be applied to total and per capita national income only if total employment would be unaffected by a shift from agriculture to nonagricultural activities.

Overallocation to nonfarm self-employment is also relevant to the analysis of differences in income levels. Nonfarm proprietors, own-account workers, and unpaid family workers made up a larger proportion of 1960 civilian nonagricultural employment in all the European countries except the United Kingdom than in the United States.[43] Esti-

37. This statement disregards hours of work. In Chapter 6 the difference between farm and nonfarm activities in hours worked per year was not permitted to influence the measure of labor input.

38. In analyzing growth rates the effect of the labor that shifted from agriculture upon the stock of labor in nonfarm industries was the major concern; here, it is a comparison between the entire stock of farm labor and the stock of nonfarm labor.

39. These differentials are, I hope, generous enough to allow for another factor that may make the estimates in Column 5, Table 16–12, a bit too large as a measure of misallocation cost. The equal productivity assumption that was applied to general government and certain other employees in measuring national income per person receives greater weight in the nonagricultural indexes than in the all-industry indexes. The calculation assumes a shift from agriculture would raise government as well as private nonfarm employment, whereas it might be better to assume only private employment is affected. An attempt was made to measure the difference between Columns 2 and 3 after eliminating activities measured on the equal productivity assumption from both aggregates. The results differed from those given in Column 4 by 0.2 percentage points or less in five of the eight European countries. The maximum differences were 0.7 points in Italy and 0.9 in Denmark.

40. If the same percentage had been used for Italy as elsewhere, the figure given in Column 6, Table 16–12, would be 20.3 instead of 19.2. The Italian estimate is much the most sensitive (with respect to its absolute size) to changes in the percentage assumed.

41. The slight negative figure shown for the Netherlands reflects unusually large farm output in 1960. In most years the same calculation would yield a slight positive figure.

42. The ratio of farm net product prices to nonfarm net product prices is much higher in Europe than in the United States, except perhaps in Denmark and France. In the remaining countries potential gains in national income measured in *national* prices are therefore smaller than in United States prices.

43. Data for Norway and the United Kingdom were adjusted before they were used for level comparisons by transferring from the wage and salary category to the unpaid family worker category one person for each four employers and own-account workers. The adjustment and the reason for it is the same as that described in the time series analysis.

mates for each European country of the differential cost of underutilization and inefficient use of labor that are approximately consistent with those used in the time series analysis are obtained in the following manner. I first compute the number of workers who would have to be transferred to wage and salary status to reduce the ratio of nonfarm proprietors and own-account workers to total civilian nonagricultural employment to the United States level of 0.1145. Then, I calculate the excess cost of misallocation on the assumption that these workers contribute only one-fourth as much to national income in United States prices as they would if they were transferred to nonfarm wage and salary worker status and contributed as much as other workers in that status. The calculation assumes that (1) no misallocation of nonlabor factors is associated with this type of labor misallocation; and (2) if the workers transferred were as productive, on the average, as present nonfarm wage and salary workers, the loss of output from their departure from their present positions would be only one-fourth that large. (Other combinations of assumptions that would yield the same estimate could, of course, be devised.) The estimates of the cost of greater misallocation than was present in the United States, expressed as a percentage of total national income excluding property income from dwellings and abroad, are given in Column 2, Table 16–13.[44] As

TABLE 16–13

Prevalence and Estimated Cost of Greater Overallocation of Labor to Nonfarm Self-Employment in Europe than in the United States, 1960

Area	Self-employed and unpaid family workers as percentage of civilian nonagricultural employment (1)	Excess cost of overallocation as a percentage of own national income[a] (2)
United States	11.5	—
Northwest Europe		.4
Belgium	18.0	3.7
Denmark	15.4	2.0
France	16.6	2.7
Germany	12.7	.6
Netherlands	14.0	1.4
Norway[b]	16.7	2.8
United Kingdom[b]	7.0	−2.6
Italy	25.9	7.7

Source: See text for derivation.
a. National income, excluding income from dwellings and international assets, measured in United States prices.
b. Employment data adjusted; see note 9, p. 205.

an indication of the degree of sensitivity to a change in assumptions, it may be noted that the estimates would be reduced by one-third if the fraction of one-fourth used in the calculation were changed to one-half. Although I have couched this description in terms of aggregate income, the estimates refer to national income per person employed and would be applicable to total national income only if a reduction in the number of proprietors and family workers did not affect total nonfarm employment.

As shown in Table 16–13, I estimate that national income per person employed (excluding income from dwellings and abroad) in the continental countries of Northwest Europe is lower than it would

---

Without this adjustment the misallocation cost estimates in Column 2, Table 16–13, would be 1.0 for Norway and −3.4 for the United Kingdom.

44. The actual mechanics of the calculation may again be illustrated by the estimates for France (employment data are given in thousands, income aggregates in millions of dollars, and average incomes in dollars):

Civilian nonagricultural employment in France was 14,458, including 12,051 wage and salary workers and 2,407 proprietors and family workers. The latter group was 751 larger than it would have been if its ratio of civilian nonagricultural employment had been the same as in the United States.

Total nonfarm national income (excluding income from dwellings and abroad) of $60,495 was multiplied by the 1960–62 labor share (excluding income from dwellings and abroad) of 0.790 (Table 4–2) to obtain an estimate of nonfarm labor earnings (including military personnel) of $47,791. Divided by actual nonfarm employment (including military) of 15,298, this yields average nonfarm labor earnings of $3,124. This figure would, however, be higher in the absence of misallocation. An adjusted employment total of 14,735 was obtained by subtracting three-fourths of 751, or 563, from 15,298; this yields an adjusted employment total of 14,735 that counts the "extra" proprietors and fam-

ily workers as the equivalent in labor input of one-fourth of other nonfarm workers.

When $47,791 is divided by 14,735, an adjusted average of $3,243.4 is obtained that represents what average earnings in United States prices would have been with no greater misallocation than in the United States. Three-fourths of the product of this adjusted average earnings figure and the number transferred, 751, yields $1,827 as the total cost of greater underutilization than in the United States.

Actual national income (excluding income from dwellings and abroad) was $65,989 and would have been $1,827 higher, or $67,816 without excess underutilization. The figure $1,827 is 2.7 percent of $67,816; this is the percentage given in Table 16–13.

have been with the United States allocation by amounts ranging from 0.6 percent in Germany to 3.7 percent in Belgium. The cost in Italy is computed to be 7.7 percent. These percentages also represent the percentage by which the national income per person employed (excluding income from dwellings and abroad) of the European countries would have fallen below that of the United States if this were the only reason for a difference to arise.

Use of the same procedure for the United Kingdom, where proprietors and family workers comprised only 7.0 percent of nonfarm employment, yields an estimate that national income per person employed was 2.6 percent *higher* than it would have been with the United States allocation. This may be a bit of an overestimate (compared to the estimates for other countries) since the gains, per person, from transferring to wage and salary status may be less when the percentage of self-employed and family workers drops from 11.5 to 7.0 than when it drops from, say, 16.0 to 11.5; but even 7.0 percent seems sufficient to accommodate what I have earlier called the core group, so that any overstatement should not be large.

Table 16-14 summarizes the estimates of the costs of both types of misallocation and converts them to the form required in this study. The estimates of the cost of misallocation in the first two columns are based on Column 6, Table 16-12, and Column 2, Table 16-13, but are expressed as a percentage of total national income instead of national income less property income from dwellings and abroad. According to the estimates for France, for example, if everything else were the same in the two countries, total national income per person employed would be 7.7 percent lower in France than in the United States because of greater overallocation of resources to agriculture, and 2.6 percent lower because of greater waste of labor of nonfarm proprietors and family workers. French national income per person would, of course, be lower for other reasons so the contribution of misallocation to the difference in output levels is smaller. To estimate the amount of the difference from the United States due to misallocation of these types, the pseudo growth rate method that was applied in Chapter 15 was used. The results are given in Columns 3 to 5, Table 16-14.

TABLE 16-14

Contribution to Differences from the United States in National Income per Person Employed Made by Greater Overallocation to Agriculture and Nonfarm Self-Employment, 1960

(*Percentage of United States national income per person employed*)

| Area | Before interaction allowance | | After interaction allowance | | |
	Agriculture (1)	Nonfarm self-employment (2)	Agriculture (3)	Nonfarm self-employment (4)	Total (5)
N. W. Europe	—	—	2.3	.3	2.6
Belgium	.3	3.6	.2	2.7	2.9
Denmark	4.1	1.9	3.1	1.5	4.6
France	7.7	2.6	5.8	1.9	7.7
Germany	5.1	.6	3.7	.4	4.1
Netherlands	−.3	1.3	−.2	1.1	.9
Norway	7.6	2.7	6.1	2.1	8.2
U. K.	−1.6	−2.5	−1.1	−1.7	−2.8
Italy	18.8	7.5	12.3	4.6	16.9

Source: See text for derivation.

Misallocation and underutilization of resources in these two forms account for a difference between Northwest Europe as a whole and the United States in national income per person employed of 2.6 percent of United States national income per person employed, which is 6 percent of the total difference.

Misallocation and underutilization explain to a much larger extent why output per person in Denmark and Germany, and especially France and Norway, is below the United States. Differences among the Northwest European countries are very large—as much as 11 points between France and Norway, which are estimated to lose most from these types of misallocation, and the United Kingdom, which has less misallocation of these types than the United States.

The potential for France and Norway, and, to a lesser extent, Denmark and Germany, to improve their relative income position by further curtailment of misallocation and underutilization was still large in 1960. Belgium had little potential in agriculture but the largest potential among all the Northwest European countries to achieve gains by reducing nonfarm self-employment. This is indicated not only by its high proportion of self-employed but also by what is probably the largest number of retail outlets per capita among all the Northwest European countries.[45] The Netherlands had the least misallocation and smallest potential among the Northwest European countries.[46]

The estimates make the outlook for the United Kingdom appear gloomy indeed, in comparison with the large continental countries. In 1960 national income per person employed was as high as in the other Northwest European countries only because the United Kingdom had long since obtained almost all of the gains available from curtailing agricultural employment and self-employment. As shown in the first half of this chapter, postwar growth rates of the continental countries exceeded the British rate partly because they were eliminating a source of waste that the United Kingdom did not have. It seems certain that this source will continue to be a major influence toward higher growth rates in most continental countries, and toward opening a growing gap in national income per person employed between the United Kingdom and both France and Germany.

The question arises, of course, as to why the level of output per unit of input is not much higher in the United Kingdom than in France and Germany if the cost of misallocation of these types is so much smaller. Discussion of this difficult question will be deferred to Chapter 20.

The estimate for Italy presented in Table 16–14 shows that, in 1960, the types of misallocation discussed in this chapter were responsible for 16.9 points out of the total difference between the United States and Italy of 60.0 points in national income per person employed, and out of the 41.3 points contributed to this difference by output per unit of input. Thus, they account for over one-fourth of the difference between the two countries in national income per person employed and two-fifths of the difference in productivity. The estimates imply that were it not for the presence of a huge (in terms of resource use though not of output) and very unproductive agricultural sector and the fact that over one-fourth of all nonfarm employment consisted of the self-employed and unpaid family workers, output per unit of total input would have been very nearly as large in Italy as in Northwest Europe. Although comparisons of levels admittedly become difficult when differences are as great as those between Italy and the other countries, there can be little doubt that this is the principal reason for the low productivity position of Italy in comparison with Northwest Europe. Italy has a great potential to narrow gradually the gap in productivity as agricultural workers and the self-employed are drawn into nonagricultural wage and salary employment.

A final reminder should be given that the analysis of differences in 1960 output levels refers to national income in United States prices, whereas the contributions to growth rates refer to national income measured in national prices. In the continental countries, except perhaps Denmark and France, the transfer of labor from agriculture to nonagricultural employment contributes more to an increase in national income in United States prices than in national income in national prices. But the main points made, and relationships indicated, in this chapter would alter little if growth rates and levels were measured in the same prices.

45. According to the United Nations Economic Commission for Europe (ECE), around 1950 Belgium had 16.9 retail food establishments per 1,000 population as against 6.2 to 9.9 in the other Northwest European countries, and 18.3 retail nonfood establishments as against 4.6 to 9.3 in the other countries (*Economic Survey of Europe in 1955*, p. 134 [I13]). Belgian census data for the end of 1961 yield much lower figures (10.0 and 8.5 for food and nonfood, respectively) which may not be comparable to those used by ECE for its international comparisons. Numbers for the other countries declined over the decade.

46. The statement would remain true if calculations were based on a more normal year for the Netherlands. Unusually large farm production in 1960 is estimated in Chapter 19 to have elevated Dutch national income per person employed by 0.7 percent.

Gains from Economies of Scale

As the size of markets increased, gains from economies of scale were an important source of productivity advance in the countries covered in this study. No pretense is made that these gains can be measured precisely or without interjection of personal judgment. But if the estimates developed are at all near the mark, economies of scale go a long way toward explaining why differences among countries in growth rates of output per unit of input were as large as they were in the postwar period.

In this chapter estimates of gains from economies of scale are developed as the sum of three components. Section I opens the discussion by supposing growth rates in all countries were computed from real national product data that used United States price weights to combine output components. It then tries to appraise the economies of scale, whether internal or external, that growth of each country's domestic economy would have permitted in the absence of independent changes in the size of local markets or in barriers to international trade. The gains measured in this section are those that would appear if national product were measured in United States prices. Section II shows that European growth rates are usually higher when national products are measured in European prices (as they are)

than they would be if measured in United States prices. The differences between the two growth rates, I argue, result mainly from economies of scale, and measure a contribution of scale economies to European growth rates that is over and above the one arrived at in Section I. The size of this additional gain is not related to total national income but to the level and increase of per capita consumption. Section II, the only one of the three sections that is based on a systematic statistical procedure, makes much the largest contribution to an explanation of differences in growth rates. Sections I and II, of course, take into account the fact that growth of national income automatically meant growth in markets that are local and regional in character as well as those that are national in scope. Section III is concerned with the impact of population shifts and increased automobile ownership that changed the size of local markets independently of changes in the size of national economies.

Two topics that are closely related to economies of scale but depend on changes in the extent to which possibilities for efficient production are grasped rather than on economic limitations upon the size of markets are deferred to Chapter 18. One is gains in efficiency made possible by *reduction* of artificial barriers to international trade, a development that extends the geographic limits of national markets. The other is changes in the size of firms or establishments that are unrelated to changes in the size of the markets they serve. The present chapter deals with gains from economies of scale in the absence of changes in barriers to international trade. Also, it does not take account of the possibility that the distribution of firms and establishments by size may move closer to or farther from an optimum distribution *given* the size of markets to be served.

I. Economies of Scale Associated with Size of National Market, Product Valued in United States Prices

The growth of a national economy and the automatically associated changes in the average size of markets when they are cross-classified by product and geographic area give rise to gains from economies of scale if the economy is operating under increasing returns. I shall first examine this subject in the United States and then in the European context.

United States Growth

In my study of the sources of American economic growth, I assumed that in the 1929–57 period the United States economy as a whole operated under increasing returns to scale. Specifically, I assumed that a 1 percent increase in inputs, or gains from reallocation of resources or any other change that would have raised the national income by 1 percent under conditions of constant returns to scale, actually increased output by 1.1 percent. This meant that cost reductions resulting from economies of scale associated with the growth of the national market were credited with being the source of one-eleventh of the growth rate of national income.

The gains covered by this assumption were intended to embrace alike gains from economies of scale associated with the size of transactions, product runs, establishments, firms, industries, product markets, and the whole economy, insofar as changes in their size were due to changes in the size of markets that were in turn related to the size of the national economy. The estimate included gains from

economies of scale in products and activities serving local and regional markets insofar as the growth of these markets was associated with the growth of the national product. Indeed, since most income arises in serving local and regional markets, and since the national market was already so large in 1929, it is here that most gains probably occurred. But the assumption did not include the effects of independent changes in the *geographic area* embraced by local markets, which are discussed in Section III of this chapter. The assumption referred, of course, to growth under the conditions actually existing in the United States with respect to the composition of output, changes in the composition of output, and the size of establishments and firms.[1]

That in 1929–57 the United States operated under conditions in which scale economies increased by 10 percent the contribution to economic growth made by all other sources was strictly an assumption. It was not based on any independent statistical investigation. I had examined the results of various studies but noted that these studies had been unable to isolate at all satisfactorily scale effects in the economy as a whole. My assumption was merely an attempt to set down a figure that was at the same time what might be termed a qualitative weighted average of views expressed by other economists and a figure that seemed reasonable to me. Gains from specialization and dealing in larger units (longer products runs, larger transactions, and so on) provide clear reason to expect increasing returns, and examples of increasing returns appear plentiful.[2] There seem to be no significant offsets. Individual

1. A special word may be needed about the implied treatment of transportation. Transportation industries, like other industries, may be subject to increasing returns from scale and these gains are intended to be included in this assumption. Transportation costs may also be reduced by advances in technology, investment, elimination of legal or union provisions requiring overmanning, or numerous other developments in the transportation industries and their supplying industries. Reduction of transportation costs from such causes may allow transport-using industries to serve wider markets and thus lead to apparent gains from economies of scale *in these industries.* From the standpoint of the *economy as a whole,* however, increases in national income resulting from advances of knowledge, investment, the elimination of obstacles to the most efficient use of resources, and the like, in transportation should be credited to these separate sources, not to scale economies; and that is my intent.

2. The literature discussing the reasons to expect gains from economies of scale, and examples, is abundant. Bela Balassa (*The Theory of Economic Integration,* Chapters 5–7 [B5]) has provided an adequate general review of this

establishments and firms can become too large for efficiency, but their number can be multiplied without limit. With land counted as an input, reasons to expect decreasing returns in an economy as a whole or even for a product, and significant examples of products produced under conditions of decreasing returns, are almost entirely lacking. While the figure of 10 percent was arbitrary, it did appear to me that the correct percentage must exceed zero by an appreciable amount. No upper limit can be stated short of a much-too-large figure (41 percent on the basis of the 1929–57 estimates given in the *Sources of Economic Growth*) that would ascribe to scale economies all of what I have estimated to be the contribution of "advances of knowledge," in addition to my estimate of scale economies. But I think it safe to say most economists believe that in the United States the number can hardly be higher than, say, 20 percent at the outside. Larger gains for certain capital costs are, to be sure, sometimes considered reasonable.[3] But when econometric studies imply larger reductions in total costs, even for large sectors of the United States economy such as manufacturing, most economists reject them as unreasonable.[4]

A second question concerned the relationship be-

tween the size already attained by the United States economy at a point in time and further gains from economies of scale: Does the percentage by which gains from economies of scale amplify the effect of other sources of growth on national income change as an economy becomes bigger?

I accepted the view that percentage gains from economies of scale would diminish as the size of the national market increases if technological and managerial knowledge did not change. From studies like that of J. S. Bain it appeared that further gains from *internal* economies of scale decline as the size of an establishment or firm increases.[5] It seemed

---

literature. His, and other, discussions of the types of economies of scale and the reasons for believing them to be important make unnecessary such a review on my part. A sampling of views concerning the nature and importance of economies of scale can be found in E. A. G. Robinson (ed.), *Economic Consequences of the Size of Nations* [B93].

3. I refer particularly to the literature pertaining to the ".6 rule" which states that the increase in capital cost is given by the increase in capacity raised to the 0.6 power. See, for example, Moore in *Quarterly Journal of Economics*, May 1959, pp. 232–45 [P34].

4. An exception is Romesh K. Diwan who accepts a figure of 29 percent that he obtained for the nonfarm sector in the United States (in *Economica*, November 1966, pp. 450–52 [P18]).

Studies based on international comparison of industries also have sometimes yielded larger results. For example, George J. Stigler (in *Output, Input and Productivity Measurement*, pp. 47–63 [B103]) arrived at an estimate of 34 percent for manufacturing based on a comparison of the United States and the United Kingdom. I noted in my American study that "(partly because of data problems) the result was not considered acceptable by other students nor, it appeared, defended very seriously by Stigler himself, who refers to it as 'embarrassingly large.' I believe, in fact, it is untenably large" (*Sources of Economic Growth*, p. 181 [B25]).

It now appears to me that there is a question as to what the result means, in addition to questions concerning its reliability. The Paige-Bombach estimates of comparisons of output in 1950 may be used to illustrate the point (Stigler

himself used Marvin Frankel's data for 1947–48). Paige and Bombach found that in manufacturing, GNP per worker in the United States was 292 percent of British GNP per worker when output is valued in United Kingdom prices and 256 percent when it is valued in United States prices (OEEC, *A Comparison of National Output and Productivity of the United Kingdom and the United States* [I22]). If, in manufacturing, capital and land together were 2.5 times as large per worker in the United States as in Britain, and they are given a 0.3 weight and employment were given a 0.7 weight, British output per unit of input (unadjusted for quality differences in inputs) was 50 percent of United States output per unit of input in British prices but 57 percent in United States prices. Stigler's results imply that British output per unit of input would be 34 percent larger if British manufacturing industries were as large as American industries, but would this apply to output valued in United States or British prices? Suppose it applies to output valued in British prices and suppose also (as I shall argue in the following section to be largely the case), the difference between output comparisons based on the two sets of weights is itself associated with economies of scale. Then the 34 percent increase in total factor productivity measured in British prices that would be obtained if British manufacturing were as large as American would raise output per unit from 50 to 67 percent of the American figure, but this includes the difference between the two measures. The increase in American prices would be from 57 to 67 percent of the American figure—an increase of only 17.5 percent. In that case, the 34 percent figure, even if correct, would be inappropriate for an appraisal of the gains from economies of scale in manufacturing that occur with growth of United States manufacturing (with output valued in United States prices).

5. Bain, *Barriers to New Competition: Their Character and Consequences in Manufacturing Industries* [B3]. However, reference should be made to an as yet unpublished econometric study by Zvi Griliches which obtains the surprising and apparently conflicting result that among manufacturing establishments there are no economies of scale *internal to the establishment* until establishments reach the size of about 250 employees, but thereafter increasing returns become sizable (about 9 percent) and are roughly constant with increasing size, except that the data are not good enough to indicate whether this rate decreases for very large sizes. Griliches does caution that difficulties of placing a value on family labor in the very small establishments may influence the results ("Production Functions in Manufacturing: Some Preliminary Results," paper presented to the Conference on Research in Income and Wealth, October 15–16, 1965 [B44]).

likely that gains from *external* economies would also have a tendency to decline as scale increases or at the least would not rise so as to provide an offset. But I also accepted the view that as markets and the scale of output grow, technology and business organization develop in such a way as to adapt themselves to the new situation and opportunities for scale economies are constantly replenished. My specific assumption was that the latter tendency did not quite offset the former, and that whereas economies of scale added 10 percent to national income growth in 1929–57, the corresponding figure in 1909–29 was 11 percent and in 1960–80 it would be 9. These differences were merely intended to give quantitative recognition to the qualitative judgment just expressed.

Studies implying estimates of the importance of economies of scale in the United States have continued to be made, but none that I have seen either provides a firmer underpinning for, or would cause me to change, the assumptions adopted in my American study.[6] I shall suppose that in 1950–62 econo-

6. The papers presented by Zvi Griliches and Marc L. Nerlove to the Conference on Research in Income and Wealth, October 15–16, 1965, provide a comprehensive review of "production function" studies.
Balassa (in *The Theory of Economic Integration* [B5]) reviews various studies that have tried to appraise the relationship between scale and efficiency. In addition to appraisals like Bain's that are based on study of plant and firm size in individual industries, these include international comparisons and time series analyses of individual industries within a country. The latter have rather consistently shown a pronounced tendency for long-term changes in total production and in productivity (and usually in employment as well) to be positively correlated. Balassa cites particularly P. J. Verdoorn, Colin Clark, and an article by John W. Kendrick. To the studies Balassa cites, the following at least should be added: Kendrick's book (*Productivity Trends in the United States* [B57]) in which he worked independently with two industrial classifications (a 33-way breakdown of most of the private economy, and an 80-way breakdown of manufacturing); W. E. G. Salter's studies of British and American manufacturing, mining, and public utilities (*Productivity and Technical Change* [B95]); Solomon Fabricant's study of fifty-one American manufacturing industries (*Employment in Manufacturing, 1899–1939* [B32]); and Victor Fuchs' study of time series for seventeen United States retail trade and service industries (in *Review of Income and Wealth*, September 1966, pp. 211–44 [S10]). The international comparisons are mainly confined to United Kingdom and United States manufacturing data, although the Paige-Bombach data have permitted broader industry coverage. Reference should be made, too, to the international comparison of retail trade lines by Margaret Hall and John Knapp (in *Economic Journal*, March 1955, pp. 72–78 [P17]). All these studies show a decided association between changes or differences in productivity and changes or differences in total output.

mies of scale associated with the growth of the national economy added 10 percent to the contribution of all other factors to the United States growth rate, and were therefore the source of one-eleventh of the total growth rate.[7]

European Growth

I should like, of course, to use assumptions for the European countries consistent with the one used for the United States. These are not easy to establish, and I approach the problem in two stages. I defer to Section II consideration of the large complication introduced by the fact that relative prices of products and the composition of national product by type of expenditure differ among countries, and proceed in the present section as if relative prices and quantities were the same in Europe as in the United States. Discussion here can then proceed as if the distribution of total national income among final products was the same in all countries so that if country A has half the national income of country B, it spends half as much on each product.

Other things being equal, the larger the size of existing markets the smaller, presumably, are gains from economies of scale as markets expand. How much larger are American markets than European markets? It would be absurd, of course, to suppose that if the American national product is 4.5 times as large as that of Germany, for example, the average American product market is also 4.5 times as large, and that one can consider economies of scale as if that were the case. The size of few markets coincides with national borders. The situation is not parallel to that of changes over time within the borders of a country. A doubling of the size of American national product from 1929 to 1953 could be taken, as a first approximation, to mean that the average size of markets for individual products within individual marketing areas doubled. No similar assumption is possible in international com-

A study for the United Kingdom similar to Bain's is now being undertaken by the University of Cambridge Department of Applied Economics. Results for four industries are given in Pratten and Dean, *The Economics of Large-Scale Production in British Industry: An Introductory Study* [B89].
7. Literal adherence to the assumptions of the *Sources of Economic Growth* would imply a figure a trifle below one-eleventh for the 1950–62 period.

parisons. Geography is at least as favorable to large markets in Western Europe (including countries not analyzed in this study) as in North America (defined, say, to include the United States and Canada). In Western Europe comparable productive resources and output are concentrated within a smaller territory. Only insofar as the division of Western Europe into many countries affects marketing patterns may one expect European markets to be appreciably smaller than American markets so that percentage gains from economies of scale with the increase of markets may be greater.

TYPES OF PRODUCTS OR INDUSTRIES. To proceed further, it is useful to distinguish three or four types of products or industries.

1. In industries where output is measured by input, economies of scale do not contribute at all to growth rates of, or international differences in, national income as measured. The contribution of economies of scale is the same (nothing) in all countries. In the United States these industries accounted for about 12 percent of GNP and more than that of national income in 1950; the percentages increased in later years.[8]

2. A great deal of production is for markets limited to a local area. The size of local markets is not related to the size of countries but instead depends on such factors as population density and local transportation. There is no reason to suppose local markets are bigger in large countries than in small countries—in the United States than in France, or in France than in Holland—just because the national markets are bigger. The higher level of per capita income in the United States than in Northwest Europe (and in Northwest Europe than in Italy) would tend to cause the size of local markets to be larger if population density and other relevant factors were equal, but population density is greater in Europe (except Norway). Detailed international comparisons of the size of local markets cannot be attempted in the present study.[9] The gen-

eral situation seems to be that the proportion of the population living in urban areas with a population of 100,000 or more is much larger in the United States than in Europe except for the United Kingdom, but the remainder of the United States population is much more widely dispersed geographically than the remainder of the European populations with the exception of Norway (Table 17–1). There is no particular correspondence between total population and population density or population concentration. It seems a reasonable first approximation to suppose that productivity in industries serving local markets does not vary among the countries in this study because of differences in the size of local markets. (See, however, the discussion of automobile ownership in Section III.) If it does vary, it is not because of differences in total national products. Norway probably is actually at a disadvantage in this respect, not because it has the smallest population and national income among the countries covered but because its population is most dispersed.

Even industries producing for local markets no doubt gain something from economies of scale that

kets of three sizes ranging downward from class A to class C (many more classes would presumably be required in practice) and that the distribution of sales among them in two countries is known. Suppose also that among industries supplying local markets the importance of economies of scale is such that if output per unit of input in class A markets is taken as 100, it would be 97 in class B markets and 93 in class C markets. An index could then be computed as follows:

Size of market	Percentage of business		Economies of scale index	Products		
	In country A	In country B		Columns (2) × (4)	Columns (3) × (4)	Ratio of Columns (5) to (6)
(1)	(2)	(3)	(4)	(5)	(6)	(7)
Class A	50	30	100	50.0	30.0	—
Class B	30	40	97	29.1	38.8	—
Class C	20	30	93	18.6	27.9	—
Total	100	100		97.7	96.7	1.010

One could then say that the size of local markets was 1 percent more favorable to productivity in industries supplying local markets in country A than in country B.

An actual study would, of course, encounter great difficulties in setting boundaries for marketing areas, which usually overlap; it would require weights corresponding to Column (4); and it would have to take into account that in some industries, such as assemblers of farm products, the availability of local supplies or suppliers is more important than that of local buyers.

8. European percentages of GNP, which were higher than the percentage in the United States, are given in Table 3–1.

9. I have not tried to define an appropriate summary measure of the size of local markets precisely, but it would clearly require not only some way of delimiting market areas but also knowledge of the importance of economies of scale for weights. Given complete information a measure might be computed somewhat as follows. Suppose that there are mar-

TABLE 17–1

Population: Density and Percentage Distribution by Size of Community, 1960[a]

Population density	United States	North-west Europe	Bel-gium	Den-mark	France	Ger-many	Nether-lands	Nor-way	United King-dom	Italy
Total (in thousands)	180,684	182,462	9,154	4,581	45,685	55,433	11,486	3,585	52,539	49,642
Population per square mile	50[b]	320	777	276	215	578	888	29	558	427
Percentage Distribution[a]										
Total	100.0	100.0	100.0	100.0	100.0	100.0	100.0	100.0	100.0	100.0
Urban agglomerations of 100,000 or more	50.7	39.4	28.6	32.0	34.6	37.5	35.6	20.3	49.9	24.9
500,000 or more	37.6	25.7	18.1	27.5	19.5	23.4	21.2	16.1	36.5	14.5
100,000–500,000	13.1	13.6	11.5	4.5	15.1	14.1	14.4	4.2	13.4	10.4
Other urban	19.2	n.a.	36.8	39.9	28.4	n.a.	44.4	36.9	28.3	22.8
Rural	30.1	n.a.	33.6	25.9	37.0	n.a.	20.0	42.9	21.7	52.3

Sources: United Nations, *Demographic Yearbook 1964* [I1]; OECD, *Manpower Statistics, 1954–1964* [I32]; United Kingdom: Central Statistical Office, *Annual Abstract of Statistics, 1964* [G36]; OSCE, *Basic Statistics for Fifteen Countries: Comparison with the United States and the Union of Soviet Socialist Republics* [I51]; Belgium: National Institute of Statistics, unpublished data, November 1965.
a. Percentage distributions are for the census years nearest to 1960; Belgium, Germany, United Kingdom, and Italy: 1961; France: 1962; other countries: 1960.
b. Sixty if Alaska and Hawaii are excluded.
n.a. Not available.

depend on the size of national markets as distinct from local, regional, and international markets. Such gains would probably be mainly from external economies, but may even include economies of scale internal to the firm (as distinct from the establishment) since some firms whose establishments serve only local markets operate on a national but not an international basis. It is difficult to believe, however, that these gains can be at once important enough and sensitive enough to the size of the country to introduce appreciable differences in productivity advances among countries.

In short, there is little reason to suppose that in industries serving local markets economies of scale permit a much larger addition to the output gains (measured in United States prices) that would be attained under constant returns to scale in large countries than in small (and I have no satisfactory way to distinguish countries on the basis of other characteristics). This conclusion does not rest on any supposition that economies of scale are less important in industries serving local markets than in industries serving wider markets, or that further gains do not decline as markets increase in size, but on the belief that the size of local markets is not related to the size of national markets in interspatial comparisons. This situation contrasts sharply with

that within a country; when its national economy grows, the size of local markets automatically increases.

Production for local markets may be about as large as combined production for markets covering broad regions, nations, groups of nations, and the world. At least, when the experiment was made of classifying broad industries in the United States in 1960 in local and nonlocal groups in accordance with what seemed to be their main characteristics, national income originating in the local group was almost as large as that originating in the other group.[10]

10. From the classification of the Office of Business Economics, I classified in the regional, national, and international group all of the twenty-eight industry groups in the divisions "agriculture, forestry, and fisheries," "mining," and "manufacturing"; all in the "transportation" division except "local and highway passenger transportation"; three industries—"security and commodity brokers, dealers and exchanges," "finance, n.e.c. [not elsewhere classified]," and "insurance carriers"—in the "finance, insurance and real estate" division; two industries—"hotels and other lodging places," and "engineering and other professional services, n.e.c.," in the "services" division; and "federal-government enterprises." I classified in the local group all industries in the divisions "contract construction," "wholesale and retail trade," and "communications and public utilities"; all industries not classified in the nonlocal group in the "finance, insurance, and real estate," and "transportation" divisions; all industries in the "services" division that were not classified in the nonlocal group except "private households," "educational services, n.e.c.," "nonprofit membership organiza-

3. Probably something over two-fifths of United States national income originates in industries where establishments serve regional, national, or international markets. These types of industries or products fall into two groups:

(a) Much of this production—but even a guess at the proportion is absent—is contributed by establishments (and, in most such cases, firms) that, though selling well beyond the limits of a local area, supply regional markets no larger than the markets provided within the borders of the large European countries or even the small countries. Similarly, there must be many such establishments and firms in France or Germany that supply regional markets no larger than are provided by the national markets of Denmark or Holland.

(b) The final group of industries serves national or international markets. If the size of nations creates a difference among the countries in gains from economies of scale that are reflected in the growth rates of national income measured in United States prices, the difference ought to be concentrated in industries that serve national or international markets. These are mainly commodity-producing industries. Comparisons of the size of countries in 1960 based on total national income and on total inputs are given in Table 17–2. As measured by total inputs the United States was three times as large as Germany, and Germany in turn was sixteen times as large as Norway. Differences between the United States and the European countries in total national income were still greater. Such ratios, however, greatly exceed typical or average differences among countries in the relative sizes of the product markets that industries in this group serve.

SIGNIFICANCE OF NATIONAL BOUNDARIES. Even for products that sell in national markets in some or all European countries, and for which these national

TABLE 17–2

Size of National Income and Total Input, and Importance of Foreign Commerce

Country	Total national income as a percentage of total U. S. income, 1960[a] (1)	Total input as a percentage of total U. S. input, 1960 (2)	Foreign trade as a percentage of GNP (1957–59 average)[b]		
			Imports plus exports (3)	Imports (4)	Exports (5)
United States	100.0	100.0	9	5	5
Large European countries					
Germany[c]	22.3	32.8	36	17	20
United Kingdom	21.0	32.1	42	21	21
France	16.7	25.1	27	14	13
Italy	11.9	23.7	28	14	14
Simple average	18.0	28.4	34	16	17
Small European countries					
Netherlands	3.9	5.9	95	47	48
Belgium	3.1	4.6	63	31	32
Denmark	1.8	2.7	67	33	34
Norway	1.3	2.0	86	43	42
Simple average	2.5	3.8	78	38	39

Sources: Column (1): Table 2–4; Column (2): computed from Tables 5–1 and 15–6; Columns (3)–(5): see Appendix N for derivation.
a. Comparisons based on national income measured in United States prices.
b. Imports and exports of goods and services exclude factor income. Percentages are based on data in national prices.
c. Original trade data adjusted by application of 1960 ratios to include the Saar and West Berlin.

markets are insufficient to exhaust scale economies, much of the significance of the size of a national economy depends on the presence of artificial barriers to commerce that crosses national boundaries. To be sure, borders do have some tendency to restrict both product markets and the size of firms even in the absence of artificial economic barriers. Differences in national tastes, laws, and customs make it more expensive to market the same volume in two or three countries than in one. Language differences intensify difficulties, although these do not always conform to national boundaries. There are even a few products for which national boundaries automatically limit a product; Canadian news broadcasts are excellent but inappropriate, as a steady diet, for American listeners. National frontiers also impose a certain barrier to the expansion of firms, although when the gains are important it is very often surmounted in Europe. But it is artificial barriers that presumably are most important.

---

tions, n.e.c.," and the hospital portion of "medical and other health services"; and "state and local-government enterprises." (Industries classified in neither group are those where output is measured by input.) Some of my classification decisions might be questioned. In any case the industrial classification used is so broad that many activities classified in the local group clearly serve primarily regional, national, and international markets while many activities classified in the nonlocal group actually depend on local markets. The offsets need not be of the same size. The exercise was intended only to provide a rough "feel" for relative weights.

Only if a large and a small country impose equal obstacles to international trade can it be reasonably certain that the level of productivity in the small country will suffer from its size, and that the small country will gain more from an expansion of the domestic market than the large one. As between two countries of the same size, productivity in the country with the greater trade barriers must be expected to gain more from an expansion of the domestic economy.

These obvious points are important because it cannot be assumed that the level of protection is independent of the size of the country. Small countries offset the disadvantage of small size (which usually is accompanied by a lack of diversity in natural resources) by greater recourse to international trade. Countries sacrifice efficiency to protect domestic interests but not without limit.

Appraisals of the level of European tariffs on industrial products in 1958, just prior to the formation of the European Economic Community (EEC) and the European Free Trade Association (EFTA), suggest that the United Kingdom, Italy, and France had the highest levels of protection. They were followed by Norway; then by West Germany, Belgium, and the Netherlands, all at about the same level; and finally, by Denmark with the lowest tariffs in Europe.[11] (The position of Belgium and the Netherlands is based on Benelux tariffs; the absence of tariffs on trade *within* Benelux should also be taken into account.) Except that German tariffs were rather low (prior to 1956 they had not been), tariffs in the large countries exceeded those in the small countries.

Table 17–2 ranks the countries by size of total national income and total inputs in 1960 and shows their total imports, exports, and the two combined as a percentage of GNP in 1957–59, about the middle of the 1955–62 period.[12] The percentages, as expected, are much larger in all the small European countries (for imports plus exports, 63 to 95; average, 78) than in any of the large ones (27 to 42; average, 34), and the latter are much higher than the United States percentage (9). Thus, there is a strong tendency among these countries for small size to be partly compensated for by greater participation in international trade.[13] The comparisons would not differ enough to alter this statement if other years were substituted for 1957–59.

The small countries do not attempt to match the range of products produced by the large countries. They meet a larger proportion of domestic requirements by imports and their exports tend to be more concentrated in a limited number of detailed products.[14] The importance of this offset to small size is clearly very great. Foreign trade is concentrated in products for which the gains from international trade, including the gains from economies of scale, are largest. Protection is avoided on products where it would impose a very large cost.

Finally, it should be noted that even for products whose markets are regional, national, or international in scope, part of the gains from economies of scale are associated with the size of the local economy. The specialized services available in a large metropolis are often factors in determining the location of establishments. Large metropolitan areas like London, New York, and Paris act as magnets for more reasons than their cultural attractions.

The preceding discussion leads me to conclude that if 10 percent is used as the estimate of gains in national income from economies of scale when the national market grows in the United States, then a percentage above but not greatly above 10 percent for the European countries should be used as an estimate of the gains they would obtain if the composition of their output were the same as in the United States and their national incomes were valued in United States prices.

11. See, for example, J. A. Wartna in OSCE, *Statistical Information*, No. 2, 1966, pp. 11–54 [I49]; R. Bertrand in *Cahiers de l'ISEA*, Series R, February 1958, p. 10 [P10]; and the discussion by Lawrence B. Krause in a forthcoming Brookings publication [B62].

12. These percentages are not adjusted to eliminate imported raw materials and components used in the production of products for export. For this reason they cannot be used to judge the importance of industries producing for international markets in the economy of a country.

13. The tendency is not powerful enough to yield a regular relationship between size and foreign commerce *within* the groups of large and small European countries. Size differences within these groups are less pronounced than between groups, and are overborne by differences in diversity of natural resources, protection, location, and other factors.

14. Even calculations based on a broad 3-digit (150-group) classification show three of the four small countries have a greater commodity concentration of exports than any of the five large ones. The exception is the Netherlands (see Michaely, *Concentration in International Trade*, p. 12 [B76]).

I shall make the specific assumption that during the 1950–62 period the countries were operating under increasing returns to scale such that a 1 percent increase in total inputs or any other change (except a change in scale economies themselves) that would yield a 1 percent increase in national income (valued in United States prices) under constant returns to scale, actually increased national income (valued in United States prices) by 1.10 percent in the United States, 1.11 percent in the large Northwest European countries, 1.115 percent in Italy (which had a smaller national income and rather high level of protection), 1.12 percent in the small European countries except Norway, and 1.13 percent in Norway.[15] It has not seemed necessary to make a distinction either among the large or among the small Northwest European countries except in the case of Norway. Norway has the smallest total national income and total inputs, had the highest level of tariff protection among the small countries, and has by far the lowest population density and (by implication) smallest local markets; it seemed desirable to recognize these circumstances. In principle, larger allowances are called for in 1950–55 than in 1955–62 because economies were smaller and the level of trade barriers greater, but such a refinement seems unwarranted.

The assumption implies that gains in national income in United States prices from economies of scale as an economy grows are 10 percent larger in the big Northwest European countries than in the United States, 15 percent larger in Italy, 20 percent larger in Belgium, Denmark, and the Netherlands, and 30 percent larger in Norway. These refer, of course, to the economies of these countries as a whole. It implies that differences are much bigger in branches of these economies producing for markets that differ significantly in size among the countries. I do not, therefore, think the differences should necessarily be regarded as conservative. On the other hand, estimates of the contribution of this source to the growth rate would in no case be changed as much as one-tenth of a percentage point if economies of scale were assumed to amount to

15. It must be remembered that these estimates do *not* include gains from relaxing international trade barriers, including European integration, which are discussed in Chapter 18.

TABLE 17–3

Economies of Scale Associated with Size of National Market: Contributions to Growth Rates of Total National Income and to Differences from the United States in National Income per Person Employed

(*In United States prices*)

Area	Contribution to growth rate of national income (percentage points)			Contribution to difference from United States in national income per person employed, 1960 (index points)	
	1950 –62 (1)	1950 –55 (2)	1955 –62 (3)	Before allowance for interaction (4)	After allowance for interaction (5)
U. S.	.30	.38	.24	—	—
N. W. Europe	.41	.47	.37	4.1	3.0
Belgium	.33	.36	.32	5.0	3.9
Denmark	.35	.20	.47	5.0	3.8
France	.44	.42	.45	4.0	2.9
Germany	.63	.86	.46	4.0	2.8
Netherlands	.48	.64	.37	5.0	3.9
Norway	.38	.44	.35	5.5	4.2
U. K.	.22	.23	.21	4.0	2.8
Italy	.55	.62	.51	4.5	2.7

Source: See text for derivation.

10 percent in all of the countries regardless of their size.

Columns 1 to 3, Table 17–3, show the resulting estimates of the contributions of "economies of scale associated with the growth of the national economy" to the growth rate of national income *measured in United States prices*. They are computed by multiplying the growth rate of national income measured in United States prices by 0.10/1.10 for the United States, 0.11/1.11 for the large Northwest European countries, 0.115/1.115 for Italy, 0.12/1.12 for Belgium, Denmark, and the Netherlands, and 0.13/1.13 for Norway.[16]

16. To be precise, the growth rates to which these fractions are applied are the growth rates in each country's own prices as given in Table 15–3 minus the contributions of economies of scale associated with income elasticities of consumption goods as given in Table 17–7 below. This means that only consumption is reweighted in United States prices in the series used. Use here of series based on United States prices permits the estimates derived in Tables 17–3 and 17–7 to be added.

Level of National Income per Person Employed

To what extent were international differences in the levels of national income per person employed (measured in United States prices) in 1960 due to differences in the size of markets served by producers? Only an attempt to arrive at orders of magnitude based on combining some rational guesses is possible. Suppose, for example, that three-fourths of production in the United States and Germany is in industries that (1) are measured on the equal productivity assumption or (2) typically serve markets—local, regional, or international—that are similar in size in the United States and Germany. Suppose, also, that in the latter industries any German advantage from greater population density and any American advantage from external economies associated with the size of the country, as such, are small and offsetting. Suppose that in the remaining one-quarter of the economy, differences in the size of markets due to the size of the country, and not offset by international trade, were sufficient to make real unit costs in Germany 20 percent higher than in the United States if all other determinants were equal. Economies of scale would then suffice to make output per unit of input in the economy as a whole (with output valued at United States prices) about 4 percent lower in Germany than in the United States. These suppositions cannot be confirmed or contradicted in the present state of ignorance and so can be juggled a good deal. For example, one-third rather than one-fourth of the economy might be assumed to be affected by differences in market size, and the cost differential between the two countries put at 25 instead of 20 percent. This would change the result from about 4 to 6.6 percent. However, somewhere around 4 percent of the United States figure seems to me to be a reasonable guess—and it is a guess—as to the effect of size of country on output per man in comparing the United States and the large Northwest European countries.

This factor, I surmise, is much less important in creating differences between the large and small European countries because international trade should prevent differences in unit costs in the relevant part of the economy from being nearly so large. There is an additional reason for believing that the small European countries do not suffer a great deal more than the large European countries from diseconomies of scale. If, as the size of countries declined, unit costs for the economy as a whole increased at a sharply increasing rate, national income per unit of input would be a great deal lower in the small European countries than in the large ones.[17] It was found in Chapter 15 that this is not the case, except that productivity in Norway, the smallest country, is somewhat lower than elsewhere. In a study of the sources of difference in national income per person employed I hesitate to use this line of argument but the facts, which of course have not gone unobserved by others, can hardly be ignored.

I shall assume that if there were no other reasons for differences, economies of scale associated with the size of the national market would have caused national income in United States prices, per unit of input and therefore per person employed, to be lower than in the United States by 4.0 percent in France, Germany, and the United Kingdom, 4.5 percent in Italy, 5.0 percent in Belgium, Denmark, and the Netherlands, and 5.5 percent in Norway. These are the estimates given in Column 4, Table 17–3.[18] These estimates are converted, in Column 5, to estimates of the contribution of economies of scale associated with the size of the national market to differences in the level of national income per person employed. The procedure, based on the use of pseudo growth rates, is identical to that followed in the derivation of Table 15–8.

The assumptions underlying these estimates do not take into account the probability that a larger economy tends to be more competitive than a smaller economy that is protected from outside

17. D. S. Pearson compared per capita national income with the size of population, land area, and population density in seventy countries and found no statistical relationship between size and per capita income. He does not find this surprising, however, in view of the diversity of the countries in other respects (in *Economic Development and Cultural Change*, July 1965, pp. 472–78 [P16]). The European countries are much more homogeneous than the countries Pearson compared.

18. The reason for isolating Italy and Norway are those stated in setting differential effects on growth rates (see p. 233). It may be useful to point out again why these percentages bear no direct relationship to those used in analyzing growth rates. Doubling the national income of a country within fixed boundaries about doubles the average size of markets within a country. But if the United States has a national income 32 times that of Belgium it does not mean markets on the average are 32 times as large.

competition, and that firms subjected to greater competitive pressure may be driven to adopt more efficient methods. But size is only one influence on the strength of competition within a country and it would be idle even to speculate here about its separate impact.

All the estimates in this section are no more than what I hope are rational guesses. But such guesses cannot be avoided until some satisfactory basis for estimation is devised.

II. Price Weights and Changing Consumption Patterns

Growth rates of different countries might be regarded as not comparable to one another because the weights used to combine different product components to obtain the national product are not the same. In a comparative study such as this, all growth rates might be based on national product estimates that are recomputed with the use of a uniform set of price weights before analysis of the sources of growth is begun. In this section I estimate that if in all countries consumption, which comprises most of net product, were uniformly valued in United States prices, European growth rates would be reduced by amounts that range from 0.1 percentage points in Belgium, Norway, and the United Kingdom to 0.5 points in France, 0.6 in Italy, and 0.9 in Germany over the 1950–62 period as a whole. The amounts differ sharply between the two subperiods in most countries.

The reader who prefers to do so may interpret this section simply as an attempt to estimate these adjustments. However, I shall argue that the amounts of the adjustments are not random statistics but have significance in themselves. They measure a contribution of economies of scale to the growth rates of the national products of the European countries that appears when their products are weighted by their own prices but not when products are weighted by United States prices.

The Argument Summarized

As per capita income and consumption increased sharply in Europe and moved closer to the Ameri-

can level, consumption and production of products for which consumer demand is particularly responsive to changes in income increased much more than total consumption, while consumption and production of products with low income elasticity increased much less than total consumption. In Europe income-elastic products are produced in quantities that fall much farther below American quantities than does the average quantity of all products. They also sell at prices that are much higher, compared to the average price of all consumer goods and services, than they do in the United States. The reverse is true of products with low income elasticity. Because of their higher relative prices in Europe the fast-growing, income-elastic products receive greater weight, per unit, in the measurement of national product in Europe than they do in the United States. Similarly, the slow-growing products with low income elasticity receive less weight in Europe. Consequently, total consumption in most European countries increased much more measured in their own prices than it would if United States prices were used to value its components.

The probable importance of this point was brought to my attention by the estimates and analysis of Gilbert and Associates for 1950. When they compared per capita consumption of the nine countries under review, these authors found the gap between the United States and each of the European countries to be larger when the comparison was based on European prices than on American prices. The statistical reason that the position of each country appears better when the other country's price weights are used is, of course, that small per capita consumption of a product and high relative prices usually go together. The differences were large. For example, per capita consumption of the United States exceeded that of Germany by 256 percent based on German prices and by 144 percent based on American prices. If American consumption had not changed, German per capita consumption would have had to increase by 256 percent in German prices but by only 144 percent in American prices to catch up to the United States. Moreover, as will be shown below, the larger the gap between per capita consumption in the United States and in a European country, the more the results of comparisons based on United States and national European price weights usually differed from one another. This meant that the greater the gap in per capita consumption between the United States and a European country the greater was the difference in consumption patterns and price relationships. It suggested that as European countries closed the gap with the United States the two measures would, in fact, converge. This implied that growth rates of the fast-growing countries would be much reduced if United States price weights were substituted for European price weights in the measurement of consumption.

Gilbert and Associates' own analysis of their data showed that consumption patterns differ mainly because of differences in (1) income level and (2) relative prices, and not to any comparable extent, or systematically, because of differences in national tastes or needs. (Their findings are described more fully below.) Moreover, since products consumed in relatively large quantities have relatively low prices at least in part because of economies of scale in production and distribution, differences among countries in relative prices are themselves at least in part the indirect result of differences in income level (although they may also be affected by factor proportions and special factors). There is strong reason to believe that if per capita consumption in Europe were to catch up with per capita consumption in the United States at some future date, a comparison would then show it to be about the same in the two areas whether European or American price weights were used in the comparison. Even if there is only a strong tendency for European-weighted and United States-weighted comparisons to converge as incomes converge, it must be the case that the growth rate of consumption in the fast-growing European countries is higher when measured (as it is) in European prices than it would be if measured in United States prices. Evidence will be presented that this is indeed the case.

The reader who accepts this finding may yet wonder why it is important except in the context of making growth rates comparable. Economists are accustomed to finding that growth rates of consumption in a country, including the United States, are usually lowered when the price weights of a later year are substituted for those of an earlier

year.[19] According to the above reasoning, substitution of United States weights for recent European weights is similar to the substitution of European weights at some distant future date for recent European weights.[20] The analytical difference, I suggest, is in the cause of differences in relative prices.

The United States has for a long time had both the largest national income and the highest per capita income in the world. As markets for particular products expanded, some more than others because of differences in income elasticities as well as because of differential rates of technological progress and the introduction of new products, the technology for larger scale operations was developed gradually, and often at substantial cost; it did not stand ready for use. While even in the United States productivity gains in the long run tended to be greatest where production increased most, there is no presumption that the increase in total production would have been less had consumption increases been concentrated in some different group of products—for example, if relative income elasticities of various products had been quite different from what they were.

What distinguishes postwar Europe is that increases in output in the fast-growing countries have systematically been particularly marked in those products that Europe produced only on a small scale and at high cost *compared to the United States* in the early 1950's, and for which techniques for lowering costs with an increase in the scale of production already existed in the United States and did not need to be developed gradually and expensively as markets expanded. As incomes rose in Europe, demand for and production of these income-elastic products rose sharply and their unit costs were reduced by applying American techniques that could

19. However, in the United States the amounts involved are usually rather small unless years very far apart are selected. For example, a computation provided at my request by the Office of Business Economics showed that from 1950 to 1960 personal consumption expenditures increased by 37.9 percent when valued in 1950 prices and by 36.8 percent when valued in 1960 prices, with reweighting done in the full detail in which estimates are prepared (which is still limited, particularly for the food group). These data refer to the estimates as they stood prior to the revision published in the *Survey of Current Business*, August 1965 [G63].

20. The shift to a different base year within the postwar period by a European country would be expected to change growth rates very little compared to a shift to United States weights, which involves a far more drastic change in weights.

not have been adopted until per capita incomes were sufficient to provide a market. Some adaptation to European conditions was often made, but this was a much less difficult process than new development. In rather a large number of cases the transference of technology was carried out by American firms themselves, but this was not an essential ingredient of the process.[21] The foregoing argument presupposes that *in a given state of knowledge* further gains from scale economies typically decline as output of individual products increases. It also presupposes that the "state of knowledge" is at least as advanced in the United States as in Europe. Both presumptions seem to correspond to reality.[22]

Automobiles and other consumer durables provide classic and obvious examples of the process but it was quite pervasive and, I believe, applied to a great range of detailed products. The patterns revealed by the Gilbert comparisons of purchasing power parities can be explained to only a moderate extent by consumer durables, and very incompletely even by average price relationships among broad types of consumer expenditures.

Such concentration of output increases enabled European countries to achieve much larger gains in total output, measured by the use of European price weights, than would have been possible if the demand for all products had increased proportionately

or if, alternatively, it had been necessary to develop the technology for larger scale output *de novo*.

This line of reasoning does not depend on any lag of European technology or management behind that of the United States but rather on the disproportionate allocation of increased purchasing power to products where, once the markets became available, existing techniques for larger scale output could be adopted with an above-average reduction in unit costs. Neither is this special aspect of economies of scale advanced as something that could have raised European output *by itself;* it was a condition that permitted what would otherwise have been substantial growth rates to be still higher. Sufficient stimulus was required from other growth sources to raise per capita consumption sharply. This factor is particularly important in the present study because it was present in Europe but not in the United States, and to a much greater extent in some European countries than in others.

The gains from economies of scale made possible by the situation described are additional to those discussed in Section I, which referred to the gains that might have been expected if the composition of European products and European price relationships were the same as in the United States. Measurement of this special aspect of economies of scale will now be attempted in terms of differences from the United States. Data needed to quantify its effects are unfortunately incomplete. This forces use of an indirect approach to measurement that greatly complicates the presentation of the evidence that *is* available, and necessitates a number of checks on underlying assumptions, procedures, and results.

21. Since American technology had developed in an environment where capital was more abundant than in Europe, the fact that capital was increasing rapidly in Europe during the postwar period (in some cases through direct investment by American firms) facilitated the transference of technology and reduced the amount of adaptation that would otherwise, or previously, have been required.

22. Bertrand de Jouvenel, taking off from the price analyses of Jean Fourastié and G. Devaux, has also pointed out the great importance of the correlation between income elasticity and the responsiveness of costs to changes in volume—his "opportunity index"—as a determinant of the growth of measured consumption and of welfare (in *Bulletin* SEDEIS, Supplement I, January 10, 1964, p. 24 [P6]).

Bela Balassa (in *The Theory of Economic Integration*, p. 107 [B5]) has also stressed that the products with high income elasticity are those in which large gains from economies of scale are concentrated in Europe and the consequent importance of rising per capita income in determining gains from economies of scale in Europe.

Léon H. Dupriez has observed the movement of the price structure in the Common Market countries toward the American price structure as Common Market income levels drew closer to the American level (in *Revue d'Economie Politique*, May–June 1966, p. 432 [P39]). Georges Szapary has traced the approach of prices and costs in three European countries toward United States levels (in *Diffusion du Progrès et Convergence des Prix*, pp. 259–492 [S7]).

Relationship Between Levels and Changes in Consumption Measured in European and United States Prices

In the following discussion I estimate the amounts by which income-induced differences between the United States and Europe in consumption patterns and relative prices have caused European growth rates of consumption valued in each country's own prices to exceed the rates that would be obtained if European consumption were valued in United States prices. European consumption grows faster in European than in American price weights only insofar as items of consumption that have higher relative prices in Europe than in the United States have also increased by more-than-average amounts.[23]

The difference in growth rates will be interpreted as a measure of the gains from the special cause of economies of scale just discussed. This interpretation rests on the proposition that systematic association between high relative prices and large increases in consumption is due mainly to economies of scale, working through the income elasticity mechanism.[24] Factor proportions provide a possible additional explanation. But this explanation would require that international price ratios reflect different mixes of

23. The index of consumption in a European country would be the same whether its own or United States price weights were used if (1) all components of consumption increased at the same rate in that country; or (2) the ratio of the European price to the American price were the same for all commodities; or (3) there were no correlation between growth rates for individual consumption items and the international price ratios.

24. The analysis of this chapter is based on end products rather than industries. This choice is dictated by the data that are available, but it is also very much preferable since it eliminates numerous intractable problems.

factor inputs (including skill mixes as well as the ratios of labor, capital, and natural resources to one another); that international differences in these mixes be correlated with level of per capita consumption; that factor proportions in different countries converge over time; that this lead to convergence of relative prices; and that this, in turn, cause consumption patterns to converge. To some degree such a process may have been present but the required associations are hard to discern. If they are present I believe they are too weak and the cost differentials among products that are associated with factor proportions too small for this process to explain very much of the difference between growth rates measured in United States and in national prices. But it should be noted that the fact that capital was becoming more abundant at the same time as markets for income-elastic products were expanding facilitated the transfer of American technology.

Random factors also might cause *true* European-weighted and United States-weighted series for consumption to diverge in any particular country, but the indirect procedure I shall use for the calcula-

TABLE 17-4

Comparison of Indexes of per Capita Consumption, 1950[a]

(United States = 100)

Country	Per capita consumption based on United States price weights (1)	Per capita consumption based on price weights of European country (2)	Ratio of columns (2) to (1) (3)	Per capita consumption based on United States price weights estimated from the formula (4)	Ratio of Columns (2) to (4) (5)
Italy	30.0	17.8	.595	29.8	.597
Germany	41.0	28.1	.685	41.3	.680
Netherlands	48.3	35.7	.738	48.8	.732
France	52.0	37.7	.725	50.8	.742
Norway	57.2	45.4	.793	57.9	.784
Belgium	59.9	51.2	.855	63.1	.811
Denmark	64.5	51.3	.795	63.1	.812
United Kingdom	65.0	51.3	.789	63.2	.812

Sources: Columns (1) and (2): for Belgium, Denmark, the Netherlands, and Norway, the indexes are computed directly from dollar estimates given in Gilbert and Associates, OEEC, 1958, pp. 99–105 [I17]. Similar data for the United Kingdom, France, Germany, and Italy are given in Gilbert and Kravis, OEEC, 1954, Tables 27–30 [I18]. These were slightly revised when the Gilbert and Associates volume was prepared, and the revised indexes in whole numbers are given on page 97. The purchasing power ratios are not given but the range (arising from rounding, and fairly wide) within which they must fall can be computed from the quantity estimates. All the ratios computed from Gilbert and Kravis lie within these ranges, so were assumed to be unaffected by the revisions. In the present table, the rounded per capita quantity indexes were used for the indexes based on United States weights, and the European-weighted index computed from the price ratios. Column (4): computed from the formula described in the text.

a. Based on factor cost weights.

tions (although not the data provided as a check) omits the effect of such chance factors.[25]

Available data provide estimates of the change from 1950 to later years in each European country's per capita consumption weighted by its own prices. But time series for consumption are not nearly detailed enough, nor are the published Gilbert price data (the only available source for weights) sufficiently detailed, to allow European consumption indexes satisfactorily to be recomputed directly with the substitution of United States prices as weights. Hence, an indirect procedure is adopted. Direct information confirming the reasonableness of the general results obtained is, however, provided.

CROSS-SECTIONAL RELATIONSHIPS: GILBERT'S DATA. The indirect method of estimation adopted in this section rests on the 1950 international comparisons made by Gilbert and Associates. Their estimates, which derive from a very detailed classification of expenditures, are given in Table 17–4. In Column 1 the various components of consumption in the United States and each European country are weighted by United States prices. In Column 2 they are weighted by the European country's prices; these price weights are different for every European country. Column 3 shows that the ratio of European-weighted to United States-weighted consumption rises strongly as per capita consumption rises although the relationship is not, of course, a perfect one.

In every country there was a larger per capita consumption gap between the United States and the European country with European price weights than with American price weights, showing that commodities used in relatively small quantities tend to have high relative prices. The rationale for the indirect method rests on the observed *fact* that the greater the gap between two countries in per capita consumption, the more indexes based on national European weights tend to differ from indexes based on United States weights, and on the *interpretation*

that this relationship arises because differences in *total* per capita consumption (or income) are the dominant cause of systematic differences in consumption patterns. Different income elasticities for products produce different consumption patterns when total per capita consumption differs, and this initial income effect is reinforced by a price effect due to the tendency for high relative quantities to result in low relative prices.

Gilbert and Associates themselves examined the reasons for international differences in the per capita consumption of different products. They noted that differences can, in principle, occur for many reasons. In addition to the level of per capita consumption and relative prices, they mention differences in national tastes, in needs imposed by climate and geography, in age distribution, and in consumer stocks of durables. There may also be random differences, including those resulting from errors of estimation.

They found, however, that total per capita consumption and relative prices paid by consumers explained most of the international variation in the per capita consumption of various types of goods and services. These two factors explained 90 percent or more of the variation among countries in per capita consumption of one-fourth of the product groups separately distinguished, more than 85 percent of the variation for just over one-half of the product classes, and at least two-thirds of the variation for three-quarters of the product classes. Thus, for most products the part of the variation in consumption not explained by current income and prices was relatively small.[26]

These percentages refer to the intercountry variation in the absolute quantity of per capita consumption for different products. Total per capita consumption and relative price explain more of this variation than of the variation in the *percentage* of total consumption devoted to products because per capita consumption of nearly all products rises to some extent when total consumption rises. However, for most commodity groups the authors also compare, in chart form, (a) the ratio of consump-

25. From the standpoint of the present discussion, differences among countries in monopoly power in particular products and differential gaps in the state of knowledge may be regarded as random factors—unless changes in monopoly power and changes in the knowledge gap for different products in Europe are correlated both with European–American price ratios and with changes in consumption.

26. Gilbert and Associates, OEEC, 1958, p. 65 [I17]. It may be noted that this analysis was conducted on the basis of much less commodity detail than was used in the weighting scheme, but this should not affect the conclusions quoted here.

tion of each product in each country to total consumption with (b) the ratio that would emerge if total per capita consumption and relative price were the only factors determining the ratio. It is apparent from inspection of these charts, and from the authors' verbal summary, that total per capita consumption and relative price also explain a high proportion of the intercountry differences in consumption *patterns*.[27]

Total per capita consumption alone exercises a strong independent role in the joint effects of consumption level and price. This is evident from the Gilbert charts. It was to be expected because the income elasticities computed by Gilbert and Associates differ greatly from product to product.

The importance of the level of per capita income in determining consumption patterns is supported by other studies that have found income elasticities are similar in different countries and differences in consumption patterns reflect differences in income levels. Thus the European organization, ASEPELT, sponsored studies and projections of consumption in eight European countries (those covered in the present study minus Denmark and plus Sweden).[28] J. Sandee states "the main conclusion is . . . that consumption functions are nearly the same all over Europe." He also notes that where forecasts of strong increases for certain items are foreseen for 1970 on the basis of the analysis, the comparisons show that richer countries have already reached the high levels foreseen.[29]

I believe, as already stated, that to a large extent the price influence also indirectly reflects income elasticities. It is certain, of course, that the relative prices of products and their share in total consumption are negatively correlated. This is shown directly by the fact that consumption in the European countries is lower, relative to the United States, when their own price weights are used than when United

States price weights are used. It may also be observed for individual product groups, both as between Europe and the United States and among the European countries, from the charts presented by Gilbert and Associates.[30]

The causation responsible for this relationship could run either way. Large consumption could yield low relative prices because of economies of scale, or relative prices that are low for any reason could induce large consumption because of the price elasticity of demand. No doubt causation to some extent actually runs both ways. However, economies of scale, working through the income elasticity mechanism as it affects consumption patterns, provide the simpler and stronger explanation for a systematic tendency for price patterns of the countries to converge as per capita consumption levels converge. Insofar as causation runs from price ratios to consumption patterns, such convergence can be explained only to the extent that both relative prices and level of per capita consumption are correlated with factor proportions.

In any case, the level of total per capita consumption, counting both its direct effect via income elasticities and its indirect effect through relative prices, is certainly a very important determinant of international differences in consumption patterns and price patterns. This is the only reasonable explanation for a finding that the divergence between international indexes of per capita consumption based on United States price weights and national European price weights is systematically and substantially greater the larger the international gap in per capita consumption. This tendency, moreover, results chiefly from differences among European countries in their consumption patterns rather than in their price structures; it would still be present in comparisons between indexes based on United States prices and *average* European prices. Thus, whatever factor proportions may contribute to the differences in price ratios, they contribute very much less to the tendency of the indexes to converge as per capita consumption rises.

Column 3, Table 17–4, shows that this tendency toward convergence is present and strong. The

27. *Ibid.*, pp. 68–74. In the charts of Figure 8 of Gilbert and Associates, comparison is between Lines A and B.

28. Association Scientifique Européenne pour la Prévision Economique à Moyen et à Long Terme (European Scientific Association for Medium- and Long-Term Forecasting).

29. J. Sandee (ed.), *Europe's Future Consumption*, pp. 9, 13 [B96]. A study of income elasticities in Denmark, the country missing from this study, was made by Erling Jorgensen but the large food group is unfortunately not subdivided (in Statistical Department, *Income-Expenditure Relations of Danish Wage and Salary Earners* [G10]).

30. This is based on a comparison of Lines A and D in their Figure 8.

higher is total per capita consumption in a European country, the higher tends to be the ratio of the consumption index weighted by the European country's prices to the index weighted by United States prices.[31] This relationship is well described by the following linear logarithmic formula:

$$\log y = 0.5871 + 0.7096 \log x$$

In this formula, the quantities x and y equal per capita consumption in the lower consumption country (always the European country in these data) as a percentage of per capita consumption in the higher consumption country (the United States) based on price weights of the poorer country and the richer country, respectively. In Table 17–4, Column 1 is y, Column 2 is x, and Column 3 is x/y. The standard error of estimate (S_y) is 1.49 and r^2 is .983. The value of r^2 indicates that over 98 percent of the squared deviations of the value of the United States-weighted indexes from their mean is "explained" by the European-weighted indexes. Belgium contributes most of the unexplained variation. However, this r^2 does not measure the ability of per capita consumption to explain the effects of different price weights alone because the same quantities for individual components of consumption enter into the computation of both indexes. This difficulty does not apply to a comparison of the ratios of x to y that are implied by the formula results with the actual ratios of x to y. Column 5 gives the ratios implied by the United States-weighted indexes estimated from the formula. The summed squares of the deviations of the actual ratios from these estimated ratios is only 7.0 percent as large as the summed squares of the deviation of the actual ratios from the

mean of the ratios of the eight countries, so a measure analogous to r^2 is .930 (and r to .964). This is a high value for a cross-sectional analysis, even though there are only eight cases.[32]

The small size of the standard error of y (1.49 percentage points) suggests that within the range of observation indexes of per capita consumption in United States price weights can be estimated fairly well from indexes in national European price weights. Differences in consumption patterns and price ratios that are *not* related to the level of total per capita consumption have only a moderate influence on the relationship between the two indexes. For the purpose of estimation it does not matter whether this is because other differences in consumption patterns and price ratios are not very important or because they are not correlated with one another.

The formula has to be used somewhat beyond the range of the 1950 observations to produce estimates for later years, however. It was computed from values of x ranging from 18 to 51, and will be used in estimation for values ranging up to 58 (for Denmark in 1962). It is therefore necessary to ask whether the formula yields reasonable results when applied to higher values.[33] The simplest case to consider is the extreme one of two countries with about equal per capita consumption—that is, where x or y equals about 100. Unless the formula is greatly in error at that high level, not much error is likely to be introduced by the small extension of the range that is required for our calculations.

The formula implies that the two indexes draw steadily together as European consumption rises toward the American level. It indicates that the two

---

31. These ratios are also the ratios of the purchasing power equivalents (at factor cost) of foreign currencies in buying consumption goods based on the European country's quantity weights to those based on United States quantity weights. If P represents price and Q quantity, and if s represents United States weights and e European weights, then in Table 17–4:

$$\text{Column 2} = \frac{\Sigma Qe\,Pe}{\Sigma Qs\,Pe} \qquad \text{Column 1} = \frac{\Sigma Qe\,Ps}{\Sigma Qs\,Ps}$$

and

$$\frac{\text{Column 2}}{\text{Column 1}} = \frac{\Sigma Qe\,Pe/\Sigma Qs\,Pe}{\Sigma Qe\,Ps/\Sigma Qs\,Ps} = \frac{\Sigma Pe\,Qe/\Sigma Ps\,Qe}{\Sigma Pe\,Qs/\Sigma Ps\,Qs}$$

This fact makes possible the use as a check of the data cited below from the Statistical Office of the European Communities and the German Federal Statistical Office.

32. To test the significance of the regression the standard F statistic was calculated with one degree of freedom for the numerator and six degrees of freedom for the denominator. The hypothesis that the regression was not significant was rejected at the 0.1 percent probability level.

33. This question is particularly important because alternative formulas can be derived that also give good fits within the range of observation (though not quite so good as the one used) but yield estimates that begin to diverge from it when used beyond the range of observation. This is the case, for example, of the following formulas cast in arithmetic or ratio form:

$$y = 13.25 + .979x$$
$$x/y = .4958 + .00633x$$

For both these formulas, the standard error of estimate (S_y) is 1.57 and r^2 is .981.

indexes are close (and closest) to one another when per capita consumption is about equal in two countries. Yet it satisfies the condition always observed in international comparisons that the comparison is always most favorable to each country when the other's weights are used.[34]

CHECKS ON CROSS-SECTIONAL RELATIONSHIP. The Gilbert computations themselves provide no check on the formula's implication that when two countries among those examined have about the same per capita consumption level, it will make only a small difference which country's weights are used. This is because bilateral comparisons among the European countries, some of which were at about the same consumption level, were not made. Two other sets of data do permit a rough check on this assumption and give some support to it, as well as to the more general observation that the indexes converge as per capita consumption converges.

The Statistical Office of the European Communities made a special investigation of the consumption patterns of workers in the steel, coal mining, and iron mining industries, and of the prices they paid in 1958. It computed purchasing power parities of the currencies of Belgium, France, Germany (excluding the Saar), the Saar, the Netherlands, Luxembourg, and Italy.[35] Each of the three groups of workers in each country was compared with the same group in each of the other countries, using the expenditure pattern of the workers in that industry for each country. For every bilateral comparison,

the ratio of the purchasing power parity based on one country's quantity weights to parity based on the other country's quantity weights (which is the same, with the countries reversed, as the ratio of real consumption ratios based on alternative price weights) can therefore be computed. I have averaged the ratios for the three groups of workers (or as many as were present in each comparison) to obtain the results given in the following paragraph.[36] Differences in real incomes of workers in these countries, except for Italy, were not extreme but incomes were by no means identical.[37]

In the fifteen bilateral comparisons of the six countries other than Italy, the difference in purchasing power parities, and hence in real income comparisons, that resulted from using country B's weights rather than country A's averaged only 6 percent.[38] Appreciable though unknown income effects remain in the comparisons since incomes were not identical, and the difference would presumably be less if they could be eliminated. As anticipated, the six comparisons of other countries with Italy, which was at a considerably lower income level, showed a much larger average difference—14 percent.

The second body of data provides comparisons of Germany with other countries. It consists of comparisons by the German Federal Statistical Office of purchasing power parities for consumer expenditures of the deutsche mark and other currencies.[39] Calculations were made using weights for both Germany and the other country. Unlike the Common Market study, the comparisons were not based on special surveys but in large part on data collected for national price indexes and the results should perhaps be viewed to a greater extent as approximations. The comparisons refer to various

34. The formula implies that when the European-weighted index reaches 98 the United States-weighted index reaches 100. For a short distance above that point there is ambiguity as to which is the high income country. When the European-weighted index is 100, the United States-weighted index reaches 101.5. When the indexes average 100 they differ by 2 percent. If European per capita consumption were to rise above the American, the calculation would be switched and parallel results obtained, with the two indexes drawing apart as European consumption rises farther above the American.

So long as United States per capita consumption exceeds that of a European country, with the United States designated by s and the European country by e,

$$x = \frac{\Sigma Qe\,Pe}{\Sigma Qs\,Pe} \quad \text{and} \quad y = \frac{\Sigma Qe\,Ps}{\Sigma Qs\,Ps}$$

If per capita consumption of a European country were to exceed that of the United States

$$x = \frac{\Sigma Qs\,Ps}{\Sigma Qe\,Ps} \quad \text{and} \quad y = \frac{\Sigma Qs\,Pe}{\Sigma Qe\,Pe}$$

35. OSCE, Social Statistics, No. 2, 1960 [152].

36. Belgium, the Netherlands, and the Saar had no iron mines, and Luxembourg no coal mines.
37. The report gives comparisons of real income for workers in a variety of different situations so that it is difficult to summarize the real income results. Moreover, whereas it is the real consumption of these workers that is relevant to consumption patterns, it is the real consumption of the population at large that is relevant to price relationships. Hence, for the present purpose the data cannot be used with precision but only as an indication of the situation when countries at very roughly similar income levels are compared.
38. The range was from 2 percent to 12 percent.
39. Federal Statistical Office in Preise, Löhne, Wirtschafts-rechnungen, 1966, pp. 12–14.

dates. The only comparisons with areas covered in the present study that are not already represented in the results summarized in the preceding paragraph are those of Germany with Denmark, Norway, the United Kingdom, and the United States. If the first three of these are added to the sample of fifteen comparisons of Northern European countries summarized in the preceding paragraph, the average weighting difference remains 6 percent.

The choice of weights affects the Federal Statistical Office comparisons of Germany with other countries covered in the present study by the following percentages of the higher index at the most recent date available: Denmark, March 1958, 5 percent; Netherlands, November 1960, 7 percent; France, October–November 1958, 11 percent; United Kingdom, May–June, 1961, 11 percent; Norway, June 1960, 12 percent; Belgium, July 1953, 13 percent; Italy, April 1952, 17 percent; and United States, March 1953, 28 percent. In the consideration of the last three comparisons it should be noted that in 1952–53 per capita consumption in Germany was far below that in Belgium, and farther below that in the United States and a little closer to that of Italy than it was in 1958–61, when the other comparisons were made. (This statement is based on interpolation of data in Table 17–6.) Differences between Germany and the remaining Northwest European countries in levels of per capita consumption were quite important at the dates to which the data refer, but even so the average effect of the choice of weights on comparisons of Germany with the five Northwest European countries except Belgium was only 9 percent, as against 13 with Belgium, 17 with Italy, and 28 with the United States.[40]

Both sets of data strongly support the view that the choice between country A's or country B's weights makes a sharply diminishing difference as real per capita consumption converges. The former set, and a combination of the two, suggest that on the average the difference is moderate (not necessarily quite so small as the formula implies) when consumption is about equal, although some individual differences may be appreciable.[41]

APPLICATION OF RELATIONSHIP TO TIME SERIES. I now turn to the calculations in which the formula is used.

Time series for per capita consumption based on the use of each country's own price weights are readily available, and shown in Columns 1 to 3, Table 17–5.[42] These indexes are used to extend Gilbert's 1950 international comparisons of per capita consumption based on national European prices to 1955, 1960, and 1962. The calculation is made by simply multiplying the 1950 international index for each country by the time series index, and recomputing with the United States equal to 100.[43]

41. Although this study's concern is primarily with what happens when differences in consumption levels are smaller than those between the United States and the European countries in 1950, it is of some interest that Wilfred Beckerman (in OECD, *International Comparisons of Real Incomes,* p. 13 [I42]) finds that, at the other extreme, William Hollister's comparisons of United States and Chinese consumption in American and Chinese prices fit a formula derived from the Gilbert data.

42. These are not based on 1950 weights but generally on weights for years around 1958. (The basic, detailed computations are for various nearby years.) It is necessary to assume that this difference in base years does not affect these indexes much or else that it does so by the same amount in all countries. This assumption probably leads to slight overestimation of the effect upon consumption indexes of shifting from European to American weights because there was presumably a slight convergence in weights between 1950 and around 1958. If the Gilbert data referred to the same year as the base year for deflation of time series, there would be no problem. The bias resulting from the difference in base years should not be large because not much of the 1950 consumption gap between Europe and America had been closed by around 1958.

43. The procedure assumes the United States index would be the same in the prices of each European country as in United States prices; there is no *a priori* basis for assuming it would rise either more or less and available data do not permit a direct recomputation. Even a rough check by reweighting such as is subsequently attempted for most European countries is barred since the United States publishes a division of consumption in constant prices among only eleven broad groups. Among these groups there is no tendency for changes in consumption from 1950 to 1962 to be associated with differences between United States and European price weights.

40. The German Federal Statistical Office comparisons of Germany and four of the other Common Market countries can be matched with the comparisons of Germany with the same countries in 1958 that were included in the comparisons of the Statistical Office of the European Communities. The percentages (with the OSCE results given first and the Federal Statistical Office results given second) are as follows: Belgium, 8 and 13; the Netherlands, 6 and 7; France, 10 and 11; and Italy, 17 and 17. The 28 percent difference in the United States comparison for 1953 can also be compared with the 31.5 percent difference obtained by Gilbert and Associates for 1950. If allowance is made for the convergence of Belgian and German consumption levels between 1953 and 1958, and of German and American consumption between 1950 and 1953, all the results are reassuringly similar.

TABLE 17–5

Time Series Indexes of per Capita Consumption in National European and United States Price Weights, and Differences in Growth Rates

Area	Indexes of per capita consumption (1950 = 100)						Reduction in growth rate of per capita consumption when U.S. price weights are substituted for national price weights		
	In national price weights			In U.S. price weights					
	1955 (1)	1960 (2)	1962 (3)	1955 (4)	1960 (5)	1962 (6)	1950–62 (7)	1950–55 (8)	1955–62 (9)
United States	109.2	115.2	119.4	109.2	115.2	119.4	—	—	—
Northwest Europe	120.8	141.9	152.7	117.9	134.4	143.1	.56	.51	.60
Belgium	108.8	119.1	126.2	109.4	117.9	124.2	.13	−.12	.31
Denmark	103.5	119.6	135.5	105.2	118.4	130.6	.32	−.33	.78
France	122.3	141.9	156.1	118.3	133.5	144.5	.66	.70	.64
Germany	144.5	184.0	202.7	133.1	160.5	173.7	1.35	1.75	1.07
Netherlands	111.5	126.1	138.2	110.9	123.7	132.6	.36	.11	.54
Norway	106.9	119.3	128.0	107.7	118.3	125.5	.17	−.15	.40
United Kingdom	109.7	123.0	126.1	109.6	120.7	124.2	.15	.02	.24
Italy	120.6	144.9	165.9	118.2	135.5	150.6	.84	.41	1.14

Sources: Indexes in national prices computed from OECD and national statistics. Data conform to OECD definitions except that the United States personal consumption expenditures are those published in *Survey of Current Business*, August 1965 [G63].
Indexes in United States prices are derived from the formula described in the text; they differ from the indexes based on national prices only because of systematic relationships and do not purport to take account of the effects of random influences.

The estimates are given in Columns 1 to 4, Table 17–6.

These international indexes in national European prices are then inserted in the formula to obtain estimated international indexes for 1955, 1960, and 1962, based on United States price weights; the estimate given by the formula is adjusted by the ratio of the actual index in 1950 to that which the formula yields. For example, in 1950 the formula yields an index for France of 50.8, whereas the actual estimate is 52.0 (Table 17–4). For 1962 the formula yields an estimate of 61.5, which is adjusted to 62.9 on the assumption that the percentage discrepancy persisted. These international indexes in United States prices are given in Columns 5 to 8, Table 17–6.

To obtain time series for per capita consumption in the European countries based on United States

TABLE 17–6

Indexes of per Capita Consumption in National European and United States Price Weights

(United States = 100)

Area	National European price weights				United States price weights			
	1950 (1)	1955 (2)	1960 (3)	1962 (4)	1950 (5)	1955 (6)	1960 (7)	1962 (8)
United States	100.0	100.0	100.0	100.0	100.0	100.0	100.0	100.0
Northwest Europe								
Belgium	51.2	51.3	52.9	54.1	59.9	60.0	61.3	62.3
Denmark	51.3	48.7	53.3	58.2	64.5	62.2	66.3	70.6
France	37.7	42.2	46.4	49.3	52.0	56.3	60.3	62.9
Germany	28.1	37.2	44.9	47.7	41.0	50.0	57.1	59.6
Netherlands	35.7	36.5	39.1	41.3	48.3	49.1	51.7	53.7
Norway	45.4	44.5	47.0	48.7	57.2	56.4	58.8	60.1
United Kingdom	51.3	51.5	54.8	54.2	65.0	65.2	68.1	67.6
Italy	17.8	19.7	22.4	24.7	30.0	32.5	35.3	37.8

Source: See text for derivation.

price weights, the international indexes based on United States price weights are multiplied by the United States time series index. These series, expressed with 1950 equal to 100, are given in Columns 4 to 6, Table 17–5.

The object of all these calculations, it will be recalled, was to try to determine the change in the movement of consumption that would be introduced by substituting United States for national European price weights. In Table 17–5 the indexes are compared, and Columns 7 to 9 show the amounts by which growth rates of per capita consumption would be reduced by substituting United States for national weights. In the 1955–62 period all European growth rates would be reduced, but the amounts range from 0.2 percentage points in the United Kingdom to about 1.1 percentage points in Germany and Italy. These amounts are generally larger the larger the increase in per capita consumption because the methodology assumes that the larger was the rise in total per capita consumption the greater was the spread among increases in products classified by income elasticity; the substitution of United States price weights reduces the weight placed on fast growing items with high income elasticities. The effect of differences among European countries in relative prices only slightly modifies this statement.

CHECKS ON TIME SERIES RESULTS. It would have been desirable to measure directly the effect on time series of substituting United States for European weights. If income elasticity is as dominant an influence as I believe, some correspondence between the formula results and those of direct reweighting should emerge, despite the fact that other factors also would influence the latter calculation. Such a test would require the use of detail similar to that of the Gilbert study, which in effect assigned separate prices and weights to several hundred product groups. Nothing approaching this detail is available.

It was decided, nevertheless, to test the effect of reweighting by whatever detail was available in each country for which *any* considerable amount of detail could be obtained. It was expected that, if the approach adopted here were valid, even reweighting on a summary and unsatisfactory

basis would usually yield some reduction in growth rates where the formula indicated the reduction to be substantial. It was obvious in advance that the amount of the reduction could not be measured in this way, however, and also that the results for individual countries could not be directly compared with one another since the detail available for reweighting varied.

Gilbert's summary distributions of 1950 consumption in national and in United States prices provided the starting point for these calculations. Volume indexes for the components of consumption were then used to carry Gilbert's 1950 estimates in United States and national prices to 1955 and 1962. Gilbert's estimates themselves are published by only a 29-way breakdown for the large countries and a 25-way breakdown for the small countries. When necessary, his categories were combined to correspond to classifications for which volume indexes over time were available for the individual countries, further reducing the detail in which reweighting could be attempted.[44] To make the calculations at all it was necessary to approximate some required detail, to adjust national classifications to those of Gilbert, to overlook some classification differences completely, and usually also to omit from the calculations certain items of consumption provided by government. For most countries, twenty or more consumption categories were distinguished.[45] The categories were not the same in any two countries and the size of the categories differed substantially. The results unfortunately are quite sensitive to the number and size of categories distinguished and the particular combinations used.[46]

---

44. For convenience in using national series that were more detailed for particular groups and not summarized, Gilbert's estimates were sometimes subdivided by using national proportions in 1950 to divide both the national and United States weights; this, of course, does not introduce any additional reweighting.

45. Dutch consumption in constant prices is available on a rather limited classification that in some categories corresponds poorly with Gilbert's. To obtain detail required to make necessary reclassifications it was necessary to divide some of the broader categories among detailed components on the assumption that the percentage division in 1958 prices in 1950, 1955, and 1962 was the same as in current prices.

46. Indexes of total per capita consumption in national price weights used in the formula estimates are not in all countries entirely consistent with those implied by the data used in the reweighting test, both because of differences in

Lack of any but the most summary consumption data forced abandonment of any attempt to make a comparison for Germany and for Italy and Denmark as well in the 1950–55 period.[47] This was unfortunate because these include cases for which the formula yields large and diverse effects of reweighting.[48]

The results for the 1955–62 period were about as consistent with the results from the formula as could be reasonably expected, given the great limitations of the data. The reductions in growth rates indicated by the two procedures are compared below; but it must be remembered that the estimates under the "direct calculation" column cannot be considered comparable from country to country:

	Direct calculation	Formula
Belgium	.18	.31
Denmark	.43	.78
France	.51	.64
Netherlands	.47	.54
Norway	.35	.40
United Kingdom	.21	.24
Italy	.57	1.14

In all cases both the formula and the direct calculations showed that substitution of United States weights would reduce growth rates. In all cases, also, the direct calculation yielded smaller reductions, which was to be expected since the amount of detail implied by the formula much exceeded the amount that could be used in direct calculation. In most countries the differences are not very great, however.

Among these countries, both calculations showed the reduction to be smallest in Belgium, Norway, and the United Kingdom, and largest in Italy. The amount calculated by direct reweighting fell below the formula estimate by the largest absolute amount in Italy; this was to be expected since the detail available for reweighting was least in Italy.

The results as a whole confirm the supposition that use of United States price weights would substantially lower growth rates of consumption in the European countries that enjoyed substantial rises in per capita consumption. They cannot be used to check the magnitudes of the estimates, however.

---

scope (mainly with respect to public consumption) and because the former are sometimes based on later data. In the reweighting test the same data were of course used in the computation of indexes in national and United States prices, since it is only the difference between the two that is of interest. However, these differences may differ from those that would be obtained if data fully consistent with those used in the estimates from the formula could have been used.

47. Only nine consumption categories can be distinguished in the German data and one of these (which includes food) accounts for half the total. Two-thirds of the total in 1950 was represented by three categories. Each of these in the aggregate comprised virtually the same percentage of total consumption in United States as in German prices, so that reweighting by these groupings is useless. (The weights of the detailed components, for which time series were not available, of course differed greatly.) If a recalculation by the use of these summary data is nevertheless attempted, about all that emerges is the fact that rent, which receives a larger weight in United States than in German prices (9 percent, as against 6) rose less than total consumption from 1950 to 1955 and more than the total from 1955 to 1962.

For Italy and Denmark detailed consumption data begin only with 1953. Even thereafter Italian estimates are less detailed than those for other countries. The Italian data suffer an additional shortcoming in that while revisions of total consumer expenditures are published, the detailed components are published only once. Hence there may be significant discrepancies between the totals used in the formula and the details used in this discussion.

48. The primary sources of consumption indexes in constant prices used to extrapolate the Gilbert estimates for 1950 follow. Procedures for required adjustments are not described.

BELGIUM: 1953–62: National Institute of Statistics, *Bulletin de Statistique*, July–August 1965, Table III.5 [G3]; 1950–53: *Cahiers Economiques de Bruxelles*, No. 19, 1963 [P9].

DENMARK: 1953–59: Statistical Department, *Nationalregnskabsstatistik, 1947–1960*, Table 19 [G7]; 1960 and 1961: Statistical Department, *Statistiske Efterretninger*, No. 7, 1964, and No. 5, 1965, Table 18 [G9]; 1962: estimated by applying detailed 1961 distributions to 1962 data for broader groups from *Statistiske Efterretninger*, No. 5, 1965, Table 5. A 1950 distribution (used only to bridge the gap from 1950 to 1953) was estimated by applying detailed 1953 distributions to data for broader groups from *Nationalregnskabsstatistik, 1947–1960*, Tables 19 and 17. Estimates for 1950 and 1962 had also to be adjusted to include public consumption.

FRANCE: 1950–1961: *Consommation*, No. 3–4, 1961, Tables, pp. 72–82 and No. 1, 1963, Table B, pp. 94–102 [P13]; 1959–1962: *Etudes et Conjoncture*, August–September 1963, Table 54 [G14].

NETHERLANDS: 1950–62: Central Bureau of Statistics, *Nationale rekeningen, 1964*, Table 43, and *1961*, Table 44 [G25].

NORWAY: 1950–62: detailed data kindly made available by the National Accounts Division of the Central Bureau of Statistics.

UNITED KINGDOM: 1950–62: Central Statistical Office, *National Income and Expenditure, 1964* and *1965*, Table 19, 1958 prices, except detailed food components which were extrapolated to 1950 from 1955 by data from *National Income and Expenditure, 1961* [G38].

ITALY: 1950–58: SVIMEZ, *Stime sui consumi privati in Italia nel prossimo decennio*, p. 49 [G22]. Extrapolated to 1962 by national accounts data in *Relazione Generale sulla Situazione Economica del Paese* (several issues) [G20]. For food, a detailed breakdown starting with 1953 was available in early issues of *Relazione*. The distribution of total food expenditures in 1950 among detailed components (used only to bridge the gap from 1950 to 1953) was assumed to be the same as in 1953.

For the 1950–55 period, direct calculations could be attempted for only five countries, and the data for most of them were less satisfactory than for the 1955–62 period. The early period was also a disturbed one and it would not be surprising if income elasticity effects were obscured by those of special developments. The reductions indicated by the two procedures follow:

	Direct calculation	Formula
Belgium	.04	−.12
France	.58	.70
Netherlands	.20	.11
Norway	−.65	−.15
United Kingdom	.35	.02

The results are tolerably consistent for France, the Netherlands, and Belgium; although the two results for Belgium have opposite signs, both calculations show the effect of reweighting to be small. Both calculations for Norway, where per capita consumption rose less than in the United States, show that use of United States weights would *raise* the 1950–55 growth rate of Norwegian consumption, but the magnitudes obtained are quite different. For the United Kingdom the formula indicates that the income elasticity factor would cause no significant change from substitution of United States weights, whereas direct reweighting lowers the British growth rate by 0.35 points. There is no way to determine whether these differences reflect use of inadequate or inaccurate detail in the direct estimates, the results of changes unrelated to income elasticities, or errors in the formula estimates.

DETAILED EXAMINATION OF TWO COUNTRIES. Among the countries for which the effect of reweighting over the 1950–62 period as a whole is estimated from the formula to be large, the detail available for reweighting was most satisfactory in the case of France. Also, the test yielded estimates for France quite consistent with the formula. The French data are therefore particularly appropriate for more detailed examination.

The Gilbert and Kravis summary table for 1950 divides French consumption into 29 groups, the largest of which (meats) accounts for 13 percent of total consumption. Their data indicate that groups for which the choice of price weights affects the group's percentage of total consumption by more than one-half (the first and last categories in the following table) are responsible for most (84 percent) of the total difference in weights. In 1950, consumption in the last category was about 80 percent larger than that in the first category in French prices, whereas consumption in the first category was about 80 percent larger than that in the last category in United States prices.

	Share of 1950 French consumption	
	Measured in U.S. relative price weights	Measured in French relative price weights
Commodity groups with a share in consumption that is:		
Higher in United States price weights by more than half (excluding education)	33.64% (29.27)	19.59% (17.12)
Higher in United States price weights by less than half	27.75	23.70
Higher in French price weights by less than half	20.06	21.65
Higher in French price weights by more than half	18.55	35.06
	100.00	100.00

The first category in the table includes product groups whose relative prices in 1950 were much lower in France than in the United States. They are: cereal and cereal products; alcoholic beverages; housing services; domestic service; education; and "miscellaneous." From 1950 to 1962, per capita consumption of items included in these groups (other than education for which data are lacking) increased only 19 percent whether they are combined by American or French weights.

The last category in the table includes those product groups whose relative prices were much higher in France than in the United States. They are: fats and oils; sugar; footwear; clothing and household textiles; fuel, light, and water; household goods; purchases of transportation equipment; operation of transportation equipment; and books, newspapers, and magazines. In contrast to the 19 percent increase in the first category from 1950 to 1962, per capita consumption of these groups increased by 74 percent if they are combined by United States price weights, and by 79 percent if they are combined by French price weights.

These groups are broad enough to conceal much of the change that was occurring. "Purchases of transportation equipment," for example, includes both bicycles, which were cheap in France and declining in importance, and automobiles, which were expensive in France and increasing in importance. Household goods include a variety of dissimilar items such as soap, appliances, rugs, furniture, and toys. Nevertheless, the classification gives some feel for the general character of the shifts that were occurring. The first category, consisting of groups that receive a particularly heavy weight in United States prices and whose share in consumption was declining sharply, is dominated by products that appear to be peculiarly unlikely to be subject to significant scale economies with increases in production. For some of them, in fact, the method of estimating output precludes any possibility that scale economies can raise productivity as measured. The last category, whose share in consumption was increasing sharply, includes a preponderance of commodity groups in which scale economies appear likely to be important and the transference of technology for large-scale production feasible as output increases from a low level. The groups involved in the shift of the composition of consumption from the first to the fourth category thus seem consistent with the thesis of this chapter.

United Kingdom data are also detailed enough to make closer examination worthwhile, although much greater difficulty was encountered in matching the British classification with that of Gilbert. For the earlier years, backward extrapolation was required, using detail subsequently deleted from the official estimates. From the formula I inferred that a shift to United States weights would reduce the growth rate much (0.51 percentage points) less in the United Kingdom than in France over the 1950–62 period. Direct reweighting yielded a much smaller difference (0.27 points) between the two countries.

United Kingdom price weights in 1950 differed less from United States weights than the French weights.[49] This was presumably because British per

capita consumption was closer to the American level in 1950 (Table 17–4). As one would therefore expect, groups with an equally extreme divergence from the United States in relative prices account for a smaller fraction of the total divergence between Gilbert's British and American weights than was the case in the French comparison.

	Share of 1950 United Kingdom consumption	
	Measured in U.S. relative price weights	Measured in U.K. relative price weights
Commodity groups with a share in consumption that is:		
Higher by more than half in United States price weights	8.66%	14.66%
Higher by less than half in United States price weights	27.85	36.55
Higher by less than half in United Kingdom price weights	40.23	34.59
Higher by more than half in United Kingdom price weights	23.26	14.20
	100.00	100.00

The product groups in the first category, whose relative prices were much lower in the United Kingdom than in the United States, are: housing services; domestic service; public transport services; and hotels, restaurants, and cafes. Except for public transport services this is, again, an unlikely set of categories in which to expect productivity to be responsive to the size of the national market.

The product groups in the last category, whose relative prices were much lower in the United States than in the United Kingdom, are: tobacco; household goods; purchases of transportation equipment; operation of transportation equipment; and books, newspapers, and magazines. Although only four groups appear in the last category in both France and the United Kingdom, while six appear in only one list (five in the French and one in the British), all ten groups had substantially higher relative prices

49. From the text tables presented it can be computed that expenditure groups with higher relative prices in France than in the United States accounted for 61.4 percent of French consumption valued in French prices and 43.3 per-

cent of French consumption valued in United States prices, a difference in weights of 18.1. (The difference for expenditure groups with higher relative prices in the United States is, of course, the same.) Expenditure groups with higher relative prices in the United Kingdom than in the United States accounted for 63.5 percent of United Kingdom consumption valued in United Kingdom prices and 48.4 percent in United States prices, a difference of 14.7.

in both France and the United Kingdom than in the United States.[50] The large clothing and household textiles group was just over the 50 percent dividing line in France and just under in the United Kingdom. Thus, the groups whose weight is greatly reduced by substitution of United States prices, and in which commodities offering the greatest possibilities for special gains from economies of scale are presumed to be concentrated, are much the same in the two countries.

From 1950 to 1962, per capita consumption in the first British category rose 7 percent (when component groups are combined by either American or British weights) and per capita consumption in the fourth category, 63 or 67 percent (when combined by American or British weights, respectively). A more interesting comparison with France is obtained by using the same expenditure categories that were compared for France. Because per capita consumption rose much less in the United Kingdom than in France, we should expect and, in fact, find much less absolute difference between the behavior of the groups. In the United Kingdom per capita consumption rose 9 or 7 percent (based on American or British weights, respectively) in the expenditure groups included in the first French category (again excluding education) and 39 or 44 percent in the fourth. In France, it will be recalled, the corresponding percentages were 18 or 18, and 74 or 79.

This completes the presentation of the evidence supporting the procedures adopted in this section and the interpretation placed upon the results. I regard it as sufficient to establish the reality and importance of the phenomenon under investigation. The specific estimates derived from the formula I shall use as the best I can derive, but additional direct evidence would be needed to establish their accuracy or permit their modification.

CONTRIBUTION TO GROWTH. The next step is to calculate the effect of the differences between per capita consumption growth rates based on national weights and United States weights (shown in Columns 7 to 9, Table 17–5) upon national income growth rates. This is done in each case by (1) ad-

justing from a per capita consumption to a total consumption basis (a slight adjustment) and (2) multiplying by the average ratio of consumption to net national product in each period. The latter ratios range from 0.64 to 0.78. The resulting estimates are presented in Table 17–7.[51]

TABLE 17–7

Economies of Scale Associated with Income Elasticities: Contribution to Growth Rates of Total National Income[a]

(*In percentage points*)

Area	1950–62	1950–55	1955–62
United States	—	—	—
Northwest Europe	.46	.50	.43
Belgium	.11	−.08	.24
Denmark			
calculated	.23	−.25	.57
adjusted	.23	−.20	.54
France	.49	.53	.46
Germany	.91	1.21	.70
Netherlands	.23	.07	.35
Norway	.12	−.10	.27
United Kingdom	.09	.01	.15
Italy	.60	.32	.80

Source: See text for derivation.
a. Represents estimated excess of contribution to European growth rates over contribution to United States growth rates.

It will be noted that the estimates for Belgium, Denmark, and Norway are negative in the 1950–55 period. Negative estimates result from an increasing spread between European and American per capita consumption, and imply that income-induced shifts in the composition of consumption ran counter to the possibility of large gains from economies of scale. There is nothing wrong with negative estimates, but the one for Denmark in 1950–55 is improbably large. It exceeds the estimate (made in Section I of this chapter) of the gains from economies of scale that would be reflected in a measure based on United States price weights; hence, the two estimates combined imply that the Danish economy was operating under decreasing returns to scale from 1950 to 1955. The slow 1950–55 rise

50. Four of the five groups that are listed in the first category in one country but not in the other also had lower relative prices in the latter than in the United States, but not much lower.

51. The estimates for Northwest Europe were obtained by constructing indexes for the component countries (with 1960 equal to 100) from the growth rates, weighting the indexes with 1960 weights to obtain a Northwest European index, and computing the contribution for Northwest Europe from this index.

and subsequent rapid 1955–62 rise in Danish consumption that produces this result was partly due to the fact that underutilization of resources increased from 1950 to 1955 and decreased from 1955 to 1962. (The actual turning point was 1957.) Although there is a short-run sense in which the adverse effect of underutilization on productivity can be described as due to economies of scale, this sense is not related to the subject of this chapter and cyclical incomparability will be separately allowed for in Chapter 19. Because of changing underutilization, the contrast between the estimates for the two periods indicated by the unadjusted figures in Table 17–7 is too great. I have introduced a small and minimum timing adjustment by assuming that in 1950–55 the adverse effect of shifts in the composition of consumption in Denmark was equal to the contribution ascribed to economies of scale with national product valued by United States price weights, so that the estimate for the two together is zero. I have retained the orginal estimate for the 1950–62 period as a whole, and readjusted the estimate for the 1955–62 period to make it consistent with the other two periods. The absence of an adjustment for "cyclical" influences in the per capita consumption indexes is a general, though usually not a very large, source of possible error in the estimates for all the countries, particularly for the subperiods.[52] However, a systematic allowance for these factors appeared impractical and arbitrary adjustments, beyond that for Denmark, unwise.

One other estimate, that for Germany in 1950–55, stands out as exceptional. The recovery aspect (from the war) of the 1950–53 rise in German per capita consumption may cause the German estimate for 1950–55 to be somewhat too large as a measure of gains from economies of scale (viewed in the long-run sense) as such, although there is no special reason to believe it overstates the effect of reweighting. The 1950–55 period in Germany, as noted earlier, is an extraordinarily difficult one to analyze from all standpoints.

If the set of estimates shown in Table 17–7 are at

all close to the truth, and I think they are, they provide an important part of the explanation for the large size of international differences in postwar growth rates. Viewed from the standpoint of the United States, they do not explain why growth rates of national income in Northwest Europe as a whole and in most of the individual countries have been higher than the United States rate, but they do help to explain why they are so much higher.

From the standpoint of the European countries, the discussion here implies that the increase in national income that results from any change that raises national income per capita is enlarged by the income elasticity-economies of scale effect, provided that at least part of the income gains are devoted to consumption. I classify the gains from this source as a separate source of growth. But they could, alternatively, be distributed back to the other sources, raising the contribution allocated to each. Unlike the redistribution of gains from economies of scale estimated in Section I of this chapter, this reallocation would be rather complicated. It could not be done mechanically because it would have to be made proportional to the initial effect on per capita consumption rather than on total income. Also, if one were attempting to estimate the increase in the growth rate of national income in a European country that could be achieved by any action to stimulate it, the method of estimate that I used for the United States in the *Sources of Economic Growth* would have to be modified to allow for this supplementation.

Gains from economies of scale that were made possible by shifts in consumption patterns in response to income elasticities and resulted from application of known technology are thus judged an important source of growth of national income, valued in national prices, in most European countries. It would not be a source of growth if national income were valued in United States prices, but rather explains the divergence between growth rates calculated by using the two sets of weights.[53]

52. H. S. Houthakker, among others, stresses the difference between short-run elasticities obtained, for example, by calculations based on year-to-year changes within a country and elasticities obtained by international comparisons which he believes also measure long-run elasticities within countries (in *Econometrica*, April 1965, pp. 277–88 [P14]).

53. This chapter has taken no account of shifts in the composition of the national product except shifts within the consumption aggregate. This is not to deny that other changes may conceivably be important. But there is, in general, no *a priori* reason to suppose they would cause a divergence between aggregates based on national and United States weights. An exception to this statement may be noted for products used both by consumers and producers, par

TABLE 17–8

Economies of Scale Associated with the Growth of the National Market: Contribution to Growth Rates of Total National Income Valued in National Prices

(*In percentage points*)

Area	1950-62	1950-55	1955-62
United States	.30	.38	.24
Northwest Europe	.87	.97	.80
Belgium	.44	.28	.56
Denmark	.58	.00	1.01
France	.93	.95	.91
Germany	1.54	2.07	1.16
Netherlands	.71	.71	.72
Norway	.50	.34	.62
United Kingdom	.31	.24	.36
Italy	1.15	.94	1.31

Sources: Tables 17–3 and 17–7.

Table 17–8 combines the estimates given in Tables 17–3 and 17–7. It provides my final estimates of the contribution of economies of scale associated with the growth of the national market to growth rates of national income valued in national prices.

Over the whole period from 1950 to 1962, economies of scale associated with the growth of national economies contributed 0.3 percentage points to the growth rate in the United States and almost three times as much in Northwest Europe. The variation among the individual European countries was extreme. Even in 1955–62, which excludes the abnormal German recovery period, the range of contributions among individual countries was from 0.24 percentage points in the United States and 0.36 in the United Kingdom to 1.01 in Denmark, 1.16 in Germany, and 1.31 in Italy.

For the most part, differences among countries and periods are in the same direction as differences in growth rates of national income, and these results provide an important part of my explanation of the size of differences in growth rates, both as between the United States and Northwest Europe and among the individual countries and time periods. There are exceptions, however, and among these the Nether-

lands provides a striking case. The growth rate of Dutch national income was 6.0 in 1950–55 and 3.8 in 1955–62. I nevertheless estimate the contribution of economies of scale at 0.7 points in both subperiods. This result is possible because per capita consumption, in contrast to national income, increased much more in 1955–62 than in 1950–55. From 1950 to 1955 the ratio of consumption to national income dropped radically in the Netherlands.

The source of growth identified in this section as "economies of scale associated with income elasticities" has no counterpart in the sources of international difference in 1960 levels of national income per person employed when national income is valued in United States prices; hence, there is nothing to be added to the estimates given in the last two columns of Table 17–3. Nor does European growth from this source help to close the gap between levels of national income per person employed measured in United States prices.

III. Independent Growth of Local Markets

Growth of national income automatically led to growth of local markets; the gains are included in the estimates of Table 17–8. But local markets, especially for retail and wholesale esablishments and for consumer and business services, have also expanded as a result of population shifts and extension of the geographic area covered by a market. In my American study I briefly discussed this growth source and guessed at its importance in the United States in the 1929–57 period:

Both the increasing concentration of population in metropolitan areas and, especially, the acquisition of automobiles by most of the population must have been of great importance in increasing the size of local markets. The latter prevented market shrinkage in many areas losing population. Although automobile ownership was widespread (and the basic road and street network established) by 1929, it has subsequently increased significantly as has the pervasiveness of driving by women, who do most of the shopping. More importantly, adjustment of markets to the automobile by construction of large stores and service establishments, particularly in shopping centers, mainly occurred after 1929 and has only recently become fairly complete. It would seem reasonable to

ticularly passenger cars, their repair and maintenance, and gas and oil. In such cases gains noted for consumption would also be present for products purchased for business use. The detail needed for direct reweighting of product components other than consumption (beyond the very broad reweighting used in Tables 2–4 and 2–5) is not available.

assume, as I shall, that these independent developments were half as important an element in increasing "true" productivity as the growth of the national economy [from 1929 to 1957]. However, the distinction between the "true" and the measured product is necessary and important here since, as discussed above, much of the benefit from changes in the *organization* of retail and consumer service establishments (but not wholesale and business service establishments) is omitted from the growth rate of the measured national product.

I make the specific assumption that of the presumed benefits of the independent growth of local markets half were reflected in the measured growth rate. Hence, I assume they counted for .07 percentage points, or 2 per cent, of the growth rate of the measured national product from 1929 to 1957.

Adjustment of the trade and service industries to general ownership of the automobile appears to be mostly completed, and the proportion of the population shifting annually into larger trading areas must slacken. I set the contribution to the growth rate of the independent growth of local markets in the 1960–80 period at .05 percentage points as against the previous .07.[54]

There was, it is apparent, little basis for the size of these estimates but for uniformity I shall use 0.06 as the figure consistent with them in the 1950–62 period. European countries measure changes in real consumption by a different procedure from the United States. The reason for halving the contribution to analyze the growth rate of measured product does not apply to continental estimates or to the food component of expenditures in the United Kingdom.[55] If the real effects were the same as in the United States, twice as big a contribution to the growth rate of measured national income should therefore be allowed in the continental countries and an intermediate amount in the United Kingdom.

Automobile ownership has brought economies of scale in distribution not only by broadening geographic markets but also by contributing to an increase in the average size of retail transactions, since the motorized shopper tends to buy more at one time. It has the further effect of facilitating reduction or elimination of home delivery. The reduction of the costs of home delivery as consumers carry a larger proportion of their purchases contributes to an increase in productivity so long as

establishments still offer delivery service.[56] In Europe complete elimination of delivery service by an establishment, or replacement of an establishment that offers home delivery by one that does not, raises measured productivity even more than its curtailment but, paradoxically, it may not raise it at all in the United States because of the way price indexes used to deflate consumer expenditures are constructed.

Urbanization of the population has proceeded rapidly in all countries. But in both prevalence and growth of car ownership, Europe and the United States differ entirely. In 1963, 77 percent of American households and about 32 percent of Northwest European households owned one or more automobiles. Percentages in the Northwest European countries ranged from 26 to 40. In Italy the percentage was only 20. Table 17–9 provides such percentages for all but two of the nine countries and, as an auxiliary indicator, the total population per registered car (including business-owned and second cars) in all the countries. The two indicators are compatible with respect to a comparison of Europe as a whole with the United States, and both show France holding the highest and the Netherlands about the lowest positions, with respect to car ownership, among the Northwest European countries covered in this study. However, they do not rank all the individual European countries in the same order.[57] Northwest Europe as a whole had 7.3 persons per registered automobile in 1963, a position reached by the United States in 1924.[58] Table 17–9 shows data for a few other countries, including Sweden and Luxembourg in Europe, that have more car ownership than the European countries covered in this study.

Trends in car ownership in Europe and the United States have also differed greatly since 1950.

54. *Sources of Economic Growth*, pp. 176–77 [B25].
55. See pp. 29–30.

56. Although gains from eliminating home delivery are not really an economy of scale effect, but rather result from substituting the consumers' time and capital for that of the retailer, it is convenient to consider them here.
57. Car ownership data are, of course, only approximations. Alternative estimates of the percentage of households owning a car in the Common Market countries can be derived from an OSCE survey. The percentages, which refer to 1963–64, are: Belgium, 38; France, 50; Germany, 32; the Netherlands, 27; Italy, 20; and Luxembourg, 43 (OSCE, *General Statistical Bulletin*, No. 1, 1967 [I48]).
58. United States data are from *Automobile Facts and Figures, 1952*, p. 20 [B2].

TABLE 17-9

Automobile Ownership, 1963

Area	Percentage of households owning one or more cars	Population per car registered (persons)
United States	77	2.8
Northwest Europe	32[a]	7.3
Belgium	30	9.2
Denmark	n.a.	7.6
France	40	6.7
Germany	26	7.3
Netherlands	26	13.6
Norway	n.a.	10.0
United Kingdom	32[b]	6.8
Italy	20	12.9
Addendum		
Canada	68[c]	3.8
New Zealand	n.a.	4.0
Australia	n.a.	4.4
Sweden	n.a.	5.0
Luxembourg	48	6.2

Sources: Data for European countries in the first column are from *The European Common Market and Britain*, a marketing survey sponsored by the Reader's Digest, Table 3 [B91]. (Copyright 1963 by the Reader's Digest Association, Inc. Reproduced with permission.) Other data are from Automobile Manufacturers' Association, *Automobile Facts and Figures, 1965*, pp. 26–27, 41, 47 [B2], except the Canadian figure which is from the *1961 Housing Census* [G75].
a. Excluding Denmark and Norway.
b. Great Britain.
c. 1961.
n.a. Not available.

Percentages of households owning cars in France, where car ownership is most advanced, compare as follows with the United States:[59]

	1950	1955	1960	1962	1964
France	13.6	21.3	30.1	35.3	41.0
United States	62.5	73.5	75.5	77.1	78.1

Since the early 1950's, when the wartime backlog was overcome, the American percentage has only inched up. Meanwhile French ownership has been increasing at a rate reminiscent of (though slower than) that of American ownership after World War I.

While the impact of automobile ownership on market structure had passed its peak in the United

59. The French estimates are from *Etudes et Conjoncture*, June 1965, pp. 21 and 23 [G14]. The 1964 figure is preliminary. United States estimates are from the "National Automobile and Tire Survey, 1965," sponsored by *Look* magazine, conducted by Alfred Politz Research, Inc., except that 1950 was extrapolated from 1954 by the Survey Research Center series for families (*Automobile Facts and Figures, 1966*, p. 45, and *Automobile Facts and Figures, 1964*, p. 35 [B2]).

States before the period reviewed here, my traveler's impression from watching the European housewife making her almost daily rounds from small shop to small shop was that in 1962 the largest impact in Europe was still in the future. This seems probable from other considerations. *The Economist* in 1962 noted that "the heavy losses reported for the multi-storey car park attached to the Teaco discount store at Leicester rather confirms the belief that the British have yet to become car-borne shoppers."[60] Even by 1963 only about one-third of Northwest European households owned automobiles.[61] The proportion had recently been far smaller, and the readjustment of production and distribution channels to the automobile requires time. Further, in the important field of food distribution the availability of capacious refrigeration facilities in the home is a prerequisite to full adoption of American buying practices. The proportion of households with refrigerators has been increasing dramatically. In France it rose from 7.5 percent in 1954 to 31 in 1960, 39.5 in 1962, and 52 in 1964, and is expected to reach 81 percent in 1970.[62] But, as yet, most refrigerators in European homes are small and few have deep-freeze compartments capable of storing adequate amounts of frozen food.

For the automobile's potential to be realized important changes in business structure are required. Retail trade is only one of the many industries affected but it is the largest single industry and changes in retailing have an important indirect impact upon wholesale trade as well. It appears that by 1962 reorganization had progressed further in some European countries than in others—more in Germany than in the United Kingdom, relatively little in Belgium, France, and Italy—but that in all of them most of the revolution in retail trade organi-

60. September 1, 1962, p. 840 [P19].
61. The importance of automobile-owning households as customers does, of course, exceed their numbers. The average income of French car-owning families in 1962 is estimated to be 41 percent above that of all families (which compares with 71 percent in 1950). Estimates are from *Etudes et Conjoncture*, June 1965 [G14].
62. *Etudes et Conjoncture*, September 1965. In the United Kingdom the proportion of families owning refrigerators is estimated to have increased from 7 in 1954 to 23 by 1960 (*Frozen Foods*, May 1961, p. 320 [P21]) and to 40 by 1966 (*Business Week*, September 10, 1966, p. 118 [P8]). By 1964 about one-half of the families in Northwest Europe as a whole had refrigerators. The fraction was apparently highest in Germany.

zation still lay ahead. Some comments on the re-organization of retail trade and the importance of size in that industry are presented in Appendix M.

In the United States, the motorized housewife loads her car with a week's supply of food, household supplies, and assorted other items at a self-service supermarket, and fills most of her remaining needs at adjacent stores and service establishments in the same shopping center.[63] If the center is miles from her home or if she happens to need an unusual item or service from a highly specialized establishment serving a wider area that is on the other side of town, she gives no second thought to the trip involved.[64] Whether general ownership of automobiles will ever make this pattern as common in Europe remains to be seen. Greater congestion may prove an obstacle, and large home refrigerators will be required to accommodate a week's supply of perishable commodities. But some large shopping centers have appeared—especially in Sweden, the European nation where incomes and car ownership most closely approach American standards—and this suggests the pattern may eventually be adopted.

The independent growth of local markets, resulting from population shifts and rising automobile ownership, seems unlikely to have contributed nearly as much to European as to American growth before 1955, or as much even during the 1955–62 period, despite the sharper rise in car ownership.[65] Actually, a major break in the pace of change in Europe seems to have occurred about 1958. I shall assume contributions of 0.09 in 1955–62, three-quarters of the assumed "true" contribution in the

United States, and contributions of 0.04 in 1950–55. Unlike the American contributions, those for the continental countries need not be halved to allow for deflation procedures. The United Kingdom deflation procedure is similar to that in the United States except for food stores. I reduce the contributions for that country by one-fourth to allow for this (obtaining 0.07 and 0.03).[66]

These estimates have a counterpart in explaining differences in the level of national income per person employed. If only the impact of the automobile were involved, the following procedure would provide an estimate of its importance that would be roughly consistent with the time series estimates for the United States. In Northwest Europe in 1960, automobile ownership was similar to that in the United States around 1922. From 1929 to 1957, United States national income per person employed increased at an annual rate of 1.6 percent a year; 0.07 percentage points, or 4.38 percent, of this rate was ascribed to the independent growth of local markets. Assume that these rates would be about the same for the longer period 1922–60. It can then be calculated that if there had been no independent growth of local markets since 1922, United States national income per person employed in 1960 would have been 2 percent smaller than it was.[67] But the difference would have been larger— 4 percent if the underlying assumptions are taken literally—if the deflation procedures in the United States were the same as those used on the continent and in all the international comparisons of the level of national product. On this basis economies of scale made possible by general availability of automobiles would be responsible for reducing Northwest European national income per person employed 4 percent below the American figure in

63. Let me confess immediately, in self-protection from any female American reader, that I exaggerate, of course. Moreover, the purchase of clothing and other greatly diversified products does not fit this stereotype at all.

64. Transportation costs are incurred, of course, but these are counted as final products in national accounting whereas the costs of moving commodities to (or nearer to) the housewife, rather than the housewife to the commodity, are counted as intermediate products.

65. Not only was automobile ownership small in the earlier period but changes in retail organization were observably small. Christina Fulop's observation that in the immediate postwar period in Britain "retailing operated in a straitjacket of rationing, building restrictions and financial controls, rendering it virtually impossible for the introduction of innovations on a large scale," also applies to the continent (in *Competition for Consumers*, p. 17 [B39]). Harper W. Boyd, Jr. and Ivan Piercy say the British retail structure has veered toward American practices since 1950 but especially since 1958 (in *Business Horizons*, Spring 1963, p. 80 [P7]).

66. Use of the same estimates for, say, France and Germany implies that if greater progress in reorganizing trade has been made in Germany than in France, as appears to be the case, this reflects a more rapid adoption of American business practices in Germany than in France given the possibilities offered by the markets available, not greater expansion of opportunities because of greater market growth. With automobile ownership higher in France, the alternative hypothesis seems improbable.

67. A growth rate of 1.6 percent would raise national income per person employed from an index of 100 to 182.8 in 38 years. If 4.38 percent of the increase had not occurred, the index would be 179.2 and national income per person employed would have been (179.2 ÷ 182.8) or 98.0 percent as large as it actually was.

1960 (without allowance for interaction). How-ever, the American time series estimate was in-tended to include also gains from the increasing concentration of population. It is true that in the absence of the extension of automobile ownership, increased concentration of population would not have been an unmixed blessing even from the stand-point of economies of scale, since the gains in urban areas would have been somewhat counterbalanced by losses in rural areas. Even so, a substantial re-duction is in order, and the 4 percent figure itself seems generous; I shall use an estimate of 2.5 in Northwest Europe and 3.0 in Italy. Differences among the Northwest European countries in 1960 seem probably too small to warrant a distinction among them in view of the crudeness of the figure.

Table 17–10 sets out in tabular form the esti-mates described in this section, and the contribution to differences in levels of national income per per-son employed after allowing in the usual way for the interaction factor.

TABLE 17–10

Economies of Scale Associated with the Independent Growth of Local Markets: Contributions to Growth Rates of Total National Income and to Differences from the United States in National Income per Person Employed

Area	Contribution to growth rate[a] of national income (percentage points)			Contribution to difference from United States in national income per person employed, 1960 (index points)	
	1950–62	1950–55	1955–62	Before inter-action allow-ance	After inter-action allow-ance
U. S.	.06	.06	.06	—	—
N. W. Europe	.06	.04	.08	2.5	1.9
Belgium	.07	.04	.09	2.5	2.0
Denmark	.07	.04	.09	2.5	1.9
France	.07	.04	.09	2.5	1.9
Germany	.07	.04	.09	2.5	1.9
Netherlands	.07	.04	.09	2.5	2.0
Norway	.07	.04	.09	2.5	2.0
U. K.	.05	.03	.07	2.5	1.8
Italy	.07	.04	.09	3.0	1.8

Source: See text for derivation.
a. Differences among countries reflect in part different methods of deflating national product.

Economies of Scale and the Growth Rate

The tables of this chapter have emphasized the contributions of economies of scale expressed in percentage points. The question may be asked: By what percentage were growth rates higher than they would have been if the countries had been operat-ing under constant returns to scale? The answer implied by the three sets of estimates presented in this chapter can be readily calculated. For example, the Dutch growth rate was 4.73 from 1950 to 1962. It was estimated in this chapter that 0.78 points of this amount represented gains from scale econo-mies; hence, the growth rate would have been 3.95 under constant returns to scale.[68] The Dutch growth rate, my estimates thus imply, was 20 percent (0.78 ÷ 3.95) higher than it would have been if the Dutch economy had operated under constant returns to scale. It should be recalled that gains from relaxa-tion of barriers to international trade are not counted as gains from economies of scale. It should also be understood that the estimates refer to the gains that would have been achieved if the distribu-tions of firms and establishments by size in 1950 were as appropriate, given the size of markets in 1950, as were the distributions in 1962, given the size of markets in 1962.

The percentages by which scale economies raised the growth rate, as implied by my estimates, were:

	1950–62	1950–55	1955–62
Germany	28	27	30
Italy	26	18	32
France	26	26	25
Northwest Europe	24	22	27
Denmark	23	3	29
Norway	20	11	28
Netherlands	20	14	27
Belgium	19	11	26
United Kingdom	19	13	23
United States	12	12	13

Large differences in some countries between the two subperiods are mainly due to differences in the speed with which consumption patterns were esti-mated to have been changing.

The fact that the general level of these percent-ages in all countries is dependent upon assumptions made for the United States must be stressed again; and, also, the general inadequacy of information.

68. The figure of 0.78 is the sum of 0.71 from Table 17–8 and 0.07 from Table 17–10.

CHAPTER EIGHTEEN

Allocation and Use of Resources:
Some Additional Aspects

A contribution to growth may be obtained during a transition period if the actual allocation of resources moves closer to the situation—itself constantly changing—that would yield a maximum national income. This may occur if institutional restrictions that prevent the equilibrium allocation from coinciding with the income-maximizing allocation are removed or weakened.[1] It may also occur if the actual allocation is brought closer to the equilibrium as a result of improved foresight or increased mobility. A contribution to growth may also be obtained if institutional restrictions against the efficient use of resources in the use to which they are actually put weaken. In practice, the same conditions—absence of competitive pressures, for example—are likely to be unfavorable to efficiency in both allocation and utilization of resources.

The reduction of overallocation to agriculture and self-employment has already been examined (in Chapter 16); so has the allocation of capital (in

Chapter 12). This chapter considers some additional topics that relate to the allocation or to the efficient use of resources, but it must be understood that examination of all the changes that might have influenced the efficiency with which resources are allocated and used in each of nine countries would be an impossible task.[2] Only a few will be mentioned, and even for these, information and technique are grossly inadequate to yield quantitative estimates of contributions to growth.[3] Only for the first topic considered, obstacles to international trade, are numerical estimates even attempted.

2. One aspect of resource allocation is of little importance in a study of measured economic growth. Changes in the composition of output that occur because the *equilibrium* price structure moves closer to or farther from the structure that would maximize economic welfare obviously increase or reduce economic welfare. But they do not, in general, change the measured national product in constant prices unless they also affect the efficiency of production where resources are actually used. By this statement I mean only that if two products have the same factor cost per unit in the base year, 1 million units of product will yield the same constant dollar national product in any other year no matter how output is distributed between the two products.

3. The discussions of international trade barriers and size of firm and establishment involve in part the effect of changes in institutional obstacles upon the degree to which economies of scale potentially available are actually realized. Gains from such changes were not included in the estimates of gains from economies of scale presented in the preceding chapter.

1. As noted in Chapter 1, attention by suppliers of the factors of production to considerations other than maximum earnings also prevent the equilibrium allocation from being an income-maximizing allocation. Changes in the weight attached to nonmonetary considerations are most likely to be of importance, if at all, among the self-employed considered in Chapter 16.

Obstacles to International Trade

Restrictions against international trade prevent full realization of its potential advantages of concentrating production of commodities in countries having the greatest comparative advantage in their production and of broadening markets and thus allowing more specialization.[4] Changes between two dates in artificial barriers to trade can consequently add to or subtract from growth rates between those dates. Calculation of this contribution to the growth rate would require knowledge of the amount of trade that would have taken place at one date with the barriers of the other date and of the increased costs that were imposed because that trade did not take place.

Costs of Protection

In my earlier study I guessed, perhaps generously, that in 1957 the total cost of all artificial barriers to exports and imports was around 1.5 percent of national income in the United States. I concluded that the cost in 1929 probably did not differ from the cost in 1957 by as much as one-fifth, the approximate amount that would have been required to affect the growth rate of national income by as much as 0.01 percentage points over the twenty-eight-year period from 1929 to 1957.[5] Unless, as I consider unlikely, my guess at the total cost of protection is much too low, changes in trade barriers could not have had any appreciable effect upon the United States growth rate in the 1950–62 period either. There were changes but they were not large enough, on balance, to have more than a trivial effect on growth.[6]

Western Europe as a whole represents a market area about as large as the United States but it is divided among many countries. Trade that would be internal in the United States is international in Europe and the cost of artificial barriers to trade is surely higher. Various studies suggest that even in Europe the cost of protection is not a very large percentage of national income.[7] But I believe the cost has been big enough to allow room for large changes in trade barriers to affect short-term growth rates by significant amounts.

Postwar Trend Toward Liberalization

Large changes in trade barriers did occur in Europe during the postwar period. In the late 1940's pent-up domestic demand and low production induced a demand for imports much larger than European countries could finance by exports or reduction of their foreign exchange reserves. In response to this situation, countries rationed imports and conducted trade under bilateral agreements that

4. I am not concerned in this section with other possible effects of trade barriers and changes in them. (One, the effect on competitive pressure, is pointed out later in this chapter.) Neither am I concerned with all the consequences of associations such as EEC or EFTA. These associations may influence the behavior of a number of growth determinants.

5. *Sources of Economic Growth*, p. 189 [B25]. The estimate in that study referred to changes in the costs of barriers to trade rather than to the cost of changes in barriers. The costs of barriers may change for reasons other than changes in the barriers themselves. However, in the United States neither could have been appreciable in growth rate terms.

6. During the 1950's nontariff restrictions on American exports were being removed in Europe. Toward the end of the 1950–62 period nontariff protection at home was increasing and formation of EEC and EFTA introduced a new form

of discrimination against United States exports. One of the American restrictions that was most costly in a real sense, the tying of foreign aid, reduced the quantity of goods that could be obtained with aid dollars but did not adversely affect the measured growth rate because of the deflation procedure utilized in the United States national accounts.

7. Indeed, estimates of the potential gains from European integration made by Tibor Scitovsky and Harry Johnson and of the welfare cost of tariffs by L. H. Janssens are so small—a small fraction of 1 percent of Western European national income in the case of Scitovsky, and of Italian national income in the case of Janssens, a maximum of 1 percent for Britain in the case of Johnson—as to suggest the total costs of protection can hardly be large enough for their elimination to make much of a contribution to growth (Scitovsky, *Economic Theory and Western European Integration*, p. 67 [B98]; Janssens, *Free Trade, Protection, and Customs Unions*, p. 132 [B53]; Johnson in *Manchester School of Economics and Social Studies*, September 1958, pp. 247–55 [P28]). However, such estimates exclude potential gains from economies of scale within the countries that are already the most efficient producers of products. Also, more recent writings on the cost of protection seem to imply higher costs although aggregate estimates are not provided. (See, for example, Balassa in *Journal of Political Economy*, December 1965, pp. 573–94 [P25], and, for an evaluation of the effects of integration on selected industries, EEC Commission, Eighth and Ninth General Reports on the Activities of the Community [I58].) This is not to say that costs are *very* large. Illustrative calculations, such as one by James E. Meade, are still illuminating. Meade notes that even if free trade with EEC increased British imports by 25 percent of national income, which would more than double *total* imports, and if the gain were 10 percent of the value of the additional imports, national income would be only 2.5 percent higher (Meade, *U.K., Commonwealth and Common Market*, pp. 13–16 [B75]).

TABLE 18-1

Exports and Imports as a Percentage of Gross National Product
at Market Prices, 1950–63

(*In current and constant 1958 prices*)

Type of trade	Belgium	Denmark	France	Germany	Nether-lands	Norway	United Kingdom	Italy
A: Current Prices								
Total exports								
1950	.248	.272	.157	.097	.406	.386	.226	.108
1951	.329	.329	.166	.132	.476	.468	.295	.124
1954–56	.311	.326	.144	.173	.470	.410	.218	.126
1961–63	.340	.301	.142	.192	.469	.398	.192	.165
Manufactured products only								
1950	n.a.	n.a.	n.a.	.064	n.a.	n.a.	.138	n.a.
1951	.257	.060	.083	.096	.160	.119	.149	.071
1954–56	.229	.065	.063	.120	.161	.099	.120	.052
1961–63	.257	.089	.076	.138	.185	.118	.111	.088
Total Imports								
1950	.280	.306	.145	.109	.477	.440	.232	.117
1951	.310	.338	.168	.116	.500	.451	.295	.140
1954–56	.315	.327	.135	.146	.480	.433	.225	.136
1961–63	.348	.314	.133	.176	.469	.423	.197	.174
Manufactured products only								
1950	n.a.	n.a.	n.a.	.023	n.a.	n.a.	.035	n.a.
1951	.125	.154	.034	.022	.206	.210	.052	.071
1954–56	.147	.149	.030	.034	.206	.219	.043	.041
1961–63	.200	.179	.047	.058	.246	.224	.051	.073
B: Constant 1958 Prices								
Total exports								
1950	.228	.290	.127	.100	.333	.393	.205	.092
1951	.248	.328	.142	.118	.356	.349	.199	.096
1954–56	.296	.321	.136	.162	.423	.375	.204	.117
1961–63	.374	.342	.150	.209	.527	.467	.202	.168
Manufactured products only								
1950	n.a.	n.a.	n.a.	.064	n.a.	n.a.	.128	n.a.
1951	n.a.	n.a.	n.a.	.085	n.a.	n.a.	.126	n.a.
1954–56	.219	n.a.	.081	.112	.147	.090	.117	.046
1961–63	.284	n.a.	.103	.149	.206	.132	.114	.095
Total Imports								
1950	.274	.344	.112	.084	.400	.461	.242	.105
1951	.266	.322	.121	.080	.370	.389	.254	.104
1954–56	.318	.349	.123	.130	.438	.412	.250	.126
1961–63	.393	.399	.146	.204	.545	.495	.264	.185
Manufactured products only								
1950	n.a.	n.a.	n.a.	.020	n.a.	n.a.	.030	n.a.
1951	n.a.	n.a.	n.a.	.017	n.a.	n.a.	.036	n.a.
1954–56	n.a.	n.a.	.032	.034	n.a.	.228	.036	n.a.
1961–63	n.a.	n.a.	.058	.074	n.a.	.318	.055	n.a.

Source: See Appendix N.
n.a. Not available.

balanced exports and imports between individual countries. Marshall Plan aid, establishment of the nondiscrimination principle in the General Agreement on Tariffs and Trade (GATT), founding of the Organisation for European Economic Co-operation pledged to trade liberalization, the European devaluations of September 1949, and the effective beginning of the European Payments Union in October 1950, all created a favorable background for progressive elimination of bilateralism, quantitative import restrictions, and exchange restrictions as European production rose and demand backlogs wore off. Successive decisions by OEEC required each country to eliminate restrictions on imports from other European countries (including trade with the sterling and franc areas) on commodities representing 50 percent of its total imports by December 1949, 75 percent by February 1951, and 90 percent by October 1955. Individual countries exceeded these standards but there were also departures from them.[8] The percentage of effective trade liberalization by the seventeen OEEC members at mid-year was 56 in 1950, 65 in 1951, 84 in 1955, 91 in 1960, and 94 in 1961.[9] Restrictions against imports from the dollar area were more persistent, but by December 1955 OEEC was able to recommend relaxation of quantitative restrictions. From 11 percent at the beginning of 1953 and 44 percent in September 1954, "effective liberalization" of restrictions against imports from the dollar area reached 54 percent at the beginning of 1956 and 89 in May 1961.[10] By 1960 quantitative restrictions on imports from all areas to the eight European countries covered in this study had almost vanished except for agricultural products, coal, and oil. OEEC also initiated liberalization of invisible transactions and in 1959 adopted a Code of Liberalization of Capital Movements. Convertibility of currencies was completed at the time of the French devaluation in December 1958.

So long as quantitative restrictions were decisive, changes in tariff rates, such as the reductions negotiated under GATT in 1947–49 and 1951, were less important than usual in influencing trade. But by 1956–57, the volume of trade responded sharply when Germany cut tariffs on industrial products by more than half.

Other tariff developments were associated with the European integration movement. The Benelux customs union was established in 1948 and the European Coal and Steel Community began operations in 1953. The EEC made its first tariff changes in January 1959 and EFTA in July 1960. Both agreements provided for gradual elimination of internal tariffs (except on agricultural and fishery products in the case of EFTA). EEC also provided for establishment of a common external tariff for industrial goods. In 1962, 70 percent of the internal EFTA tariffs remained until March and during the rest of that year, 60 percent; 60 percent of the tariff on internal EEC trade remained until July, and thereafter, 50 percent; and 70 percent of the difference between national tariffs and the EEC common external tariff reduced by 20 percent remained in effect.[11]

In spite of some setbacks, it can be stated safely that European trade barriers were reduced from 1950 to 1955 and again from 1955 to 1962.

Trade Related to GNP

Table 18–1 shows what happened to trade in relation to GNP. Total exports and total imports of goods and services (excluding factor incomes) are shown as a percentage of GNP in both current and constant prices. Current and constant price ratios are also given for manufactured products separately when they are available. To iron out short-term fluctuations, which are often associated with stock accumulation or liquidation that has little productivity significance, I use 1954–56 averages to represent 1955 and 1961–63 averages for 1962. Actual percentages are given for 1950 because the situation was changing so rapidly from 1949 to 1951

8. Progress toward liberalization was periodically interrupted as countries temporarily resorted to "clauses of derogation" to meet payments difficulties. Ten member countries, including France, Germany, and the United Kingdom, did so for parts of the 1951–53 period. France did not return to 75 percent liberalization until 1955, and again departed from the standard (then 90 percent) in 1957–58.

9. OEEC, *Twelfth Annual Economic Review*, p. 185 [I14]. The 1960 and 1961 percentages include Spain.

10. *Ibid.*, p. 186.

11. By January 1967, the EFTA countries had completed transition to an industrial free trade area. EEC internal tariffs were down to 20 percent of their 1957 level and a unified agricultural market was in effect for several products.

that the actual data appear to represent the 1950 situation better than a three-year average; however, 1951 percentages are also shown. The 1961–63 data treat the Saar and West Berlin as part of Germany, and the original data for France and Germany in the earlier years were adjusted when necessary to provide changes in the percentages that are significant.[12]

Prices of internationally traded goods and services moved very differently from GNP prices so there is little resemblance between changes in the current and constant price percentages. Constant price percentages generally rose more or fell less than current price percentages over the periods shown, although there are some exceptions. Analysis will center on the constant price data because changes in the terms of trade do not directly affect growth rates. But for the purposes of this study, the changes in price relationships are doubly unfortunate. First, they make it more difficult to infer missing constant price ratios from available current price ratios. Second, the changes in relative prices must themselves have had effects on trade and domestic resource utilization that I cannot isolate.

Contribution of Trade Relaxation to Growth

The relaxation of trade barriers in Europe was accompanied by an increase in trade. I think it safe to assume that it affected efficiency in production favorably and contributed to growth. But to suggest amounts I can only offer some experimental calculations. These require estimates of (1) the additional trade that would have taken place in one year with the restrictions of the other, and (2) the costs imposed by the absence of this trade.

Consider first the 1955–62 period, and specifically manufactured products. Restrictions against imports of manufactured products clearly were smaller in 1962 than in 1955. Intra-European trade is so important that it is safe to assume restrictions against exports of the European countries also declined in this period. One would therefore expect ratios of trade in manufactured products to GNP to be higher in 1961–63 than in 1954–56 unless changes in the domestic economy were very strongly in the direction of reducing gains potentially avail-

12. See Appendix N.

able from international trade. All the percentages for manufactured products except that for British exports did in fact rise in both constant and current prices. Changes in the constant price percentages, including estimates where data are lacking, were as follows:

	Export ratio	Import ratio
Belgium	6.5	(9.5)
Denmark	(3.8)	(7.0)
France	2.2	2.6
Germany	3.7	4.0
Netherlands	5.9	(12.2)
Norway	4.2	9.0
United Kingdom	–.3	1.9
Italy	4.9	(6.0)

In this table, figures not in parentheses are computed from Table 18–1. Figures in parentheses are crude estimates inferred from changes in manufactured goods ratios in current prices, changes in total trade in current and constant prices, and relationships among these data in other countries.

Do these changes measure the additional trade that would have taken place in 1954–56 if trade barriers had been at 1961–63 levels? They do so only if the ratios would have been unchanged in the absence of changes in trade barriers (including inappropriate exchange rates). For manufactured goods I shall assume this condition to be met. I do so only for lack of a better procedure.

R. Bertrand puts the 1953–55 average of tariffs on industrial products at about 13.5 percent in Germany, 9 in Benelux, 19 in France, and 18 in Italy, while P. J. Verdoorn in 1954 put the weighted average level of tariffs on industrial products at 12.4 in the United Kingdom and 9.7 in the Scandinavian countries.[13] I assume the tariff rate faced by manufactured goods exports of each country was 12.5 percent.[14] Tariff percentages are at best only a very

13. Bertrand in *Cahiers de l'*ISEA, Series R, February 1958, p. 10 [P10] (figures given are based on an average of his groups IV and V), and Verdoorn in *World Politics*, July 1954, p. 489 [P50]. The Verdoorn estimates are further discussed in Scitovsky, *Economic Theory and Western European Integration*, pp. 64–67 (B98). Verdoorn also gives estimates for other countries, including a very high figure of 33.5 for Germany, which appears to be inappropriately weighted for the purposes here. Reference may also be made to estimates referring to more recent years by Wartna, OSCE, *Statistical Information*, No. 2, 1966, pp. 11–54 [I49].

14. The average, weighted by value of imports, of the import rates just given is 12.7 percent. Scitovsky (*Economic Theory . . .*, p. 66 [B98]) used 12 percent as the average rate of European exports to non-European countries.

rough guide to costs of protection because tariffs may be higher than are needed for protection. Moreover, these rates do not refer specifically to products not traded in 1955 that would have been traded with 1962 restraints; they do not take exchange rates into account; and they do not reflect quantitative restrictions that in 1955 were still of some importance in intra-European trade and of even more importance with respect to imports from the United States. There are also more subtle difficulties. For the following calculations I assume the costs in 1955 of not importing or exporting manufactured goods that would have been traded with 1962 restrictions were a percentage of their value equal to two-thirds of the average tariff rate given above.[15]

The calculation of the contribution to growth on the stated assumptions may be illustrated with French data. The assumptions imply that if trade barriers had been the same in 1955 as in 1962 France would have imported in 1955 additional manufactured goods equal to 2.6 percent of her national product and exported additional manufactured goods equal to 2.2 percent of her national product.[16] Absence of the additional imports cost her 12.6 percent of their value, or 0.33 percent of national product, and absence of the additional exports cost her 8.3 percent of their value, or 0.18 percent of her national product. The total 1955 cost of greater restrictions on trade than existed in 1962 was then 0.51 percent of national product. If French national product had been 0.51 percent higher in 1955, the French growth rate from 1955 to 1962 would have been 0.07 percentage points lower, so the contribution made by the elimination of restrictions was 0.07 percentage points. The results of similar calculations for the other countries are given in the first column of the following table. The cal-

culations assume average tariff rates on imports to have been one-fourth lower in Denmark and one-fourth higher in Norway than the "Scandinavian rate" given by Verdoorn.[17]

Calculations of the contribution to the 1955–62 growth rate of changes in trade barriers, based on changes in ratios to GNP of trade in:

	Manufactured goods	All goods and services
Belgium	.16	.16
Denmark	.09	.06
France	.07	.06
Germany	.10	.15
Netherlands	.16	.21
Norway	.15	.20
United Kingdom	.02	.01
Italy	.16	.16

For lack of anything better I shall use these estimates despite their flimsy basis.

The second column of the same table shows, for comparison, the results of mechanically applying the same procedure (including the same cost ratios) to changes from 1954–56 to 1961–63 in the ratios to GNP of exports and imports of all goods and services. For most countries the results are rather similar. However, this calculation is less plausible. Ratios to GNP of trade in nonmanufactured goods and services rose in some countries and fell in others so that the second column is sometimes larger and sometimes smaller than the first.[18] Changes in these ratios were too much dominated by influences unrelated to trade barriers for even the most tolerant standards to allow their use as indicators of the effects of changes in trade barriers. I shall use as estimates of the total gains from relaxation of trade barriers in 1955–62 those derived for manufactured products.[19]

15. Insofar as exports and imports of manufactured products would have been higher by the same amount, the cost of foregoing this trade is the product of this amount and the sum of the assumed export and import cost ratios. The latter sum is 21 percent for France, for example (two-thirds of the sum of 19 + 12.5). The calculations thus imply that diversion of resources from home production to export production up to the 1962 level would have enabled France to obtain imports with a value (in constant French prices) 21 percent greater than the same resources actually produced in 1955.

16. It will be noted that the calculation is the same whether a rise in the import or export ratio was from, say, 3 percent to 6 percent or from 23 percent to 26 percent.

17. This adjustment was introduced on the basis of the evidence cited on p. 232 which indicates Norwegian tariffs to have been higher than those of Sweden and Denmark, and Danish tariffs to have been lower than those of Norway and Sweden.

18. This is not surprising since, in contrast to manufactured products, it is not clear that obstacles to trade in nonmanufactured products were strongly and generally reduced from 1955 to 1962. Nonagricultural raw materials were not, in general, subject to much protection at either date. Fuel imports were persistently restricted, mainly to protect domestic coal mines; Germany and Belgium even increased protection. Restrictions on trade in agricultural products are complex, but appear to have been somewhat relaxed in most countries. Restrictions on services generally declined.

19. This decision eliminates the possibility of double counting the gains from reducing the overallocation of resources to agriculture, which were estimated in Chapter 16.

Similar calculations for the 1950–55 period following the same procedures and using the same cost ratios can be made for Germany and the United Kingdom for manufactured goods, and for all countries for total exports and imports.

Calculations of the apparent contribution to the 1950–55 growth rate of changes in trade barriers based on changes in ratios to GNP of trade in:

	Manufactured goods	All goods and services
Belgium		.16
Denmark		.06
France		.04
Germany	.11	.18
Netherlands		.20
Norway		−.11
United Kingdom	−.01	.01
Italy		.09

Except for Germany and the United Kingdom, 1950 estimates of manufactured goods imports and exports in constant prices were not available. Even current price ratios for manufactured products could generally be pushed back only to 1951.

However, the 1950–55 period was so abnormal that, even aside from data problems, the meaning of any such calculations is dubious. Restrictions on trade that were present in 1950 but not in 1955 were not imposed for the usual reasons of protecting domestic interests or increasing self-sufficiency, but to insure that scarce foreign exchange secured the most necessary items. Special attention was given to imports most needed for production, especially production for export. Under 1950 conditions European production would probably have been lower, not higher, in the absence of import controls. Marshall Plan aid in 1950 further complicates interpretation. It seems more realistic to say that from 1950 to 1955 recovery and growth made possible freer trade than to say that the removal of trade restrictions as such contributed to growth. The freeing of trade was an integral part of the postwar recovery and resumption of normal economic patterns that complicate the entire analysis of this period.

For these reasons I was tempted to omit any estimate for the 1950–55 period. But this would introduce an unacceptable discontinuity in the analysis of growth sources for the two periods. To avoid this discontinuity I shall simply assume the same con-

TABLE 18–2

Contribution of Changes in Trade Barriers to Growth Rates of Total National Income

(In percentage points)

Area	1950–62[a]	1950–55[a]	1955–62
United States	.00	.00	.00
Northwest Europe	.08	.08	.08
Belgium	.16	.16	.16
Denmark	.09	.09	.09
France	.07	.07	.07
Germany	.10	.10	.10
Netherlands	.16	.16	.16
Norway	.15	.15	.15
United Kingdom	.02	.02	.02
Italy	.16	.16	.16

Source: See text for derivation.
a. Assumed to be the same as 1955–62.

tributions in 1950–55 as in 1955–62 (Table 18–2). Numerically, the results of calculations based on manufactured goods are similar in the two periods for the two countries, Germany and the United Kingdom, where they are available. It happens that the calculations based on total imports and exports are also similar in the two periods in all countries except Norway and Italy, where they are lower in the first period. The estimates for 1950–55 are better interpreted as estimates of gains from the elimination of the conditions that compelled restrictive trade barriers in 1950, rather than from the elimination of the barriers themselves.[20]

I do not attempt to isolate the effects of trade barriers on differences in the *level* of national income per person employed. These effects are already covered (or nearly so) by previous estimates. In the estimation of the effect of economies of scale on the level of productivity (Section I, Chapter 17), existing trade barriers were assumed, and in the calculation of the costs (to national income in United States prices) of overallocation of resources to agriculture, overallocation due to trade barriers was not eliminated. Any additional allowance would introduce double-counting.

20. The difference between the two periods in the calculations based on total exports and imports in constant prices is large in Norway. If this happens also to be true of manufactured goods, for which I lack 1950 data, it may mean that the Norwegian estimate for 1950–55 is very poor. However, it would hardly seem sensible to suppose that Norwegian productivity was suffering, as the 1950–55 calculation shows, rather than gaining from changes in trade barriers.

Obstacles to Efficient Transportation

A number of obstacles to the transport of people and commodities between and within countries by the most efficient methods and carriers have been lessened or removed.

Movement across national boundaries in Europe has been greatly eased by international agreement. Customs inspection and immigration have been simplified and costly waiting times at borders reduced. Agreements referring to drivers, vehicles, roads, and safety regulations have facilitated international transportation by road. Others provide for joint use of railroad equipment, with a joint pool of freight cars and a joint financing agency, and for "through rates" on coal and steel products moving among the Common Market countries. A European system of air navigation control was established. A specialized agency promoted interconnection of electricity networks.[21]

Internally, the degree of success in ensuring "freedom of choice to the user . . . at the least cost to the nation as a whole" (the explicit aim of a French decree dated November 1949) has varied. In most countries rate structures have been brought more closely into line with costs, and discrimination against trucking to protect the railroads has been reduced. The Benelux treaties of 1947 and 1958 not only eliminated national discrimination against citizens of other member countries but also established the principle of the viability of all transport undertakings (which forbids discrimination against one carrier to protect another). They have particularly affected Belgian policy. Not all changes, of course, have been improvements. For example, German transport legislation of 1952–53 effectively limited own-account transport by a "deliberately high transport tax, which in effect taxed own-account operations nearly seven times as heavily as those of carriers for hire. As a result the long distance own-account transport fleet hardly increased

in size between 1953 and 1964."[22] Unremunerative railroad services were not quickly discontinued as the need for them declined, and this contributed to the large deficits of nationalized railroads, particularly those of Belgium and Germany. Nevertheless, the adverse effect of discriminatory pricing policy has been generally reduced.

Mobility and Use of Labor

There can be little doubt that before World War II mobility of labor was greater in the United States than in Europe, whether one considers geographic, occupational, industrial, or almost any other important aspect of mobility. In the postwar period the difference has apparently narrowed. Extended labor shortages have both brightened the prospects for a European worker to improve his situation by changing jobs and reduced his reluctance to give up the security of an established job.[23] Changes in attitudes of both workers and employers have made European labor markets more fluid.

Most European countries have had short-term training and retraining programs for adults, directed either at making the unemployed and disadvantaged employable or (as in France and the Netherlands) at training well-qualified younger persons for occupations in which labor shortages were acute. Numbers involved were not large but some contribution was made to mobility.[24] In the United States adult programs were greatly expanded after the 1950–62 period.

Hilde Wander reports that the international movement of European workers greatly increased from 1950 to 1962, both among the industrial countries and between the southern and northern countries.[25] Charles P. Kindleberger notes that "Italian

---

21. See Bayliss, *European Transport* [B9]; Despicht, *Policies for Transport in the Common Market* [B29]; de Ferron, *Le Problème des Transports et le Marché Commun* [S5]; Owen in Dewhurst, Coppock, Yates, and Associates (eds.), *Europe's Needs and Resources,* pp. 282–83 [B31]; European Coal and Steel Community, *C.E.C.A. 1952–1962,* pp. 382–411 [160]; and OECD *Observer,* November 1962, pp. 10–12 [136].

22. Despicht, *Policies for Transport in the Common Market,* pp. 88–89.

23. German time series "confirm [the inference from United States data] that voluntary mobility increases on a tight labor market" (OECD, *Wages and Labor Mobility,* p. 67 [141]).

24. Margaret S. Gordon describes the programs in most countries in *Retraining and Labor Market Adjustments in Western Europe* [G72]. A discussion of policies to cope with structural unemployment of various types will be found in OECD, *Active Manpower Policy in the United States, Canada, and Europe* [I25].

25. "Communication on the Origin and Destination of Recent Migration in Western Europe." Paper presented at the Population Conference, Council of Europe, Strasbourg, 1966 [I62].

and other Mediterranean workers in the North are mobile where the local population is not, and in economics it takes only a small movement at the margin to change the price of a large inframarginal mass."[26] Extension of social security coverage, elimination of restrictive regulations, and international agreements, such as those among the Benelux and Scandinavian countries, have also favored international movement.[27]

In 1950 housing shortages and rent control adversely affected geographic mobility in Europe (except possibly in Belgium) and in diminishing degree have done so up to the present time. A shortage of dwellings in the places where additional labor was wanted most, especially the large cities, hampered attainment of an optimal geographic distribution of the labor supply. One means of alleviating this difficulty, where feasible, was to continue use of housing where it existed, even though far from the job, but this led to long travel times between home and work.[28] Moreover, even where no *net* population movement was involved, normal movement of individual workers from place to place in response to individual employment opportunities was, and still is, curtailed by the difficulty of obtaining accommodations. When accommodations could be found at all, a large increase in housing costs was often encountered. Rent control, rather than a housing shortage as such, is the main reason for the latter difficulty.[29] Improvement in the housing situation has favored increased mobility and contributed to growth.

A special factor impairing geographic mobility in Italy until early 1961 was statutory restraint of the internal migration of labor through the state employment control system. Its importance is debatable. George H. Hildebrand stresses it as a cause of structural unemployment, especially in the South, as well as of misallocation, and finds that only after 1961 could labor mobility "begin to make an effective contribution to the task of welding together a long divided national economy."[30] Luigi Spaventa, however, believes that legal restraints "never prevented migration whenever job opportunities were available" and points to the heavy migration from 1959 to 1961 "when the boom gathered speed and the unemployment rate fell considerably."[31]

To a degree that varies widely from country to country, and that is particularly great, though for different reasons, in Italy, the United Kingdom, and perhaps France, dismissal of unneeded workers is made difficult and expensive by a combination of public opinion, employers' feeling of responsibility toward permanent employees, laws requiring costly dismissal benefits, and the resistance of labor organizations.

It is likely that during the period under review redundancy declined in all the continental countries. It is also possible that at the end of the period more individuals were working where their capabilities were best utilized than at the beginning. Both developments, if they really occurred, must have contributed to an increase in European productivity, although the costs imposed by labor turnover should perhaps be considered a partial offset. It is not probable that such gains were realized in the United States; working in the other direction up to 1962 were excessive unemployment, persisting for several years at the end of the period; continuing growth of private pension plans, though this was ameliorated by a trend toward greater vesting; rising dismissal costs; and an increase in the benefits to be gained from seniority. I should not like to convey the impression, however, that any adverse effect on the growth rate was appreciable, nor that offsetting benefits, even to growth, were necessarily absent. In the mid-sixties tighter labor markets brought an increase in job shifting.

26. *Europe and the Dollar*, p. 42 [B59]. The UN Economic Commission for Europe (*Economic Survey of Europe in 1965*, p. 78 [I13]) also stresses the responsiveness of foreign workers to changes in the regional pattern of the demand for labor.

27. Agreements among the Common Market countries are described in Mark J. Fitzgerald, *The Common Market's Labor Programs*, Chapter 7 [B33].

28. This has sometimes had peculiar consequences. To try to resolve the geographic incompatibility of available housing and jobs, the Dutch instituted a premium pay system for certain categories of workers who had to travel long distances. This ultimately made commuting long distances attractive to some workers.

29. Aside from their effect on the allocation of labor, long continued control of rents imposed a substantial direct social cost by misallocating available housing. However, this is not a factor in the analysis of the growth rate of measured national product.

30. *Growth and Structure in the Economy of Modern Italy*, pp. 187, 351–65 [B50].

31. Review of the Hildebrand book in *American Economic Review*, December 1966, p. 1297 [P1].

Fear of unemployment or destruction of the value of skills sometimes leads workers to oppose the introduction of more efficient techniques as well as to require employment of more workers than the tasks to be performed require. In the United States and in most other countries this has typically been an important obstacle to efficiency only in industries and occupations with declining employment; the railroads offer an illustration in many countries. When unemployment is high in an economy as a whole, however, restrictive practices may become more widespread and they sometimes persist even after labor markets have tightened. Whether successful employee resistance to change contributed positively or negatively to the 1950–62 growth rate of any country depends on whether, over its whole economy, actual practices departed more from those that would have prevailed in the absence of such restrictions in 1950 or in 1962. Although descriptive information is available for particular situations —for example, concerning the greater success of French than of British railroads in combating restrictive practices—data that would permit estimates for economies as a whole are lacking.

As indicated in Chapter 9, there is a widespread belief that in the United Kingdom employee opposition to change is stronger, more prevalent, and more persistent than in other countries and that British employers have not combated restrictions as vigorously as other employers. Insofar as this is correct, employee resistance to change adversely affects the level of British productivity and also has a greater potential to affect the growth rate than is the case elsewhere. Organization of British unions on a craft basis evidently contributes importantly to redundancy. As Gertrude Williams writes, "[The United Kingdom] is the only European country in which the unions believe they are protecting their members by refusing to allow one worker to undertake the jobs normally done by another, for this policy depends directly upon the British trade union structure."[32]

Competition and Efficiency

A private enterprise economy relies upon the profit motive and competition among firms to secure efficiency in production and distribution. The carrot of profit is an incentive to efficiency with or without competition. But the stick of competition may be equally important. In theory, firms that provide customers with desired goods and services of good quality at low prices will profit, survive, thrive, and grow; those who do not will be replaced by those who do.

This process has worked rather well in the United States where the force of law has generally supported competition. Of course, there are few American markets in which all firms face horizontal demand curves, the textbook definition of pure competition. But neither are there many firms so sheltered from competition that they can survive and prosper for long periods if they continuously fail to give attention to providing customers with good values—which usually means giving attention to costs. In Western Europe competitive pressures to produce at low cost or be displaced by those who will do so has been less intense. One manifestation has been a lower rate of attrition among business firms and a lower rate of formation of new firms. Stronger competition is almost surely one reason that output is higher in the United States but I am unable to isolate this effect.

Possible Inconsistency of Competition and Large-Scale Production

The competitive solution to cost minimization encounters a dilemma if decreasing costs, internal to the firm, continue over a range of output so large relative to the size of markets that vigorous competition and optimum size of firm are inconsistent with one another. In such situations some of the benefits to efficiency of one or the other must be sacrificed.[33] An inherent advantage of the American economy is the large size of the country. Situations

---

32. *Apprenticeship in Europe*, p. 204 [B109]. P. J. D. Wiles found the United Kingdom to be the only country covered in a survey of international employers in Europe where restrictive trade union practices were "commonly complained of" (in *Oxford Economic Papers*, June 1951, p. 167 [P33]).

33. A similar dilemma is encountered in the typical public utility case in which multiplication of facilities—such as electricity and telephone lines, gas and water mains, or subway tracks—would impose unacceptable additional costs. Neither recourse to regulated private monopoly, the usual American

in which markets are too small to allow vigorous competition among a number of firms that are of sufficient size to secure all or almost all of the potential gains from economies of scale are fewer than in Europe. The discussion in Chapter 17 suggests that if there were no obstacles to international trade this natural European disadvantage of smaller national economies would not be very great and in any case it is present only in production for markets of more than national size. But whatever emphasis is placed on limitations imposed by size of markets, it is clear that European countries have been a long way from making the best of their situations. Historically, most of them have tolerated cartels and restrictive agreements generally among small and medium-sized firms and firms that, though large in terms of their aggregate operations, have only a small output of individual products. These have prevented either the full benefits of competition or, where they were potentially present, the benefits of larger enterprise from being obtained.

In recent years the situation has been changing. Integration is at once · broadening markets geographically, making *possible* in an industry the existence of a larger number of firms of efficient size that can compete with one another, and also changing the legal structure that has supported monopoly in the past. In addition, Europe is trying to face up more explicitly to the problem of minimizing the adverse effects in situations where competition and sufficient size to obtain minimum costs appear irreconcilable. Most of the impact of these changes had yet to be felt in 1962.

The formation of the European Economic Community as a large free trade area is probably the most important development affecting competition in Europe. Many observers see the invigoration of firms through increased competition and the possibility of supporting several large competing firms as the most important economic benefits of the Common Market. Firms in each of the member countries are exposed in their home markets to the competition of firms domiciled in the other five countries, and are offered the opportunity to fight for expansion in the markets of the other five on

equal terms with domestic producers. The scope of markets that are too small to support enough large enterprises to provide effective competition is reduced. The European Free Trade Association has a similar effect toward increasing competition among its members but on a smaller scale. The need for intensification of competition in the United Kingdom has been the principal economic argument adduced by most supporters of the British application for Common Market membership.

The need to establish competition where its absence does not contribute to efficiency and the problem of reconciling competition and optimum size where they are inconsistent have come to be widely recognized in principle. The British government has recently been trying to distinguish between good and bad concentration, relying heavily on efficiency as a criterion. It favors and has even offered to promote those mergers that it believes would stimulate greater efficiency while opposing others. The EEC treaty takes a slightly different approach. To quote a summary by the CED research staff, "monopolies ... are not outlawed but monopoly action inimical to the interests of other producers or consumers is forbidden. These provisions apply equally to public monopolies and public enterprises."[34] The EEC treaty also deals with agreements among firms. Again quoting the CED research staff, "the general principle is that all agreements between enterprises, and decisions by associations of enterprises, and concerted practices which prevent, restrict or distort competition and which affect commerce between states are forbidden.[35] There is a large exception to this principle, however. Agreements which contribute to the improvement of production or distribution or which promote technical or economic progress are permitted if the consumer receives a fair share of the benefits and if a monop-

---

expedient, nor to public ownership, the typical European practice, provides an automatic substitute for competition as a guarantee of efficiency.

34. Committee for Economic Development, *The European Common Market and Its Meaning to the United States*, p. 99 [B21].
35. In July 1966 the Court of Justice of the European Communities outlawed an agreement made in 1957 by which Grundig, a German radio-TV manufacturer, made Consten, a French distributor, its exclusive distributor for France, and prohibited Consten from representing competing German manufacturers or from selling Grundig products outside France. Both the German and Italian governments had filed briefs supporting the agreement (reported in *Business Week*, July 23, 1966, p. 32 [P8]). The decision, hailed as of great importance in stimulating price competition, was of course far too late to affect the period under review.

oly position is not established thereby."[36] The provision in the EFTA agreement dealing with restrictive business practices is very brief and general but further, or different, provisions may be adopted by the Council of Ministers after review in the light of experience. Domestic law was also changing. The change was earliest in Germany, where the military government regulations on cartels, followed by the 1957 Act Against Restraint of Competition, introduced a major departure from the prewar legal situation. All the other Northwest European countries made some move during the 1950–62 period to weaken restrictive practices or, more often, to limit their abuse.[37] But all these changes appear minor if one takes as a standard the difference between European and American law.

Two other developments have been of importance in most or all of the European countries. First, quite apart from and preceding the formation of EEC and EFTA, international competition was strengthened by the freeing of trade that resulted from elimination of quantitative restrictions and in some cases the reduction of tariffs, by the creation of a common market in steel and, in Belgium and the Netherlands, by the formation of the Benelux customs union. Second, in all countries the growth of branches and subsidiaries of American firms was tending to invigorate competition. In a number of individual industries the impact has been considerable.[38]

Changes in France

Among the large countries the effect of restrictive agreements by small and medium-sized firms is usually said to have been most damaging in France. French law, like most European law, condoned and even enforced both domestic and international cartels.[39] The French businessman has been more comfortable with "live and let live" arrangements assuring the survival of firms than with the opportunities and risks of vigorous competition. In this respect he was perhaps no different from most American businessmen, but in France the renegade —the unpopular price-cutter who makes the system work—was apparently rarer and he lacked the support of law.

During the 1950–62 period the French situation was changing in several ways. First, the French government, and particularly the French Planning Commission, used its not inconsiderable influence to promote the reorganization of French industry into larger units. According to R. Plaisant, the French fiscal law also gives great advantages to mergers to help concentration.[40] Second, rapid growth of the French economy was itself facilitating increases in the size, as measured by output, of French business units. Third, after 1959 the Common Market exposed the French manufacturer to increased competition from producers in other member countries. Fourth, French businessmen were both pleased and somewhat surprised to find they could compete on equal terms. Not only did the Common Market have direct economic effects; it also led industrialists to wish to increase their individual freedom of action.[41] Fifth, the provisions of the EEC charter dealing with agreements among enterprises and discrimination had some effect, ap-

36. Committee for Economic Development, *The European Common Market . . .* [B21]. These provisions are interpreted in EEC Commission, *Ninth General Report on the Activities of the Community*, pp. 59–83 [I58].

37. A review of the legal situation in all the European countries covered in this study will be found in Edwards, U.S. Department of State, Bureau of Intelligence and Research, *Cartelization in Europe* [G73]. See also Zijlstra, EEC, *Politique Economique et Problèmes de la Concurrence dans la CEE* [I59], and de Gaay Fortman, *Theory of Competition Policy: A Confrontation of Economic, Political, and Legal Principles*, Chapter VI [S6].

38. Tibor Barna's study of British manufacturing led him to the interesting observation that two foreign firms may be required to significantly increase competition in an industry. One may be content to obtain high profits with limited sales, especially since it may often be reluctant to assume a dominant position in another country's market. Entry of a second foreign firm often increases competitive pressure throughout the industry (*Investment and Growth Policies in British Industrial Firms*, pp. 52–53 [B6]).

Christopher Layton notes there is "a world of difference" between a situation in which a *single* American (or foreign European) firm dominates a sector of the economy and one in which, though American firms may have the largest share

of an industry, they compete vigorously with each other. He indicates there is likely to be more vigorous competition in "American-dominated" sectors than "where European industries compete together on their own" (*Trans-Atlantic Investments*, p. 82 [B68]).

39. For a discussion in English of competition and restraints upon it, see Baum, *The French Economy and the French State*, Chapter 10 [B8].

40. In U.S. Congress, Senate Subcommittee on Antitrust and Monopoly of the Committee on the Judiciary, *Antitrust Developments in the European Common Market*, p. 241 [G47].

41. Balassa in *Quarterly Journal of Economics*, November 1965, pp. 545–46 [P34].

parently slight up to 1962, upon national laws and practices. Except for the first of these, similar changes pointing toward greater competition have been present in varying degree in the other continental countries during the postwar period.[42]

Competition and Growth

So long as the intensity of competition does not change in a country, the degree of competitive pressure can be regarded as part of the general framework within which the economy operates rather than as an active ingredient in the growth process itself. But if competition changes, this may affect efficiency and hence the growth rate. In my American study I concluded that changes in the intensity of competition during the time period covered were insufficient to affect the growth rate, and I believe this also to have been the case in 1950–62.

There is a voluminous literature on competition and its absence in postwar Europe, but quantitative evaluations of the effect on efficiency are lacking. Even evaluations of changes in competition differ but the general impression created by a variety of materials presented in *Antitrust Developments in the European Common Market*[43] is that in most countries there was some change in law and attitude during the postwar period but the effect on actual practice was not very profound and therefore could not have contributed very much to growth. This is also my impression from most discussions with informed individuals. In the case of France, however, John Sheehan stresses the importance to the postwar success of French industry of a revival of competition "in automobiles and probably a number of other consumer goods industries" and "the development of effective substitutes for its absence in some of the concentrated industries."[44]

Charles P. Kindleberger also emphasizes invigoration of the competitive spirit among large French firms, which are no longer willing to restrict output and hold a price umbrella over small firms but now believe their interests lie in "lower prices, expanded output, and larger markets."[45] I suspect that in most if not all of the European countries there was some increase in competition during the 1950–62 period; that this helped to increase pressure on prices and costs; that this effect probably was greatest in the last years of the period and has subsequently been increasing; and that the effect on the growth rate was not appreciable up to 1962 although France may have been an exception.

Cost of Units of Inefficient Size

Competition is relied upon to eliminate inefficient firms, and efficiency presumably implies firms of efficient size, operating establishments of as efficient size, as the extent of markets permits.[46] An increase in competition, or a deliberate program directed to this end as in France, may move the size distribution of firms toward the distribution that would be most efficient. Unfortunately, there is no accurate way of identifying an optimal distribution. What is optimal at any given time depends on a host of factors, not least of which is the managerial talent available; it is probable that a variety of different combinations of firm and establishment size, product specialization, and vertical and horizontal integration may be about equally efficient. Neither is there any way to measure comprehensively the costs or the prevalence of departure from an optimum distribution.

Some appraisals of the total cost or the prevalence of small size without distinguishing the reasons for small size have been attempted. Jan Tinbergen has made a "wild guess" that "say 80 percent of production is already going on, in countries such as Sweden and Holland, in enterprises of opti-

---

42. This in no way implies a decrease in *concentration* within individual countries. For example, a German study showed a "marked growth in concentration" from 1954 to 1960 (in *Cartel*, October 1964, pp. 170–72 [P12]; this is a summary of the "Report on the Results of an Inquiry into Concentration in the German Economy"). A Belgian study suggests a slight increase in concentration from 1947 or 1955 to 1962 (Demeulenaere in *Reflets et Perspectives*, December 1964, pp. 431–42 [P36]).

43. Report of the Senate Subcommittee on Antitrust and Monopoly [G47].

44. *Promotion and Control of Industry in Postwar France*, p. 21 [B100].

45. In Hoffmann and others, *In Search of France*, pp. 141–42 [B60].

46. A qualification is introduced by the fact that markets in general are growing and the size of establishments is somewhat conditioned by investment that must be of discrete amounts and will be used for some period of time. Optimum efficiency does not, therefore, imply exactly the size that would be most efficient given the size of markets at a point in time.

mal size, but that in 20 percent either the size of the unit or the length of the run [is sub-optimal so that an increase in size of unit or run] can lead to substantial cost reductions, say of one-quarter." This implies the possibility of "an overall reduction in production costs of, say, five percent."[47] The guess seems to refer to manufacturing, although it has been applied elsewhere to the economy as a whole. If the *total* cost is no greater than this in small countries, differences among countries or changes over time in the *part of the cost* in manufacturing that is not imposed by the size of markets (and therefore not covered in my estimates of gains from economies of scale) could not be very great.

Joe S. Bain has attempted international comparisons of the importance of suboptimal plants in manufacturing.[48] In twenty United States manufacturing industries he studied, at least 70 percent of employment was in establishments large enough for unit costs to be not more than 3 or 4 percent above unit costs in establishments of optimum size. For the purpose of making international comparisons, he assumed this was the case in all United States manufacturing industries. He further assumed that minimum size for reasonable efficiency (costs not more than 4 percent above the minimum), as measured by employment, was the same in other countries as in the United States. By the 4 percent criterion, and on the first assumption stated, no United States manufacturing industry, of course, had less than 70 percent of employment in plants of reasonably efficient size. By the same criterion, in the United Kingdom 32 percent of manufacturing industries (of twenty-two examined) had less than 70 percent of employment in establishments of at least reasonably efficient size. The corresponding percentages were 75 in France (of twenty industries examined) and 91 in Italy (of twenty-three industries examined). In the industries with less than 70 percent of employment in establishments of a size big enough for reasonable efficiency, the mean percentage of employment in too small plants was 46 in the United Kingdom, 52 in France, and 58 in Italy. Bain's findings indicate that among these

countries the costs of having small establishments—whether because of small markets or because establishments are smaller than necessary given the size of markets—are greatest in Italy, followed by France, the United Kingdom, and the United States in that order.

Bain's estimates clearly imply that the fraction of employment in too small plants in even the large European countries is greater than the 20 percent assumed by Tinbergen for small countries. Moreover, Bain gives valid reasons to believe his estimates are conservative. However, he does not provide estimates of the total *cost* of too small plants, and his estimates do not necessarily imply higher costs than Tinbergen's 5 percent for Sweden and the Netherlands since Bain's criterion for inefficiency is a cost disadvantage of only 5 percent or more.

Bain also computed average employment in the twenty largest establishments for a sample of manufacturing industries. The median ratio of average employment in European countries to average employment in the United States was 0.78 in the United Kingdom, 0.39 in France, and 0.29 in Italy. Bain found, further, that seller concentration among the largest companies in manufacturing was about the same in the United States and the United Kingdom, substantially greater in France, and still greater in Italy. Thus, among these four countries, superfluity of too small plants, smallness of large plants, and high seller concentration tend to go together.

Such detailed industry comparisons as Bain has made are not available for the other countries, and not much can be inferred from distributions of establishments for manufacturing as a whole. One is likely to be more impressed by the similarity of such distributions in different countries than by the differences, even among countries where Bain found differences.[49] At least this is so when all establish-

---

47. In *International Trade and Finance: A Collected Volume of Wicksell Lectures, 1958–1964*, p. 234 [B105].
48. *International Differences in Industrial Structure*, Chapters 3 and 4 [B4].

49. An EEC expert commission, discussing nonmanufacturing as well as manufacturing activities, concluded "it seems . . . to be arguable that, if there are differences among the economies of the Community in the total degree of concentration, this is above all due to the uneven shares held by the various industries and services; on the other hand there are no essential differences of structure in each of these branches taken individually" (EEC Commission, *Report on the Economic Situation in the Countries of the Community*, p. 51 [I54]).

TABLE 18-3

Percentage Distributions of Employment in Manufacturing Establishments
by Size of Establishment, Various Years Around 1955

Size of establishment by number of workers	United States	Belgium	France	Germany	Netherlands[a]	United Kingdom	Italy
Establishments with 50 or more workers							
50– 99	11.3	14.5	14.7	11.3	14.1	9.7	14.9
100–499	34.7	38.5	41.9	35.7	34.3	35.8	37.9
500–999	15.0	15.8	15.8	15.1	15.8	15.4	16.4
1,000 and over	39.0	31.2	27.6	37.9	35.8	39.1	30.8
	100.0	100.0	100.0	100.0	100.0	100.0	100.0
All establishments							
0– 49	16.4	28.0	19.0	15.0	24.0	—	21.0
50– 99	9.4	10.4	11.9	9.6	10.7	—	11.7
100–499	29.0	27.2	34.0	30.3	26.2	—	30.0
500–999	12.5	11.4	12.8	12.8	11.9	—	12.9
1,000 and over	32.6	23.0	22.3	32.3	27.2	—	24.4
	100.0	100.0	100.0	100.0	100.0	—	100.0

Sources: United States: U.S. Bureau of the Census, *1954 Census of Manufactures* [G59]; United Kingdom: 1958 data from Armstrong and Silberston in *Journal of the Royal Statistical Society*, Series A, Pt. 3, 1965, p. 408 [P26]; other countries: Mandy and de Ghelinck in *Revue Economique*, May 1960, pp. 406–7 [P40]. Estimates of employment in European establishments with less than 50 employees are approximations by Mandy and de Ghelinck intended to improve comparability. They sometimes differ from data reported elsewhere. Details may not add to totals because of rounding.
a. Distributions refer to enterprises rather than establishments, hence concentration in the Netherlands is overstated compared to the other countries.

ments with 1,000 or more workers are classified together.[50] Table 18–3 gives estimates referring to the mid-fifties for six of the European countries and the United States.[51] The similarity is rather pronounced if establishments with less than 50 employees are excluded. However, manufacturing employment is somewhat more concentrated in larger establishments in the United States, Germany, and the United Kingdom than in the other countries; this suggests that Germany would be closer to Britain than to France in a study like Bain's. Small establishments with less than 50 employees are more important in Belgium and the Netherlands than in the larger countries, according to these estimates. (The estimates for such establishments are rough, and inclusion of handicraft establishments might change the comparisons appreciably.)

50. Because of this grouping and the fact that the data refer to establishments rather than to firms, the greater importance of very large firms in the United States than in Europe is not brought out by Table 18–3.
51. Small differences among countries should not be considered significant. Particular mention may be made of the fact that in the United Kingdom concentration in large establishments was much greater in 1958 (the year shown) than in 1951. Data for other countries refer to an intermediate date.

Classification by employment size minimizes differences between the United States and Europe. If distributions of employment when classification is by employee size are similar in the United States and a European country, greater proportions of value added are created by establishments with value added above a stated amount in the United States than in Europe because value added per worker is greater. In addition, it is widely accepted that American establishments typically produce fewer types of products, and fewer varieties of each type, than European establishments of similar size. If so, European establishments tend to produce less of an individual product than American establishments with the same total output.

The French government, as noted, has promoted business consolidation. From 1954 to 1962 the size distribution of manufacturing establishments, classified by number of employees, shifted upward in France, but the change was not dramatic.[52] The upward shift would be larger if classification were by

52. Data are provided in INSEE, *Les Etablissements Industriels et Commerciaux en France, 1954* and *1962* [G13]. Similar distributions of firms are not available.

deflated value added. Even so, it would not be so great as to rule out the possibility that, with growth of the economy, the optimal distribution was changing about as rapidly as the actual distribution so that France was no nearer an optimum position in 1962 than in 1954.[53] This is also the case with respect to the other countries, where distributions were also shifting toward the larger sized firms.[54]

In summary, I suspect that although in the 1950–62 period there was some reduction in monopoly power leading to greater efficiency in use of resources, and although there may have been some slight movement in the size distribution of firms toward the optimum (in addition to the elimination of small family enterprises, largely in trade and the services, that was discussed in Chapter 16), up to 1962 these were not very important factors in European growth. If any country is an exception, it is most likely to be France.

Resale Price Maintenance and Other Restrictions in Retailing

Resale Price Maintenance (RPM), or Fair Trade, helps to keep inefficient retailers in business, deprives low-cost distributors of the market expansion their superior efficiency would otherwise bring, and results in the use of more resources in retailing than are needed to perform the function of distribution.

Introduction of Fair Trade laws in the American states, which was concentrated in the 1937–39

period, was estimated to have deducted 0.04 percentage points from the United States growth rate in the 1929–57 period.[55] In 1950–62, in contrast, Fair Trade laws were becoming weaker in the United States, a change slightly favorable to growth. American laws allow a retailer to contract with a manufacturer (or sometimes with a wholesaler) of a branded product to sell it at a price that then becomes the minimum legal price for all retailers. In Europe this is called "individual" RPM.

In 1950 Resale Price Maintenance was even more restrictive in Europe than in the United States. Groups of manufacturers were permitted to act jointly to establish and enforce retail prices. This practice, called "collective" RPM, has been continuously prohibited in the United States under the Sherman Act of 1890. The presence of RPM was particularly adverse at a time of great potential change in distribution channels in Europe because it discouraged customer acceptance of new types of distributors by preventing them from underselling established shops on price-fixed items.

Percentages of retail sales covered by RPM in the early 1950's were on the order of 25 to 40 in Denmark, Norway, and the United Kingdom, 12 in Germany (1954), 10 in France (and the United States), and still less in Italy. Since 1950 the tendency has been to weaken or eliminate RPM. Legal measures to do so became effective in France in 1953 (with additional ordinances and decrees being enacted almost annually), in Denmark in 1955, in Germany and Norway in 1958, and in the Netherlands and the United Kingdom in 1956 and (after the period covered here) 1964.[56] Such measures

---

53. In his chapter on "Scale and Competition" in *Economic Growth in France and Britain, 1851–1950* (p. 181 [B58]), Charles P. Kindleberger says, "This is an easy field in which to generalize. But the generalizations are not worth much." One can only add, "Amen."

54. In the United Kingdom, where there was no strong government pressure toward consolidation, the distribution of manufacturing employment among establishments with 10 or more workers did move rather sharply toward the larger establishments from 1951 to 1958, and a similar shift is noted for a distribution of firms (Armstrong and Silberston in *Journal of the Royal Statistical Society*, Series A, Pt. 3, 1965 [P26]). W. G. Shepherd also finds increased concentration among firms (in *Oxford Economic Papers*, March 1966, pp. 126–32 [P33]). Data for German industry, available annually in the *Statistisches Jahrbuch* [G16], show a gradual increase in the share of employment held by establishments with 1,000 or more employees from 35.3 percent in 1952 to 39.6 percent in 1962, with the offsetting reductions in the under 100 and 200 to 499 size classes. Data for the seventeen manufacturing industries in the Netherlands show the percentage of employment in firms with 500 or more employees was 42 in 1950, 44 in 1953, 47

in both 1957 and 1961, and 51 at the end of 1964 (*Brief van de Staatssecretaris van Economische Zaken*, Parliamentary Session 1965–66, No. 3, January 7, 1966, pp. 3–31 [S3]). From 1953 to 1962 the number of enterprises with 1 to 4 workers declined (*Amsterdam-Rotterdam Bank Economic Quarterly Review*, September 1965, p. 19 [P2]).

Similarly, Belgian data for 1955 and 1960 show a decline, though slight, in the number of establishments with 1 to 4 workers and a small shift in the distribution of employment by size of establishment toward the larger size classes (National Institute of Statistics, *Etudes Statistiques et Econométriques*, No. 6, 1964, p. 63 [G4]).

55. *Sources of Economic Growth*, p. 193 [B25].

56. Reviews of RPM and legislation affecting it are given in Yamey (ed.), *Resale Price Maintenance* [B110], and Gammelgaard, OEEC, *Resale Price Maintenance* [I16]. The extent to which RPM had been relaxed in the United Kingdom by mid-1966 is discussed in the *Statist* ("An Unconscionable Time A-dying"), July 1, 1966, pp. 11–13 [P43]. Belgium,

contribute to efficiency and growth. Suzanne Berger states that only the 1953 decree stipulating a manufacturer's refusal to sell to a retailer could be punished by a jail sentence saved the life of the low-price Leclerc stores in France.[57] Recently, according to F. D. Boggis, the importance of RPM has been greatly eroded throughout the Common Market area.[58] But estimates of the contribution of these changes would partially overlap estimates already presented of the gains from reducing the number of nonfarm proprietors and own-account workers. I shall merely note that these gains would have been smaller in the absence of relaxation of RPM, and

that they do not reflect all of the gains from weakening RPM.

On the continent a great range of other regulations has restricted entry into retailing, discriminated among types of distributors, and blocked the sale of a full range of products by individual stores. These have been greatly relaxed since 1950, or since 1955 in some areas, and this has improved efficiency. But even today, "laws are slow, cumbersome and often arbitrary. In an era of rapid retail development they lead to prolonged litigation, delay innovations, and make it unnecessarily difficult for retailers to take the changing requirements of their customers into account."[59] I have not tried to estimate the effect of changes in such regulations.

---

where RPM was strong, and Italy, where it was restricted to pharmaceuticals (but other types of restrictive practices in retailing are prevalent), were exceptions to the tendency to weaken the legal status of RPM in the postwar period.

57. In *Yale Review*, Autumn 1965, p. 97 [P52].

58. In Yamey (ed.), *Resale Price Maintenance*, pp. 215–16 [B110].

59. Fulop, *Competition for Consumers*, p. 214 [B39]. See also Jefferys, Hansberger, and Lindblad, OEEC, *Productivity in the Distributive Trade in Europe, Wholesale and Retail Aspects*, Chapter VIII [I20], and Jefferys and Knee, *Retailing in Europe*, pp. 57 and 70 [B55].

Effect of Irregular Fluctuations on Growth Rates of Output per Unit of Input

Growth rates of national income per unit of input were calculated from data for the individual years 1950, 1955, and 1962. Because the intervening periods are so short, special influences affecting these particular years can significantly affect the computed growth rates. This chapter examines the two main sources of irregular fluctuations. One is the pressure of demand. The other is farm output, which is subject to the vagaries of nature. These factors did not have much effect on the growth rates of output per unit of input over the 1950–62 period as a whole except in Denmark and the Netherlands, where they contributed 0.2 percentage points. However, they greatly influenced growth rates in the 1950–55 and 1955–62 subperiods, and especially the differences between these subperiods, in the United States, Denmark, the Netherlands, and the United Kingdom. Their effect was largest in Denmark, where they are estimated to have subtracted 0.5 from the 1950–55 growth rate and added 0.6 to the 1955–62 rate.

The irregularities discussed in this chapter have no fundamental significance for the study of long-term growth but are of considerable importance to an interpretation of the computed growth rates shown in Table 2–1. If they were not taken into account their influence would be wrongly ascribed to some other growth source. I shall classify the influence of short-run fluctuations in demand and weather upon output per unit of input as sources of growth, but the estimates could equally well be viewed as adjustments that should be made to the computed growth rates of output per unit of input before allocating them among the other sources of growth.

Demand Pressure and Fluctuations in Productivity

In the United States there is a clear tendency for output per unit of input to be higher in periods when the pressure of demand upon resources is strong than in periods of weaker demand. This presumably is a reflection of fluctuations in the intensity with which employed resources are used, although this cannot be proven directly since there is no satisfactory direct measure of the intensity of input utilization. In the United States output per unit of input tends to be lower the higher is the unemployment rate, the most widely used indicator of demand pressure. At least this is so as long as the unemployment rate remains above the 4 percent level that has been considered in the United States to represent "high employment." In addition to being inversely correlated with the *level* of the unemployment rate, productivity is affected by the phase of the business cycle.[1] For example, productivity tends to be higher, after adjustment for trend, just at the time when unemployment is being reduced to about 4 percent than it does after the unemployment rate has been at this level for a period of time.

Why should national income per unit of input be low when demand is low in relation to productive potential? One reason is that capital and land input are measured by the stock of capital and land without adjustment for fluctuations in their use. A decline in production therefore necessarily reduces output per unit of capital and land input in the short run. Quantitatively more important is the fact that labor input, though measured for wage and salary workers by actual man-hours worked (with adjustment for quality change), nonetheless contains a substantial overhead component. Employers often hesitate to dismiss experienced workers when labor requirements fall if they expect to need these workers again in the near future. Dismissal itself may entail costs or difficulties; it is always unpleasant. There is also an important element of short-run indivisibility of labor in a going concern; some positions must remain filled so long as the firm operates at all.[2] Employment expansion during an upswing may be restrained and work intensity be temporarily increased until it becomes clear that a rise in orders is not temporary. Cyclical changes in product mix may contribute to a small extent to the fluctuation in total productivity, and no doubt there are other causes as well. Although there are offsets, they are apparently outweighed. The exact relationships are, in fact, poorly understood.[3]

1. For manufacturing and certain other industries, changes in man-hours per unit of input at different phases of the cycle are analyzed in Hultgren, *Cost, Prices and Profits: Their Cyclical Relations* [B51].

2. This includes positions held by nearly all proprietors. In addition, most proprietors and unpaid family workers do not vary their hours with fluctuations in demand. In the present study no allowance was made even for any fluctuations that may occur in actual hours worked by proprietors and family workers.

3. It is not obvious, for example, why fluctuations in productivity should be associated in the United States with changes in unemployment rather than with changes in employment or total hours worked, nor is it even certain that this is, in fact, the case.

Comparisons of 1950, 1955, and 1962

If the growth rate of output per unit of input is computed between two years that are not comparable with respect to the pressure of demand upon productive potential, and if output per unit of input is sensitive to demand pressure, then the growth rate of output per unit of input between those years will be affected by this incomparability. Such an effect must then be considered as itself a source of growth over the particular time period examined.

Estimates of the size of this effect are difficult to make but they are essential to avoid gross errors of interpretation. Thus, I estimate that United States national income per man-hour worked was 1.95 percent higher in 1955 and 0.45 percent lower in 1962 than it would have been if the rate of utilization of resources had been the same in these years as it was in 1950. The same percentages may be applied to the measures of national income per unit of total input.[4] These estimates imply that differences in the intensity of utilization of inputs added 0.39 percentage points to the 1950–55 growth rate of national income per unit of input and subtracted 0.34 percentage points from the 1955–62 rate. The difference between the two periods is 0.73 points. The main reason that national income per unit of input rose more rapidly in 1950–55 than in 1955–62 is thus cyclical incomparability of the years compared. Incomparability of 1950 and 1962 affects the growth rate over the whole period from 1950 to 1962 by only −0.04. This estimate is smaller partly because 1950 and 1962 were more comparable to one another than they were to 1955 and partly because the period was longer. The longer the period, the less sensitive are growth rates to differences in cyclical position of end years.

Before the estimates for the European countries are examined, certain general points should be stressed.

This chapter is concerned only with the effect of differences between 1950, 1955, and 1962 in the intensity of utilization of inputs upon the compara-

4. In principle, the percentages should differ a trifle because cyclical changes in hours worked were not distinguished from other changes in computing quality adjustment indexes.

bility of output per unit of input when inputs measure employed resources (subject to the qualifications already noted). Differences in the intensity of utilization are presumed to arise because of fluctuations in the pressure of demand upon potential output when the latter is viewed in a short-run sense. The rate of unemployment is one of the indicators that may be used to infer demand pressure but it is relevant only insofar as low unemployment of resources and intensive use of employed resources can be assumed to accompany one another. Only insofar as the unemployment rate in years compared differs because the pressure of demand relative to short-term output potential differs is unemployment an appropriate indicator. This is not the case when there is a change in structural unemployment. The steady decline of the German unemployment rate from 7 percent in 1950 to under 1 percent in 1962, or of the Italian rate from nearly 8 percent in 1950 to 3 percent in 1962, does not indicate that the pressure of demand upon short-run productive capacity was much greater in 1962 than in 1950 or that employed resources were being used progressively more intensively. Unemployment in 1950 would not have been 1 percent in Germany and 3 percent in Italy if demand pressures in 1950 had been much stronger than they were. The persistent declines in unemployment in these countries are viewed as reductions in structural unemployment. That structural unemployment probably would have declined less if the general level of demand throughout the period had been weaker is irrelevant to the present topic. This chapter is not concerned with long-term effects of sustained high demand.

It should also be understood that the effects of variations in short-term demand pressures on total national income and product are typically much greater than the effects upon output per unit of input, with which this chapter is exclusively concerned. An analysis by Arthur M. Okun, which has been used by the President's Council of Economic Advisers, may be used to illustrate the point.[5] Okun assumes, I believe correctly, that the percentage of the labor force structurally unemployed has not varied in the United States so that differences in the

5. Okun, *Potential* GNP: *Its Measurement and Significance* [B84].

TABLE 19–1

Contribution Made by Differences in Pressure of Demand to Growth Rates of National Income per Unit of Input

(*In percentage points*)

Area	1950–62	1950–55	1955–62
United States	−.04	.39	−.34
Northwest Europe	−.01	.06	−.07
Belgium	.00	.00	.00
Denmark	.22	−.10	.44
France	.00	.00	.00
Germany	.00	.00	.00
Netherlands	.19	.34	.09
Norway	.00	.00	.00
United Kingdom	−.09	.16	−.29
Italy	.00	.00	.00

Sources: See text and Appendix O for derivation.

actual rate of unemployment are demand-induced. For unemployment rates above 4 percent, he estimates that on the average a difference of 1 percentage point in the unemployment rate is associated with a difference of 3.2 percent, in the opposite direction, in total GNP. Of this amount, 1.8 percent is due to effects on average hours of work and on employment (counting both the unemployed who become employed and an induced net addition to the labor force) and 1.4 percent to the effect on GNP per man-hour worked.[6] This chapter is concerned only with the latter effect.

Table 19–1 presents estimates for all the countries similar to that already described for the United States. For each it was necessary to ask two questions. Did the pressure of demand upon productive potential differ among the years considered? Was output per man-hour affected by differences in demand pressure, presumably through effects on the rate of utilization of employed inputs? Unless the answer to *both* questions was affirmative, no adjustment was required and the estimate was zero. If, as in the United States, both questions were answered affirmatively it was then necessary to estimate the size of the effect on output per man-hour.

According to Table 19–1, in only four countries did the effect of differences in the intensity of resource utilization affect growth rates of output per

6. This statement is intended to indicate the principle involved. Adjustments were made to the Okun formula in applying it to actual United States data; see Appendix O.

unit of input. More intensive utilization of resources in 1955 than in 1950 contributed strongly to the computed 1950–55 rise in national income per unit of input in the United States, the Netherlands, and the United Kingdom. In the Anglo-Saxon countries greater resource utilization in 1955 than in 1962 subtracted from the growth rate of output per unit of input computed for 1955–62. In the Netherlands the contribution was still positive in this period, but much smaller than in 1950–55. In all three countries, consequently, this factor tended to make the 1950–55 growth rate higher than the 1955–62 growth rate; the contrast was greatest by far in the United States and least in the Netherlands. The situation in Denmark was the reverse of that in the other three countries. Changes in the rate of utilization of resources subtracted a little from the 1950–55 growth rate and contributed heavily to the 1955–62 rate.

Over the *whole* 1950–62 period this "source" contributed about 0.2 points to the Danish and Dutch growth rates. It subtracted 0.1 from the British rate and a smaller amount from the American growth rate.

Differences among 1950, 1955, and 1962 in the rate of resource utilization did not appear to influence the growth rate of national income per unit of input in the five remaining countries. Either the three years appeared to be comparable with respect to the intensity of demand pressures or else output per unit of input was insensitive to differences in demand pressures within the relevant range of variation. In most of these countries both conditions held, or nearly so. These three particular years appeared to be closely comparable with respect to the intensity of demand and, in addition, productivity showed no systematic tendency to vary cyclically during the 1950–62 period. The latter finding, where it applies, may result in part from the fact that demand was never or rarely seriously deficient. The Okun formula for the United States, it will be recalled, refers to fluctuations below the "high employment" level.

The estimates presented in Table 19–1 rest heavily on personal judgments. The basis for these judgments is described in Appendix O. The main questions, I believe, concern the *size* of the adjustments where adjustments were made and the decision to introduce no adjustment for Belgium. Where adjustments were made, both the need for an adjustment and its direction in each subperiod seem obvious, except possibly for the small positive adjustment to the Dutch growth rate in 1955–62. Other investigators might, however, arrive at considerably different estimates of magnitudes. I had little difficulty in concluding that no adjustment was appropriate for France, Germany, Norway, or Italy, and I do not believe adjustments of substantial size would appear warranted to anyone else examining data for these countries. As explained in Appendix O, the conclusion that no adjustment was required for Belgium was less easily reached.

The preceding paragraph presupposes that, in the short run, stronger demand was always either favorable to or neutral toward, and never adverse to, high output per unit of input. One can visualize a situation in which demand is so strong that shortages and bottlenecks develop, or workers become indifferent to performance, to such an extent that the favorable effects of fuller utilization of inputs are overborne; some commentators believe Germany was in this position in the mid-sixties. I do not believe this describes the situation in the three years compared in any of the nine countries.[7]

Comparisons of 1960 Levels

The year 1960 is a relatively satisfactory one for international comparisons of the level of national income per unit of input.

Nowhere on the continent does it appear that productivity was depressed appreciably by short-run underutilization and would have been higher if demand in that year had been stronger than it was. In Denmark, France, Germany, Norway, and Italy, the unemployment position in 1960 was favorable and in all these countries GNP per person employed was in line with other years. In the Netherlands and Belgium unemployment was not quite so low as at cyclical peaks but it was declining sharply. In the

---

7. Again I stress that I am concerned only with short-term fluctuations. The question is, for example, whether British productivity would have been different from what it was in 1962 if demand had been different in 1962, not whether it would have been greater or less if demand and unemployment had been different throughout, say, the preceding decade.

Netherlands GNP per worker was exceptionally high in 1960, even when allowance is made for an especially favorable farm output.[8] The position in Belgium is less clear but an adjustment is not clearly indicated.

In the United Kingdom 1960 was a business cycle peak, but unemployment was not so low as it had been in some other years. I estimated that in 1960 output per unit of input might have been 0.7 percent higher than it actually was if demand pressure had been as strong as in 1955 when the unemployment rate was at its postwar low.[9]

The year 1960 was also a business cycle peak in the United States, but it was the peak of a cycle in which recovery was interrupted before unemployment due to deficient demand had been eliminated. The unemployment rate in 1960 averaged 5.6 percent. A variation of the Okun formula suggests that if demand in 1960 had been sufficient to reduce the unemployment rate to 4 percent, national income per unit of input would have been higher than it actually was by 2.4 percent.[10]

I conclude that in 1960 national income per unit of input would have been higher by 2.4 percent in the United States and by 0.7 percent in the United Kingdom if the pressure of demand on the utilization of employed resources had been adequate and comparable to that in the remaining countries. The concept and measurement are admittedly imprecise, but this factor cannot be omitted from the analysis. The United States could raise output per unit of input from its position in 1960 merely by increasing demand pressure, and by 1965–66 it had actually done so, whereas this opportunity was not available to the continental countries.

These percentages imply that if there had been no other differences among the countries, national income per person employed would have been 2.4 percent higher in all the continental countries than it was in the United States, and 1.7 percent higher in the United Kingdom than in the United States.

8. The percentage of wage and salary workers unemployed in the Netherlands was 1.5 in 1960 compared to a previous low of 1.3 in 1956 and to 0.9 in 1962. It had fallen from a high of 3.0 in 1958.

9. See Appendix O, note 5, p. 443.

10. This calculation identifies a 1 percentage point difference in the unemployment rate with a difference of 1.5 percent in national income per unit of input. See Appendix O, pp. 442–43.

TABLE 19–2

Irregularities in Pressure of Demand and in Farm Output: Contribution to Differences from the United States in National Income per Person Employed, 1960

(*In index points*)

Area	Before interaction allowance		After interaction allowance	
	Demand pressure (1)	Farm irregularities (2)	Demand pressure (3)	Farm irregularities (4)
United States	—	—	—	—
Northwest Europe	−2.2	.0	−1.6	.0
Belgium	−2.4	.0	−1.8	.0
Denmark	−2.4	.0	−1.8	.0
France	−2.4	.0	−1.7	.0
Germany	−2.4	.0	−1.7	.0
Netherlands	−2.4	−.7	−1.8	−.5
Norway	−2.4	.0	−1.8	.0
United Kingdom	−1.7	.0	−1.3	.0
Italy	−2.4	.0	−1.4	.0

Source: See text for derivation.

These estimates are shown in the first column of Table 19–2, and estimates of the contributions after allowing for interaction effects are given in the third column.

Irregular Fluctuations in Farm Output

Farm output jumps up and down from year to year. Variations in weather and other natural conditions that are independent of any of the sources of long-term growth considered elsewhere in this study are largely responsible. In Denmark 1950 and 1962 were good years for agriculture and 1955 an exceptionally bad year. This reduced the calculated growth rate of output per unit of input from 1950 to 1955, raised the rate from 1955 to 1962, and distorts a comparison of the two periods. Differences among 1950, 1955, and 1962 with respect to agricultural output were also present in other countries.

To estimate the amounts by which growth rates were affected, an adjusted "normal" farm GNP was substituted for actual farm GNP in constant prices in each of the three years. The amount by which this substitution would change growth rates of total gross product was then computed. The effect on the growth rate of national income was assumed to be the same as that on gross product.

The estimates of the "contribution" of this factor to growth rates depend on the estimates of the amount by which actual farm GNP departs from "normal." The "normal" amount for each year was arrived at by examining the data for earlier and later years; some average was ordinarily used. No statistical procedure was found that could be uniformly applied in all countries and at all dates with satisfactory results; the estimates are *ad hoc* in character and rest on judgment. Another investigator would, however, be unlikely to reach different conclusions as to the signs of the estimates, even though he would not arrive at identical figures.

Table 19–3 gives my estimates. In view of the approximate character of the procedure, no estimate was introduced for a country unless it appeared that the effect on the growth rate would exceed 0.05 percentage points in some period. Estimates for the United States, Belgium, and the United Kingdom (which are the countries in which agriculture is least important) are omitted for this reason. Irregularities in farm output have their greatest effect upon a comparison of 1950–55 and 1955–62 growth rates in Denmark. They are also fairly substantial in comparisons of these periods in

the Netherlands, Norway, and Italy. The influence on the growth rate over the whole 1950–62 period was less than 0.1 in all countries.

Special mention must be made of Germany. Gross product in agriculture (including forestry) in the early 1950's (in billions of deutsche marks at 1954 prices) was as follows:

	DM (billions)		DM (billions)
1950	11.61	1953	13.45
1951	13.29	1954	13.76
1952	13.40	1955	13.67

Data prior to 1950 are unavailable, but collateral information on farm production suggests the sharp 1950–51 increase was a continuation of a similar rise in the earlier postwar years. I interpret this rise as a recovery from wartime disruption. If it is estimated that in the absence of this disruption farm gross product in 1950 would have been higher by, say, 1.50, then this factor alone contributed nearly 0.3 percentage points to the German growth rate from 1950 to 1955. (Actual 1955 farm GNP was estimated to be practically normal.) This adjustment, if made, would be quite different from those introduced for the other countries, which stem primarily from the influence of the forces of nature. It seems better not to introduce such an adjustment in this context but to leave it combined with other effects of German recovery in this period.[11]

No allowance for the effect of abnormal weather conditions on the comparison of levels of national income per person employed in 1960 appears to be required except in the Netherlands, where 1960 was an extraordinarily favorable year. It appears that national income per person employed was raised about 0.7 percent by this circumstance (Table 19–2).[12]

TABLE 19–3

Contribution to Growth Rates of National Income per Unit of Input Made by Irregularities in Farm Output

(*In percentage points*)

Area	1950–62	1950–55	1955–62
United States	.00	.00	.00
Northwest Europe	.00	.01	−.01
Belgium	.00	.00	.00
Denmark	−.07	−.43	.19
France	−.01	.07	−.07
Germany	.00	.00	.00
Netherlands	.02	.19	−.10
Norway	−.02	−.21	.11
United Kingdom	.00	.00	.00
Italy	.01	.11	−.07

Source: See text for derivation.

11. To a small extent it duplicates the allowance already made in Chapter 12 for the "balancing of the capital stock," but most of the item is included in the "residual" line for Germany when allocation of growth sources is completed.

12. Estimates given in Appendix L indicate that, in 1960, 6.0 percent of Dutch GNP in United States prices consisted of farm GNP and that farm GNP in 1957–63 averaged 11.1 percent less than the 1960 volume. Substitution of this average would therefore lower Dutch product per person by 0.7 percent.

Advances of Knowledge
and Other Residual Sources

This chapter has two related purposes. One is to discuss "advances of knowledge," a source of growth that is important but that cannot be measured directly. The second is to present and attempt to interpret the residuals that are obtained when the contributions of all sources previously estimated are deducted from growth rates. These residuals include, but are not confined to, the contributions of advances of knowledge and the related growth source, the "change in the lag in the application of knowledge." Residual differences in the level of national income per person employed in 1960 are also considered.

Advances of Knowledge
as a Source of Growth

As knowledge relevant to production advances, the output that can be obtained from a given quantity of resources rises. In the very long run changes in the "state of the arts" and gains from economies of scale, insofar as the latter are not due to changes in artificial restrictions upon markets, are the fundamental sources of growth in output per unit of in-

put. Other sources reflect changes in the extent to which actual output falls below what it would be if resources could be allocated and used with perfect efficiency. They can contribute to growth only during a transition period, although this period may in fact be long.

The scope of advances of knowledge that are relevant to this study is greatly limited by the fact that my analysis is confined to the growth of *measured* national income. The consequences of three characteristics of national income measurement described in Chapter 3 are especially pertinent. (1) Advances of knowledge cannot contribute at all to measured growth in activities where output is measured by input. (2) The treatment of quality change imposes a still more important restriction. The introduction of new and improved final products provides the user with a greater range of choice or enables him to meet his needs better with the same use of resources, but it does not, in general, contribute to growth as measured; it results in "noneconomic" or "unmeasured" quality change.[1] In general, as a consequence, only those advances of knowledge that reduce the unit costs of end prod-

1. See also *Sources of Economic Growth,* Chapters 14 and 21 [B25].

279

ucts already in existence contribute to measured growth. It is conceivable that the omitted benefits of new knowledge make a greater contribution to individual welfare than those that are reflected in the growth rate although there is no way to compare the benefits of the two. (3) The development of new forms of business organization in retail trade does not affect the measured national income in the United States or in nonfood lines in the United Kingdom.

Technological and Managerial Knowledge

With the crucial exceptions noted, the advance of knowledge must be construed comprehensively.[2] It includes, of course, what may be termed technological knowledge—knowledge concerning the physical properties of things, and of how to make, combine, or use them in a physical sense. It also includes what I call "managerial knowledge," that is, knowledge of techniques of management, construed in the broadest sense, and of business organization. Advances in managerial knowledge may easily contribute as much or more to measured growth as advances in technological knowledge, but again there is no way to provide a quantitative comparison.

It should be noted that growth rates and my estimates of the contribution of "advances of knowledge" to growth embrace gains from reductions in the unit costs of obtaining end products as a consequence of "noneconomic" quality improvement

in intermediate products.[3] These include structures and equipment and, hence, as explained in Chapter 12, they incorporate what is sometimes called "embodied" technical progress.

Advances of knowledge differ from other growth sources in one highly important respect. Any scientific discovery, theory, or knowledge of any new materials, machines, techniques, procedures, and practices that arises anywhere in the world quickly spreads to all industrialized countries. Secrets are few and temporary. By accelerating its own contribution to advances of knowledge, one industrialized country cannot expect to gain more than a temporary advantage over the others with respect to knowledge available for use, and in growth rate terms the differential gains are small.[4] Of course, as Jacob Schmookler has found, the demand or prospective gain from inventions greatly influences what is invented; the prospective gain is likely also to influence other types of advances of knowledge.[5] Individual inventors and firms are most familiar with and best able to exploit potential markets in their own country. Hence, insofar as the pattern of opportunity varies among countries, advances of knowledge may on the average have greater applicability in the country of origin than abroad. But this point does not greatly qualify the idea that knowledge is an international commodity.

The best practice possible with the knowledge *available* at any given time must, however, be dis-

---

2. Any attempt at direct measurement of changes in the state of knowledge (if this is conceivable at all) would encounter much the same type of difficulties in delimiting its scope as are encountered in defining research and development in measurement of R&D expenditures. At some level of detail, "knowledge" becomes part of the production process. It would not be desirable, for example, to count as part of the state of knowledge an employer's information that Mr. X regularly has a headache on Monday mornings and should not be given important assignments at that time, while Mr. Y is dependable on Mondays but is likely to be absent on the opening day of the baseball season. A general awareness that Blue Monday and Opening Day must be considered as possible factors affecting attendance and performance could be considered part of the "state of knowledge," but some might consider even this information too specific. Similarly, the designing of valves for use in particular applications—if no new principles are involved—will ordinarily not be considered to advance knowledge but to be part of the problem-solving activity inherent in production. The distinction is necessarily fuzzy, and I shall not attempt a precise delineation.

3. See *Sources of Economic Growth*, p. 243 [B25].
4. International trade analysts often stress the importance in international competition of just such leads in product improvement. They believe the ability of a national industry to stay a year or two ahead of its competitors in product improvement may be vital to its success in export markets. (For this reason, it is sometimes inferred, small countries should concentrate their limited research effort in a small number of industries.)
This view may be correct but I believe it has only trifling relevance to the analysis of the growth of total measured national income, provided a nation keeps its resources fully employed. If resources can earn more in an industry under consideration than they could in other industries, after deducting the costs of staying ahead of international competitors, then a change in this ability leading to a redistribution of the nation's resources may add to or subtract from the growth rate, but only by the amount of the differential. Of course, one can visualize a relationship between competitive ability based on this factor and the general position of a country's balance of payments, and between the balance of payments and policies that affect some other growth determinants, but the same can be said about anything else that affects the balance of payments.
5. *Invention and Economic Growth*, Chapters V–VII [B97].

tinguished from the average practice actually in use. Translating this distinction into a classification suitable for growth sources, one may distinguish in principle between the contribution of "advances of knowledge" and the contribution (positive or negative) that may be made by a change in the lag of average practice behind the best known. This is an essential distinction, especially in the present study, and a common one, but it is difficult to give it precision. It seems necessary to conceive of the techniques that would be used each year by the most advanced enterprises or other producing units anywhere in the world if they were free to adopt the techniques they regarded as most efficient, without restrictions imposed from outside or by their own past actions (including investment actions). The increase that would take place in output per unit of input because of advances of knowledge if all firms were in this position then corresponds to my conception of the contribution of "the advance of knowledge."[6] The actual technique used on the average by all enterprises in a country will always be below or behind this standard, and average practice may improve more or less rapidly than the best if average practice moves closer to or farther from the best. The difference between the contribution actually made by changes in average practice and the contribution that would be made if all producers could and did always use the best practice I regard as the contribution of the "change in the lag in application of knowledge." If the lag or differential between best and average practice does not change, there will be no contribution from this source.[7]

I have no way to isolate the various reasons that average practice is below the best or that the margin of difference changes. The reasons may be simple

6. This falls somewhere between the first and second (but closer to the second) of three definitions suggested by Abramovitz in *American Economic Review*, September 1962, p. 776 [P1].

The problem of defining "knowledge," as well as the process of obtaining and diffusing it, is also discussed by Nelson, Peck, and Kalachek in *Technology, Economic Growth, and Public Policy* [B83].

7. If the rate at which knowledge advances is approximately constant (my estimate of the situation over the past several decades, although this is inferred from changes in actual practice in the United States), a reduction in the differential between average and best practice will correspond to a reduction in the time span between the dates at which the most advanced firms would reach any level of costs under the assumed conditions and the date at which average costs reach this level.

TABLE 20–1

Contribution of Residual Sources
(Including Advances of Knowledge)
to Growth Rates of Total National Income
(In percentage points)

Area	1950–62	1950–55	1955–62
United States	.76	.76	.76
Northwest Europe	1.30	1.77	.99
Belgium	.84	.95	.77
Denmark	.44	.05	.75
France	1.51	1.48	1.56
Germany	1.56	2.55	.87
Netherlands	1.20	1.79	.75
Norway	.90	.76	.97
United Kingdom	.79	.70	.87
Italy	1.65	2.12	1.30

Sources: Data obtained by deducting from the contribution of output per unit of input (Table 15–3) the contribution of all separately estimated sources except advances of knowledge; see tables in Chapter 21 for a summary of these sources in each area.

ignorance of best practice on the part of firms and the inability to start afresh each year. Again, it may relate to the ability and effort devoted by management to obtaining maximum efficiency. Still again, it may relate to institutional conditions or attitudes that prevent management from securing maximum efficiency; overmanning may often result from this inability.

The Residual in Growth Rates

The contribution to growth rates made by advances of knowledge and changes in the "lag" cannot be estimated directly, not even if the two series are combined. All that I can offer are residual estimates obtained by deducting from the growth rates of national income the contributions made by all the sources for which estimates were attempted. These residuals are shown in Table 20–1.[8] They pick up the net error (positive or negative) in the other estimates as well as the net contribution (positive or negative) of other sources for which no estimate was attempted; many of these were discussed in earlier chapters.

RESIDUALS FOR THE UNITED STATES. For the United States I arrive at an estimate that advances

8. These residuals include the "interaction" between the contribution of factors included in the residual and other growth sources but it is too trifling—nowhere more than 0.02 points—to impair comparisons. The contributions of the other sources are summarized in the tables in Chapter 21.

of knowledge and any change in the lag, together with errors and omissions, contributed 0.76 percentage points to the growth rate of national income in both the 1950–55 and 1955–62 periods. In my earlier study I arrived at an estimate of 0.59 for the 1929–57 period, but this estimate would be raised to about the same level as I now obtain for 1950–62 if procedural changes introduced in the present study were incorporated.[9] (Another calculation, a rough estimate for the 1925–60 period based on a combination of data from the present study for 1950–60 and adjustment of estimates from the earlier study for 1925–50, yields about 0.6.) There is no indication in these data of appreciable acceleration or deceleration in the amounts that advances of knowledge and changes in the lag in its application, together with errors and omissions, have been contributing to the United States growth rate over a rather long time span.

The stability of these estimates is consistent with and most plausibly explained by an approximately constant rate of advance in knowledge and little change in the lag. However, a sizable change in the lag of average practice behind the best known would also be consistent with these estimates if it were very smooth and continuous. A different consideration suggests to me that it is unlikely to have been very important. Advances of knowledge, according to these estimates, raise national income about 0.75 percent a year and reducing the lag by 1 year would raise national income about the same amount. At this rate a change of 1.6 years over a twelve-year period in the lag of average practice behind the best known would be required for the change to contribute even as much as plus or minus 0.1 points to the growth rate. In the world's most advanced, efficient, and diversified economy, this would seem to me to be a very large change.[10]

In my American study I inserted an estimate of 0.01 points for the contribution of the change in the lag of average practice behind the best known in the 1929–57 period. This token estimate was in-

troduced to emphasize the possibility of such a change and to express my judgment that any change was slight. In the present study I shall use the residual estimate of 0.76 as the contribution of advances of knowledge as such, allowing nothing for a change in the lag. Since it is a residual, the estimate is subject to the possibility of a substantial margin of error.

Because knowledge is an international commodity, I should expect the contribution of advances of knowledge—as distinct from changes in the lag—to be of about the same size in all the countries examined in this study. Admittedly this does not, *a priori,* have to be the case if the rate at which knowledge relevant to production advances differs greatly among activities. Individual new inventions, discoveries, management techniques, or methods of business organization that affect unit costs may have applications in only one or a group of industries or, at least, be of greater importance in some industries than others. Even in the same industry, some advances may have greater application when production is at one volume than at another, or with one set of factor proportions than another, or (particularly in the case of the natural resource and transport industries) under some natural conditions than under others.

It is sometimes suggested that one reason the United States growth rate has been below that of Europe is that services have a greater weight in the national product. Services, it is supposed, are less amenable than commodities to productivity increase through advances of knowledge. The point may have some validity but I do not believe it can be of large quantitative importance. Relative price changes provide one indication of relative productivity changes over long periods. Although the price of services, excluding rent and those measured on the equal productivity assumption, has risen more than that of commodities in the United States during the postwar years, this was not the case over the longer 1929–57 period.[11] Also, Victor R. Fuchs found that much of the differential in the rate of increase in output per man between commodity-producing and distributive and service industries is explained by differential changes in the quality of

9. These changes refer mainly to the contribution of increased experience and better utilization of women workers and the "days" adjustment in the education estimates. See Chapter 9, note 4, and Appendix F, p. 383.

10. United States enterprises are not, of course, the first to adopt widely every improvement in technique. Everyone knows of exceptions. But it is rather obvious that they *are* exceptions.

11. See *Sources of Economic Growth,* pp. 220–22 [B25].

labor and in the use of capital and by the shift from agriculture.[12] There are, moreover, at least two offsets to any remaining differential. First, the United States engages in more research than the European countries and this is presumably concentrated on the activities and types of situations that are important in the United States. Second, the activities in which output is measured by input, so that advances of knowledge have no opportunity to affect the measured growth rate, receive somewhat less weight in the United States than in Europe (Column 1, Table 15–1).

The contribution of "advances of knowledge" as such is not likely, in my view, to differ a great deal among the countries covered in this study. The possibility remains that changes in the "lag" may differ importantly. The average level of technique in Europe is generally considered to be below and behind that in the United States. This appears to be particularly true of the technique of management and the organization of business as distinct from technology more narrowly defined. As shown later in this chapter, the present study yields an estimate that, whatever the reasons, output per unit of input in Northwest Europe in 1960 was more than one-quarter below the United States even after eliminating the effects of economies of scale, overallocation of resources to agriculture and self-employment, and differences in the rate of utilization. Thus, there appears to be opportunity for the European countries to add substantial increments to their growth rates by imitating and adopting American practices.

During the 1950–62 period, there was a concentrated and deliberate effort to seize this opportunity. This effort had its origins in the Marshall Plan. Teams of European businessmen and experts were sent to the United States to study and evaluate American practices; France and the United Kingdom sent the largest numbers of such teams. Under the sponsorship of the European Productivity Agency, a specialized agency of OEEC, productivity centers were established throughout Western Europe to spread the gospel of European backward-

ness and the advantages to be seized by emulating the United States. In addition to participating in formal efforts by governments and international agencies to stimulate the rise in productivity, the European businessman or manager was exposed to a wave of articles, speeches, and books stressing the need and opportunity to raise productivity. It was often presented as a patriotic duty, especially for those in the export industries. Under these conditions, a finding that the European countries have secured a substantial increment to growth by narrowing the gap between European and American practices would not be a surprise.

RESIDUALS FOR EUROPE. The residuals shown in Table 20–1, however, show little trace of the effects of any such catching-up upon productivity in the economy as a whole except in France and perhaps Italy.[13] These residuals, of course, do not provide a direct measure. It must be stressed again that they include not only the contributions of advances of knowledge and changes in the lag of average practice behind the best known but also the net effect of errors in the growth rates themselves, of errors in estimates of the contributions made by other sources of growth, and of omission of all sources not specifically estimated. However, some of these sources, such as changes in the quality of management (not due to amount of education) and changes in the general efficiency with which resources are allocated and used (except for changes in overallocation to agriculture and self-employment, and in misallocation due to trade barriers), might reasonably be regarded as part of a catching-up process.

The residuals (in percentage points) in the 1955–62 period are as follows:

France	1.56
Italy	1.30
Norway	.97
Germany	.87
United Kingdom	.87
Belgium	.77
United States	.76
Denmark	.75
Netherlands	.75

The figures for seven of the nine countries—all except France and Italy—lie within so narrow a range that it is impossible to attach much significance to

12. *Productivity Trends in the Goods and Service Sectors, 1929–61: A Preliminary Survey* [B38]. Elsewhere, however, Fuchs has seemed to place some stress on the remaining differential in foreseeing a possible slowdown in the measured growth rate as services increase in importance.

13. I refer to "catching-up" in ways not measured in other growth sources. See p. 286.

the differences. Differences are trifling compared to the size of the growth rates from which the residuals were obtained. This does not prove conclusively that changes in the "lag" were not an important source of difference between the growth rates of the United States and those of the six European countries, or among these European countries themselves; but the pattern does establish some presumption that this was not the case.

The residual for Italy exceeds those for the other seven countries by 0.33 to 0.55 percentage points. I should certainly not wish to suggest that this is a significant difference, especially in view of the fact that, both for statistical reasons and because the Italian economy is so different from the others, estimates for Italy are probably less reliable than the others.[14] On the other hand, the frequent error must be avoided of supposing that a difference is not significant because it cannot be shown that it is significant; in other words, I have no basis for an opinion.

The residual for France in 1955–62 is approximately three-fourths of a percentage point higher than that for the United States and much above those for the other Northwest European countries. About the same margin over the United States is also shown below to appear in the 1950–55 period and therefore, of course, over the whole 1950–62 period. These results suggest that France may have been obtaining an appreciable increment to its growth rate from some source not measured in previous chapters and which neither the United States nor the other European countries were obtaining in comparable degree. I do not entirely rule out the possibility that the higher residual obtained for France is simply the result of incomparabilities in statistics or inadequate estimates of the other growth sources distinguished, but I think it more likely that it is not. If the differential does represent something "real," perhaps the most likely source is an increase in productivity stemming from a reduction of the gap between American and French management practices and technology.

The French productivity program, started in late 1949 under the Marshall Plan, grew quickly into "the largest and most varied" in Europe, with the establishment of regional centers in nearly every important French provincial town, with the creation of thirty-two separate industry productivity boards, and with the opening of business and management institutes at fifteen universities. Modernization committees were set up in nearly all industries as part of the planning mechanism. (The National Productivity Board and the National Planning Board were merged in 1960.) It is possible that this French program had an impact that the less formal and comprehensive devices adopted elsewhere did not.[15]

There are, of course, numerous other possibilities. The impact of planning upon resource allocation and the possibility of a greater increase in competitive pressure than occurred elsewhere cannot be ruled out. Others include a reduction in redundancy among wage and salary workers in response to tight labor markets, and better utilization of individual workers as the labor market became more fluid, but these aspects of postwar labor markets were not confined to France.

As stressed at the outset of this study, the period from 1950 to 1955 was an abnormal one in Europe and some odd results should be expected and are, in fact, obtained. For five of the nine countries, nevertheless, the residuals are close to those secured in 1955–62.

The residuals (in percentage points) obtained for the 1950–55 period are as follows:[16]

Germany	2.55
Italy	2.12
Netherlands	1.79
France	1.48
Belgium	.95
Norway	.76
United States	.76
United Kingdom	.70
Denmark	.05

I have already noted that the residual for the United States was the same in 1950–55 as it was in

---

14. Also, the Italian residual would be reduced by about 0.1 points if the recent revision of the growth rate of national income noted in Appendix A does not imply revisions of the contributions of other sources.

15. The quotation is from U.S. Department of State, International Cooperation Administration, *European Productivity and Technical Assistance Programs: A Summing Up (1948–1958)*, pp. 139–40 [G74]. I emphasize in this paragraph developments undertaken early enough to affect productivity in the 1950–62 period. Efforts to raise productivity have continued (see *Ve Plan, 1966–1970: Rapport Général de la Commission de Productivité* [S1]).

16. These residuals do not include estimates of 0.10 percentage points assigned as the contribution of shortening the average age of capital in Denmark, Germany, and Norway.

1955–62. Residuals for Belgium, Norway, and the United Kingdom in 1950–55 are close to that for the United States, as they were in 1955–62, and also close to the residuals obtained for the same countries in 1955–62. The largest difference between the subperiods is about 0.2 percentage points, an amount to which significance can hardly be attached.

The residual estimates for France in 1950–55 and 1955–62 were close to each other and in both cases about three-fourths of a percentage point above that obtained for the United States. Although I place greater stress on the results for the 1955–62 period, the consistency of these results with those for 1950–55 adds a little weight to the likelihood that France was obtaining additional growth from some source not measured in earlier chapters.

The residuals obtained for Germany and Italy in 1950–55 are large in comparison with those obtained for countries mentioned thus far or for Germany and Italy themselves in 1955–62. These are the two countries that were defeated in World War II and had returned least nearly to normal economic life by 1950. This characterization applies more strongly to Germany than to Italy. The strong probability is that the large residuals are picking up an abnormal increase in efficiency in the early fifties that was associated with recovery from wartime disruption and that my techniques are unable to capture.[17] Indeed, except for the special allowance for balancing the capital stock in Germany no effort was made to estimate this effect.[18] Although I have not attempted annual estimates of the sources of growth, it is apparent that the German residual is largest at the beginning of the 1950–55 period. It was in these early years that the recovery aspect was strongest.[19]

The 1950–55 residuals for two of the small countries, Denmark and the Netherlands, are also out of line with those for other countries in 1950–55 and for these countries in the later period. For Denmark I obtain only 0.05, and for the Netherlands the large figure of 1.79. For these results I have no special explanation. It is likely that they reflect no more than errors in the estimation of growth rates or in the contributions of other sources, but again there is no way to be sure.

It is perhaps worth noting that among the eighteen observations (nine countries in two subperiods) the highest growth rates of national income and the largest residuals were obtained for Germany, Italy, and the Netherlands in 1950–55, and the smallest growth rate and residual for Denmark in 1950–55. Thus, the other factors examined fell short of wholly explaining the most extreme growth rates.

The general pattern of the residuals, particularly those for the period after 1955, suggests that with the probable exception of France and possible exception of Italy the higher growth rates obtained by most European countries than by the United States were not due in any large measure to a catching-up of technique to that of the United States. This is so even though the residuals include gains from reducing the prevalence of redundant labor and any tightening up of cost control generally. I must confess that I would not have been particularly surprised by a different result. Residuals for the continental countries generally in the 1955–62 period somewhat like those actually obtained for France would not have seemed unreasonable. (That some of the residuals in 1950–55 would probably be erratic was, of course, foreseen.) The opportunity for gains by duplicating American practice clearly was large, and most descriptive evidence, except perhaps that pertaining to the United Kingdom, suggests that gains from imitation have been present.[20] Most observers, I think, have assumed that some catching-up was taking place. The literature is full of examples of the adoption of American practices by

17. In the case of Italy, reference should also be made to the discussion on pages 115–16 and in Appendix G, where it is suggested that the improvement in nutrition may have contributed significantly to Italian growth.

18. Aside from the estimate of 0.3 in the 1950–55 growth rate for recovery in agriculture that remains in the German residual.

19. Norman Macrae characterized "Germany in 1945–48" as "the most extreme example of an economy that was misutilizing its resources in the most completely ridiculous directions," and discussed the return to rational production, in *The Economist*, October 15, 1966, A Special Survey, pp. i–xxxii [P19].

20. A flood of articles appearing in early 1967 in which reference was made to a *growing* technological gap between America and Europe does not constitute a real exception. This literature stressed a few science-based industries in which technology has recently been advancing most rapidly, and had limited relevance to a comparison of whole economies. The stress, moreover, was on quality improvement in end products that does not affect output measures.

European firms. Much of the descriptive evidence refers to situations, of the type discussed in Section II of Chapter 17, in which expansion of markets made possible the application of American techniques that were not relevant to the European scene until markets for income-elastic products became sufficiently large. The gains from this source, which are substantial in some countries, are classified in this study under the general heading of "economies of scale." They are not included in the residuals nor regarded as gains from a reduction in this "lag." But not all the descriptive evidence can be dismissed on grounds of classification. It may be that most observers have been overly impressed by isolated cases or that insufficient weight has been given to the fact that American productivity has itself continued to rise with advances in the "state of the arts." Although the evidence of the residuals is not conclusive it is the only quantitative evidence that exists. It does not rule out *some* catching-up in most European countries and, in the case of France and perhaps Italy, it even suggests that this was a significant factor. But it does suggest that catching-up in technique was not a major factor in explaining European growth generally up to 1962.

It is possible that the situation has changed materially since 1962. Descriptive evidence, and illustrative data such as those given in Appendix M for the spread of self-service stores and supermarkets, suggests that only at the very end of the period were many changes becoming sufficiently general to importantly affect productivity in whole economies. The new generation of managers has only recently begun to attain positions of responsibility in a number of countries.[21] A repetition of this study for the decade of the sixties might yield appreciably larger residuals. But I can deal here only with the period covered by my estimates.

Contribution of Advances of Knowledge

To interpret European postwar growth, and especially to use the results of postwar European experience to attempt to appraise the future, it seems

to me essential to distinguish the contribution made by advances of knowledge from the contribution of changes in the "lag" and the remaining elements caught in the residuals. This seems to me so necessary as to justify use of a bold procedure to incorporate in the tables the best appraisal of this contribution I can make. To do this requires two assumptions.

First, the residual estimate obtained for the United States is assumed to measure accurately the contribution of advances of knowledge in the United States. This implies that in the United States there was no important change in the "lag." It also implies that no net contribution, positive or negative, was made by omitted factors and by errors in the estimates for other growth sources; here I rely heavily upon the likelihood of offsetting errors. This assumption is admittedly a strong one. But an estimate of the contribution of advances of knowledge, as such, can be better obtained by the residual method in the United States than in any other country. The United States has the most "advanced" and highly diversified economy. It is also the country for which data are most nearly adequate, in which the sources whose contributions were most difficult to appraise are of the least importance, and in which omitted factors (other than advances of knowledge) are likely to be of least importance.

Second, the contribution made by advances of knowledge to growth is assumed to have been the same in the European countries as it was in the United States.[22] As noted earlier, this second assumption can be in error insofar as there is a correlation between (a) differences in the "mix" of the economies with respect to industries or products, factor proportions, scale, and the like, and (b) differences in the rate at which knowledge pertinent to production in different situations advances. I ignore the effects of any such intercorrelation but I

21. See, for example, "U.S. Business in the New Europe," a special report in *Business Week*, May 7, 1966, pp. 94–120 [P8], and Bignami in *Proceedings, CIOS XIII International Management Congress*, pp. 406–09 [B12].

22. More precisely, my assumption is that the contribution of advances of knowledge would be the same if this were the *only* factor affecting growth. Elimination of the interaction term drops this contribution from 0.76 to 0.75 in the United States in both subperiods. This estimate was imputed to the European countries and the interaction reintroduced separately for each. This results in estimates of the contribution of advances of knowledge that occasionally differ by 0.01 or 0.02 from those for the United States. This procedure is required to maintain consistency with the procedures followed for other sources.

should be surprised if they were large relative to growth rates. They would have to alter by one-third the rate at which knowledge relevant to production in a particular country advances to change the contribution of the "advances of knowledge" (0.75 in the United States) by as much as one-quarter of a percentage point. This strikes me as improbable even in the smaller and more specialized European economies.

In the following chapter I shall use as my estimate of the contribution of advances of knowledge in all countries the residual shown for the United States in Table 20–1, slightly adjusted where necessary for differences in the interaction term. This estimate is the same in the United States in both the 1950–55 and 1955–62 subperiods, and as indicated earlier would also be approximately the same over a time span reaching back to the 1920's. From the residuals shown in Table 20–1 for each country in each time period I deduct this contribution to obtain an ultimate residual. I shall term this ultimate residual the contribution of "other changes in the lag in the application of knowledge, general efficiency, and errors and omissions."[23]

Efforts To Promote Advances of Knowledge

Have the European countries been doing more than the United States to obtain growth by promoting advances of knowledge? As already noted, knowledge is an international commodity and an individual country can scarcely gain more than a temporary advantage in growth through its own contributions, although some allowance should be made for the possibility of concentrating effort on those activities or situations that are especially important in that country.

The question might be amended to ask which area has been doing more to stimulate growth in all countries. But the foundation for a firm answer is still lacking because there is no breakdown, by type or origin, of the advances of knowledge that have been contributing three-quarters of a percentage

point to growth rates. There is, therefore, no way to know the relative importance of different types of activity.

Some advances of knowledge contributing to measured growth originate in organized research that results in the reduction of costs. Costs may be reduced either directly, by reducing costs of enterprises by or for whom research is undertaken, or indirectly, by improvement of intermediate products—materials, supplies, or capital goods—sold by enterprises to others, thereby reducing their customers' costs. Some advances in science and in general knowledge of broad principles have wide applicability for cost reduction.

Total research expenditures are larger in the United States than in any of the European countries or in all of them combined. They are also larger in relation to population, employment, GNP measured in national prices and, with the possible exception of the United Kingdom, GNP measured in United States prices. C. Freeman and A. J. Young attempted a comparison of total research and development expenditures in 1962 in the United States and the Northwest European countries studied here except Norway and Denmark.[24] The latter area had about the same population as the United States and 10 percent more employment. The United States spent four times as much as Northwest Europe if expenditures are equated by exchange rates and 2½ times as much if a "research exchange rate" is used. The "research exchange rate" results from an attempt to price inputs used in research and development; it does not consider differences in productivity in research which, the authors give some reason to believe, may be higher in the United States. It implies that R&D costs were higher in the United States than in Europe and by a wider margin than prices in general.

Freeman and Young found the expenditure ratios in military and space research were 7 to 1 at exchange rates and 4 to 1 at a "research" rate. The ratio for other types of research was about 2½ to 1 at exchange rates and 1½ to 1 at the "research rate." The percentages of GNP at factor cost devoted to research and development, based on each country's own prices as is proper in measuring

23. "Other" refers only to the allowance made in three countries for the effects of changes in the average age of capital in the 1950–55 period, which is not included here.

24. OECD, *The Research and Development Effort* [I44].

"effort," were 3.5 in the United States, 2.5 in the United Kingdom, 1.8 in France, 1.7 in the Netherlands, 1.5 in Germany, and 1.2 in Belgium.[25] Uniform use of United States prices (including the "research rate" for R&D) would not bring the European ratios up to the United States level except perhaps in the United Kingdom. The United States had 2.2 times as many persons and 3.0 times as many scientists and engineers engaged in research and development as Northwest Europe (excluding Denmark and Norway). R&D expenditures increased in both areas after 1950 but a reliable comparison of changes over time is not available.

Figures such as these are impressive and suffice to show that the United States was devoting more effort than the European countries to R&D.[26] Their relevance to an analysis of measured growth is remote, however. They refer to inputs into research and tell nothing of what is learned. The purpose of most—probably the bulk—of R&D expenditures, moreover, is such that it does not affect the growth rate no matter how successful it may be.[27] The growth rate would have been the same (aside from any slight indirect effort on the quantity or quality of labor input) whether antibiotics were developed or not.[28] It would have been the same if the effort to reach the moon by 1970 had not been made and, instead, the same resources had been used to build and stockpile battleships. It will be the same whether the moon is or is not reached by 1970. Finally, there is no way of knowing whether those fruits of organized research that do affect the measured growth rate contribute 0.1, 0.7, or any intermediate amount to the total contribution of advances of knowledge. The fact that expenditures for research and development have expanded so much in the

United States while estimates of the contribution of advances of knowledge have not may suggest that organized R&D is not very important to measured growth. But even this remark must be qualified by noting that we do not know how large has been the increase in R&D expenditures of the types that are relevant to measured growth.

In the field of management and business organization, the United States appears to do much more than the European countries to promote new advances of knowledge. This, at least, is a widespread impression that I believe to be correct. Much of the European effort is devoted to learning, adapting, and promoting American practices. One visible difference has been the scarcity of European institutions corresponding to the schools of business administration in American universities. In the past decade a number of new European institutions have appeared. Almost nothing can be said about other sources of advances of knowledge except that increments resulting from observation and application of ingenuity on the job by workers at all levels seem more likely to occur where actual practice is already most advanced.

In principle, a country has a much greater opportunity to gain an advantage in the growth rate race by reducing the gap between average and best practice than by advancing the frontiers of knowledge. To disseminate information and push innovation, the United States relies mainly on private channels, such as: salesmen; buyers; books; trade, business, and professional journals, and a myriad of specialized publications; associations; meetings; advice of bankers; research departments of firms; exchange of information among businessmen and employees; and the alertness of managers and employees. All of these are backed by the force of competition. The government has not been passive. It has long made a major effort in agriculture through the Agricultural Extension Service. In the postwar period it has made some effort to be helpful to small business and has tried to make foreign information available to American businessmen in usable form. But the government's role is a secondary one, except in defense research where an elaborate structure to exchange, channel, and evaluate information is supported.

The main channels and mechanisms in Europe

25. The percentage in Norway, which is not given in the Freeman-Young study, was lower than in any of these countries in 1960, according to data given in National Council of Scientific Policy, *Recherche et Croissance Economique*, p. 65 [G1].

26. It is unnecessary to ask to what extent this is due, in addition, to defense expenditures, to differences in industrial structure, and to size of firms.

27. See *Sources of Economic Growth*, pp. 241–44 [B25], for an attempt to analyze United States R&D expenditures in accordance with its relevance to measured growth.

28. These comments, of course, have nothing whatever to do with the question of how much ought to be spent on research and development. They are made strictly within the context of what contributes to growth rates as they are measured and why these rates differ.

are, of course, similar to those in the United States but, as noted earlier, government participation through the productivity centers, and in France through the modernization committees (which have been paid the compliment of imitation by the British "Little Neddies"), are additional features.[29] Participation in production by foreign firms through ownership, or through licensing agreements accompanied by technical and managerial advice, are much more important in disseminating foreign practices in Europe than in America. In Chapter 18 I commented on the likelihood that the "stick of competition" is probably less effective in forcing efficiency and modernization, but that its use may have increased somewhat and thus have made some contribution toward a "catching-up."

If France, Italy, or—despite the evidence of the residuals—some other European countries did obtain substantially more growth than the United States by reducing the gap between average and best practice, I think it is fair to assert that this was primarily because there was a larger gap to be eliminated and the opportunities were accordingly greater.[30] I turn now to the extraordinarily difficult problem of appraising the difference.

The Residuals in Level Comparisons

Chapter 15 compared output per unit of total input in the various countries in 1960. It also provided estimates of the contributions of output per unit of input to differences in the level of national income per person employed, after taking into account the interaction between output per unit of input and total input per person employed. The amounts (positive or negative) that were due to several particular

29. "Neddy" is a nickname for the National Economic Development Council. "Little Neddies" are its regional and industrial offshoots.

30. This is not, of course, to deny the possibility that the United States could accelerate its own growth by measures that would reduce the gap between average practice and the best known. Programs to do so in the private sector would presumably be designed: (1) to further improve the dissemination of information (and the right to use it if patent law is an obstacle) and the provision of advice to smaller or backward firms; (2) to make it easier to displace poor management in publicly held firms; or (3) to intensify competition so that inefficient firms would be more quickly driven out of existence.

TABLE 20-2

Contribution of Residual Sources to Differences from the United States in National Income per Person Employed, 1960

(*Percentage of United States national income per person employed*)

Area	Before interaction allowance	After interaction allowance
Northwest Europe	28.0	23.7
Belgium	26.4	23.4
Denmark	26.2	22.4
France	23.1	19.1
Germany	24.3	19.8
Netherlands	30.3	27.5
Norway	25.9	22.9
United Kingdom	33.7	29.3
Italy	30.2	21.3

Source: See note 31, p. 290 for derivation.

sources have now been estimated. These include overallocation of resources to agriculture and self-employment, economies of scale, use of shift work, differences in the intensity with which resources were used in the year 1960 because of the strength of demand pressures, and the happenstance that in the Netherlands 1960 was an especially favorable year for farm production. The contribution of all the factors not yet considered to the difference between each of the European countries and the United States in national income per person employed is given in the second column of Table 20–2. It is obtained as a residual.

For Northwest Europe as a whole, the starting point, Table 2–4, was a finding that national income per person employed, valued in United States prices, was 41 percent below the United States level in 1960. Of this difference a net amount of 11.3 points was due to differences in factor input per person employed, and a net amount of 6.0 points to differences in determinants of output per unit of input that were explicitly estimated and have just been enumerated. This leaves 23.7 points, the figure given in the second column of Table 20–2, as the net contribution of all remaining sources of difference. Thus, an amount equal to more than half of the original difference remains unexplained. The importance of the unexplained factors can be considered more conveniently if effects of their interaction with other sources are eliminated. Such estimates are shown in the first column of Table 20–2.[31] They indicate that if all the income-determining factors whose effects were measured in previous chapters were the same in the United States and Northwest Europe, national income per person employed would still be 28 percent lower in Northwest Europe than in the United States because of differences in determinants whose effects have not been measured. For brevity, I shall refer to this amount as the difference in residual productivity.

Exploration, Qualification, and Interpretation

Several observations about the estimates of residual productivity are appropriate.

1. The estimates refer, strictly speaking, to nonfarm activities. The procedure adopted in Chapter 16 to measure the cost of overallocation of labor to agriculture implied that if the ratio of output per unit of total input in a European country to output per unit of total input in the United States was different in agriculture and nonagricultural activities, this difference was due to differences in the extent of overallocation to agriculture; and it has been so classified.

2. It must be remembered that the percentages shown in Table 20–2 reflect only the differences in output per person employed that remain after taking account of most of the explanations for differences in the level of output that are at all mea-

surable. It is especially important that this be recognized in comparing Italy with Northwest Europe. I have already taken account of such facts as Italy's large and unproductive agricultural sector, large number of nonfarm self-employed, low level of education, and relatively small capital resources. There is no important a priori reason to feel confident that productivity is lower in Italy than in Northwest Europe for reasons whose effects have not been measured.

3. The "state of knowledge" is regarded in my classification as being the same by definition in all countries except insofar as the appropriate weights to apply to different kinds of knowledge may vary among countries because of differences in industry mix, etc., or because information is literally unavailable to certain countries. Conceptually, therefore, the residuals obtained in the level comparisons are approximately comparable to the ultimate residuals obtained in the growth rate analysis after the contribution of advances of knowledge is deducted, and they reflect the effects of the same bundle of sources.

4. There is, however, no reason at all to expect any correspondence between the importance of individual unmeasured factors in accounting for the residuals in the level comparisons and their importance in accounting for the ultimate residuals obtained in the analysis of growth. For example, I quoted in Chapter 9 the opinion that Americans simply work harder than Europeans and that this may be an important element in accounting for the difference in level of output per man. If so, this is the source of a large fraction of the 28 percent residual differential between the United States and Northwest Europe at which I have arrived. But if the intensity of work did not change in either area during the 1950–62 period (except in response to changes in hours of work), the same factor had no effect at all on growth rates. In Chapter 9, I suggested the possibility that work effort might have increased on the continent but not in the Anglo-Saxon countries.[32] If this surmise were correct, changes in the intensity of work would have con-

31. These estimates were computed as follows. For each of the other determinants of output per unit of input, the estimate of the percentage difference between a European country and the United States in output per unit of input that would be present if it were the only source of difference was converted to index form (United States equals 100). For example, according to Table 17–3, economies of scale associated with the size of the national market would make output per unit of input in Belgium 5 percent lower than in the United States if this were the only difference between the countries. This means it would be 95 percent as high. To obtain data for the first column of Table 20–2, the product of the six indexes for each area thus computed from Tables 16–14, 17–3, 17–10, and 19–2, and the corresponding index for shift work (p. 173) was divided into the index of output per unit of input given in Table 15–6.

Although the text describes the second column of Table 20–2 as a residual to stress its essential characteristic, the precise procedure was to apply the pseudo growth rate method simultaneously to each of the factors determining output per unit of input, including the residual factor, in order to treat the interaction term in a fashion identical to that followed in arriving at the contribution of inputs.

32. The residuals in Table 20–1 give little support to this supposition but any such effect might, of course, have been offset by something else.

tributed to growth in Northwest Europe and to the difference between continental and Anglo-American growth rates, but no correspondence between its *importance* in growth and level differences could be expected.

5. The residuals obtained in Table 20–2 result from the use of United States weights in the measurement of national income and in the evaluation of the contribution of each source that has been considered to the difference in national income. Use of national European weights to measure output yielded a difference in income per person employed between Northwest Europe and the United States of 54 percent of the United States figure instead of 41 percent, and a difference between the United States and Italy of 76 percent instead of 60 percent. The amounts that would be ascribed to many of the sources identified would also be larger if European weights were used. How the residual productivity differences given in the first column of Table 20–2 would change if European weights were employed instead of American weights has not been measured. But it must be recognized that my results rest on the use of only one of the possible alternative weighting systems.

6. Throughout this study I have stressed that the difficulties of interspatial comparison are far greater than those encountered in intertemporal comparisons over a short time span unless (as, for example, in Germany in 1950–55) the time period is a very disturbed one. Errors in the comparisons both of national income itself and of the contributions of sources evaluated directly are likely to be more substantial in interspatial than in intertemporal comparisons so that residuals are almost sure to provide a less reliable measure of the combined contribution of all sources that were not explicitly estimated.

7. It is even more difficult in interspatial than in intertemporal comparisons to select from all the income determinants not directly measured those that seem to have a potential to contribute importantly to differences in the residuals. In time series analysis it is often possible to rely upon general information to conclude that some condition has not changed much and therefore cannot have contributed an appreciable positive or negative amount to the growth rate. General information and impres-

sions are much less likely to be sufficient in interspatial comparisons.

After these comments, what can be said about the meaning of the residuals? The main positive statement that can be based upon them is that sources for which no specific estimate was made are responsible for a large difference in output per man between the European countries generally and America. My view is that the residuals are accurate enough for their large size to support this statement.

This conclusion is in harmony with the "conventional wisdom." There is a voluminous literature in which opinions or impressions are offered on the amount by which productivity differs among countries in situations that are sufficiently similar to be identified with my measure of "residual productivity." Case studies are also numerous. Both the impressions of observers and the case studies overwhelmingly support two views: that there is a large gap in output per man that cannot be ascribed to differences in capital, labor quality, or scale; and that such a gap is present in almost all industries or activities that are compared and is not confined to certain sectors of the economy. The most comprehensive comparison of output per man by industry so far attempted—the OEEC study by Paige and Bombach[33]—also supports the latter conclusion.

There is also extensive though largely impressionistic literature on the reasons for the productivity gap. Much of this deals specifically with international differences in management and labor attitudes and practices, but it can hardly be said that a consensus emerges.[34]

For individual countries the arithmetic of the calculations produces estimates that *if all the*

---

33. *A Comparison of National Output and Productivity of the United Kingdom and the United States* [I22].

34. To cite or summarize here, even on a selective basis, opinions and studies dealing with the amount of or the reasons for the productivity gap is impossible, but a fair sampling of the more careful studies was reported, summarized, or reviewed in the *Productivity Measurement Review*, organ of the European Productivity Agency [I23] until its suspension of publication in 1965. David Granick's *The European Executive* [B43] is a particularly interesting study of management in Great Britain, France, Belgium, and Germany, written from an American background. Dunning has investigated reasons for differences in profitability between British firms and American firms operating in Britain. His preliminary findings are reported in *Business Ratios*, Autumn 1966 [S9].

income-determining elements for which specific esti-mates were made were the same as in the United States, national income per person employed and per unit of total input in United States prices would be below the United States by 23 percent in France, 24 in Germany, 26 in Belgium, Denmark, and Nor-way, 30 in the Netherlands and Italy, and 34 in the United Kingdom. The smaller differences among the Northwest European countries (such as that between France and Germany or even these coun-tries and Belgium, Denmark, and Norway) can be dismissed as without probable significance; the orig-inal comparisons of national income per person employed are themselves not likely to be accurate enough for differences within this range to be re-garded as significant.[35] Unhappily, it is hazardous to suppose that the larger differences that emerge among the European countries either are or are not a reflection of real and significant differences. How-ever, the gap between France and Germany on the one hand and the United Kingdom on the other is so substantial that I doubt if it can be dismissed. (I shall return to that comparison shortly.) Several unusual features of the Dutch society and economy that affect its position with respect to output per person employed were noted in earlier chapters, and it is of some interest that by this ultimate measure of residual efficiency, the Netherlands finishes rather low on the list of countries. The comparison of Italy with the Northwest European countries was more difficult than comparisons of the Northwest Euro-pean countries with one another at almost all points of this study, and an even larger margin of error in the estimate of residual efficiency must be presumed. Sensitivity of the Italian position to the choice of price weights is also especially high. For what they are worth, the results for Italy suggest that, after the effect of all the factors separately estimated is eliminated, the influence on productivity of the re-maining factors is within, or at least close to, the range of the Northwest European countries.

Any attempt to judge the quantitative impor-tance of the reasons that residual productivity is lower in Europe than in the United States is sheer

35. It should also be recalled that the relative positions of these countries in income per person employed are consid-erably affected by the choice of price weights for the com-parisons.

speculation. My own enumeration of the factors that are likely to be most important would empha-size the following: the lag in the application of knowledge, especially managerial knowledge; the quality of management; less intense competitive pressures; how hard people work; institutional re-straints not only against the dismissal of employees and reassignment of their duties but also against a great variety of business practices that could raise productivity; and the adequacy of industrial organi-zation, including the efficiency with which financial institutions allocate savings.

Imperfect communications, whereby European enterprises are simply unaware of superior Ameri-can practices, is doubtless one element. In the field I have termed "technological knowledge" a gap presumably exists but I have difficulty in supposing that it is of great importance. In the field of "man-agerial knowledge" it is probably futile to distin-guish between what management knows and what management does with the knowledge it has; but somewhere in this area, I suspect, lies an important part of the explanation for the productivity differen-tial. Businessmen with experience in both Europe and the United States believe this to be the case; that American firms operating in Europe typically earn more than their local competitors—or at least are widely believed to—suggests it is so; the heavy emphasis that publications for European business-men place upon American practices supports this implication; and floods of case studies show produc-tivity to be lower (or man-hours required for a par-ticular operation higher) in Europe for reasons that cannot be identified with capital or with the skills of workers. Less competition means that inefficient firms and inefficient management are under less pressure to minimize costs and less likely to be dis-placed by those who can do better. The pace of work at all levels is apparently slower than in the United States and employee resistance to dismissal for redundancy and to reassignment of duties as requirements change is more effective. In the United Kingdom, at least, resistance to new methods and machines is generally greater.

It is often said that attitudes of European buyers affect the characteristics of both final and interme-diate products in ways that impinge upon produc-tivity. One aspect is the greater attention devoted by

European manufacturers, particularly durable goods producers, to finish. Perfection of the finish is carried to lengths considered absurd and redundant by American producers but regarded by European buyers as a visible indication of the quality of performance and length of service to be anticipated from the product. A report by an American firm of management consultants, Serge A. Birn Company, points out that the "fetish over appearance"—the propensity of European managers and consumers to confuse appearance and quality—even carries over to parts that are invisible.[36] Rather similar is the apparent necessity of making capital goods heavy and solid to persuade industrial buyers that they will give long and satisfactory service.[37] It is an open question whether these attitudes are an expression of immutable preferences of Europeans, or (as I suspect) they are prevalent because the real alternatives have yet to be made clear.[38]

My guess is that most of the difference in residual productivity is ascribable to some combination of the elements mentioned in this chapter, but I have touched on other possibilities in earlier chapters and doubtless there are still others I have ignored.

36. The report states: "Examples are legion, but to take a specific: the 'appearance requirements' of ultimately invisible parts for a well-known German compact car force one of their suppliers to perform the *completely useless* operation of removing metal and blemishes on perfectly sound parts no one will ever see! Another specific: some 'appearance requirements' of the same popularly priced German compact are *higher* than those for Cadillac!" (*A Survey of International Labor Productivity: Are European Costs Really Lower?* p. 10 [B13]).

37. If European industrial buyers happened to be correct not only in their method of appraising durability but also in paying a premium for it, this attitude would, of course, contribute toward a higher rather than a lower national income in Europe. When one considers not only obsolescence but also the fact that future services of a capital good must be discounted to the present in order to decide what is the best buy, it is apparent that the buyers can be correct only if a great increase in durability can be obtained at little cost. (In *Sources of Economic Growth*, p. 119 [B25], I argue that there is probably opportunity to increase productivity in the United States by reducing the durability of capital goods.)

38. Another claim, that European consumers demand and obtain a greater variety of goods than American consumers and that this results in less standardization and higher costs, strikes me as improbable. At least, I have never seen any indication that a greater variety of products is offered in Europe than in America. It appears to be true that individual producers try to offer a greater variety of products—that is, there is less specialization—and that this contributes to higher unit costs. However, this cannot be ascribed to limitations imposed by consumer tastes.

The British Question

Estimates presented in Chapter 16 showed that in United States prices national income per person employed in nonagricultural industries in the United Kingdom was 15 percent lower than it was in France in 1960, 10 percent lower than in Germany, 8 percent below the lowest of the remaining Northwest European countries (Belgium), and only 5 percent above Italy. The influence of all the factors I have attempted to measure directly does not account for the relatively low British position. I arrive at a residual productivity index for the United Kingdom that is 14 percent below that for France, 12 percent below Germany, and 5 percent below both the lowest of the other Northwest European countries (the Netherlands) and Italy.[39] Although real national income per person employed in all industries in the United Kingdom was still about as high as in the rest of Northwest Europe in 1960, this was only because the gains which could be made by reducing overallocation of resources to agriculture and self-employment had already been largely achieved. As the other countries reduce the amount of such overallocation they obtain higher growth rates than the United Kingdom and improve their relative positions.

If they accepted these estimates as reasonable approximations to the truth, many observers of the British scene would have a ready explanation for the unfavorable state of affairs.[40] They believe that the United Kingdom suffers far more from overmanning and all that goes with it than the other countries. Such respected journals as *The Economist* and the *Statist* have repeatedly stressed this

39. The percentages are derived from the first column of Table 20–2; the indexes referred to are simply 100 minus the percentages shown. Thus, the United Kingdom index of 66.3 is 14 percent below the French index of 76.9, and so on.

40. Despite all the difficulties of comparison, I do not think the calculation can seriously misrepresent the position of the United Kingdom relative to the other major Northwest European countries unless the original national income comparisons in Table 2–4 understate the British position. This comparison, it will be recalled, showed that, in United States prices, *per capita* income in the United Kingdom was second only to Germany among the European countries, and by only 1 point. This seems plausible enough but only a new international comparison of the type conducted by Gilbert and Kravis could provide a check sufficient to establish more conclusively that British per capita income was not far above the other countries.

type of inefficiency.[41] If their evaluations are reasonable, this type of resource waste may be of an order of magnitude comparable to that associated with agriculture and self-employment in France and Germany.[42] Indeed, it is difficult to explain why output per unit of input in the United Kingdom economy as a whole was not well above that in France and Germany in 1960 unless unaggressive management, labor resistance to change, and restrictive practices have combined to prevent the United Kingdom from realizing as fully as the other countries the potential for reducing labor requirements as technology has advanced and the quantity of capital and the scale of operations have increased. If the extra cost of overmanning in the United Kingdom is really comparable to that of excessive agricultural employment and nonfarm self-employment in France and Germany, Britain has an opportunity to obtain comparable gains and to maintain its relative position by eliminating this cost. British government agencies are counting heavily upon doing so and use the results of the Fawley agreement to buttress their view of the possibilities.[43] But this is a much more difficult type of waste to eliminate than that facing France and Germany. It requires a change of attitudes, practices, and habits that is not readily made.[44] In contrast the movement of labor from agriculture and self-employment to nonagricultural wage and salary employment is already in progress and is as nearly inevitable and unstoppable as any economic change can be; further gains are merely a matter of time.

This plausible explanation for low residual productivity in the United Kingdom can hardly be tied to postwar developments, however. If the United Kingdom was not realizing the fruits of progress as much as other Northwest European countries in the postwar period, substantially smaller residuals should appear for the United Kingdom in Table 20-1. In the period beginning with 1955, they do not, except to a moderate extent in the comparison with France. In the 1950-55 period a much larger residual is shown for Germany but the obvious explanation is that Germany was recovering from wartime disruption and that this did not constitute an element in long-term growth. If this evidence and interpretation is accepted, an explanation of the low *level* of British nonagricultural productivity, relative to the continental countries, that rests on unprogressive labor and management cannot depend mainly on postwar changes. It must suppose that this was a much longer term factor and that "residual productivity" in the United Kingdom had been low for this reason, relative to the continent, for many years. Indeed, *whatever* explanation may be offered for the low level of British nonagricultural productivity, the evidence of the growth rate residuals suggests that it must be a condition of long standing. Let me stress that this conclusion does not conflict with any substantial evidence. Indeed, one of the most careful comparisons of the efficiency of British manual labor with that of labor in other countries was made in 1948. P. J. D. Wiles concluded from a 1948 study of the experience of international firms that British manual labor was inferior to Swiss and Swedish labor and even more inferior to Belgian labor.[45] He expressed the view

41. Random examples are *The Economist* articles: "At Half Efficiency?" (March 7, 1964, pp. 863–65); "Britons Will Be Slaves" (December 26, 1964, pp. 1411–13); and "Overmuch Overtime" (May 28, 1966, pp. 931–32) [P19]; and *Statist* articles: "Britain's Hidden Unemployed" (January 7, 1966, p. 5) and "Getting Down to Productivity at Last" (April 29, 1966, pp. 1057–58) [P43].

42. It is perhaps illicit to quote the guesses of others when I cannot make a direct estimate myself, but it may be of interest to note an estimate of 2 million jobs, or 8 percent of British employment ("by Mr. William Allen, the managing director of Emersons, the consultants," quoted by Frank Broadway in *Statist*, January 28, 1966, p. 213 [P43]). In the *Sunday Times* (June 12, 1966, p. 49 [P44]), Allen suggests that "the manufacturing industries, on average, are overmanned by a factor of two" and gives estimates for many individual industries to show British productivity is low compared not only to the United States but also to continental Europe.

43. Reference to the "Fawley agreement" has become shorthand recognized throughout the United Kingdom for the increase in productivity that aggressive management working sympathetically with cooperative unions can achieve. For a description see Flanders, *The Fawley Productivity Agreements* [B34]. As the situation is developing, inefficiency seems to be becoming a marketable commodity that unions can on occasion sell to employers in collective agreements. See, for example, Bonar in *Wall Street Journal*, March 7, 1966 [P48]; and Carpenter in *Statist*, October 14, 1966, pp. 908–09 [P43].

44. The *Statist* article by Frank Broadway cited in note 42 is illustrative of a growing literature that suggests that such changes may very well *not* be made.

45. Wiles' comparisons are intended to refer to "willingness or manageability" and "the amount of physical effort put in" but not to skill (in *Oxford Economic Papers*, June 1951, pp. 158–80 [P33]).

that British management was equally inferior though, he says, the evidence is much less reliable. And even in 1946 *The Economist* was making observations similar to those I have cited in more recent issues.[46]

46. In *The Economist*, June 29, 1946, pp. 1033–35 [P19].

This discussion has supposed that the difference between residuals for the United Kingdom and for the other large countries correctly indicates the relative position of the United Kingdom with respect to factors not directly measured. I regard it as highly probable but not certain that it does so.

The Sources of Growth and the Contrast Between Europe and the United States

Examination of the individual growth sources has been completed and the time has come to attempt comprehensive answers to the broader questions with which this book is concerned: What was the division of growth in each country among the sources? How much similarity was there among countries? What sources have most often been important? Why do growth rates differ? Can the techniques employed in this and my earlier study explain most of the variation in growth rates? How do growth rates differ among countries if the effects of special transitory influences are eliminated? Why do income levels differ among countries? What relationships can be discerned between level and growth of income? Was postwar Europe securing faster growth than the United States by narrowing gaps between the two areas in the determinants of income? If so, in what determinants? Given that income per person employed in Northwest Europe in 1960 was about the same as in the United States in 1925, how did the determinants of income compare? Was postwar Europe doing more than the United States to obtain growth? Or was Europe obtaining faster growth as a result of differences in the environment in which growth was taking place? These and a number of subsidiary questions are the subjects of this final chapter which both summarizes and assesses postwar expansion in nine countries.

Any reader who has omitted earlier chapters is warned that the particular numbers used in this analysis range from satisfactory estimates to guesses based only on general information or impressions. The cautions and qualifications pertinent to each figure were provided when they were derived and cannot be repeated in this summary. I note again that the use of two decimal points to present estimates in tables and text is not an indication of precision. It is imposed by the necessity of avoiding annoying rounding discrepancies at all points and preventing the introduction of large percentage errors in small items. It will also facilitate the task of readers who may wish to rearrange the estimates.

The Sources of Growth

I begin with capsule summaries of the sources of growth of national income in each country. The estimates are presented in the odd-numbered tables from 21–1 through 21–19. Twenty-three different growth sources in addition to subtotals and totals are distinguished, though a few do not appear in all countries. These tables refer to the sources of growth of actual measured national income between the particular years compared: 1950, 1955, and 1962. The meaning and scope of each growth source have been described in earlier chapters and cannot be repeated here.

Two of the twenty-three sources simply quantify the incomparability with data for other countries that special deflation procedures used for government and construction, respectively, introduce into the growth rates for Belgium and France. Two other sources measure the effect upon growth rates of output per unit of input, measured between the terminal years of the periods, of (1) irregular fluctuations in farm output and (2) incomparabilities between these years with respect to the intensity of utilization of resources. For some purposes it is useful to deduct the contributions of these four sources to obtain adjusted growth rates. The adjusted growth rates and the contribution of output per unit of input to these rates are shown at the bottom of these tables. They will be used frequently in this chapter. Deduction of the two items referring to deflation techniques is solely to improve international comparability. Deduction of the effects of irregular fluctuations in farm output removes a random influence that affects the particular years compared but has no longer term significance. Deduction of the effects upon output per unit of input of differences in the intensity of resource utilization associated with demand pressures is a step toward eliminating the influence of cyclical fluctuations upon changes in actual national income and thus moving toward an analysis of changes in "potential" national income.[1] However, the effect of cyclical incomparability upon inputs remains. In the absence of cyclical differences, changes in employment and hours of work between the years compared would have been different than they actually were. The estimated gains from economies of scale may also have been affected. The adjusted estimates for national income per person employed are much more nearly free of cyclical influences than those for total national income because cyclical influences on employment itself do not affect the results.

1. "Potential national income" is used in the restricted sense customary in the United States. See Chapter 19.

Summaries by Country

Percentage distributions of the adjusted growth rates by sources of growth are provided for each area in the even-numbered tables from 21–2 through 21–20. In order to compare the importance of growth sources within each area, the country summaries that follow emphasize these percentage distributions. It must be remembered, however, that the same absolute contribution to growth represents a different percentage of the total growth rate in each country. For example, as explained in the previous chapter, I have estimated that advances of knowledge contributed almost identical amounts to the growth of total national income in all countries (0.75 to 0.77 percentage points, the differences reflecting only the interaction term). In the 1950–62 period this represented only 10 percent of the total adjusted growth rate in Germany but 32 percent in the United Kingdom.

The verbal summaries are designed only to remind the reader of the growth rates themselves; to indicate the broad division of the adjusted growth rates of total national income over the whole period among the contributions of labor, capital, and output per unit of input; to point out the six to nine individual sources that contributed or deducted amounts equal to 5 percent or more of the growth rate over the whole period; to remind the reader of a few of the contrasts between the subperiods; and to note where the estimates do not seem to be wholly consistent. Only scattered comments on national income per person employed are offered. International comparisons are deferred, except for a few obvious comments, until later in the chapter.

For a fuller classification of the sources of growth in each country the reader is referred to the tables themselves.

UNITED STATES. The growth rate of actual national income in the United States was 4.23 percent from 1950 to 1955 and 2.67 percent from 1955 to 1962 (Table 21–1). Most of the difference is due to the fact that the resources potentially available were used more fully in 1955 than in 1950 or 1962. If the effect of differences among terminal years in the degree of utilization of *employed* resources is eliminated, as in the adjusted growth rates at the bottom

TABLE 21-1

United States: Sources of Growth of Total National Income and
National Income per Person Employed, 1950–62

(*Contributions to growth rate in percentage points*)

Sources of growth	Total national income			National income per person employed		
	1950–62	1950–55	1955–62	1950–62	1950–55	1955–62
National income	**3.32**	**4.23**	**2.67**	**2.15**	**2.74**	**1.73**
Total factor input	**1.95**	**2.30**	**1.70**	**.79**	**.82**	**.77**
Labor	1.12	1.32	.97	.22	.19	.24
Employment	.90	1.13	.73	—	—	—
Hours of work	−.17	−.13	−.20	−.17	−.13	−.20
Age-sex composition	−.10	−.12	−.08	−.10	−.12	−.08
Education	.49	.44	.52	.49	.44	.52
Capital	.83	.98	.73	.60	.67	.55
Dwellings	.25	.26	.25	.21	.22	.21
International assets	.05	.03	.06	.04	.02	.05
Nonresidential structures and equipment	.43	.54	.35	.29	.34	.25
Inventories	.10	.15	.07	.06	.09	.04
Land	.00	.00	.00	−.03	−.04	−.02
Output per unit of input	**1.37**	**1.93**	**.97**	**1.36**	**1.92**	**.96**
Advances of knowledge	.76	.76	.76	.75	.75	.75
Improved allocation of resources						
Contraction of agricultural inputs	.25	.25	.24	.25	.25	.24
Contraction of nonagricultural self-employment	.04	.09	.01	.04	.09	.01
Reduction of international trade barriers	.00	.00	.00	.00	.00	.00
Economies of scale						
Growth of national market measured in U.S. prices	.30	.38	.24	.30	.38	.24
Independent growth of local markets	.06	.06	.06	.06	.06	.06
Irregularities in pressure of demand*	−.04	.39	−.34	−.04	.39	−.34
Adjusted Growth Rates						
National income	3.36	3.84	3.01	2.19	2.35	2.07
Output per unit of input	1.41	1.54	1.31	1.40	1.53	1.30

Sources: Tables 15–3, 15–5, 16–10, 17–3, 17–10, 18–2, 19–1, 19–3, and 20–1 except for slight differences between contributions to national income and national income per person employed due to interaction.
* Contributions of this source are excluded from adjusted growth rates.

of the table, the rates for the subperiods become 3.84 and 3.01. The difference in cyclical position also affected the contribution made by changes in labor input and this, together with effects on economies of scale, accounts for much of the remaining difference between the subperiods. The adjusted rate of 3.36 percent for 1950–62 as a whole is hardly affected by difference in cyclical position because 1950 and 1962 were not very different and the greater length of the period dissipates the influence of the difference that did exist. This rate places the United States among the countries with the lowest growth rates.

The percentage distributions shown in Table 21–2

show that over the 1950–62 period the increase in labor input from all causes contributed 33 percent, the increase in capital input of all types 25 percent, and the increase in output per unit of input from all causes 42 percent of the adjusted growth rate of total national income. Thus expressed as a percentage of the growth rate, the contribution of labor was larger and the contribution of output per unit of input smaller than in any other country studied.

Employment alone contributed 27 percent while hours subtracted 5 percent. In the United States—unlike other countries—the negative contribution of hours reflects almost entirely an increase in the prevalence of part-time employment. There was al-

TABLE 21-2

United States: Percentage Distributions of Growth Rates of Adjusted National Income and National Income per Person Employed Among the Sources of Growth, 1950–62

(*In percentages*)

Sources of growth	Total national income			National income per person employed		
	1950–62	1950–55	1955–62	1950–62	1950–55	1955–62
Adjusted national income	**100**	**100**	**100**	**100**	**100**	**100**
Total factor input	**58**	**60**	**56**	**36**	**35**	**37**
Labor	33	34	32	10	8	12
Employment	27	29	24	—	—	—
Hours of work	−5	−3	−7	−8	−6	−10
Age-sex composition	−3	−3	−3	−5	−5	−4
Education	15	11	17	22	19	25
Capital	25	26	24	27	29	27
Dwellings	7	7	8	10	9	10
International assets	1	1	2	2	1	2
Nonresidential structures and equipment	13	14	12	13	14	12
Inventories	3	4	2	3	4	2
Land	0	0	0	−1	−2	−1
Output per unit of input	**42**	**40**	**44**	**64**	**65**	**63**
Advances of knowledge	23	20	25	34	32	36
Improved allocation of resources	9	9	8	13	14	12
Contraction of agricultural inputs	7	7	8	11	11	12
Contraction of nonagricultural self-employment	1	2	a	2	4	a
Reduction of international trade barriers	0	0	0	0	0	0
Economies of scale	11	11	10	16	19	14
Growth of national market measured in U.S. prices	9	10	8	14	16	12
Independent growth of local markets	2	2	2	3	3	3

Source: Computed from Table 21–1. Details may not add to subtotals because of rounding.
a. Less than 0.5 percent.

most no change in the annual hours of full-time workers. If the employment estimates were recast on a full-time equivalent basis, the increase in employment could be regarded as contributing approximately 22 percent of, and changes in hours of full-time workers as deducting almost nothing from, the growth rate. Other individual sources of growth that accounted for as much as 5 percent of the total are advances of knowledge (23 percent); the increase in the education of the labor force (15 percent); the increase in the stock of nonresidential structures and equipment (13 percent); economies of scale associated with the growth of the national market (9 percent); the increase in dwellings (7 percent); and the reduction of the costs of overallocation of resources to agriculture (7 percent). As noted in earlier chapters, I have treated economies of scale associated with the growth of the national market as a separate source of growth but their con-

tribution could, alternatively, be reallocated among the other sources in proportion to their contributions as shown.

Contributions to the 2.19 percent adjusted growth rate of national income per person employed in 1950–62 are, of course, rather different. Employment disappears from the accounting and the contributions of other inputs depend upon changes in their quantities relative to the change in employment. The increase in labor input per person employed contributed 10 percent, the increase in capital 27 percent, and the increase in output per unit of input 62 percent.[2] The largest individual sources were:

2. If employment had been treated on a full-time equivalent basis the contribution of labor input—the change in the quantity and quality of work represented by a year of employment—would have been larger. As shown, it includes a contribution of −8 percent for the reduction in hours of work which is almost entirely the result of the increase in part-time employment.

TABLE 21-3

Northwest Europe: Sources of Growth of Total National Income and
National Income per Person Employed, 1950-62

(*Contributions to growth rate in percentage points*)

Sources of growth	Total national income			National income per person employed		
	1950-62	1950-55	1955-62	1950-62	1950-55	1955-62
National income	**4.76**	**5.68**	**4.11**	**3.80**	**4.46**	**3.34**
Total factor input	**1.69**	**1.77**	**1.62**	**.73**	**.57**	**.85**
Labor	.83	1.12	.62	.12	.21	.05
Employment	.71	.91	.57	—	—	—
Hours of work	−.14	.03	−.26	−.14	-.03	−.26
Age-sex composition	.03	−.04	.08	.03	−.04	.08
Education	.23	.22	.23	.23	.22	.23
Capital	.86	.65	1.00	.65	.41	.83
Dwellings	.07	.05	.08	.04	.04	.05
International assets	−.03	−.12	.03	−.04	−.13	.03
Nonresidential structures and equipment	.64	.56	.70	.51	.38	.59
Inventories	.18	.16	.19	.14	.12	.16
Land	.00	.00	.00	−.04	−.05	−.03
Output per unit of input	**3.07**	**3.91**	**2.49**	**3.07**	**3.89**	**2.49**
Advances of knowledge	.76	.76	.76	.76	.76	.76
Changes in the lag in the application of knowledge, general efficiency, and errors and omissions						
Reduction in age of capital	.02	.04	.00	.02	.04	.00
Other	.54	1.01	.23	.54	.99	.23
Improved allocation of resources						
Contraction of agricultural inputs	.46	.52	.42	.46	.52	.42
Contraction of nonagricultural self-employment	.14	.18	.12	.14	.18	.12
Reduction of international trade barriers	.08	.08	.08	.08	.08	.08
Balancing of the capital stock	.08	.20	.00	.08	.20	.00
Deflation procedures*	.07	.04	.08	.07	.04	.08
Economies of scale						
Growth of national market measured in U.S. prices	.41	.47	.37	.41	.47	.37
Income elasticities	.46	.50	.43	.46	.50	.43
Independent growth of local markets	.06	.04	.08	.06	.04	.08
Irregularities in pressure of demand*	−.01	.06	−.07	−.01	.06	−.07
Irregularities in agricultural output*	.00	.01	−.01	.00	.01	−.01
Adjusted Growth Rates						
National income	4.70	5.57	4.11	3.74	4.35	3.34
Output per unit of input	3.01	3.80	2.49	3.01	3.78	2.49

Sources: Same as Table 21-1 for lines included in that table; "Income elasticities" line: Table 17-7; "Advances of knowledge" and "Changes in the lag . . .": Table 20-1 and pp. 283-84; other lines are derived from country estimates given in Tables 21-5, 21-7, 21-9, 21-11, and 21-15.
* Contributions of this source are excluded from adjusted growth rates.

advances of knowledge, 34 percent; increased education of the labor force, 22 percent; economies of scale associated with the growth of the national market, 14 percent; the increase in nonresidential structures and equipment per person employed, 13 percent; the reduction in the waste of resources in agriculture, 11 percent; the increase in dwellings per person employed, 10 percent; the reduction in annual hours or, more properly, the increase in

part-time work, −8 percent; and changes in the composition by age and sex of man-hours worked, −5 percent.

NORTHWEST EUROPE. Tables 21-3 and 21-4 give similar data for Northwest Europe. However, in this section discussion is confined to the individual countries.

BELGIUM. The Belgian growth rate was 3.25 in

TABLE 21-4

Northwest Europe: Percentage Distributions of Growth Rates of Adjusted National Income and National Income per Person Employed Among the Sources of Growth, 1950–62

(*In percentages*)

Sources of growth	Total national income			National income per person employed		
	1950–62	1950–55	1955–62	1950–62	1950–55	1955–62
Adjusted national income	**100**	**100**	**100**	**100**	**100**	**100**
Total factor input	**36**	**32**	**39**	**20**	**13**	**25**
Labor	18	20	15	3	5	1
Employment	15	16	14	—	—	—
Hours of work	−3	1	−6	−4	1	−8
Age-sex composition	1	−1	2	1	−1	2
Education	5	4	6	6	5	7
Capital	18	12	24	17	9	25
Dwellings	1	1	2	1	1	1
International assets	−1	−2	1	−1	−3	1
Nonresidential structures and equipment	14	10	17	14	9	18
Inventories	4	3	5	4	3	5
Land	0	0	0	−1	−1	−1
Output per unit of input	**64**	**68**	**61**	**80**	**87**	**75**
Advances of knowledge	16	14	18	20	17	23
Changes in the lag in the application of knowledge, general efficiency, and errors and omissions	12	19	6	15	24	7
Reduction in age of capital	a	1	0	1	1	0
Other	11	18	6	14	23	7
Improved allocation of resources	14	14	15	16	18	19
Contraction of agricultural inputs	10	9	10	12	12	13
Contraction of nonagricultural self-employment	3	3	3	4	4	4
Reduction of international trade barriers	2	1	2	2	2	2
Balancing of the capital stock	2	4	0	2	5	0
Economies of scale	20	18	21	25	23	26
Growth of national market measured in U.S. prices	9	8	9	11	11	11
Income elasticities	10	9	10	12	11	13
Independent growth of local markets	1	1	2	2	1	2

Source: Computed from Table 21-3. Details may not add to subtotals because of rounding.
a. Less than 0.5 percent.

1950–55 and 3.18 in 1955–62 (Table 21–5). No adjustment of output per unit of input for incomparability of the years compared was indicated. Only deduction of the effects of a special procedure used in Belgium to deflate government production is required to obtain the adjusted growth rates, which were 3.16 in 1950–55, 2.95 in 1955–62, and 3.03 in 1950–62. Like the United States, Belgium is among the low growth rate countries.

The estimates for Belgium, like those for all the other European countries, include two sources of growth that are not present in the United States estimates. One is gains from economies of scale associated with the especially large magnitude of increases in income-elastic consumption components. The great expansion of markets for these products made possible special gains by adoption of existing techniques for large-scale production. These gains appear in estimates of national income valued in European prices but would not contribute to growth if national income were valued in United States prices. They are distinguished in the tables from the contribution of economies of scale associated with the growth of the national market that would appear if growth rates were uniformly based on valuation of national income in United States prices. This topic was discussed at length in Chapter 17. The second new item includes gains or losses from

TABLE 21–5

Belgium: Sources of Growth of Total National Income and
National Income per Person Employed, 1950–62

(*Contributions to growth rate in percentage points*)

Sources of growth	Total national income			National income per person employed		
	1950–62	1950–55	1955–62	1950–62	1950–55	1955–62
National income	**3.20**	**3.25**	**3.18**	**2.64**	**2.55**	**2.70**
Total factor input	**1.17**	**1.33**	**1.06**	**.62**	**.64**	**.60**
Labor	.76	.90	.66	.36	.39	.33
Employment	.40	.51	.33	—	—	—
Hours of work	−.15	−.04	−.22	−.15	−.04	−.22
Age-sex composition	.08	.01	.12	.08	.01	.12
Education	.43	.42	.43	.43	.42	.43
Capital	.41	.43	.40	.28	.27	.28
Dwellings	.02	.04	.01	−.01	.00	−.02
International assets	−.06	−.03	−.08	−.06	−.03	−.08
Nonresidential structures and equipment	.39	.37	.40	.31	.28	.33
Inventories	.06	.05	.07	.04	.02	.05
Land	.00	.00	.00	−.02	−.02	−.01
Output per unit of input	**2.03**	**1.92**	**2.12**	**2.02**	**1.91**	**2.10**
Advances of knowledge	.76	.76	.76	.76	.76	.75
Changes in the lag in the application of knowledge, general efficiency, and errors and omissions						
Reduction in age of capital	.00	.00	.00	.00	.00	.00
Other	.08	.19	.01	.07	.18	.01
Improved allocation of resources						
Contraction of agricultural inputs	.20	.23	.18	.20	.23	.18
Contraction of nonagricultural self-employment	.15	.17	.13	.15	.17	.13
Reduction of international trade barriers	.16	.16	.16	.16	.16	.16
Government deflation procedure*	.17	.09	.23	.17	.09	.23
Economies of scale						
Growth of national market measured in U.S. prices	.33	.36	.32	.33	.36	.31
Income elasticities	.11	−.08	.24	.11	−.08	.24
Independent growth of local markets	.07	.04	.09	.07	.04	.09
Adjusted Growth Rates						
National income	3.03	3.16	2.95	2.47	2.46	2.47
Output per unit of input	1.86	1.83	1.89	1.85	1.82	1.87

Sources: Same as Table 21–1 for lines included in that table; "Income elasticities" line: Table 17–7; "Advances of knowledge" and "Changes in the lag . . .": Table 20–1 and pp. 283–84; "Government deflation procedure": p. 27.
* Contributions of this source are excluded from adjusted growth rates.

changes in the lag of average practice behind the best known anywhere, changes in efficiency for other unidentified reasons, and the net result of errors and omissions in the estimates of other growth sources. This component is obtained as a residual. In Belgium it is a small item.

Over the 1950–62 period as a whole, 25 percent of the adjusted Belgian growth rate of total national income was contributed by labor input, 14 percent by capital, and 61 percent by output per unit of input (Table 21–6). The individual items that con-

tributed as much as 5 percent were: advances of knowledge, 25 percent; increased education of the labor force, 14; increased employment, 13; non-residential structures and equipment, 13; economies of scale associated with growth of the national market in United States prices, 11; improvement in the allocation of resources by reducing overallocation to agriculture, 7; by reducing the waste of labor in nonfarm self-employment, 5; and by reducing international trade barriers, 5; and the reduction in working hours, −5. The two subperiods were fairly

TABLE 21–6

Belgium: Percentage Distributions of Growth Rates of Adjusted National Income and National Income per Person Employed Among the Sources of Growth, 1950–62

(*In percentages*)

Sources of growth	Total national income			National income per person employed		
	1950–62	1950–55	1955–62	1950–62	1950–55	1955–62
Adjusted national income	100	100	100	100	100	100
Total factor input	39	42	36	25	26	24
Labor	25	28	22	15	16	13
Employment	13	16	11	—	—	—
Hours of work	−5	−1	−7	−6	−2	−9
Age-sex composition	3	a	4	3	a	5
Education	14	13	15	17	17	17
Capital	14	14	14	11	11	11
Dwellings	1	1	a	a	0	−1
International assets	−2	−1	−3	−2	−1	−3
Nonresidential structures and equipment	13	12	14	13	11	13
Inventories	2	2	2	2	1	2
Land	0	0	0	−1	−1	a
Output per unit of input	61	58	64	75	74	76
Advances of knowledge	25	24	26	31	31	30
Changes in the lag in the application of knowledge, general efficiency, and errors and omissions	3	6	a	3	7	a
Reduction in age of capital	0	0	0	0	0	0
Other	3	6	a	3	7	a
Improved allocation of resources	17	18	16	21	23	19
Contraction of agricultural inputs	7	7	6	8	9	7
Contraction of nonagricultural self-employment	5	5	4	6	7	5
Reduction of international trade barriers	5	5	5	6	7	6
Economies of scale	17	10	22	21	13	26
Growth of national market measured in U.S. prices	11	11	11	13	15	13
Income elasticities	4	−3	8	4	−3	10
Independent growth of local markets	2	1	3	3	2	4

Source: Computed from Table 21–5. Details may not add to subtotals because of rounding.
a. Less than 0.5 percent.

similar, but in the second period employment contributed less, the reduction in hours subtracted much more, and gains from economies of scale associated with income elasticities contributed 8 percent of the total.

DENMARK. The Danish growth rate was far lower in 1950–55, when it was only 1.58 percent, than in 1955–62, when it reached 4.92 (Table 21–7). Even the adjusted rates of 2.11 and 4.29 show a sharp contrast. On either basis, the Danish rate in 1950–55 is the lowest encountered in any country in any period, while the 1955–62 rate is among the highest. My estimates account for most but not all of the difference between the two periods. That I have

not fully succeeded in explaining why the 1950–55 rate was so low is indicated by the −0.70 percentage points obtained in that period as the residual for the contribution made by changes in the "lag" in the application of knowledge and in general efficiency, together with errors and omissions. In the absence of any other likely explanation, I must assume that this figure results from errors in either the growth rate or the estimates for other sources in 1950–55. This difficulty greatly qualifies the significance of the 1950–55 percentage distributions. The problem is not so acute when the entire 1950–62 period is examined, but the residual still amounts to −0.32 percentage points, or −10 percent, of the adjusted growth rate of 3.36 percent.

TABLE 21-7

Denmark: Sources of Growth of Total National Income and National Income per Person Employed, 1950–62

(Contributions to growth rate in percentage points)

Sources of growth	Total national income			National income per person employed		
	1950–62	1950–55	1955–62	1950–62	1950–55	1955–62
National income	**3.51**	**1.58**	**4.92**	**2.56**	**1.11**	**3.62**
Total factor input	**1.55**	**1.38**	**1.67**	**.62**	**.91**	**.40**
Labor	.59	.47	.68	−.11	.12	−.27
Employment	.70	.35	.95	—	—	—
Hours of work	−.18	.04	−.34	−.18	.04	−.34
Age-sex composition	−.07	−.06	−.07	−.07	−.06	−.07
Education	.14	.14	.14	.14	.14	.14
Capital	.96	.91	.99	.77	.81	.73
Dwellings	.13	.14	.12	.10	.12	.09
International assets	.02	.01	.03	.02	.01	.03
Nonresidential structures and equipment	.66	.64	.66	.53	.58	.49
Inventories	.15	.12	.18	.12	.10	.12
Land	.00	.00	.00	−.04	−.02	−.06
Output per unit of input	**1.96**	**.20**	**3.25**	**1.94**	**.20**	**3.22**
Advances of knowledge	.76	.75	.76	.75	.75	.75
Changes in the lag in the application of knowledge, general efficiency, and errors and omissions						
Reduction in age of capital	.04	.10	.00	.04	.10	.00
Other	−.32	−.70	−.01	−.31	−.70	−.01
Improved allocation of resources						
Contraction of agricultural inputs	.41	.29	.49	.40	.29	.48
Contraction of nonagricultural self-employment	.18	.16	.19	.18	.16	.19
Reduction of international trade barriers	.09	.09	.09	.09	.09	.09
Economies of scale						
Growth of national market measured in U.S. prices	.35	.20	.47	.35	.20	.47
Income elasticities	.23	−.20	.54	.22	−.20	.53
Independent growth of local markets	.07	.04	.09	.07	.04	.09
Irregularities in pressure of demand*	.22	−.10	.44	.22	−.10	.44
Irregularities in agricultural output*	−.07	−.43	.19	−.07	−.43	.19
Adjusted Growth Rates						
National income	3.36	2.11	4.29	2.41	1.64	2.99
Output per unit of input	1.81	.73	2.62	1.79	.73	2.59

Sources: Same as Table 21-1 for lines included in that table; "Income elasticities" line: Table 17-7; "Advances of knowledge" and "Changes in the lag . . .": Table 20-1 and pp. 283–84; "Reduction in age of capital": Table 12-6.
* Contributions of this source are excluded from adjusted growth rates.

As shown in Table 21–8, the increase in labor input contributed 18 percent, capital 29 percent, and output per unit of input 54 percent to the adjusted 1950–62 growth rate of total national income. These percentages would become 16, 27, and 57 if the "residual" were added both to the growth rate and to the contribution of output per unit of input. On either basis, the proportionate contribution of capital was larger in Denmark than in any of the other countries.

The individual sources making the biggest contributions to Danish growth in 1950–62 were: advances of knowledge, 23 percent; employment, 21; nonresidential structures and equipment, 20; reduction of the excessive allocation of resources to agriculture, 12; economies of scale associated with the national market in United States prices, 10; the residual estimate which in Denmark I regard as largely errors and omissions, −10; economies of scale associated with income elasticities, 7; the re-

TABLE 21-8

Denmark: Percentage Distributions of Growth Rates of Adjusted National Income and National Income per Person Employed Among the Sources of Growth, 1950–62

(*In percentages*)

Sources of growth	Total national income			National income per person employed		
	1950–62	1950–55	1955–62	1950–62	1950–55	1955–62
Adjusted national income	**100**	**100**	**100**	**100**	**100**	**100**
Total factor input	**46**	**65**	**39**	**26**	**55**	**13**
Labor	18	22	16	−5	7	−9
Employment	21	17	22	—	—	—
Hours of work	−6	2	−8	−7	2	−11
Age-sex composition	−2	−3	−2	−3	−4	−2
Education	4	7	3	6	9	5
Capital	29	43	23	32	49	24
Dwellings	4	7	3	4	7	7
International assets	1	a	1	1	1	1
Nonresidential structures and equipment	20	30	15	22	35	16
Inventories	4	6	4	5	6	4
Land	0	0	0	−2	−1	−2
Output per unit of input	**54**	**35**	**61**	**74**	**45**	**87**
Advances of knowledge	23	36	18	31	46	25
Changes in the lag in the application of knowledge, general efficiency, and errors and omissions	−8	−28	a	−11	−37	a
Reduction in age of capital	1	5	0	2	6	0
Other	−10	−32	a	−13	−43	a
Improved allocation of resources	20	26	18	28	33	25
Contraction of agricultural inputs	12	14	11	17	18	16
Contraction of nonagricultural self-employment	5	8	4	7	10	6
Reduction of international trade barriers	3	4	2	4	5	3
Economies of scale	19	2	26	27	2	36
Growth of national market measured in U.S. prices	10	9	11	15	12	16
Income elasticities	7	−9	13	9	−12	18
Independent growth of local markets	2	2	2	3	2	3

Source: Computed from Table 21–7. Details may not add to subtotals because of rounding.
a. Less than 0.5 percent.

duction of nonfarm self-employment, 5; and reductions in annual working hours, −6. The distribution in the 1955–62 period of rapid growth was substantially different. The reader is referred to Table 21–8 for a comparison as well as for distributions of national income per person employed.

FRANCE. The French growth rate has been high and stable. The unadjusted rate for total national income was 4.77 in 1950–55 and 5.03 in 1955–62 (Table 21–9). After adjustment (mainly for a different method of deflating construction), rates of 4.55 in 1950–55, 4.82 in 1955–62, and 4.70 in 1950–62 are obtained.[3] There was very little change

3. If one is concerned only with analysis of French

in employment in France so that the sources of growth of national income per person employed are similar to those of total national income.

The classification of sources of growth in France includes a rather large contribution in both subperiods from "changes in the lag in the application of knowledge, general efficiency, and errors and omissions." As stated in Chapter 20, I lean to the belief that in France this residual represents a real change in efficiency from sources not elsewhere

growth itself, independent of international comparisons, there is no particular reason to make the construction adjustment. In that case the contribution shown for "advances of knowledge" should be raised.

TABLE 21-9

France: Sources of Growth of Total National Income and
National Income per Person Employed, 1950–62

(*Contributions to growth rate in percentage points*)

Sources of growth	Total national income			National income per person employed		
	1950–62	1950–55	1955–62	1950–62	1950–55	1955–62
National income	**4.92**	**4.77**	**5.03**	**4.80**	**4.65**	**4.91**
Total factor input	**1.24**	**1.17**	**1.28**	**1.13**	**1.06**	**1.17**
Labor	.45	.46	.44	.37	.38	.35
Employment	.08	.08	.09	—	—	—
Hours of work	−.02	.02	−.06	−.02	.02	−.06
Age-sex composition	.10	.08	.12	.10	.08	.12
Education	.29	.28	.29	.29	.28	.29
Capital	.79	.71	.84	.76	.68	.82
Dwellings	.02	.00	.03	.02	.00	.03
International assets	.02	.02	.02	.02	.02	.02
Nonresidential structures and equipment	.56	.52	.59	.53	.49	.57
Inventories	.19	.17	.20	.19	.17	.20
Land	.00	.00	.00	.00	.00	.00
Output per unit of input	**3.68**	**3.60**	**3.75**	**3.67**	**3.59**	**3.74**
Advances of knowledge	.76	.76	.76	.76	.76	.76
Changes in the lag in the application of knowledge, general efficiency, and errors and omissions						
Reduction in age of capital	.00	.00	.00	.00	.00	.00
Other	.75	.72	.80	.74	.71	.79
Improved allocation of resources						
Contraction of agricultural inputs	.65	.59	.69	.65	.59	.69
Contraction of nonagricultural self-employment	.23	.25	.22	.23	.25	.22
Reduction of international trade barriers	.07	.07	.07	.07	.07	.07
Construction deflation procedure*	.23	.15	.28	.23	.15	.28
Economies of scale						
Growth of national market measured in U.S. prices	.44	.42	.45	.44	.42	.45
Income elasticities	.49	.53	.46	.49	.53	.46
Independent growth of local markets	.07	.04	.09	.07	.04	.09
Irregularities in agricultural output*	−.01	.07	−.07	−.01	.07	−.07
Adjusted Growth Rates						
National income	4.70	4.55	4.82	4.58	4.43	4.70
Changes in output per unit of input	3.46	3.38	3.54	3.45	3.37	3.53

Sources: Same as Table 21–1 for lines included in that table; "Income elasticities" line: Table 17–7; "Advances of knowledge" and "Changes in the lag . . .": Table 20–1 and pp. 283–84; "Construction deflation procedure": p. 27.
* Contributions of this source are excluded from adjusted growth rates.

specified, including changes in the "lag," rather than to errors in the growth rate or estimates for other sources.

In the 1950–62 period the increase in labor input contributed 10 percent, capital 17 percent, and output per unit of input 74 percent—the largest percentage among the nine countries—to the adjusted growth rate of total national income (Table 21–10). No individual source of growth (by my classification) contributed more than 16 percent, the small-

est such figure among the nine countries. The principal sources were: advances of knowledge, 16 percent; the reduction in the "lag" and increase in general efficiency, 16; reduction of the excessive allocation of resources to agriculture, 14; nonresidential structures and equipment, 12; economies of scale associated with income elasticities, 10; economies of scale associated with growth of the national market measured in United States prices, 9; increased education of the labor force, 6; and the

TABLE 21–10

France: Percentage Distributions of Growth Rates of Adjusted National Income and National Income per Person Employed Among the Sources of Growth, 1950–62

(*In percentages*)

Sources of growth	Total national income			National income per person employed		
	1950–62	1950–55	1955–62	1950–62	1950–55	1955–62
Adjusted national income	100	100	100	100	100	100
Total factor input	26	26	27	25	24	25
Labor	10	10	9	8	9	7
Employment	2	2	2	—	—	—
Hours of work	a	a	−1	a	a	−1
Age-sex composition	2	2	2	2	2	3
Education	6	6	6	6	6	6
Capital	17	16	17	16	15	17
Dwellings	a	0	1	a	0	1
International assets	a	a	a	a	a	a
Nonresidential structures and equipment	12	11	12	12	11	12
Inventories	4	4	4	4	4	4
Land	0	0	0	0	0	0
Output per unit of input	74	74	73	75	76	75
Advances of knowledge	16	17	16	17	17	16
Changes in the lag in the application of knowledge, general efficiency, and errors and omissions	16	16	17	16	16	17
Reduction in age of capital	0	0	0	0	0	0
Other	16	16	17	16	16	17
Improved allocation of resources	20	20	20	21	21	21
Contraction of agricultural inputs	14	13	14	14	13	15
Contraction of nonagricultural self-employment	5	5	5	5	6	5
Reduction of international trade barriers	1	2	1	2	2	1
Economies of scale	21	22	21	22	22	21
Growth of national market measured in U.S. prices	9	9	9	10	9	10
Income elasticities	10	12	10	11	12	10
Independent growth of local markets	1	1	2	2	1	2

Source: Computed from Table 21–9. Details my not add to subtotals because of rounding.
a. Less than 0.5 percent.

reduction of nonfarm self-employment, 5. The contributions of the various sources were rather similar in the two subperiods in both absolute and relative terms.

GERMANY. Adjusted and unadjusted growth rates are the same in Germany. The rate for total national income was 9.93 in 1950–55 and 5.39—still very high—in 1955–62 (Table 21–11). In the 1950–55 period a large (1.78 point) residual is obtained for the contribution of "changes in the lag in the application of knowledge, general efficiency, and errors and omissions." The large size of this residual is most likely to be due to a general increase in efficiency as wartime distortions were eliminated. An additional 0.63 points of the 1950–55 growth

rate is ascribed to the balancing of the capital stock and 0.10 points to reduction in the average age of capital. Both these sources were aftermaths of the war. Thus German experience in 1950–55 was quite special. Estimates for the 1950–62 period as a whole are averages of two subperiods in which both the total growth rate and the sources of growth were very different.

Over the whole 1950–62 period, 19 percent of German growth was contributed by labor, 19 percent by capital, and 62 percent by output per unit of input (Table 21–12). The main individual sources were: employment, 21 percent; nonresidential structures and equipment, 14; the residual, interpreted as mainly postwar recovery, 11; advances of knowledge, 10; the shift of excessive resources

TABLE 21-11

Germany: Sources of Growth of Total National Income and
National Income per Person Employed, 1950–62

(*Contributions to growth rate in percentage points*)

Sources of growth	Total national income			National income per person employed		
	1950–62	1950–55	1955–62	1950–62	1950–55	1955–62
National income	**7.26**	**9.93**	**5.39**	**5.15**	**7.06**	**3.81**
Total factor input	**2.78**	**3.19**	**2.51**	**.72**	**.44**	**.94**
Labor	1.37	1.99	.94	−.12	−.02	−.19
Employment	1.49	2.01	1.13	—	—	—
Hours of work	−.27	−.01	−.45	−.27	−.01	−.45
Age-sex composition	.04	−.12	.15	.04	−.12	.15
Education	.11	.11	.11	.11	.11	.11
Capital	1.41	1.20	1.57	.93	.59	1.20
Dwellings	.14	.12	.16	.12	.10	.14
International assets	−.08	−.13	−.05	−.08	−.12	−.05
Nonresidential structures and equipment	1.02	.85	1.14	.66	.39	.87
Inventories	.33	.36	.32	.23	.22	.24
Land	.00	.00	.00	−.09	−.13	−.07
Output per unit of input	**4.48**	**6.74**	**2.88**	**4.43**	**6.62**	**2.87**
Advances of knowledge	.76	.77	.76	.75	.76	.75
Changes in the lag in the application of knowledge, general efficiency, and errors and omissions						
Reduction in age of capital	.04	.10	.00	.04	.10	.00
Other	.80	1.78	.11	.79	1.75	.11
Improved allocation of resources						
Contraction of agricultural inputs	.77	1.01	.59	.76	.99	.59
Contraction of nonagricultural self-employment	.14	.24	.07	.14	.23	.07
Reduction of international trade barriers	.10	.10	.10	.10	.10	.10
Balancing of the capital stock	.26	.63	.00	.26	.62	.00
Economies of scale						
Growth of national market measured in U.S. prices	.63	.86	.46	.62	.84	.46
Income elasticities	.91	1.21	.70	.90	1.19	.70
Independent growth of local markets	.07	.04	.09	.07	.04	.09
Adjusted Growth Rates						
National income	7.26	9.93	5.39	5.15	7.06	3.81
Output per unit of input	4.48	6.74	2.88	4.43	6.62	2.87

Sources: Same as Table 21–1 for lines included in that table; "Income elasticities" line: Table 17–7; "Advances of knowledge" and "Change in the lag . . .": Table 20–1 and pp. 283–84; "Reduction in age of capital" and "Balancing of capital stock": Table 12–6.

from agriculture, 10; economies of scale associated with income elasticities, 13; and economies of scale associated with growth of the national market measured in United States prices, 9.

Sources of growth in the less disturbed 1955–62 period are of greater general interest. The largest contributions to the 1955–62 growth rate in Germany were made by: the increase in nonresidential structures and equipment, 21 percent; employment, 21; advances of knowledge, 14; economies of scale associated with income elasticities, 13; the shift of

excessive resources from agriculture, 11; economies of scale associated with the national market measured in United States prices, 9; reduction in annual working hours, −8; and the increase in enterprise inventories, 6.

Germany had a very large employment expansion so the sources of growth of national income per person employed were considerably different from those of total national income. Germany was unusual in that the contribution of labor input was negative. The increase in education was estimated to

TABLE 21-12

Germany: Percentage Distributions of Growth Rates of Adjusted National Income and National Income per Person Employed Among the Sources of Growth, 1950–62

(*In percentages*)

Sources of growth	Total national income			National income per person employed		
	1950–62	1950–55	1955–62	1950–62	1950–55	1955–62
Adjusted national income	**100**	**100**	**100**	**100**	**100**	**100**
Total factor input	**38**	**32**	**47**	**14**	**6**	**25**
Labor	19	20	17	−2	a	−5
Employment	21	20	21	—	—	—
Hours of work	−4	a	−8	−5	a	−12
Age-sex composition	1	−1	3	1	−2	4
Education	2	1	2	2	2	3
Capital	19	12	29	18	8	3
Dwellings	2	1	3	2	1	4
International assets	−1	−1	−1	−2	−2	−1
Nonresidential structures and equipment	14	9	21	13	6	23
Inventories	5	4	6	4	3	6
Land	0	0	0	−2	−2	−2
Output per unit of input	**62**	**68**	**53**	**86**	**94**	**75**
Advances of knowledge	10	8	14	15	11	20
Changes in the lag in the application of knowledge, general efficiency, and errors and omissions	12	19	2	16	26	3
Reduction in age of capital	1	1	0	1	1	0
Other	11	18	2	15	25	3
Improved allocation of resources	14	14	14	19	19	20
Contraction of agricultural inputs	10	10	11	15	14	15
Contraction of nonagricultural self-employment	2	2	1	2	3	2
Reduction of international trade barriers	1	1	2	2	1	3
Balancing of the capital stock	4	6	0	5	9	0
Economies of scale	22	21	23	31	29	33
Growth of national market measured in U.S. prices	9	9	9	12	12	12
Income elasticities	13	12	13	17	17	18
Independent growth of local markets	1	a	2	1	1	2

Source: Computed from Table 21–11. Details may not add to subtotals because of rounding.
a. Less than 0.5 percent.

have been smaller in Germany than in any other country and its effect on labor quality was more than offset by the largest reduction in hours. In 1955–62 improved allocation of resources by contraction of inputs in agriculture, nonfarm self-employment, and trade barriers together contributed 20 percent of the growth of national income per person employed and economies of scale from all sources contributed 33 percent.

NETHERLANDS. The growth rate of the Netherlands was 6.00 in 1950–55 and 3.83 in 1955–62 (Table 21–13). The adjusted rates are 5.47 and

3.84. Just as I was unable wholly to explain why the Danish rate was so low in 1950–55, I am unable to explain fully why the Dutch rate was as high as it was in that period. The residual of 1.03 points I obtain in 1950–55 is not readily attributed to omitted factors; my guess is that errors in the growth rates or in the estimates for the contributions of other sources are responsible. Though the residual is much smaller in the 1950–62 period as a whole, it still accounts for 10 percent of the total adjusted growth rate (Table 21–14).

Labor accounted for 15 percent, capital for 23 percent, and output per unit of input for 58 percent

TABLE 21-13

Netherlands: Sources of Growth of Total National Income and
National Income per Person Employed, 1950–62

(*Contributions to growth rate in percentage points*)

Sources of growth	Total national income			National income per person employed		
	1950–62	1950–55	1955–62	1950–62	1950–55	1955–62
National income	**4.73**	**6.00**	**3.83**	**3.65**	**4.86**	**2.78**
Total factor input	**1.91**	**2.33**	**1.62**	**.86**	**1.23**	**.59**
Labor	.87	1.15	.68	.09	.34	−.08
Employment	.78	.81	.76	—	—	—
Hours of work	−.16	.03	−.29	−.16	.03	−.29
Age-sex composition	.01	.06	−.03	.01	.06	−.03
Education	.24	.25	.24	.24	.25	.24
Capital	1.04	1.18	.94	.78	.90	.68
Dwellings	.06	.04	.07	.04	.02	.06
International assets	.10	.39	−.10	.09	.37	−.11
Nonresidential structures and equipment	.66	.52	.76	.49	.34	.58
Inventories	.22	.23	.21	.16	.17	.15
Land	.00	.00	.00	−.01	−.01	−.01
Output per unit of input	**2.82**	**3.67**	**2.21**	**2.79**	**3.63**	**2.19**
Advances of knowledge	.76	.76	.76	.75	.75	.75
Changes in the lag in the application of knowledge, general efficiency, and errors and omissions						
Reduction in age of capital	.00	.00	.00	.00	.00	.00
Other	.44	1.03	−.01	.43	1.01	−.01
Improved allocation of resources						
Contraction of agricultural inputs	.21	.19	.23	.21	.19	.23
Contraction of nonagricultural self-employment	.26	.25	.27	.26	.25	.27
Reduction of international trade barriers	.16	.16	.16	.16	.16	.16
Economies of scale						
Growth of national market measured in U.S. prices	.48	.64	.37	.47	.63	.36
Income elasticities	.23	.07	.35	.23	.07	.35
Independent growth of local markets	.07	.04	.09	.07	.04	.09
Irregularities in pressure of demand*	.19	.34	.09	.19	.34	.09
Irregularities in agricultural output*	.02	.19	−.10	.02	.19	−.10
Adjusted Growth Rates						
National income	4.52	5.47	3.84	3.44	4.33	2.79
Output per unit of input	2.61	3.14	2.22	2.58	3.10	2.20

Sources: Same as Table 21–1 for lines included in that table; "Income elasticities" line: Table 17–7; "Advances of knowledge" and "Changes in the lag . . .": Table 20–1 and pp. 283–84.
* Contributions of this source are excluded from adjusted growth rates.

of the adjusted Dutch growth rate in 1950–62. The detailed sources that contributed large amounts were: employment, 17 percent; advances of knowledge, 17; nonresidential structures and equipment, 15; economies of scale associated with the national market, 11; the residual factor, 10; the reduction of excessive nonfarm self-employment, 6; economies of scale associated with income elasticities, 5; increased education of the labor force, 5; and contraction of agricultural inputs, 5.

NORWAY. The growth rate of total national income in Norway was 3.69 in 1950–55 and 3.27 in 1955–62 (Table 21–15). After the effects of irregularities in farm output are eliminated, the adjusted growth rates become 3.90 in 1950–55, 3.16 in 1955–62, and 3.47 in the 1950–62 period as a whole.

Over the whole period the increase in labor input contributed only 4 percent of the adjusted Norwegian growth rate, the smallest percentage obtained for any country (Table 21–16). Capital con-

TABLE 21–14

Netherlands: Percentage Distributions of Growth Rates of Adjusted National Income and National Income per Person Employed Among the Sources of Growth, 1950–62

(*In percentages*)

Sources of growth	Total national income			National income per person employed		
	1950–62	1950–55	1955–62	1950–62	1950–55	1955–62
Adjusted national income	**100**	**100**	**100**	**100**	**100**	**100**
Total factor input	**42**	**43**	**42**	**25**	**28**	**21**
Labor	19	21	18	3	8	−3
Employment	17	15	20	—	—	—
Hours of work	−4	1	−8	−5	1	−10
Age-sex composition	a	1	−1	a	1	−1
Education	5	5	6	7	6	9
Capital	23	22	24	23	21	24
Dwellings	1	1	2	1	a	2
International assets	2	7	−3	3	9	−4
Nonresidential structures and equipment	15	10	20	14	8	21
Inventories	5	4	5	5	4	5
Land	0	0	0	a	a	a
Output per unit of input	**58**	**57**	**58**	**75**	**72**	**79**
Advances of knowledge	17	14	20	22	17	27
Changes in the lag in the application of knowledge, general efficiency, and errors and omissions	10	19	a	12	23	a
Reduction in age of capital	0	0	0	0	0	0
Other	10	19	a	12	23	a
Improved allocation of resources	14	11	17	18	14	24
Contraction of agricultural inputs	5	4	6	6	4	8
Contraction of nonagricultural self-employment	6	5	7	8	6	10
Reduction of international trade barriers	4	3	4	5	4	6
Economies of scale	17	14	21	22	17	29
Growth of national market measured in U.S. prices	11	12	10	14	15	13
Income elasticities	5	3	9	7	2	13
Independent growth of local markets	2	1	2	2	1	3

Source: Computed from Table 21–13. Details may not add to subtotals because of rounding.
a. Less than 0.5 percent.

tributed 26 percent and output per unit of input 70 percent. The principal individual sources were: increases in nonresidential structures and equipment, 23 percent; advances of knowledge, 22; contraction of the overallocation of resources to agriculture, 16; economies of scale associated with the national market measured in United States prices, 11; increased education of the labor force, 7; reduction of the overallocation of labor to nonfarm self-employment, 7; and the residual factor, 5.

As in most countries, the reduction in hours subtracted importantly from growth after 1955. In Norway the deduction was sufficient to make the contribution of labor input as a whole slightly negative in 1955–62. Economies of scale associated with

income elasticities were much more important in 1955–62 than over the whole period.

UNITED KINGDOM. The actual growth rate of national income was low and about the same in the two subperiods: 2.32 in 1950–55 and 2.27 in 1955–62 (Table 21–17). The similarity of the actual rates was partly happenstance. Elimination of the effect of differences in demand pressures yields adjusted growth rates of 2.16 in 1950–55 and 2.56 in 1955–62. The difference between the adjusted growth rates in the two subperiods is more than accounted for by income from international assets, which subtracted 0.36 points in 1950–55 and contributed 0.17 in 1955–62. This source had only a small (−0.05

TABLE 21–15

Norway: Sources of Growth of Total National Income and National Income per Person Employed, 1950–62

(*Contributions to growth rate in percentage points*)

Sources of growth	Total national income			National income per person employed		
	1950–62	1950–55	1955–62	1950–62	1950–55	1955–62
National income	**3.45**	**3.69**	**3.27**	**3.27**	**3.48**	**3.11**
Total factor input	**1.04**	**1.55**	**.69**	**.86**	**1.35**	**.53**
Labor	.15	.41	−.03	.02	.27	−.16
Employment	.13	.14	.13	—	—	—
Hours of work	−.15	.06	−.31	−.15	.06	−.31
Age-sex composition	−.07	−.03	−.10	−.07	−.03	−.10
Education	.24	.24	.25	.24	.24	.25
Capital	.89	1.14	.72	.85	1.09	.69
Dwellings	.04	.05	.04	.04	.05	.04
International assets	−.07	−.04	−.09	−.07	−.04	−.09
Nonresidential structures and equipment	.79	.93	.68	.76	.89	.67
Inventories	.13	.20	.09	.12	.19	.07
Land	.00	.00	.00	−.01	−.01	.00
Output per unit of input	**2.41**	**2.14**	**2.58**	**2.41**	**2.13**	**2.58**
Advances of knowledge	.76	.76	.75	.76	.76	.75
Changes in the lag in the application of knowledge, general efficiency, and errors and omissions						
Reduction in age of capital	.04	.10	.00	.04	.10	.00
Other	.14	.00	.22	.14	−.01	.22
Improved allocation of resources						
Contraction of agricultural inputs	.54	.72	.41	.54	.72	.41
Contraction of nonagricultural self-employment	.23	.24	.23	.23	.24	.23
Reduction of international trade barriers	.15	.15	.15	.15	.15	.15
Economies of scale						
Growth of national market measured in U.S. prices	.38	.44	.35	.38	.44	.35
Income elasticities	.12	−.10	.27	.12	−.10	.27
Independent growth of local markets	.07	.04	.09	.07	.04	.09
Irregularities in agricultural output*	−.02	−.21	.11	−.02	−.21	.11
Adjusted Growth Rates						
National income	3.47	3.90	3.16	3.29	3.69	3.00
Output per unit of input	2.43	2.35	2.47	2.43	2.34	2.47

Sources: Same as Table 21–1 for lines included in that table; "Income elasticities" line: Table 17–7; "Advances of knowledge" and "Changes in the lag . . .": Table 20–1 and pp. 283–84; "Reduction in age of capital": Table 12–6.
* Contributions of this source are excluded from adjusted growth rates.

percentage points) effect upon the adjusted growth rate of 2.38 over the period from 1950 to 1962 as a whole.

Over the entire period the increase in labor input contributed 25 percent of the adjusted growth rate, capital 21 percent, and output per unit of input 53 percent (Table 21–18). The individual sources making the largest contributions were: advances of knowledge, 32 percent; employment, 21; nonresidential structures and equipment, 18; economies of scale associated with the national market measured

in United States prices, 9; and hours reduction, −6. The effect of hours reduction is somewhat magnified by an increase in part-time female employment, but the amount was not nearly so large as in the United States.

The distinctive feature of the growth experience of the United Kingdom was the small size of gains from the improved allocation of resources and—partly as a consequence of this—the small size, relative to other European countries, of gains from economies of scale.

TABLE 21-16

Norway: Percentage Distributions of Growth Rates of Adjusted National Income and National Income per Person Employed Among the Sources of Growth, 1950–62

(*In percentages*)

Sources of growth	Total national income			National income per person employed		
	1950–62	1950–55	1955–62	1950–62	1950–55	1955–62
Adjusted national income	**100**	**100**	**100**	**100**	**100**	**100**
Total factor input	**30**	**40**	**22**	**26**	**37**	**18**
Labor	4	11	−1	1	7	−5
Employment	4	4	4	—	—	—
Hours of work	−4	2	−10	−5	2	−10
Age-sex composition	−2	−1	−3	−2	−1	−3
Education	7	6	8	7	7	8
Capital	26	29	23	26	30	23
Dwellings	1	1	1	1	1	1
International assets	−2	−1	−3	−2	−1	−3
Nonresidential structures and equipment	23	24	22	23	24	22
Inventories	4	5	3	4	5	2
Land	0	0	0	a	a	a
Output per unit of input	**70**	**60**	**78**	**74**	**63**	**82**
Advances of knowledge	22	19	24	23	21	25
Changes in the lag in the application of knowledge, general efficiency, and errors and omissions	5	3	7	5	2	7
Reduction in age of capital	1	3	0	1	3	0
Other	4	0	7	4	a	7
Improved allocation of resources	27	28	25	28	30	26
Contraction of agricultural inputs	16	18	13	16	20	14
Contraction of nonagricultural self-employment	7	6	7	7	7	8
Reduction of international trade barriers	4	4	5	5	4	5
Economies of scale	16	10	22	17	10	24
Growth of national market measured in U.S. prices	11	11	11	12	12	12
Income elasticities	3	−3	9	4	−3	9
Independent growth of local markets	2	1	3	2	1	3

Source: Computed from Table 21–15. Details may not add to subtotals because of rounding.
a. Less than 0.5 percent.

ITALY. The Italian growth rate was 6.30 in 1950–55 and 5.71 in 1955–62 (Table 21–19). After elimination of the effects of irregularities in farm output, adjusted rates of 6.19 in 1950–55, 5.78 in 1955–62, and 5.95 in the 1950–62 period as a whole are obtained. The growth rates and the contributions of several growth sources were quite similar in the two subperiods but the contributions of others were not. Employment contributed 12 percent in 1950–55 and 3 percent in 1955–62 (Table 21–20). Economies of scale of all types contributed 16 percent in 1950–55 and 24 percent in 1955–62. The residual item covering "changes in the lag in the application of knowledge, general efficiency, and errors and omissions" accounted for 22 percent (1.36 points)

of the growth rate in 1950–55 and 9 percent (0.54 points) in 1955–62. Whether the residual in 1955–62 represents a real increase in efficiency from unmeasured factors, as I have surmised it did in France, or is simply the result of errors in other estimates, I cannot even hazard a guess; the Italian economy was the most difficult to analyze throughout the study. It seems likely that at least the *difference* between the residuals in the two subperiods reflects a general recovery of efficiency from war-induced distortions in the early postwar period, similar to that which is presumed to have taken place in Germany.

Over the 1950–62 period as a whole labor contributed 16 percent to the adjusted growth rate,

TABLE 21-17

United Kingdom: Sources of Growth of Total National Income and
National Income per Person Employed, 1950–62

(*Contributions to growth rate in percentage points*)

Sources of growth	Total national income			National income per person employed		
	1950–62	1950–55	1955–62	1950–62	1950–55	1955–62
National income	**2.29**	**2.32**	**2.27**	**1.63**	**1.41**	**1.79**
Total factor input	**1.11**	**1.05**	**1.15**	**.45**	**.15**	**.68**
Labor	.60	.95	.35	.10	.26	−.02
Employment	.50	.69	.37	—	—	—
Hours of work	−.15	.05	−.30	−.15	.05	−.30
Age-sex composition	−.04	−.06	−.02	−.04	−.06	−.02
Education	.29	.27	.30	.29	.27	.30
Capital	.51	.10	.80	.37	−.08	.71
Dwellings	.04	.02	.06	.02	.00	.04
International assets	−.05	−.36	.17	−.06	−.37	.17
Nonresidential structures and equipment	.43	.38	.46	.35	.27	.41
Inventories	.09	.06	.11	.06	.02	.09
Land	.00	.00	.00	−.02	−.03	−.01
Output per unit of input	**1.18**	**1.27**	**1.12**	**1.18**	**1.26**	**1.11**
Advances of knowledge	.76	.76	.76	.75	.75	.75
Changes in the lag in the application of knowledge, general efficiency, and errors and omissions						
Reduction in age of capital	.00	.00	.00	.00	.00	.00
Other	.03	−.06	.11	.04	−.06	.11
Improved allocation of resources						
Contraction of agricultural inputs	.06	.07	.05	.06	.07	.05
Contraction of nonagricultural self-employment	.04	.05	.04	.04	.05	.04
Reduction of international trade barriers	.02	.02	.02	.02	.02	.02
Economies of scale						
Growth of national market measured in U.S. prices	.22	.23	.21	.22	.23	.21
Income elasticities	.09	.01	.15	.09	.01	.15
Independent growth of local markets	.05	.03	.07	.05	.03	.07
Irregularities in pressure of demand*	−.09	.16	−.29	−.09	.16	−.29
Adjusted Growth Rates						
National income	2.38	2.16	2.56	1.72	1.25	2.08
Output per unit of input	1.27	1.11	1.41	1.27	1.10	1.40

Sources: Same as Table 21-1 for lines included in that table; "Income elasticities" line: Table 17-7; "Advances of knowledge" and "Changes in the lag . . .": Table 20-1 and pp. 283–84.
* Contributions of this source are excluded from adjusted growth rates.

capital 12 percent, and output per unit of input 72 percent. Capital contributed the smallest percentage of growth among the nine countries. The biggest individual source of growth was the reduction of the excessive allocation of resources to agriculture (17 percent). This was followed by the residual item to which I have just referred (15 percent), advances of knowledge (13), economies of scale associated with income elasticities (10) and with the national market measured in United States

prices (9), nonresidential structures and equipment (9), the increase in employment (7), and the increased education of the labor force (7).

The Principal Sources of Growth

The results of this investigation fully document the expectation expressed in Chapter 1 that there are many sources of growth and that their relative importance varies greatly from period to period

TABLE 21-18

United Kingdom: Percentage Distributions of Growth Rates of Adjusted National Income and National Income per Person Employed Among the Sources of Growth, 1950–62

(*In percentages*)

Sources of growth	Total national income			National income per person employed		
	1950–62	1950–55	1955–62	1950–62	1950–55	1955–62
Adjusted national income	**100**	**100**	**100**	**100**	**100**	**100**
Total factor input	**47**	**49**	**45**	**26**	**12**	**33**
Labor	25	44	14	6	21	−1
Employment	21	32	14	—	—	—
Hours of work	−6	2	−12	−9	4	−14
Age-sex composition	−2	−3	−1	−2	−5	−1
Education	12	12	12	17	22	14
Capital	21	5	31	22	−6	34
Dwellings	2	1	2	1	0	2
International assets	−2	−17	7	−3	−30	8
Nonresidential structures and equipment	18	18	18	20	22	20
Inventories	4	3	4	3	2	4
Land	0	0	0	−1	−2	a
Output per unit of input	**53**	**51**	**55**	**74**	**88**	**67**
Advances of knowledge	32	35	30	44	60	36
Changes in the lag in the application of knowledge, general efficiency, and errors and omissions	1	−3	4	2	−5	5
Reduction in age of capital	0	0	0	0	0	0
Other	1	−3	4	2	−5	5
Improved allocation of resources	5	6	4	7	11	5
Contraction of agricultural inputs	3	3	2	3	6	2
Contraction of nonagricultural self-employment	2	2	2	2	4	2
Reduction of international trade barriers	1	1	1	1	1	1
Economies of scale	15	12	17	21	22	21
Growth of national market measured in U.S. prices	9	11	8	13	18	10
Income elasticities	4	a	6	5	1	7
Independent growth of local markets	2	1	3	3	2	3

Source: Computed from Table 21–17. Details may not add to subtotals because of rounding.
a. Less than 0.5 percent.

and from place to place. I have attempted to identify and quantify the contributions of twenty-three sources (or twenty-one if two "statistical" sources are omitted) and all of them play a significant role in the explanation of growth rates, though not in all places or periods. I have discussed but not attempted to measure the contribution of various other sources, and one of the twenty-three sources shown —the residual estimate—is a basket containing the effects of many different influences whose effects could not be isolated.

There is no unambiguous answer to the question: What are the principal sources of growth? It has meaning, first of all, only within the framework of some particular classification. The type of classification adopted is one that I consider informative and useful, but it represents a certain degree of "ultimateness." I have tried to measure the contributions of employment, of capital, and of the reduction in the waste of resources in agriculture, to take a few examples; but it could be asked with regard to each of the sources measured: Why did it change as it did? There is no room in my classification for such more ultimate influences on growth as birth control, tax structures, the spirit of enterprise, or planning—to name only a few. These must operate to influence growth by affecting one or more of the sources considered in this study, but their impacts have not been assessed here.

Even within the type of classification used, the

TABLE 21–19

*Italy: Sources of Growth of Total National Income and
National Income per Person Employed, 1950–62*

(*Contributions to growth rate in percentage points*)

Sources of growth	Total national income			National income per person employed		
	1950–62	1950–55	1955–62	1950–62	1950–55	1955–62
National income	**5.96**	**6.30**	**5.71**	**5.36**	**5.28**	**5.42**
Total factor input	**1.66**	**1.92**	**1.48**	**1.07**	**.93**	**1.19**
Labor	.96	1.35	.68	.54	.63	.48
Employment	.42	.72	.20	—	—	—
Hours of work	.05	.09	.03	.05	.09	.03
Age-sex composition	.09	.15	.05	.09	.15	.05
Education	.40	.39	.40	.40	.39	.40
Capital	.70	.57	.80	.57	.37	.73
Dwellings	.07	.02	.11	.05	.02	.09
International assets	−.03	.00	−.05	−.03	.00	−.05
Nonresidential structures and equipment	.54	.47	.59	.45	.32	.55
Inventories	.12	.08	.15	.10	.03	.14
Land	.00	.00	.00	−.04	−.07	−.02
Output per unit of input	**4.30**	**4.38**	**4.23**	**4.29**	**4.35**	**4.23**
Advances of knowledge	.76	.76	.76	.76	.75	.76
Changes in the lag in the application of knowledge, general efficiency, and errors and omissions						
Reduction in age of capital	.00	.00	.00	.00	.00	.00
Other	.89	1.36	.54	.88	1.36	.54
Improved allocation of resources						
Contraction of agricultural inputs	1.04	.84	1.18	1.04	.83	1.18
Contraction of nonagricultural self-employment	.22	.17	.26	.22	.17	.26
Reduction of international trade barriers	.16	.16	.16	.16	.16	.16
Economies of scale						
Growth of national market measured in U.S. prices	.55	.62	.51	.55	.61	.51
Income elasticities	.60	.32	.80	.60	.32	.80
Independent growth of local markets	.07	.04	.09	.07	.04	.09
Irregularities in agricultural output*	.01	.11	−.07	.01	.11	−.07
Adjusted Growth Rates						
National income	5.95	6.19	5.78	5.35	5.17	5.49
Output per unit of input	4.29	4.27	4.30	4.28	4.24	4.30

Sources: Same as Table 21–1 for lines included in that table; "Income elasticities" line: Table 17–7; "Advances of knowledge" and "Changes in the lag . . .": Table 20–1 and pp. 283–84.
* Contributions of this source are excluded from adjusted growth rates.

contribution of individual sources depends on the amount of detail that is distinguished at each point in the classification. For example, the contribution of capital is divided into four components, but a more or a less detailed division might have been adopted. Finally, of course, any answer must refer to a particular time and place.

Having said all this, I still think it of some interest to note the sources, based on my most detailed classification, that most often contributed

heavily to or subtracted heavily from growth rates in the nine countries examined in the period covered. Table 21–21 shows a count of the number of countries in which each source appears among the five sources contributing most (positively or negatively) in the 1950–62 period, and repeats the tabulation for the 1955–62 period. In the compilation of this list the four sources whose contributions were deducted from growth rates to obtain "adjusted" growth rates were omitted as having only

TABLE 21-20

Italy: Percentage Distributions of Growth Rates of Adjusted National Income and National Income per Person Employed Among the Sources of Growth, 1950–62

(*In percentages*)

Sources of growth	Total national income			National income per person employed		
	1950–62	1950–55	1955–62	1950–62	1950–55	1955–62
Adjusted national income	**100**	**100**	**100**	**100**	**100**	**100**
Total factor input	**28**	**31**	**26**	**20**	**18**	**22**
Labor	16	22	12	10	12	9
Employment	7	12	3	—	—	—
Hours of work	1	1	1	1	2	1
Age-sex composition	2	2	1	2	3	1
Education	7	6	7	7	8	7
Capital	12	9	14	11	7	13
Dwellings	1	a	2	1	a	2
International assets	−1	0	−1	−1	0	−1
Nonresidential structures and equipment	9	8	10	8	6	10
Inventories	2	1	3	2	1	3
Land	0	0	0	−1	−1	a
Output per unit of input	**72**	**69**	**74**	**80**	**82**	**78**
Advances of knowledge	13	12	13	14	15	14
Changes in the lag in the application of knowledge, general efficiency, and errors and omissions	15	22	9	16	26	10
Reduction in age of capital	0	0	0	0	0	0
Other	15	22	9	16	26	10
Improved allocation of resources	24	19	28	27	23	29
Contraction of agricultural inputs	17	14	20	19	16	21
Contraction of nonagricultural self-employment	4	3	4	4	3	5
Contraction of international trade barriers	3	3	3	3	3	3
Economies of scale	21	16	24	23	19	26
Growth of national market measured in U.S. prices	9	10	9	10	12	9
Income elasticities	10	5	14	11	6	15
Independent growth of local markets	1	1	2	1	1	2

Source: Computed from Table 21-19. Details may not add to subtotals because of rounding.
a. Less than 0.5 percent.

special or short-term significance. The number of times each remaining source stands first, second, third, fourth, and fifth is also shown in the table. Ties are counted as fractions.

Eight different sources appear on the list in 1950–62 and two additional sources in 1955–62. Among these ten, five different sources made the largest single contribution in at least one instance.

With a single exception in the 1950–62 period in each case, advances of knowledge and the increase in the stock of nonresidential structures and equipment stood always among the five largest sources in all countries. The former was the largest single source in 4 of the 9 countries in 1950–62 and 4⅓

in 1955–62.[4] Employment is among the five largest sources of growth in 6 of the 9 countries in each period, and the largest single source in 3 countries over the full period and in 1⅓ in 1955–62. Other sources appearing on the list are economies of scale associated with the national market measured in United States prices, economies of scale associated with income elasticities, the reduction of overallocation to agriculture, the increase in the education of the labor force, the "residual" bundle of sources

4. The contribution of advances of knowledge expressed in percentage points was assumed to be the same in all countries (see page 282). This assumption, of course, greatly influences but does not in itself determine this result.

TABLE 21-21

Sources of Growth of Adjusted Total National Income: Frequency with Which Each Source Ranks Among the Five Largest Sources in the Nine Countries

Sources of growth	Number of appearances in each position					Number of appearances in first five
	First	Second	Third	Fourth	Fifth	
1950–62						
Advances of knowledge	4	3	1	0	0	8
Nonresidential structures and equipment	1	1	3	3	0	8
Economies of scale: growth of national market measured in U.S. prices	0	0	0	2	5	7
Employment	3	2	1	0	0	6
Contraction of agricultural inputs	1	0	2	1	1	5
Education	0	1	1	1	1	4
Unmeasured sources, errors, omissions	0	2	0	1	1	4
Economies of scale: income elasticities	0	0	1	1	1	3
1955–62						
Advances of knowledge	4⅓	2⅓	2⅓	0	0	9
Nonresidential structures and equipment	1⅓	2⅓	2⅓	3	0	9
Employment	1⅓	2⅓	1⅓	1	0	6
Contraction of agricultural inputs	1	0	2	0	2	5
Economies of scale: income elasticities	0	1	0	2	2	5
Education	0	1	1	½	½	3
Economies of scale: growth of national market measured in U.S. prices	0	0	0	2	1	3
Unmeasured sources, errors, omissions	1	0	0	0	1	2
Hours of work	0	0	0	½	1½	2
Dwellings	0	0	0	0	1	1

Sources: Compiled from odd-numbered Tables 21–1 through 21–19. Note that ties are counted as fractions.

TABLE 21-22

Sources of Growth of Adjusted National Income per Person Employed: Frequency with Which Each Source Ranks Among the Five Largest Sources in the Nine Countries

Sources of growth	Number of appearances in each position					Number of appearances in first five
	First	Second	Third	Fourth	Fifth	
1950–62						
Advances of knowledge	6½	½	1	1	0	9
Nonresidential structures and equipment	½	3½	0	3	1	8
Contraction of agricultural inputs	1	0	4	0	2	7
Economies of scale: growth of national market measured in U.S prices	0	0	3	3	1	7
Unmeasured sources, errors, omissions	0	3	0	1	1	5
Education	0	2	1	0	1	4
Economies of scale: income elasticities	1	0	0	1	1	3
Hours of work	0	0	0	0	1	1
Contraction of nonagricultural self-employment	0	0	0	0	1	1
1955–62						
Advances of knowledge	6	2	1	0	0	9
Nonresidential structures and equipment	1	3	3	2	0	9
Contraction of agricultural inputs	1	0	2	2½	½	6
Economies of scale: growth of national market measured in U.S. prices	0	0	1	2½	2½	6
Economies of scale: income elasticities	0	2	1	1	2	6
Hours of work	0	0	½	½	3	4
Education	0	2	½	½	0	3
Unmeasured sources, errors, omissions	1	0	0	0	1	2

Sources: Compiled from odd-numbered Tables 21–1 through 21–19. Note that ties are counted as fractions.

(referred to in Tables 20–21 to 20–26 as "unmeasured sources, errors, omissions") and (in 1955–62 only) the reduction in hours of work and the increase in dwellings.

Table 21–22 shows a similar compilation based on contributions to growth rates of national income per person employed. Except that employment disappears from the list, the frequencies are not very different from those obtained for total national income. "Advances of knowledge" is the largest source of growth in 6½ countries in 1950–62 and 6 in 1955–62. Only one new source, the reduction in the excessive allocation of labor to nonfarm self-employment, is added to the list.

Based on this particular classification, these tables identify the sources that exerted the strongest influence on growth rates most frequently in this particular set of 9 countries in 1950–62 and 1955–62. The 1950–55 period, taken by itself, was too disturbed by special factors to have similar interest.

Why Growth Rates Differ

Over the whole period examined in this study we have encountered growth rates of total national income that ranged from 2.3 percent to 7.3 percent, and growth rates of national income per person employed that ranged from 1.6 to 5.4. Even more extreme rates were observed in 1950–55. Differences in growth rates have no simple general explanation. Growth is the net consequence of many changes, and the countries with high growth rates have by no means enjoyed larger contributions from all sources than those with low growth rates. Neither do the individual high growth rate countries differ from the individual low growth rate countries in a uniform fashion. A complete explanation of differences can therefore be conveniently provided only in tabular form. Nevertheless, some important general observations emerge. These appear more clearly when the sources of growth are arranged in an order slightly different from that followed previously.

Tables 21–23 through 21–26 show the difference between the contribution provided by each source to growth in Northwest Europe and in each European country and the contribution that it provided to United States growth. The differences are given for total national income and for national income per person employed, first for the 1950–62 period as a whole, and then for the 1955–62 subperiod.

Total National Income

I begin with the growth of total national income in 1950–62, for which Table 21–23 provides the data. In this period the United States growth rate of 3.32 percent was exceeded by 1.44 percentage points in Northwest Europe as a whole, 1.60 points in France, 3.94 in Germany, and 2.64 in Italy; the United Kingdom rate was lower than that of the United States by 1.03 points. The smaller countries lie in intermediate positions—the Netherlands close to France, the others to the United States—so the extreme range is 5 percentage points: that between the United Kingdom and Germany. The following discussion is focused on Northwest Europe as a whole and the large countries, though not to the exclusion of the smaller nations.

Consider first contributions that would have been made by changes in the eight input components under conditions of constant returns to scale (Lines 1–8). Four of these sources contributed less and four contributed more to Northwest European than to United States growth.

From increased employment all of the European countries except Germany gained less than the United States. For Northwest Europe the deficiency is only 0.19 percentage points but it is 0.82 points in France, 0.40 in the United Kingdom, and 0.48 in Italy, whereas Germany gained 0.59 points *more* than the United States. The increase in the quality of labor resulting from changes in the educational level of the labor force contributed less to growth in all European countries than it did in the United States. The deficiency was 0.26 points in Northwest Europe, 0.20 in France, 0.38 in Germany, 0.20 in the United Kingdom, and 0.09 in Italy; it was smallest, at 0.06, in Belgium. The increase in the services of dwellings also contributed less to growth in all European countries than it did in the United States; differences were 0.18 in Northwest Europe as a whole, 0.23 in France, 0.11 in Germany, 0.21 in the United Kingdom, and 0.18 in Italy. The earnings of international assets is the remaining source classified as an input that contributed less to European than to United States growth; it did so in all European countries except the Netherlands. The deficiency was 0.08 points in Northwest Europe, 0.03 in France, 0.13 in Germany, 0.10 in the United Kingdom, and 0.08 in Italy.

Changes in two aspects of labor quality added more to or subtracted less from European than United States growth. Changes in hours of work did so except in Denmark and Germany. The difference was 0.03 in Northwest Europe as a whole, 0.15 in France, −0.10 in Germany, 0.02 in the United Kingdom, and 0.22 in Italy. Changes in the distribution of man-hours worked by age, sex, and military or civilian status were more favorable in all European countries than in the United States. Contributions were larger by 0.13 points in Northwest Europe, 0.20 in France, 0.14 in Germany, 0.06 in the United Kingdom, and 0.19 in Italy. The results for both sources were influenced by the large increase in the voluntary part-time employment of women and minors in the United States. This development reduced average American working hours and combined with an increase in full-time female employment to reduce the weight of males in the prime working ages in total man-hours worked in the United States. Hours of full-time workers were little changed in the United States and France, while they were substantially reduced in Germany and, to a lesser extent, in the United Kingdom and Italy. In Italy there was a large shift from part-time to full-time work as employment opportunities expanded.

Increases in two capital components, nonresidential structures and equipment and inventories, each contributed more in all European countries except Belgium and the United Kingdom than in the United States. For these two types of capital combined, the differences were 0.29 percentage points in Northwest Europe, 0.22 in France, 0.82 in Germany, −0.01 in the United Kingdom, and 0.13 in Italy.

Line 9, Table 21–23, shows differences from the United States in the total contribution of changes in inputs, and therefore the differences among countries in growth rates that would have emerged if growth depended only on inputs and if all countries operated under conditions of constant returns to

scale.[5] In that case the United States growth rate would have been 1.95. Only the German rate would have been higher, by 0.83 points. The rate would have been lower than in the United States by 0.26 points in Northwest Europe, by 0.71 points in France, by 0.84 points in the United Kingdom, and by 0.29 points in Italy. Germany would have held a unique position as *the* high growth country due to the extraordinary increases in employment and in enterprise capital.[6] After Germany would have come the United States and the Netherlands, followed by Italy and Denmark. The low growth rate countries—falling as far below the United States and the Netherlands as those countries did below Germany—would have been Belgium, France, Norway, and the United Kingdom. The extreme range in growth rates—between Norway and Germany—would have been only 1.7 percentage points in this situation as against the 5.0 points actually observed.

Even under constant returns to scale, differences in the contributions of inputs would have been affected by differences in local conditions—specifically by international differences in factor proportions and relative marginal products. Under American conditions the changes in factor inputs that occurred in Europe would, in general, have contributed less to growth than they actually did in Northwest Europe, and still less than in Italy. United States weights for education groups would have reduced the contribution of education by 0.05 percentage points in Northwest Europe—the range is from 0.02 in Germany to 0.07 in France and 0.08 in Belgium and the United Kingdom—and by 0.18 points in Italy. Use of United States earnings weights to evaluate the contributions of labor and of capital in the form of nonresidential structures and inventories would have reduced the contributions of inputs in Europe because capital increased faster than labor and receive a larger weight in Europe than in America. The difference in weights presumably reflects differences in factor proportions between the two areas. There are partial offsets in

5. I ignore in this paragraph the fact that the calculated contributions of inputs include a small factor for interaction with other sources of growth. It is too trifling to affect the comparisons.

6. This would also have been the case in the 1955–62 subperiod alone, as shown in Table 21–25.

TABLE 21–23

Contributions of the Sources to Growth of Total National Income, 1950–62:
Differences from the United States

(*In percentage points*)

	Sources of growth	North-west Europe	Bel-gium	Den-mark	France	Ger-many	Nether-lands	Nor-way	United King-dom	Italy
1	Employment	−.19	−.50	−.20	−.82	.59	−.12	−.77	−.40	−.48
2	Hours of work	.03	.02	−.01	.15	−.10	.01	.02	.02	.22
3	Age-sex composition	.13	.18	.03	.20	.14	.11	.03	.06	.19
4	Education	−.26	−.06	−.35	−.20	−.38	−.25	−.25	−.20	−.09
5	Dwellings	−.18	−.23	−.12	−.23	−.11	−.19	−.21	−.21	−.18
6	International assets	−.08	−.11	−.03	−.03	−.13	.05	−.12	−.10	−.08
7	Nonresidential structures and equipment	.21	−.04	.23	.13	.59	.23	.36	.00	.11
8	Inventories	.08	−.04	.05	.09	.23	.12	.03	−.01	.02
9	Total factor input, Lines 1 to 8	−.26	−.78	−.40	−.71	.83	−.04	−.91	−.84	−.29
10	Advances of knowledge	.00	.00	.00	.00	.00	.00	.00	.00	.00
11	Contraction of agricultural inputs	.21	−.05	.16	.40	.52	−.04	.29	−.19	.79
12	Contraction of nonagricultural self-employment	.10	.11	.14	.19	.10	.22	.19	.00	.18
13	Reduction of international trade barriers	.08	.16	.09	.07	.10	.16	.15	.02	.16
14	Economies of scale: growth of local markets	.00	.01	.01	.01	.01	.01	.01	−.01	.01
15	Total, Lines 9 to 14	.13	−.55	.00	−.04	1.56	.31	−.27	−1.02	.85
16	Reduction in age of capital	.02	.00	.04	.00	.04	.00	.04	.00	.00
17	Balancing of the capital stock	.08	.00	.00	.00	.26	.00	.00	.00	.00
18	Unmeasured sources, errors, omissions	.54	.08	−.32	.75	.80	.44	.14	.03	.89
19	Total, Lines 15 to 18	.77	−.47	−.28	.71	2.66	.75	−.09	−.99	1.74
20	Economies of scale: growth of national market measured in U.S. prices	.11	.03	.05	.14	.33	.18	.08	−.08	.25
21	Economies of scale: income elasticities	.46	.11	.23	.49	.91	.23	.12	.09	.60
22	Adjusted national income	1.34	−.33	.00	1.34	3.90	1.16	.11	−.98	2.59
23	Irregularities in pressure of demand	.03	.04	.26	.04	.04	.23	.04	−.05	.04
24	Irregularities in agricultural output	.00	.00	−.07	−.01	.00	.02	−.02	.00	.01
25	Deflation procedures	.07	.17	.00	.23	.00	.00	.00	.00	.00
26	Total national income	1.44	−.12	.19	1.60	3.94	1.41	.13	−1.03	2.64

Sources: Derived from odd-numbered Tables 21–1 through 21–19.

the European weights for land and dwellings. The point made in this paragraph does not play a major part in my analysis but it is not without significance.

The next item listed in Table 21–23 is advances of knowledge (Line 10). This is an important source of growth in all countries but in my evaluation plays no part in explaining differences in growth rates. It refers to the gains from advances of knowledge that would be obtained if all enterprises always followed the most efficient practices anywhere or, alternatively stated, that would be realized if there were no change in the ratio of average to best practice.

The next three entries refer to gains from the re-allocation of resources. They bear a large part of the burden of explaining growth rate differentials. All European countries except the United Kingdom, Belgium, and the Netherlands gained more than the United States by reducing the overallocation of resources to agriculture and all except the United Kingdom gained more by reducing the number of self-employed and unpaid family workers in nonagricultural industries.

Both of these entries measure gains realized by transferring resources (almost exclusively labor) from activities from which their departure deducted little from the national income to activities in which their addition made a substantial contribution. Together, these two improvements in resource allocation added 0.31 points more to growth rates in the Northwest European countries than they did in the United States. The difference was 0.59 points in France, 0.62 in Germany, and 0.97 in Italy. The United Kingdom gained less than the United States by 0.19 points. Belgium gained only 0.06 points more than the United States. The differential gains in the other small countries were intermediate: 0.18 points in the Netherlands; 0.30 in Denmark; and 0.48 in Norway. In Chapter 16 I stressed that differences in the size of these gains had hardly anything to do with each country's success in reducing the misallocation with which it started; in this respect, great differences among the countries were not observed. Rather, the size of the gains depended upon the amount of overallocation to agriculture and to fringe nonfarm self-employment that was present in each country at the beginning of the period. In 1950 all countries had too large a proportion of their labor forces allocated to agriculture and to nonfarm self-employment but these proportions varied enormously.

The third source of gains from resource allocation was reduction in barriers to international trade (Line 13). The estimates are not satisfactory—in Chapter 18, I describe them as illustrative—and, in addition, they were actually derived for 1955–62 but used also for the whole period. In consequence any difference between 1950–62 as a whole and 1955–62 becomes part of the "residual." This caution may be especially pertinent to Germany, where a resumption in normal trade relations was occurring in 1950–55 and may have been contributing substantially to efficiency. My estimate for the United States of gains from changes in international trade barriers was zero. The estimates, such as they are, indicate gains of 0.08 in Northwest Europe, 0.07 in France, 0.10 in Germany, 0.02 in the United Kingdom, 0.16 in Italy, and 0.09 to 0.16 in the small countries. I have not tried to compare these gains with the costs of trade barriers country by country but it is apparent that the costs, and therefore the opportunities for gain, were much greater in Europe than in the United States.

The gain from economies of scale associated with the independent growth of local markets differed by no more than 0.01 from the gain in the United States, and this source is grouped with gains from reallocation.

The contributions from reallocation of resources of the types enumerated are added to the contributions of factor inputs in Line 15. A pattern now begins to emerge. Germany gained greatly from reallocation and its original margin over the United States is raised to 1.56 percentage points. Italy gained even more, and emerges as another high growth rate country with a margin of 0.85 points over the United States. The United Kingdom gained the least of all countries from reallocation and Belgium the least among the continental countries. When the contributions of inputs and reallocation are combined, these two countries stand last, which is also their final position in actual growth rates. Reallocation gains were also very large in France, but suffice only to explain why the French growth rate of total national income was not lower than that of the United States, not why it is higher. The contributions of inputs and reallocation alone would produce a Danish growth rate the same as the United States, a Dutch growth rate moderately higher (by 0.31 points), and a Norwegian growth rate moderately lower (by 0.27 points).

The two sources that follow are special to the early postwar period. In Denmark, Germany, and Norway I allowed for a contribution in the earlier years from a reduction in the lag in the application of knowledge as a result of the reduction in the average age of capital (Line 16). (The reasons for believing this factor to be of negligible importance in other countries and periods are discussed in Chapter 12.) When spread over the whole 1950–62 period, this contribution amounted to only 0.04 percentage points in these three countries and to 0.02 in Northwest Europe as a whole. The item I call "balancing the capital stock" (Line 17), on the other hand, made a contribution to German growth in 1950–55 that was sufficient to add 0.26 percentage points to the German growth rate even over the 1950–62 period as a whole, and 0.08 to the Northwest European rate.

Line 18 represents the combined contribution of changes in the lag of average practice behind the best known (except from changes in the age of capital), increases in efficiency from all sources not explicitly measured, omissions from the measure-

TABLE 21-24

Contributions of the Sources to Growth of National Income per Person Employed, 1950–62:
Differences from the United States

(*In percentage points*)

	Sources of growth	North-west Europe	Bel-gium	Den-mark	France	Ger-many	Nether-lands	Nor-way	United King-dom	Italy
1	Hours of work	.03	.02	−.01	.15	−.10	.01	.02	.02	.22
2	Age-sex composition	.13	.18	.03	.20	.14	.11	.03	.06	.19
3	Education	−.26	−.06	−.35	−.20	−.38	−.25	−.25	−.20	−.09
4	Dwellings	−.17	−.22	−.11	−.19	−.09	−.17	−.17	−.19	−.16
5	International assets	−.08	−.10	−.02	−.02	−.12	.05	−.11	−.10	−.07
6	Nonresidential structures and equipment	.22	.02	.24	.24	.37	.20	.47	.06	.16
7	Inventories	.08	−.02	.06	.13	.17	.10	.06	.00	.04
8	Land	−.01	.01	−.01	.03	−.06	.02	.02	.01	−.01
9	Total factor input, Lines 1 to 8	−.06	−.17	−.17	.34	−.07	.07	.07	−.34	.28
10	Advances of knowledge	.01	.01	.00	.01	.00	.00	.01	.00	.01
11	Contraction of agricultural inputs	.21	−.05	.15	.40	.51	−.04	.29	−.19	.79
12	Contraction of nonagricultural self-employment	.10	.11	.14	.19	.10	.22	.19	.00	.18
13	Reduction of international trade barriers	.08	.16	.09	.07	.10	.16	.15	.02	.16
14	Economies of scale: growth of local markets	.00	.01	.01	.01	.01	.01	.01	−.01	.01
15	Total, Lines 9 to 14	.34	.07	.22	1.02	.65	.42	.72	−.52	1.43
16	Reduction in age of capital	.02	.00	.04	.00	.04	.00	.04	.00	.00
17	Balancing of the capital stock	.08	.00	.00	.00	.26	.00	.00	.00	.00
18	Unmeasured sources, errors, omissions	.54	.07	−.31	.74	.79	.43	.14	.04	.88
19	Total, Lines 15 to 18	.98	.14	−.05	1.76	1.74	.85	.90	−.48	2.31
20	Economies of scale: growth of national market measured in U.S. prices	.11	.03	.05	.14	.32	.17	.08	−.08	.25
21	Economies of scale: income elasticities	.46	.11	.22	.49	.90	.23	.12	.09	.60
22	Adjusted national income	1.55	.28	.22	2.39	2.96	1.25	1.10	−.47	3.16
23	Irregularities in pressure of demand	.03	.04	.26	.04	.04	.23	.04	−.05	.04
24	Irregularities in agricultural output	.00	.00	−.07	−.01	.00	.02	−.02	.00	.01
25	Deflation procedures	.07	.17	.00	.23	.00	.00	.00	.00	.00
	National income per person employed	1.65	.49	.41	2.65	3.00	1.50	1.12	−.52	3.21

Sources: Derived from odd-numbered Tables 21–1 through 21–19.

ment of inputs (for example, of the effects of health and of work intensity upon labor quality), and errors in the growth rates themselves and in the contribution of all the sources explicitly estimated. The residual contributes relatively little to the difference in growth between the United States and Belgium, Norway, and the United Kingdom. To aid in interpreting the differences in the other countries, I can only refer to surmises offered in Chapter 20 and in the country summaries above.

The case of France is the most interesting. It is only the residual of 0.75 percentage points that raises France from the position of a medium to a high growth rate country. My surmise is that France actually was obtaining a substantial increase in productivity from sources that I have not attempted to measure separately. One can only speculate (as in Chapter 20) on what these sources may have been, or on their relative importance.

The residual added 0.80 percentage points to the already high growth rate of Germany and 0.89 to the already high rate of Italy. In Germany the residual was only 0.11 points in 1955–62 but it was 1.78 in 1950–55. My surmise is that it mainly represents gains in efficiency associated with recovery from World War II. In Italy the residual was 0.54

even in 1955–62. The difference of 0.35 points between 0.54 and 0.89 may suggest the size of similar recovery gains upon the 1950–62 growth rate of Italy. But I have no guess as to whether the remaining 0.54 points represent a real contribution to efficiency from sources I have not isolated or results from errors in the other estimates.

The residual contributed 0.44 points to the Dutch growth rate and subtracted 0.32 points from the Danish rate. In each country this was a significant item only in 1950–55; the residual in each was −0.01 in 1955–62. My surmise is that contributions of the residual reflect mainly some combination of errors in the growth rates or in the estimated contributions of other sources.

The change in the age of capital and balancing of the capital stock together contributed 0.10 percentage points and the residual contributed 0.54 points to the difference between growth rates of Northwest Europe as a whole and the United States. If my surmises are reasonably correct, about half of these 0.64 points (the 0.10 contributed by the first two factors and nearly all of the German contribution to the residual) resulted from recovery from wartime distortion that did not exist in the United States. The rest reflects mainly an increase in French productivity from unidentified sources that had the effect of narrowing the productivity gap between France and the United States.

When differences in the contributions of these three sources are added to those of inputs and improved allocation, as in Line 19, Table 21–23, the ranking of the countries begins to resemble that in actual growth rates as shown in Line 26. There are interchanges between France and the Netherlands, and among the United States, Denmark, and Norway, but the differences within each of these groups are moderate both in Line 19 and in actual growth rates. Line 19 provides, in fact, estimates of the differences in *adjusted* growth rates (the term is used in the same sense as before) that would appear if all countries operated under constant returns to scale.

Economies of scale greatly magnify the amounts by which growth rates differ. To some extent they also affect the relative position of countries. The components distinguished in Lines 20 and 21 must be examined separately.

Line 20 refers to the amounts that economies of scale would have contributed to the growth rate of each country if the national incomes of all of the countries were uniformly valued in United States prices. Since the expansion of markets depends on the growth rate, and gains from economies of scale depend on the expansion of markets, gains from economies of scale are naturally greater the higher is the growth rate.[7] The estimates also allow for the probability that gains are greater in the European countries than in the vastly larger United States economy, and greater in the small European countries than in the large; but the quantitative effects of this allowance are not great. Economies of scale associated with the growth of the national market, measured in United States prices, are estimated to have contributed 0.11 percentage points more to growth in Northwest Europe as a whole than to growth in the United States. They contributed 0.14 more in France, 0.33 more in Germany, 0.08 less in the United Kingdom, and 0.25 more in Italy than in the United States. Their main effect is to widen the differences in growth rates that would exist under constant returns to scale.

The source of growth listed in Line 21 as economies of scale associated with income elasticities increases the spread among growth rates by much larger amounts. The numbers on this line represent estimates of the amount by which growth rates of national products valued in each country's own prices exceed the growth rates of national products that would be obtained if the components of consumption were uniformly valued in United States prices. This line could thus be regarded as merely a statistical adjustment required to make growth rates of the various countries comparable.[8]

For reasons explained in Chapter 17 I believe Line 21 has greater significance than this, however. Viewed from the standpoint of the European countries, it represents additional gains from economies

7. The relationship reflected is, however, to growth rates of national income valued in United States rather than European prices.

8. However, its statistical derivation takes account only of divergences for systematic reasons related to the relationship between European and American price ratios and changes in the composition of consumption associated with income elasticities.

TABLE 21-25

Contributions of the Sources to Growth of Total National Income, 1955–62:
Differences from the United States

(*In percentage points*)

	Sources of growth	North-west Europe	Bel-gium	Den-mark	France	Ger-many	Nether-lands	Nor-way	United King-dom	Italy
1	Employment	−.16	−.40	.22	−.64	.40	.03	−.60	−.36	−.53
2	Hours of work	−.06	−.02	−.14	.14	−.25	−.09	−.11	−.10	.23
3	Age-sex composition	.16	.20	.01	.20	.23	.05	−.02	.06	.13
4	Education	−.29	−.09	−.38	−.23	−.41	−.28	−.27	−.22	−.12
5	Dwellings	−.17	−.24	−.13	−.22	−.09	−.18	−.21	−.19	−.14
6	International assets	−.03	−.14	−.03	−.04	−.11	−.16	−.15	.11	−.11
7	Nonresidential structures and equipment	.35	.05	.31	.24	.79	.41	.33	.11	.24
8	Inventories	.12	.00	.11	.13	.25	.14	.02	.04	.08
9	Total factor input, Lines 1 to 8	−.08	−.64	−.03	−.42	.81	−.08	−1.01	−.55	−.22
10	Advances of knowledge	.00	.00	.00	.00	.00	.00	−.01	.00	.00
11	Contraction of agricultural inputs	.18	−.06	.25	.45	.35	−.01	.17	−.19	.94
12	Contraction of nonagricultural self-employment	.11	.12	.18	.21	.06	.26	.22	.03	.25
13	Reduction of international trade barriers	.08	.16	.09	.07	.10	.16	.15	.02	.16
14	Economies of scale: growth of local markets	.02	.03	.03	.03	.03	.03	.03	.01	.03
15	Total, Lines 9 to 14	.31	−.39	.52	.34	1.35	.36	−.45	−.68	1.16
16	Unmeasured sources, errors, omissions	.23	.01	−.01	.80	.11	−.01	.22	.11	.54
17	Total, Lines 15 and 16	.54	−.38	.51	1.14	1.46	.35	−.23	−.57	1.70
18	Economies of scale: growth of national market measured in U.S. prices	.13	.08	.23	.21	.22	.13	.11	−.03	.27
19	Economies of scale: income elasticities	.43	.24	.54	.46	.70	.35	.27	.15	.80
20	Adjusted national income	1.10	−.06	1.28	1.81	2.38	.83	.15	−.45	2.77
21	Irregularities in pressure of demand	.27	.34	.78	.34	.34	.43	.34	.05	.34
22	Irregularities in agricultural output	−.01	.00	.19	−.07	.00	−.10	.11	.00	−.07
23	Deflation procedures	.08	.23	.00	.28	.00	.00	.00	.00	.00
24	Total national income	1.44	.51	2.25	2.36	2.72	1.16	.60	−.40	3.04

Sources: Derived from odd-numbered Tables 21–1 through 21–19.

of scale, in excess of those covered by Line 20, that were made possible because the rise in per capita consumption in Europe, which narrowed the consumption gap between the United States and Europe, concentrated the increase in consumption in products with high income elasticity. These income-elastic products were much more expensive, relative to other consumer products, in Europe than they were in the United States because in Europe they were produced in small volume at high unit cost. As markets for these products became large enough to warrant large-scale production, substantial cost reductions could be achieved by the adoption of known technology that was previously inapplicable.

The size of gains from this source is related to the growth rates of per capita consumption, not to those of total national income. A ranking of countries by the former rates can differ from a ranking by growth of national income, and in the 1950–55 and 1955–62 subperiods there are some marked differences. This source, consequently, cannot only widen the gaps between countries in growth rates of national income but also shift their relative positions. Over the whole period from 1950 to 1962, however, countries with very high or low growth rates of national income also had very high or low growth rates of per capita consumption, so that the main impact of economies of scale associated with income elasticities was to greatly widen the growth rate differentials among countries with relatively little change in their rank. However, all European countries had a larger percentage increase in per capita consumption than the United States so that even those with lower growth rates had some differential gain from this source.

Northwest Europe as a whole gained an advantage over the United States of 0.46 points, France of 0.49, Germany of 0.91, and Italy of 0.60, whereas the United Kingdom gained only 0.09. The small countries with the lowest growth rates, Belgium and Norway, gained only 0.11 and 0.12, and Denmark and the Netherlands each gained 0.23.

When the contributions from both of these types of economies of scale are added to the contributions of other sources computed without allowance for economies of scale I arrive, in Line 22, at the growth rates of adjusted national income.

Growth rates of actual national income differed from those of adjusted national income insofar as a comparison of output per unit of input in 1950 and 1962 is distorted by the effect of weather and similar factors on farm output, or by the effect of differences in the pressure of aggregate demand upon the intensity with which employed resources were used. Together, these incomparabilities added 0.19 percentage points more to the growth rate of Denmark and 0.25 points more to the growth rate of the Netherlands than to that of the United States. Compared to the United States, they added 0.03 points in France, 0.04 in Germany, and 0.05 in Italy, and deducted 0.05 in the United Kingdom. Observed growth rates are also affected by differences in statistical procedure. The low growth rate of Belgium was raised about 0.17 percentage points by a unique method used to deflate income originating in government, and the already high growth rate of France was raised an estimated 0.23 points, in comparison with the United States, by an allowance for rising productivity in on-site construction.[9] Addition of differences in these items yields the differences in growth rates of actual national income as measured.

9. I have not attempted the impossible task of quantifying the effects of all differences in statistical procedure upon growth rates. The two I have isolated are those that I was aware of and that also seemed to have a sizable effect. I have not attempted to adjust for the differences between the United States, the United Kingdom, and the other countries in the procedure for handling shifts in retail distribution

The general observations that emerge from this review of the 1950–62 period might be summarized as follows. Among the countries examined, special influences associated with recovery from World War II, incomparabilities of the terminal years compared, and differences in statistical procedures to measure national income considerably influenced relative growth rates. Aside from such special factors, the basic standing of the countries in growth rates was largely determined by (1) the extent to which inputs were increased and (2) the size of gains from shifting the distribution of labor from farm employment and nonfarm self-employment to nonfarm wage and salary employment. Reduction of trade barriers also had some influence. The ranking of France (and to a lesser extent, and with a larger question mark, the ranking of Italy) apparently was raised substantially by productivity gains from sources that were not isolated and from which other countries did not benefit, as least not to a comparable extent. Therefore, the *ranking* of the countries is established by the special factors first enumerated, inputs, resource allocation, and these differential productivity gains from unidentified sources. The *size* of the differentials in growth rates between countries was greatly magnified by economies of scale, especially those associated with differences in the degree to which consumption patterns changed as a result of rises in per capita consumption. If this generalization of experience differs from most analyses, it is in the heavy importance attached to gains from reallocation of labor as a determinant of growth rates and to economies of scale as a factor accentuating international differences.

National Income per Person Employed

Table 21–24 analyzes differences in the growth rates of national income per person employed, a measure that is perhaps of even greater interest than total national income. In 1950–62 the United States

channels (see p. 29f.) except to take it into account in measuring gains from the independent growth of local markets. Neither have I included an adjustment for the small contribution to the German growth rate made by imputation of a productivity increase in government (see p. 27).

TABLE 21–26

Contributions of the Sources to Growth of National Income per Person Employed, 1955–62: Differences from the United States

(In percentage points)

	Sources of growth	North-west Europe	Bel-gium	Den-mark	France	Ger-many	Nether-lands	Nor-way	United King-dom	Italy
1	Hours of work	−.06	−.02	−.14	.14	−.25	−.09	−.11	−.10	.23
2	Age-sex composition	.16	.20	.01	.20	.23	.05	−.02	.06	.13
3	Education	−.29	−.09	−.38	−.23	−.41	−.28	−.27	−.22	−.12
4	Dwellings	−.16	−.23	−.12	−.18	−.07	−.15	−.17	−.17	−.12
5	International assets	−.02	−.13	−.02	−.03	−.10	−.16	−.14	.12	−.10
6	Nonresidential structures and equipment	.34	.08	.24	.32	.62	.33	.42	.16	.30
7	Inventories	.12	.01	.08	.16	.20	.11	.03	.05	.10
8	Land	−.01	.01	−.04	.02	−.05	.01	.02	.01	.00
9	Total factor input, Lines 1 to 8	.08	−.17	−.37	.40	.17	−.18	−.24	−.09	.42
10	Advances of knowledge	.01	.00	.00	.01	.00	.00	.00	.00	.01
11	Contraction of agricultural inputs	.18	−.06	.24	.45	.35	−.01	.17	−.19	.94
12	Contraction of nonagricultural self-employment	.11	.12	.18	.21	.06	.26	.22	.03	.25
13	Reduction of international trade barriers	.08	.16	.09	.07	.10	.16	.15	.02	.16
14	Economies of scale: growth of local markets	.02	.03	.03	.03	.03	.03	.03	.01	.03
15	Total, Lines 9 to 14	.48	.08	.17	1.17	.71	.26	.33	−.22	1.81
16	Unmeasured sources, errors, omissions	.23	.01	−.01	.79	.11	−.01	.22	.11	.54
17	Total, Lines 15 and 16	.71	.09	.16	1.96	.82	.25	.55	−.11	2.35
18	Economies of scale: growth of national market measured in U.S. prices	.13	.07	.23	.21	.22	.12	.11	−.03	.27
19	Economies of scale: income elasticities	.43	.24	.53	.46	.70	.35	.27	.15	.80
20	Adjusted national income	1.27	.40	.92	2.63	1.74	.72	.93	.01	3.42
21	Irregularities in pressure of demand	.27	.34	.78	.34	.34	.43	.34	.05	.34
22	Irregularities in agricultural output	−.01	.00	.19	−.07	.00	−.10	.11	.00	−.07
23	Deflation procedures	.08	.23	.00	.28	.00	.00	.00	.00	.00
24	National income per person employed	1.61	.97	1.89	3.18	2.08	1.05	1.38	.06	3.69

Sources: Derived from odd-numbered Tables 21–1 through 21–19.

growth rate of 2.15 percent was exceeded by 3.21 points in Italy, 3.00 in Germany, 2.65 in France, 1.65 in Northwest Europe as a whole, 1.50 in the Netherlands, 1.12 in Norway, 0.49 in Belgium, and 0.41 in Denmark, while the United Kingdom rate was 0.52 points lower.

The contributions of total inputs differed much less than they did in total national income. As shown in Line 9, their contribution was biggest in France, where it was 0.34 percentage points larger than in the United States, and smallest in the United Kingdom, where it was 0.34 points less than in the United States. Thus, the extreme range is 0.68 points. That the range is as limited as this results

from the fact that differences in the contributions of individual inputs tended to be offsetting. In the case of France, for example, five components contributed 0.75 points more than in the United States while three contributed 0.41 points less. In Northwest Europe as a whole the contribution of inputs was 0.06 points less than in the United States, but this net figure cancels four components contributing 0.46 percentage points more against four components contributing 0.52 points less.

All the European countries obtained *larger* contributions than the United States from the increase in nonresidential structures and equipment and all except Belgium larger contributions from the increase in inventories.[10] With Germany a decided exception, differences in the contributions of these types of capital to growth of national income per person employed were more favorable to Europe than were differences in their contributions to growth of total national income. Changes in the composition of man-hours by age and sex also were more favorable to growth in all the European countries than in the United States. The amounts were 0.20 percentage points in France, 0.14 in Germany, 0.06 in the United Kingdom, and 0.19 in Italy. From changes in annual hours France obtained 0.15 percentage points more than the United States, Italy 0.22 points more, and Germany 0.10 points less; in other countries the differences were slight and usually positive.[11] All the European countries obtained *smaller* contributions from education, from dwellings, and, with the exception of the Netherlands, from international assets.

The contributions of all of the components of output per unit of input to the growth rates of na-

tional income per person employed are the same, when expressed in percentage points, as their contributions to the growth rates of total national income except for small differences due to "interaction" with employment. There is therefore no need to discuss them again in detail. The cumulative subtotals do, however, bring out one point of particular interest. When the contributions of inputs and the reallocation of resources, but no other sources, are cumulated in Line 15, France already stands second only to Italy; thus, in contrast to total national income, France would have ranked high in growth of national income per person employed even in the absence of large gains in efficiency from sources that have not been isolated.

Tables 21–25 and 21–26 compile differences in the sources of growth in the 1955–62 subperiod. This period has the decided advantage over 1950–62 of being relatively free of the effects of recovery from World War II and also of sizable entries for the "residual" item that are inexplicable. It has the decided disadvantage that a much larger intrusion is made by incomparabilities in cyclical position (for which inputs have not been adjusted at all and for which the adjustment of output per unit of input, though made, was difficult) and by irregularities in farm output. Differences in cyclical position importantly affected the United States itself, the base from which differences are computed.

10. In Chapter 13 I noted that the Belgian inventory series is suspect; Belgium may be an exception only because of errors in the inventory series.

11. The impact of the great increase in part-time work on the United States results should again be noted. If output were measured on a full-time equivalent basis the United States growth rate of national income per person employed would be higher and most of the change would appear in the hours of work component. (The contributions of capital input components would be raised slightly.)

TABLE 21–27

Differences from the United States in Growth Rates of National Income per Person Employed and in Contributions of Selected Sources

(*In percentage points*)

Area	Contributions of selected sources		Adjusted growth rates[a]		Actual growth rates	
	1955–62 (1)	1950–62 (2)	1955–62 (3)	1950–62 (4)	1955–62 (5)	1950–62 (6)
Italy	2.45	2.04	3.52	3.23	3.69	3.21
France	1.99	1.83	2.66	2.41	3.18	2.65
Germany	.92	.88	1.84	3.08	2.08	3.00
Northwest Europe	.73	.84	1.29	1.63	1.61	1.65
Norway	.69	1.05	1.07	1.21	1.38	1.12
Netherlands	.41	.36	.88	1.20	1.05	1.50
Belgium	.22	.18	.53	.38	.97	.49
Denmark	.18	.23	.94	.24	1.89	.41
United States	—	—	—	—	—	—
United Kingdom	−.23	−.31	−.11	−.37	.06	−.52

Sources: Derived from Tables 21–24 and 21–26; see text for explanation of sources included and adjustments made for Columns (1) and (2).
a. Excludes the contribution of international assets in addition to the sources excluded from adjusted growth rates in Tables 21–1 to 21–20.

Table 21–27 uses information from both periods to try to gain some additional insight into postwar growth differentials. It represents an attempt to abstract from the special disturbing influences of war, incomparabilities of years with respect to cyclical position and agricultural output, and unexplained aberrations. This analysis is confined to national income per person employed, which is less affected than total national income by differences in cyclical position.

Column 1, Table 21–27, shows the contribution, expressed as a difference from the contribution in the United States, that was made to 1955–62 growth rates of national income per person employed by (1) all factor inputs except international assets; (2) improvements in resource allocation; and (3) the residual item.[12] The reason for omitting the contribution of income from international assets, which affects the numbers appreciably only in the United Kingdom and the Netherlands, is that in the United Kingdom at least the timing of changes in this item was dominated by quite special factors.[13] Column 2 shows the contributions of the same sources in 1950–62. However, one important adjustment has been made. For the actual 1950–62 residuals I have substituted the 1955–62 residuals. My reasoning is that the 1955–62 residuals are mostly small, and where they are not they are likely to measure genuine contributions to productivity from otherwise unmeasured but persistent sources. In contrast, the *difference* between the 1950–55 and 1955–62 residuals (which is large in Denmark, Germany, the Netherlands, and Italy) is most likely to reflect recovery from wartime conditions, simple errors in the estimates, or a combination of the two.

Columns 1 and 2 thus represent an effort to compare international differences in the contributions made by domestic inputs, improved allocation of resources, and other sources of increased efficiency not related to recovery from the distortions of war. International differences in the contributions made by these sources over the whole period were strik-ingly similar to differences in the 1955–62 subperiod except in Italy and Norway. Italy's advantage over the United States was greater in 1955–62 than in 1950–62, mainly because of a more rapid shift of resources out of agriculture after 1955 than before, and because of acceleration of the growth, per person employed, of enterprise capital. Norway's margin over the United States was smaller in 1955–62 than over the whole 1950–62 period chiefly because of the movement of hours of work and of the shift from agriculture. With these exceptions, the contributions to differences in growth rates made by the rather basic sources combined in these columns were much the same whether the longer or shorter period is viewed.

The first two columns of Table 21–27 provide a *ranking* of countries that measures as well as I am able the underlying trend in domestic national income per person employed in the postwar period up to 1962.[14] If Belgium and Denmark, which are very close in both periods, are counted as tied for sixth place, there is only one difference in rank between the 1955–62 and 1950–62 periods. In 1955–62 the ranking is Italy, France, Germany, Norway, the Netherlands, Belgium and Denmark (tied), the United States, and the United Kingdom. Based on 1950–62, Norway stands above Germany.

The differences in the contributions of these sources alone may be compared with differences in "adjusted" growth rates (from which the contribution of income from international assets has been eliminated in this comparison) and with actual growth rates; these are given in Columns 3 to 6, Table 21–27.

In the 1955–62 period the adjusted growth rates in Column 3 rank the nine countries in the same order, except for Denmark, as do the contributions of the selected sources shown in Column 1. The differentials in the adjusted growth rates are, however, much larger because they are increased by gains from economies of scale. This increase in the differentials is not, to be sure, altogether uniform; gains from economies of scale associated with the growth

---

12. The contribution of the small component, economies of scale associated with the "growth of local markets," is included as are the occasional differences of 0.01 in the contribution of advances of knowledge that arise because of the interaction term.

13. See p. 131.

14. It is admittedly questionable whether great significance can be attached to the notion of an underlying trend of growth from which the influence of special and temporary factors is eliminated, but if related to a particular time span I believe this concept has some value.

of the national market depend on the contributions of all growth sources, not only those selected in Column 1, and gains associated with income elasticities depend upon the growth of per capita consumption which may have still a different movement. Gains from economies of scale—or in any event my estimates of them based on growth from all sources—are also responsible for the Danish aberration in 1955–62.[15] In 1950–62 Denmark's rank in adjusted growth rates (Column 4) is about the same as would be expected from Column 2. (It is somewhat lowered by the unexplained residual.) On the other hand, over the longer period recovery from war distortions elevated the adjusted growth rate of Germany above that of France, and the large unexplained residual in the Netherlands, though it did not cause the rank of that country to diverge, did make the adjusted rate higher than the sources measured in Column 2 would lead one to expect. For obvious reasons (including, in this table, the contributions of international assets) the actual growth rates show much more erratic relationships than the adjusted rates.

Is European Experience Incompatible with My Analysis of United States Growth?

The most important objective of my previous study of growth in the United States was to estimate the size of the change in any income determinant that would be required to alter the American growth rate by any given amount, and to provide a "menu of choices" for raising the rate. In that study requirements for altering future growth rates and the sources of past growth were estimated by consistent procedures. In Chapter 1 the question was raised as to whether the high postwar growth rates actually obtained by some of the European countries were an indication that I had overstated the requirements for raising the growth rate of the United States. One chief purpose of the present study was to see whether European experience was compatible with my procedures and conclusions.

15. Denmark had little growth from 1950 to 1955, and my estimates assign the entire contribution of scale economies realized from 1950 to 1962 to the second subperiod. In the absence of sources not included in Column 1, gains from scale economies would have been smaller in 1955–62 and Denmark would have stood lower in Column 3.

One test of procedures is their ability to explain differences in growth rates. This study deals, at the most detailed level, with eighteen growth rates of national income: those for nine countries in the 1950–55 and 1955–62 periods. (Rates for Northwest Europe and rates for 1950–62 as a whole are, in effect, averages of these rates.) The eighteen rates ranged from 1.58 to 9.93 percent and had a standard deviation of 1.90 percentage points. The estimates used to move from actual to "adjusted" growth rates in Tables 21–1 to 21–20 are largely irrelevant to the present question, but the standard deviation of the *adjusted* growth rates was still 1.82 points. The sources whose contributions were independently estimated in this study accounted for nine-tenths of this amount; the standard deviation of the residuals was only 0.18.[16] I have no independent means of knowing how much of the deviation *should* be left in the residuals to measure variations in the gains from productivity due to sources not directly estimated, but it is clear that the great bulk of the variation in growth rates can be explained without reference to these sources.[17] Thus, the general methodology followed in my American study, adapted as necessary to take account of European conditions, can successfully cope with the wide range of experience observed in these nine countries.

Two supplementary observations may be made. First, the analysis has given quite as much attention to growth sources that contributed most to growth where growth rates were low as to sources that contributed most where rates were high; it was not confined to searching for sources that accounted for differences in rates. Second, the residuals obtained in Table 20–1 could not be foreseen when the contributions of other sources were estimated and no adjustments were made subsequent to initial estimation in order to obtain more reasonable residuals. Once obtained the residuals were not altered.[18]

16. The result is the same whether the calculation is based on the residuals before or after deduction of the contribution of advances of knowledge since that was taken to be the same amount in all countries.
17. Almost all of the variation remaining in the residuals arises from the inability of the sources directly estimated to explain wholly the most extreme rates—those for Denmark, Germany, the Netherlands, and Italy in 1950–55—and the French rate in both subperiods.
18. I do not suggest that reviewing and revising the estimates in an attempt to reduce differences in the residuals

The question concerning the relationship between European experience and my analysis of the requirements to alter the United States growth rate may also be answered in a broader and less statistical fashion. Rather than indicating that my estimates of the yield from various steps that might be envisioned to accelerate United States growth are too small, the very high growth rates obtained by some of the European countries show that the conditions of growth were different in Europe and America; the United States could not have matched these rates with any combination of reasonable measures, much less by duplicating what the European countries were doing. Aside from irrelevancies such as recovery from World War II and differences in cyclical position that simply inject confusion into comparisons, the conditions differed, first, in that the opportunity to raise national income by reallocation of resources was far greater in the fast-growing continental countries than in the United States—or, for that matter, in the United Kingdom. Second, the conditions differed in that the opportunity to raise productivity by bringing the average of prevailing practice closer to that of the world's most efficient enterprises was far greater in Europe than in the United States, and it is something of a surprise that according to the evidence of the residuals only in France and perhaps Italy was much gained from this source in the period covered. The conditions differed, third, in that economies of scale, and particularly those labeled as "associated with income elasticities," are such that any change of a type that raises the national income does so by a substantially larger percentage in Europe than in the United States.[19] This third difference implies, of course, that if one were to appraise the size of measures required to raise the growth rates for European countries by any given amount, as I did for the United States in my earlier study, he would find that these measures would be

smaller in Europe than in the United States. Other relevant differences, including those in factor proportions, have been noted in this study and they are not negligible, but the three just cited seem to be the crucial ones.

Income Levels and Growth Rates

To assist in the interpretation of international differences in growth rates and the sources of growth this study has devoted a great deal of attention to comparisons of the positions of the countries at a point in time. The additional difficulties of international comparisons of this type have been stressed, but even crude estimates can provide additional perspective for the evaluation of growth rates. This information will now be introduced into the analysis.

Sources of Differences in Income Levels in 1960

In 1960 national income per person employed in Northwest Europe as a whole was 41 percent lower than it was in the United States. My estimates of the amount and the sources of the differences between each of the European countries and the United States in national income per person employed in 1960 are shown in Table 21–28.[20]

The differences in national income per person employed shown in this table are those that appear when the output of all countries is valued in United States prices; differences would be larger if comparisons were based on European prices. The contributions of the sources also are based, for consistency, on the use of United States values and

---

would be improper, but that procedure would reduce the significance of the standard deviations in the context of the paragraph.

19. Alternatively, one could substitute for this statement, with respect to income elasticities, the more firmly established statement that price weights are such that changes in Europe raise national income more when national income is measured in European prices than when it is measured in United States prices.

20. To facilitate comparison of these estimates with sources of growth the pseudo growth rate method described in Chapter 15 was used to handle the difficult problem of the "interaction" among the sources. This method makes the results as comparable as possible to those for growth rates. The method yields equal values for (1) the percentage contribution of any source to the 1960 difference between levels of output per person in a European country and the United States and (2) the percentage of the growth rate of national income per person employed, valued in United States prices, that would be ascribed to that source over a twenty-year period if, at the end of twenty years, all of the factors determining income per person were the same as they were in the United States in 1960.

weights. In this respect the analysis of levels differs from that of growth rates, which is based on each country's own prices and weights. Because of this, one of the largest European growth sources, economies of scale associated with income elasticities, has no counterpart in Table 21–28. This source does not contribute to differences in income levels measured in United States prices. It contributes to European *growth* when national income is measured in European prices but not when it is measured in United States prices, and growth from this source does not help to narrow the gap between Europe and the United States in income level. The differences between United States and European weights also introduce incomparability between estimates of the contributions of other sources to growth and to level, but not to such an extent as to hamper greatly broad comparisons.

I shall first examine the sources of differences in income and then attempt to relate them to growth rate experience.

As shown in Table 21–28, two sources were more favorable to high national income per person employed in all European countries than in the United States in 1960. One was the inadequacy of aggregate demand in the United States that led to a low rate of utilization of employed resources in 1960. This differential had been eliminated by 1965–66, and its elimination contributed to the favorable United States growth record in the 1960's.[21] The second was hours of work. Hours are an unusual example of an income determinant that typically

21. Exceptionally large farm output in the Netherlands in 1960 was also a favorable factor in the Dutch level of output of 1960 and depressed the subsequent Dutch growth rate if the calculation is started in 1960. The effect on Northwest Europe as a whole was negligible.

TABLE 21–28

Contributions to Differences from the United States in National Income per Person Employed, 1960

(*Percentage of United States national income per person employed*)

Sources of difference	North-west Europe	Bel-gium	Den-mark	France	Ger-many	Nether-lands	Nor-way	United King-dom	Italy
Total difference	**41.0**	**39.0**	**42.0**	**41.0**	**41.0**	**35.0**	**41.0**	**41.0**	**60.0**
Total factor input	11.3	8.5	11.0	11.0	14.0	2.8	5.3	11.0	18.7
Labor	1.1	1.0	2.8	1.0	2.5	−4.7	−.4	.6	4.4
Hours of work	−3.9	−3.2	−3.5	−4.1	−3.9	−5.9	−3.4	−3.1	−4.9
Age-sex composition	1.2	.1	2.2	1.1	2.3	−.9	.1	.7	.8
Education	3.8	4.1	4.1	4.0	4.1	2.1	2.9	3.0	8.5
Capital	9.7	6.9	7.7	9.6	11.0	7.0	5.2	9.9	13.8
Dwellings	1.9	2.1	1.8	2.1	1.9	1.9	2.1	1.6	3.2
International assets	.4	.3	.5	.5	.7	.2	1.0	.0	.6
Nonresidential structures and equipment	6.6	3.5	4.8	6.1	7.4	4.8	1.5	7.5	8.7
Inventories	.8	1.0	.6	.9	1.0	.1	.6	.8	1.3
Land	.5	.6	.5	.4	.5	.5	.5	.5	.5
Output per unit of input	29.7	30.5	31.0	30.0	27.0	32.2	35.7	30.0	41.3
Overallocation to agriculture	2.3	.2	3.1	5.8	3.7	−.2	6.1	−1.1	12.3
Overallocation to nonagricultural self-employment	.3	2.7	1.5	1.9	.4	1.1	2.1	−1.7	4.6
Use of shift work	.1	.1	.1	.1	.1	.2	.2	.2	.0
Economies of scale: national market[a]	3.0	3.9	3.8	2.9	2.8	3.9	4.2	2.8	2.7
Economies of scale: local markets	1.9	2.0	1.9	1.9	1.9	2.0	2.0	1.8	1.8
Irregularity in pressure of demand	−1.6	−1.8	−1.8	−1.7	−1.7	−1.8	−1.8	−1.3	−1.4
Irregularity in agricultural output	.0	.0	.0	.0	.0	−.5	.0	.0	.0
Lag in the application of knowledge, general efficiency, and errors and omissions	23.7	23.4	22.4	19.1	19.8	27.5	22.9	29.3	21.3

Sources: Tables 15–8, 16–14, 17–3, 17–10, 19–2, and 20–2; "Use of shift work" derived from estimates on p. 174 by the usual procedure for handling "interaction."
a. Includes effects of barriers to international trade.

becomes less favorable to high income per person employed as income rises to high levels. This clearly has been the case with respect to hours of full-time workers. In the United States part-time employment has also increased.

All the remaining income determinants contributed toward lower national income per person employed in Northwest Europe as a whole than in the United States. In the absence of the offsets just noted, these sources would have produced a differential of 46.5 percent between Northwest Europe and the United States. All of these sources also contributed positively to the income gap between the United States and each of the individual European countries with the following exceptions: age-sex composition in the Netherlands; the overallocation of resources to agriculture in the Netherlands and the United Kingdom; and the overallocation of labor to nonfarm self-employment in the United Kingdom. As stressed in earlier chapters, the exceptions noted for the United Kingdom are extremely important to interpretation of that country's relative position with respect to both level and growth.

Of the 46.5 points contributed by sources making a positive contribution to the income difference between the United States and Northwest Europe, 22.8 points, or about half, were divided among a large number of sources. Five points were due to two aspects of labor quality—1.2 points to a less favorable age-sex composition of man-hours worked in Europe and 3.8 points to less education. Nearly twice this much, 9.7 points, was due to less capital per worker, including 6.6 points ascribed to nonresidential structures and equipment and smaller amounts to each of the other components. Land contributed 0.5 points. Greater overallocation of resources to agriculture contributed 2.3 points and greater overallocation of labor to nonfarm self-employment 0.3 points.[22] Less use of shift work contributed 0.1 points. Economies of scale associated with the size of local markets contributed 1.9 points (mainly because automobile use was less prevalent than in America) and economies of scale

associated with national markets 3.0 points. The latter estimate includes the greater cost in Europe of barriers to international trade; in the level comparisons I did not try to distinguish natural from artificial limits on the size of markets.

The remaining 23.7 points, or about half of the difference contributed by all factors unfavorable to income in Northwest Europe and 58 percent of the net difference, is due to lower output per unit of input for reasons that have not been isolated—that is to say, reasons other than the broad types of misallocation I have tried to measure, economies of scale, and special characteristics of the year 1960.

The United States in 1925 and Northwest Europe in 1960

I noted in Chapter 2 that by 1925 national income per person employed in the United States had already reached the 1960 Northwest European level. This level was 41 percent below the level in the United States in 1960. The question was raised as to whether the reasons for the shortfall were the same. Table 21–29 compares the sources that were responsible for the United States in 1925 and Northwest Europe in 1960 falling below the United States of 1960 by equal amounts.[23] Small differences between the positions of Northwest Europe in 1960 and the United States in 1925 cannot be stressed but the comparison can be revealing if some caution is used.

The first point to be noted is that the average quality of a year's work was much higher in Northwest Europe in 1960 than in the United States in 1925. Labor quality was responsible for 20 percent of the difference between United States output per man in 1925 and 1960 but only 3 percent of the difference between the United States and Northwest

---

22. Outside the United Kingdom the importance of these two components was much greater; among the Northwest European countries the figures for the two combined were particularly large in Germany (4.1), Denmark (4.6), France (7.7), and Norway (8.2).

23. The 1925 United States estimates were obtained (for procedural comparability) by applying a percentage distribution of the sources of growth of national income per person employed in the 1925–60 period to the difference in level. The growth rate estimates were obtained by combining the 1950–60 estimates from the present study and 1925–50 estimates from my earlier study. The earlier data were not completely reworked for full consistency with the present study but the obvious adjustments were made. However, in measuring the contribution of inputs, 1960–62 United States income share weights were used in the United States-European comparison whereas shifting weights were used to analyze United States growth over the 1925–60 period.

TABLE 21-29

Sources of Differences from United States, 1960, in National Income per Person Employed: Northwest Europe in 1960 and the United States in 1925

Sources of difference	Percentage of United States national income per person employed, 1960		Percentage of differences	
	Northwest Europe 1960	United States 1925	Northwest Europe 1960	United States 1925
Total difference from U.S. level in 1960	**41.0**	**41.0**	**100**	**100**
Total factor input	11.3	13.5	28	33
Labor	1.1	8.1	3	20
Hours of work	−3.9	−4.6	−10	−11
Age-sex composition	1.2	.0	3	0
Education	3.8	12.7	9	31
Capital	9.7	6.5	24	16
Dwellings	1.9	2.2	5	5
International assets	.4	.3	1	1
Nonresidential structures and equipment	6.6	3.5	16	9
Inventories	.8	.5	2	1
Land	.5	−1.1	1	−3
Output per unit of input	29.7	27.5	72	67
Overallocation to agriculture	2.3	3.2	6	8
Overallocation to nonagricultural self-employment	.3	.5[b]	1	1[b]
Use of shift work	.1	n.a.	[d]	n.a.
Economies of scale: national market[a]	3.0	7.0	7	17
Economies of scale: local markets	1.9	1.9	5	5
Irregularity in pressure of demand	−1.6	−1.0	−4	−2
State of knowledge, lag in application of knowledge, general efficiency, and errors and omissions	23.7	15.9[c]	58	39[c]

Sources: Northwest Europe: Table 21-28; United States: see text for derivation. Details may not add to subtotals because of rounding.
a. Includes effects of barriers to international trade.
b. Includes cost of resale price maintenance.
c. Includes use of shift work.
d. Less than 0.5 percent.
n.a. Not available.

Europe in 1960.[24] The difference between 3 percent and 20 percent is much more than accounted for by the education of the labor force; Northwest European workers of 1960 had considerably more education than American workers of 1925. There was a slight offset in hours of work—the combined effect of differences in full-time hours and the prevalence of part-time employment—and a larger offset in age-sex composition, which was more favorable in the 1925 United States.

The 1960 Northwest European worker's advantage in labor quality over the 1925 American worker was largely offset by the fact that he had less capital and land to work with. Capital was responsible for 24 percent of the difference between

24. Because the absolute difference is the same—41 percent of the United States level in 1960—comparisons can be made in terms of percentages without being misleading.

Northwest Europe and the United States as against 16 percent of the difference between 1925 and 1960 in the United States. It must be remembered that in measurement of capital in the form of nonresidential structures and equipment, different types of capital goods are equated by production cost at a common date, not by ability to contribute to production; "unmeasured" or "noneconomic" quality differences are not taken into account. This means that as advances of knowledge enable capital goods that are more productive to be obtained with the same use of resources (if both were produced at a common date), the effect on income is classified as due to the state of knowledge, not to the quantity of capital. No precision attaches to the comparison, which is an extraordinarily difficult one, but it does appear fairly clear that by the definition followed, Northwest Europe in 1960 had yet to provide as much capital per worker as the United States was already providing in 1925. According to the series used in my previous study, nonresidential structures and equipment capital per worker in the United States in 1925 was already about four-fifths as large as in 1960. The particular magnitudes attached to land in the comparison are dubious but it is clear that, per worker, the United States in 1925 was far better endowed with agricultural land, fuels, and mineral resources than Europe in 1960.

When all inputs are combined they account for 11.3 points of the interspatial gap and 13.5 points of the intertemporal gap, according to the estimates shown. Given the difficulties of estimation, the difference should not be stressed.

Differences between the two sets of estimates with respect to the cost of misallocation to agriculture and to self-employment are relatively minor; so is the effect of cyclical incomparability. The combination of the procedures that were used to compare economies of scale associated with the size of national markets (including the effects of barriers to international trade) across countries in 1960 and over time in the United States yields a larger difference. To this source is ascribed only 3 points, or 7 percent, of the interspatial difference in national income per person employed but 7 points, or 17 percent, of the intertemporal difference in the United States. This results from very crude assumptions and, though tenable, may be greatly in error.

It is the last line of Table 21–29 that provides the really striking result. It shows that when inputs are measured as comprehensively as possible, and the effects of resource allocation and economies of scale on output per unit of input are eliminated, residual productivity was even lower in Northwest Europe in 1960 than it was in the United States in 1925. This comparison is very crude indeed. But the margin is so large that it is unlikely that better data or methods would lead to a finding that residual productivity was *higher* in 1960 Northwest Europe than in the 1925 United States. Apparently some combination of sources not isolated (but speculated about in the previous chapter) was so adverse to high productivity in Europe as to offset the benefit of being able to draw upon 35 years' accumulation of advances in managerial and technological knowledge, including advances embodied as quality improvement in capital goods. The contribution of this residual to the difference between output per person employed in the United States in 1925 and 1960 is ascribable, I believe, to advances of knowledge. Since knowledge available to the United States in 1960 was also, by and large, available to Europe in 1960, the contribution of this residual to the difference between the United States and Northwest Europe in 1960 must be ascribed to other causes that have not been isolated. Thus the line has quite a different meaning in the two comparisons.

The results imply that the enormous advantage of Northwest Europe in 1960 over the United States in 1925 with respect to available knowledge was offset, or more than offset, by lower efficiency. Thus the comparison of the residuals, together with the findings with respect to capital and labor, make clear that although the United States in 1925 and Northwest Europe in 1960 had the same national income per person employed, they were obtaining this income in decidedly different ways.

The Relationship Between Income Levels and Growth

Is the fact that some of the European countries have had much higher growth rates of national income per person employed than the United States somehow related to their much lower levels of income? Have these countries been obtaining faster growth than the United States by reducing gaps between themselves and the United States with respect to the determinants of income or in some different fashion? If so, in what determinants? Is the convergence of the European and American positions general? Or is it concentrated on certain income determinants?

Table 21–30 is designed to help answer these questions. For Northwest Europe as a whole and the three large continental countries, it compares percentage distributions of (1) the sources of difference from the United States in growth rates of adjusted national income per person employed in 1955–62 and (2) the sources of difference from the United States in adjusted levels of national income per person employed in 1960. In addition to the sources eliminated to arrive at adjusted growth rates in Tables 21–1 to 21–20, in this table the contributions to growth of economies of scale associated with income elasticities were deducted because they have no counterpart in the differences in income levels measured in United States prices.[25] This deduction eliminates from the growth analysis a source that has greatly accentuated differences in observed growth rates.

The 1955–62 period, though not ideal, is the best available for such a comparison as is attempted here. The three European countries shown separately are those with the highest adjusted growth

25. This brings the adjusted growth rates, and their breakdown among the sources of growth, much closer than the original adjusted rates to what they would be if national income were uniformly measured in United States prices; it does not, of course, go all the way.

rates of income per person employed in this period before or after elimination of the contribution of economies of scale associated with income elasticities.

The reader is cautioned that Table 21–30 stretches the use of the estimates very far and the results are very sensitive to even minor errors. One percent of the amount by which the adjusted growth rate of Northwest Europe as a whole or Germany differs from the United States rate is only about one-hundredth of a percentage point; even for France and Italy it is only between two and three one-hundredths of a point.[26] It must also be stressed

26. It should be remembered that it is Table 21–25, not 21–30, that is appropriate for comparisons of *absolute* dif-

TABLE 21–30

Adjusted National Income per Person Employed in Selected European Areas:
Comparison of Percentage Distributions of the Sources of Difference from the United States
in Level, 1960, and Growth Rate, 1955–62[a]

Sources of difference in level or growth	Northwest Europe		France		Germany		Italy	
	Level	Growth rate	Level	Growth rate	Level	Growth rate	Level	Growth rate
Difference in level (percent of United States)	42.6	—	42.7	—	42.7	—	61.4	—
Difference in growth rates (percentage points)	—	.84	—	2.17	—	1.04	—	2.62
PERCENTAGE DISTRIBUTIONS OF DIFFERENCES								
Total	100	100	100	100	100	100	100	100
Total factor input	27	10	26	18	33	16	30	16
Labor	3	−23	2	5	6	−41	7	9
Hours of work	−9	−7	−10	6	−9	−24	−8	9
Age-sex composition	3	19	3	9	5	22	1	5
Education	9	−35	9	−11	10	−39	14	−5
Capital	23	33	22	12	26	62	22	7
Dwellings	4	−19	5	−8	4	−7	5	−5
International assets	1	−2	1	−1	2	−10	1	−4
Nonresidential structures and equipment	15	40	14	15	17	60	14	11
Inventories	2	14	2	7	2	19	2	4
Land	1	−1	1	1	1	−5	1	0
Output per unit of input	73	90	74	82	67	84	70	84
Overallocation to agriculture	5	21	14	21	9	34	20	36
Overallocation to nonagricultural self-employment	1	13	4	10	1	6	7	10
Use of shift work	0	0	0	0	0	0	0	0
Economies of scale: national market[b]	7	25	7	13	7	31	4	16
Economies of scale: local markets	4	2	4	1	4	3	3	1
State of knowledge, lag in application of knowledge, general efficiency, and errors and omissions	56	27	45	36	46	11	35	21

Sources: Derived from Tables 21–26 and 21–28; details may not add to subtotals because of rounding.
a. Level comparisons are in United States prices. The contribution of irregularities in the pressure of demand was eliminated before the percentages were computed. Growth rates are in national prices, and correspond to the adjusted growth rates of Tables 21–1 to 21–20, *except* that the contributions of economies of scale associated with income elasticities have been deducted to approximate more closely the sources of growth in United States prices and to achieve greater comparability with the level comparisons.
b. Includes effects of barriers to international trade.

that the contribution of each source is expressed as a percentage of the *net* contribution of all sources. In Germany, eight sources contributed an amount equal to 185 percent of the adjusted growth rate differential while five sources contributed an amount equal to −85 percent.

Table 21–30 reveals a very mixed situation with respect to the relationship between level and growth. Several points of interest emerge. Most of these have implications for future differentials in the growth of national income per person employed. I shall try to point these out, and shall also comment here on prospects for eliminating gaps between Europe and the United States.

1. The most striking single fact revealed by this table is that the reduction in the costs of misallocation of resources made a contribution to more rapid growth in Europe than in America out of all proportion to its contribution to differences in income levels. The fast growing countries were reducing this source of difference in levels very rapidly. This was true of Northwest Europe as a whole, and of each of the three large fast growing countries separately, with respect to both agriculture and nonfarm self-employment. The position was similar with respect to the combined contributions of "economies of scale associated with the national market" and "barriers to international trade"; in this combination it was mainly though not entirely the reduction of barriers to international trade that accounted for the difference. If the first two or all three of these sources are combined, the following tabulation of percentage contributions is obtained.

	Two sources: contribution to net difference from the United States in		Three sources: contribution to net difference from the United States in	
	Level	Growth	Level	Growth
Northwest Europe	6	34	13	59
France	18	31	25	44
Germany	10	40	17	71
Italy	27	46	31	62

ferentials. Differences from the United States in the contributions of education, for example, were −0.23 percentage points in France and −0.41, or less than twice as much, in Germany but when expressed as percentages of the total differential in each country the numbers become −11 in France and −39, or three and one-half times as much, in Germany.

The great importance of resource allocation to more rapid growth of income per person in Europe than in America during 1955–62, and in the postwar period as a whole, has implications for the future. Reduction of agricultural employment and nonfarm self-employment will continue to provide the European countries with large differential gains for some time—perhaps a decade or two in Germany, longer in France, and perhaps for several decades in Italy.[27] But in all probability the differential will be diminishing in amount as the labor remaining in agriculture and self-employment contracts, and eventually it will nearly disappear. Future changes in trade barriers are yet to be determined but, as of 1966, the cost of barriers is hardly large enough to permit further relaxation to provide annual gains over a long period of time (through economies of scale and better resource allocation) as large as were obtained in 1955–62.

Resource reallocation of these types will continue to be a major source of higher European growth in the intermediate run but it cannot be in the very long run.

2. All the European countries except Belgium narrowed the percentage gap between themselves and the United States in capital stock position and obtained more growth from the increase in capital per worker than the United States. In Germany capital was far more important in explaining the differential in growth rates than in income levels, so that Germany's rapid growth was due in disproportionate measure to narrowing the gap in capital. Mainly due to the weight of Germany, this was also true, but in much smaller degree, of Northwest Europe. It was not the case in France or Italy. In these two countries capital as a whole contributed less to the differential in growth than in level; nonresidential structures and equipment and inventories together contributed about as much to growth as to level differences in Italy and contributed more in

27. If the percent of total employment devoted to agriculture is added to the percent of nonfarm employment consisting of proprietors and own-account workers, the difference between the sum of the European percentages and the sum of the United States percentages is found to have been cut by 41 percent in the 14 years from 1950 to 1964 in France, by 64 percent in Germany, and by 35 percent in Italy (where the original gap was largest). This comparison gives a very crude indication of the speed with which the excess cost (over the cost in the United States) of misallocation in Europe was contracting.

France, but dwellings and international assets contributed much less.

The period from 1955 to 1962 was one in which the United States stock of nonresidential capital was increasing rather slowly so that it was especially easy for Europe to narrow the gap between the United States and Europe; subsequently, the growth of capital of this type accelerated in America.

In 1960 the gap between Northwest Europe and the United States in dwellings, nonresidential structures and equipment of enterprises, inventories, and international assets, was equal to almost 1½ years of Northwest European GNP (in United States prices). It could be eliminated over a period of a few decades if a large differential between European and American net saving rates could be developed and maintained. This differential would have to be sufficient to remain large after allowance for the higher relative price of capital goods in Europe, if this price relationship persists.[28] Realistically, it seems that *if* there is any reason to expect the European capital-labor ratio to move toward the American ratio, this reason will remain operative for rather a long time in the future.

3. The education of the labor force occupies a unique position among major growth sources. The American labor force was better educated than the Northwest European labor force in 1960 and its education was increasing more rapidly. Consequently, education makes a positive contribution to the differential in income levels and a negative contribution to the differential in growth rates. Education's contribution to the differential in levels was equal to 14 percent of the total differential in Italy and to 9 or 10 percent in France, Germany, and Northwest Europe as a whole, while its contribution to the differential in growth rates was equal to −5 percent of the total differential in Italy, −11 in France, −35 in Northwest Europe, and −39 in Germany. The European countries as a group are likely to continue to obtain less growth from education than the United States. The differential is likely to continue to be much greater in Germany than in France or Italy.

The difference between the education of the labor force of the United States and that of Northwest Europe is not enormous. But to close the gap in a period measured by less than generations would be extraordinarily difficult because the present tendency is for the gap to widen rather than narrow, and because the education that an individual receives in his youth usually determines his educational background for nearly half a century of labor force participation.[29]

4. Hours of work make a negative contribution to differentials in income levels between Europe and the United States. In 1960 this stemmed both from the difference in full-time hours and from the greater prevalence of part-time employment in the United States. One might expect full-time hours also to make a negative contribution, on the average and under normal conditions, to growth rate differentials as European hours move toward the American standard. But part-time employment not only is much more prevalent in the United States; it also is increasing much more rapidly.

Full-time hours tend to change discretely rather than continuously and can therefore be very important or unimportant in short periods. It has been seen that in 1950–55 there was little change in any of the nine countries. In 1955–62, the period currently under review, there was little change in full-time hours in the United States or France, a substantial decline in all of the remaining European countries, and a very large decline indeed in Germany. The fact that average hours in the United States were being reduced by expansion of voluntary part-time employment and in Italy raised by contraction of involuntary part-time employment further affects the comparisons. In the 1955–62 period the net result of these changes was that hours had a quite different effect in different countries. Their contribution was equal to 9 percent of the adjusted growth rate differential in Italy, 6 percent in France, −7 percent in Northwest Europe as a whole, and −24 percent in Germany.

28. This condition need not be met for capital to contribute to higher growth rates in Europe measured in European prices than in the United States measured in United States prices.

29. In Chapter 8 I noted that the heavy concentration of the European labor force at levels determined by the legal school leaving age is a disadvantage compared to the wide dispersion of educational backgrounds of American workers. This disadvantage will probably be diminishing in countries such as Belgium and France where there has been a postwar upsurge in voluntary school attendance.

One cannot expect this experience to be repeated. German hours are not likely again to be reduced so much in so short a time.[30] French weekly hours are not likely to continue indefinitely to hold at their present level. In Italy remaining involuntary part-time employment is small and the experience of the 1950's cannot be repeated. The increase in voluntary part-time employment is continuing in the United States, has become of some importance in the United Kingdom, and sooner or later may become significant in other countries.

5. The distribution of total hours worked between men and women and among age groups rather surprisingly had a big enough effect in these sensitive comparisons to require mention. This source of difference in average labor quality contributed much more to higher European growth than to the shortfall in European income levels. The comparisons are 19 percent of the growth differential as against 3 of the level differential in Northwest Europe as a whole, 9 percent against 3 in France, 22 percent against 5 in Germany, and 5 against 1 in Italy. The general explanation concerns labor force participation rates. In the United States employment of women and part-time employment of students have been rising. In Europe there has been little increase in the percentage of work done by females, part-time employment of students is unimportant, and increased school attendance has reduced the labor of young people. These trends may well continue for some time. In addition, the age distribution of the population may importantly affect short-term movements. The international movement of labor, particularly the large inflow from East Germany, did so in Germany in the 1950's. The large German differential of 1955–62 is not likely to persist, but short-term aberrations in individual countries are likely.

In all European countries except the Netherlands and Norway, age-sex composition was both less favorable than in the United States to high income per person employed in 1960 and contributed more to growth in both 1955–62 and 1950–62 than it did in the United States. Thus it seems, on statistical

grounds, that with respect to this source a gap is being closed. But this seems to be only coincidence. If there are fundamental factors toward convergence, they are not obvious.[31]

6. Residual productivity—the productivity difference not due to sources separately estimated—and errors and omissions accounted for over half the 1960 difference between the United States and Northwest Europe in adjusted national income per person employed. Among the individual Northwest European countries, including those not shown in Table 21–30, the percentage ranged from 45 in France up to 70 in the United Kingdom. It was smaller, at 35 percent, in Italy only because the absolute gap in other sources—especially resource allocation, education, and capital—was much larger.

In sharp contrast to the dominance of residual productivity in determining differences from the United States in income levels, none of the six countries not shown separately in Table 21–30, nor Germany, appears to have gained appreciably, nor held any important advantage over the United States, in growth from this source from 1955 to 1962. According to the table, to be sure, an amount equal to 11 percent of the net German advantage in growth over the United States (though only 6 percent of the gross contribution made by sources making a positive contribution) stemmed from this source. Even if correct this percentage is small when compared with the 47 percent of the difference in level due to residual productivity. And in absolute terms it amounts to only 0.11 percentage points in the growth rate, or a total gain of 0.8 percent in seven years.[32] Since the net effect of errors in other estimates and omissions from the measure of inputs are included in this amount, the true gain in residual productivity may have been smaller or larger.

In Italy and France the estimates for residual productivity are bigger. The statistical results show that this source, with errors and omissions included, accounted for 21 percent of the growth differential as against 35 percent of the level differential in

---

30. However, the possibility cannot be altogether dismissed. One projection anticipates a 6 percent reduction in hours from 1965 to 1970 (EEC, *Perspectives de Développement Economique dans la* CEE *Jusqu'en 1970*, p. 65 [157]).

31. In particular, there was no tendency for the percentages of females in total employment in the various countries to converge during the period analyzed.

32. Among the countries not shown in the table only the residual for Norway (0.22 points) is larger than this in absolute terms.

Italy, and for 36 percent as against 45 percent in France. For Northwest Europe as a whole I obtain a 27 percent contribution to the growth rate differential—mostly due to the weight of France—and a 56 percent contribution to the differential in level.

Although changes in residual productivity were important in growth only in France and Italy in the 1955–62 period, in all the European countries this source dominates the difference from the United States in levels of national income per person employed. My inability to decompose residual productivity or analyze it satisfactorily is surely the greatest gap in the present study. Any projection of future European growth must be critically affected by the investigator's judgment as to whether this productivity gap will be reduced in the future and, if so, how much and how fast.

On the surface, to reduce the gap greatly would not seem very difficult if the businessmen, workers, and governments of a country really wished and were determined to do so. The American model exists, and American firms and the American government have been quite willing to expose American business operations, institutional arrangements, and all other aspects of the American economy to European observers. These have in fact been widely studied and observed. International organizations have also promoted the diffusion of knowledge. Of course there are costs of transferring American practices and of adapting them to European conditions, but they seem small compared to the potential gains. No one would expect American productivity to be matched overnight, but the time required for change would not seem to be a block to rapid progress. In contrast to this *a priori* impression of possibilities, the historical record up to the early 1960's, at least, suggests that either the desire is lacking or imitation is a very difficult thing; most countries seem to have made little progress. Lack of greater progress cannot be ascribed to ignorance of the international productivity gap; there has been widespread awareness of it throughout the postwar period. Although a comprehensive quantitative study to isolate residual productivity differences in the way attempted here had not been made, there was general recognition that much of the gap between America and Europe in output per man could not be explained by differences in capital, labor quality,

resource allocation, and economies of scale. Such an awareness was present not only with respect to economies as a whole but also with respect to very particular situations; yet little was achieved except in France and perhaps Italy.[33] Even in France the rate at which the gap was closing was rather slow in comparison to the apparent possibilities.[34] Whether European integration or other means of intensifying competition, or government intervention modeled on the French pattern, or some other force, has already begun to overcome this inertia or will do so in the future remains to be seen.

Two general points emerge from this discussion. First, the answer to the question, have the fast growing European countries been getting more growth per person employed than the United States by reducing differentials between themselves and the United States, is obviously "yes"—provided that growth rate differences that disappear when the output of all countries is uniformly valued in United States prices are eliminated, and that the effects of short-term disturbances are also disregarded. Since every income determinant except hours of work contributed to the gap between adjusted American and European income levels, this conclusion would hold no matter what sources had contributed to

33. Two issues of the OEEC *Productivity Measurement Review* [123] contain an interesting study of shirt manufacturing in the Netherlands that seems to illustrate this point. The August 1955 issue reports a detailed study, by department, of the man-minutes used to produce a shirt in 16 United States, 6 Danish, and 15 Dutch establishments. The study was made in the early 1950's. Man-minutes per shirt were greatest in the Netherlands in all four components of labor time distinguished: the cutting room, the sewing department, pressing and packing, and indirect labor. The total time used averaged 33.7 minutes in the United States, 54.5 in Denmark, and 92 in the Netherlands. The *least* efficient plant took 46.1 minutes in the United States and 61.8 in Denmark while the *most* efficient Dutch plant used 75 minutes. The Dutch firms were fully aware of the facts. A team of efficiency experts studied the Dutch factories to see what could be done to raise productivity and how much time could be saved by actions that management could take without making any new investment. A general productivity drive was carried out in the industry.

The August 1956 issue carries quarterly time series from the second quarter of 1952 through the third quarter of 1955 for productivity in each of nine Dutch factories. No extraordinary improvement had occurred.

34. If residual productivity in France was 23 percent below the United States in 1960, a continuous contribution to the French growth rate from this source of 0.80 points (my estimate for the 1955–62 period) would eliminate the gap in the year 1994. The calculation is intended only to give perspective.

faster European growth. But Europe was not narrowing the gap in *all* income determinants; education is a major exception.

Second, the size of the contributions of individual sources to differences in growth rates was not at all similar to the size of their contributions to differences in income levels. The major differences are concerned with resource allocation, capital, education, hours of work, age-sex composition, and residual productivity. The first and last of these seem to me of greatest importance and interest. Reallocation of resources contributed to higher European growth out of all proportion to its contribution to differences in income levels. The situation was the reverse with respect to residual productivity. The great importance of resource allocation stands out if one is considering periods of intermediate length. The course of residual productivity will also be crucial over the decades immediately ahead; in the longer run it will be decisive. Suppose that all other reasons for which European and American incomes per person employed differ were to disappear, but that the residual productivity ratio were to remain as it was in 1960. National income per person employed in Northwest Europe (measured in United States prices) would still be 28 percent below that of the United States.[35]

This section has been concerned with national income per person employed valued in United States prices. Economies of scale associated with income elasticities will continue to be an important determinant of actual growth rates valued in national prices. The future growth of *total* national income will also be greatly influenced by changes in employment. In the United States the labor force will expand even more rapidly than in the past, much more rapidly than in any of the European countries and more than twice as much as in any except the Netherlands. The German and French positions will be interchanged. From 1955 to 1962 Germany had the largest employment increase among all the countries while France had scarcely any increase at all. From 1965 to 1980 the French labor force is expected to increase by 13.5 percent, that of Germany by only 2.9 to 5.5 percent, the range representing alternative assumptions

35. The first column of Table 20–2 gives estimates for individual countries.

about immigration. German employment expansion had already become small by 1963. Norway, like France, had little labor force growth up to 1962 but will be getting appreciable increases. Prospective changes in trend are less pronounced in the other countries. Italy had a small decline in the labor force but a small increase in employment from 1955 to 1962. From 1965 to 1970 a further small decline in the labor force is anticipated and from 1965 to 1980 a small increase is foreseen.[36]

Specific projections of national income are outside the scope of this study. But one can hardly fail to note that in France the employment outlook, the large gains yet to be realized by curtailing agriculture and nonfarm self-employment, the rapid extension of education beyond the compulsory level, and the apparent French ability to cut into the residual productivity gap combine to provide an especially favorable prospect for future rapid growth of national income insofar as the fundamental factors are concerned—although hours changes are likely to become adverse at some point.

Nor can one fail to note that the United Kingdom's uniquely small opportunity to gain by contracting agricultural employment and self-employment, coupled with continuation of small labor force increases, will continue to make it difficult to match continental growth rates unless and until the United Kingdom starts to curtail the gap in residual productivity—a gap that apparently exists between the United Kingdom and not only the United States but also France and Germany.

The basic factors affecting Germany's outlook are quite mixed: Capital was unusually important to German growth in the period analyzed in this study and may continue to be; employment expansion, so important in that period, has nearly stopped; education was and, in comparison to other

36. Labor force projections for the countries covered in this study, except Belgium and Denmark, are given in OECD, *Demographic Trends 1965–1980 in Western Europe and North America*, p. 60 [I24]. The implied growth rates of the projected labor force from 1965 to 1980 are: United States 1.74; Netherlands 1.21; France 0.85; Norway 0.64; United Kingdom 0.29; Germany 0.19 or 0.36; Italy 0.11. Simple extrapolation of the male and female labor forces of Denmark by projected population of working age yields 0.41. The implied rate for Northwest Europe, excluding Belgium, is 0.46 or 0.41, depending on which German rate is used. A study by F. Rogiers implies a Belgian labor force growth rate from 1965 to 1975 of 0.41 (*Revue belge de Securité sociale*, December 1965, p. 30 [P38]).

major countries, will continue to be an unfavorable factor; gains from resource reallocation will continue to be sizable for a time but they can hardly be so large as in the period analyzed; hours reduction, which significantly curtailed growth in the period analyzed, is unlikely to be as adverse again in the future.

The outstanding feature of the Italian position is the very large gain yet to be realized from contraction of agriculture and nonfarm self-employment. Italy should be able to continue to narrow the gap between herself and Northwest Europe in income per person employed, and perhaps to do so more rapidly as the opportunities for further gains from reallocation of resources diminish in other countries. The outlook is also for a good rise in the educational qualifications of the labor force. Employment changes will continue to be negligible.

So long as the opportunity to gain from reallocation of resources remains large, continental Western Europe as a whole should be able to obtain larger increases than the United States in national income per person employed, measured in United States prices. If Europe finds ways to reduce the gap in residual productivity higher growth rates will be possible for a very long time. And whatever differentials are present when national income is measured in United States prices, they will continue to be much magnified when each country measures national income in its own prices.

An Epilogue for American Readers

In the first of the television debates between John F. Kennedy and Richard M. Nixon that were held during the Presidential election campaign of 1960, then-candidate Kennedy stated that he was not satisfied with the lowest rate of growth among all industrialized nations, that it was time to get America moving again. This theme recurred throughout his campaign.

At that time Kennedy drew no distinction between the changes in potential output that determine long-term growth and the short-term changes in actual output that accompany the phases of the business cycle. In the autumn of 1960 the United States was entering a period of recession and comparisons of year-to-year and other short-term changes, which his speeches featured, were especially unfavorable to the United States. Since 1960 the United States has been in a period of rapid expansion. Underutilization of labor and capital were being eliminated and comparisons of national income increases became particularly favorable to the United States. They have led some to observe that whereas Americans formerly looked to Europe for guidance as to how to obtain rapid growth, the shoe is now on the other foot. But comparisons of short periods that begin with 1960 or thereabouts are as irrelevant to growth of productive potential or long-term growth as comparisons that ended at that time.

If comparisons are made over a period long enough to iron out fluctuations in the business cycle, but not extending back beyond the postwar period, Kennedy's original statement that United States growth was the lowest among industrialized countries needs little amendment. Among countries covered in this study, only the United Kingdom and perhaps Belgium are exceptions (the position of Belgium depends on the exact period compared). In the period ahead, comparisons will be influenced by the accident that age distributions will yield a much larger employment increase in the United States than in Europe, but the United States can match European growth rates of income *per person employed* over an *extended* period only if Europe fails dismally to grasp its opportunities.

The analysis of this book indicates that the low past and prospective standing of the United States in the "International Growth Rate League" is not an indication of poor economic performance. Rather, it has come about because the same sort of changes produce larger percentage increases in national income in Europe than they do in the United States and, in addition, there are opportunities to increase efficiency in European countries that do not exist to the same degree in the United States.

The European countries have higher growth rates but they have not, on balance, done more in any relevant sense to obtain growth. It is worth recapitulating some of the data that support this conclusion.

Consider labor, which represents 75 or 80 percent of total input. From 1950 to 1962 the United States increased employment more than any other country except Germany. Insofar as changes in employment simply reflect changing numbers in the working ages, this is, to be sure, hardly germane. But the employment increase in the United States was so big only because large numbers of women and children and young people who were also attending school entered the labor force. Given the demographic factors, the American people were doing more to add to the numbers at work than the people of any other country.[37]

Hours of work and education are key determinants of the quality of a year's work and both can be altered by individual and social decisions. Only France did not reduce the hours of full-time workers appreciably more than the United States.[38] No European country matched the increase in the education of the labor force that was achieved by the United States. For all the Northwest European countries this is shown by any measure I can devise, and Italy is an exception only if comparisons are based on the percentage change in years of education, a very poor measure.[39] It is possible that the

gap between the pace of work on the continent and that in the United States has been reduced by increased fluidity and improved motivation on the continent; but even if this speculation is correct, it indicates only that the continental countries were eliminating a deficiency in comparison with the United States.

Consider capital, which represents 15 or 20 percent of total input. Here, the situation was mixed. Percentage increases in the stock of nonresidential structures and equipment and inventories were generally larger in the European countries than in the United States and Europe obtained more growth from this source. The difference was accentuated by particularly low capital formation in the United States during the period of deficient demand from 1958 to 1962—a deficiency subsequently remedied—but it would probably have been present in any case. One cannot easily judge the extent to which larger percentage increases in the stock of this type of capital in Europe stem from the difference between European and American conditions. The much lower capital-labor ratio in Europe is perhaps relevant, and in earlier chapters the complications introduced by differences in the absolute level of the stock and by differences in relative prices were discussed. By any simple test, however, the United States has done less than Europe to stimulate growth by investment in nonresidential structures and equipment and inventories. This appears to be the only important field in which the United States was doing less.[40]

---

37. The large employment increase in Germany was due to a combination of the age distribution, elimination of unemployment which was very large in 1950 as a result of wartime dislocation, and a very large influx of workers from East Germany, supplemented by admission of foreign workers. Except that the United States could have had a freer immigration policy, the German experience reflects conditions not present in the United States.

38. The entry into the labor force of women and student workers of course depressed United States labor quality indexes for both hours and age-sex composition, but nevertheless made a net contribution to total labor input and to total and per capita national income, though it subtracted from income per person employed.

39. Education of the labor force reflects changes in educational effort over a long period of time. The difference between the education of those leaving the labor force and those entering it determines the movement of these measures.

The education of the labor force changed from 1950 to 1962 primarily because workers who reached retirement age in the intervening period were replaced by young persons. Consequently, changes in the education of the labor force are determined by changes in the education of young people that took place over more than half a century.

However, the reader is also reminded of the comparison attempted between the amount of education being received by young people in recent years and the amount held by the average member of the labor force. The education of young people exceeds that of labor force members more in the United States than it does in any of the European countries except Italy, where the educational level of the labor force is very low, the legal school leaving age has been greatly increased, and compliance with school attendance laws much improved.

40. The contribution of nonresidential structures and equipment and inventories to the 1950–62 growth rate was much the largest in Germany, where it was 0.8 percentage points greater than in the United States. (Nowhere else did the difference exceed 0.4 points.) It should be noted that the United States growth rate would not have been 0.8 points

The United States had exceptionally large increases in the stock of dwellings and in international assets, and obtained more growth than any of the European countries from these sources. Over the 1950–62 period these sources almost entirely offset the bigger contribution from domestic business capital obtained by Northwest Europe as a whole, and the offset was more than half in all the individual countries except Germany and the Netherlands. Investment in dwellings contributed less to growth, as measured, than an equal amount of investment in enterprise capital might have but it is not clear that it contributed less to welfare. The contribution made by international investment should not be overlooked. If, in the future, American investment in Europe is impeded by restrictions imposed in response to the American balance of payments problem, or by European opposition, it will be unfortunate for growth in both areas.

The total percentage of national income saved in the form of physical capital was higher in Europe (especially Germany, the Netherlands, and Norway) than in the United States when percentages for each country are based on output valued in its own prices, though generally not when output in all countries is valued in the same prices.[41] The former is the more appropriate measure of effort, the latter is more pertinent to raising the national income.

Consider resource allocation. The United States has been as successful as any European country and more successful than most in reducing misallocation associated with agriculture and nonfarm self-employment of a fringe character. It has not made comparable changes in barriers to international trade but the potential gains available, especially

from any action the United States could take without European reduction of barriers to United States exports, were slight.

Finally, consider advances in knowledge. The United States has devoted far more of its resources to technical research and development than any of the European countries. It also seems clear that it has devoted more attention both within business and in schools of business administration to advances in business organization and management practices. In this area the European effort has concentrated upon learning what the United States is already doing and upon adapting and stimulating the adoption of American practices.

The conclusion, I believe, is clear. Although most of the European countries have achieved higher growth rates than the United States, this was not because they were doing more to obtain growth. They were able to secure higher growth rates only because they were operating in a different environment. Conditions were very different with respect to factor proportions; to misallocation of resources; to the existing level of technology, management, and general efficiency in the use of resources; and to economies of scale. Some have supposed that the United States could have matched the growth rates of European countries if only Americans had done as the Europeans did. I conclude that this is simply not so.

Comparisons with the postwar growth rates of European countries, therefore, do not provide grounds for dissatisfaction with the American growth record. The point needs stressing because the conditions that enabled Europe to obtain higher growth rates are not exhausted. Aside from short-term aberrations Europe should be able to report higher growth rates, at least in national income per person employed, for a long time. Americans should expect this and not be disturbed by it. Nothing in this analysis suggests that the conditions making for higher European growth would continue to operate if the European countries were to reach American levels of national income per person employed.

A comparison provided earlier should be recalled for perspective. In 1960, national income per person employed was 69 percent larger in the United States than in Northwest Europe and 150 percent

---

higher than it was if the stock of these types of capital could have been increased by as large a percentage as in Germany. A better estimate is around 0.5. Capital is much more abundant relative to labor in the United States, its earnings relative to labor earnings are lower in the United States, and each 1 percent increase in capital brings a smaller increase in national income in the United States than it does in Germany.

41. In the mid-1960's the United States was in an investment boom. Mainly for this reason, but also because of retardation in some European countries, comparisons of investment ratios became more favorable to the United States than they were in the period examined in this study. The rate of investment in nonresidential structures and equipment reached in the United States in 1966 is not, however likely to be sustainable.

larger than in Italy. This is the comparison most favorable to Europe, obtained when the output of all countries is measured in United States prices. If, with equal validity, the prices of European countries are used in the comparisons, United States national income per person employed was 117 percent larger than that of Northwest Europe and 317 percent larger than that of Italy. Thus, the level of output per person employed in the United States is still far above levels in Europe. In percentage terms these differentials have been narrowing. But from 1950 to 1964 none of the eight European countries narrowed the absolute gap when output is uniformly measured in United States prices. This means, of course, that from 1950 to 1964 none achieved a larger absolute increase than the United States in national income per person employed. This situa-

tion cannot be expected to continue indefinitely and, indeed, the comparisons showed larger increases after 1955 in France and Norway than in the United States. But it will be a long time before American levels will be approached.

The performance of the American economy is not, of course, all that it might be. I doubt that inability to produce and distribute a large and rising total of goods and services—the aspect of economic life with which this book is concerned—should be listed among its defects. But an appropriate evaluation would have to be based on a comparison of United States achievements with United States possibilities. It cannot be based on casual comparisons of the United States growth rate with the rates of countries having quite different opportunities for growth.

Appendixes

≫ APPENDIX A ≪

Derivation of Growth Rates of National Income and Gross National Product at Factor Cost, Constant Prices

The growth rates shown in Chapter 2 are compound interest rates computed from indexes of national income or GNP in constant prices in the terminal years of the subperiods. Growth rates were computed for the 1950–55, 1955–62, and 1955–64 periods, and averaged, using the length of the periods as weights, to obtain 1950–62 and 1950–64 rates.[1]

It was necessary to link indexes of national income and product in several cases. German indexes for 1950–60 exclude the Saar and West Berlin whereas the 1960–64 indexes include them. United States indexes for 1950–60 exclude Alaska and Hawaii, whereas the 1960–64 indexes include them. French data are available on one statistical basis for 1950–59, and on a slightly different one for 1959–64. The series were linked at 1959. As further described below, two series for Belgium were linked at 1953.

Growth rates for the 1955–62 and 1955–64 periods are based on national product or income measured in 1958 prices. Those for 1950–55 are based on national product or income expressed in 1953 prices in Belgium, 1954 prices in Denmark,

France, Germany, the Netherlands, and Italy, 1955 prices in Norway, and 1958 prices in the United States and the United Kingdom.[2] (Detailed deflation of the original estimates by national statistical offices was based on weights for the following years: Belgium, 1953; Germany and Italy, 1954; Denmark and Norway, 1955; France, 1956 for the 1950–59 period and 1959 for 1959–64; Netherlands, United States, and United Kingdom, 1958, except that the Netherlands data for 1950–55 were based on 1953. The original data were converted, when necessary, by either the national agency or the Organisation for Economic Co-operation and Development (OECD) to a 1954 or 1958 base by reweighting only broad expenditure groups.)

Several countries derive more or less independent estimates of national product by alternative approaches (the so-called "expenditure," "income," and "output" methods). The series used here are

1. As explained in Chapter 1, the present study analyzes the period from 1950 to 1962 but growth rates are given through 1964.

2. The original intention was to use 1954 prices for 1950–55 and 1958 prices thereafter for all countries. This choice was dictated by the fact that OECD had published data in 1954 prices in OECD, *Statistics of National Accounts, 1950–1961* [139], and, when it shifted to 1958 prices the following year, provided data back only to 1955. Subsequently, several countries revised their estimates for the 1950–55 period and the revised estimates were not available in 1954 prices in accordance with OECD definitions.

those given in, or comparable to, the OECD summary tables labeled "National Product or Expenditure," except for the United Kingdom (see below).

Description of Estimates Used

National accounts data used in the computation of growth rates and for analysis throughout this book are, in general, those published by OECD and the Statistical Office of the European Communities (OSCE). National sources were used extensively for supplementary detail, and also to obtain revised data not republished by the international agencies.

For the period 1955–64, GNP data expressed in 1958 prices were obtained for all countries from OECD, *National Accounts Statistics, 1955–1964* [I35], except that French data for 1959 on the old statistical basis and German data excluding Berlin and the Saar in 1960 are from OECD, *General Statistics* (January 1965 [I28]).

For the 1950–55 period data in 1954 prices were obtained for Denmark, France, the Netherlands, and Italy from OECD, *Statistics of National Accounts, 1950–1961*. Revised data for the United States in 1958 prices conforming to OECD definitions were provided by the United States Department of Commerce. Revised data for Germany in 1954 prices conforming to OECD definitions were obtained from Federal Statistical Office, *Wirtschaft und Statistik* (October 1963, December 1963, and January 1964 [G18]). Revised data for Norway conforming to OECD definitions were obtained from Central Bureau of Statistics, *Nasjonalregnskap, 1865–1960* [G33]. For the United Kingdom, revised data in 1958 prices conforming to OECD definitions were obtained from the Central Statistical Office, *National Income and Expenditures, 1965* [G38].[3] For Belgium, revised data in 1953 prices conforming to OECD definitions for the period 1954–55 were obtained from the National Institute of Statistics, *Bulletin de Statistique* (July–August 1965 [G3]), and for 1953 were provided directly by the Institute. Official Belgian statistics begin only in 1953. The Department of Applied Economics of the Free University of Brussels (DULBEA), which

formerly prepared the Belgian national accounts, generously made available 1950–52 estimates comparable to those published for 1953 by the Institute. Since the Institute subsequently revised its 1953 estimates, it was necessary to link the DULBEA and Institute series at 1953.

Gross National Product at Factor Cost at Constant Prices was provided by OECD and other sources just described for all countries except France and Germany; for France and Germany constant price data are shown only at constant market prices.[4] For Germany, where the Statistical Office publishes by a twelve-industry breakdown (counting income from abroad) both GNP at factor cost in current prices and GNP at market prices in constant 1954 and 1958 prices, it was possible in the present study to reweight at the twelve-industry level of detail. For France, GNP at factor cost in current prices in the base year (1954 or 1958) was extrapolated, with reweighting only of net income from abroad, by GNP at constant market prices. Although OECD shows GNP at factor cost at constant prices for the United States and the Netherlands, weighting for these countries also is actually at market prices.

Two adjustments were made to OECD data for the United Kingdom: (1) for gross domestic product at factor cost in constant prices, OECD estimates obtained by the "expenditure" and "output" methods were averaged; and (2) net income from abroad in 1958 prices as given in *National Accounts Statistics, 1955–1964,* was not used. Instead, this series was obtained by deflating the OECD current price series given in that source by the index of import prices. This corresponds to the United Kingdom procedure for deflation of current price estimates based on its own definition, a procedure which OECD also followed for the United Kingdom in its publications prior to 1965. In *National Accounts Statistics, 1955–1964,* property income received from abroad was deflated by import prices and property income paid to abroad by the implicit deflator for gross domestic product; the two

---

3. See below for reference to property income from abroad.

4. OECD uses depreciation computed at market prices in deriving GNP at factor cost. The procedure causes overstatement of the level of GNP at factor cost by the amount of depreciation charged against indirect taxes (less subsidies) imposed on depreciable capital assets. The overstatement, which can hardly be large, is not present in net national product at factor cost (national income).

deflators diverge greatly and this procedure yields an appreciably larger increase in deflated net income from abroad from 1955 to 1962 than the British procedure adopted here.[5] The actual figures I use for the United Kingdom gross national product at factor cost in 1958 prices are as follows: 1950: £ 17,432 million; 1955: 19,645; 1960: 22,259; 1962: 23,184; and 1964: 25,347. For net property income from abroad in 1958 prices: 1950: £462 million; 1955: 163; 1960: 273; 1962: 388; and 1964: 439.[6]

After the statistical work for this study was completed, Italian statistics were revised. The growth rates analyzed in detail in this study were little affected. The 1955–62 growth rates of total national income and national income per person employed given in Tables 2–1 and 2–2 were each lowered by 0.1 percentage points, as was the 1955–62 growth rate of national income per capita; however, the growth rate of GNP was reduced by 0.3 points. Over the 1955–64 period, the national income growth rates—total, per person employed, and per capita— were lowered by 0.2 points. The revised data are from the Italian reply to the 1966 OECD national accounts questionnaire.

National Income at Factor Cost in Constant Prices was obtained by deducting depreciation in constant prices from GNP at factor cost in constant prices.[7] This required compilation of constant price depreciation series.

Constant price depreciation series with various base years are published in accordance with OECD definitions in the official national accounts of Denmark, Germany, the Netherlands, the United Kingdom, and Italy for all years, and unpublished estimates were also available for France, Norway (except for the single year 1950), and Belgium (except 1950–52); the gaps were filled by the author's estimates.[8] Most of these estimates were also available in 1958 prices from country submissions to OECD. When it was necessary to shift base years, these constant price series were used to extrapolate depreciation at current replacement cost in the base year desired.

For the United States, the Office of Business Economics, Department of Commerce, has prepared a variety of estimates of capital consumption, valued both at current replacement cost and at 1954 prices, based on alternative assumptions with respect to service lives and depreciation patterns. The estimates based on Bulletin F lives and straight line depreciation were selected and used in the same way as the corresponding estimates for the European countries mentioned above.[9] However, the available depreciation series were consistent with the national accounts as they stood prior to the revisions of the national accounts published in the *Survey of Current Business* (August 1965 [G63]). They were adjusted, with residential and other depreciation treated separately, by the same percentages that capital consumption estimates at "book" values were revised.[10]

---

5. Appearance of this particular OECD series was more or less an accident. The United Kingdom did not provide deflated property income from abroad in its submission for the January 1965 issue of *General Statistics* [I28]; OECD adopted its own deflation procedure which, though recommended by OECD, is not generally followed by other countries.

6. The figures given in *National Accounts Statistics, 1955–1964* [I35], in 1958 prices are: 1955: £93 million; 1960: 281; 1962: 427; and 1964: 471. (The comparable unpublished figures for 1950 are 405 at 1958 prices and 393 at current prices.)

7. The weighting implicit in this procedure is not ideal. The preferable procedure, where weighting is by industry, is to extrapolate base year national income at factor cost originating in each industry by net national product at constant market prices originating in the industry, and then to sum the industry estimates to obtain national income at factor cost at constant prices. The estimates used here are (at best) obtained by extrapolating base year GNP at factor cost in each industry by GNP at constant market prices originating in the industry; summing the industry estimates to obtain GNP at factor cost at constant prices; and then deducting depreciation at constant prices for the entire economy to obtain national income at factor cost at constant prices. However, it is not likely that the preferred procedure, which

could not be attempted here, would yield appreciably different estimates of growth rates for any economy that is covered here.

8. For Norway, the percentage increase in depreciation was assumed to be the same from 1950 to 1951 as from 1951 to 1952. For Belgium, the ratio of depreciation to gross domestic product in 1953 prices was assumed to be the same in 1950 as in 1953.

9. Bulletin F (1942 edition) of the Bureau of Internal Revenue was intended to provide guidelines of useful service lives of depreciable property that could be used for tax purposes.

10. Department of Commerce data for depreciation cover only private capital assets. OECD depreciation data for the United States include in addition an allowance for depreciation on government-owned assets; this is assumed to be equal each year to the value of new construction of public buildings (not all public construction), except buildings constructed for the Atomic Energy Commission. Accordingly, the value of such construction in constant prices was added here to the constant price series for private depreciation.

A Supplementary Note on the Treatment of Proprietors' Income in the Derivation of Labor Shares

Estimates of total proprietors' income, required in Chapter 4 for the allocation of income shares between capital and labor, were not directly available from the national accounts of the Netherlands, Norway, Denmark, Germany, and Italy. They were derived in the following manner.

Both the Netherlands and Norway provide partial estimates of proprietors' income. The Netherlands series covers agriculture and the professions. Proprietors' income in other industries is combined with directors' fees and income of pensioners in published data. The three components were obtained separately for 1957, and the 1957 percentage allocation was applied in other years to derive estimates of the separate components. The estimates of proprietors' income (about two-thirds of the total) were added to the estimates for agriculture and the professions to obtain total proprietors' income. Directors' fees were added to employee compensation. The Norwegian proprietors' income series covers agriculture, forestry and fisheries, restaurants, and substantially all the service industries (United States definition) including the professions. Proprietors' income in other industries was estimated to equal 9 percent of national income in all years, a percentage considered reasonable by a Norwegian expert.

The national accounts of Germany and Denmark combine all proprietors' income with private income in the form of interest, dividends, and net rents.[1] The ratio of dividends, interest, and net rents to national income in these two countries was assumed to be the same in each year as the simple average of the corresponding ratios for that year in Belgium, France, the United Kingdom, and the United States. Proprietors' income was then obtained by deducting estimated dividends, interest, and net rents from the combined shares.[2]

For the year 1960 the shares (as a percentage of national income) of employee compensation, estimated proprietors' income, and all other income,

1. In the case of Denmark, the published data after 1952 also combine undistributed corporate profits before taxes with these shares. These were estimated in subsequent years from independent data for the surplus, net of depreciation, of joint stock companies, and national accounts data for direct taxes on corporations, and deducted.

2. The estimate thus obtained for Germany could be compared with estimates of proprietors' "withdrawals" made by the German Central Bank. An implied estimate of "entrepreneurial saving" was calculated; over the whole period it averaged 1.5 percent of the national income (and 6.4 percent of proprietors' income). This does not seem unreasonable, but the most detailed saving series in the German national accounts that includes this item has so many other components that the comparison provides no particularly useful check.

and my derived estimate of the labor share (computed as equal to employee compensation plus 63 percent of proprietors' income except in the United States), are as follows:

	Employee compensation	Proprietors' income	All other income	Labor share
United States[a]	72.6	11.3	16.1	80.1
Belgium	57.1	26.1	16.8	73.5
Denmark	58.0	26.9[c]	15.0[c]	74.9
France	58.3	29.5	12.2	76.9
Germany	60.8	19.9[c]	19.3[c]	73.3
Netherlands	59.5[b]	22.2[d]	21.2[d]	73.5
Norway	65.2	19.9[d]	14.9[d]	77.7
United Kingdom	72.5	8.5	19.0	77.9
Italy	52.1	(31.6)[c]	(16.3)[c]	(72.0)

a. National income roughly adjusted to measure depreciation at current replacement cost.
b. Adjusted to include directors' compensation.
c. Estimated.
d. Partially estimated.

Italy is yet to be discussed. The only important income component available separately is employee compensation. This is persistently a much lower percentage of national income than in any other country. Proprietors' income is undoubtedly a high proportion of national income. If it were as high as the highest of the other countries in 1960 (29.5 percent in France), my procedure would yield a labor share of 70.7 percent, below that for any other country. Were the Italian percentage for income *other* than employee compensation and proprietors' income as low as the lowest of the other countries (12.2 in France, and much below any other), this would imply that proprietors' income is 35.7 percent of national income, and yield a labor share of 74.6 percent. Such an estimate would bring the Italian labor share within the range obtained for the Northwest European countries, but it seems on the high side. Other studies suggest there is reason to believe profits in Italy have been especially high and the labor share correspondingly low, at least until 1962.[3] As a guess I suppose the labor share in Italy to be 72 percent throughout the period. This implies (by working backward) that proprietors' income in 1960 was 31.6 percent.[4]

3. Also, as shown in Table 4–1, income from housing is larger than in most countries.
4. The assumption stated yields estimates (shown in Table 4–2) that the labor share of national income excluding dwellings and income from abroad averaged 73.1 percent in 1950–54, 74.6 in 1955–59, and 75.6 in 1960–62. Giuseppe

Agriculture is more important in Italy than elsewhere, which supports the implication of an exceptionally large percentage for proprietors' income.

The estimates of the labor share, even aside from the assumed Italian figure, are obviously crude. How bad are they likely to be because of errors in the measurement or allocation of proprietors' income? Estimates of proprietors' income are usually weak estimates in the national accounts, and for Germany and Denmark, and to some extent the Netherlands and Norway, it was necessary to estimate the amounts actually included in the national income estimates. For each percentage point error in the proprietors' income share of national income, the error in the labor share is, by the allocation procedure followed, 0.37 percentage points if the compensating error is in employee compensation, and 0.63 percentage points if it is in corporate earnings, interest, and net rent. The latter is the more likely, at least in countries for which proprietors' income is supplied either in whole or in part by the author's estimate. In such instances, an error in the proprietors' income estimate of, say, 4 percent of national income would mean 2.5 percentage points in the labor share. A larger error in my estimate of the proprietors' income actually included (explicitly or implicitly) in national income does not appear very likely. This, of course, does not take into account the possibility of error in the national estimates themselves.

The more basic question concerns the division of proprietors' income between the return for the work performed by the proprietor and unpaid members of his family, on the one hand, and the return on his investment in capital and land, together with profit or loss, on the other. Since actual data cannot exist, the only possible solution is the adoption of some conventional assumption. The assumption in the United States estimates, as stated in Chapter 4, was that the division of national income between labor and other resources was the same in unincor-

de Meo (in *Banca Nazionale del Lavoro Quarterly Review*, March 1966, p. 47 [P4]) has estimated that with government also excluded, the labor share was 74.9 in 1951–54, 79.1 in 1955–59, and 78.6 in 1960–62. His procedure assumes earnings of the independent workers to be the same as those of dependent workers "of the same occupational categories." This procedure normally yields larger labor shares than the procedure I have used in other countries.

porated firms as in corporations. As already noted, this implied that on the average in the 1950's 63 percent of proprietors' income represented a return for labor. The procedure could not be duplicated for European countries, and it was assumed that 63 percent of proprietors' income in each of them also represented a return to labor; whereas the United States figure varied from year to year, the 63 percent was applied to Europe uniformly in all years.[5]

It is of course evident that the "labor share" figures have a greater synthetic component and must be inherently less satisfactory where proprietors' income is large, as in Belgium, Denmark, and France, than where it is small, as in the United Kingdom and the United States. It is also evident that assignment of a different uniform percentage of proprietors' income to labor would affect the relative position of the countries. Since I suspect 63 percent may strike some readers as a low proportion of proprietors' income to allocate to labor, the effect of using a very much higher allocation—80 percent —may be of interest. The results of the two alter-

native allocations of labor as a percentage of national income for 1960 are as follows:

	Based on an allocation of proprietors' income to labor of	
	63 percent	80 percent
United States	79.7[a]	81.5
Belgium	73.5	78.0
Denmark	74.9	79.5
France	76.9	81.9
Germany	73.3	76.7
Netherlands	73.5	77.3
Norway	77.7	81.1
United Kingdom	77.9	79.3
Italy	72.0	77.4

a. This differs from the actual estimate of 80.1 shown above because the allocation of proprietors' income for the United States was derived independently each year.

Use of this much higher allocation would raise the 1960 labor share (and reduce the other shares) by amounts ranging from 1.4 percentage points in the United Kingdom to 5.0 points in France (and 5.4 in Italy). Differences among countries in the labor share would be narrowed. The simple average of the ratios in the nine countries would be raised 3.7 points, from 75.5 to 79.2. If the labor allocation were dropped from 63 percent to 46 percent, the change in each country would be of the same size, but in the opposite direction.

It is evident that the general level of the labor shares is not highly sensitive to even a rather large difference in allocation. Intercountry comparisons are considerably affected by the choice of an allocation percentage. In addition, of course, the correct percentage may vary among countries.

5. For the United Kingdom alone the United States procedure could have been duplicated. For 1960 (the only year tested) the percentage obtained was 57. Use of 57 rather than 63 percent to allocate proprietors' income would lower the United Kingdom share by 0.5 percentage points. I am indebted to Geoffrey Dean for this calculation.

It may be noted that H. Glesjer's estimates of the Belgian labor share in 1953 and 1957 are practically the same as those obtained by my procedure when account is taken of revisions in the Belgian national accounts subsequent to publication of his article (in *Cahiers Economiques de Bruxelles*, No. 10, 1961, pp. 304–05 [P9]).

Sources and Evaluation of Employment Statistics

The principal source of annual labor force and employment data for years beginning with 1955 is the OECD publication, *Manpower Statistics, 1954–1964* [I32]. Where it is complete, this source provides all the data shown in Table 5–1. The starting point for 1950 data is *Manpower Statistics, 1950–1962* [I32].[1] However, the data for several countries were revised between the earlier and later publications; it was necessary to obtain 1950 estimates corresponding to those for later years from national sources that originate the series (Norway and the United States) or to introduce minor adjustments (United Kingdom). The Dutch Central Planning Bureau provided in February 1966 a revised series which was used for all years.

Omissions in OECD Data

Manpower Statistics, 1950–1962 omits all statistics for Italy for the years 1950 through 1953. Moreover, I did not use the estimates of Italian civilian labor force and employment in 1954–58

given in the OECD publications. Those data are based on sample surveys of households, similar to surveys conducted monthly in the United States. This method can yield large erratic movements due to sampling fluctuation and to shifting seasonal patterns unless the annual figures are the averages of several surveys during the year. The Italian figures for 1954, 1955, 1956, and 1958 report the results of only a single survey in each instance, and those for 1957 the average of two. These surveys, furthermore, were taken in different months of the year. Prior to 1959 the data are clearly erratic. The 1959–64 figures, in contrast, are averages of four monthly surveys.

The 1950 and 1955 estimates of Italian employment and unemployment given in Table 5–1 were obtained by extrapolating backwards the 1959 data in *Manpower Statistics, 1954–1964*. The series used for farm and nonfarm employment, excluding casual workers, were prepared by the Society for the Industrial Development of South Italy (SVIMEZ).[2] Estimates of casual workers and unemployment are unpublished estimates by the Italian Social Science

---

1. These sources omit all Danish data for 1950–54 and most of the details for later years, but figures comparable to those that are published in *Manpower Statistics* were obtained directly from Danish sources (except for estimates of the armed forces).

2. *L'aumento dell'occupazione in Italia dal 1950 al 1957* [G21]. Estimates for 1958 and 1959 were obtained from the Italian SSRC study group.

Research Council study group. Data published by OECD for 1955 were used to divide casual workers between farm and nonfarm components.

OECD also omits 1950 data for France. The 1955 estimates of the French labor force and employment were extrapolated to 1950 using data of unpublished series furnished by the National Institute of Statistics and Economic Studies (INSEE).

The OECD publications provide only fragmentary data for Denmark; but for the 1950–60 period, all data were available, by sex, from Danish sources, except for data for the armed forces. Numbers in the armed forces were estimated and deducted from published figures for total employment and nonagricultural wage and salary employment to obtain civilian components. After 1961 full detail needed for the estimates was not available and some detailed components are the author's estimates.[3]

For the Netherlands, data provided by the Central Planning Bureau in February 1966 were used for all years. The series is a statistical revision of that carried in *Manpower Statistics, 1950–1962*. Breakdowns by sex and the division between proprietors and unpaid family workers are the author's estimates, except that the 1962 breakdown of the total labor force by sex is taken from *Manpower Statistics, 1954–1964*. It is the only year in which the two sources are in agreement for total labor force.

Manpower Statistics, 1954–1964, includes the Saar with Germany throughout the period, and West Berlin beginning with 1960. Table 5–1 also incorporates both areas beginning with 1960 but, for comparability with national income data, both are excluded prior to that date. Data excluding the Saar and Berlin were available for 1950–59 in *Wirtschaft und Statistik* (January 1960 and October 1960 [G18]). To obtain similar estimates for 1960, which are needed for an overlap with the 1960–64 series, I used the same figures for employment in the Saar as were used by the Federal Statistical Office for 1959. The estimates excluding the Saar and West Berlin are given for 1960 in Table C–1.

Certain other details were also missing from

3. The principal aggregates for Denmark are published in Labor Market Council, *Beretning om Arbejdsmarkedsrådets Virksomhed* [G5]. Supplementary data were obtained by correspondence in January and April 1966.

TABLE C–1

Labor Force and Employment Data for 1960 Comparable to 1950 and 1955

Labor force category	United States[a]	Northwest Europe[b]	Germany[b]
Total labor force	**72,820**	**81,349**	**25,098**
Male	49,317	53,748	15,807
Female	23,503	27,601	9,291
Unemployment	3,913	1,034	232
Total employment	68,906	80,315	24,866
Armed forces	2,514	1,984	290
Civilian employment	66,392	78,331	24,576
Male	44,303	51,059	15,360
Female	22,088	27,272	9,216
Agriculture, forestry, hunting, and fishing	5,696	10,214	3,575
Wage and salary workers	1,839	2,415	524
Employers and own-account workers	2,802	4,030	1,154
Unpaid family workers	1,055	3,769	1,897
Male	433	992	376
Female	621	2,777	1,521
Nonagricultural activities	60,697	68,118	21,001
Wage and salary workers	53,740	60,251	18,313
Employers and own-account workers	6,344	6,589	2,015
Unpaid family workers	613	1,278	673
Male	91	230	89
Female	522	1,048	584

Sources: United States: *Special Labor Force Report*, No. 14, April 1961 [G70]; unpublished data provided by the Bureau of Labor Statistics; author's estimates based on detailed data for Alaska and Hawaii in one month. Northwest Europe: Table 5–1C except Germany. Germany: author's adjustment, to exclude Saar employment, of data given in OECD, *Manpower Statistics, 1954–1964* [I32].
a. Excludes Alaska and Hawaii.
b. Excludes the Saar and West Berlin.

Manpower Statistics data.[4] Such details were estimated using whatever scattered sources were available. Since these omissions often result from inability of the national source to provide data on a basis comparable to the OECD statistics, it is evident that most of these estimates are crude.

4. For Belgium, proprietors and unpaid family workers are combined in the breakdown between agricultural and nonagricultural industries. (OECD, *Manpower Statistics, 1950–1962* [I32] actually classifies all unpaid family workers in nonagricultural activities, but the Belgian population census shows most of them actually employed in agriculture in 1947. OECD, *Manpower Statistics, 1954–1964* [I32] dropped the division.)
For France, the division between employers and own-account workers, and unpaid family workers, is given only for 1954 and 1962.
For the Netherlands, employers and own-account workers are combined with unpaid family workers throughout. In addition, breakdowns by sex are given only for 1954–57.
The breakdown of unpaid family workers by sex is omitted in the OECD compilation for 1950 and missing in several countries in later years.

Comparability of National Data

The general level of all the estimates—except the Dutch and, in part, the British—is based upon censuses or sample surveys of the population. Hence, the estimates correspond to the labor force concept which counts people rather than jobs.[5] The labor force and employment definitions and data are, nevertheless, only approximately comparable from country to country. There may be appreciable differences in the criteria actually applied to determine who is to be counted in the labor force, as well as in the enumeration of unemployment.

The greatest source of possible incomparability in employment estimates relates to the counting of unpaid family workers, and some analysts have supposed this difficulty to be so great that they have rejected the use of employment data for international comparisons.

In Table C–2 the number of unpaid family workers in the employment totals is related to the total population of working age and to the total labor force. These percentages vary greatly from country to country. Differences stem from several sources with different implications.

Some countries omit certain categories entirely, but in each case the reason is that their number is thought unimportant. In Denmark, only working wives are classified as unpaid family workers but this does not mean that others are omitted from total employment. Rather, children and other unpaid relatives (who are believed to be rare because there are tax advantages in paying male family workers) are classified as wage and salary workers. Norway counts no unpaid family workers outside agriculture because they "are of rather small importance" and difficult to estimate. The United Kingdom omits all unpaid family workers from the estimates reported for *Manpower Statistics* because,

5. The Dutch estimates represent estimates of man-years of employment somewhat similar to the American series for "persons engaged in production." In addition to adjusting to full-time equivalence, the Dutch further reduce the number of female unpaid family workers by one-third. Nonetheless, the Dutch employment estimates appear to run slightly higher than estimates based on the labor force concept rather than lower, as might be supposed. This is similar to American experience, based on a comparison of "persons engaged in production" (which altogether omits unpaid family workers) with employment (after deducting unpaid family workers) as reported in the U.S. Bureau of Labor Statistics, *Monthly Report on the Labor Force* [G68].

TABLE C–2
Unpaid Family Workers and Labor Force Participation Rates, 1960

Area	Unpaid family workers as a percentage of		Total labor force as a percentage of population aged 15 to 64 years
	Population aged 15 to 64 years	Total labor force (including armed forces)	
United States	1.5	2.3	67.8
Northwest Europe	4.3	6.2	70.2
Belgium	2.9	4.8	61.2
Denmark	5.1	6.9	74.8
France	6.6	9.4	69.6
Germany	7.1	9.9	71.2
Netherlands[a]	2.4	4.1	59.8
Norway	5.4	8.2	65.9
United Kingdom[b]	0.0	0.0	73.2
Italy	9.3	14.8	62.9

Sources: OECD, *Manpower Statistics, 1954–1964* [I32] and author's estimates given in Table 5–1C.
a. In the Netherlands data, the estimated number of female unpaid family workers is reduced by one-third. Without this adjustment these percentages would be 2.9, 4.8, and 60.3, respectively.
b. Unpaid family workers are excluded from the United Kingdom estimates. If included on the basis of the Central Statistical Office 1951 population census, these percentages would be 0.2, 0.2, and 73.4, respectively.

according to the United Kingdom submission to OECD, their number is believed negligible. This is supported by the 1951 British population census, which found only 51,000 unpaid family workers, equal to 0.2 percent of the labor force. In Britain farming is unimportant, there are but few proprietors of unincorporated firms, and there are legal advantages in paying family members. The United States excludes family workers who work less than 15 hours a week.

Aside from such relatively clear cases, it is difficult to tell to what extent the large differences shown in Table C–2 stem from: (1) differences in legal, institutional, and industrial structure that cause workers of a type who would appear as unpaid family workers in one country to appear in other employment categories elsewhere; (2) actual differences in labor force participation; and (3) differences among countries in reporting procedure that result in similar persons being reported as unpaid family workers in some countries and out of the labor force in others.

In a sense, it is only the third category that impairs international comparisons. However, even if absolutely uniform reporting could be achieved, the number in the second category, and hence the relative size of labor forces in different countries, would be sensitive to the exact definition adopted.

That variations in reporting procedure and definition *can* substantially affect the results is confirmed by United States experience. The numbers of unpaid family workers reported in the censuses of agriculture and the censuses of business have consistently, but inexplicably, been several times as large as the comparable numbers reported by respondents in the censuses of population or in the relevant issues of the *Monthly Report on the Labor Force*.[6] This is so even though, for family farms and businesses, respondents are family members in both cases. The numbers reported in the *Monthly Report on the Labor Force* have themselves proven sensitive to the exact wording of the question asked by the enumerator.

I have experimented (as others have) with attempts to test and improve international comparability by uniformly omitting all unpaid family workers, or certain categories or fractions of categories, from the estimates. Such exclusions did not produce more comparable labor force participation rates because countries with large numbers of reported unpaid family workers are not consistently those with high participation rates. This is apparent from comparison of the first and last columns of Table C–2. Thus Italy, with the most unpaid family workers, has one of the lowest participation rates. The United Kingdom, with no unpaid family workers included, has next to the highest participation rate. When analysis is based on rates for detailed age-sex classes, especially for males in the prime working ages where little variation is to be expected, it becomes still clearer that any uniformly applied downward adjustment of unpaid family workers increases rather than decreases the international variation in participation rates.

For the Common Market countries the 1960 estimates of unpaid family workers shown in Table 5–1 can be compared with estimates for early autumn 1960 obtained on what was intended to be a

consistent basis from household surveys conducted under the auspices of the Statistical Office of the European Communities (OSCE).[7] The proportions of civilian employment represented by unpaid family workers are as follows:

	Percentages for 1960, derived from Table 5–1C	OSCE percentages for early autumn, 1960
Italy	15	14
Germany	10	10
France	9	10
Belgium	5	5
Netherlands	4	5

The similarity of the two columns provides some assurance that the differences among these countries implied by the data I use are largely genuine rather than the result of data incomparability.

Unpaid family workers were 2.3 percent of total employment in the United States and 6.2 in Northwest Europe. If the difference were wholly statistical and, on a comparable basis, the percentage of unpaid family workers in the United States were really the same as in Northwest Europe, this would raise the 1960 index of European national income per man in United States prices (United States equals 100) from 59 to 61.4. But the OSCE survey used the same definition as the United States, so that any such upward adjustment does not appear to be warranted.

Inconsistencies of reporting are not, of course, confined to the counting of family workers, although this is the most difficult group.[8] Nonetheless, my judgment is that the big differences in labor force participation rates among the European countries are largely genuine, so that use of employment in productivity comparisons is much better than adoption of the statistical expedient, occasionally used in other studies, of substituting total or adult population or some uniformly standardized set of participation rates.

The previous comments refer to the general level

---

6. See Denison in *Trends in the American Economy in the Nineteenth Century*, pp. 402–03 [B27].

7. Results reported in OSCE, *Statistical Information*, No. 2 bis, 1963 [I49]. For exact dates, see Appendix D.

8. Mention may also be made of the fact that a large number of children under 14 years of age are included in the Italian labor force (many as unpaid family workers). The number was as large as 272,000 in 1960, then dropped to 180,000 in 1962, and 27,000 in 1964. So few children under 14 have been employed in the other countries that their complete omission (which is customary outside Italy) has little effect on comparability with Italy.

of the series. To estimate changes in total employment and labor force, various methods are followed. The United States, Germany, and Italy rely on sample surveys of the population (but I have used these Italian data only since 1959). To interpolate and extrapolate periodic census of population data (often adjusted in one way or another), other countries rely on estimates of total population, classified by age and sex, and estimated labor force participation rates; on social insurance statistics and establishment reports, supplemented by estimates for uncovered groups; or on a combination of these two approaches. Any of these methods may develop biases, but there is no general reason to suppose one approach yields estimates biased upward or downward over time relative to another.

The United States labor force estimates presently under discussion, and to varying degrees the European data, have a limitation for computations of intertemporal changes in output per man: The employment statistics are largely independent, statistically, of the national income and product series. This difficulty was absent in my United States study, which used the Department of Commerce series for "persons engaged in production." This series is compiled as an integral part of national income estimation. Any errors (except in deflation) tend to be common to both employment and national income, greatly reducing the possible error in estimates of income per person employed.[9] In the present study, which focuses on international differences, I use the household survey results because they are more comparable to European statistics and provide necessary detail. However, the "persons engaged" series may provide a more accurate measure of changes in national income per person employed in the United States itself.

9. See Denison in *Output, Input, and Productivity Measurement*, pp. 359–72 [B28].

⇛ A P P E N D I X   D ⇚

Derivation of Estimates of Hours of Work

This appendix first describes estimates of hours worked in 1960 and then the 1950–62 indexes of hours worked in each country.

Tables 6–1 and 6–2: Average Weekly Hours, Early Autumn 1960

Estimates in Table 6–1 for the United States and the five Common Market countries included in the study are based on comprehensive sample surveys of households.[1] They are believed to be reasonably comparable although subject to sampling errors and possibly to the influence of unknown differences in reporting procedures and special characteristics of the sample weeks. The hours data presented here refer to persons at work during the survey week; persons with a job but not at work have been excluded in the computation of these averages. Data for the United Kingdom and Norway derive from establishment reports that are representative of nearly all manual employment in the United Kingdom, but only of manual employment in manufacturing and mining in Norway. They have been

adjusted in an effort to arrive at hours estimates for all civilian employment on the labor force concept, comparable to those for the other countries. Hours information for Denmark was too sparse to use in deriving this table. Instead, average hours for each component labor force group were assumed to be the same as in Norway, where legal restrictions on hours are the same. The Danish estimates differ from those shown for Norway (themselves based in part on experience in other countries) only because of differences in labor force composition.

Although the exact definition of a full-time worker varies from country to country in this table, the differences should not appreciably affect the average hours computed for full-time workers.[2] Differences in definition and procedures are likely to have a greater effect upon the average hours of part-time workers. Part-time workers include both persons who usually work part-time and those who

---

1. The survey for Germany includes the Saar but not West Berlin.

2. This is, of course, a factual statement based on examination of the actual hours data analyzed, not a statement of general principles. The main conclusion from the analysis of full-time workers is that hours differentials between the United States and Western Europe are much smaller for full-time workers than for all workers combined. If differences in classification and procedure bias the results at all, it is in the direction of overstating, not understating, the remaining differential.

usually work full-time but worked only part-time during the survey week.

UNITED STATES. Data refer to September 1960 and are from the *Monthly Report on the Labor Force* [G68].[3] Full-time workers are taken to be those working 35 hours or more. For each category of employment the number of full-time and part-time workers was available. The Bureau of Labor Statistics provided unpublished tabulations of average hours of all persons at work (full-time and part-time combined) based on exact hours reported in individual returns; from these, total hours worked were calculated. The Bureau also provided distributions of persons at work by number of hours worked; these were in class-interval groupings. Average hours of part-time workers were computed from data for numbers at work grouped in four hours classes (1–14, 15–21, 22–29, 30–34) and multiplied by their number to obtain total hours. Average hours of full-time workers in each category were obtained by deducting total hours of part-time workers from total hours worked and then dividing by the number of full-time workers. Any error in the computation of average hours of part-time workers from grouped data could scarcely affect averages for full-time workers by more than one-tenth of an hour.

BELGIUM, FRANCE, GERMANY, NETHERLANDS, AND ITALY. Data are derived from surveys conducted under the auspices of the Statistical Office of the European Communities (OSCE). Results are reported in *Statistical Information*, No. 2 bis, 1963 [I49]. Definitions appear to parallel closely those in the United States. German and Italian data refer to October 24–30, 1960. In the other countries the population was sampled over a period of several weeks. The bulk of the data in France and Belgium refer to weeks in the period from September 26 to October 30, and in the Netherlands from October 17 to November 20. Average hours of employed persons as published were recomputed to exclude those reporting no hours worked. The latter group corresponds to those reported in United States statistics as "employed but not at work."

3. September was chosen rather than October to avoid the Columbus Day holiday.

As full-time workers I have counted: (1) all those working 45 hours or more; (2) all those working less than 45 hours who reported that they regularly worked a shorter workweek because of a collective agreement; and (3) half of the small group reporting they regularly worked less than 45 hours because of the nature of the work. The numbers in the second and third groups are known but the survey's distributions of employed persons by hours of work do not differentiate them from those groups of workers employed less than 45 hours for reasons other than those mentioned here. Workers in these groups were assumed to be at the top of the hours distributions for workers employed less than 45 hours. The effect of this treatment was typically (but not uniformly) that all workers employed 40 hours a week or more and part of those employed 35 to 39 hours were counted as full-time workers.

Some additional estimation was required to calculate average hours of full-time nonfarm wage and salary workers by sex, but the procedures appear unlikely to introduce much error. Together with sampling errors in the original surveys (which are indicated in the source) and the possibility of differences in reporting despite efforts at uniformity, they nevertheless make it unwise to attach significance to small differences.

UNITED KINGDOM. Estimates for nonfarm wage and salary workers refer to the second pay week in October 1960. Original data are collected from a large sample of employers in Great Britain. The sample refers to manual workers at work in most nonfarm activities; results are reported in the *Ministry of Labour Gazette* (February 1961 [G42]). Two adjustments were made to these data: (1) In an effort to shift to a labor force concept by allowing for dual job holding, hours of full-time males were multiplied by 1.0208 and hours of full-time females by 1.008. These are United States ratios derived from data on dual job holders. (2) To include salaried employees, hours of male manual workers were multiplied by 0.996 and hours of females by 1.009. These ratios are simple averages of the ratios of average hours of wage and salary workers to those of wage earners only in the five Common Market countries. Thirty hours or more is considered full-time work in the British statistics. The basic data by age group for nonfarm wage and salary workers as reported and adjusted are as follows:

	Reported hours per week	*Adjusted* hours per week
Men, 21 years and over		
Full-time	48.0	48.8
Part-time	17.8	17.7
Youths and boys, under 21 years	44.3	45.0
Women, 18 years and over		
Full-time	40.5	41.2
Part-time	21.7	22.1
Girls, under 18 years	41.4	42.1

Average weekly hours of hired "whole-time" farm workers (50.2 for men, 48.9 for youths under 20 years, and 46.0 for women and girls) refer to the period from October 1960 to March 1961. They are given in the *Ministry of Labour Gazette* (February 1964).

Farm proprietors and own-account workers, and nonfarm proprietors and own-account workers, were each assumed to work the same average hours (and to be divided between full- and part-time workers in the same proportions) as in the combined Common Market countries. Together, these groups represented only 7.5 percent of United Kingdom employment. Males and females in these small groups were assigned the same hours.

Data for total employment, by sex, for farm and nonfarm wage and salary workers, and for farm and nonfarm proprietors, were available for the United Kingdom for use as weights. For nonfarm wage and salary workers (90 percent of the total), the proportions working full-time and part-time were based on proportions from the Ministry of Labour sample for Great Britain (with some minor estimating required). For the other groups, the proportions were based on the Common Market countries.

NORWAY. The only usable data are for average hours of manual workers employed in manufacturing and mining (representing about one-third of all wage and salary employment) during full weeks (weeks without holidays or vacations) in 1960. These were 42.9 for males and 38.1 for females, about the lowest for these categories of employ-

ment in 1960 among the European countries covered here. They most closely resembled hours in Belgium.

Data for manual workers' hours in manufacturing and mining in the other European countries were compared with finally adjusted estimates of average hours for all nonfarm wage and salary workers at work. For males, it was found that in five countries (Germany, France, Belgium, Italy, and the United Kingdom), those in the latter category worked 1.2 to 2.0 hours more than those in the former category, averaging 1.6 more hours.[4] The difference in Belgium, the only country with male manufacturing and mining hours as short as Norway, was about the same as the average (1.7). The Norwegian figure for manufacturing and mining was therefore raised 1.6 hours to arrive at an estimate for all nonfarm wage and salary workers at work. For females, the patterns in other countries were less uniform but among the three countries with the shortest female hours (France, Belgium, and the United Kingdom) differences were small. In these three countries average hours of all female nonfarm wage and salary workers exceeded those of employed female manual workers in manufacturing and mining by 0.5 to 0.9 hours, averaging 0.6. This adjustment was used for Norway.

Hours of *full-time* male nonfarm wage and salary workers were estimated by applying the average differential, 1.5 hours, between hours of full-time male workers and hours of all male workers in Germany, France, Belgium, Italy, and the United Kingdom. (The differential in Belgium was 1.7.) For females, the average differential in France, Belgium, and the United Kingdom (which was close to the average for all six countries and the same as that for Belgium) was used.

Nonfarm wage and salary workers account for 69 percent of Norwegian civilian employment. For nonfarm proprietors, farm proprietors, and farm wage and salary workers, the same hours were used as in the United Kingdom. For unpaid family workers in agriculture, a group not present in United Kingdom statistics, averages for the Common Market countries were used.

---

4. The Netherlands, where the difference was 0.7 hours, is omitted from this comparison.

The estimates indicate that, in 1960, hours in Norway were about the shortest among the European countries covered. This appears consistent with information of a nonstatistical character for various groups of salaried and other employees.

DENMARK. Available information was insufficient to attempt a direct estimate of the 1960 level of hours. However, laws governing hours are the same as in Norway. Hours of male and female nonfarm wage and salary workers were assumed to be the same as in Norway. For other groups the same hours estimates were used as in Norway. Hours of unpaid family workers in nonagricultural activities, a group not present in the Norwegian employment estimates, were based on hours in the Common Market countries.

Table 6–3: Hours Adjusted to an Annual Basis

The hours data just described refer to persons actually at work during a full workweek in early autumn. Absence of comparable annual data forces one to assume, for full-time and for part-time persons at work separately, that the ratio of hours worked during a full workweek in early autumn to the annual average for such weeks throughout the year is the same in all countries. However, before the international hours indexes given in Table 6–2 can be used in connection with annual average employment estimates (which include persons with a job but not at work), allowance must be made for certain other sources of international incomparability.

For persons at work, holidays reduce average weekly hours over the year below those worked in full weeks. Vacations do the same when they cut into the calendar week, and drive a wedge between employment and persons at work when the vacation extends over an entire calendar week. The *Westminster Bank Review* [P49] has published a compilation of the number of public holidays and the typical length of vacation periods in days. The estimates are consistent with international comparisons given in the British *Ministry of Labour Gazette* and various other sources. They are reproduced in Table D–1 and, with some estimation, are used

TABLE D–1

Adjustment of 1960 Weekly Hours Data for Holidays and Vacations

Country	Number of public holidays (1)	Days of vacation (2)	Estimate of average weeks of vacation (3)	Percentage of time lost by holidays and vacations (4)	Required percentage adjustment of hours indexes (5)
U. S.	8	10–20	2.5	7.0	—
Belgium	10	12+	2.6	7.7	−.7
Denmark	10	18	3.0	8.5	−1.5
France	10	18–24	3.25	9.5	−2.5
Germany	11	12–24	2.5	8.8	−1.8
Netherlands	8	12–15	2.12	6.5	.5
Norway	10	18	3.0	8.5	−1.5
U. K.	7	12+	2.12	6.3	.7
Italy	17	10+	2.12	9.0	−2.0

Sources: Columns (1) and (2): *Westminster Bank Review*, November 1962, p. 33 [P49], except Belgium, *Ministry of Labour Gazette*, February 1962, p. 59 [G42].

Column (3): estimated from Column (2), using appropriate number of workdays. Where ranges are given in Column (2), a figure one-fourth of the way from the lower to the higher figure is used. A slight allowance is made for the "pluses" in the United Kingdom and Italy; a larger allowance is made in Belgium partly to allow for local holidays (the figure given in Column (1) is for legal national holidays).

Column (4): [Column (1) ÷ 365] + [Column (3) ÷ 52]. The absolute percentages are probably overstatements.

Column (5): United States percentage less European percentages in Column (4).

there to calculate the percentage of time lost as a result of holidays and vacations. The absolute percentages are probably overstated, mainly because important categories do not take vacations (while remaining in an employed status). The figure of 2.5 weeks used for the United States, for example, compares with an apparent actual average of only 1.4 weeks for all employed persons estimated for 1960 from the *Monthly Report on the Labor Force*.[5] The differentials among countries appear plausible, however, and while no claim to accuracy is made, it is probably better to use the estimates

5. Over the year, persons with a job but not at work because they were on vacation averaged 2.37 percent of the total number employed. Of all persons who usually worked full-time in nonagricultural industries, 0.48 percent worked part-time because of vacation in an average week. Assuming they were on vacation half the week, this is a loss of 0.24 percent. The total loss is then about 2.61 percent, which translates into an average of 1.36 weeks. This may be an underestimate, however, since only two of the twelve sample weeks fall in the main summer vacation period, which extends more than two months, and vacations taken between Christmas and New Year's Day are missed.

TABLE D-2

Adjustment of 1960 Weekly Hours Data for Time Lost from Sickness

Country	Percentage of employed not at work due to sickness[a] (1)	Column (1) adjusted to average for year (2)	Estimated percentage working no hours (3)	Required percentage adjustment of hours indexes (4)
U. S.	2.5	2.8	1.4	—
Belgium	3.5	3.9	2.0	−.6
Denmark	—	—	1.8	−.4
France	3.6	4.0	2.0	−.6
Germany	1.6	1.8	.9	.5
Netherlands	1.9	2.1	1.1	.3
Norway	—	—	1.8	−.4
U. K.	—	—	1.8	−.4
Italy	2.5	2.8	1.4	—

Sources: Column (1): United States: *Monthly Report on the Labor Force* [G68]; Common Market countries: OSCE, *Statistical Information*, No. 2 bis, 1963 [I49]. (The United States percentage is for a week in October; the percentage for September, the month used in Tables 6-1 and 6-2, is 2.3.)

Column (2): United States: *Monthly Report on the Labor Force*; Common Market countries: estimated on the assumption the ratio of Column (2) to Column (1) is the same as in the United States.

Column (3): United States: *Monthly Report on the Labor Force*; Common Market countries: estimated on the assumption the ratio of Column (3) to Column (2) is the same as in the United States; other countries: average for Belgium, France, and Italy.

Column (4): United States percentage less European percentage in Column (3).

a. This percentage includes persons working less than full time on account of sickness. Data refer to the same week as those for Tables 6-1 and 6-2, except that the United States figure is for October.

than to ignore the problem.[6] Vacations and holidays appear to reduce hours in five European countries more, and in three less, than in the United States. The indexes in Table 6-2 (United States equals 100) have to be adjusted by amounts ranging from −2.5 percent in France to +0.7 percent in the United Kingdom if they are to be used with employment data (Column 5, Table D-1).

Sickness is a second source of incomparability. Data from the *Monthly Report on the Labor Force* show that in the United States employed persons not at work because of illness averaged 1.4 percent of employment during 1960. Persons who usually work full-time but worked only part-time during

6. In most European countries where typical vacations are long, vacations for wage and salary workers are required by law, which probably brings the average vacation closer to the "typical" vacation than in the United States. This is offset by the use of the full international differentials in typical vacations rather than reducing them by the ratio of average to typical vacations in the United States, a possible alternative procedure.

the survey week because of sickness also averaged about 1.4 percent. If they lost 40 percent of their normal work time, this represents about 0.6 percent of available time, yielding a total of 2.0 percent of available time.[7] The percentage of employed persons who worked either none or only part of (a survey) week in October 1960 is given for the United States and the Common Market countries in Column 1, Table D-2.

If the autumn data are typical, any international differences in part weeks lost are already reflected in the weekly hours data and adjustment is required only for full weeks. The October data are multiplied by the ratio of the annual average percentage to the October percentage in the United States on the assumption that international differences in October are typical of the year. Half this group in the United States represented persons not working at all during the survey weeks, and the fraction is assumed to be the same in the Common Market countries. This yields, in Column 3, the percentage of time lost from full weeks of sickness that is required to adjust the data used here. The estimates are not intended for analysis of time lost due to sickness as such. For the United Kingdom, Norway, and Denmark, I assume a figure equal to the simple average of those for Belgium, France, and Italy.[8]

I have no alternative but to assume that time lost

7. This, of course, is not the total time lost because of sickness. It does not include persons who are not employed at all, or who hold only part-time jobs, because of sickness.

8. I am aware that John and Sylvia Jewkes give 4.5 percent as a minimum estimate of time lost from sickness by employed persons in Great Britain that is comparable to the 2.0 percent for the United States mentioned in the text. This implies a larger differential between the two countries in full weeks lost than I use here. Their estimate for Great Britain is based on sickness insurance statistics (*Value for Medicine*, Chapter 2 [B56]). However, on the basis of sickness insurance statistics, Philip E. Enterline finds that rates for most other European countries are also high by comparison with the United States. In his table, time lost from sickness in 1956 is even higher in France, Germany, and Norway than in the United Kingdom (in *Industrial Medicine and Surgery*, October 1964 [P24]).

One can scarcely mix the two sources in estimating work loss in the European countries; either United States data based on labor force statistics must be compared with similar European data on the evidence of only one month, as I have done here, or else United States labor force data must be compared with sickness insurance data for all European countries. It is entirely possible, even probable, that the latter comparison is correct in showing much higher sickness rates in Europe than in America. Nevertheless, use of the same source from which weekly hours are computed appears likely to give a better basis for adjusting the hours data used here.

by employed persons because of bad weather was about the same in all countries over the course of the year. In the United States the percentage can be estimated at 0.7 percent of available time in 1960. However, in the particular autumn week on which Table 6–2 is based, there were differences among the United States and the Common Market countries. In Italy, 6.7 percent of employed persons worked less than full-time hours because of bad weather, whereas the percentage was 1.3 in the United States and France, and less elsewhere. The difference does not systematically affect the average hours of full-time workers in the survey week, but reduces Italian hours for all workers by increasing the proportion classified as part-time workers. I assume the affected workers lost an average of one-third their normal work hours. On this assumption, the index of average hours for full-time and part-time workers combined in Italy must be raised by 1.8 percent, and the indexes for Germany, the Netherlands, and Belgium reduced by negligible amounts. Table D–3 shows the calculations. No adjustment for the United Kingdom, Denmark, and Norway is indicated.

Time lost as a result of industrial disputes was less than 0.1 percent of available time in the United States. It is known to be negligible, except in rare years, in the other countries.[9] It was also negligible in the survey weeks. Time lost for miscellaneous personal reasons can be estimated at 1.2 percent in the United States in 1960; comparable European data are not available and I shall assume the percentage to be the same. In addition, time is lost by employed persons because insufficient work is available, but if the survey week is typical of the year, this is already taken into account in the average hours data.

Thus, the only adjustments which it is both necessary and feasible to make are those for holidays

9. See *Westminster Bank Review*, November 1962, p. 33 [P49]; and OSCE, *Statistical Information*, No. 2 bis, 1963 [I49]. According to International Labour Organisation data, the number of working days lost because of industrial disputes for the period 1950–62 averaged 30.5 million a year in the United States and 9.2 million in the Northwest European countries; these averages were higher in 1950–54 (34.3 million and 9.8 million) than in 1955–62 (28.1 million and 8.9 million). In Italy, man-days lost by strikes, already relatively high at 5.4 million a year in 1950–54, increased to 8.3 million in 1955–62 (ILO, *Year Book of Labour Statistics, 1957* and *1963* [I12]).

TABLE D-3

Adjustment of 1960 Weekly Hours Data for Time Lost due to Bad Weather

Country	Percentage of employed not working full-time because of bad weather (1)	Estimated percentage of available time lost (2)	Required percentage adjustment of hours indexes (3)
United States	1.3	.4	—
Belgium	.6	.2	−.2
Denmark	—	—	—
France	1.3	.4	.0
Germany	.3	.1	−.3
Netherlands	.2	.1	−.3
Norway	—	—	—
United Kingdom	—	—	—
Italy	6.7	2.2	1.8

Sources: Column (1): United States: *Monthly Report on the Labor Force* [G68]; Common Market countries: OSCE, *Statistical Information*, No. 2 bis, 1963 [I49].
Column (2): one-third of Column (1).

and vacations, illness, and bad weather. The last is required only for average hours of full-time and part-time workers combined, the others also for average hours of full-time workers. Table D–4 summarizes the required percentage adjustments for the several countries. These are applied to the indexes in Table 6–2 to arrive at Table 6–3. The same adjustments are applied to all categories of workers shown. This is no doubt incorrect, but the adjust-

TABLE D-4

Total Adjustments of 1960 Weekly Hours Indexes to Annual Basis

Country	Adjustment for holidays and vacations (1)	Adjustment for sickness (2)	Total adjustment for full-time workers (3)	Adjustment for bad weather (4)	Total adjustment for full-time and part-time workers (5)
U. S.	—	—	—	—	—
Belgium	−.7	−.6	−1.3	−.2	−1.5
Denmark	−1.5	−.4	−1.9	—	−1.9
France	−2.5	−.6	−3.1	.0	−3.1
Germany	−1.8	.5	−1.3	−.3	−1.6
Netherlands	.5	.3	.8	−.3	.5
Norway	−1.5	−.4	−1.9	—	−1.9
U. K.	.7	−.4	.3	—	.3
Italy	−2.0	—	−2.0	1.8	−.2

Sources: Columns (1), (2), and (4): Tables D–1, D–2, and D–3; Column (3): Columns (1) + (2); Column (5): Columns (3) + (4).

ments are not large enough to distort the indexes appreciably.

Table 6–5: Indexes of Average Hours Worked by Nonagricultural Wage and Salary Workers, 1950–62

Time series data for average hours actually worked generally take one of three forms: (1) Directly suitable for indexes of annual hours per person employed are averages of hours worked per week or month computed from data collected for (or adjusted to represent) all weeks during the year. The data used for Belgium, Denmark, Germany, and Italy, and Norwegian data for "hours worked per calendar week," are of this type. (2) A second type measures hours worked during full weeks not affected by holidays and vacations. The data used for France, the Netherlands, and the United Kingdom, and Norwegian data for "hours worked per full week," are of this type. If changes occur in the number of holidays, or in the length of vacations, data of this type require adjustment to allow for these changes. (The number of hours per week reported in this type of series is, of course, greater than in the first type but our concern here is only with movements.) (3) A third type represents average hours during a sample of weeks in which the number of weeks containing holidays varies from year to year. Annual averages for the United States from the *Monthly Report on the Labor Force* are of this type and for comparability require adjustment, first, to a full-week basis, and, second, to allow for holidays and vacations.

All three types measure hours actually worked. Various other series—hours paid for, normal hours, and the like—also are often available, and some collateral use has been made of them.

Where possible, separate series are developed for males and females. Otherwise, series covering both sexes are used for each separately. For the United States and Italy, and for women in the United Kingdom, separate series are developed for all workers and for full-time workers. Data with the broadest possible industrial and occupational coverage within the nonfarm wage and salary worker category were used, but the scope of available data varies among countries and it was generally neces-

sary to assume changes in hours of the covered groups were representative of the total. Derivation of the series for the individual countries is described below.

UNITED STATES. Data refer to hours worked by all nonagricultural wage and salary workers, based on information from the *Monthly Report on the Labor Force*. For each sex, separate estimates were prepared for all workers and for full-time workers. The procedure entailed three steps:

1. Data were first obtained for persons at work during a full workweek in May. Average hours of full-time and part-time workers combined, by sex, were provided by the Department of Labor. Average hours of full-time workers (those employed 35 hours or more) were computed from unpublished data giving the number of persons at work classified by detailed number-of-hours classes. The same procedure of estimating part-time hours and obtaining full-time hours as a residual that was used for September 1960, and described on page 361, was followed. The May data for hours per week, referring to nonagricultural wage and salary workers, are as follows:

	1950	1955	1960	1962
All males and females	40.4	40.0	39.2	39.3
All males	41.8	41.9	41.4	41.7
Full-time males	44.3	44.4	44.4	44.9
All females	37.4	36.3	35.4	35.1
Full-time females	42.0	41.7	41.7	41.5

2. The May data for persons at work were adjusted to an annual-average basis for full weeks by adding to each category 0.1 hours in 1950 and 1955 and 0.2 hours in 1960. No adjustment was indicated in 1962. These adjustments were based on the difference between annual-average hours in full weeks and May hours of *all* persons at work in nonagricultural industries. The May data are published in *Hours of Work*, Hearings before the House Select Subcommittee on Labor [G49]. The annual data, unpublished, are those prepared (in connection with its productivity studies) by the Department of Labor. They are obtained by adding to hours worked the estimated number of hours lost because of holidays during the survey weeks (the holidays vary from year to year).

3. The full-week data were then adjusted to an

actual or "calendar week" basis for employed persons. The ratio of (a) the number of persons with a job but not at work (for any reason, including vacation) plus one-half the number working less than 35 hours because of vacation to (b) employment was computed. Full-week hours were reduced by this ratio. In addition, a further reduction was made for holidays, based on data for paid holidays granted manual and salaried workers in most nonfarm industries in eighteen cities in 1952–53 and 1961–62. (The average number of holidays increased less than one day over this period.)

The ratio of actual hours over the year per employed person to full-week hours of persons at work dropped about 1 percent from 1950 to 1962 for each sex.

BELGIUM. S. Mendelbaum has provided estimates, separately for wage earners and salaried employees (other than civil servants), of average employment, average annual hours worked (adjusted for vacations and holidays), and total hours worked, for each year from 1948 through 1962.[10] Mendelbaum's total man-hours of wage and salary workers combined were divided by his total employment of wage and salary workers to obtain average annual hours. These estimates required no adjustment for use in the present study.

Mendelbaum obtained average annual hours worked by wage earners from the National Institute of Statistics. They are based on data covering 35 percent of all wage earners in 1950 and 50 percent thereafter. His estimates for salaried employees were prepared by H. Maes, who adjusted estimated full-time hours for time lost due to holidays, vacations, sickness, and other causes.

Mendelbaum's series corresponds closely to one I had previously developed. This series was based on an analysis of changes in normal hours, vacations, and the like, in Belgium, and on the assumption that the relationship between actual and normal hours was similar to that in the Netherlands.

DENMARK. Available data refer to manufacturing industries and are based on a sample that, by 1962, covered employers of five or more workers and

10. Mendelbaum in *Cahiers Economiques de Bruxelles,* No. 21, 1964, pp. 77–92 [P9].

represented two-thirds of total manufacturing employment. The original data yield annual hours, already adjusted for changes in vacations and holidays. (The main change in vacations was to extend them from two to three weeks between 1950 and 1955.)

The procedure is to cumulate total man-hours worked during the twelve months of each year and to divide by average employment on the last day of each month. Data for 1955, 1960, and 1962 are from various issues of the Statistical Department's *Statistiske Efterretninger* [G9]. The 1950 figure is extrapolated from 1960 by use of data compiled from the same source by Angus Maddison (in *Economic Growth in the West,* p. 228 [B71]); the product of Maddison's "working weeks per year" and "weekly working hours" was used.

FRANCE. Data refer to wage and salary earners employed in enterprises with ten employees or more in industrial and commercial activities (that is, nearly all branches of the nonfarm economy). They are averages of the last week in each quarter that contains no holidays, hence are of the "full week" type. Data are published in ILO, *Year Book of Labour Statistics, 1963* [I12], and in OSCE, *Social Statistics,* No. 4, 1963 [I52].

There have been no changes in holidays but substantial changes in vacations. These were 2 weeks (12 days) in 1950 under a statute which was unchanged from 1936 to 1956. In 1955 major collective bargaining agreements provided for 3 weeks, and a law of March 1, 1956, made 3 weeks compulsory. In 1961 a collective agreement in the automobile industry set a 4-week pattern, which quickly became widespread. I assume an average vacation of 2 weeks in 1950, 2.5 in 1955, 3 in 1960, and 3.6 in 1962, and adjust the full-week hours index accordingly. The vacation adjustment converts a 2.4 percent increase in full-week hours from 1950 to 1962 to a decline of 0.8 percent in annual hours.

GERMANY. The German indexes are estimates for all nonfarm wage and salary workers. They were constructed in three steps:

1. Average annual hours worked (taking account of vacations and holidays) by wage earners in manufacturing and mining (both sexes combined)

were available for all years. For 1950–64 they are given directly in publications of the German Institute for Economic Research (Berlin).[11] They can also be computed from data for aggregate hours and employment given in various issues of *Statistisches Jahrbuch für die Bundesrepublik Deutschland* [G16].

2. Separate indexes for males and females were constructed for the same group of workers by use of the ratio of hours for each sex to hours for the two sexes combined based on data for average hours performed (1957–62) or hours paid for (1950–57). The resulting indexes for males and females are very similar. The source is the *Statistisches Jahrbuch*.

3. Indexes of "tariflichen" (normal) work hours were available for wage earners and for salary workers in most of the nonfarm economy, as well as for wage earners in manufacturing and mining industries. In general, changes in hours of all workers were very similar to those of industrial wage earners between the years that are analyzed in this study, but the comparison suggested the former dropped about 0.6 percent less than the latter from 1955 to 1960. This adjustment was incorporated into the indexes for hours actually worked that were obtained in Step 2. Data are from the German statistical yearbooks for 1961 and 1963.

THE NETHERLANDS. Data for 1958 to 1962 refer to hours worked in full weeks in April and October by wage earners in enterprises in manufacturing, mining, electricity, and water employing ten or more persons, and those in construction with five or more. To these were linked similar 1950–58 October data for male wage earners in manufacturing. Data are taken from OSCE, *Social Statistics*, No. 4, 1963, and from ILO, *Year Book of Labour Statistics, 1963*.

There were no changes in holidays during the period. Through 1960, vacations were generally 12 days (2 weeks) under collective bargaining agreements (though only 6 days were required by law). When the 5-day week was introduced at the end of

11. *Produktionsvolumen und Produktionsfaktoren der Industrie im Gebiet der Bundesrepublik Deutschland*, "Statistische Kennziffern, 1958 bis 1964" and "1950 bis 1960" [B30].

1960 and in early 1961, the 12 days of vacation were retained, automatically raising the vacation to 2.4 weeks.[12] In addition, collective agreements providing for 13 to 15 days began to appear, which I assume further raised the 1962 average to 2.6 weeks as against 2 weeks from 1950 through 1960. The difference represents 1 percent of annual hours so the 1962 index for full-week hours was reduced 1 percent to allow for the increase in vacations.

NORWAY. Available data refer to wage earners in manufacturing and mining. For each sex, two series were available from 1957 through 1962: (1) actual hours per calendar week (that is, the average for all weeks); and (2) actual hours per week without vacation and public holidays. The latter data were also available for 1951 and 1955. An earlier series provided both types of data for 1950 and 1951 for the two sexes combined, but not on a basis directly comparable to those for subsequent years.

For each sex, series (1), actual hours per calendar week, was used for 1960 and 1962 and estimated for 1951 and 1955 on the assumption that it fell short of series (2) by the same amount (4.0 hours for males and 3.5 hours for females) as it did in 1957. (In 1962 the differences were 3.8 and 3.4; there was no upward trend.) Vacation periods were unchanged at 3 weeks, and compulsory, from 1947 to January 1, 1965, so this assumption appears appropriate. The earlier series indicated an increase from 1950 to 1951 of 0.1 hours per calendar week for both sexes combined, and this was assumed to apply to each sex separately.

It may be noted that the estimates show male hours exceeded female hours by 3.0 in 1950 and 2.8 in 1955; the differential increased to 4.4 in both 1960 and 1962 after having reached 5.3 in 1957.

The data used are compiled from establishments by the Norwegian Employers Confederation and published by the Central Bureau of Statistics in various issues of the *Statistisk Årbok for Norge* [G35], and *Lønnsstatistikk* [G32].

UNITED KINGDOM. Available data for full-time workers refer to wage earners in most nonagricultural industries. Indexes for this group were

12. Normal hours consisted of a 6-day (48-hour) week until that time and thereafter of a 5-day (45-hour) week.

assumed to be typical of all full-time nonfarm wage and salary workers. Data for average hours actually worked in a full workweek (without holidays) by full-time adult males and full-time females are available for October in each year, and for April beginning with 1956. For 1960 and 1962, averages of April and October data were used. For 1950 and 1955 the October data were multiplied by the 1956 ratio of the April–October average to the October figure. Data are from the *Ministry of Labour Gazette* (February 1964), and the Central Statistical Office, *Annual Abstract of Statistics, 1955* [G36].

To develop an index of full-week hours for full-time and part-time females combined, the proportion of women who worked part-time and their average hours had to be estimated. The main problem was to estimate the proportion of women who worked part-time since their average hours do not change very much. For 1960 and 1962 fairly complete information covering both wage and salary workers was available. For earlier years the estimates had to be carried back by use of data covering only manufacturing wage earners.

The percentage of female wage and salary workers who worked part-time was 6.0 in October 1960 and 6.9 in October 1962 in all industries covered by the Ministry of Labour reports, which were taken to be representative of all female nonfarm wage and salary workers. Among the *wage earners* reported in these industries, 18.2 percent of females worked part-time in 1960 and 20.8 in 1962 (averages of April and October). In salaried employment part-time work was much less common but has been increasing. Average hours of part-time female wage earners were available beginning with 1956.

For the early part of the period, only data for female wage and salary workers in manufacturing were available and these were used to extrapolate the later data backward. The percentage who worked part-time was 11.8 in 1950, 11.4 in 1955, and 11.9 in 1959, according to the old classification, and 11.7 in 1959, 13.2 in 1960, and 13.8 in 1962, according to the new classification. Of all females covered by the manufacturing data in 1962, only one-fourth were in administrative, technical, and clerical occupations and three-fourths were wage earners, which apparently accounts for the high proportion of part-time workers among females in this industry.

June employment data for all nonfarm wage and salary earners were used to compute average hours of both sexes combined in Table 6–6.

There was no *general* change in the number of holidays or in the length of vacations (2 weeks) over the period (except for some movement toward two additional holidays in Scotland). To allow for scattered changes, however, I assume increased vacations and holidays cut annual hours by 0.1 percent every two years, or 0.6 percent over the 1950–62 period, and have adjusted all the indexes accordingly.

ITALY. Data for full- and part-time workers combined refer to wage earners in enterprises employing ten or more in mining, manufacturing, electricity, gas, and water industries. Data are collected on a monthly basis every month. Consequently, when annual averages are converted to a weekly basis they are on a "calendar week" basis, that is, they automatically allow for holidays and vacations (as well as time lost for other reasons). The adjustment to a weekly basis made by OSCE, which eliminates the effect of leap year in 1960, was accepted.

There was a sharp reduction over the period in involuntary part-time employment as the slack in the labor market was taken up. The percentage working less than 40 hours a week is available each year; it dropped from 15.2 in 1950 to 3.3 in 1962. Estimates were therefore made of the average hours worked by those employed 40 hours or more to better indicate the movement of hours worked by full-time workers. This was done by estimating the hours worked by part-time workers from frequency distributions and the ratio of average hours in this survey to those shown in Table 6–1; the average after eliminating part-time workers was then computed.

Data (all referring to the same series) were taken from various issues of *Rassegna di Statistiche del Lavoro* [S11]; from OSCE, *Social Statistics*, No. 4, 1963; from Vera Lutz, *Italy: A Study in Economic Development*, p. 77 [B69]; and from EEC, *Exposé sur l'Evolution de la Situation Sociale dans la Communauté en 1963*, p. 139 [I53].

→>> A P P E N D I X   E <<←

Derivation of Estimates by Age, Sex, and Military Status

Distributions of Man-Hours, 1960 (for Tables 7–2 and 7–6)

Derivation of the 1960 man-hours distributions (Table 7–2) from the 1960 employment distributions in Table 7–1 required estimates for each country of hours differentials among the labor force groups.[1]

For the United States, average hours worked by the civilian age-sex groups in 1962, based on the *Monthly Report on the Labor Force* [G68], were used. Data are given in Column 4, Table E–1. Hours of the armed forces were set conventionally at the same level as those of civilian males 20 to 64 years of age.

For the European countries average hours of male and female civilians were available; the international indexes of average annual hours given, by sex, in Table 6–3 were simply applied to the United States data. However, differentials in hours between age groups were not generally available. Percentage differentials between the 65 and over and 20–64 age groups were assumed to be the same, for each

sex, as in the United States. The percentage hours differential between persons under 20 and persons 20–64 in the European countries was assumed to be half as large, for each sex, as in the United States. It is clear that average hours of young people are much closer to those of adults in Europe than in the United States, where the young groups are dominated by part-time workers.[2] Indeed, data for some countries suggest there may be no significant hours differential between teenagers and adults. If this is the general situation, percentages given for hours worked by persons under 20 in Europe are understated and the quality indexes for the European countries given in Table 7–5 are overstated. If there were no differential at all the overstatement would, on the average, be about 1 percent. Hours of members of the armed forces are assumed to be the same in Europe as in the United States.

---

1. The 1960 employment distributions given in Table 7–1 were derived by procedures similar to those for other years described in the next section of this appendix.

2. In the United States in 1955, 49 percent of teenage boys at work, and 44 percent of teenage girls at work, worked part-time (annual averages). Almost half the 14- to 19-year-olds in the labor force were also in school, usually full-time (see U.S. Bureau of Labor Statistics, *Population and Labor Force Projections for the United States, 1960 to 1975*, pp. 42–43 [G69]). When European teenagers both work and attend school, it is normally schooling that is the part-time activity, whether attended on a released-time or after-work basis.

TABLE E-1

United States: Derivation of Earnings Differentials of Civilians
by Sex and Age, and of Military Personnel, 1960[a]

Status, sex, and age group (in years)	Average 1960 money income of year-round full-time workers		Estimated average hourly earnings of all workers, 1960 (males 20 to 64 years = 100) (3)	Average hours worked per week by all persons at work, 1962 (4)	Average weekly earnings per employed person (males 20 to 64 years = 100) (5)
	Dollars (1)	Index (males 20 to 64 years = 100) (2)			
Civilians					
Males					
Under 20	1,994	31.8	31	27.9	19
20 to 64	6,272	100.0	100	44.8	100
65 and over	5,455	87.0	82	35.6	65
Females					
Under 20	2,327	37.1	40	26.2	24
20 to 64	3,465	55.2	59	36.5	48
65 and over	2,966	47.3	47	32.1	34
Military personnel	—	—	69	—	69

Sources of civilian data: Column (1): unpublished data collected for U.S. Bureau of the Census, *Current Population Reports* [G57]; Column (2): computed from Column (1); Column (3): derived from Column (2) as described in text; Column (4): unpublished data collected for U.S. Bureau of Labor Statistics, *Monthly Report on the Labor Force* [G68]; Column (5): product of Columns (3) and (4), converted to index form.
Sources of military data: Column (3) is the product of: (a) the ratio of the average compensation of military personnel to average labor income of all persons engaged in production (as estimated by the author from Office of Business Economics data) and (b) the weighted (by total hours) average index for the civilian components of Column (3). Hours are taken to be the same as for civilian males aged 20 to 64 years, hence Column (5) is the same as Column (3).
a. Hours data for 1962 were used in Column (4) in the absence of 1960 data.

Distributions of Man-Hours in 1950, 1955, and 1962 (for Table 7-7)

Computation of Table 7-7 required distributions of man-hours worked in 1950, 1955, and 1962 among the seven groups similar to those for 1960. Employment distributions were first assembled. Distributions of employment among civilian males, civilian females, and the armed forces were available from Table 5-1. Age distributions of employed male and female civilians in the United States were directly available from the *Manpower Report of the President*, 1965, p. 201 [G50]. Age distributions in most European countries had to be estimated in all years because the employment and labor force data used were not available by age. This was done by applying to detailed age-sex distributions of the population estimated participation rates usually based on interpolation or extrapolation of census or sample-census data. This required the use of many national sources, supplemented by the annual Demographic Yearbooks of the United Nations [I1], and *Demographic Trends 1956–1976 in Western Europe and in the United States* [I24] of the Or-ganisation for European Economic Co-operation. The trends of average annual hours for each sex were taken from Chapter 6; within each sex the same hours index was applied to each of the three age groups. Military hours were held constant.

Earnings Differentials in the United States, 1960 (Table 7-3)

The starting point for these estimates is the arithmetic mean annual money income in 1960 of civilians who were employed full-time throughout that year. The data are given in the first column of Table E-1. In the second column they are expressed as percentages of the average income of males 20 to 64 years of age.

These percentages require several adjustments to convert them to indexes, given in Column 3, of average *earnings* per *hour* worked during 1960 by *all* persons in each of the age-sex groups:

1. The income data include money income other than earnings. The proportion of such income prob-

ably rises with age, and especially affects the group 65 years and over. It must be recalled that only persons working full-time throughout the year are included in the tabulation, so the bias is far less than it would be if the whole population were under consideration. Even so it must operate to make the indexes for the 65 years and over age groups too high. Indexes for the latter were lowered by 5 percent (not percentage points) to allow for this.

2. Full-time female workers work shorter hours than full-time males. All the indexes for females were raised by 10 percent (based on Table 6–1) to allow for this. There is no information suggesting that there is an appreciable hours differential among age groups within each sex for full-time, year-round workers.

3. The age classification is as of spring 1961. The under 20 age group consequently excludes those who were nearly 20 while working during 1960; it is approximately equivalent to an "under 19¼" group in terms of age while working during 1960. Since 19-year-olds earn more than younger workers, income indexes for the under 20 groups are understated on this account and were raised by 5 percent.

4. Full-time, year-round workers earn more per hour than other workers (full-time workers who do not work the whole year and part-time workers). I assume the earnings differential per hour within each age-sex group to be 10 percent. (Available data indicate it is not greater than 20 percent but do not yield an exact figure.) The proportion of total hours in each age-sex group that was worked by full-time, year-round workers could be approximated. Since full-time, year-round workers contribute a higher percentage of total hours worked among adult males than among the other groups, this adjustment lowers all the other indexes by varying amounts.

The hourly earnings indexes derived by these adjustments are shown in Column 3, Table E–1. The main *net* changes from the indexes for annual earnings of year-round, full-time workers are a higher index number for females 20 to 64 and a lower figure for males 65 and over.

Although hourly earnings provide the weights needed in Chapter 7, weekly earnings per person employed are also of interest in this study. Average weekly hours during the year 1962 for persons at work (full-time and part-time combined) are shown for each group in Column 4, Table E–1. The product of Columns 3 and 4, reconverted to index form, yields in Column 5 indexes of average earnings per person employed in each group that are consistent with average monthly employment data.

Education: Derivation of Estimates and Supplementary Material

This appendix supplements Chapter 8, and general explanations given in that chapter are not repeated here. The appendix is divided into four sections: the first describes the selection of earnings weights for the various education levels; the second, the derivation of quality indexes and estimates of average years of education; the third, time spent in school by recent students; and the fourth, time spent in part-time day education under released time and similar programs.

I. Weights for Education Groups

The chief purpose of this section is to review the scattered and fragmentary information available concerning European earnings differentials by amount of education. Comparisons with the United States are attempted but the difficulties are great. Though detailed and fairly lengthy, this section has the limited objective of arriving at a single set of weights that can reasonably be used to compute quality indexes for Northwest European labor. I do not pretend to know whether apparent differences among European countries are real, or reflections of noncomparability or inaccuracy in the estimates.

Earnings data presented in this section refer to males. They are expressed as percentages (indexes) of the earnings of those with some stated level of education (8 years of education or the nearest level available). Unless otherwise indicated the indexes presented are unweighted averages of similar indexes for each of four age groups: 25–34, 35–44, 45–54, and 55–64. This procedure largely removes the effect of correlation between age and amount of education.

It may be noted that, above the 8-year education level, earnings differentials between education groups typically increase with age. Differentials are much smaller in the 25–34 age group than at higher ages. Table F–1 shows the earnings pattern for American males in 1959, which is typical.

United States

Table F–2 gives an assortment of income differentials for American males, including some shown only because they are useful for comparisons with data available for other countries. Columns 1 and 2 give the differentials based on 1949 income that were used in this study, before and after reduction

TABLE F–1

United States: Indexes of Mean 1959 Earnings of Males[a] with Earnings, by Age and Years of School Completed[b]

(*Earnings at 8 years of education = 100*)

Years of school completed	Age groups (in years)				
	25–34	35–44	45–54	55–64	Average of four age groups
0	52	46	50	58	51
Elementary					
1–4	62	61	58	62	61
5–7	82	83	83	84	83
8	100	100	100	100	100
High school					
1–3	114	116	117	119	116
4	128	135	136	141	135
College					
1–3	139	166	175	178	165
4 or more	168	230	272	270	235
4	166	211	237	249	216
5 or more	170	253	314	297	258

Sources: Computed from U.S. Bureau of the Census, *Census of Population, 1960*: "Occupation by Earnings and Education," pp. 2–3 [G56], except that indexes for the groups with less than 8 years of elementary school are based on the total income of males with income and were computed from distributions given in *ibid.*, "Educational Attainment," pp. 88–89 [G55].
a. Males in the experienced civilian labor force in 1960.
b. Age and years of school completed as of 1960.

for associated differences in ability and the like (see Chapter 8, pp. 83–84). Columns 3 and 4 give similar differentials computed from 1959 earnings, based on Table F–1. They are almost the same as Columns 1 and 2 except that the earnings of high school graduates are a bit lower relative to the other groups. Column 5 differs from Column 3 in that "farmers and farm managers" and "farm laborers and foremen" have been excluded to provide data comparable with those available for most other countries. Exclusion of agriculture narrows earnings differentials. Column 6 shows the differentials in median earnings that correspond to the differentials in arithmetic means given in Column 3; above the 8-year level differentials in medians are much smaller than in means.

Canada

Although Canada is excluded from this study, it is discussed because usable data are available for so few advanced countries that all indications of the amount of variation among countries in earnings

TABLE F–2

United States: Indexes of Income by Years of School Completed, 1949 and 1959[a]

(*Income or earnings at 8 years of education = 100*)

Years of school completed	All males, based on mean income in 1949		Males[b] with earnings in 1959				
			Based on 1959 mean earnings			Based on 1959 median earnings, total employment, not reduced
			Total employment		Nonfarm employment only, not reduced	
	Not reduced[c] (1)	Reduced to three-fifths[d] (2)	Not reduced (3)	Reduced to three-fifths[d] (4)	(5)	(6)
0	50	70	51	71	80	43
Elementary						
1–4	65	79	61	77		55
5–7	80	88	83	90		82
8	100	100	100	100	100	100
High school						
1–3	115	109	116	110	114	113
4	140	124	135	121	134	125
College						
1–3	165	139	165	139	160	141
4 or more	235	181	235	181	220	183
4	—	—	216	170	208	178
5 or more	—	—	258	195	248	189

Sources: Columns (1) and (2): Denison, *Sources of Economic Growth*, p. 68 [B25]; Column (3): Table F–1; Column (4): derived from Column (3); Columns (5) and (6): derived from U.S. Bureau of the Census, *Census of Population, 1960*, "Educational Attainment," pp. 88–89 [G55].
a. All indexes are simple averages of similar indexes for four 10-year age groups from 25 to 64, except that in computing the first three rows of Column (6) the 25–34 group is represented by the average of similar indexes for the 25–29 and 30–34 age groups.
b. Males in the experienced civilian labor force in 1960.
d. Estimates represent indexes of earnings after reducing differences from the 8-year level by two-fifths.

TABLE F-3

*Comparative Indexes of Mean Earnings Differentials
of Males in Nonfarm Labor Force by
Education Level: Canada, 1960–61, and
United States, 1959*

(*Earnings at 5–8 years of education = 100*)

Canada, 1960–61			United States, 1959
Education category (with years completed)	Index	Index	Education category (with years completed)
Elementary, 5–8	100	100[a]	Elementary, 5–8
Secondary, 1–3	123	123	High school, 1–3
Secondary, 4–5	153	146	High school, 4
University, no degree	171	176	College, 1–3
University, degree	258	250	College, 4 or more

Sources: Canadian indexes computed from J. R. Podoluk, *Earnings and Education*, pp. 43 and 69 [G76]. Indexes are averages of indexes for age groups 25–34, 35–44, 45–54, and 55–64. United States indexes are computed from Table F–2 on the assumption that earnings of the 5–8-year group are 94 percent of the 8-year group.
a. Estimated.

differentials are of interest.[1] The distribution of the Canadian labor force by years of school completed shares certain characteristics of both the United States and Northwest European distributions. Like the European countries, Canada has much smaller percentages than the United States at the high school graduate level and beyond. In general, the Canadian distribution is lower pitched than that of the United States but does not share the extreme concentration of the European distributions. Among males in the labor force in 1961, 7 percent had less than 5 years of education, 68 percent had 5–11 years, 15 percent were high school graduates, 4 percent had some university training, and 5 percent had a university degree. If the difference between the United States and Northwest European distributions affects relative earnings, this should show up in less intense form in the Canadian data.

Canadian earnings data, which were obtained in the decennial census enumeration, exclude agricultural workers. I therefore compare them with non-agricultural data for the United States. The chief difficulty in a comparison is that Canadian earnings

data combine those with 5 through 8 years of education. It appears that a comparable United States figure would be about 94 percent of 8-year earnings, and Table F–3 makes the comparison on that basis.

The main impression from the comparison is that differentials are rather similar in the United States and Canada. The differential between the 5–8-year group and the high school graduate group is about one-seventh larger in Canada. The differential between the high school and college graduate groups is about the same in the two countries. The comparisons are slightly affected by the fact that Canadian high school graduates in certain provinces (including Quebec) have an extra year of education. What seems to come out of the comparison is that, overall, Canadian differentials are larger but very little larger.

France

Data for France are much the most satisfactory among those available for European countries. They refer to earnings of wage and salary workers in 1962. They were collected in a special survey by the National Institute of Statistics and Economics (INSEE). The report of the survey has not yet been published but some summary results have generously been made available by Edmond Malinvaud and are shown on the left side of Table F–4. Amount of education is measured by age at leaving school. The number of years of education is approximately equal to this age minus 6.[2]

Table F–4 also attempts a rough comparison of differentials in France and the United States. The comparison is made with American data from which agricultural workers have been eliminated. French workers who left school at age 14 or less include those with complete or incomplete elementary education; Table F–10 indicates (after allowance for the difference in dates) that the bulk of them had 7 or 8 years of schooling. Table F–4 assumes that earnings of a comparable United States group would be 95 percent of the earnings of those with 8 years of education. Those leaving school at 15–18

---

1. The order in which these countries are discussed is dictated by the suitability of the data for the purposes of this study. Canada and France have by far the most appropriate data.

2. The French earnings indexes are standardized by age, but the precise method is unknown to me.

TABLE F-4

*Comparative Indexes of Mean Earnings Differentials of Males
in Nonfarm Labor Force by Education Level:
France, 1962, and United States, 1959*[a]

(Earnings at education level indicated = 100)

| Age at leaving school (in years) | France, 1962 | | | United States, 1959 | | |
	Approximate years of school completed	Index		Index	Education category (with years completed)
14 or less	7 or 8 (a few have less)	100		100	Assumed to be 95 percent of earnings at elementary, 8
15–18	9–12	150		121[b] / 143[b]	High school, 1–3 / High school, 4
19–21	13–15	190		170	College, 1–3
22 and over	16 or more	260		235 / 263	College, 4 or more / College, 5 or more

Sources: France: INSEE unpublished data from special survey; United States: see Table F-1. See text for explanation.
a. French data cover male nonfarm wage and salary workers and United States data cover male nonfarm workers with earnings in 1959.
b. With the two groups weighted by United States numbers, the combined index is 133; with the groups weighted by French numbers, the combined index is 127.

years in France are divided in roughly equal proportions among those with 9, 10, 11, or 12 years of schooling. They correspond to United States students attending high school with or without completion, but a larger proportion of the Americans than of the French in the group had completed 12 years of schooling.

The French differential between elementary and university groups (the first and last groups in the table) is about the same as the American differential between those with a comparable elementary education and those with 5 or more years of college, or less than one-fifth larger if the comparison is made with Americans with 4 or more years of college. Most, though not all, French university graduates have 17 or more years of education. The earnings of the intermediate groups in France are considerably higher than in the United States relative to both the elementary and university graduate groups. The general picture—a spread between elementary and university levels not much greater than in the United States but with higher earnings at the intermediate levels—is similar to but more accentuated than that shown in the comparison with Canada.

Data available for the remaining countries are much less suitable for the purpose at hand than those for Canada and France.

Netherlands

Available information for the Netherlands refers to wage and salary workers in manufacturing, coal mining, construction, banking, and insurance.[3] Workers are classified among five educational levels according to type of certificate or degree held. Medians and first and third quartile values, but not arithmetic means, are available for earnings. Indexes of medians are given in Table F–5.[4] Indexes of the average of the first, second, and third quartile values are nearly the same.

Each of the Dutch education groups covers a fairly wide span of years of education and there is some overlapping. Estimates of the average numbers of years can be given, however.[5]

To match the Dutch and American education levels is particularly difficult but some rough comparisons with median earnings of all American male members of the experienced labor force with earn-

3. Data are from *Maandschrift van het Centraal Bureau voor de Statistiek*, June 1964, p. 554 [G24].
4. The Dutch indexes given in Table F–5 are averages of indexes for 5-year age classes in the age span from 25–49 and of a single 15-year age class in the 50–64 age span. Indexes for each of the 5-year classes were given a weight of 1; those for the 50–64 age span a weight of 3. Data for the age groups used elsewhere are not available.
5. They were computed from data given in Section II of this appendix.

TABLE F-5

Comparative Indexes of Median Earnings Differentials of Males by Education Level: Netherlands, 1962, and United States, 1959[a]

(Earnings at education level indicated = 100)

Netherlands, 1962			United States, 1959		
Education category[b]	Average years of education	Index	Index	Education category (with years completed)	
Elementary	7	100	100	Assumed to be 94 percent of earnings at elementary, 8	
			106	Elementary, 8	
Upper lower	10.5	112	120	High school, 1–3	
			133	High school, 4	
Middle	13.7	146	150	College, 1–3	
Semi-higher	16	174	189	College, 4	
			201	College, 5 or more	
Higher	20	295			

Sources: Netherlands: *Maandschrift van het Centraal Bureau voor de Statistiek*, June 1964, p. 554 [G24]; United States: see Table F-1. See text for explanation.

a. The Netherlands data cover selected industries and the United States data cover males (with earnings in 1959) in all industries.

b. The twenty-two Dutch education categories listed in the description of Netherlands estimates in Section II of this appendix collapse into these five groups in the following way: elementary, group 1; upper lower, groups 2–5; middle, groups 6–12; semi-higher, groups 13–20; and higher, groups 21 and 22.

ings are nevertheless attempted in Table F–5. The two distributions do not seem to be greatly different. If anything, Dutch differentials look smaller than the American. The Dutch index for those with higher education is above that for Americans with 5 or more years of college but the Dutch group had longer education than this American group. Also, it excludes teachers and other employees of government agencies and nonprofit organizations, whose inclusion probably reduces the differential in the United States.

United Kingdom

United Kingdom data are drawn from a survey of 6,500 male heads of households, age 20 or more, in Great Britain.[6] Mean income is available for only two broad education groups: those leaving school at age 15 or under, and those leaving school at ages 16–18. The former group presumably had 10 years or less of school; Table F–19 suggests that the bulk had 8 or 9 years. The second group presumably had about 11–13 years; the concentration is at the bottom of this span. The mean income of

6. They were collected in the National Readership survey by Mark Abrams and reported in *New Society*, July 9, 1964, p. 26, then retabulated and adjusted by D. Henderson-Stewart and presented in an appendix to M. Blaug in *Manchester School of Economic and Social Studies*, September 1965, pp. 252–54 [P28].

the second education group was 78 percent above that of the first, based on the usual procedure of averaging indexes for four 10-year age classes. However, Henderson-Stewart suggests that the average income of the first group equaled its average earnings while the average income of the second group exceeded its earnings by 10 percent. If so, the earnings differential is reduced to 62 percent. If it is assumed that earnings of a United States group comparable to the first British group would be 4 percent above earnings of those with 8 years of education, and that Americans with 4 years of high school are equivalent to the second British group, the comparable American differential is 30 percent.

Median income is also available for those leaving school at age 19 or over but only for the broad age groups 20–44 and 45–64. (I disregard a 65-plus group.) Based on the average for these two age groups, the median income of the top education group was 51 percent above that of the middle group. In the United States, the median earnings of college graduates exceeded those of high school graduates—roughly equivalent education groups—by 47 percent.[7]

The comparisons given in Table F–6 are very crude, but seem to imply a much bigger differential

7. Those leaving at age 19 and over in Great Britain had 14 or more years of schooling, but perhaps three-fifths had 17 years or more (see Table F–19).

TABLE F-6

Comparative Indexes of Mean and Median Earnings Differentials of Males by Education Level:
Great Britain, 1963, and United States, 1959[a]

(Income or earnings at education level indicated = 100)

Great Britain, 1963					United States, 1959		
Age at leaving school (in years)	Years of school completed	Mean income (based on four age groups)	Mean earnings (based on four age groups)	Median income (based on two age groups)	Mean earnings	Median earnings	Education category (with years completed)
15 or less	10 or less	100	100	100	100	100	Assumed to be 104 percent of earnings at elementary, 8
16–18	11–13	178	162	169	130	120	High school, 4
19 and over	14 and over			257	226	176	College, 4 or more

Sources: Great Britain: M. Blaug in *Manchester School of Economic and Social Studies*, September 1965, pp. 252–54 [P28]; United States: see Table F–2, Columns (3) and (6); see text for explanation.
a. British data cover male heads of households and United States data cover males in the labor force with earnings in 1959.

between workers with elementary and secondary education, and a slightly smaller differential between those with secondary and higher education, in Britain than in the United States.

A survey to be conducted by the Unit for Economic and Statistical Studies on Higher Education at the London School of Economics and the Department of Applied Economics at the University of Cambridge should provide more usable information for Great Britain in the future.

Belgium

The Working Group for the Study of Human Capital at the Free University of Brussels (of which Max Frank is Chairman) undertook a study of the contribution of education to Belgian growth broadly similar to mine for the United States.[8] They divided the male Belgian labor force among five occupational categories, based on skill and earnings levels, and estimated the usual or average earnings of each level. They then set down the educational certificates or degrees typically held by members of each class. For example, those in Class I typically have a 6-year primary education and 1 or 2 years of lower secondary education. Those in Class V typically have a university education. In Table F–7 the

8. *Cahiers Economiques de Bruxelles*, No. 24, 1964, pp. 501–23 [P9].

degrees are translated into approximate years of education and the indexes are given.[9]

These differentials are far wider than those found to exist in any of the other countries. I do not know why this is so. It may reflect the fact that Belgian data actually refer to occupational differentials and educational differentials are inferred, whereas all the others are based on actual classification by education. The Belgian investigators were aware of and tried to avoid the danger of overstating differentials on this account but may not have succeeded. It is possible that differentials actually are much larger in Belgium than elsewhere. However, if the

TABLE F-7

Belgium: Occupational Earnings Differentials

(Mean income of Group I = 100)

Occupational group	Typical years of school completed	Mean income
I	7–8	100
II	9	130
III	12	251
IV	14–16	349
V	16 or more	502

Source: *Cahiers Economiques de Bruxelles*, No. 24, 1964, pp. 501–23 [P9]; see text for explanation of occupational groups.

9. The Belgian earnings patterns are presumed to refer to a year in the early 1960's.
The indexes are not age standardized, which would ordinarily cause differentials to be understated. Given the actual procedures followed in the study, this bias seems unlikely to be significant.

differentials given in the table are assumed to be comparable to those in other countries, it must also be supposed that in absolute terms the real earnings of all the education groups except the lowest are much higher than in the other European countries and, in the case of the top three groups, even higher than in the United States.

Because these Belgian differentials are so far out of line with those for other countries I decided, though with some misgivings, to disregard them entirely in arriving at uniform education weights for Europe.

Summary

For a general examination of the information that was assembled it was necessary, despite all difficulties, to try to convert the differentials described to a scale in which the earnings of persons with 8 years of education is taken as 100, in which all differentials represent mean earnings, and in which the various education groups are identified by years of education on the scale used for the United States. Differentials of all groups from the 8-year level were then reduced by two-fifths. The results are given in Table F–8. The chief assumptions or procedures follow (numbers given refer to the estimates before the two-fifths reduction was introduced):

1. Earnings of the lowest education group shown in the preceding tables were estimated to be the

following percentages of what they would be at 8 years of education: Canada, 94; France, 95; Great Britain, 104; Netherlands, 94.

2. Dutch indexes of medians were multiplied by American ratios of means to medians at corresponding education levels to try to convert them to indexes of means. A similar adjustment was made for the British differential between the second and third education levels.

3. Canadian education levels were assumed to be directly comparable to United States levels except that a slight downward adjustment in earnings was made at the high school graduate level because some had completed 5-year high schools.

Frenchmen who left school at age 22-plus were equated with Americans with 16 or more years of schooling, and those leaving at 19–21 with Americans with 13–15 years. Those leaving at age 15–18 were equated with Americans completing 9–12 years of education. Separate French differentials for the 9–11 and 12-year subgroups were computed by assuming: (1) the ratio of earnings of those with 12 years of schooling to those with 9–11 years was the same (1.22) as the ratio between Canadians with 4, and 1–3, years of high school, respectively; and (2) that 74 percent of the French in this group had 9–11 years and 26 percent, 12 years.

British males leaving school at age 16–18 (11–13 years of education) were considered comparable to Americans with 12 years' schooling, those leaving at age 19 or over with Americans having 13 or more years. Estimates of subgroups were then made on the assumptions: (1) that the ratios of earnings of those with 16 years and those with 17-plus years to those with 14–15 years were the same as in the United States;[10] and (2) that 30 percent had 14–15 years; 15 percent, 16 years; and 55 percent, 17-plus years. The 16 and 17-plus groups were then recombined using British weights for their numbers.

Netherlands males with "upper lower" education were directly compared with Americans having 9–11 years of education and the middle group with Americans having 13–15 years. Indexes for the semi-higher and higher groups were weighted by the numbers in each group in the Netherlands, and

TABLE F–8

Education Weights Derived from Data for Five Countries[a], *Selected Dates, 1959–63*

(*Earnings at 8 years of education = 100*)

Years of school completed	Derived weights				
	United States 1959	Canada 1960–61	France 1962	Great Britain 1963	Netherlands 1962
8	100	100	100	100	100
9–11	110	111	122	—	105
12	121	126	139	141	—
13–15	139	140	152	176	138
16 or more	181	191	194	242	208

Source: See text for derivation.
a. Estimates represent indexes of earnings after reducing differences from the 8-year level by two-fifths.

10. For these calculations a United States index of 175 was used for the 14–15-year group as compared with 165 for the 13–15-year group.

the resulting weighted average compared with Americans with 16 or more years of schooling.

4. The indexes for Canada, France, and the Netherlands were multiplied by the ratios of the corresponding indexes in the United States when agriculture is included to the indexes when agriculture is excluded.

After examination of these indexes and the comparisons discussed earlier, the decision was made to use the French indexes for all the European countries. This was chiefly because, among the European countries, the original French data were much the most suitable for the purpose at hand. They were obtained in a survey designed for the purpose, arithmetic means were available, and the only major adjustment introduced was to subdivide the 12–15 year education group.

The British differential between the 8- and 12-year levels is about the same as the French. For higher education levels the British statistics yield larger differentials but the original statistics for these higher levels are wholly inadequate for the purpose of this study; it is just not possible to state whether or not differentials are really larger than in France. The Dutch statistics suggest a differential over the whole span reasonably close to that in France but much lower indexes at intermediate points. If the index for the 9–11 level is somewhat understated (which is not unlikely), the Dutch distribution appears rather similar to that for Canada and not greatly different from that for the United States. The Dutch statistics are not satisfactory for our purpose because of their restricted industrial scope and the necessity of adjusting medians, but it is doubtful that these factors in themselves account for the finding of lower indexes at the intermediate levels than in France; a relatively large concentration of the Dutch labor force at this level may be partly responsible.

The main contribution of the Canadian, Dutch, and even the British data is to confirm the conclusion from the French data that, despite the relative scarcity of individuals with higher education, differentials over the whole education span do not *greatly* exceed those in the United States. Except for the Dutch data they support the finding that, in comparison with the United States, earnings are particularly high at the high school graduate level.

II. Education Quality Indexes and Average Years of Schooling of the Labor Force

This section describes distributions of the labor force by years of education (some of which are presented in Table 8–1); the quality indexes over time given in Tables 8–5 and 8–6; the 1960 quality indexes for comparison of countries, based on years of education, given in Column 1, Table 8–7; and the average years of education, given in Table 8–12. If estimates for the specific years shown in these tables are not discussed for a particular country, they were obtained by interpolation or extrapolation of data for years described.[11] Where estimates or projections for years not needed in this study were readily available, they have been included for the convenience of others engaged in research in this area.

United States

TIME SERIES. Time series estimates were derived by the following procedure:

1. Percentage distributions of the civilian labor force 18 years of age and over, classified by highest school grade completed, were obtained for each sex for the seven dates shown in Table F–9. Data are from the Bureau of the Census, *Current Population Reports* (Series P–50, Nos. 14, 49, and 78 [G57]), and from the Bureau of Labor Statistics, *Special Labor Force Reports* (Nos. 1, 30, 53, and 65 [G70]).[12]

2. For each sex the average number of years of education of persons in the labor force at each date was calculated from the distributions (Table F–9). The class-interval means used in these calculations for all dates were obtained by dividing the numbers in each class interval in every age-sex group in the labor force in 1957 among 1-year education classes

11. I depart from the usual order in describing the country estimates by putting France first among the European countries. This facilitates description of the estimates.
12. The original data for October 1948 exclude persons who were unemployed or 65 years or more of age. They were adjusted for comparability with later years on the basis of October 1952 relationships. At the earlier dates some detailed education classes at the bottom of the distribution were combined in the original sources, and estimation was required to subdivide them.

TABLE F-9

United States: Percentage Distributions of the Civilian Labor Force,
18 Years of Age and Over, by Sex and Years of School Completed,
and Mean Years Completed, Selected Dates, 1948–65

Sex and date	Years of school completed								Mean years completed
	0	1–4	5–7	8	9–11	12	13–15	16 or more	
Males									
October 1948	2.0	6.6	14.5	20.8	20.2	22.6	6.8	6.4	9.5
October 1952	1.8	6.5	13.5	19.4	18.9	23.7	8.1	8.1	9.9
March 1957	1.4	5.7	12.1	17.2	19.6	26.2	8.3	9.5	10.1
March 1959	1.2	4.9	11.1	15.9	20.2	27.2	9.1	10.5	10.4
March 1962	1.0	4.4	10.0	14.2	19.6	28.7	10.4	11.7	10.7
March 1964	.7	3.7	9.0	13.6	19.4	31.1	10.6	12.1	10.9
March 1965	.6	3.8	8.5	12.8	19.4	32.0	10.5	12.5	11.0
Females									
October 1948	1.5	4.5	11.4	17.7	17.4	32.7	8.0	6.7	10.1
October 1952	1.3	4.2	10.0	15.6	18.3	34.0	8.9	7.7	10.4
March 1957	.9	3.4	9.0	13.9	18.8	36.5	9.2	8.3	10.7
March 1959	.7	2.8	8.6	12.9	19.1	38.1	9.7	8.0	10.8
March 1962	.5	2.5	7.3	11.5	18.8	38.7	11.2	9.5	11.1
March 1964	.4	2.0	6.9	10.9	18.8	40.9	10.6	9.5	11.2
March 1965	.4	2.0	6.1	10.4	18.8	41.9	10.4	10.0	11.3

Source: See text for derivation. Percentages may not add to 100.0 because of rounding.

in proportion to the numbers in the corresponding age-sex groups in the whole population in 1960, as reported in the *Census of Population, 1960* [G54].

3. Preliminary quality indexes for each sex that took account only of years of education were calculated by applying to the distributions the United States earnings weights given in Table 8–3.

4. For later use, both average years and preliminary quality indexes were computed for those of each sex falling within the 1–12 years of education range. Comparison of these series showed that for each sex the ratio of the percentage increase in the quality index from October 1948 to March 1962 to the percentage increase in the average number of years of education was 0.48, and approximately 0.48 also in the various subperiods. It was inferred that each 1 percent increase in the average number of years of education would raise the quality index by about 0.48 percent within the 1–12 year range of the distribution.

5. All the series described in Steps 2, 3, and 4 were estimated for the middle of 1950, 1955, 1960, and 1962 by interpolating between the months for which data were available.

6. The preliminary quality indexes computed in Steps 3 and 5 (and shown in Table 8–5) would be

correct if a year of education had the same meaning over time. However, as indicated in Chapter 8, the number of days in school represented by each year has greatly increased over time. Steps 7, 8, and 9 describe the adjustment of the quality indexes for this development.

7. The average days attended per year, per enrolled pupil, at the time each age group was attending elementary and secondary school was estimated from Office of Education data. It was assumed that days per year in higher education have not changed. From these estimates, and distributions of the labor force by age, sex, and years of education, the average number of days of education per year, per enrolled pupil, was calculated for males and females in the labor force, 18 years of age and over, in 1960. It was further assumed that those who completed one year or more of college *at any date* had averaged 158 days a year in elementary and secondary school, so that the increase in days per year resulted entirely from those who did not complete one year of college.[13] This assumption permitted the average

13. Persons who completed one or more years of college in the past are thought usually to have attended regularly either school systems with a full-length school year or equivalent private schools, or else to have made up any deficiency by additional precollege training (usually at academies con-

days per year to be calculated for males and for females in the labor force in 1960 who had not completed one year of college.

8. Similar calculations of average days for all males 25 or more years of age (both for the entire education range and the range from 1 through 12 years of education) were made for 1950, 1960, and 1970.[14] These were used to extrapolate to 1950 and 1970 the male and female labor force averages for 1960, and other dates were set by interpolation. The change in average days of school attendance occurred at a steady rate. Thus, use of the same movement for the labor force as for males 25 and over and the use of the interpolation procedure should introduce, at most, only slight error despite the fact that labor force series for average days of attendance tend to lead those for males 25 and over by several years.

9. For members of the labor force with 1–12 years of education, it was initially assumed that a given percentage increase in the average number of days of education per year had the same effect on the quality of labor as a similar percentage increase in average years of education. The quality indexes for this group were therefore initially adjusted upward 0.48 percent (Step 4 above) for each 1 percent increase in the average days of education per year, and recombined with the indexes for the groups with no education or more than 12 years. This yielded a "semifinal" set of quality indexes for males and females.

10. It appeared, however, that this initial adjustment was likely to be too large for several reasons:

First, and least important, the data used for days-per-year may have a small upward bias over time. The original data used refer to days attended per pupil enrolled rather than per pupil in average daily class membership, which would be preferable.[15]

The ratio of true average daily membership to reported enrollment may have increased.

This would occur as nominal enrollments declined with better enforcement of attendance laws and improvement of school statistics. However, there may be an offset. Some students drop out during the year, remaining in enrollment but not in membership and average daily attendance. Other things being equal the ratio of dropouts during a year to total enrollment declines as the average number of years of school attended rises.

Second, the procedure followed is, strictly speaking, appropriate for adjustment of an original series based on years of school attended rather than on highest school grade completed. Although the distinction is, over all, of no great importance, data for highest school grade completed implicitly allow for reduced absenteeism insofar as respondents with scanty attendance failed to achieve promotion to a next recognized grade and so report, or based their response to the highest-school-grade-completed question on the "reader" they had last finished.

Third, at any point in time absenteeism is greater in elementary schools than in secondary schools. The increase in the proportion of secondary school pupils would thus have raised the average number of days attended by all pupils even without a change in each separate grade. The influence of this factor ought to be removed.

Fourth, even after elimination of those who went on to college, there must have been some tendency for students who reached the higher school grades to have been among those who had the most regular school attendance records in the lower grades. If so, the procedure described in Step 9 would lead to an overestimate of the increase in the quality index since the absolute earnings differentials per additional year of school are, in general, larger as one moves up the education levels.

It is impossible to calculate the precise effect of these several factors, but I have reduced the initial adjustment for the increase in school days described in Step 9 by one-third in an attempt to allow for them. This adjustment seems to me ample.

11. The final quality indexes for males and females (education at the 8-year level equals 100) were expressed as indexes with 1960 equal to 100. They were combined, by use of 1960 earnings

nected with the colleges). Hence, college graduates and those with 1–3 years of college may be considered to have had an equivalent education at all times. Consequently, the adjustment required to allow for extension of the school term outside the large cities and for reduced absenteeism is presumed to apply only to those with 1–12 years of education.

14. The basic estimates for these calculations had been made for my study of United States growth.

15. Average daily membership is not available for earlier years. The Office of Education has estimated that in 1957–58 average daily membership equaled just under 96 percent of enrollment.

weights given in Table 8–4, to obtain an index for the civilian labor force, and with a series for the armed forces, held constant at 100, to obtain a final combined index for the entire labor force. These series are shown in Table 8–5.

12. The procedures used here differ in two important respects from those followed in my American study of the sources of economic growth:

(a) The calculations are based on distributions of the civilian labor force age 18 and over, by years of education, with indexes for males and females combined by 1960 earnings weights, whereas the earlier calculations were based on distributions of all males 25 years of age and over.[16] In itself, this change would have had little effect on the 1950–60 increase in the quality index.

(b) The total adjustment for changes in days of school attended per year has been cut by about half. The earlier estimates assumed the effect of a change in average days to be the same as that of an equal percentage change in average years of education, based on the labor force as a whole. The present estimates assume the change in days per year affected are mainly those in the lower portion of the educational distribution, where absolute differentials in the weights applied to education groups are smallest.[17] The reduction was also intended to allow for a probable bias (in the use to which I put them) in the data used. The total reduction in the "days" adjustment from my original estimate was deliberately generous in response to several comments on the earlier study, and may be too large.

The quality index for civilians increases 7.6 percent from 1950 to 1960 as compared with an increase of 10.3 percent projected in my American study and 9.6 percent calculated in my OECD paper.

LEVEL IN 1960. The weighted average of the preliminary quality indexes for male and female civilians described in Step 4 above was 118.9 in 1960 (educational quality of individuals with 8 years of

education equal to 100). Since the assumptions were made in Column 1, Table 8–7, that (1) the same number of years of education in the United States and Europe have *recently* been equivalent, and (2) a year of education of older Americans represents less education than that of recent students, this figure must be reduced for comparison with other countries. Procedures similar to those described for the time series yield an estimate that the educational quality of civilian labor in 1960 was 94.5 percent of what it would have been if each year of education of the labor force represented the same number of days of schooling as it did for recent students (taken as 158 days per student enrolled on the Office of Education basis). The adjusted quality index for the United States is then 112.4 for civilians in 1960.

France

Principal reliance is placed on an unpublished study by Michel Debeauvais, Jacqueline Pillet, Pierre Maes, and Nicolas Panayotakis of the Institute for the Study of Economic and Social Development.[18]

ESTIMATE FOR 1954. For the year 1954 the Institute developed two distributions of the occupied population by years of education. One is derived from the response to a question in the 1954 census which asked: "Up to what age did you regularly attend school?" The number of years of education was taken to be the age of leaving school minus 6 years. The second estimate was derived by examining school enrollment ratios at the time labor force members in each age group were attending school. The estimates derived from the census and those derived from enrollment statistics are compared in Table F–10, separately for males and females. The distributions from enrollment statistics are higher pitched and yield means for the number of years of school completed that exceed the census-based means by 0.7 years or 9 percent for males, and 0.3 years or 4 percent for females.

The authors note that the census-based figures show a large number with 6 years of schooling and

16. Exclusion of persons under 18 years of age introduces a formal incomparability with the European estimates but improves real comparability because those under 18 in the United States are mainly schoolchildren with part-time jobs who should receive almost no weight in the calculation.

17. The need for some such change was suggested by Edmond Malinvaud (in OECD, *The Residual Factor and Economic Growth*, pp. 64–65 [I43]), and by Mary Jean Bowman (in *Journal of Political Economy*, October 1964, p. 457 [P25]).

18. "L'éducation de la population française et son évolution de 1850 à 1980," Paris: Institut d'Etude du Développement Economique et Social, August 1963 (mimeo.).

TABLE F-10

*France: Percentage Distributions of the Labor Force
by Sex and Years of School Completed, 1954;
Alternative Estimates*

Years of school completed	Males			Females		
	Derived from the census	Derived from enrollment statistics	Adopted in this study for international comparisons	Derived from the census	Derived from enrollment statistics	Adopted in this study for international comparisons
0–4	2.9	3.0	2.7	2.7	2.8	2.6
5	3.9	0.3	3.6	3.6	0.2	3.6
6	17.1	0.5	15.6	16.7	0.4	16.4
7	23.1	29.5	21.1	23.0	44.2	22.6
8	30.4	34.0	27.8	28.4	24.7	27.9
9	5.0	8.1	4.6	5.6	6.3	5.5
10	4.8	4.1	4.1	6.5	5.1	5.1
11	4.0	6.5	6.5	5.2	5.8	5.8
12	3.8	5.4	5.4	4.1	4.3	4.3
13 or more	5.0	8.6	8.6	4.1	6.2	6.2
	100.0	100.0	100.0	100.0	100.0	100.0
Mean years	7.90	8.64	8.30	7.96	8.30	8.10

Source: See text for derivation.

an appreciable number with 5, whereas the enrollment-based estimates show negligible numbers at these levels but larger percentages with 7 or 8 years of schooling.[19] They suggest that in the past, and especially in the rural zones, some of the 12- and 13-year-olds continued to be registered as pupils but did not attend school (at least not regularly) leading to overestimation of educational achievement in the enrollment-based estimates. The census-based figures are apparently to be preferred in this range. The reason that the figures derived from the enrollment statistics are higher than those from the census for the upper end of the distribution, the authors suggest, may be explained by a misunderstanding of the census question. Those who left school and then resumed their studies may have reported the age at which their studies were interrupted. Evidently the enrollment-based data are superior at the top of the distribution.

In view of these comments, I have adopted the following procedure to establish the level of education of the French labor force in 1954. The enrollment-based percentages were used for the groups with 10 years or more of education. The percentage

19. Education was compulsory for 7 years from 1882 to 1936, and for 8 years thereafter.

remaining for those with less than 10 years of schooling was distributed among detailed classes in proportion to the census-based data. The resulting means are about midway between those obtained from the two sets of original distributions.[20]

The distributions shown in Table F-10 contain an open-end class for those with 13 years or more of education. For both sexes combined, it contains 8.1 percent of the labor force (8.6 percent of the males and 6.2 percent of the females). In addition to school leaving age, the census collected information on degrees received. When adjusted to labor force coverage, the Institute report found that 3.0 percent had the "baccalauréat" and 2.1 percent "brevets professionnels" (each requiring 13 or 14 years of study), while 2.3 percent held a higher degree, requiring 16 or more years. The sum of these (7.4 percent) is not far from the 8.1 percent with 13 or more years of schooling derived from enrollment statistics. I made a proportionate adjustment, obtaining estimates that 2.5 percent of the whole

20. Means given here assume 4 years for those with 1–4 years' schooling and 14 for those with 13 years or more, corresponding approximately to the Institute's practice. (Its report used 4 years for those with 0–4 years; I assumed in all distributions that 0.3 percent had no education; the difference in the mean is 0.01 years.)

labor force had 16 or more years of schooling and 5.6 percent 13 to 15 years.

The implied number with 16 years or more exceeds only slightly the census figure for the total number of persons with a diploma of "l'enseignement supérieur" (general or technical). If it is assumed that the number of females in the labor force with 16 years or more of education equals four-fifths of the total number of females with this diploma, then 1.2 percent of females and 3.2 percent of males in the labor force would have had 16 years or more of education. With this breakdown and the use of 0.3 percent as the proportion with no years of education (from the Institute study), and some consolidation of classes, the distributions shown in Table F–11, which correspond to those for the United States, are obtained.

When the United States earnings weights are applied, indexes of 101.9 for males and 99.7 for females are obtained for 1954, when the educational

TABLE F–11

France: Percentage Distributions of the Labor Force by Sex and Years of School Completed, 1954

Years of school completed	Males	Females
0	0.3	0.3
1–4	2.4	2.3
5–7	40.3	42.6
8	27.8	27.9
9–11	15.2	16.4
12	5.4	4.3
13–15	5.4	5.0
16 or more	3.2	1.2
	100.0	100.0

Source: See text for derivation.

TABLE F–12

France: Derivation of Education Estimates at Selected Dates, 1936–81

Item	1936	1946	1950	1954	1955	1960	1961	1962	1965	1970	1975	1981
Mean years of education of the labor force (enrollment-based estimates)												
Both sexes	7.70	8.15	—	8.57	8.59	—	8.90	—	9.13	9.47	9.95	10.55
Males	—	—	—	—	8.68	—	8.96	—	—	—	—	—
Females	—	—	—	—	8.49	—	8.85	—	—	—	—	—
Difference from 1954												
Males[a]	−.87	−.42	—	.00	.02	—	.30	—	.53	.91	1.39	1.99
Females[a]	−.87	−.42	—	.00	.02	—	.36	—	.61	.95	1.43	2.03
Estimated indexes of educational labor quality (persons with 8 years of school completed = 100)												
United States weights												
Males[b]	94.8	98.5	—	101.9	102.1	104.0	104.4	—	106.3	109.4	113.4	118.4
Females[b]	92.6	96.3	—	99.7	99.9	102.2	102.7	—	104.8	107.6	111.5	116.5
Northwest European weights												
Males[b]	98.1	102.9	—	107.3	107.5	109.9	110.4	—	112.8	116.8	121.9	128.2
Females[b]	93.8	98.5	—	102.9	103.2	106.1	106.7	—	109.3	112.9	118.0	124.3
Estimated indexes of educational labor quality (1960 = 100)												
United States weights												
Civilian labor force[c]	91.0	94.6	96.2	97.9	98.1	100.0	100.4	100.9	102.2	105.2	109.0	113.8
Total labor force[d]	91.3	94.7	96.4	98.0	98.1	100.0	100.4	100.8	102.2	105.0	108.7	113.3
Northwest European weights												
Civilian labor force[c]	89.1	93.4	95.4	97.4	97.6	100.0	100.5	101.0	102.7	106.3	110.9	116.7
Total labor force[d]	89.5	93.6	95.6	97.5	97.7	100.0	100.5	101.0	102.6	106.1	110.5	116.1

Source: See text for derivation.
a. Prior to 1955 and after 1961 the changes for males and females are assumed to be the same as for the two sexes combined.
b. The 1954 index was computed from distributions in Table F–11. Other years were calculated on the assumption that a change of 1 year in the mean years of education changes the quality index by 8¼ points with United States weights and by 10½ points with Northwest European weights. Estimates for 1960 were by interpolation. The *level* of the European-weighted indexes shown here is based directly on the enrollment-based education estimates, and is higher than that based on my compromise estimates. A downward adjustment was made in the European-weighted comparison with the United States.
c. Weighted average of indexes for males and females converted to the base, 1960 = 100. Weights are 78.4 percent for males and 21.6 percent for females, corresponding to their importance in civilian labor input in 1960. Estimates for 1950 and 1962 are by interpolation.
d. Weighted average of indexes for civilians and constant indexes of 100 for armed forces. Weights are 96.5 percent for civilians and 3.5 percent for armed forces.
Note: One additional decimal point was used in the calculations.

quality of individuals with 8 years of schooling is taken as 100. Calculations based on the unadjusted enrollment-based and census-based estimates each fall within 3 percent of these figures for males and 1.1 percent for females.

CHANGES OVER TIME AND THE LEVEL IN 1960. The Institute has developed enrollment-based estimates and projections for several dates. Distributions needed for the computation of quality indexes are not given in the report but the mean years of education are shown and reproduced in Table F–12. In the absence of distributions, changes in the quality indexes were estimated from changes in the average number of years of education.

For 1954 it was possible to compute mean years of education and quality indexes, by sex, not only for the entire labor force but also for various age groups (based on the enrollment-based estimates). It appeared that, within each sex, a difference of 1 year in the mean years of education corresponded to a difference of around 8¼ points in the quality index based on United States weights, with persons with 8 years of schooling taken as 100.[21] Estimates of the quality indexes for other years were computed on the assumption that this relationship held over time,[22] since these changes essentially result from the turnover of age groups in the labor force. Estimates for 1960 were obtained by interpolating between the 1955 and 1961 indexes.

The Institute investigated changes in school days per year in France and found that there had been no change in the percentage of students attending classes since 1900; the proportion was constant at about 90 percent.[23] Prior to 1900, it found, the proportion was lower and slight downward adjustments in the average years of education were introduced in the 1936 and 1946 estimates to compensate for this; thereafter no adjustment was required.[24] The

series therefore needs no adjustment on this account.[25]

The 1960 United States-weighted index for civilians (with the quality of persons with 8 years of education equal to 100) is obtained by combining the indexes for males (104.0) and females (102.2) by earnings weights; it is 103.6. The similarly computed index for the United States (after downward adjustment from 118.9 to allow for the change in days of education per year) is 112.4. The average quality of the French civilian labor force in 1960, as affected by education, is therefore put at 92.2 percent of the American labor force. Setting the quality of the armed forces in the two countries as equal, and using the French earnings weight of 3.5 percent, I obtain 92.5, the figure given in Column 1, Table 8–7, as the percentage for the entire labor force.

Time series, based on United States weights, for the civilian labor force and the total labor force were constructed by converting the indexes for male civilians, female civilians, and the armed forces (taken as 100 throughout) to a base where 1960 equals 100, and applying 1960 earnings weights to them.

A time series based on Northwest European weights was constructed by a parallel procedure. The only difference is that the comparison of the enrollment-based distributions for various age groups in 1954 led to the conclusion that a difference of 1 year in average education corresponded to a difference of about 10½ index points (eighth grade equals 100) in the quality index as against 8¼ when United States weights were used. The European-weighted index is at a higher level, so the difference in sensitivity is less than this comparison might suggest. The increase in the United States-weighted civilian index from 1950 to 1962 is 80 percent as large as that in the Northwest European-weighted index.

Belgium

E. Raymaekers has constructed estimates and projections of the stock of education of the Belgian

---

21. However, comparisons involving the 65 and over age group, separately, did not conform to this relationship.

22. The assumption is likely to bias the indexes downward when applied to the projections far into the future.

23. It is not clear to me whether this is altogether consistent with the statement, quoted on page 384 above, that some children probably were enrolled in school but did not attend classes, at least not regularly.

24. The 1936 estimate appears to have been reduced from 7.77 to 7.70 years and the 1946 estimate from 8.30 to 8.15 to allow for this.

25. The Institute also notes that there has been some increase in vacation periods, hence, reduction in scheduled days per year, but considers that this has not affected the quality of a year's education.

labor force based on past enrollment statistics, a technique similar to that followed in obtaining the French enrollment-based estimates.[26] He stresses the inadequacy of the basic data. His estimates yield the figures given in the first two columns of Table F–13, Part A, for the average number of years of schooling held by the Belgian labor force at different dates.

The level of the estimates in 1960 is close to that for France. The increase after 1950 is greater than in France. I have constructed quality indexes for Belgium by assuming, for each sex, that when the quality of individuals with 8 years of education is taken as 100, a difference from France, and from one date to another, of 1 year in the mean years of education is equivalent to 8¼ points in the index based on United States weights, and to 10½ points in the index based on Northwest European weights. These are the relationships derived for France. The resulting quality adjustment indexes for Belgium, converted to 1960 equals 100, and with the armed forces weighted in, are given in the last two columns of Part A, Table F–13. The same assumptions yield an estimate of the quality of Belgian labor in 1960 relative to the United States—93.9 in United States weights.

The procedures for combining males, females, and the armed forces are the same as those followed for France. Estimates for 1955 and 1962 given in Chapter 8 are interpolations.

Certain checks on both the level and movement of the Raymaekers' estimates can be made. The Belgian census collected data as of December 31, 1961, on the age at which the Belgian population had left school.[27] Data were not provided for the labor force as such, but they have been tabulated for all males 14 years of age and over who were not in school. Of this group 96.2 percent were in the labor force. The average number of years of education for this group was 8.9 years if years of education are taken as age of leaving school minus 6. This calculation is based on a tabulation by single years of education; grouped data are shown in Part B of

26. Raymaekers' estimates are given in "The Educational Stock of the Active Population in Belgium for 1940, 1950, 1960 and 1970" (1963), an unpublished memorandum prepared for OECD.
27. Tabulations were kindly made available by the Belgian National Statistical Institute.

TABLE F–13

Belgium: Mean Years of Education, Quality Indexes, and Percentage Distributions of Males by Years of School Completed

A. Education estimates for the labor force, 1940–70

Year	Mean years of education		Quality indexes (1960 = 100)	
	Males (1)	Females (2)	United States weights (3)	Northwest European weights (4)
1940	7.51	7.47	90.7	89.4
1950	7.98	7.95	94.3	93.5
1960	8.74	8.65	100.0	100.0
1970	9.68	9.46	107.0	108.3

B. Percentage distribution of males 14 years of age and over who were not in school, by years of school completed, December 31, 1961

Years of school completed	Percentage
0	.8
1–4	2.5
5–6	12.7
7	2.4
8	45.9
9	6.2
10	7.8
11	5.4
12	6.1
13–15	5.7
16 or more	4.5

Sources: Part A, Columns (1) and (2): E. Raymaekers in OECD unpublished memorandum, 1963; see text for explanation of derivation of Columns (3) and (4) and Part B.

Table F–13. An interpolation of Raymaekers' estimates for 1960 and 1970 yields the same average, 8.9 years, for males in the labor force at the end of 1961.

Use of Raymaekers' estimates yields for Belgium a larger increase in the education quality index than was obtained for any of the other Northwest European countries. This result, too, appears entirely plausible. Age groups retiring from the labor force had two years less schooling than those entering the labor force. In addition, the proportion of children continuing school beyond the compulsory school age has been large and sharply rising. In 1957–58 the proportion of the 15–19 year age group attending school was higher in Belgium than in any of the other countries except Norway, where the age of starting school is higher. (The proportion in the 5–14 age class was higher than in any other country except the United Kingdom, where the starting age is lower.)

Denmark

Estimates for Denmark are based upon a large representative sample survey of households conducted by the Danish National Institute of Social Research.[28] Interviewing took place in the winter of 1961–62; data refer to the year 1961. The sample used in my calculations, after eliminating persons for whom some necessary information was not available, covered 10,542 males and 11,069 females 15 years of age or over who were not in school. These individuals were cross-classified by sex, age, and education completed. The age groups distinguished were as follows: 15–19; 20–29; 30–39; 40–49; 50–59; 60–69; and 70 and over.

Six education groups were distinguished, based on type of school or examination, and it was necessary to equate these groups with the number of years of full-time education completed. The groups and the number of years assigned were as follows:

Type of school[a]	Years of schooling assigned
1 "7-årig folkeskole" (7 years' elementary school)	7 years for age group 15–69; 4 years for age group 70 and over
2 "8, 9 klasse, eller 2–3 år i mellemskole" (5 years' elementary + 2 or 3 years' intermediate school)	33%, 7 years; 66%, 8 years
3 "7-årig folkeskole + efterskole/højskole" (elementary school + special rural school)[b]	25%, 7 years; 75%, 8 years
4 "Mellemskoleeksamen" (intermediate school certificate)	9 years
5 "Real-eller praeliminaereksamen" ("real" school)	10 years
6 "Studentereksamen" (high school diploma)	12 years or more

a. English translations are only approximate.
b. The efterskole provides a full-time course for young people, especially those from rural districts, for about five months during the winter. It may be attended more than one winter. The division I have made here is an attempt to place the distribution at about the right level without dealing in fractional years.

The period of compulsory education in Denmark has been unchanged at 7 years since 1903.

The tables actually used from the survey do not distinguish between persons who were in the labor

28. Madsen, Pedersen, and Elgaard, *Nogle Tabeller om Uddannelse Erhverv og Helbred*, 1966 [B72]. Data referring to the labor force (mentioned below) are unpublished tabulations provided by the Institute.

force and those who were not. However, a tabulation of the total labor force classified by education but not cross-classified by age and sex was available. This was compared with the estimated distributions derived by sex that are described in the following paragraphs. The agreement was so close that no adjustment was required.

A distribution of the total Danish labor force (universe estimates) by age (14 and over) and sex was available for 1960 (and used as representative of labor force composition in 1961). To obtain preliminary distributions of the labor force, persons in the labor force in each age-sex group were distributed by years of education in the same proportions as persons in the same age-sex group in the sample used. These distributions are given for each sex in the third and fourth columns of Table F–14.

The cohort method was used to derive similar distributions for the labor force in 1951. A distribution of the 1951 labor force by age and sex was available. Each age-sex group from age 20–59 in 1951 was distributed by education levels in the same proportion as the age group 10 years older (that is, the same cohort) in 1961. The entire age group 60 and over in 1951, of each sex, was distributed like the age group 70 and over in 1961. The distributions for the age group under 20 in 1951 were estimated on the assumption (to which some adjustments were made) that the differences between the distributions for this age group and the next highest age group were similar in 1951 and 1961. The resulting preliminary 1951 estimates are given in Table F–14.

It was necessary to subdivide the highest education group, and some minor adjustments also appeared appropriate.

For the late fifties and early sixties, the ratio of the numbers graduating from Danish universities to the numbers obtaining the "studentereksamen" (high school diploma) four or five years earlier were computed. The ratios obtained were 0.625 for males and 0.145 for females. These proportions of the total numbers with 12 years or more of education were allocated to the 16-plus education class. The remainder of the 12-plus class was divided between 12 years and 13–15 years in the same proportions as in the United Kingdom distributions.

For females, the percentages obtained for each

TABLE F–14
Denmark: Percentage Distributions of the Labor Force, by Sex and Years of School Completed, 1951 and 1961

Years of school completed	Unadjusted distributions				Adjusted (final) distributions			
	1951		1961		1951		1961	
	Males	Females	Males	Females	Males	Females	Males	Females
0	—	—	—	—	.3	.3	.3	.3
1–4	5.1	3.1	.6	.4	5.1	3.1	.6	.4
7	72.9	71.8	72.0	69.4	72.6	70.5	71.7	67.8
8	7.1	8.4	8.4	10.1	7.1	8.4	8.4	10.1
9	3.4	3.9	4.3	4.0	3.4	3.9	4.3	4.0
10	8.3	10.9	10.7	13.5	8.3	10.9	10.7	13.5
12	3.2[a]	1.9[a]	4.0[a]	2.6[a]	.6	1.2	.8	1.6
13–15	—	—	—	—	.6	1.3	.7	1.7
16 or more	—	—	—	—	2.0	.4	2.5	.6
	100.0	100.0	100.0	100.0	100.0	100.0	100.0	100.0
Mean years	—	—	—	—	7.49	7.57	7.79	7.81

Source: Danish National Institute of Social Research, sample survey of households; see text for explanation of derivation.
a. Twelve years or more.

group with 12 years or more of education were then raised by half, in the belief that highly educated women were more likely than others to be in the labor force. Also, a nominal 0.3 percent of the labor force of each sex was placed in the "no education" category. Offsets were taken at the 7-year level. The final distributions are given in the last four columns of Table F–14. The concentration at the 7-year level, which corresponds to compulsory education, is probably somewhat exaggerated at the expense of the 5- or 6-year and perhaps, also, slightly higher levels, but it is surely not very great. It seems possible, too, that the percentages at the top of the distribution might be understated, but there was no basis for further adjustment.

Quality indexes for 1951 and 1961 were computed from the distributions in the usual way. (Because of the extreme concentration at particular years, the detailed weights given at the bottom of Table 8–3 were used in the 5–11 years of education range.) Estimates for other years are interpolations or extrapolations.

Germany

Distributions of the labor force by years of schooling were prepared for April 1964. These rest upon the "Vocational Training" follow-up survey

to the "Microcensus" (sample survey of households) for that date. Results were published in Federal Statistical Office, *Wirtschaft und Statistik* (No. 3, 1966 [G18]).[29]

A table on page 178 of that report divides the German labor force 14–64 years of age, excluding foreign workers, among four education groups. Percentage distributions for all males and females covered, and for the separate male age groups, are shown in Lines 1, 4, 5, and 6 of Table F–15.[30] A second table (on page 167* of the statistical annex to the report) was used to obtain an approximate subdivision of two of the groups. This table shows (among other entries) the percentage of the labor force that received its occupational training "only" from "Berufsbildende Schule" (full-time career training schools), as distinct from practical experience, subdivided by type of school among "Berufsfach-, Verwaltungs-, Fachschule" (vocational, clerical, and administrative training schools), "Technikerschule" (technical schools), "Ingenieurschule" (engineering training schools), "Pädagogische Hochschule" (teacher training schools), and "Universität, Hochschule" (advanced education institu-

29. Additional results are to be published subsequently; this was the only report available at the time of writing (1966).
30. Distributions were recomputed from those published after eliminating the "unknowns."

TABLE F-15

Germany: Percentage Distributions of the Labor Force, 14–64 Years of Age,
by Sex and Type of School, April 1964[a]

	Years of school assigned		Males by age group (In years)				Males	Females
Type of school departure[b]	Class	Mean	14–29	30–39	40–49	50–64	Total	Total
1 "Abitur" (including evening "Abitur")			2.6	7.2	8.0	6.5	5.6	2.8
2 Higher education completed	16 or more	17	(1.5)	(4.2)	(4.4)	(4.3)	(3.4)	(1.9)
3 Other	13–15	14	(1.1)	(3.0)	(3.6)	(2.2)	(2.2)	(.9)
4 "Nach Erreichen der mittleren Reife jedoch vor dem Abitur"	10–11 and 12	11.5	.6	.8	.9	1.0	.8	.8
5 "Nach Erreichen der mittleren Reife"	10–11	10	8.2	7.8	9.1	8.0	8.2	10.3
6 "Volkschule bzw. vor mittleren Reife"			88.6	84.2	82.0	84.4	85.4	86.1
7 "Berufsfach-, Verwaltungs-, Fachschule"	10–11	10[c]	(4.5)	(6.5)	(7.1)	(6.6)	(6.0)	(11.9)
8 "Technikerschule" and "Ingenieurschule"	10–11	11	(.7)	(1.2)	(1.2)	(1.1)	(1.1)	(.0)
9 Other	7 and 8	7.5	(83.4)	(76.5)	(73.6)	(76.7)	(78.2)	(74.1)
10 All categories			100.0	100.0	100.0	100.0	100.0	100.0

Sources: Federal Statistical Office, Wirtschaft und Statistik, No. 3, 1966, p. 178 [G18]; figures in parentheses are derived from ibid., p. 167*; see text for explanation of derivation. Terms in quotes are those used in the original source.
a. Excluding foreign and refugee workers.
b. Approximate English translations of the education categories covered are as follows: Line 1: high school graduates (including those graduating from evening courses); Line 4: intermediate school graduates without completion of high school; Line 5: intermediate school graduates; Line 6: elementary school graduates without completion of intermediate level; Line 7: vocational clerical, and administrative training schools; Line 8: technical and engineering training schools.
c. Eleven years for those educated in the postwar period but probably less for those educated earlier.

tions).[31] The last two of these were considered to represent higher education and to be included in the "Abitur" (high school diploma) group in the first classification; the remainder of the "Abitur" group in the original classification was obtained by subtraction. The first three of these groups were considered subdivisions of the "Volkschule" (elementary school) group in the original classification.[32] The correspondence of the two tables is imperfect but the procedure should not introduce major errors in this study's results.

Table F-16 converts these distributions into distributions by years of education. The number of

31. English translations are merely rough indications of the type of schooling covered.
32. The table also shows the percentage (23.3 for all males and 12.4 for all females) who received their training "both" from "Berufsbildende Schule" and from practical experience. It was assumed that those in this group received only part-time education (see Section IV below) whereas those receiving training "only" from "Berufsbildende Schule" received full-time education.

TABLE F-16

Germany: Percentage Distributions of the Labor Force
by Sex and Years of School Completed,
Mean Years of Education and Quality
Indexes, 1964

Years of school completed	Males	Females
0	0.4	0.4
1–4	0.8	0.8
5–6	1.1	1.1
7	38.3	36.3
8	38.2	36.2
10–11	15.4	22.1
12	0.4	0.4
13–15	2.2	0.9
16 or more	3.3	1.8
	100.0	100.0
Mean years	8.29	8.23

Quality indexes (persons with 8 years of education = 100)
United States weights	102.9	102.1
Northwest European weights	106.5	106.5

Source: See text for derivation.

years of schooling assigned to each of the seven education groups (for all age groups combined) is shown in Table F–15. Persons included in Line 4, Table F–15, were divided equally between 11 and 12 years, and those in Line 9 between 7 and 8 years, in the distributions in Table F–16.

A comment on the latter group, which includes over three-fourths of the total and consists of those receiving only compulsory education, is necessary. Full-time education is required in Germany up to age 14 (except that recently it has been 15 in Bremen, Hamburg, Schleswig-Holstein, West Berlin, and Lower Saxony). The starting age is 6, which nominally yields compulsory education of 8 years (9 recently in the excepted areas). The leaving age of 14 was included in the Constitution of 1919, and has actually been in effect in Germany throughout the period relevant to these calculations, although it presumably was somewhat less well enforced in earlier years.

In 1958, 80.2 percent of German children 5 through 14 years of age were in school. This is much the lowest percentage among all the countries covered in this study except for Norway and Denmark, where the starting age is higher than elsewhere. It implies that German children were receiving an average of 8.02 years of education while they were in this 10-year age bracket. This includes the years of education received by students continuing their education through their fourteenth year, either voluntarily or because by 1958 it was required in certain areas. Because it includes those continuing voluntarily, the average for those corresponding to the lowest group in the labor force distribution must have been appreciably under 8 years. For example, if even one-third of the 14-year-olds were obtaining two-thirds of a year of voluntarily extended education while they were 14, the average for the remainder (including those living where compulsory education was 9 years) was 7⅔ years. The average when the labor force was being educated must have been lower. I assign half of this group 7 years and half 8 years, implying an average of 7½ years. Small percentages actually have 9 or less than 7 but any other reasonable division that held the average at 7½ would yield practically the same quality indexes.

To complete the distributions shown in Table

F–16 the 3 percent of the German labor force that was 65 and over was distributed like the entire 14–64 group, and the 2.4 percent that consisted of foreign workers excluded from the survey was distributed like the Italian labor force with 7 years or less of education. Mean years and quality indexes (8 years equals 100) are also shown in the table.

CHANGES OVER TIME. The 1964 Microcensus data are cross-classified by sex and age. The age brackets are very broad, with only four classes distinguished (14–29, 30–39, 40–49, and 50–64) and no data provided for those 65 and over (who would have been 51 and over in 1950). These limitations of the tables block their use to derive an accurate distribution for an earlier date by use of the cohort method. The data given in Table F–15 show, however, that there is very little difference in the educational distributions of the four age groups distinguished, once allowance is made for the fact that the lowest age group excludes persons not in the labor force because they were still in school.[33] The absence of any consistent and pronounced tendency for the educational distribution to move up as age declines is a remarkable feature of the data. Moreover, in the absence of any significant change in the legal school leaving age, the younger age groups within an education category can have but little more education than the older age groups. The clear implication is that the education of the German labor force has increased very little since 1950, and less than in any other country considered.

A completely independent set of data confirms that the difference between age groups is smaller in Germany than elsewhere. The age at which full-time education ended was obtained in a marketing survey conducted by the Reader's Digest in 1963. The percentages of the population (male and female combined) that had left school at ages 15 and under, 16–17, 18–20, and 21 and over were tabulated for the age groups 21–29, 30–39, 40–54, and

33. In fact, there is the extraordinary situation that the 50–64 year male age group apparently had more education, as measured by either a quality index or average years of school, than the male labor force as a whole. This calculation assumes that education *within* each of the seven categories distinguished in Table F–15 does not vary with age and may therefore overstate the position of the 50–64 group, but this group could not have had much less education than the labor force as a whole.

55 and over. The data refer to the whole population (male and female combined) rather than to the labor force; the top age bracket is open-ended above 55 and therefore includes older individuals than those in the oldest age group in Table F–15.

Part A of the table shown below indicates the difference between the 30–39 and the 55 and over age groups with respect to the percentage who completed full-time education at each age. For example, in Belgium 54 percent of persons 30–39 and 80 percent of persons 55 or older left school at age 15 or less. The difference of −26 percentage points is the first number in the table. Part B shows a similar comparison of the 21–29 and the 55 and over groups. Since some in the 21–29 group had not completed their education, this comparison is less satisfactory. By either comparison, however, Germany shows the smallest differences between age groups.

Age when full-time education ended
(in years)

	15 and under	16–17	18–20	21 or more

Part A. Percentage in 30–39 age group minus percentage in 55 and over age group

Belgium	−26	11	11	4
France	−10	7	3	1
Germany	−4	4	0	1
Netherlands	−18	10	3	5
Great Britain	−7	6	1	0
Italy	−6	1	1	4

Part B. Percentage in 21–29 age group minus percentage in 55 and over age group

Belgium	−39	17	16	6
France	−27	13	8	5
Germany	−13	10	3	0
Netherlands	−25	17	3	2
Great Britain	−22	10	10	3
Italy	−23	3	9	11

Source: Derived from *The European Common Market and Britain*, Table 49 [B91]. Copyright 1963 by the Reader's Digest Association, Inc. Data used with publisher's permission. Numbers for Germany in Part B were obtained after a redistribution, with Reader's Digest Association permission, of the data for the 21–29 age group among the four educational levels to eliminate the small "no answer" category. The correction of a printing error in the Italian data was also provided by the publisher.

General considerations also point to an extraordinarily small increase in the education of the German labor force. An increase in the education of the labor force requires that those entering it have more education than those who leave it. This may result from one of three causes: First, the legal school leaving age may have been raised. But in Germany no significant increase occurred in the

relevant period. (Only the Scandinavian countries shared this characteristic.) Second, enforcement of school attendance laws may have improved. But strict enforcement was characteristic of Germany even in the nineteenth century and improvement could not have been as great as in most other countries. Third, voluntary education beyond the school leaving age may have occurred. But in 1957–58, Germany had a radically lower proportion of the crucial 15–19 age group in full-time school than Belgium, France, the Netherlands, or Norway. The proportion was a little below Denmark. It was only the same as in the United Kingdom where children start school at an earlier age. Since in all the European countries voluntary school attendance was small at the turn of the century, voluntary attendance cannot have increased as much in Germany as in the other countries.

Still another indication that the rise in German education has been exceptionally small is the fact that the difference between the average years of schooling of the labor force and the average years of education currently being received in Germany in 1957–58 was exceptionally small (see page 107).

The increase in education in Germany appears to be similar to but even less than that in Denmark which, in turn, was much below the other countries. (The increase for Germans alone was probably a little smaller than in Denmark, and the inflow of foreign workers since 1950 further depresses the index.) For males and females I estimate the increase in both average years of school and quality indexes in Germany after 1950 to have been four-fifths as large as in Denmark.

For a comparison with the United States in 1960, the 1964 indexes (8 years equals 100) were carried back to 1960, using the same annual change as in 1950–62. When males, females, and the armed forces are combined by the usual procedure, this yields the estimate, given in Column 1, Table 8–7, that the quality index for the German labor force, based on United States weights, was 90.9 percent as high as in the United States.

Netherlands

Estimates for the Netherlands were derived from data collected in the census for May 31, 1960. The Dutch census classified the labor force, by age and sex, among twenty-two education groups. Classification is in accordance with the highest level certificate obtained. The large proportion of pupils who drop out before obtaining a final leaving certificate for the type of education in which they are last enrolled are classified at the next lower certificate. There is, in general, no standard number of years of education required to obtain a given certificate and there is a wide difference between the minimum and the typical length of study. This, according to P. J. Verdoorn, is due to three factors:

a) the number of grades varies within each type of education, some primary schools have 6 grades, some 8, a secondary modern school can have 3 or 4 grades, etc.;

b) doubling of grades is normal in a selective education system; as a consequence it takes on the average about 6 years to complete the 5 grades of a modern grammar school;

c) admittants to a certain type of school may have chosen different ways to obtain admission: about 15 percent of the pupils admitted to grammar school education have received some years of secondary modern education.[34]

Verdoorn also provided me with the following estimates of the average number of years of education for each of the census categories, based on statistical and other information. The averages, and the percentage of the labor force in each group, are given in the following list:

Census category number	Average years	Percentage of labor force	Census category number	Average years	Percentage of labor force
1	7	56.1	12	15	0.7
2	10.5	4.8	13	15	0.8
3	10	14.1	14	18	0.1
4	10.5	3.5	15	15	0.1
5	11	11.0	16	16	0.3
6	13	0.5	17	18	0.1
7	15.5	0.4	18	17	0.2
8	13	3.0	19	16.5	0.3
9	14	2.3	20	17	0.1
10	14.5	0.1	21	21	0.04
11	16	0.1	22	20	1.3

Verdoorn used these estimates to compute the average number of years of education of the labor force in 1960 as 9.0 years for males and 8.9 years for females.

34. Memorandum provided by P. J. Verdoorn, January 1965.

Netherlands: Percentage Distributions of the Labor Force by Sex and Years of School Completed, Mean Years of Education and Quality Indexes, 1950 and 1960

(*In percentages of total by years of school completed*)

Years of school completed	Males		Females
	1950	1960	1960
5	4.7	.9	
6	21.0	11.9	
7	29.1	30.1	54.1
8	10.8	13.8	
9	—	—	—
10–11	25.5	32.5	36.6
12	—	—	—
13–15	6.3	7.6	7.9
16	0.6	0.8	0.6
17 or more	2.0	2.4	0.8
	100.0	100.0	100.0
Mean years	8.43	9.00	8.91

Quality indexes (persons with 8 years of education = 100)

U. S. weights	103.4	106.5	105.6
N. W. European weights	109.1	113.8	113.4

Source: See text for derivation and explanation of gaps at 9 and 12 years.

Table F–17 shows distributions of males and females in the labor force in 1960 by years of education. These were obtained by combining census data for the numbers in each category with Verdoorn's estimates of the years of schooling held by individuals in each category. All those in each education category, except the first, were either assigned the same number of years of education as the average for their group (if the average was a whole number) or divided equally between years of education classes (if the average was in half-years). Thus, all those in group 3 were assigned 10 years of education while those in group 2 were divided equally between 10 and 11 years. Since there is actually considerable dispersion in each education group, this results in a distribution with overly discrete changes and with complete gaps at 9 and 12 years that obviously do not exist in fact; but this should not significantly affect the quality indexes to be computed.

The same procedure could have been used for the very large first (elementary) group if interest were confined to 1960.[35] But the 1960 data for males, classified by age, were also needed to construct a 1950 estimate and the average number of years in this first group varies with age. The minimum legal school leaving requirement was 5 years of education or less for those approximately 72 years of age and over in 1960, 6 for those 52–71, 7 for those 17–51, and 8 for those 16 and under. Verdoorn informs me that each change in the law legalized a situation that had developed spontaneously. Actual changes were gradual, and the legal changes came into force at a time when some 80 to 90 percent of the age group concerned were already enrolled in the grades affected by the legal change. I have assumed that males in group 1 who were 65 and over had an average of 5.63 years of education, those 45–64 had 6.53 years, and those 44 and under had 7.43 years. These averages comply with the need for a weighted average of 7 years for all age groups, given the numbers in each age class. Each age class in group 1 was then treated like the other education groups. For example, of those 65 and over, 37 percent were assigned 5 years and 63 percent 6 years.

For males, the 1960 distributions by years of education were constructed separately for each age group distinguished in the census (14–24; 25–34; 35–44; 45–54; 55–59; 60–64; 65 and over). These distributions were then used to build up a 1950 distribution by use of the cohort method. Those 35–44 years of age and 45–49 in 1950 were assumed to be distributed among education classes like those 45–54 and 55–59, respectively, in 1960. In younger groups it was necessary to allow for students in school and in older groups for differences in labor force participation by educational level. This was done by examining the 1960 patterns. The resulting 1950 distribution for males is shown in Table F–17.

Table F–17 also shows mean years of education and quality adjustment indexes (8 years equals 100) in 1950 and 1960 for males and in 1960 for females.[36] It is almost impossible to apply the co-

hort method directly to labor force data for females and no 1950 estimate was attempted. Instead, the 1950–60 change in the quality index for females was assumed to be the same as for males. Since females receive only 12.4 percent of the total weight in the Netherlands (less than in any other country), little error should be introduced into the Dutch quality index by this assumption.

The 1950–60 change in the quality index for civilians was thus assumed to be the same, in United States and Northwest European weights, as that for males. It was weighted with a constant index for the armed forces to obtain an index for the entire labor force. Estimates for 1955 and 1962 were obtained by straight line interpolation or extrapolation.

The weighted index for male and female civilians in United States weights in 1960 is 106.4 (8 years equals 100) or 94.7 percent of the corresponding index for the United States. With allowance for the armed forces the educational quality of the Dutch labor force, based on years of schooling, is put at 94.8 percent of the United States in 1960.

Norway

The 1950 Norwegian census reported the highest general education attained after primary school, and all examinations taken at other schools normally lasting 5 months or more. Anne-Marie Arnesen used these data to estimate the average years of education of the employed population, by sex and age group, in 1950.[37] She then used the cohort method to obtain estimates for 1930, 1960, and 1970.[38] Arnesen arrived at the estimates of the average years of education of the occupied population given in Table F–18.

I have used these estimates to derive quality indexes for Norway, which are also given in the table (with the constant military index included). The procedures were identical with those followed in the case of Belgium; that is, they rely on the French

---

35. The quality adjustment indexes (8 years of education equals 100) would have been the same.

36. Weighting was carried out in the same detail as is shown in Table F–17. Females in the first group were actually divided by single years but the weighting system is such that the index would be the same if they were all put at 7 years.

37. A. M. Arnesen's estimates are given in "Measuring the Educational Stock of the Labor Force" (1963), an unpublished memorandum prepared for OECD.

38. The 1960 census results became available after the Arnesen study was completed. An attempt to check her estimated change from 1950 to 1960 by comparison of the two censuses was unsuccessful because I was unable to duplicate the Arnesen 1950 estimates.

TABLE F-18

Norway: Mean Years of School Completed by the Labor Force, by Sex, and Education Quality Indexes, 1930, 1950, 1960, and 1970

	Mean years of education		Quality indexes (1960 = 100)	
Year	Males	Females	United States weights	Northwest European weights
1930	7.6	7.4	94.3	92.6
1950	7.9	7.7	96.7	95.7
1960	8.3	8.2	100.0	100.0
1970	8.8	8.6	103.8	105.0

Sources: Mean years: A. M. Arnesen, OECD unpublished memorandum, 1963; see text for explanation of derivation of quality indexes.

relationship between differences in average years and differences in quality indexes.

It may be noted that compulsory school attendance in Norway has been 7 years, starting at age 7, throughout the period relevant to these calculations. (In 1959 it was raised to 9 years, but the change is being extended over the country gradually; it is expected to be complete by 1970.) Hence, none of the increase shown is due to a change in compulsory education.

United Kingdom

The education data used derive ultimately from the 1951 and 1961 censuses. They refer only to Great Britain, and no adjustment to include Northern Ireland, which has only a small weight, was attempted.

Rose Knight prepared the following estimates and projections of the mean years of education held by the labor force:

	Original estimates[a]		Revised estimates[a]	
	Males	Females	Males	Females
1931	8.72	9.14	—	—
1951	9.42	9.67	9.44	9.68
1961	9.88	10.05	9.89	10.03
1971	10.57	10.58	—	—

a. The "original" estimates are from "Educational Stock of the British Labour Force" (1963), an unpublished memorandum prepared for OECD. Revised estimates were provided in May 1966.

The base year of her original estimates is 1951. The census for that year asked each person how old he was when he finished full-time education. Knight assumed that the number of years of full-time edu-

cation equaled that age minus 5 years, the usual school starting age. She computed mean years not only for the total male and female labor force but also for each age-sex group within it. She then estimated the average years of schooling completed by the labor force as of 1931, 1961, and 1971 by use of the cohort method. The average education of each year of birth class that had completed its education in both 1951 and the other year was taken to be the same in the other year as in 1951. The average for other classes was estimated from enrollment or other outside data. When the 1961 census became available she recomputed the 1951 and 1961 data. The new and old estimates are almost identical. I have used her data for the new 1951–61 changes and her original 1931–51 and 1961–71 changes.[39]

For 1951 it is possible, by turning to the census, to obtain distributions of the labor force by years of education that correspond exactly to Rose Knight's assumptions, and that are consistent with her calculations of mean years. The distributions are given in the first two columns of Table F–19.

I have made two adjustments of these distributions for use in the present study; the adjusted distributions are also given in Table F–19:

1. The Robbins Committee on Higher Education has estimated (largely from past school records) the percentage of the working population that has had higher education after full-time courses.[40] Their estimates for 1951 and 1961 are as follows:

	1951		1961	
	Males	Females	Males	Females
Universities (number holding degrees)	1.7	1.4	2.3	1.4
Teacher training	0.5	2.0	0.6	2.3
"Further education"	(0.2)[a]	(0.0)[a]	0.4	0.1
Total	2.4	3.4	3.3	3.8

a. These are my rough estimates; the Report provides none prior to 1961. The percentages must have been much smaller in 1951 than in 1961 because of the recency of most advanced level programs of full-time higher education (see *Higher Education*, pp. 16 and 29–34 [G40]).

39. The increase projected from 1961 to 1971 may be a little too large because of a delay in raising the compulsory school leaving age. Since I use this estimate only to arrive at changes from 1961 to 1962 this can scarcely affect my estimates.

40. *Higher Education*, Cmnd. 2154–IV, 1963, pp. 126, 128, 130 [G40]. The Robbins Committee percentages refer to the working population age 20 and over, hence are slightly too high.

TABLE F–19

Great Britain: Percentage Distributions of the Labor Force by Sex and Years of School Completed, 1951

Years of school completed	Distributions derived from the census		Adjusted distributions used in this study	
	Males	Females	Males	Females
0[a]	.2	.1	.2	.1
1–4[a]	.2	.1	.2	.1
5–7[a]	2.0	1.0	4.8	2.9
8	8.4	5.7	27.2	23.5
9	64.8	59.2	45.1	42.3
10	10.5	16.1	8.4	12.9
11	7.3	8.9	7.3	8.9
12	2.5	3.4	2.5	3.4
13	1.4	1.9	1.4	1.9
14	.4	.6	.4	.6
15	.4	1.1	.4	1.1
16	.4	.9	.4	.9
17 or more	1.5	1.0	1.7	1.4

Source: See text for explanation of derivation.
a. Persons leaving school before age 13, corresponding to these groups, were combined in the census data. The means used by Rose Knight indicate nearly all of these would fall in the 7-year class except for those over 65 years of age who were assigned 5 years.

The 1.7 percent of males and 1.4 percent of females with university education exceed the 1.5 percent and 1.0 percent with 17 years or more of education derived from data on age at leaving school. I have adjusted the 17-plus groups up to the university percentages.[41] The percentages with teacher training or advanced "further education" (0.7 for males and 2.0 for females) are almost identical with the percentages (0.8 and 2.0) having 15 or 16 years of education. No exact correspondence is to be expected but the comparison suggests the data are roughly consistent.

2. I believe the procedure followed to convert age of leaving school to years of school completed slightly overstates educational achievement at the legal school leaving age, where the great bulk of the British labor force is concentrated. British children normally have started school in the September following their fifth birthday. During the period under review, almost all of those who left school at age 13 and 14, and most of those who left at age 15, left school at what was the minimum legal school leaving age at the time they left school. They were thus credited with 8, 9, or 10 years of education. However, the student could leave at the end of the school

41. The offset was taken at the 9 years of education level.

term (third of a school year) in which he reached the school leaving age.[42] Nearly all of those who did not intend to continue their education the following year actually left school as soon as possible, without completing the year. For greater comparability with estimates for the United States, which count only school years completed, and on the continent, where it is customary to leave school at the end of a school year, I have dropped by one year one-third of those originally classified as having 8 or 9 years of education, and one-fifth of those originally classified as having 10 years of education. The effect of this adjustment is not to disregard part years (which would provide formal comparability with the United States data based on school years completed) but to give them a fractional weight; those with part years are divided between the next lower and the next higher full-year class. Corresponding changes were made in the estimates of the average number of years of education.

Quality indexes were then computed for the adjusted 1951 distribution. Thereafter the procedure closely followed that used for France. Calculations for various age groups in 1951 were used to establish a relationship between differences in mean years of education and in the quality index. It was estimated that, on Rose Knight's basis, a difference of 1 year in the mean was equivalent to 6¼ points in the quality index for each sex based on United States weights (8 years of education equals 100), and to 10 points in the quality indexes based on Northwest European weights.[43]

ADJUSTMENT FOR ABSENTEEISM. John Vaizey studied absenteeism in Britain and concluded that average school attendance has risen substantially in the last half century because of the decline in truancy and improvement in child health.[44] He has indicated in correspondence that truancy dropped dramatically during the period from 1910 to 1920

42. Prior to 1918 the student could leave on his birthday. Recently (too recently to affect these data) the number of dates at which he could leave school has been cut from three to two a year.
43. A 1961 distribution could be derived directly from the 1961 census. Because the census labor force distribution by age of leaving school is condensed, a study based on more detailed data for the whole population by age and sex is required to do so. Data became available only at the last moment and this study could not be undertaken.
44. *The Economics of Education*, p. 81 [B106].

while the decline in child illness occurred mainly from 1925 to 1940, and he has suggested use of absenteeism figures of around 15 percent in 1910, 5 percent in the late 1930's, and somewhat less after 1945. Guided by these estimates, and with the assumption of 96 percent attendance throughout the postwar period and a minimum of 80 percent by the small group who were 75 years of age and over in 1951, I assigned attendance percentages to each age cohort. These estimates led to a calculation that the male labor force of 1951 had averaged 89.95 percent attendance and the 1961 male labor force 92.3 percent attendance during the period of compulsory education, and that the corresponding percentages for the female labor force were 91.3 and 92.7.[45] The increase over 10 years was 2.6 percent for males and 1.5 percent for females. Other years in the 1950–62 period were estimated by straight line interpolation and extrapolation.

My final estimates for the United States implied that a 1 percent increase in the average number of days attended per year by persons with 1–12 years of education raised the quality index with United States weights (8 years of education equals 100) by 0.27 percent. The same relationship was assumed to hold in the United Kingdom. This led to estimates that, in United States weights, the increase in atten-

45. Estimates of average years of school adjusted to postwar attendance equivalence were computed by multiplying average years by the ratio of these percentages to 96; they are shown in Table F–20.

dance raised the quality of labor from 1950 to 1962 by 0.85 percent for males, 0.51 percent for females, and 0.77 percent for the two together (based on earnings weights). The same estimate was used in Northwest European weights since those affected are at the lower end of the distribution where the weights are the same.

The time series estimates obtained by weighting males, females, and the armed forces by 1960 earnings weights are summarized in Table F–20. Those shown for 1950, 1955, 1960, and 1962 are interpolations.

COMPARISON WITH THE UNITED STATES. With those at 8 years taken as 100, quality indexes for the United Kingdom and the United States compare as follows for civilians:

	United Kingdom	United States
Adjusted for school attendance	108.8	112.4
Not adjusted for school attendance	110.0	118.9

The British index is 96.8 percent of the United States when both countries are adjusted for the difference between school attendance when the labor force was educated and attendance in recent years. With the armed forces weighted in, this becomes 96.9 percent, and this is the figure carried into Table 8–7. If data for neither country were adjusted for differences in school attendance this percentage would be 92.7. If only the United States were adjusted it would be 97.9.

TABLE F–20

Great Britain: Derivation of Education Estimates at Selected Dates, 1931–71

Item	1931	1950	1951	1955	1960	1961	1962	1971
QUALITY INDEXES (1960 = 100)								
Total labor force (United States weights)	—	96.8	97.3	98.5	100.0	100.3	100.7	—
Civilian labor force	—	96.8	97.2	98.5	100.0	100.3	100.8	—
Civilian before attendance adjustment	94.0	97.4	97.8	98.8	100.0	100.3	100.6	104.0
Total labor force (Northwest European weights)	—	95.8	96.2	97.9	100.0	100.4	101.2	—
Civilian labor force	—	95.7	96.1	97.8	100.0	100.4	101.1	—
Civilian before attendance adjustment	90.9	96.4	96.6	98.1	100.0	100.4	100.9	106.1
AVERAGE YEARS OF SCHOOL COMPLETED								
Males	8.49	9.16	9.19	—	—	9.64	9.71	10.33
Females	8.93	9.43	9.46	—	—	9.81	9.86	10.34
Adjusted to postwar equivalence for attendance								
Males	—	8.56	8.61	—	—	9.27	9.36	—
Females	—	8.96	9.00	—	—	9.47	9.54	—

Source: See text for derivation.

Italy

The Italian census for 1951 provides distributions by level of education of the labor force, classified by sex,[46] and of the population, classified by age and sex. Percentage distributions based on these data are shown in Table F–21. (The census detail for the university graduate group [laureati] is condensed in this table.) It was necessary, for application of the weighting system, to translate these data into distributions by years of school completed.

The number of years ordinarily required for each certificate or degree was known, but not the number who had started but did not complete the next level of school; in general these were considered small in number. The "analfabeti" (illiterates) and "alfabeti privi di titolo di studio" (literates without school certificate) presumably had less than 3 years of school (although some of the latter may have had

3 or 4). The percentages of each census category that I assigned to each years-of-schooling group are given in Table F–21.

These allocations yielded distributions of males and females in the civilian labor force by years of education in 1951. From them education quality indexes (8 years equals 100) could be computed directly.

For the construction of time series indexes, the following procedure was followed. Synthetic distributions for 1951 of the total labor force, and each age-sex group within it, were derived on the assumption that within each age-sex group the percentage distribution of the labor force by years of school completed was the same as the distribution of the total population in the same age-sex group. The detail by age thus obtained permitted use of the cohort method to distribute the male and female labor force in 1931, 1961, and 1971. Estimation of the oldest age groups in 1931 was mainly based on extrapolation of the patterns shown by year-of-birth

46. Data for the experienced labor force (which excludes those seeking a first job) were used in these calculations.

TABLE F–21

Italy: Allocations Used To Convert 1951 Italian Census Education Categories to Years of Full-Time Education

Education category[a]	Percentage of total labor force		Percentage allocation by years of schooling
1 "Analfabeti"	11.3		0 years, 90; 1 year, 5; 2 years, 5
2 "Alfabeti privi di titolo di studio"	12.4		0 years, 75; 1 year, 12½; 2 years, 12½
3 "Forniti di titolo di studio di scuòla elementare			
3ª elementare	28.9		3 years, 80; 4 years, 20
5ª elementare"	35.4		5 years, 80; 6 years, 10; 7 years, 10
Line 3, subtotal		64.3	
4 "Forniti di Licenza di scuòla media inferiore"	6.2		8 years, 80; 9 years, 6⅔; 10 years, 6⅔; 11 years, 6⅔
5 "Diplomati			
Licèo classico e scientifico	0.7		13, 14, 15, 16 years, 25 each
Istituto magistrale	1.4		12 years, 90; 13 years, 5; 14 years, 5
Istituto tecnico	1.7		13 years, 67; 14, 15, and 16 years, 11 each
Scuòla artistica	0.1		12 years, 50; 13, 14, and 15 years, 16⅔ each
Altri istituti o scuòle"	0.04		13 years, 100
Line 5, subtotal		3.9	
6 "Laureati			
Medicina e chirurgia	0.3		19 years, 100
Ingengeria e architettura"	0.2		19 years, 75; 17 years, 25
[All others]	1.3		17 years, 100
Line 6, subtotal		1.8	

Source: See text for derivation.

a. Approximate English translations are as follows: Line 1, illiterates; Line 2: literates without a school certificate; Line 3: graduates with elementary school certificates at third and fifth grades; Line 4: intermediate school graduates; Line 5: graduates with diplomas from the Liceo in classics and science, and from teacher training and technical institutes, art schools, and other institutes or schools; Line 6: university graduates in medicine and surgery, engineering and architecture, and other fields.

groups present in 1951, while estimates for the youngest age groups in 1961 and 1971 were largely deduced from recent enrollment data.

For the percentages thus derived for 1961 at the top of the distribution (laureati, diplomati, and forniti di Licenza di scuòla media inferiore) were substituted percentages estimated by SVIMEZ from surveys by the Central Institute of Statistics (ISTAT). Percentages for 1961 are given, for the two sexes combined, in OECD, *The Mediterranean Regional Project: Italy*, p. 36 [I33]. Separate estimates for males and females were derived by use of October 20, 1960, data from "Rilevazione Nazionale delle Forze di Lavoro."[47] The 1961 estimates are not exactly comparable to those for 1951 (especially for the separate sexes) but the incomparability is not serious. (The 1961 distribution for males is shown in Table 8–1.)

The 1951 index was extrapolated to 1931, and the 1961 index to 1971, by indexes computed for all four years from the unadjusted cohort estimates. The 1931 and 1971 estimates have but little effect on the 1950–62 indexes used in this study.

The weighting of indexes for the two sexes, and for military personnel, and the use of interpolation to obtain indexes for 1950, 1955, 1960, and 1962, was similar to that for other countries.

There can be little doubt that, by the standards of Northwest Europe, absenteeism of enrolled pupils is high in Italy, and that it has declined over the period relevant to this study, so that the number of days attended per year of school has risen.[48] If the

basic data used for the estimates referred to the number of years of school attended, or school leaving age, a substantial downward adjustment of the level and upward adjustment of the trend of the quality indexes would be required similar to the adjustments introduced for the United States. The actual estimates are derived from information concerning degree or certificate received and, for those without a certificate, literacy. Insofar as persons of different ages holding the same degree or certificate had received the same amount of education regardless of the number of years over which it was spread, for degree and certificate holders the procedure followed automatically adjusts the distributions for changes in days.[49] The problem may not be very serious for these groups except that it may be doubted that the older age groups with 3-year certificates had spent as much time in school as did the younger age group with 5-year certificates in their first three years. To offset the remaining biases, and to take account of those without certificates, I have allocated larger proportions of both the literates without school certificate and the illiterates to the no school category than would be warranted if consideration were literally given to the number of years enrolled in school irrespective of attendance record, and assigned none of them more than 2 years of education. This introduces an implicit allowance for irregular attendance into the quality indexes (with respect both to level and movement) by reducing the estimates to something approaching a full-year equivalent basis. This admittedly is not satisfactory. It is not unlikely that the quality adjustment indexes still understate the increase in, and perhaps overstate the level of, the educational quality of Italian labor in comparison with other countries. But if a bias remains, it seems unlikely to be large.

III. Derivation of Table 8-8

This table shows time spent in school by recent students, and possible alternative adjustments to

---

47. In recent years data have been collected annually, on a sample basis, in ISTAT surveys and published once a year in Ministerio del Bilancio, *Relazione Generale sulla Situazione Economica del Paese* [G20]. They appear to be generally in line with the estimates used here.

48. Vera Lutz says "even today many children never attend school, and still larger numbers do not attend regularly up till the officially recognized school leaving age of 14. Many of these relapse into illiteracy in later years. Poor attendance is due, in many cases, to the poverty of the parents: among the farming population children are frequently integrated into the family labor team at a very early age. In some mountain areas, attendance is made difficult by the long distances between the children's homes and the nearest school. Another factor affecting educational standards is poor school accommodation.... In all these respects the situation is, on the average, worse in the South of Italy than in the North" (*Italy: A Study in Economic Development*, p. 238 [B69]).

During the postwar period there has been a substantial rise in the ratio of enrollments to population in the compulsory school ages (OECD, *The Mediterranean Regional Project:*

Italy, p. 36 [I33]). Under these circumstances a decline in absenteeism on the part of enrolled pupils seems probable.

49. The number repeating a grade is high in Italy; the OECD report (*ibid.*, p. 43) considers it to be "in fact one of the most worrying aspects of the system."

1960 education quality indexes. As stressed in the text, the table is only an approximation, and the possibility of substantial errors in some numbers is not ruled out. It was derived as follows.

Columns 1, 2, and 3: Scheduled Days and Hours

The starting point for these estimates was information contained in UNESCO, *The Organization of the School Year: A Comparative Study* [I5], which reported the answers to an inquiry directed to governments. Information presumably refers to 1961 or thereabouts. This source unfortunately has some omissions and contains a number of ambiguities, inconsistencies, incomparabilities, and unrepresentative figures. I have interpreted, corrected, and filled gaps in the information by consultation with individuals in the countries concerned and in the United States Office of Education, but significant errors may remain. Three gaps were filled by the assumption of similarity to other countries, as noted in footnotes to the table.

Aside from rounding, Column 3 (annual hours) equals the product of Columns 1 (days per year) and 2 (hours per day). Estimates of annual hours for some countries were actually constructed in this way. More often the number of school weeks (with vacations and holidays eliminated) was multiplied by weekly hours to obtain annual hours. Multiplication of total weeks by days per week provided days per year, and their division provided the number of hours per day.

School schedules vary by grade level. Columns 1 and 2 are averages, weighted by enrollment, of averages for the age groups 5–14, 15–19, and 20–24. For ages 5–14 the simple average for grades 1–9 (United Kingdom 1–10), and for ages 5–19 the simple average for grades 10–14 (United Kingdom 11–15) were used. To combine actual data for grades 13 and up with the lower grades would be meaningless. The convention was adopted of using 180 days, 6 hours a day (the United States averages for high schools), for grades 13 and up in all countries (hence, also for the age group 20–24). These grades receive negligible weight in the European averages.

Although differences among countries in days

and hours as shown in Table 8–8 reflect variations in the composition of enrollment among (but not within) the three broad age groups as well as differences in days or hours at the same grade level, all the figures shown are in fact close to the averages for grades 1–9, which dominate the calculations.

Data on hours per year (Column 3) are in general more accurate, and certainly more significant for comparisons, than Columns 1 or 2 taken separately.[50] The number of scheduled weeks, with proportionate reduction for holidays and for vacations embracing part weeks, would perhaps be more significant than the number of scheduled days, but was not calculated for all countries.

Low figures for hours per day and high figures for days per year shown for Germany and Italy reflect the fact that hours are uniform, though short, for the six days of the week, hence, these countries are counted as being on a full 6-day week. The principal schools in other countries were counted as having a 5- or 5½-day week. Data are based on regular primary and secondary schools (which implies that full-time vocational schools are equated with them by years of school).

Column 4: Average Years per Student

Ratios of school enrollment to population in the age groups 5–14, 15–19, and 20–24 in 1957 or 1958 are given by Ingvar Svennilson, in association with Friedrich Edding and Lionel Elvin, in OECD, *Policy Conference on Economic Growth and Investment in Education*, Vol. II: "Targets for Education in Europe in 1970" (1962, p. 108 [I46]). Column 4 is the sum of the products for the three age classes of enrollment ratios and the number of years in the age class. Thus, in the United States 89.9 percent of persons 5–14 were in school so children aged 5–14 were presumably receiving (10×0.899) or 8.99 years of school on the average. From 15–19, 66.2 percent were in school for an average of (0.662×5) or 3.31 years. From 20–24, 12.0 percent were in school for an average of (0.120×5) or 0.60 years. This totals 12.90 years. Data for the

50. This is partly because it was not always clear what to count as a whole day and what to count as a half day, and because in some systems there are local variations in the distribution of the same number of weekly hours among the days of the week.

United States, France, Germany, and the Netherlands refer to 1958, those for other countries to 1957.

Although the averages obtained in this way refer to no single age cohort, they should provide a reasonably comparable measure of the amount of education being provided as of 1957–58. Differences in age distribution by single years within the broad age classes distinguished, especially the 15–19 class, could introduce small errors in the calculation.

Columns 5 to 9

Column 5 is the product of Columns 3 and 4.

Column 6 was computed by multiplying average years in the United States by Column 7 (unrounded) to obtain a United States-equivalent number of years based on hours attended.

Columns 7 and 8 are computed from Columns 4 and 5, respectively.

Column 9 was obtained by multiplying the difference between Column 4 and Column 6 by six, in accordance with the estimate that a difference of 1 year would mean about a 6-point difference in the quality index.

IV. Education in Part-Time Day Schools

This section amplifies the statement on page 98 that the inclusion on a full-time equivalent basis of part-time day education of young persons would have but little effect on the average years of education of the labor force, and hence on the quality adjustment indexes.

In the United Kingdom, 21 percent of the boys and 5 percent of the girls in the 4-year age bracket, 15 through 18, obtained released time from work to attend school in 1957–58, and about two-thirds of all those obtaining released time were in this age bracket. This implies that, as of 1957–58, all boys were obtaining an average of about 1.2 years of released-time education and girls 0.3 years.[51] Re-

leased time comprises one day of the week, and may reasonably be counted as about one-fifth of full-time education.[52] This means the boys on the average were receiving 0.24 full-time equivalent years of education in this form in 1957–58, and girls 0.06 years. The figure for males was only about half as large in 1948–49 and one-tenth as large in 1938, so the education of this type held by even the 1962 labor force must have averaged less than one-tenth of a full-time equivalent year. While the percentage was rising, inclusion of such schooling in the education measures used to compute the British education quality index obviously could not have a perceptible effect on the index.[53]

Germany has the most comprehensive provision for part-time day schools. Young people not in full-time schools are required by the 1938 compulsory attendance law to attend a "Berufschule" until they reach age 18 (or complete a three-year course) and most do so, particularly the boys. In 1955–56, when attendance at these schools was at a peak, they enrolled 1.2 million boys and 1.0 million girls, including considerable numbers over 18. Most (1.0 million) of the male students and almost half (0.5 million) of the females attended as part of an apprenticeship or trainee program conducted by their employer. The ratio of males of all ages enrolled in these schools to the number of males in the 5-year age bracket, 14–18, was 0.56 and the corresponding female ratio 0.46. Multiplying by five yields estimates that on the average German males were obtaining in 1955–56 a total of about 2.8 years of such schooling and females 2.3 years. Attendance was usually 1 day (generally 6 hours) a week for 40 weeks, although it was sometimes 2 days. This was normally in addition to a 5-day working week which, as Gertrude Williams says, "puts a heavy burden on young people a little over 14 years of age."[54] If, again, a year's attendance is counted as the equivalent of one-fifth of a full-time year, this amounts to less than 0.6 full-time equivalent years for boys and 0.5 for girls. These ratios have not

51. In the single age groups from 15 through 18 the average percentage of boys in part-time day school was 20.85, implying that during this age span an average of 0.83 years (0.2085 × 4) of such education was being obtained. About half as many older boys were in the program, raising the total years to 1.2. The calculation for girls is similar.

52. One day a week produces about 220 teaching hours a year in the United Kingdom, which is often supplemented by an evening class to bring the total to about 270 hours.

53. Data for the United Kingdom are drawn from Ministry of Education, *15 to 18*, Vol. I (Report), pp. 5–6 and Chapter 31 [G39].

54. Gertrude Williams, *Apprenticeship in Europe*, p. 43 [B109].

changed much since 1955–56, were slightly lower for boys and much lower for girls in 1950, and were apparently lower still before (and during) World War II.[55]

In 1964, 23.3 percent of German males and 12.4 percent of females in the labor force, aged 14–64, had received their occupational training both from "Berufsbildende Schule" and from practical experience.[56] If this group had received 3 years (a generous estimate) of part-time education, this education amounted to an average of 0.70 part-time years for all males and 0.37 years for females, or 0.14 full-time equivalent years for males and 0.05 for females. Some workers who had received part-time training are excluded because their training was unrelated to their present work, but an extreme outside estimate of the total would not exceed twice these amounts. The average could not have increased by more than about 0.1 years from 1950 to 1962.

The French system of vocational education is often rated the finest in Europe. Most vocational education is carried on through full-time schools and the data on years of schooling include this education, but part-time schooling is also widespread.

In 1958–59, 205,000 boys and 64,000 girls were in apprenticeship programs in commerce, manufacturing, and artisan trades. The ratios of persons enrolled in these programs to a 1-year age class of the French population at the appropriate age level was about 0.73 for males and 0.24 for females. Apprentices attend daytime "theory" courses 150–180 hours a year in addition to practical course work (mainly in schools conducted by firms). The cost of training that does not represent work for the employer is met by a payroll tax on all employers. It

may be reasonable to count these programs as a higher fraction of full-time education than that allowed for part-time education elsewhere—perhaps as much as one-third. If so, on the average, French boys were receiving about 0.24 full-time equivalent years of education in this way and girls 0.08 years in 1958–59.

In addition, France requires children (boys and girls) of agricultural workers not enrolled in other schools to attend courses one day a week (a minimum of 100 hours a year) until age 18, that is, for 3 years after the end of compulsory education. Data on enrollment in these courses are not available to me. If one guesses (perhaps liberally) that one-fifth of all French children in a 3-year age bracket attend these courses, and count them (probably too generously) as the equivalent of one-fifth of full-time schooling, one concludes that this type of education adds 0.12 full-time equivalent years to the average for France. Estimates can then be obtained that part-time education adds nearly 0.4 years for boys and 0.2 years for girls to the full-time equivalent education received by French children.

Again, however, the figures for the labor force could hardly be half this large, that is, as much as 0.2 for males and 0.1 for females. The agricultural program has remote origins on a small scale but was made compulsory only in 1941 and financed and implemented only in the fifties. The apprenticeship program existed but enrolled very small numbers before World War II.[57]

The average number of years of part-time general and vocational education being received in the Netherlands can be readily computed for 4 years.[58] The averages, and the full-time equivalent numbers of years obtained by dividing these figures by five, are given in the text table on the following page.

The full-time equivalent of part-time education held by the labor force cannot be computed from these data, but it seems unlikely the figures would

55. Information on Germany is taken from EEC, "Formation professionnelle des travailleurs qualifiés dans les pays de la CEE," Brussels, 1963 (mimeo.); EEC, *La Formation Professionnelle des Jeunes dans les Enterprises Industrielles, Artisanales et Commerciales des Pays de la C.E.E.* [I55]; Wason, in Senate Committee on Labor and Public Welfare, *The Role of Apprenticeship in Manpower Development: United States and Western Europe* [G48]; ILO, *European Apprenticeship: Effects of Educational, Social and Technical Development on Apprenticeship Training in Eight Countries* [I8]; and Federal Statistical Office, *Statistiches Jahrbuch für die Bundesrepublik Deutschland, 1963* [G16].

56. Federal Statistical Office, *Wirtschaft und Statistik*, No. 3, 1966, p. 167* [G18]. By age, the percentages range from 19.7 at 50–64 to 26.0 at 14–30 for males, and from 6.7 at 50–64 to 17.5 at 14–30 for females.

57. Information for France is based on the EEC sources cited in note 55 and on "La formation professionelle," *Encyclopédie de l'Education Française*, especially around p. 18 [S2].

58. *Jaarcijfers voor Nederland, 1961–1962* [G23], gives, by sex, the percentages of the population attending part-time schools in the age groups 12–14, 15–17, 18–20, and 21–31. The percentage in each age group was multiplied by the number of years in the age group, and the products were added (and divided by 100) to obtain the figures given on the left side of the table that follows.

	Total years of part-time education		Full-time equivalent years	
	Males	Females	Males	Females
1940	1.19	.40	.24	.08
1953	1.27	.96	.25	.19
1958	1.35	1.24	.27	.25
1961	1.02	1.18	.20	.24

exceed 0.25 years for males, or be as large as 0.2 years for females, in 1962.

The Danish system is similar to that in Germany. None of the other European countries has a more extensive part-time program than France and Germany. Other countries with extensive programs, such as Belgium, have enrolled large numbers only recently, so that few members of the labor force have experienced such training. It is not likely, therefore, that in any European country inclusion of part-time day education on a full-time equivalent basis would add more than about 0.2 years to the average years of education of the labor force, or 0.1 years to the increase from 1950 to 1962.

In the United States released-time programs are of no quantitative significance for young people. Although an apprentice must be given organized instruction to provide knowledge in technical subjects related to his trade, with 144 hours annually usually considered necessary, this is provided in evening extension courses rather than on released time during the day. In any case, only 132,000 apprentices were enrolled in extension courses in 1961, which is equal to only 0.14 of a 1-year age class in the male population, 15–19.

⇒⇒⇒ A P P E N D I X   G ⇐⇐⇐

Correa's Estimates of the Effect of Calorie Intake on Labor Quality

Hector Correa has attempted to compare daily per capita calorie intake in a large number of countries with the per capita calorie consumption that would be required for the labor force to achieve 100 percent working capacity.[1] His estimates of per capita requirements take account of the different requirements of various occupational groups and of the average temperature of the country. By use of a schedule relating calorie intake to efficiency for each occupational group, he calculated that "working capacity as a percentage of full capacity" in (or about) 1958 was 96.2–97.8 in the United States, Denmark, and the United Kingdom; 90.1–92.5 in France, Germany, the Netherlands, and Norway; and 75.4 in Italy.[2] Taken at face value, these would provide quality adjustment indexes similar to those I have calculated for other factors. The difference that they indicate between the first and second group of countries is considerable, and the gap between the second group and Italy is very large indeed.

The estimates for advanced countries do not ap-

pear to be acceptable for a reason recognized by Correa himself. The main difficulty is that, in matching calorie consumption with requirements, Correa in effect assumes that the per capita calorie intake of each occupational group is the same as that of the *whole* population of the country. A deficiency always appears, therefore, unless per capita consumption of the whole population at least equals the per capita requirements of miners (4,200 calories a day). A deficiency appears for the United States even though the average intake is 3,100 and the average requirement 2,608. Correa himself states that the percentages of full working capacity for advanced countries are understated (which implies that differences are overstated) because of failure to allow for differences in consumption among groups in the population. Since his estimates of per capita calorie consumption comfortably exceed per capita requirements in all the countries under review except Italy, his estimates of requirements for every occupational group, as well as for those not employed, could easily be met if calorie intake were appropriately distributed. In addition, recent reduction of estimated calorie requirements presumably would reduce Correa's calculated shortfalls. Except for Italy, it is probable that no signifi-

---

1. *The Economics of Human Resources,* pp. 30–38 [B22].
2. Belgium is omitted from Correa's table. Per capita calorie consumption in Belgium was the same as in France, according to the United Nations, *Statistical Yearbook, 1963* [I2].

cance at all should be attached to the differences obtained by Correa for the countries studied here. They give no reason to modify the judgment expressed in Chapter 9 that, except for Italy, no significant difference in the quality of labor provided by employed persons arises from food deficiencies among the dates and countries I compare.[3]

Even for Italy it is impossible to accept Correa's estimate. The overstatement of food deficiencies arising from the assumption that everyone eats alike, and from probable overstatement of per capita requirements, applies to the Italian comparison as well as to the others. A further major qualification concerns the specific estimate of Italian requirements. Much of the computed Italian deficiency appears only because Correa puts average requirements in Italy especially high—at 2,850 calories as against (for example) 2,682 in France, even after allowing for reduced needs due to the higher average temperature in Italy. FAO, in contrast, estimates that requirements in Italy are lower than in any other country covered in the present study.[4] Still another factor would cause Correa's efficiency differentials to be greatly overstated. In his calculation all workers are weighted equally, rather than by earnings. Since the reason for calorie

deficiency is inadequate income, deficiencies must be concentrated among categories of workers whose marginal product is smallest and would be smallest even if income were sufficient to provide adequate nutrition.

Correa's estimates imply that Italian labor was at least 13 percent less efficient than Northwest European labor in 1958 because of insufficient food, and application of his procedures would appear to imply that the average quality of Italian labor had risen as much as 21 percent between 1950 and 1962 as the deficiency was reduced.[5] These are gross overestimates but if the correct figures were even one-third as large (4 percent for level in 1960, 7 percent for change between 1950 and 1962), which seems to me not altogether impossible, they would help to explain low Italian productivity and rapid Italian growth.[6]

3. In fairness to Correa, it should be noted that his main interest seems to be in underdeveloped countries.

4. FAO, *State of Food and Agriculture, 1965*, Table V–7 [I7].

5. The 13 percent is based on the ratio (0.87) of Correa's "working capacity" percentage for Italy to the lowest of his percentages for the Northwest European countries. The 21 percent is estimated by drawing a regression between the "working capacity" percentages and the ratio of calorie intake to calorie requirements for a number of countries, and reading the Italian "working capacity" percentages in other years from the regression. Italian calorie consumption was taken from the United Nations, *Statistical Yearbook, 1963* [I2], and Correa's per capita requirement for Italy in 1958 was assumed not to have changed over time.

6. An FAO report [I7] puts daily per capita calorie requirements in Italy at 2,460 and per capita consumption at 2,350 in 1948–50, 2,480 in 1951–54, and 2,860 in 1963–64 (Table V–7 and Annex Table 9–B).

Estimates of Gross Fixed Investment in United States and European Prices

This appendix describes in detail the derivation of Tables 11–2, 12–7, and 12–10. There are three steps in the estimating procedure.

Step I.

All the estimates start from total expenditures in 1950 as given by Gilbert and Associates.[1] Their estimates, based on each of three sets of price weights, are derived in Table H–1. The need for most of the calculations shown arises only because Gilbert's aggregate data are published in very rounded form. They can be reconstructed more accurately, especially for the small countries, as the product of Gilbert's population and per capita data. In three cases where this procedure yields figures a trifle outside the range of his rounded aggregate estimates, figures are substituted that are consistent with both the rounded aggregates and the rounded per capita figures as published.

Gilbert's data are raised, where necessary, to include Alaska and Hawaii with the United States, and the Saar and West Berlin with Germany. The

slight adjustments for the United States are based on statements by the U.S. Office of Business Economics as to the average size of the adjustment required. The ratios for Germany are the 1960 ratios of expenditures in each category when the Saar and West Berlin are included to expenditures when they are excluded.

The only revision of estimates published in Gilbert and Associates that has been made in Table H–1 is in residential construction in the United States. Gilbert and Associates state that they used residential construction data for 1950 given in the *Survey of Current Business*, July 1953 [G63]. This United States figure was a gross underestimate, and has since been revised upward by 39.3 percent (including the small adjustment to include Alaska and Hawaii).[2] Since Gilbert and Associates treated residential construction as a single commodity, and obtained their residential construction estimates entirely by "deflating" value data by price ratios, this

1. The reader is referred to Gilbert and Associates, OEEC, 1958 [I17], for a description of the data.

2. New data are from U.S. Bureau of the Census, *Value of New Construction Put in Place, 1946–1963 Revised*, October 1964 [G61]. Both figures include public and private nonfarm residential buildings and farm operator dwellings. The new United States national accounts show a still higher estimate because of an allowance for real estate commissions; this inclusion was not regarded as changing the volume comparisons with other countries.

TABLE H–1

Derivation of Gross Domestic Fixed Investment in 1950, Based on Alternative Price Weights

Item	United States	Belgium	Denmark	France	Germany	Netherlands	Norway	United Kingdom	Italy
1 Population (thousands)	151,032	8,640	4,271	41,945	47,462	10,114	3,264	50,373	46,356
Territorial adjustment ratios for expenditures									
2 Residential construction	1.005	—	—	—	1.056	—	—	—	—
3 Nonresidential construction	1.005	—	—	—	1.058	—	—	—	—
4 Producers' durables	1.000	—	—	—	1.052	—	—	—	—
Per capita expenditures in U.S. price weights (dollars)									
5 Residential construction	127[a]	72	59	27	67	51	87	47	18
6 Nonresidential construction	103	40	51	51	28	47	98	24	29
7 Producers' durables	151	95	79	58	49	62	86	65	23
Total expenditures in U.S. price weights (millions of dollars)									
8 Residential construction	19,242[a]	622	252	1,133	3,358	516	284	2,368	834
9 Nonresidential construction	15,634	345	218	2,151[b]	1,406	475	320	1,209	1,344
10 Producers' durables	22,806	821	337	2,433	2,447	627	281	3,274	1,049[b]
Per capita expenditures in average European price weights (dollars)									
11 Residential construction	63[a]	35	29	13	33	25	43	23	9
12 Nonresidential construction	92	30	37	46	24	37	72	21	24
13 Producers' durables	202	118	94	65	61	79	103	73	27
Total expenditures in average European price weights (millions of dollars)									
14 Residential construction	9,514[a]	302	124	551[b]	1,654	253	140	1,159	417
15 Nonresidential construction	13,964	259	158	1,909	1,205	374	235	1,058	1,113
16 Producers' durables	30,508	1,020	401	2,697	3,046	799	336	3,677	1,249
Per capita expenditures in national European price weights (dollars)									
17 Residential construction	(See	34	26	20	26	24	36	23	7
18 Nonresidential construction	Lines	24	38	38	20	34	65	28	18
19 Producers' durables	20–22)	104	90	62	61	75	108	72	33
U.S. per capita expenditures measured in price weights of country in column head (dollars)									
20 Residential construction		60[a]	55[a]	91[a]	49[a]	60[a]	53[a]	61[a]	47[a]
21 Nonresidential construction		81	107	77	86	100	94	112	76
22 Producers' durables		192	209	218	211	212	226	203	258
Total expenditures in national European price weights (millions of dollars)									
23 Residential construction	(See	294	111	839	1,303	243	118	1,159	324
24 Nonresidential construction	Lines	207	162	1,594	1,004	344	212	1,410	834
25 Producers' durables	26–28)	899	384	2,601	3,046	759	353	3,627	1,530
U.S. total expenditures measured in price weights of country in column head (millions of dollars)									
26 Residential construction		9,091[a]	8,457[a]	13,955[a]	7,400[a]	9,091[a]	7,531[a]	9,302[a]	7,189[a]
27 Nonresidential construction		12,295	16,241	11,687	13,054	15,179	14,268	17,001	11,535
28 Producers' durables		28,998	31,566	32,925	31,868	32,019	34,133	30,659	38,966

Sources: Line 1: Gilbert and Associates, p. 168 [I17]; Lines 2-4: see text for derivation; Lines 5-7: Gilbert and Associates, p. 75; Line 8: Lines 1 × 2 × 5; Line 9: Lines 1 × 3 × 6; Line 10: Lines 1 × 4 × 7; Lines 11-13: Gilbert and Associates, p. 76; Line 14: Lines 1 × 2 × 11; Line 15: Lines 1 × 3 × 12; Line 16: Lines 1 × 4 × 13; Lines 17-19: Gilbert and Associates, pp. 99-106 for Belgium, Denmark, Netherlands, and Norway; Gilbert and Kravis, pp. 113-120 [I18] for France, Germany, United Kingdom, and Italy, with the data multiplied by the ratio of expenditures in U.S. price weights as given in Gilbert and Associates, p. 76, to those given in Gilbert and Kravis, p. 37; Lines 20-22: Gilbert and Associates, pp. 99-106 for comparison with Belgium, Denmark, Netherlands, and Norway; Gilbert and Kravis, pp. 113-120 for comparison with France, Germany, United Kingdom, and Italy, with the data multiplied by the ratio of U.S. expenditures in U.S. price weights as given in Gilbert and Associates, p. 75 to those given in Gilbert and Kravis, p. 37; Line 23: Lines 1 × 2 × 17; Line 24: Lines 1 × 3 × 18; Line 25: Lines 1 × 4 × 19; Line 26: Lines 1 × 2 × 20; Line 27: Lines 1 × 3 × 21; Line 28: Lines 1 × 4 × 22.

a. United States residential construction data as given by Gilbert and Associates were raised by 39.3 percent for the aggregates and 38.6 percent for per capita figures, the difference representing the share of Alaska and Hawaii in the totals. See text for explanations.
b. Adjusted to agree with the aggregates given by Gilbert and Associates, pp. 87-88 [I17]; adjusted data are within range of rounding of per capita estimates.

revision carries directly into their international comparisons at all price weights. The United States estimates for residential construction have been raised accordingly.

Other revisions in national estimates for 1950 that have been made since Gilbert and Associates completed their study (which was published in 1958) are disregarded. To secure international comparability, Gilbert and Associates made numerous reclassifications of data published by national statistical offices and extensive use of worksheet detail and preliminary revisions. Their procedures cannot now be reproduced and it is usually impossible in any particular case to tell whether, or to what extent, revisions in published national statistics imply a need for revisions of the 1950 international comparisons.[3]

The *absolute* dollar values given in Table H–1 have limited significance even when United States price weights are used, since Gilbert tied the estimates to United States levels for 1950 that are between a factor cost and a market price valuation. At average European and national European price

weights, they have no simple meaning at all. This makes no difference for the purposes of this study. It does not affect the relative position of countries or comparisons between the types of expenditure. Weights for combining components are factor cost weights as estimated by Gilbert and Associates.

Step II.

The next step was to obtain annual series in constant prices for the three types of investment shown in Table H–1. Where a choice was conveniently available, series expressed in prices of the year on which the detailed deflation was based were selected, and linking of series in different price weights was avoided, but in no case were data not corresponding to OECD definitions, or not corresponding to the latest data revisions, used in order to implement this slight preference.[4] Where linking of series was required (usually of series expressed in 1954 and in 1958 prices), it made no difference to the calculations of the tables in Chapters 11 and 12 which series was extrapolated by the other. In several countries estimates for 1949 and especially 1948 are weak but the effect of any likely error in the 1948 and 1949 figures is small in comparison with the effect of excluding one or both of these years from the period covered.[5]

In discussion of data for individual countries below, the following numbers will be used to identify the sources indicated:

GENERAL

  1. OECD, *General Statistics*, January 1965 [I28].

  2. OECD, *Statistics of National Accounts, 1950–1961* [I39].

---

3. This is the case, for example, with respect to the United States estimate for producers' durables, which has been revised both conceptually and statistically. The Gilbert estimate of 1950 producers' durables expenditures in the United States was $22.8 billion, including $0.5 billion for public investment and $22.3 billion for private investment, the Office of Business Economics estimate at that date. The latest estimate by the Office of Business Economics for private investment in producers' durables in 1950 is $18.7 billion, a reduction of $3.6 billion, but most of the change appears to reflect changes in definition. In the earlier estimate investment was defined to include goods lasting more than one year, regardless of business accounting practice. The estimate included $2.1 billion for capital outlays charged to current account by business firms. This amount was reduced to $0.9 billion in 1955 and eliminated entirely in 1965 as the definition of investment in producers' durables was narrowed to include only items charged to capital account by business firms. Part of the remaining $1.5 billion reduction reflects two additional changes in classification made in 1965. One is the transfer of the value of second-hand producers' durables sold by business to government from private to government purchases of producers' durables. The amount was $1.2 billion in 1946 (when this item was at a maximum) and $0.6 billion in 1964; the 1950 value has not been published. The other, for which no value has been published, is the sale from business to consumers of used passenger cars; this was transferred from producers' durables to personal consumption expenditures. The net reduction in the estimate of producers' durables that business purchased and charged to capital account in 1950 (introduced by revisions in 1955, 1958, and 1965) does not appear to be very large. For a history of changes in this estimate see *Survey of Current Business*, August 1965, p. 13 [G63], and two supplements to the *Survey of Current Business*, "National Income, 1954 Edition," p. 135, and "U.S. Income and Output," 1958, p. 84.

4. Except for the United States and Belgium, data used are in the same state of revision, and in current prices correspond to those given for 1955–63 in OECD, *General Statistics*, January 1965 [I28]. Subsequent small revisions in estimates for the latest years did not warrant reworking the data. Series for the United States and Belgium are in the same state of revision as those given in OECD, *National Accounts Statistics, 1955–1964* [I35].

5. In these countries estimates for 1948 and 1949 are backward extrapolations from 1949 or 1950; the ratio of 1949 and 1950 investment to investment in later years differed radically between countries.

3. OEEC, *Statistics of National Product and Expenditure No. 2, 1938 and 1947 to 1955* [I15].

UNITED STATES

4. U.S. Bureau of the Census, *Value of New Construction Put in Place, 1946–1963 Revised,* October 1964 [G61].

5. U.S. Office of Business Economics, *Survey of Current Business,* August 1965 [G63].

BELGIUM

6. National Institute of Statistics, *Etudes Statistiques et Econométriques,* No. 11, 1965 [G4].

7. Belgian reply to United Nations National Accounts Questionnaire, 1962 edition.

8. Letter from National Institute of Statistics providing a breakdown of gross capital formation in current and 1953 prices for the 1953–64 period consistent with data contained in source 6.

DENMARK

9. The Statistical Department, *Nationalregnskabsstatistisk, 1947–1960* [G7].

10. The Statistical Department, "Nationalregnskabsstatistisk, 1960–1962," *Statistiske Efterretninger,* February 20, 1964 [G9].

11. The Statistical Department, "Nationalregnskabsstatistisk, 1961–1963," *Statistiske Efterretninger,* January 22, 1965 [G9].

GERMANY

12. Federal Statistical Office, *Wirtschaft und Statistik,* No. 10, 1964 [G18].

NETHERLANDS

13. *Amsterdam-Rotterdam Bank Economic Quarterly Review,* March 1965 [P2].

UNITED KINGDOM

14. Central Statistical Office, *National Income and Expenditure, 1963* [G38].

15. Central Statistical Office, *National Income and Expenditure, 1964* [G38].

United States (including Alaska and Hawaii)

RESIDENTIAL CONSTRUCTION IN 1957–59 PRICES. Data represent the value of new construction of residential buildings (private and public) and farm operators' dwellings from source 4. These data include Alaska and Hawaii throughout.

NONRESIDENTIAL CONSTRUCTION IN 1957–59 PRICES. Data represent total new construction from source 4 minus residential construction as above, military facilities from source 4, and estimated Atomic Energy Commission construction. The latter estimates were obtained by deflating unpublished data in current prices by the implicit deflator for nonresidential buildings. The data for 1948–57 were raised 0.5 percent to include Alaska and Hawaii.

MACHINERY AND EQUIPMENT IN 1958 PRICES. Data are from source 5; Alaska and Hawaii are included throughout.

Belgium

RESIDENTIAL CONSTRUCTION IN 1953 PRICES. Data for 1953–63 are from source 8.[6] The 1953 estimate was extrapolated to 1950–52 by the corresponding series in source 7. The estimate for 1950 was extrapolated to 1949 by residential construction in 1954 prices from source 3. The estimate for 1949 was extrapolated to 1948 by total gross domestic fixed asset formation as given in source 3.

NONRESIDENTIAL CONSTRUCTION AND MACHINERY AND EQUIPMENT IN 1953 PRICES. Difficulties with the division between construction and producers' durables necessitated a special procedure for Belgium:

1. Preliminary series for each of these components were first constructed, and they were then added for use as a control total. For each component, data for 1953–63 are from source 8. The estimates for 1953 were extrapolated to 1950–52 by the corresponding series in source 7, and the resulting 1950 estimates were extrapolated to 1949 by the corresponding series in source 3. Each of the estimates for 1949 was extrapolated to 1948 by total

6. Published data for gross capital formation in Belgium, as given in source 6 and elsewhere, include transfer taxes and commissions. Current price data for this item are carried directly into the deflated series as published. Most of the transfer taxes and commissions are allocated to residential construction. The series from source 8 used here for residential construction, nonresidential construction, and machinery and equipment exclude transfer taxes and commissions. The series used for residential construction, especially, rises much less from 1953 to 1963 than does the published series including transfer taxes and commissions.

gross domestic fixed asset formation as given in source 3.

2. Dividing the combined series into its components posed a special problem. The estimates just described implied that, in 1953 Belgian prices, nonresidential construction represented 44 percent of the combined figure in 1950. Gilbert's data, in contrast, implied it represented only 18.8 percent in 1950 Belgian prices, equivalent to 18.6 percent in 1953 Belgian prices. The difference was so large that there was the possibility of somewhat distorting the results for construction and equipment combined because of inconsistent weighting if the standard procedure for carrying Gilbert's data to later years were followed.[7] For use in these estimates, nonresidential construction in 1950 was therefore put at 18.6 percent of the combined figures for nonresidential construction and machinery and equipment. This 1950 estimate was then extrapolated by the larger series for nonresidential construction obtained in Step I, and machinery and equipment was obtained as a residual from the combined series derived in Step I. The division between nonresidential construction and equipment thus obtained is presumably quite wrong, with construction greatly understated, but the extrapolation of the two components combined should not be appreciably affected.

Denmark

ALL SERIES IN 1955 PRICES. Data were directly available on the OECD definitions from source 9 for 1948–59, source 10 for 1960, and source 11 for 1961–63.

France

ALL SERIES IN 1958 PRICES. Data for 1959–63 are from source 1. The 1959 estimate for each component was extrapolated to 1950–58 by the corresponding series in 1954 prices as given in source 2. (The linking at 1959 involved not only a shift of base year but also the linking of the "new" and "re-

vised old" French series in current prices; these differ moderately in 1959, the overlap year.) The 1950 estimate for residential construction was extrapolated to 1949 by the corresponding series in 1954 prices given in source 3. The 1950 estimate for nonresidential construction and machinery and equipment combined was extrapolated to 1949 by the corresponding series in 1954 prices given in source 3; each of the two components was then extrapolated separately by the corresponding series given in source 3, and they were adjusted proportionately to their total. The 1949 estimate for each of the three components was extrapolated to 1948 by total gross domestic fixed asset formation as given in source 3.

Germany (Including the Saar and West Berlin)

RESIDENTIAL CONSTRUCTION AND NONRESIDENTIAL CONSTRUCTION IN 1958 PRICES. Data for 1955–63 for each of the two construction components are from source 1. For each component, data for 1955–59 excluding the Saar and West Berlin were raised by the ratio of (a) the estimate including these areas to (b) the estimate excluding them in 1960. The 1955 estimate for each component was extrapolated to 1950–54 by a series in 1954 prices. These series represent, in each year, the product of (a) estimates for each component in 1954 prices as given in source 2 and (b) the ratio of total construction in 1954 prices as given in source 12 to total construction in 1954 prices as given in source 2. (Sources 2 and 12 are the same in current prices; source 12 incorporates revisions of the price deflators.) For each component the 1950 estimate was extrapolated to 1949 by the corresponding series in source 3. The 1948 estimate was based for each component on the assumption that the absolute increase from 1948 to 1949 was the same as it was from 1949 to 1950.

MACHINERY AND EQUIPMENT IN 1954 PRICES. Data for 1950 to 1962 are from source 12. Data for 1950–59 excluding the Saar and West Berlin were raised by the 1960 ratio of the estimate including these areas to the estimate excluding them. The 1962 estimate was extrapolated to 1963 by the corresponding series in 1958 prices given in source 1.

---

7. The distortion would not actually be very great because the division between nonresidential construction and equipment estimated by the procedure described in the preceding paragraph has not changed greatly over time.

The 1950 estimate was extrapolated to 1949 by the corresponding series in 1954 prices given in source 3. The 1948 estimate was based on the assumption that the absolute increase from 1948 to 1949 was the same as from 1949 to 1950.

Netherlands

ALL SERIES IN 1958 PRICES. For 1955–63 all data are from source 1. The 1955 estimate for each component was extrapolated to 1950–54 by the corresponding series in 1954 prices given in source 2. Each series was extrapolated from 1950 to 1949 by a series in 1954 prices obtained by deflating estimates given in current prices in source 13 (which is consistent with source 2) by an implicit deflator computed from source 3. All series were extrapolated from 1949 to 1948 by total gross domestic fixed capital formation in 1954 prices as given in source 3.

Norway

ALL SERIES IN 1958 PRICES. For 1951 to 1963 all data are from source 1 (1955–63) or the Norwegian submission to OECD from which data in source 1 are taken (1951–54). Each component was extrapolated from 1951 to 1950 by corresponding data in 1954 prices given in source 2, from 1950 to 1949 by corresponding data in 1954 prices given in source 3, and from 1949 to 1948 by total gross domestic fixed asset formation as given in source 3.

United Kingdom

ALL SERIES IN 1958 PRICES. All data are from sources 14 and 15. Residential construction is the sum of "dwellings" in the public and private sectors. Nonresidential construction is the sum of "other new buildings and works, etc." in the public and private sectors. Machinery and equipment is the sum of "vehicles, ships, and aircraft" and "plant and machinery" in the public and private sectors.

These combinations are used by OECD, and the percentage division between nonresidential construction and machinery and equipment in 1950 (in current prices) is close to Gilbert's (in current United Kingdom prices). Inclusion of "plant" with machinery and equipment causes the latter to be overstated, and construction understated, in comparison with the United States (and probably other countries), but does not cause difficulties in extrapolation of the Gilbert data in Step III.

Italy

ALL SERIES IN 1954 PRICES. Data for the years 1950–60 are from source 2. The 1960 estimate for each component in 1954 prices was extrapolated to 1961–63 by the corresponding series in 1958 prices from source 1. Residential construction and machinery and equipment were extrapolated from 1950 to 1949 by the corresponding series in 1954 prices from source 3, as was the sum of nonresidential construction and machinery and equipment; nonresidential construction in 1949 was obtained by subtraction. All components were extrapolated from 1949 to 1948 by total gross private domestic investment in 1954 prices as given in source 3.

Step III.

The next step was to cumulate capital expenditures of each of the three types in constant prices over each of the periods shown in the tables. The ratio of expenditures in each of these periods to expenditures in 1950 was then computed. These ratios were multiplied by 1950 expenditures in the desired prices, as shown in Table H–1, to obtain total expenditures of each of the three types in each of the periods considered. These were then divided by employment to obtain expenditures per person employed of each of the three types. The component estimates were added to obtain the totals for nonresidential construction and machinery and equipment. The figures were then converted to index form to obtain Tables 11–2, 12–7, and 12–10.

APPENDIX I

Derivation of the Contribution of Net Property Income from Abroad and Property Income from Dwellings to Growth Rates

This appendix first describes my estimates of the value of the contribution of net property income from abroad and net property income from housing to the real national income in 1950, 1955, 1960, and 1962.[1] The objective was to approximate the amounts actually included, explicitly or implicitly, in the real national income estimates for each country.[2] This description is followed by a discussion of the estimates of the contribution of changes in these magnitudes to the growth rate of real national income. For dwellings, estimates on a GNP basis are also described.

Net Property Income from Abroad in Constant Prices

Net property income from abroad in current prices, on the OECD concept, was available for all countries. Total net income from abroad (labor and property income combined) was available from OECD national accounts in both current and constant prices, so that an implicit deflator could be computed. The procedure followed was to divide the property income estimates in current prices by this deflator to obtain the desired constant price series. Exceptions to this procedure were made for Belgium (where the National Statistical Institute provides a constant price series for property income) and for Germany after 1955.

Almost no error can arise from application of the general procedure in the several countries, including the United States and the United Kingdom, where property income comprised all or almost all of income from abroad.[3] In Denmark and Italy, current and constant price estimates of income from abroad are identical, or almost so, and again no significant error seems possible. Elsewhere an error would be introduced by this procedure only if the countries apply different deflators to property and labor income, which generally is not the case. The

1. All the calculations were based on estimates expressed in the same prices as those from which the growth rates of national income were computed: that is, 1958 prices for the 1955–62 period and various prices in the 1950–55 period. See Appendix A.
2. It is apparent from the data that the deflation procedure adopted for net property income from abroad varies from country to country.

3. For a description of the series for net income (entirely property income) from abroad for the United Kingdom used in this study, see Appendix A. The series represents the current price series of OECD deflated by use of the United Kingdom deflation procedure.

estimates appeared reasonable except after 1955 in Germany. In the German national accounts both labor and property income are important, there is a net outflow of property income and inflow of labor income, and the relationship between current and constant price values for the two combined is irregular.[4] A special procedure was necessary to obtain estimates in 1958 prices. The *change* in net property income from abroad was assumed to be the same fraction of the *change* in total net income from abroad from 1955 to 1960, and again from 1960 to 1962, in constant (1958) prices as it was in current prices.

GNP at Factor Cost at Constant Prices Originating in Dwellings

This series, as included in OECD national accounts, could be accurately estimated for the European countries except the Netherlands. It is given by OECD for Belgium, Denmark, Norway, the United Kingdom, and Italy. For France and Germany, the base year figures at factor cost in current prices were obtained from national data, and these base year figures were extrapolated by GNP originating in dwellings at constant market prices, which is given by OECD. For the United States, national data permitted approximately the same procedure to be adopted. (Current price data were developed from unpublished data provided by the U.S. Office of Business Economics and deflated by a price index made available by that agency.) For the Netherlands, only current price estimates of GNP originating in dwellings at factor cost and at market prices were available. Housing GNP at current market prices was deflated by the implicit price deflator for consumer expenditures for rent to obtain very rough estimates of housing GNP at constant market prices. This series was then used to extrapolate GNP at factor cost in the base years. In general, a constant fraction, always small, representing the ratio of employee compensation to GNP originating in dwellings was eliminated to arrive at *gross property income originating in dwellings*.

4. The reason for a net inflow of labor income is that wages and salaries paid to Germans working for foreign armies are classified as income from abroad in the national accounts for Germany.

Net Property Income Originating in Dwellings at Factor Cost at Constant Prices

Data were obtained by subtracting depreciation at constant prices from gross property income originating in dwellings. Depreciation on dwellings at constant prices was available from national sources for the United Kingdom and the United States. (For the United States, adjustments were required; see p. 351.) For the other countries, depreciation on dwellings at current prices was deflated by the implicit deflator for residential construction.

Contribution to the Growth Rate of National Income at Factor Cost

The computation of the estimated contribution of net property income from dwellings and abroad to growth rates (described in Chapter 11) will be illustrated by the United States estimates for the 1950–55 period. All values given are in 1958 prices.

The growth rate of United States national income over this period was 4.23 percent. The absolute increase from 1950 to 1955 was $68.0 billion, of which $0.5 billion, or 0.7 percent, consisted of net property income from abroad; $4.2 billion, or 6.2 percent, net property income from housing; and $63.3 billion, or 93.1 percent, all other net income. These percentages were applied to the growth rate, yielding estimates that, of the total growth rate of 4.23 percent, 0.03 points were attributable to net property income from abroad, 0.26 points to net property income from housing, and 3.94 points to all other sources. This method credits a given dollar change with the same contribution to the growth rate regardless of the size of the component in which it occurs and regardless of whether the change was an increase or a decrease. Similar calculations were made for each country for each subperiod. Contributions (in percentage points) for the entire period are weighted averages of the figures for the subperiods.

For France, the housing data for 1959 are very different in the "old" and "new" series. Separate calculations were made for the 1955–59 and 1959–62 periods, and the results averaged to obtain the 1955–62 results. This procedure correctly reproduces the contribution of dwellings to the French growth rate that is being analyzed.

⇛ A P P E N D I X J ⇚

Derivation of Indexes of the Stock of Enterprise Structures and Equipment

This appendix describes the derivation of Table 12–1, which provides indexes of the average value of the gross and net stock (normally, the simple average of values at the beginning and end of the year) in the years 1950, 1955, 1960, and 1962. Net stock estimates for the end of 1963 or beginning of 1964 are also described. The latter estimates do not enter into the analysis of growth rates; they were used only to carry the capital stock estimates in United States prices back from that date to 1960 in the derivation of Tables 12–13 and 12–14.

The indexes measure the total stock of structures and equipment, other than dwellings, held by private and public enterprises. General government and consumer assets are excluded. Property of non-profit organizations is generally included (unavoidably) but can have little effect on the indexes.

Indexes of both the gross and net stock in constant prices were compiled or estimated from data provided by national sources wherever possible. The series are described in Section I. For Denmark, Norway, the Netherlands, and Italy, only net stock series could be derived from available data. The movement of the gross stock in these countries was inferred from that of the net stock. The procedure is described in Section II. A general discussion of the methodology underlying the estimates for the various countries is provided in Section III.

I. Derivation of Direct Estimates

Although absolute values of gross and net stock are given in the tables of this section, only indexes derived from them are used in Chapter 12; errors or incomparabilities in the *levels* of the national estimates have no effect on my analysis. The values shown in the tables are often rounded more than those actually used in the calculations; minor discrepancies will sometimes appear for this reason.

United States

In the *Survey of Current Business,* November 1962 [G63], George Jaszi, Robert C. Wasson, and Lawrence Grose of the Office of Business Economics provided a number of alternative gross and net stock series in 1954 prices. The article contained data for selected dates. Consistent data for other dates, and revisions of data for recent years that incorporated revisions in capital formation estimates made prior to August 1965, were obtained directly from the Office of Business Economics. The series based on Bulletin F service lives and, in the case of the net stock, straight line depreciation were selected from among the available alternatives.[1] The estimates are of the perpetual inventory type, based on a six-way breakdown of gross investment. Structures and equipment were separately estimated for manufacturing, agriculture, and all other industries combined. Assets of government enterprises are excluded but these are of minor importance in the United States. These data are shown in Part A, Table J–1. The collateral information referring to average age and the effect of changing assumed service lives that is provided in Chapter 12 and in Section III of this appendix refers to this set of estimates.

In August 1965, the Office of Business Economics published revised national product estimates. The revisions included an upward adjustment of capital expenditures in the postwar years that implied a revision of the capital stock series, and therefore had to be taken into account. The Office made available to me the new annual esti-

mates of gross capital expenditures, expressed in 1958 prices, covering as long a period as is needed for a perpetual inventory calculation. The classification was the same as that used in the construction of the original series. The average service life in 1954 for each of the six components, representing an average of the lives for the more detailed components, was also made available. For two components the service lives are substantially different from those used in the original tabulation: that for farm structures is 45 years instead of 90, and that for nonfarm manufacturing structures 32 years instead of 40.[2] This information made it possible for me to construct a new gross stock series that is based on use of the same procedures as the original Office of Business Economics study but incorporates the revised data. This series is shown in Part B, Table J–1. The movement of the new series differs from that of the old because of revisions in the capital outlay estimates, the shift from 1954 to 1958 prices, and the change in service lives. From the end of 1949 to the end of 1962, the original series rises by 50.2 percent and the adjusted series by 60.1 per-

1. Bulletin F (1942 edition) of the Bureau of Internal Revenue was intended to provide guidelines of useful service lives of depreciable property that could be used for tax purposes.

2. Service lives used for other components are: manufacturing equipment, 17 years; nonfarm nonmanufacturing equipment, 13.5 years; farm equipment, 15.9 years; nonfarm nonmanufacturing structures, 36.4 years.

TABLE J–1

United States: Estimates of Gross and Net Stock of Enterprise Structures and Equipment[a]

(Amounts in billions of U.S. dollars in 1954 or 1958 prices)

Year	Gross stock				Net stock			
	Beginning of year	End of year	Average for year	Index (1950 = 100)	Beginning of year	End of year	Average for year	Index (1950 = 100)
	A. Original Estimates (in 1954 prices)							
1950	459.2	476.8	468.0	100.0	246.3	258.8	252.6	100.0
1955	555.1	581.4	568.2	121.4	306.2	318.5	312.3	123.7
1960	662.9	672.3	667.6	142.6	353.5	360.9	357.2	141.4
1962	679.2	689.9	684.6	146.3	366.7	375.1	370.9	146.9
1963	—	699.5	—	—	—	385.0	—	—
	B. Adjusted Estimates (in 1958 prices)							
1950	485.1	505.3	495.2	100.0	260.2	274.3	267.2	100.0
1955	592.8	620.4	606.6	122.5	327.0	339.9	333.4	124.8
1960	726.7	746.2	736.4	148.7	387.5	400.6	394.1	147.4
1962	758.9	776.4	767.6	155.0	409.8	422.1	416.0	155.6
1963	—	794.3	—	—	—	437.2	—	—

Sources: U.S. Office of Business Economics, *Survey of Current Business*, November 1962 [G63]; other unpublished Office of Business Economics estimates; see text for explanation of derivation.
a. Excluding dwellings.

TABLE J-2

Belgium: Estimates of Gross and Net Stock of Enterprise Structures and Equipment[a]

(*Amounts in billions of Belgian francs in 1953 prices*)

	Gross stock				Net stock			
Year	Beginning of year	End of year	Average for year	Index (1950 = 100)	Beginning of year	End of year	Average	Index (1950) = 100
1950	783.0[b]	809.1	796.1	100.0	437.6[b]	453.6	445.6	100.0
1955	898.9	927.2	913.0	114.7	503.3	520.0	511.6	114.8
1960	1,043.2	1,076.9	1,060.1	133.2	583.3	601.0	592.2	132.9
1962	1,108.5	1,143.1	1,125.8	141.4	619.0	639.2	629.1	141.2
1963	—	1,177.7[b]	—	—	—	659.4[b]	—	—

Source: G. Labeau, *Cahiers Economiques de Bruxelles*, No. 25, 1965, pp. 5–46 [P9]; see text for explanation of derivation.
a. Excluding dwellings.
b. Author's estimate.

cent. If the old service lives for farm structures and nonfarm nonmanufacturing structures had been used with the new data, the increase would have been 57.1 percent. A similar direct recomputation of the net stock could not be attempted. The series shown in Part B was obtained by applying to the new gross stock estimates the old ratios of net to gross stock, computed from Part A.

After the present study had been completed, the Office of Business Economics itself prepared a new set of capital stock estimates, including a wide range of variants.[3] These estimates were based on the same gross investment data as were used in the preparation of Part B, Table J–1, but in its new compilations the Office introduced the use of more detail and, in some variants, distributions of retirements around the average retirement age. Because the Office of Business Economics tabulations (which consist of about 12,000 sheets of printed computer output) were completed as this book was about to go to press, I have been unable to review them comprehensively or in detail, but preliminary inspection of a few results suggests that the use of more detail and distributed retirements yields increases in capital stock that are smaller than the increases in the series I have used, especially in the 1950–55 period. Use of the new series would not, however, greatly affect my estimates of the sources of growth in the United States. Substitution for the series in Part B, Table J–1, of the new gross and net stock series

3. They are described in Grose, Rottenberg, and Wasson, *Survey of Current Business*, December 1966, pp. 34–40 [G63].

based on Bulletin F lives, the Winston S–3 distribution, deflation alternate 1 (deflation procedures similar to those used in Table J–1), and (in the case of the net stock) straight line depreciation would lower the contributions of nonresidential structures and equipment provided in Tables 12–4 (average of gross and net stock), 15–5, and 21–1 by 0.04 percentage points in 1950–62, 0.06 in 1950–55, and 0.03 in 1955–62. Use of the other variants of the new capital stock estimates I have examined would change my estimated contributions by smaller amounts.

Belgium

Annual data for the gross stock ("valeur de remplacement") and net stock ("valeur vénale") of Belgium, in 1953 prices, are taken from G. Labeau.[4]

The gross and net stock estimates used here are the sum of the appropriate series given by Labeau for agricultural equipment (Table 7), manufacturing and commercial buildings (Table 13), enterprise vehicles (Table 14), and enterprise equipment (Table 15).

The Belgian series runs from year-end 1950 through year-end 1962. To complete the estimates I have assumed increases during 1950 were the same as during 1951, and (to obtain a basis for adjusting the international comparisons of the level of the stock) that the increases during 1963 were the same as during 1962. The data are given in Table J–2.

4. *Cahiers Economiques de Bruxelles*, No. 25, 1965, pp. 5–46 [P9].

TABLE J–3

Denmark: Estimates of Net Stock of Enterprise Structures and Equipment[a]

(Amounts in billions of Danish kroner in 1955 prices)

	Beginning of year							Average for year	
	Net stock including dwellings and general government			Amounts assumed to be included for				Net stock, desired scope	
Year	Total (1)	Structures (2)	Machinery, fixtures, and transport equipment (3)	Dwellings (4)	General government (5)	Other structures (6)	Net stock, desired scope (7)	Amount (8)	Index (1950 = 100) (9)
1950	44.7	35.9	8.9	19.0	1.9	15.0	23.8	24.6	100.0
1951	47.1	37.1	10.0	19.6	2.0	15.4	25.4		
1955	56.6	42.0	14.6	22.2	2.4	17.3	31.9	32.7	132.8
1956	58.9	43.2	15.7	22.8	2.5	17.8	33.5		
1960	70.3	48.7	21.6	25.8	3.0	19.9	41.5	42.9	174.3
1961	74.4	50.7	23.7	26.8	3.2	20.7	44.4		
1962	79.1	53.0	26.1	28.1	3.4	21.5	47.6	49.4	200.6
1963	84.2	55.5	28.7	29.4	3.6	22.5	51.2		
1964	88.8	57.9	30.9	30.6	3.8	23.4	54.3		

Sources: Columns (1) to (3), and Columns (4) and (5) for 1955 only: unpublished data from Danish Statistical Department. Columns (4) to (5) except for 1955: author's estimates; see text for explanation of derivation. Column (6): Columns (2) minus (4) minus (5); Column (7): Columns (1) minus (4) minus (5).
a. Excluding dwellings.

Denmark

Only a net stock series could be constructed for Denmark. Annual estimates in 1955 prices of the net stock of structures and equipment, including dwellings as well as general government capital other than roads and bridges, were made available by the Danish Statistical Department. This series, which is too inclusive for my purposes, is given in Column 1, Table J–3. Columns 2 and 3 divide the total between "structures" and "machinery, fixtures, and transport equipment." The percentage rise in the latter is much larger than in the former. The increase in the total stock is so large—78 percent from the average of 1950 to the average of 1962—that Denmark clearly belongs among the countries with the largest increases. It is clear, moreover, that the inclusion of housing in these data depresses the index, and that its exclusion would raise it substantially.

The amounts included for dwellings and general government (which are almost entirely classified in the structures component) are known for the beginning of 1955.[5] Dwellings represented 52.9 percent of the stock of structures at that date. I have assumed (Column 4) that dwellings represented the same percentage of the stock of *structures* at all dates, implying they were a declining fraction of the total stock. General government capital is only a small part of the total stock (4.3 percent in 1955). Although it must consist largely of structures, it is believed to have increased as fast as or faster than the total stock. I have assumed (Column 5) that it was the same percentage of the *total* stock at all dates as in 1955. Deduction of these estimates for dwellings and general government leaves (Column 7) an estimated series with the desired scope, which is converted to a yearly average basis in Column 8.

It is possible that I have underestimated the increase in the dwellings and general government components (49 percent and 78 percent, respectively, from 1950 to 1962, on an annual average basis) and that the estimate of a 100 percent increase in the remaining stock is consequently too large, but if so the amount of overstatement on this account is unlikely to be great. In Column 6 I give the implied series for structures other than resi-

5. This is the base date for the Statistical Department estimates. Other years were calculated by cumulating net capital formation, using a classification that does not isolate these components.

dences and general government.[6] This increases by only 45 percent from 1950 to 1962 (on an annual-average basis) as compared with the increase of 190 percent in the machinery group which presents no problem. The increase for structures does not appear unduly large.

France

Estimates of the net capital stock in France, valued in 1956 prices, were prepared by P. Berthet, J.-J. Carré, P. Dubois, and E. Malinvaud. The series, prepared for a forthcoming economic growth study, provides annual estimates for the beginning of the years 1949 through 1963.[7] The estimates were, in general, prepared by (1) establishing base levels for each industry in 1956, founded on a comparison of three methods of estimate, and (2) carrying the estimates forward and backward by cumulating the difference between gross investment and depreciation. A full description will be contained in the French growth study.

The French study provides a series for net fixed

6. This calculation assumes all general government capital is included in structures.
7. Their data for this Social Science Research Council study were generously made available prior to publication.

reproducible capital, excluding dwellings and most types of general government capital, but including "transportation infrastructure," which consists mainly of public roads. To obtain a series with the scope desired in the present study, I have eliminated the value of the "transportation infrastructure," which is provided separately. The resulting series is given in billions of (new) French francs at 1956 prices in Column 1, Table J–4, and on an average for the year and index basis in Columns 2 and 3. An estimate for the beginning of 1964, needed to obtain the estimated level of the stock in 1960, is inserted on the assumption that the percentage increase was the same during 1963 as during 1962.

The French authors provide rough estimates of the gross stock, including transportation infrastructure, for three dates—the beginning of 1951, 1956, and 1961; these are given in Column 4. The gross value of the transportation infrastructure, which must be eliminated, is given separately only for 1956. However, the transportation infrastructure estimates are based on the observation that the road network was fully maintained, but not extended, until 1955 and increased only a little thereafter. In consequence, the *net* stock series for transportation infrastructure, which *is* available, changes only a

TABLE J–4

France: Estimates of Gross and Net Stock of Enterprise Structures and Equipment[a]

(*Amounts in billions of new French francs in 1956 prices*)

Year	Net stock (desired scope)			Gross stock					
	Beginning of year (1)	Average for year (2)	Index (1950 = 100) (3)	Beginning of year, including transportation infrastructure (4)	Beginning of year, transportation infrastructure (5)	Beginning of year, desired scope (6)	Average for year, desired scope		
							Amount (7)	Index (1950 = 100) (8)	
1950	147.62	152.06	100.0			279.36[b]	287.23[b]	100.0	
1951	156.50			435.00	139.90[b]	295.10[b]			
1955	179.05	182.42	120.0			332.73[b]	338.36[b]	117.8	
1956	185.80			484.00	140.00	344.00			
1960	231.90	228.54	150.3			398.10[b]	405.65[b]	141.2	
1961	233.88			555.00	141.80[b]	413.20[b]			
1962	246.33	253.24	166.5			431.00[b]	440.88[b]	153.5	
1963	260.15					450.76[b]			
1964	274.72[b]					471.33[b]			

Source: Unpublished data prepared by P. Berthet, J.-J. Carré, P. Dubois, and E. Malinvaud for Social Science Research Council Study; see text for explanation of derivation.
a. Excluding dwellings.
b. Author's estimate.

little over the whole period. To obtain the gross stock exclusive of transportation infrastructure at the beginning of 1951 and 1961, I have simply assumed (Column 5) that the gross stock of transportation infrastructure moved like the net stock. This assumption is unlikely to introduce appreciable error into the estimates of gross stock with the desired scope (Column 6). At this stage, estimates of the gross stock with the desired scope were available for the beginning of 1951, 1956, and 1961. The ratio of gross stock (Column 6) to net stock (Column 1) at these dates was computed and the ratio was interpolated and extrapolated to obtain estimates of the ratio at other dates. The net stock was multiplied by these ratios to obtain estimates of the gross stock at other dates (Column 6). Columns 7 and 8 present the estimates on an average for the year basis.

Germany

Wolfgang Kirner of the German Institute for Economic Research (Berlin) is developing new estimates of the value in 1958 prices of the gross and net capital stock of Germany. Kirner has previously published such estimates in 1954 prices for the beginning of the years 1950, 1955, and 1960.[8] His unpublished gross stock estimates for the other years in the 1950–61 period were made available by the Institute. Revised estimates in 1958 prices of the gross stock in manufacturing and mining industries prepared by Rolf Krengel of the same Institute have already been released.[9] For use in the present study I have tried to guess at the indexes of the capital stock at which Kirner will arrive, by combining the new Krengel data for manufacturing and mining and the earlier Kirner estimates for other industries.

GROSS STOCK. Columns 1 and 2, Table J–5, give Kirner's original estimates of the gross stock of structures and equipment (excluding dwellings and

general government capital) and the amounts included for manufacturing and mining.[10] Columns 3 and 4 show annual averages. These data exclude the Saar and West Berlin. Columns 5 and 6 give Krengel's revised estimates in 1958 prices for manufacturing and mining, with an overlap at 1960 for change in geographic coverage. The Krengel estimates indicate a slightly smaller percentage increase for manufacturing and mining from 1950 to 1955 and an appreciably smaller percentage increase from 1955 to 1960 than Kirner's. How much of the difference is due to a different base year, how much to revisions of the data, and how much to differences in procedure, is unknown.

To construct a tentative series, I have extrapolated Kirner's 1955 average for the year estimate for manufacturing and mining by Krengel's new series (Columns 5 and 6), linking in 1960 for the change in geographic coverage. For other industries Kirner's estimates were used for 1950, 1955, and 1960. The sum of the two estimates yields the total gross stock (Column 7) for these years. After the beginning of 1961 the gross stock in industries other than manufacturing and mining had to be estimated. It was noticed that Krengel's 1961–64 estimates for manufacturing and mining could be practically reproduced by applying their 1955–60 growth rate. I have assumed the growth rate in other industries after 1960 to be the same (5.68) as from 1955 to 1960 inasmuch as this procedure would give good results for the industrial sector. The absolute values in Column 7, it may be noted, are pitched at the 1954 price level and use 1954 price weights to combine sectors, except that *within* manufacturing and mining, 1958 price weights are implied. The figure for the beginning of 1964 is the average of the 1963 and 1964 annual averages.

NET STOCK. Kirner's estimates of the net stock are given in Column 9. These are comparable to his gross stock estimates in Column 1. The ratio of net to gross rises from 0.569 at the beginning of 1950 to 0.609 at the beginning of 1955 and 0.650 at the beginning of 1960. I have used straight line interpolation and extrapolation to estimate the ratios at other dates, and applied these ratios to the gross

---

8. Kirner in *Schriften des Vereins für Sozialpolitik*, New Series, Vol. 26, 1962 [P41].

9. German Institute for Economic Research, *Produktionsvolumen und Produktionsfactoren der Industrie im Gebiet der Bundesrepublik Deutschland*, "Statistitische Kennziffern 1950 bis 1960" and "Statistische Kennziffern 1958 bis 1964" [B30].

10. The series given in Column 1 is simply Kirner's total minus "Wohnungsvermietung" and "Staat."

TABLE J-5

Germany: Estimates of Gross and Net Stock of Enterprise Structures and Equipment[a]

(Amounts in billions of deutsche marks in 1954 or 1958 prices)

	Gross stock								Net stock, total, 1954 prices, excluding Saar and West Berlin		
	Kirner estimates, 1954 prices				Krengel estimates, 1958 prices, manufacturing and mining, average for year		Estimates used, total, average for year (excluding Saar and West Berlin)				
	Beginning of year		Average for year						Kirner estimates, beginning of year	Estimates used, average for year	
Year	Total (1)	Manufacturing and mining (2)	Total (3)	Manufacturing and mining (4)	Saar and West Berlin excluded (5)	Saar and West Berlin included (6)	Amount (7)	Index (1950 = 100) (8)	(9)	Amount (10)	Index (1950 = 100) (11)
1950	262.6	71.8	267.8	73.8	84.5		263.1	100.0	149.4	150.8	100.0
1951	273.1	75.7									
1955	327.4	98.8	338.6	103.6	118.0		327.4	124.4	199.5	200.8	133.2
1956	349.9	108.5									
1960	450.8	149.7	467.0	156.0	166.9	176.7	441.4	167.8	293.2	288.9	191.6
1961	483.3	162.4				190.0					
1962						204.2	498.7	189.5		334.5	221.9
1963						217.5	528.4				
1964						231.9	560.0				
1964[b]							544.2			371.7	

Sources: Columns (1)–(6) and (9): estimates derived from Wolfgang Kirner and Rolf Krengel, German Institute for Economic Research (Berlin); other columns: see text for explanation of derivation.
a. Excluding dwellings.
b. Estimates for beginning of year.

stock estimates in Column 7 to estimate the net stock. The results are given in Column 10 and, in index form, in Column 11.

Netherlands

Only a net stock series could be derived for the Netherlands.

The Netherlands Central Bureau of Statistics has itself published an annual series, given for the relevànt years in Column 1, Table J–6, for the value of the net stock of enterprise structures (excluding residences) and equipment in 1952 prices. This series runs to the end of 1958.[11] I have not used this series, since it stops in 1958, but have constructed my own seriès in 1953 prices by a similar method. The movement of the two series throughout the overlap period is very similar.

The level of my series was established for the end of 1952. At that date the net stock of enterprise

nonresidential structures, in millions of current guilders, was 14,200 and of equipment, 18,900.[12] I applied half the 1952–53 declines in the prices of gross investment in these types of assets to estimate these values in 1953 prices at 13,970 and 18,680, respectively, or a total of 32,650. The year-end figure for 1952 was moved to other dates by subtracting or adding net capital formation in 1953 prices.

For the years 1950 through 1960 net capital formation in 1953 prices (excluding construction work in progress) was calculated from data contained in the national accounts of the Netherlands for 1960. Net domestic capital formation of enterprises, including dwellings, in 1953 prices (excluding changes in work in progress) was obtained from Line 11, Table 15, of the published source.[13] From

11. Central Bureau of Statistics, Statistische en econometrische onderzoekingen, 3rd quarter, 1960, p. 114 [G27].

12. Division of National Accounts of the Netherlands Central Bureau of Statistics, in Goldsmith and Saunders (eds.), The Measurement of National Wealth, Series VIII, p. 144 [B42]. (The same figures are used in the source cited in note 11 for the series in 1952 prices.) The value of some (not all) nonfarm land is included but from internal evidence it appears the amount is not large.

13. Central Bureau of Statistics, Statistical Studies, No. 11 (English ed.), December 1961 [G28].

TABLE J-6

Netherlands: Estimates of Net Stock of Enterprise Structures and Equipment[a]

(*Amounts in billions of Dutch guilders in 1952 or 1953 prices*)

Year	Net stock in 1952 prices, year end, CBS series (1)	Net stock in 1953 prices, series used		
		Year end (2)	Average for year	
			Amount (3)	Index (1950 = 100) (4)
1949	30.4	29.87		
1950	31.6	30.96	30.41	100.0
1952	33.1	32.65		
1954	36.0	35.28		
1955	38.0	37.62	36.45	119.8
1958	45.4	44.78		
1959		46.90		
1960		49.78	48.34	158.9
1961		52.92		
1962		56.28	54.60	179.5
1963		59.54		

Sources: Column (1): Central Bureau of Statistics in Goldsmith and Saunders (eds.), *The Measurement of National Wealth*, Series VIII, p. 144 [B42]; Columns (2)–(4): author's estimates; see text for explanation of derivation.
a. Excluding dwellings.

this series net capital formation in dwellings had to be deducted. Net domestic capital formation in dwellings in *current* prices was obtained by deducting from gross capital formation (Table 24) the sum of the change in work in progress (Table 22) and depreciation allowances (Item 64, Table 32, or, for years not given, as derived in my calculation of net income from housing). This series was deflated by the implicit deflator for new construction of dwellings to obtain net capital formation in dwellings in 1953 prices.

All the current price estimates for 1959 and 1960 contained in the 1960 national accounts have subsequently been revised. The original estimates for each series in 1953 prices were adjusted in proportion to the revision in current prices.

In later publications the Central Bureau of Statistics has shifted its constant price series from a 1953 to a 1958 base. Data from the 1961, 1962, 1963, and 1964 issues of *Nationale rekeningen* [G25] were used to construct a series for net capital formation in 1958 prices by procedures parallel to those used to obtain the series in 1953 prices. From 1954 through 1960 the ratio of the net capital for-

mation estimates in 1953 prices to those in 1958 prices was almost identical each year.[14] The 1960 ratio was applied to the 1961–63 estimates in 1958 prices to obtain estimates for these years in 1953 prices. Estimates of the net stock obtained by cumulating net investment are given in Columns 2 to 4, Table J–6.

Norway

Only a net stock series was available. The Central Bureau of Statistics provides annual data for the net stock of fixed real capital in enterprises, valued in 1955 prices, for the end of the years 1949 through 1962. Deduction of the amounts included for land and forests and for dwellings provides a series with the desired scope. The data are given in Table J–7. To obtain a preliminary estimate for the end of 1963, I assumed the same increase during 1963 as during 1962.

TABLE J-7

Norway: Estimates of Net Stock of Enterprise Structures and Equipment[a]

(*Amounts in millions of Norwegian kroner in 1955 prices*)

Year	Beginning of year	End of year	Average for year	Index (1950 = 100)
1950	36,140	38,302	37,221	100.0
1955	47,271	50,036	48,654	130.7
1960	60,975	63,109	62,042	166.7
1962	65,867	68,839	67,353	181.0
1963		71,811[b]		

Source: Central Bureau of Statistics; the series used is from *Nasjonalregnskap, 1949–1962*, Table 21, Lines 6 − (6k + 7a) [G33] or, alternatively, *Statistisk Årbok, 1965*, Table 90, Line 1 less dwellings, land, and forests [G35].
a. Excluding dwellings.
b. Author's estimate.

United Kingdom

Estimates of gross and net capital stock in 1958 prices with the desired scope were provided by the Central Statistical Office.[15] They are shown in Table J–8.

14. It was, however, lower before 1954.
15. *National Income and Expenditure, 1964*, Table 68 [G38]. Geoffrey Dean, who prepared the estimates, discusses them in detail in *Journal of the Royal Statistical Society*, Series A, Vol. 127, 1964, pp. 89–107 [P26]. Dean generously made available appropriate series excluding dwellings and general government for gross and net stock.

TABLE J-8

United Kingdom: Estimates of Gross and Net Stock of
Enterprise Structures and Equipment[a]

(Amounts in billions of pounds sterling in 1958 prices)

Year	Gross stock				Net stock			
	Beginning of year	End of year	Average for year	Index (1950 = 100)	Beginning of year	End of year	Average for year	Index (1950 = 100)
1950	37.8	38.9	38.35	100.0	19.5	20.2	19.85	100.0
1955	43.2	44.6	43.90	114.5	23.0	24.0	23.50	118.4
1960	49.7	51.6	50.65	132.1	28.6	30.1	29.35	147.9
1962	53.6	55.8	54.70	142.6	31.7	33.0	32.35	163.0
1963		57.5				34.4		

Sources: Central Statistical Office, *National Income and Expenditure, 1964,* Table 68 [G38], and data provided by Geoffrey Dean.
a. Excluding dwellings.

Italy

Arnando Agostinelli has prepared estimates of the net capital stock of Italy valued in 1954 prices.[16] His estimates are based primarily on a conversion and extension of earlier estimates in 1938 prices prepared by Benedetto Barberi.[17]

16. Agostinelli's estimates are published in Central Institute of Statistics, *Annali di Statistica,* Series VIII, Vol. 15, 1965, pp 285–86 [G19].
17. Barberi's data were published in *L'Industria,* No. 3, 1960 [P22], and in Cao-Pinna, in Geary (ed.), *Europe's Future in Figures,* p. 115 [B17]; an updating of Barberi's estimates for the period 1958–62 was provided by correspondence. Comparable estimates for 1961 are given by Giannone in *Banca Nazionale del Lavoro Quarterly Review,* December 1963, p. 427 [P4].

TABLE J-9

Italy: Estimates of Net Stock of Enterprise
Structures and Equipment[a]

(Amounts in billions of Italian lire in 1954 prices)

Year	Net stock			
	Beginning of year	End of year	Average for year	Index (1950 = 100)
1950	12,360[b]	12,743	12,552	100.0
1955	14,505	14,995	14,750	117.5
1960	17,325	18,211	17,768	141.6
1962	19,369	20,688	20,028	159.6
1963		22,087		

Source: Agostinelli in Central Institute of Statistics, *Annali di Statistica,* Series VIII, Vol. 15, 1965, pp. 285–86 [G19]; see text for explanation of derivation.
a. Excluding agriculture and dwellings.
b. Author's estimate.

From Agostinelli's estimates a series covering the end of the years 1950 through 1963 can be obtained which corresponds to the scope desired in the present study with one exception. This is the omission of nonresidential structures and equipment in agriculture. In both the Agostinelli and Barberi series this value is combined with the value of land. Table J–9 shows the Agostinelli series for the value of enterprise structures and equipment, excluding dwellings and also excluding agriculture.

An estimate for the beginning of 1950 has been entered on the assumption that the percentage increase during 1950 was the same as during 1951. The last two columns show the series on an average for the year and index basis.

In the present study the assumption is made that the addition of agricultural structures and equipment to the series would not change the index.[18]

II. Inferred Gross Capital Stock Series

Indexes of both the gross and net stock were derived in Section I for the United States, Belgium,

18. Although it appears that in several European countries the agricultural stock increased less than the total, this assumption was not made for Italy because (1) the increase in the nonfarm stock was fairly moderate; (2) agricultural investment is known to have been large; and (3) the increase in the total agricultural stock of fixed capital, including land, appears to be large enough (from 12,445 to 14,715 billion lire, year-end 1950 to year-end 1962) to accommodate the assumption of a percentage increase in agricultural structures and equipment as large as in the remainder of the economy.

France, Germany, and the United Kingdom but of only the net stock for Denmark, the Netherlands, Norway, and Italy. It was necessary to try to infer the gross stock series for the four countries for which it was not available from the behavior of the net stock.

On *a priori* grounds gross and net stock may be expected to increase at about the same rate when that rate is fairly similar to past growth rates. When the growth rate has sharply accelerated the net stock can be expected to increase more rapidly than the gross because the annual increment represents a larger percentage of the total net stock than of the total gross stock. The irregular time pattern of investment prior to 1950 makes it impossible to give this statement precise content in the present context and, in any case, prewar growth rates of capital stock for the missing countries are not, in general, available on a comparable basis. To infer the missing data I was forced to fall back on the supposition that prewar growth rates were moderate and that when the growth rate of the stock in the postwar period was also moderate, indexes of the gross and net stock differed only at random but that at higher rates the net stock increased more rapidly than the gross. The estimates for four of the five countries for which both series are available support this interpretation. Over the 1950–62 period as a whole, for example, the growth rate of the gross stock in Belgium was 2.93 and that of the net stock 2.92, and in the United States (based on the original estimates) the rates were 3.22 and 3.26, respectively.[19] In contrast, in France the gross stock grew at a rate of 3.64 percent and the net stock at 4.34 percent, and in Germany the figures were 5.67 and 6.87, respectively. I shall use the experience of these countries to estimate series for the missing countries.

It will be noted that I disregard for this purpose the experience of the United Kingdom, which provides a distinct exception to the general pattern. From 1950 to 1962 the gross stock grew at a rate of only 3.00 in the United Kingdom, but the net stock grew at the much higher rate of 4.15. Though the

postwar growth rate of the gross stock in the United Kingdom was moderate by international standards, available data indicate that it was very much higher than it had been at any time in the preceding half century. This apparently accounts for the observed divergence between the postwar growth rates of gross and net stock. That the earlier growth rate of the British stock may also have been exceptionally low by international standards is indicated by the fact that the 1950 ratio of net stock to gross stock was the lowest (0.52) among the five countries for which the calculation can be made.

Based on the experience of the other four countries, the best way to fill in the missing series appeared to be to assume that the growth rates of the two series are the same when they are 3 percent or less, and that the growth rate of the net stock is greater when the rate exceeds 3 percent. How much of a difference is it reasonable to assume? The following table gives growth rates for the four countries, other than the United Kingdom, for which both rates are available in the 1950–55 and 1955–62 subperiods:

	Net stock	Gross stock
United States, 1955–62[a]	2.49	2.70
Belgium, 1950–55	2.79	2.78
Belgium, 1955–62	3.00	3.03
France, 1950–55	3.71	3.33
United States, 1950–55[a]	4.35	3.95
France, 1955–62	4.80	3.85
Germany, 1950–55	5.90	4.47
Germany, 1955–62	7.56	6.20

a. See note 19.

With rates of 3 percent or less for the net stock omitted (none of the countries that must be estimated fall in this range), the amounts by which these rates exceed 3 percent, and the ratio of the excess over 3 percent in the net to that in the gross, are:

	Net stock rate, less 3 percentage points (1)	Gross stock rate, less 3 percentage points (2)	Ratio of Columns (2) to (1) (3)
France, 1950–55	.71	.33	.46
United States, 1950–55	1.35	.95	.70
France, 1955–62	1.80	.85	.47
Germany, 1950–55	2.90	1.47	.51
Germany, 1955–62	4.56	3.20	.70
Average			.57

19. Since the purpose of this comparison is to obtain relationships based on consistent independent data, I use the original Office of Business Economics series shown in Part A, Table J–1, rather than the higher adjusted estimates shown in Part B.

The average ratio is 0.57. Rounding this figure, I have assumed that the growth rates of the gross stock in Denmark, the Netherlands, Norway, and Italy were equal to 3 percent a year plus three-fifths of the amounts by which the growth rates of their net stocks exceeded 3 percent a year.

There is no need to stress the crudeness of this procedure, nor the possibility that in individual cases the assumed differences between the indexes of gross and net stock may be wide of the mark. However, the general level of all the series and important differences between countries are determined by the independent estimates, not by this estimating procedure.

III. Some Characteristics of the Series

This final section discusses certain characteristics of the national estimates that were used in Section I.

Except for the Belgian series the estimates derive from some variant of the perpetual inventory method. When the method is used in its pure form, as in the United States estimates, gross investment is cumulated over the service life of each type of asset, assets are dropped out of the stock at the end of their service lives to obtain the gross stock, and accumulated depreciation is deducted to obtain the net stock. Both the level and the movement of the series is thus derived from past investment.

In Europe, the perpetual inventory method is commonly used to calculate annual changes in series for which the base levels were established more or less independently. Adjustments for war damage were generally required; in Germany, both extensive war damage and territorial changes had to be taken into account. In France and in the countries for which only net stock series were available, the procedure of cumulating net investment from an independent base year estimate of the net stock is generally adopted. In these countries the arithmetic of the perpetual inventory method is curtailed by deducting depreciation from gross capital formation each year and adding the resulting net capital formation estimate to the previous year's net stock. With this procedure a gross stock series does not emerge unless estimates are specially prepared. The Belgian series differs from others in that it makes

considerable use of physical indicators of the stock (such as the number of automobiles or number of buildings of different types in use) to extrapolate base year estimates of components of the stock.

Depreciation used in the calculation of capital stock estimates for the United States, Germany, the Netherlands, and the United Kingdom is computed by the straight line formula. The other countries use indirect procedures to estimate net stock that make it difficult to specify precisely what depreciation formula is implied. Most of them estimate depreciation on each type of asset as a constant fraction of net rather than of gross stock, but this appears to be due to data availability rather than to an intention to apply a different formula. It is impossible to say whether the procedure makes the net stock estimates rise more or less than would use of straight line depreciation.[20]

20. The Norwegian procedure is to estimate directly the value of the net stock, cross-classified by industry and type of asset, at benchmark dates. The only benchmark dates affecting the stock series for the period beginning with 1950 are 1939 and 1953. (Estimates after 1953 are preliminary until a new benchmark is established.) The change in net stock between benchmark dates is subtracted from gross capital formation during the intervening period as a whole to obtain depreciation during the intervening years. Depreciation in the intervening period as a whole is then allocated to individual years on the assumption that the ratio of depreciation to capital stock is the same each year. An annual series for net stock is then derived by cumulating net investment from the preceding benchmark year. Since 1953 depreciation has been calculated, by industry and type of asset, on the assumption that the ratio of depreciation to net stock has been rising slightly. This procedure, which is intended to anticipate the results of the next benchmark estimate, probably yields a somewhat faster rise in depreciation in Norway than would application of the straight line formula. How the *level* of depreciation, which determines the movement of the net stock series, compares with the results of the straight line formula is not known.

The Danish estimates are generally similar to the Norwegian estimates except that the 1955 ratio of annual depreciation to net stock has been applied (by type of asset) in all years of the period covered.

The procedure followed in the French estimates is the same as that used in Denmark (except that the base year is 1956) but the intent is to approximate the results of straight line depreciation and the estimators believe the divergence from straight line depreciation is slight.

The Italian estimates assume a constant ratio of depreciation in 1938 prices to volume of output in each industry. Depreciation almost surely rises more rapidly than it would by the straight line formula but how the average level of the depreciation series, which governs the movement of the net stock series, compares with that which would be obtained by straight line depreciation is not known. If, as Giorgio Fuà suggests, the level of the depreciation series is too high the increase in the Italian stock is presumably understated (*Notes on Italian Economic Growth, 1861–1964*, p. 50 [B37]).

The Belgian stock series are constructed without an ex-

American statisticians typically use shorter service lives than European statisticians to estimate capital stock and depreciation; there are also variations among the European countries. The estimates for the United States given in Table 12–1 are based on service lives that correspond to Bulletin F, as interpreted by Department of Commerce economists. For producers' durables, these average about 17 years in manufacturing, 13.5 years in nonfarm nonmanufacturing private industries, and 16 years in farming, and for nonresidential structures they average about 32 years in manufacturing, 36 years in nonfarm nonmanufacturing industries, and 45 years in farming. Until recently, Bulletin F lives were nearly always used in American estimates. American statisticians used them not because they wished to follow tax rules but because they believed that Bulletin F provided the best available guide to actual economic service lives—which, indeed, was its intent. Recently, however, there has been some tendency to use even shorter service lives, probably as a consequence of a 1962 change in tax regulations.

Statisticians in European countries for which information on this point is available use longer service lives.[21] The French and Belgian estimates imply average service lives of about 20 years for producers' durables and the French about 50 years for structures. The German and United Kingdom series imply service lives that average 27 to 35 years for producers' durables and upward of 50 years for nonresidential structures. Tax regulations were quite properly disregarded in arriving at these lives.[22] But, as in the United States, the evidence for arriving at correct lives is sparse.

One can hardly doubt that capital goods are, in fact, used longer in Europe than in America, but whether the difference is as great as some of the estimates imply is uncertain. It is entirely possible that part of the difference is not real, and that Amer-

TABLE J–10

United States: Alternative Estimates of Changes in Gross and Net Stock of Enterprise Structures and Equipment[a]

(Indexes, year-end 1950 = 100)

Stock and service lives	Year-end 1955	Year-end 1961	Ratio of 1961 to 1955
Gross stock, based on service lives			
40 percent shorter than Bulletin F	124.6	146.3	1.17
20 percent shorter than Bulletin F	120.2	132.3	1.10
Bulletin F	121.9	142.4	1.17
20 percent longer than Bulletin F	118.2	141.9	1.20
40 percent longer than Bulletin F	117.3	138.9	1.18
Net stock, based on straight line depreciation, and service lives			
40 percent shorter than Bulletin F	125.5	146.9	1.17
20 percent shorter than Bulletin F	124.3	142.9	1.15
Bulletin F	123.0	141.5	1.15
20 percent longer than Bulletin F	122.0	142.4	1.17
40 percent longer than Bulletin F	121.0	141.5	1.17

Source: These indexes are computed from data (some of them unpublished) developed in the study reported by Jaszi, Wasson, and Grose in *Survey of Current Business,* November 1962 [G63]. They are consistent with the series shown in Part A, Table J–1; as noted, the indexes were revised upward before use in Table 12–1.
a. Excluding dwellings.

ican capital stock estimates based on longer service lives would be more comparable to the European estimates. Fortunately, it is possible to indicate what difference it would make to American indexes over time periods close to those considered here if longer service lives had been assumed. Table J–10 provides five alternative sets of indexes for the gross stock, and five for the net stock, based on year-end figures for 1950, 1955, and 1961. The table compares the results of using service lives corresponding to Bulletin F lives with the results of using service lives uniformly 40 percent longer, 20 percent longer, 20 percent shorter, and 40 percent shorter.[23] It is evident from the table that substitution of service lives 20 or 40 percent longer in the United States would have only a small effect on the *indexes* of gross and net stock. It thus appears that even if the American estimates are based on service lives too short to be comparable to the European estimates, the substitution of considerably longer lives would not affect the comparisons very much.

plicit calculation of annual depreciation. For the most part they assume no change in the ratio of net stock to gross stock. For the stock as a whole, this appears to be consistent with use of straight line depreciation, given the calculated growth rate of the Belgian stock.

21. The Scandinavian estimates are constructed in a way that avoids any direct estimate of service lives.

22. Permissible tax lives are typically shorter in Europe than they were in the United States under Bulletin F, if estimates for manufacturing given by Peggy Brewer Richman are correct and typical of other industries (in *National Tax Journal,* March 1964, pp. 86–91 [P31]).

23. The "Bulletin F lives" used in this table correspond to those used to derive Part A of Table J–1. See p. 415.

⋙ A P P E N D I X   K ⋘

Derivation of Inventory Estimates

The first section of this appendix describes the series for inventory holdings in constant prices from which the indexes shown in Table 13–1 were derived. The indexes are based on averages of the value of inventories at the beginning and end of the year. The second section shows how the levels of inventories were obtained that are compared in Table 13–4.

1. Inventory Holdings in Constant Prices

UNITED STATES. The value of private inventories in 1958 prices was provided by the United States Department of Commerce, Office of Business Economics.

BELGIUM. The value of inventories in 1953 prices at the end of each year from 1950 through 1962 was obtained from G. Labeau, in *Cahiers Economiques de Bruxelles* (No. 25, 1965, pp. 5–46 [P9]). The series is the sum of Labeau's estimates for livestock and for other inventories. The estimate of the 1950 inventory change in 1953 prices provided by DULBEA (see page 350 above) was used to carry the year-end 1950 figure back to the beginning of the year. The change in inventories in 1953 prices shown in the

official Belgian national accounts was added to the Labeau estimate for the end of 1962 to carry the series forward.

DENMARK. The value of inventories including livestock in 1955 prices at the end of 1954 was provided by the Danish Statistical Department. Other years were obtained by cumulating the change in inventories in 1955 prices as given in the official Danish national accounts.

FRANCE. The value of inventories in 1954 was taken to be the sum of the estimates for livestock, other agricultural inventories, and inventories in manufacturing and commerce given by François Divisia, Jean Dupin, and René Roy in *Fortune de la France*, Vol. 3: "A la Recherche du Franc Perdu," p. 44 [S4]. The estimate was used as applying to the end of 1954, in 1954 prices. Other years were obtained by cumulating the change in business inventories in 1954 prices. The change in inventories in 1954 prices for the years 1950 through 1959 ("old" series, revised) was taken from OECD, *Statistics of National Accounts, 1950–1961* [I39]. For the years after 1959, the change in 1954 prices was estimated by multiplying the change in 1959 prices ("new" series) by the 1959 ratio of the change in 1954 prices to the change in 1959 prices ("old" series). The new series is provided in the national accounts.

GERMANY. The value of nonfarm inventories in 1954 prices at year-end 1954 was taken from Federal Statistical Office, *Wirtschaft und Statistik* (No. 9, 1958, p. 489 [G18]).[1] The data exclude the Saar and West Berlin. The value of farm inventories in 1954 was estimated on the assumption that the ratio of the value of inventories to the value of gross farm product in 1954 was the same as in France. The value of total inventories at year-end 1954 was obtained by adding nonfarm and farm inventories. Estimates for other years were obtained by cumulating the change in inventories in 1954 prices as reported in the German national accounts. Estimates of inventory change for 1961–62, which include the Saar and West Berlin, were reduced by the ratio of the value of inventory change in 1960 excluding these areas to the value including these areas. This procedure provided a series with consistent geographic coverage; the 1960–62 index including the Saar and West Berlin was assumed to be the same as that excluding these areas.

For comparison of the level of inventories with the United States, described below, the 1960 estimate was raised to include the Saar and West Berlin on the assumption that these areas had the same percentage of inventories as of employment.

NETHERLANDS. An annual series for the value of inventories in 1952 prices at year-end was available for the period 1948–58 from Central Bureau of Statistics in *Statistische en econometrische onderzoekingen* (3rd Quarter, 1960, p. 114 [G27]). The value of livestock was added to the value of other inventories.

A separate series in 1958 prices was constructed beginning with year-end 1958. The value in 1958 prices at the end of 1958 was approximated from the current price and constant price series given in the source cited in the preceding paragraph. Estimates for later years were obtained by cumulating the change in inventories in 1958 prices, as reported in Central Bureau of Statistics, *Nationale rekeningen, 1964*, Table 15 [G25]. As a check, this se-

ries was also carried backward; its movement was practically identical to that of the Central Bureau in 1952 prices.

The two series were linked at the end of 1958.

NORWAY. The value of inventories in 1955 prices at the beginning of the year is reported for the entire 1950–63 period in Central Bureau of Statistics, *Nasjonalregnskap, 1949–1962*, Table 31 [G33], and *Statistisk Årbok, 1965*, Table 90 [G35]. The value of livestock was included. Revisions of the estimates for inventory change in 1962, and the change in 1963 and 1964, were obtained from the national accounts and incorporated in the series used here.

UNITED KINGDOM. The value of stocks (including work in progress) at year-end in 1958 prices was provided by the Central Statistical Office for the entire period 1948–63. Strategic stocks are excluded. A year-end figure for 1964 was obtained by cumulating the inventory change shown in the national accounts.

ITALY. An estimate of the value of nonfarm inventories and livestock in 1961, valued in 1938 prices, was published by Antonino Giannone in *Banca Nazionale del Lavoro Quarterly Review* (December 1963, p. 427 [P4]). Starting from this estimate, an unofficial (and unpublished) series was privately prepared by Alberto Appetito for the value of inventories in 1954 prices for the beginning of each year from 1949 through 1964. This is the series used here. The absolute increase from 1950 through 1962 or 1964 is slightly below that obtained by cumulating inventory change as shown in the national accounts series.

For international comparison of the levels of inventories in 1960, described below, the Italian estimate was raised 5 percent to allow for the omission of farm inventories other than livestock from the Appetito series.

II. Levels in 1960

The following method was followed to obtain the comparison of the levels of inventories in 1960 given in Table 13–4:

1. The starting point was the value (average at the beginning and end of the year) of inventories in

---

1. The national accounts of Germany were subsequently revised (in 1963) but revised data for the *level* of inventories have not been released.

1960, valued in each country's own constant prices. These are the estimates just described. The constant price estimates for the several countries are expressed in prices of various years that are scattered from 1952 to 1958.

2. These estimates for 1960 expressed in assorted prices were next converted to 1955 prices.

For the United States, the values of farm and nonfarm inventories in 1960 expressed in 1958 prices were multiplied by the ratio of their 1955 values in 1955 prices to their 1955 values in 1958 prices. The farm and nonfarm components were added to obtain an estimate of $120.93 billion as the value in 1955 prices of inventories in 1960.

The estimates for Denmark and Norway were already in 1955 prices. The Belgian estimate for 1960 was converted from 1953 prices to 1955 prices by multiplying it by the ratio of the average value of inventories in 1955 in 1955 prices to the value in 1953 prices; both current and constant price estimates were available from Labeau. For the other five countries, two procedures for converting to 1955 prices were tried: One was to base the conversion on the wholesale price index; the other was to base it on the ratio of the value of the change in inventories in 1955 expressed in 1955 prices to the value of the change expressed in constant 1952, 1954, or 1958 prices. The results in all cases were very similar, and they were averaged. The amount of the price adjustment required to move from constant prices to 1955 prices was only about 1 percent or less except in the United Kingdom (where it was 5.6 percent). Because periods of large price movement were not involved in the conversion, substantial errors in this step are unlikely.

3. The final step was to convert the estimates of total inventories in 1960, valued in national prices of 1955, to estimates uniformly valued in United States prices of 1955. This, of course, required price ratios. Purchasing power equivalents for the entire GNP in 1955, based on national European quantity weights (which yield quantity comparisons based on United States price weights) were available from Gilbert and Associates.[2] These purchasing power equivalents for European currencies are presumably too large (by amounts that vary from country to country) for use in comparing inventories since they include services, which were more underpriced in Europe (relative to the United States) than were commodities. They were reduced by the ratio of the purchasing power equivalents Gilbert used for inventory change in 1950 to the purchasing power equivalents he obtained for GNP in 1950 (both with national European quantity weights).[3]

2. OEEC, 1958, p. 30 [I17]. The United Kingdom figure erroneously given as 0.272 pounds to the dollar was corrected to 0.242.

3. *Ibid.*, p. 80. Gilbert and Associates do not show purchasing power equivalents for inventories in 1955.

It may be noted that if Gilbert's 1950 purchasing power equivalents for inventory change were really accurately weighted for the components of inventory change in the year 1950, they would be quite erratic and unusable for the purpose of comparing the level of stocks. Although Gilbert and Associates do not describe their procedures, it appears evident from examination of their data that these parities actually result from an effort to obtain a purchasing power parity for commodities that enter into inventories (rather than inventory change) in 1950 and thus are appropriate for a comparison of stocks. The number of units of European currencies considered equivalent to one dollar for inventories in 1955 exceeds that for GNP by 4 percent in Norway, 11 or 12 percent in Belgium, Denmark, and Italy, and 19 to 22 percent in France, Germany, the Netherlands, and the United Kingdom.

⋙ A P P E N D I X   L ⋘

Derivation of International Comparisons of Nonagricultural National Income

This appendix describes the derivation of the 1960 indexes of national income per person employed in nonagricultural industries, measured in United States prices, that are presented in Table 16–12.

National income originating in dwellings and property income from abroad have no significant counterpart in employment. They were therefore deducted from total national income for the statistical analysis of this appendix. (The necessary data in United States prices were developed in the preparation of Chapters 2 and 11.) Indexes of national income per person employed computed after deduction of these components are shown in Column 2, Table L–2. (The indexes before their deduction, corresponding to Table 2–4, are shown in Column 1.) In the remainder of this appendix the terms "all industries" and "nonagricultural industries" will refer to the data *after* these types of income have been eliminated.

The purpose of this appendix is to determine the *difference* between national income per person employed in all industries and in nonagricultural industries. This difference is small in comparison to the level of the indexes themselves. The indexes are therefore shown here to a tenth of a point although elsewhere they are rounded to whole numbers.

To obtain national income in nonagricultural industries in United States prices in 1960, agricultural product had to be estimated and deducted from total national income. The evidence available was much too crude to offer hope that the agricultural estimates themselves would be very accurate. However, since in United States prices agriculture in the countries studied is estimated to comprise only between 2 and 8 percent of national product except in Denmark (where the percentage is 12), even rather large percentage errors in the estimates of agricultural national income have only a moderate effect upon estimates of nonagricultural national income per person employed.

Derivation of Estimates of Farm National Income

The United Kingdom had 9.73 percent as much farm GNP valued in United States prices as the United States in 1950, according to Paige and Bombach; this is the only direct comparison of a European country with the United States available in

United States prices.[1] Farm GNP of each of the two countries in 1950 was moved to 1955 by the percentage change in deflated farm GNP measured in its own prices. This produced an estimate that United Kingdom farm GNP was 9.75 percent of United States farm GNP in 1955.

A Twentieth Century Fund study valued the 1955 gross agricultural output (which is equal to farm GNP plus current purchases from other industries) of each of the European countries in Danish prices.[2] The price data covered a sample of commodities that represented two-thirds of the total value of farm output in Western Europe as a whole but as little as half in Italy. The remaining output was converted to Danish prices by use of price ratios for the sampled commodities. The Fund study also provided data that permitted the ratio of farm GNP to gross agricultural output in each country's own prices to be calculated.[3] I assumed these ratios to be the same in Danish as in national prices and applied them to the gross output estimates in Danish prices to obtain farm GNP in Danish prices. The ratio of farm GNP of each of the continental countries to farm GNP of the United Kingdom was then assumed to be the same in United States prices as it was in Danish prices. It was multiplied by the ratio (0.0975) of United Kingdom to United States farm GNP to obtain the ratio of farm GNP to that of the United States in 1955.[4] The 1955 estimates in United States prices in each country were extrapolated to 1960 by gross farm product in each country's own constant prices, a procedure that assumes that in each country the percentage change was the same in United States prices as in national prices.

The 1960 ratio of total agricultural GNP in each country to United States agricultural GNP, valued in United States prices, was then calculated.[5] The

1. Paige and Bombach, OEEC, *A Comparison of National Output and Productivity of the United Kingdom and the United States*, p. 21 [I22].
2. Dewhurst, Coppock, Yates and Associates, *Europe's Needs and Resources*, p. 1085, Table C [B31].
3. *Ibid.*, p. 1085, Table B.
4. The Twentieth Century Fund estimates include Luxembourg with Belgium. To eliminate Luxembourg the estimate was multiplied by the ratio of farm GNP in Belgium to farm GNP in the two countries combined, as shown by data given in OECD reports. However, as indicated below, the Belgian estimate was ultimately discarded.
5. Because of the starting point, the comparison is in principle in 1950 rather than 1960 United States prices; the difference is ignored.

ratios were assumed to be the same for net as for gross product, and were multiplied by United States farm national income (excluding income from farm dwellings) to obtain European agricultural national income in United States prices.

Table L–1 shows the calculated ratios of each country's total agricultural national income to that of the United States, the implied ratios of farm national income to total national income in United States prices within each country, and the implied ratios of agricultural product per person employed in agriculture to the United States figure. (The adjusted ratio shown for Belgium is described below.)

Estimates of Income in Nonagricultural Industries

Once estimates of total farm net product in United States prices were available, national income in nonfarm industries could be obtained by subtraction. Indexes of nonfarm national income per person employed in nonagricultural industries

TABLE L–1

Estimates of Agricultural National Income in United States Prices, 1960

Area	Total agricultural national income as percentage of		Agricultural national income per person employed as percentage of United States
	United States	Own national income (excluding dwellings and income from abroad)	
Calculated			
United States	100.00	3.9	100
Northwest Europe	85.20	4.7	47
Belgium	4.36	5.3	97
Denmark	5.49	11.7	70
France	36.43	8.3	50
Germany	20.36	3.5	32
Netherlands	6.09	6.1	81
Norway	1.59	4.8	35
United Kingdom	10.88	2.0	59
Italy	19.63	6.0	17
Adjusted			
Northwest Europe	83.08	4.6	46
Belgium	2.24	2.8	50

Source: See text for derivation.

TABLE L-2
Indexes of Total and Nonagricultural National Income per Person Employed and Reference Indexes, 1960

Area	National income per person employed (United States = 100)				Nonagricultural indexes minus indexes for all industries[a]	
	All industries		Nonagricultural industries[a]			
	Including dwellings and international assets (1)	Excluding dwellings and international assets (2)	Estimates (3)	Reference indexes (4)	Estimates (5)	Reference indexes (6)
	Calculated					
United States	100.0	100.0	100.0[b]	100.0	—	—
Northwest Europe	59.4	59.9	62.3	—	2.4	—
Belgium	61.2	61.9	60.4	61.6	−1.5	−.3
Denmark	58.3	58.7	62.8[b]	63.4	4.1[b]	4.7
France	59.5	60.2	67.1[b]	65.2	6.9[b]	5.0
Germany	58.9	59.7	63.7[b]	61.7	4.0[b]	2.0
Netherlands	64.6	65.1	65.1[b]	65.9	0.0[b]	.8
Norway	59.2	60.5	66.7[b]	63.9	6.2[b]	3.4
United Kingdom	58.9	58.7	57.3[b]	57.4	−1.4[b]	−1.3
Italy	40.4	41.4	54.7[b]	48.1	13.3[b]	6.7
	Adjusted					
Northwest Europe	59.4	59.9	62.4[b]	—	2.5[b]	—
Belgium	61.2	61.9	62.0[b]	—	0.0[b]	—

Source: See text for derivation.
a. Excluding income from dwellings and international assets.
b. Estimates used in Table 16–12.

(based on data for nonagricultural employment, including military personnel, from Table 5–1) are given in Column 3, Table L–2. Column 5 shows the differences between indexes of national income per person employed in all industries and national income per person employed in nonagricultural industries.

Examination and Adjustment of the Estimates

The procedure for deriving the estimates of farm national income per person employed is so roundabout that it is necessary to examine the results and judge whether they are reasonable.

The estimates of agricultural product per person employed in Table L–1 provide one basis for doing so. I shall examine them shortly but will state now that they led me to reject the Belgian farm estimates as implausibly high and to substitute estimates shown at the bottom of the table.

As a second test, an effort was made to compute the ratio of net farm product to net nonfarm product in national prices. In conjunction with similar ratios based on United States prices computed from Table L–1, this would have permitted the implied ratio of net product prices in agriculture to net product prices in nonagriculture in each country to be compared with the United States price ratio. In practice, only very crude comparisons could be obtained. Because of lack of data on a really comparable basis for net product at factor cost by industry in national prices, it was necessary to utilize gross product figures at either factor cost or market prices. The comparisons showed the ratio of farm to nonfarm product prices in Denmark and France to be only moderately higher than in the United States. In the other countries, except Belgium, it was higher by amounts ranging upward from over 50 percent in Germany and the Netherlands to over 100 percent in Norway and even more in Italy. This pattern appeared broadly reasonable since it seemed certain that the price ratio in Denmark and France was in fact much lower than in the other European countries, and that the ratio was much higher in all of the other European countries than in the United States. However, the implied Belgian price ratio was only about 25 percent above the United States ratio which is implausibly low in comparison with the other countries (especially the Netherlands) and gave further reason to reject the Belgian estimate.

As a third basis for comparison it seemed useful to compute the indexes of nonagricultural product per person employed that would emerge if, in United States prices, the ratio of national income per person employed in agriculture to national income per person employed in nonagricultural industries were the same in each European country as in the United States. This is the same as supposing that in United States prices, European indexes of output per person employed (United States equals 100) were the same in agriculture and in nonagricultural industries. Indexes that would result from this supposition are given in Column 4, Table L–2. These reference indexes are not presented as alternative or reasonable estimates but only as a guide for comparison. The differences between nonfarm and all-industry indexes, shown in Column 6, reflect only differences in employment composition whereas Column 5 also reflects differences among countries in farm-nonfarm differentials in income per person employed. For a European country, Column 5 should exceed Column 6 algebraically if, in *United States prices,* the ratio of farm to nonfarm production per person was lower than in the United States.

UNITED KINGDOM AND DENMARK. The estimate for the United Kingdom is clearly the most reliable since it derives most directly from the study by Paige and Bombach. It is almost the same as the reference index.[6] This was expected. Paige and Bombach found that in 1950 the ratio of British to American output per person in United States prices was about the same in agriculture as it was in nonagricultural industries. They also found that the British ratio of farm to nonfarm GNP was much (56 percent) higher in British than in American prices.

The direct estimate for Denmark is also fairly close to the reference index. This implies that in United States prices the Danish-American ratio of output per man in agriculture does not differ greatly from (it is actually estimated to be somewhat higher than) that in nonagriculture. Farm output per worker is estimated to be 70 percent of the United States, which is above that for any of the large European countries. Danish agriculture is quite efficient and the estimate seems plausible; so does the implication of a relatively low ratio (for Europe) of farm to nonfarm prices.

FRANCE, GERMANY, NORWAY, AND ITALY. The estimates of farm national income per person employed rank these four countries, compared with one another and with the United Kingdom and Denmark, in an order that in general corresponds with usual impressions.[7] (I ignore Belgium and the Netherlands for the moment.) All four lie below the United Kingdom and Denmark, France is much above Germany and Norway, and they in turn are much above Italy. That Germany is actually below Norway as the indexes show (32 against 35) is dubious. But if it were assumed the German index should be 40 instead of 32, and the estimate of total German farm product were therefore raised by one-fourth, this would lower the German index of output per man in nonfarm industries only from 63.7 to 63.2.

For all these countries the direct estimates of nonfarm national income per person employed are above the reference indexes. The implication that output per person is farther below the United States in agriculture than in nonagriculture seems reasonable enough.

The difference between the all-industry and the nonfarm estimates of income per person employed is much larger in Italy than in any other country— 13.3 points. So, in absolute terms, is the difference between the estimate of nonfarm income per person employed and the reference index. Also, as noted earlier, the implied ratio of farm to nonfarm product prices is very high. None of these results seemed implausible, but they did suggest the desirability of testing the sensitivity of the Italian estimate of non-

---

6. Statements like this refer both to Columns 3 and 4 and to Columns 5 and 6, Table L–2, but the differences under discussion can be seen more clearly in Columns 5 and 6.

7. In trying to judge what is reasonable, I have checked my impressions with those of a colleague much better informed than I about European agriculture.

farm product per man to possible error in the estimate of farm product in United States prices. This was done by supposing total Italian farm product in United States prices was really 50 percent higher or lower than estimated (29.45 percent or 9.82 percent of the United States farm product instead of 19.63 percent). Even these drastic alterations would lower or raise the index of nonfarm national income per person employed by only 1.8 points and, consequently, reduce or increase the difference between the indexes of nonfarm and total income per person by the same amount. Thus, the large estimate of the difference between the nonfarm and all-industry indexes is not very sensitive even to gross changes in the farm national income calculation.[8]

NETHERLANDS. The figure implied for farm product per person employed in the Netherlands—81 percent of the United States figure—is well above those for the other European countries (except the original calculation for Belgium). This is partially due to the fact that farm GNP was exceptionally large in 1960, higher by far than in other years during the period under review. In addition, Dutch employment data eliminate one-third of the number of female unpaid family workers. Substitution of the 1957–63 average for actual 1960 farm GNP would reduce the Dutch index from 81 to 72 and undoing the family worker adjustment, in addition,

8. Farm employment, and therefore farm product per person employed, in Italy is sensitive to the definition of employment. Use of a narrower definition for employment would yield a higher index for output per man in Italian farming. The selection of a farm employment estimate also affects total national income per person employed, but it does not affect national income per person employed in non-agricultural industries. The higher the Italian farm employment estimate used, the greater is the gap between the United States and Italy in income per person employed to be explained and, properly, the larger is the amount of the gap that must be ascribed to overallocation of labor to agriculture.

would bring the index to 70. The true figure is unknown but 70—the same as for Denmark—does not seem so implausibly high as to warrant its rejection.

A sensitivity test shows that if (improbably) the index should be only the same as France (50) on this adjusted basis (implying 58 as the *actual* 1960 figure), the index of output per person in nonagricultural industries would be raised from 65.1 to 66.3, and the difference between the nonfarm and all-industry indexes from zero to 1.2. This would still leave the Netherlands with much the smallest difference between nonfarm and all-industry indexes among the continental countries, except for Belgium.

BELGIUM. The directly calculated Belgian index of farm product per person employed, 97 percent of the United States figure, is altogether improbable. (Farm product in 1960 was not out of line with other years.) So, as indicated earlier, is the implication of a price ratio much below the Dutch ratio. Rejection of the directly calculated index seemed indicated. I have assumed that the correct index for farm product per person employed was 50, the same as France, and therefore reduced the estimate of farm GNP in United States prices by 49 percent. The Belgian index of nonfarm product per person employed is, fortunately, not highly sensitive to errors in the farm estimate. This huge farm adjustment changes the calculated index of nonfarm product per person employed from 60.4 to 62.0, and the difference between the nonfarm and all-industry indexes from −1.5 to zero. Use of an index for farm product per person employed of 40 or 60 instead of 50 would change the adjusted result by only 0.3 points. The adjusted estimates for Belgium are shown at the bottom of Tables L–1 and L–2.

≫≫ A P P E N D I X   M ≪≪

Supplementary Note on the Independent Growth of Local Markets and the Reorganization of Retail Trade

Section III of Chapter 17 points out that while the independent growth of local markets provides the opportunity for productivity gains, their actual realization requires major changes in business organization. Retail trade is the most important single industry affected by the independent growth of local markets resulting from the combination of population shifts and increased automobile ownership by customers. In the United States great changes have been occurring in this industry for several decades.[1] In Europe the revolution in distribution is taking place much later.

The total gains from retail reorganization in the United States have been large. David Schwartzman of the National Bureau of Economic Research has been studying productivity in retail and wholesale trade intensively. Like other authors, he stresses the organizational and size aspects of the rise of productivity in distribution; the great magnitude, and the importance to productivity, of the rise in the average size of retail transactions, especially in food

distribution; and the key role of automobile ownership and refrigeration in making changes possible. Also like other authors, he notes that expansion of the size of retail outlets increases the size of wholesale transactions, bringing important savings in wholesaling.[2]

European studies reinforce the findings of American studies concerning the importance of the size of the transaction and the store, and also of delivery costs, as determinants of unit costs in retailing. S. C. Bakkenist and D. E. Beutick (of Bakkenist, Spitz and Company, management consultants) conducted an intensive investigation of costs in a sample of Dutch food stores in 1948; the sample excluded both chains and cooperatives on the one hand

---

1. I do not mean, of course, to trace these changes exclusively to the growth of markets. New concepts of business organization and practice—"advances of knowledge" in my classification of growth sources—were present and would have brought changes in the absence of any change in the size or character of markets.

2. Schwartzman's book has not yet been completed but major findings are given in his sections of the 1964, 1965, and 1966 (44th, 45th, and 46th) annual reports of the National Bureau of Economic Research [B80]. Changes in output per person and productivity in retail trade by type of store developed in the National Bureau project have been presented by Victor Fuchs (in *Review of Income and Wealth*, No. 3, September 1966, pp. 211–44 [S10]. However, advances in productivity as measured by the National Bureau omit much of the gain from reduction in cost per unit of sales that has resulted from reorganization of the industry in the same sense and for the same reason that United States national product estimates do so (see "Differences in Channels of Retail Distribution," pp. 29–30).

and very small stores on the other.[3] They found the average number of items bought by each customer was only three, and that the average customer spent only 1.52 to 2.56 guilder (florins) in middle-class shops, and 1.06 to 2.30 guilder in lower-class shops. (The guilder was then worth 38 U.S. cents at exchange rates.) They found that the amount of the sale and (especially for unpackaged commodities) the size of the purchase of an individual commodity were of great importance in determining the unit costs of the retailers they studied.[4] They also found that delivery costs amounted to almost 12 percent of total costs. These conclusions were based on detailed analysis of the operations of individual stores. Another Dutch study examined wholesalers in confectionery and allied goods in 1958–59 by a similar procedure.[5] The size of order was found to be a crucial cost determinant in wholesaling as well as retailing. Larger retailers ordinarily mean larger orders to wholesalers.

Margaret Hall and John Knapp compared British and American retailing around 1950 and suggested the American advantage in real sales per person engaged—it was about the same (over two to one at the time) as the advantage in manufacturing production per worker—might be largely ascribable to the smaller average size of sale per customer in Britain.[6] Average sales per store were also much smaller than in the United States, notably so for chain stores which were more common in the United Kingdom. It may be observed that, within a line of trade, large stores and large transactions generally seem to go together both between and within countries, so the separate effects of store size and transaction size can hardly be distinguished except in studies of the Dutch type.[7] However, it is clear that changes which simultaneously increase the size of store, the size of sale per customer, and the average quantity of each individual item sold can greatly reduce the cost of moving a given volume of commodities to consumers. Introduction of self-service, elimination of home delivery, and more prepackaging also exert a powerful downward influence on costs. Shopping by automobile facilitated nearly all of these changes.

Because drastic changes in business structure are required for the automobile's potential to be realized, a brief showing that such changes have been occurring in Europe at an accelerating pace, and

3. In OEEC, *Productivity Measurement Review*, Special Number, July 1957 [I23].

4. They also found great variability in the profitability of different items and, in general, that packaged goods were profitable and unpackaged goods unprofitable. Even in the Netherlands in 1948, unpackaged goods were dwindling in importance. In the American supermarket, they scarcely existed. Packaging provides an interesting example of a shift of productive activity from retailer to manufacturer that may distort comparisons of productivity change by industry.

5. Van der Post in OEEC, *Productivity Measurement Review*, February 1962, pp. 47–48 [I23].

6. The analysis of Hall and Knapp might suggest expansion of the role assigned in Section II of Chapter 17 to per capita income and consumption (as distinguished from total income) as determinants of scale economies. Their analysis suggests that the average size of retail transactions rises with per capita income. The number of stores does not, at least proportionately; therefore, a rise in per capita income raises both the average size of store and the average size of transaction, and greatly reduces costs per dollar of sales. These authors have written extensively on the general subject. References here are to an article in *Productivity Measurement Review*, February 1957, pp. 22–38 [I23], and to their book (with Winsten), *Distribution in Great Britain and North America* [B46].

Schwartzman also found a significant relationship between sales per person engaged and family income (as well

as automobile usage) in a comparison of 188 metropolitan areas in the United States. He interpreted this as demonstrating the importance of transaction size (in National Bureau of Economic Research, *The Task of Economics*, 45th Annual Report, pp. 49–50 [B80]).

It may be noted that great emphasis on transaction size as a factor explaining the Anglo-American productivity differential in retail trade is in seeming conflict with the view of at least one observer. William H. Starbuck believes the two-to-one advantage of the United States over Britain cited in the text did not arise in "clerking activities" involving direct contact with customers but in "backing activities" which he estimates to have been twelve to eighteen times as high per dollar of sales in Britain as in the United States (*Emerging Concepts in Marketing*, pp. 212–19 [B102]).

7. This is shown in a striking way for retail grocery stores in Puerto Rico in a table provided by J. K. Galbraith and R. H. Holton (*Marketing Efficiency in Puerto Rico*, p. 17 [B40]). Both sales per employee and the average sale per customer transaction rose very strongly with size of store. The figures for the average sale per transaction are striking. From $0.38 in the smallest stores with a monthly volume under $500, it rose regularly to $1.77 when monthly volume was $4,000 to $9,999, and to $4.00 in the largest stores where volume was $10,000 to $40,000 a month. The implied figure for number of transactions per month per employee was about the same (630 to 731, the variation being irregular) in each of the four smallest size classes; it jumped to 839 in the second largest class, and fell to 475 in the largest size class.

Estimates given by W. G. McClelland imply the average sale in British supermarkets was around 1.7 times as large as the average sale in grocery shops around 1961 (*Studies in Retailing*, p. 44 [B70]). Schwartzman (in *The Task of Economics*, p. 49 [B80]) compares the average sale of $4.58 in American supermarkets in 1958 with the average sale of about $0.50 in American food stores in the 1930's. (Food prices approximately doubled between these dates.)

that in 1962 (and probably even in 1966), the bulk of the reorganization had yet to occur, may be appropriate. Data on size of store and size of transaction after eliminating very small stores (because the important gains from eliminating underemployment of the self-employed are considered separately in Chapter 16) would be most relevant to the discussion of Section III, Chapter 17, but are not generally available. However, the shift from counter service to self-service in food stores, for which information is available (Table M–1), at least illustrates the rate at which changes in retail organization are occurring in Europe. At the beginning of 1950, there were only 431 self-service stores in Northwest Europe. From the beginning of 1950 to the beginning of 1955, the number rose by 600 a year; from 1955 to 1960, by 5,100 a year; from 1960 to 1962, by 10,000 a year; from 1962 to 1964, by 13,300 a year; and from 1964 to 1966, by 14,500 a year. The increase in the four-year period from 1962 to 1966 was larger than that in twelve years from 1950 to 1962. The increase from 1950 to 1955 was trifling in absolute terms compared to the 1955–62 increase. The pattern of increase was somewhat similar in the different countries but conversion to self-service began earlier and was much further advanced by 1962 in some countries than others. Since 1960 about three-fifths of all the self-service outlets in Northwest Europe were in Germany. Italy was still far behind all the Northwest European countries.

If value of sales is inferred from number of outlets where the former type of data is absent, the incomplete data in Table M–1 suggest that the increase from 1950 to 1962 in the proportion of total food sales made by self-service stores was a substantial proportion of total food sales in Germany, the Netherlands, Norway, and the United Kingdom, but probably not elsewhere. In absolute terms most of the change occurred after 1957 and very little before 1955.

Self-service food stores in Europe should not be equated with American supermarkets; large supermarkets are a still more recent development. They were still scarce in Europe in 1962 and even in 1966, although their numbers were growing rapidly. Table M–2 gives the number of supermarkets for recent years; they are defined as food self-service stores with a minimum sales area of 400 square meters (300 in Italy after 1962) which, besides the

TABLE M–1
Self-Service Food Stores in Europe, 1950–66

| Area | Number of self-service stores[a] | | | | | | Self-service stores as a percentage of all food stores | | | | | |
| | | | | | | | By number[a] | | By value of sales | | | |
	1950	1955	1960	1962	1964	1966	1960	1963	1957	1959	1962	1965
Northwest Europe	431	3,651	29,114	49,177	75,711	104,591	n.a.	n.a.	n.a.	n.a.	n.a.	n.a.
Belgium	10	53	289	573	1,074	1,529	.3	1.1	2.9	n.a.	10.0	n.a.
Denmark	2[b]	207	645	1,592	2,524[c]	4,040	3.2	n.a.	n.a.	n.a.	n.a.	n.a.
France	1	380[b]	1,663	2,691	5,312	9,957	.9	n.a.	n.a.	n.a.	n.a.	13.9
Germany	1	326	17,132	30,680	46,794	62,714	11.8	27.6	6.9	25.0[b]	45.0	60.0
Netherlands	2	204	1,565	2,779	4,267	5,701	7.4	15.0	13.0	25.0	n.a.	n.a.
Norway	15[b]	480	1,470[d]	1,650	2,611[e]	2,800	11.5[d]	n.a.	18.9	n.a.	n.a.	n.a.
United Kingdom	400[b]	2,000[b]	6,350	9,212	13,129	17,850	4.3	7.7	10.1	17.0	36.7	43.9[f]
Italy	1	1[b]	250	n.a.	309	404[g]	.1	n.a.	n.a.	n.a.	n.a.	n.a.

Sources: 1950–59: OEEC, *The Economic Performance of Self-Service in Europe* [I19]; 1960–64: Henksmeier, *Self-Service, 1964*, Tables II and VIII [B48], and *Selbstbedienung und Supermarkt*, No. 11, 1965, p. 53 [P42]; 1965–66: Netherlands: unpublished data provided by The Ministry of Agriculture and Fisheries; other countries: *Techniques Marchandes Modernes*, September 1966, pp. 9–21 [P45]. Data from Henksmeier refer to Great Britain rather than the United Kingdom.
a. Data refer to the beginning of the year.
b. Indicated in the source to be partly estimated.
c. Average of estimates at July 1, 1963, and July 1, 1964.
d. Number refers to one year earlier than indicated in column head.
e. Estimate obtained by interpolation of data referring to January 1, 1963, and May 5, 1965.
f. Average of estimates for three periods in 1965 from the *Statist*, October 21, 1966, p. 981 [P43].
g. Data at July 1, 1965.
n.a. Not available.

TABLE M-2
Number of Supermarkets in Europe, 1961-66[a]

Area	1961	1962	1963	1964	1966
Northwest Europe[b]	486	793	1,285	1,930[c]	3,200[c]
Belgium	19	44	77	125	157
Denmark	87	104	160	230	410
France	49	121	207	323	584
Germany[d]	250	350	500	719	1,300
Netherlands	7	44	63	96	169
Norway[d]	n.a.	n.a.	15	n.a.	30
Great Britain	74	130	278	n.a.	n.a.
Italy	18	36	45	141	214

Sources: Henksmeier, *Self-Service, 1964* [B48] and also by correspondence; *Techniques Marchandes Modernes*, April and September 1966, and March 1967 [P45].
a. Data refer to the beginning of the year.
b. Data exclude Norway and Northern Ireland.
c. Includes estimate for Great Britain; British figure in 1967 was 919.
d. Indicated as estimate in the sources cited.
n.a. Not available.

usual assortment of foodstuffs, also sell fresh fruit, vegetables, meat, and other articles of daily use.

Although self-service stores are larger on the average than counter-service stores, many are small establishments and do not necessarily even carry a full line of food products. This was notably true in the earlier years when they were first being introduced.[8] A period of consolidation into larger establishments is to be expected.

What in Europe is sometimes called "concentrated commerce" (chain stores, department stores, mail order, cooperatives, and the like) is too inclusive a category for changes in its importance to be as instructive with respect to changes in retail distribution as one might suppose. Very small chain and cooperative establishments are included. However, it is noteworthy that "concentrated commerce" still accounted for only 14 to 16 percent of retail sales in 1960 in all the European countries covered in this study except the United Kingdom, where the percentage was 42, and Italy, where it was 5.[9] In France, it increased only from 10.2 percent in 1950 to 14.0 in 1960, but it was 16.4 in 1962.[10] The British percentage was already 35 to 40 percent in 1950, so the distributive pattern from which changes have been occurring in the United Kingdom differed decidedly from that on the continent.[11] The British figure for "concentrated commerce" even exceeded that in the United States, a fact partially responsible for the relatively small number of nonfarm self-employed in the United Kingdom that is noted in Chapter 16. However, the stores included in this category were much different in type and, on the average, had very much smaller sales in the United Kingdom than in the United States.[12] It is indicative, for example, that in 1965 stores described as "supermarkets" accounted for about 16 percent of British and 80 percent of American food sales.[13]

The development of shopping centers on the American pattern is so recent in Europe that it plays no role in an analysis of the 1950-62 period.

With regard to the United Kingdom, *The National Plan* [G45] seems to run counter in one respect to the judgment that the greatest impact of retail reorganization is still ahead in Europe. It suggests that the peak rate of introduction of supermarkets (though not of shopping centers) had been passed by 1964. It states that: "The last five years saw the large scale introduction of supermarkets, and although their expansion has still some way to go, especially in the less prosperous regions, their rate of introduction should now slow down. Other potential developments, such as out-of-town shopping centres, seem unlikely to catch on very widely before 1970."[14] *The National Plan* unfortunately does not give a reason to expect supermarket ex-

8. Jefferys, Hausberger, and Lindblad, in OEEC, *Productivity in the Distributive Trade in Europe, Wholesale and Retail Aspects*, p. 75 [I20]. In 1960 the *average* self-service food shop in Europe had more than 2.5 times as many persons engaged as, and higher sales per head than, the average counter shop (Jefferys and Knee, *Retailing in Europe*, p. 107 [B55]).
9. Jefferys and Knee, *Retailing in Europe*, p. 65 [B55].
10. The percentages for food sales were 10.5 in 1950 and 14.6 in 1960, for nonfood sales 9.8 in 1950 and 13.3 in 1960.

Data cited are from Quin in *Consommation*, 1962, No. 2, p. 50 [P13], and Quin, *Physionomie et Perspectives d'Evolution de l'Appareil Commercial Français, 1950-1970*, p. 343 [B90].
11. Jefferys, Hausberger, and Lindblad in OEEC, *Productivity in the Distributive Trade in Europe, Wholesale and Retail Aspects*, p. 107 [I20].
12. Hall, Knapp, and Winsten, *Distribution in Great Britain and North America*, pp. 144-45, 149 [B46]. However, in both food and nonfood retail trade the percentages of total retail trade personnel employed in establishments with total personnel of ten or more were similar in Great Britain in 1950 and the United States in 1948, and much higher than in the continental countries. See United Nations, Economic Commission for Europe (ECE), *Economic Survey of Europe in 1955*, p. 134 [I13].
13. *New York Times*, January 21, 1966 [P32].
14. *The National Plan*, presented to Parliament by the First Secretary of State and Secretary of State for Economic Affairs, Pt. I, pp. 60-61 [G45].

pansion to slow down and the supporting industry report does not repeat the statement.[15] Two years earlier, the National Economic Development Council had stated: "The introduction of labour saving methods is expected to be marked in many industries. . . . In retail distribution there will be [in 1963–66] a more rapid spread of supermarkets and self-service food shops, in which sales per person are typically over 50 per cent higher than they are in counter-service shops."[16] At that time the share of the "food sector represented by self-service (including supermarkets)" was expected to rise from 15 to 20 percent in 1961 to 48 percent in 1966.[17] The share of chains, mail order houses, and department stores in nonfood lines was also expected to rise.

15. *Ibid.*, Pt. II, pp. II-225–32.

16. *Growth of the United Kingdom Economy to 1966,* p. 27 [G43].

17. *Ibid.*, p. 147. The 48 percent was actually reached in mid-66, according to the *Statist,* October 21, 1966, p. 982 [P43].

⋙ A P P E N D I X N ⋘

Exports and Imports as Percentages of GNP

This appendix describes the derivation of Table 18–1 and the last three columns of Table 17–2.

Total Exports and Imports (Excluding Factor Income) at Current Prices

Most of these data were readily available. Series for Germany were linked at 1960, and for Belgium at 1953, to adjust earlier years for comparability with later data. For the Common Market countries, data are from the Statistical Office of the European Communities (OSCE), *General Statistical Bulletin*, 1965, No. 11; 1964, No. 11; 1962, No. 12; and 1961, No. 12 [I48], except that Belgian data for 1950 and 1951 were estimated by procedures consistent with those used in Chapter 2 and that Germany's 1950 and 1951 data come from the Federal Statistical Office, *Wirtschaft und Statistik*, 1963, No. 10 [G18]. Data for the United Kingdom are from the Central Statistical Office, *National Income and Expenditure, 1965* [G38]. Data for Norway for 1950–60 are from the Central Statistical Office, *Nasjonalregnskap, 1865–1960* [G33]; data for 1961–64 were provided by that Office. For Denmark, factor incomes from the Statistical Department, *Nationalregneskabsstatistik, 1947–1960* [G7], and *Statistiske Efterretninger* 1965, No. 7 [G9],

were deducted from export and import totals from OECD sources described in Appendix A.

Total Exports and Imports (Excluding Factor Income) at Constant 1958 Prices

The 1958 current price data for these items were multiplied by indexes of the volume of exports and imports, obtained from national sources, in the cases of Belgium, Denmark, the Netherlands, Norway, and the United Kingdom. These indexes were not necessarily based on 1958 prices. For France, Germany, and Italy, constant price time series including factor incomes were derived from the OSCE, *General Statistical Bulletin* data, and were multiplied by the ratio at current prices of exports and imports excluding factor incomes to exports and imports including them.

Manufactured Goods Exports and Imports at Current Prices

Manufactured goods are Standard International Trade Classification (SITC) categories 5, 6, 7, and 8.[1]

---

1. SITC categories are defined by OECD in *Trade by Commodities* [I40].

Belgian, German, Dutch, and British data in the currencies of these countries were available from national sources for the individual categories 5, 6, 7, and 8. Danish, French, Norwegian, and Italian data in dollars were available from OECD trade statistics and were converted to national currencies by use of current exchange rates.

Belgium's manufactured goods exports and imports include the joint trade of the Belgium-Luxembourg economic union; the GNP of Luxembourg was added to that of Belgium for the computation of the ratios. Trade between Belgium and Luxembourg is omitted.

France's manufactured goods exports and imports prior to July 1959 were adjusted as well as data permitted to exclude the trade of the Saar, which is incorporated with the French statistics until that date.[2] The procedure followed was to take total French SITC 5, 6, 7, 8 exports, subtract Saar exports of manufactured goods to Germany and one-half of total Saar exports to countries other than France and Germany, and add half of the Saar's total imports from France. On the import side, from total French SITC 5 to 8 imports were subtracted two-thirds of total Saar exports to France, Saar imports of manufactured goods from Germany, and half of total Saar imports from countries other than France and Germany.

The original German trade data included West Berlin throughout the period but excluded the Saar until July 1959. An adjustment to include the Saar was made prior to that date. From total German SITC 5 to 8 exports, Saar manufactured goods imports from Germany were subtracted and half of total Saar exports to France were added. To Ger-

many's SITC 5 to 8 imports half of total Saar imports from France were added and Saar manufactured goods exports to Germany were subtracted.

Manufactured Goods Exports at Constant 1958 Prices

The 1958 current price estimates were multiplied by volume indexes. Volume indexes were available for the period 1954–65 for Belgium-Luxembourg, France, Germany, the Netherlands, the United Kingdom, and Italy from the United Nations, *Monthly Bulletin of Statistics,* September 1963 and June 1966 [I3]. For the United Kingdom, *Annual Abstract of Statistics, 1958* [G36], carries the series back to 1950. For Germany, the *Statistisches Jahrbuch* [G16] carries indexes of semi-finished and finished manufactured goods back to 1950; the weighted average of these indexes was used to extend the German time series back to 1950. OECD, *Trade by Commodities,* Series B [I40], provided an index of manufactured goods exports for Norway for the period 1953–64.

Manufactured Goods Imports at Constant 1958 Prices

The 1958 current price estimates were multiplied by volume indexes. OECD, *Trade by Commodities,* Series B [I40], provides indexes for imports of France, Germany, Norway, and the United Kingdom back to 1953. The series for Germany and the United Kingdom were extended to 1950 in the same way as their export time series.

The import and export ratios for France and Germany prior to July 1959 were adjusted in the same proportion as in current prices to exclude and include the Saar, respectively.

2. Saar trade with Germany was available separately for manufactured products, but only total Saar trade with other areas was known. All the trade statistics for the Saar were taken from the German statistical yearbooks for 1959 and 1960 [G16].

Contribution to Growth Rates of National Income per Unit of Input Made by Differences Among Selected Years in the Pressure of Demand

This appendix describes the estimates presented in Table 19–1. To facilitate the explanation, the countries are discussed in a different order from that usually followed. First to be considered are the four countries for which an adjustment of output per unit of input for differences in demand pressures was deemed necessary: the United States, the United Kingdom, the Netherlands, and Denmark. They are followed by the five countries for which I concluded that no adjustment was required, grouped according to the reasons for reaching this conclusion: France and Norway; next, Germany and Italy; and finally, Belgium.

United States

Fluctuations in unemployment in the United States have been associated with the adequacy of demand.[1] The percentage of the civilian labor force unemployed was 5.3 in 1950, 4.4 in 1955, and 5.6 in 1962. All three years fell in periods of business cycle expansion but this does not imply complete comparability with respect to the phase of the cycle.

Arthur M. Okun has estimated that in the post-

war period each percentage point above 4 percent in the unemployment rate was associated on the average with a difference of −1.4 percent in GNP per man-hour worked.[2] Since the absolute amount of depreciation is (virtually) unaffected by current unemployment, national income is a little more sensitive on a percentage basis. Okun's −1.4 percent in GNP was changed to −1.5 percent to refer to national income. This relationship would imply that national income per man-hour worked was 1.35 percent higher in 1955 and 0.45 percent lower in 1962 than it would have been if unemployment had been at the 1950 level. The Okun adjustment works well in most years but not, it appears to me, in the 1955–56 period. Output per man-hour was exceptionally high in 1955. It scarcely rose from 1955 to 1956 even though the two years were approximately equal with respect to cyclical *level*.[3]

---

1. The reduction of the unemployment rate to the 4 percent level in the winter of 1965–66 largely disposed of the view that there had been a substantial increase in structural unemployment after 1957.

2. Okun, *Potential* GNP: *Its Measurement and Significance* [B84]. The −1.4 percent estimate is a by-product of Okun's estimate that a difference of 1 point in the unemployment rate is associated with a difference of −3.2 percent in total GNP.

3. In consequence, if the Okun formula is used to adjust output per man-hour to a high employment level, comparisons of growth rates of GNP per man-hour in the earlier and later periods are considerably altered if the division of periods is made at 1956 rather than at 1955.

(Unemployment was even slightly lower in 1956, at 4.2 percent as against 4.4 in 1955, but average hours of work were slightly shorter in 1956.) Application of the Okun formula to each separate year would indicate there was no trend increase in output per man-hour from 1955 to 1956. It is more plausible to conclude that the impact of cyclical position was more favorable in 1955 than in 1956 despite the similarity of the unemployment rates. Because 1955 was a year of rapid cyclical advance, when high employment was just being reached, I believe that in 1955 the intensity of utilization of employed resources was greater than it is on the average when unemployment is 4.4 percent.

I was tempted to substitute an estimate for 1955 based on the plausible assumptions that (1) the Okun adjustment is appropriate for the years 1955 and 1956 together but not separately, and (2) the increase in private output per man-hour from 1955 to 1956, after eliminating cyclical influences, was the same as the average increase between the cyclical peak years 1953 and 1957. This would yield an estimate that output per man-hour in 1955 was not 1.35 percent but 2.4 percent higher than it would have been under 1950 demand conditions (if no similar adjustment of the Okun result is made in 1950). Instead, I adopted the assumption that, for comparison with 1950 and 1962, the cyclical position of output per man-hour in 1955 could be taken as that which is ordinarily associated with a 4 percent, rather than the 4.4 percent, unemployment rate. I therefore estimated that national income per man-hour worked was 1.95 percent higher in 1955 (and 0.45 percent lower in 1962) than it would have been under 1950 demand conditions.

The contribution of differences in cyclical position to the growth rate of output per unit of input thus becomes 0.39 in 1950–55, −0.34 in 1955–62, and −0.04 in 1950–62.

United Kingdom

The intensity of demand has been analyzed by British economists, particularly those associated with the National Institute of Economic Research and with the Social Science Research Council growth project. Peaks in demand occurred *during* 1951, 1955, and 1960, and troughs *during* 1952, 1958, and 1962. On an *annual* basis the United

Kingdom unemployment rates and the "excess demand for labor" series indicate that peaks in demand occurred in 1951, 1955, and 1961, and troughs in 1952, 1958 or 1959, and 1963.

Series such as unemployment, "excess demand" for labor, and hours worked that indicate demand pressures were compared with series such as output per man, output per man-hour, and assorted variants of "output per unit of input" that indicate productivity. The comparisons led to the conclusion that national income per unit of input in the United Kingdom was sensitive to demand pressures, and that it was lower in 1950 and lower by at least twice as much in 1962 than it would have been if demand pressures had been as strong as in 1955. To estimate the amounts involved is difficult, however.

The percentage of the civilian labor force unemployed was 1.5 in 1950, 1.1 in 1955, and 2.0 in 1962.[4] Application to British unemployment rates of the adjusted Okun formula for the United States, according to which a 1 percentage point difference in unemployment rates yields a −1.5 percent difference in national income per hour worked, would yield the result that output per unit of input was lower by 0.6 percent in 1950 and by 1.35 percent in 1962 than it would have been at the 1955 cyclical position. However, the much lower level of the unemployment series (partly due to differences in definition) and the probability that there is a greater tendency to retain workers when work becomes slack, provide *a priori* grounds for believing output per man-hour may be more sensitive to absolute differences in the unemployment rate in Britain than in America. Examination of year-to-year movements in various productivity series also suggested that the adjustments should be larger than the Okun ratio yields at least as between 1955 and 1962. On a judgmental basis, national income per unit of input

4. This series represents the ratio of average monthly registered unemployment in the United Kingdom, as reported in the *Ministry of Labour Gazette* [G42], to the midyear civilian labor force, as reported by OECD in its *Manpower Statistics* [I32] reports. In 1960 this series stood at 1.6 percent, the frequently used series representing the ratio of registered unemployment to employed *wage and salary workers* plus the unemployed in *Great Britain* stood at 2.0, and a series adjusted to United States definitions by Neef (in *Monthly Labor Review*, March 1965, p. 258 [G67]) stood at 2.4. Movements of the three series are quite similar when all are available (Neef's series starts only in 1959 so could not be used for cyclical adjustment in this study).

in 1962 was estimated to be 2.0 percent rather than 1.35 percent lower than it would have been under 1955 demand conditions. This corresponds approximately to the definitional difference between the levels of the British and American unemployment series.[5] This implied that a 1 percentage point difference in the unemployment rate was associated with a 2.22 percent difference in national income per man-hour. The same ratio was applied to obtain an adjusted estimate that national income per man-hour in 1950 was 0.89 percent lower than it would have been with 1955 demand pressure; this maintains consistency between the 1950 and 1962 estimates. These estimates imply that the difference in cyclical position contributed 0.16 to the growth rate of national income per unit of input in 1950–55, −0.29 in 1955–62, and −0.09 in 1950–62.

The Netherlands

From 1948 through 1964 the annual unemployment rate experienced two periods of uninterrupted rise and two periods of uninterrupted decline.[6] The percentage of wage and salary workers unemployed

5. The following roundabout procedure also yields approximately this result (2.2). The years 1955 and 1960 were both at or near cyclical peaks in Britain. Although 1955 was a more buoyant year than 1960, gross domestic product per man-hour in 1960 was quite high in comparison with adjacent years. The Okun adjustment is probably adequate to adjust for the effect of differences in demand pressure between 1955 and 1960. It indicates that 1960 output per hour was 0.7 percent lower than it would have been with 1955 demand pressure. Output per man-hour in 1962 was about 1.5 percent lower than it would have been if it had increased from 1960 at the rate Godley and Shepherd estimated from 1951–62 data to be the trend after eliminating the effect of cyclical variation (Godley and Shepherd in *National Institute Economic Review*, August 1964, p. 30 [P30]). If cyclical factors were responsible for dropping the 1960 figure 0.7 percent below the 1955 figure and that for 1962 1.5 percent below the one for 1960, the difference between 1955 and 1962 was 2.2 percent.

The estimate that output per hour was 1.5 percent lower in 1962 than in 1960 for cyclical reasons implies that the underlying increase in productivity, after eliminating cyclical influences, was much smaller from 1960 to 1962 than from 1962 to 1964. The unemployment rate was the same in 1960 and 1964 so these years may be regarded as cyclically comparable. If one supposed that after eliminating cyclical influences the growth rate of productivity was really constant between 1960 and 1964, my 1962 adjustment for demand pressure would have to be doubled. However, this assumption is entirely inconsistent with the annual changes. Productivity increased more in both 1963 and 1964 than in either 1961 or 1962 even though both pairs of years included a year of rising and a year of declining unemployment.

6. Except that the rate was the same in 1962 and 1963.

rose from 1.6 in 1948 to 4.7 in 1952, fell to 1.3 in 1956, rose to 3.0 in 1958, then fell to 0.9 in 1962 where it remained (except for a dip to 0.8 in 1964) through 1965.[7] The rate was 2.8 in 1950, 1.7 in 1955, and 0.9 in 1962. The year 1950 fell in a period of rising unemployment, 1955 in a period of declining unemployment, and 1962 in a period of slightly declining unemployment.

There was a definite tendency for GNP per person employed to increase most in years when unemployment declined from the preceding year:

Change in unemployment rate (percentage points)	Number of years	Average change in unemployment rate (percentage points)	Average percentage increase in GNP per person employed
−0.4 to −1.3	7	−.8	4.3
−0.1 or 0.0	3	−.1	3.2
3.0 to 1.5	5	.5	1.4

Simple correlation indicates that on the average a difference of 1 point in the change in the unemployment rate was associated with a difference of −1.8 points in the percentage change in GNP per man. Variations in average hours may contribute a little to the sensitivity of this relationship. The adjusted Okun formula for the United States, according to which a difference of 1 point in the level of the unemployment rate (due to deficiency in demand) is associated with a −1.5 percent difference in national income per man-hour may be a reasonable approximation for the Netherlands as well as for the United States.

The 1955 unemployment rate was 1.1 points lower in 1955 than in 1950 and I assume this resulted from the difference in demand pressure.[8] In 1962 the rate was 0.8 points lower than in 1955. However, the rate in 1955 was only 0.4 points higher than in 1956, and 1956 was a year of extreme demand pressure, resulting in bottlenecks in production, balance of payments deficits, high wage in-

7. I rely here on a series provided by C. A. van den Beld which is a revision and extension of that given in Hickman (ed.), *Quantitative Planning of Economic Policy*, p. 150 [S8]. Ratios of unemployment to wage and salary workers were regarded as giving a better indication of cyclical position at different dates in the Netherlands than ratios to the total labor force.

8. Insofar as unabsorbed repatriates from the East Indies swelled 1950 unemployment this may be an overstatement.

creases, and the lowest unemployment rate in the whole 1948–60 period.[9] Unemployment due to deficient demand in 1955 can therefore hardly be put above 0.4. I assume that unemployment associated with intensity of demand, expressed as a percentage of the labor force, was 0.4 points higher in 1955 and therefore 1.5 points higher in 1950 than in 1962. Using the −1.5 ratio, I estimate that output per man-hour was 0.6 percent lower in 1955 and 2.25 percent lower in 1950 than it would have been with demand pressure similar to 1962. The contribution to the growth rate was then 0.34 points in 1950–55, 0.09 in 1955–62, and 0.19 in 1950–62.

Short-term fluctuations in GNP per man seem reasonably consistent with these results. GNP per man actually dropped from 1949 to 1950, and the actual 1950 figure was 1.4 percent *below* the average of 1949 and 1951. In contrast, the 1955 figure was 0.5 percent *above* the average of 1954 and 1956, and the 1962 figure was 0.8 percent *above* the average of 1961 and 1963. Thus, the adjustments for differences in cyclical position derived in the preceding paragraph happen to be rather similar to those that would result from substituting for actual output per unit of input in each year the average of the values for the preceding and following year.

Denmark

The unemployment rate in Denmark averaged 4.9 percent from 1948 through 1958.[10] During this period there were appreciable fluctuations, with unemployment peaks (business cycle troughs) falling in 1949, 1952, and 1956 and unemployment lows in 1950 and 1954. From its 1956 peak unemployment had fallen back only to 4.9 percent, the 1948–58 average, by 1958. Thereafter, it dropped sharply to 1.9 percent in 1961, and continued downward to a new low of 1.6 in 1964. The estimated unemployment rates in 1950, 1955, and 1962 were 4.3, 4.8, and 1.7, respectively.

An annual series for gross domestic product per person employed in nonagricultural industries was

computed. (Agricultural product is so large and erratic in Denmark that its elimination was essential.) This showed a decided tendency for the size of annual changes in output per man to be inversely related to changes in the unemployment rate. A simple correlation yielded an estimate that a difference of 1 point in the change in the unemployment rate was associated with a difference of −1.11 points in the percentage change in nonfarm GNP per man. This is a lower ratio than was used for the countries described previously. Application of this ratio to the differences in the unemployment rate indicated that nonfarm GNP per man was 0.58 percent lower in 1955 and 3.01 percent higher in 1962 than it would have been at the 1950 unemployment rate. After allowance for the weight of agriculture, estimates of 0.49 percent and 2.63 percent were used for the economy as a whole. These translate into estimates that the difference in cyclical position contributed −.10 points to the growth rate in 1950–55, 0.44 in 1955–62, and 0.22 in 1950–62. Even though the cyclical adjustment utilized is not a very sensitive one, it is possible that the estimate for the 1955–62 period is too large. This might be the case if part of the unemployment eliminated from 1955 to 1962 were structural in character.[11] On the other hand, comparison of the actual index for nonfarm GNP per person with a "cyclically adjusted" index computed from the regression formula shows the bulk of the divergence between the two series occurred in 1959 and 1960, a short period to eliminate a substantial amount of structural unemployment.

France

No adjustment for differences in cyclical position was made for France.[12] French growth was remarkably steady throughout the period. Significant retardations or declines (which were followed by periods of quick recovery) occurred only from January

---

9. Van den Beld in *Quantitative Planning of Economic Policy*, p. 148 [S8].

10. In this paragraph I rely on an unpublished, and admittedly approximate, series.

11. It is perhaps relevant that although unemployment in the early 1950's looks high from the perspective of the 1960's, at the time it was regarded as low and satisfactory. See, for example, Pedersen, in Lundberg (ed.), *The Business Cycle in the Post-war World* [B86].

12. In considering whether an adjustment was required, I have benefited from an analysis of changes in demand by the French economists associated with the Social Science Research Council growth project.

to December 1952 and from about March 1958 to March 1959. The years 1950, 1955, and 1962 fall outside both the decline and recovery periods.[13] The unemployment rate was 1.4 in 1950 (estimated), 1.4 in 1955, and 1.2 in 1962. Examination of annual output data does not suggest the course of productivity has been influenced by differences of such trifling size in the unemployment rate.

Norway

No adjustment was made for Norway. Except for 1958–59, when the unemployment rate rose to 1.5 percent and price and output increases temporarily dwindled, and perhaps 1952, Norway has operated under strong demand conditions throughout the postwar period. Unemployment was very low, ranging on an annual-average basis from 9,000 to 15,000 except in 1958–59.

The years 1955 and 1962 appear to be comparable. Unemployment was 0.9 percent of the labor force in 1955 and 1.0 percent in 1962. Increases from the preceding year in consumption prices were 3.7 percent and 4 percent. Although in both years GNP per man was below the average of the preceding and following years, unemployment and price data over these periods do not suggest this was due to fluctuations in the pressure of demand.

Demand pressures were probably even stronger in 1950 than in 1955 and 1962. The unemployment rate in 1950 was only 0.6 percent. The increase from the prior year in consumption prices was 12.3 percent, by far the largest in the postwar period, and the rise in total production from the prior year was also extraordinary. However, demand was so strong in 1955 and 1962 that it is unlikely that still stronger demand pressure would have lifted national income per unit of input appreciably in those years.[14]

13. For this reason the conclusion that no adjustment is required does not necessarily conflict with the finding of an increase in capacity utilization from the "early fifties," inferred from information first collected in May 1953, to 1957 (see ECE, *Economic Survey of Europe in 1961*, Pt. 2, "Some Factors in Economic Growth in Europe during the 1950s," Chap. IV, pp. 20–21 [I13]).

14. Since 1950, 1955, and 1962 are regarded as comparable, it is unnecessary to ask whether productivity is responsive to changes in demand pressure in Norway but one study suggests that it is, at least in industry (Ministry of Labor and Municipalities, *Virkninger av arbeidstidsforkortelsen fra 48 til 45 timer*, pp. 28–29 [G30]).

Germany

No adjustment was made for Germany. The protracted decline in unemployment was not interpreted as inducing a corresponding persistent rise in the intensity of utilization of employed inputs and in output per unit of input that would require adjustment of the 1950, 1955, and 1962 data for comparability.[15] The possibility that the years reviewed in this study were significantly out of line with adjacent years was considered. However, examination of annual data for unemployment and for such productivity measures as GNP per worker and the German Institute for Economic Research (Berlin) estimates of net production value in industry per worker and per hour worked did not suggest this to be the case.

Italy

The situation appeared to be similar to that in Germany and no adjustment was made. The unemployment rate declined without interruption (except that 1951 and 1952 were the same) from 7.6 percent in 1950 to 6.3 in 1955, 2.9 in 1962, and 2.5 in 1963, then increased to 2.7 in 1964. The persistent decline in unemployment was not interpreted as giving rise to the type of productivity fluctuations with which Chapter 19 is concerned. Examination of annual data for series such as the unemployment rate (annual average), the number "occasionally employed," and GNP per worker did not suggest that the years that concern this study were out of line with the other years.

Belgium

Belgium experienced swings in unemployment superimposed upon a trend that was generally level from 1949 to 1954 and thereafter downward. The unemployment rate was 4.9 percent in 1950, 3.8 in 1955, and 2.1 in 1962. Each of these years fell within periods of declining unemployment (from peaks in 1949, 1954, and 1959). In the first part of the following discussion I shall argue that although the evidence is not entirely clear, relevant short-term demand pressures probably were not nearly so

15. The decline in the unemployment rate from 7.3 in 1950 to 3.9 in 1955 and to 0.7 in 1961 was uninterrupted, except that the 1957 and 1958 rates were the same. From 1961 through 1964 the rate stabilized at 0.6 or 0.7 percent.

different in these years as the variations in unemployment rates might suggest, hence, even if an adjustment were required it would not be large. The second part of the discussion indicates that, with the possible exception of years of severe recession, output per unit of input was not sensitive to short-run demand pressures. This is the basis for the conclusion that no adjustment should be made.

1. Although the unemployment rate was 1.7 points higher in 1955 than in 1962, only perhaps half—0.8 points—of this difference seems to be due to a difference in short-term demand pressures. This estimate is obtained by regarding the average of the prosperous years 1956 and 1957 as cyclically comparable to the average of the years 1963 and 1964, even though unemployment was higher in 1956–57. Price increases were about the same in 1956–57 and 1963–64; they exceeded those in any other years except 1951–52. Unemployment in 1956–57 was the lowest over the whole period from 1949 through 1960 and in 1963–64 the lowest in the whole postwar period. The 1955 unemployment rate was 1.25 points above the 1956–57 average, and the 1962 rate was 0.45 points above the 1963–64 average. The 0.8 estimate is the difference between the two figures. The years 1955 and 1962 were at about the same phase of the cycle: Each was the second of four consecutive years of declining unemployment and the year in which employment increased most during each expansion.

The 1950 unemployment rate was 2.1 points above the 1955 rate but only 0.6 above the 1951 rate. The pressure of demand on resources was at least as strong in 1951 as in 1956–57 and 1963–64. Both the increase in the GNP price deflator and the increase in employment in 1951 were the largest of the whole postwar period. The armed forces were doubled from 1950 to 1951, contributing to tightness in the labor market. Employment reached a peak in 1951 that was not regained until 1955. The 0.6 difference between the 1950 and 1951 unemployment rates might be regarded as a measure of unemployment due to short-run demand deficiency that is comparable to the figures of 1.25 for 1955 and 0.45 for 1962. The inference that unemployment due to deficient demand was less in 1950 than in 1955 is questionable, however, because various

indicators referring to the years 1950 and 1955 themselves do not suggest that 1950 was a year of as strong demand pressure as 1955. Whether the difference between 1950 and 1955 in unemployment due to deficient demand was positive or negative, it probably was much less than the total difference in the unemployment rate of 2.1 points.[16]

2. Annual changes in GNP per person employed were compared with changes in the unemployment rate. The average increase in GNP per man was 3.1 percent in seven years in which the unemployment rate declined 0.5 points or more (averaging a decline of 0.7 points) and almost the same, 2.9 percent, in eight years in which the unemployment rate increased or declined 0.3 points or less (averaging an increase of 0.2 points). Moreover, among all of the eight individual years in which unemployment increased or declined least, the productivity increase was of below-average size only in 1952 and 1958, the years in which the unemployment rate rose most.[17] I conclude that there is no positive relationship between fluctuations in demand and fluctuations in productivity except in periods of sharp unemployment increases, whereas 1950, 1955, and 1962 were all years in which unemployment was falling.[18]

An additional and more specific point may be mentioned. From 1955 to 1957 the productivity increase was not especially large although unemployment was sharply reduced. An assumption that productivity in 1955 was cut to any considerable extent by less intensive use of resources would leave very little productivity advance from 1955 to 1957 for reasons other than the increase in utilization.

16. The preceding discussion implies that the decline in unemployment from the early 1950's to the 1960's resulted in part from a reduction in structural unemployment. The earliest year for which an unemployment estimate is available is 1948. The estimated unemployment rate in that year was only 2.4. If this is an accurate figure it raises some question as to whether this implication is correct.

17. In each of the other six years the percentage increase in GNP per man was within the range of 3.0 to 4.7, and it averaged 3.8.

18. This judgment appears to differ, though perhaps not greatly, from that adopted in the OECD report, *Economic Growth, 1960–1970: A Mid-decade Review of Prospects*, p. 106 [I27]. In a comparison of 1960, 1965, and a projection for 1970 its authors assumed a one point difference in the unemployment rate was associated with a 2 percent difference in total GNP. The extra 1 percent includes the effects of lower unemployment on labor force participation and hours of work in addition to effects on GNP per man-hour worked.

List of Sources

List of Sources

Series G: Government Publications

Belgium

Conseil National de la Politique Scientifique (National Science Policy Council), Brussels

G1 *Recherche et Croissance Economique* (R&D and Economic Growth). Report on certain aspects of industrial R&D with relation to economic growth. 1965.

Institut National de Statistique, Ministère des Affaires Economiques (National Institute of Statistics, Ministry of Economic Affairs), Brussels

G2 *Annuaire Statistique de la Belgique* (Belgian Statistical Yearbook). Vols. 82–86, selected issues, 1961–65.

G3 *Bulletin de Statistique* (Statistical Bulletin). Vol. 51, No. 7–8, July-August 1965.

G4 *Etudes Statistiques et Econométriques* (Statistical and Econometric Studies)

"Evolution de la concentration industrielle, variation du rendement, des rémunérations, de la valeur ajoutée et des investissements avec la dimension des établissements industriels" (Development of Manufacturing Concentration; Changes in Rates of Return, Earnings, Value Added, and Investments and the Size of Manufacturing Establishment), No. 6, 1964, pp. 44–87.

Les Comptes Nationaux de la Belgique, 1953–1964 (Belgian National Accounts, 1953–1964). No. 11, 1965.

Denmark

Arbejdsmarkedsrådets Virksomhed (Labor Market Council), Copenhagen

G5 *Beretning om Arbejdsmarkedsrådets Virksomhed: I Perioden 1.4.1961 til 30.6.1962* (Report of the Labor Market Council: April 1, 1961, to June 30, 1962). Nordlundes, 1962.

Det Statistiske Departement (The Statistical Department), Copenhagen

G6 *Børneskolen, 1957–61* (Children's Schools, 1957–61). Statistiske Meddelelser, 1964.

G7 *Nationalregnskabsstatistik, 1947–1960* (National Accounts Statistics, 1947–1960). Statistiske Undersøgelser Nr. 7, 1962.

G8 *Statistik Årbog* (Statistical Yearbook). Selected issues, 1951–65.

G9 *Statistiske Efterretninger* (Statistical Bulletin)

"Nationalregnskabsstatistik 1960–1962" (National Accounts Statistics 1960–1962), 56 Årgang, No. 7, February 20, 1964.

"Nationalregnskabsstatistik 1961–1963" (National Accounts Statistics 1961–1963), 57 Årgang, No. 5, January 22, 1965, and No. 7, February 4, 1965.

G10 Jørgensen, Erling. *Income-Expenditure Relations of Danish Wage and Salary Earners.* "Statistical Inquiries" series published by the Statistical Department in collaboration with the Institute of Statistics and the Institute of Economics of the University of Copenhagen. 1965.

France

Ministère de l'Industrie, Direction des Industries Mècaniques et Electriques (Ministry of Industry, Department of Mechanical and Electrical Industries), Paris

G11 *Le Parc de Machines-Outils dans les Industries Mécaniques et Electriques: Fin 1960* (Inventory of Machine Tools in the Mechanical and Electrical Industries: Year End 1960). Second Survey. 1961.

Ministère des Affaires Sociales (Ministry of Social Affairs), Paris

G12 *Revue Française du Travail* (French Labor Review)

"L'enquête trimestrielle sur l'activité économique et les conditions d'emploi de la main d'œuvre" (Quarterly Survey of Economic Activity and Conditions of Employment of the Labor Force), Vol. 4, No. 9–10, September-October 1950, pp. 451–65.

"Enquête sur l'activité et les conditions d'emploi de la main d'œuvre au 1er avril, 1960" (Survey of Conditions of Employment of the Labor Force up to April 1, 1960), Vol. 14, No. 2, April-June 1960, pp. 99–126.

"Répartition des ouvriers selon le mode de rémunération en 1960" (Distribution of Workers According to Payment System, 1960), Vol. 15, No. 2, April-June 1961, pp. 33–38.

"Le travail en équipes du personnel ouvrier dans les différents secteurs de l'industrie et du commerce au 1er juillet 1963" (Use of Shift Work in Manufacturing and Commercial Activities, Wage Earners, July 1, 1963), Vol. 19, No. 2, April-June 1965, pp. 87–93.

"Etude des incidences économiques et sociales de la réduction de la durée du travail" (Study of the Economic and Social Effects of the Reduction of Hours of Work), Vol. 20, No. 1, January-March 1966, pp. 361–93.

Institut National de la Statistique et des Etudes Economiques, Ministère des Finances et des Affaires Economiques (INSEE—National Institute of Statistics and Economic Studies, Ministry of Finance and Economic Affairs), Paris

G13 *Les Etablissements Industriels et Commerciaux en France en 1954* and *en 1962* (Manufacturing and Commercial Establishments in France in 1954 and in 1962). Imprimerie Nationale, 1955 and 1963.

G14 *Etudes et Conjoncture, Revue Mensuelle de l'I.N.S.E.E.* (Studies of Economic Activity, INSEE Monthly Review). Paris: Presses Universitaires de France

Rault, C. "L'équipement des ménages en décembre 1962" (Household Equipment, December 1963), Vol. 20, No. 12, December 1965, pp. 3–46.

Van Grevelinghe, G. "Projection de la consommation des ménages en 1970" (Projection of Household Consumption in 1970), Vol. 20, No. 6, June 1965, pp. 3–63.

Vincent, L. A. "Productivité et prix relatifs dans 15 branches de l'économie française (1949–1963)" (Productivity and Relative Prices in 15 Sectors of the French Economy, 1949–1963), Vol. 21, No. 2, February 1966, pp. 74–75, 81.

"Rapport sur les comptes de la nation de l'année 1962" (Report on the National Accounts for 1962), Vol. 18, No. 8–9, August-September 1963, pp. 662–63.

"Projection de la consommation des ménages en 1970: les dépenses d'habitation" (Projection of Household Consumption in 1970: Housing Expenses), Vol. 20, No. 9, September 1965, pp. 3–73.

"Les salaires dans l'industrie, le commerce et les services en 1963" (Wages and Salaries in Manufacturing, Commercial, and Service Industries, 1963), Vol. 20, No. 11, November 1965, pp. 62–65.

Germany

Statistisches Bundesamt (Federal Statistical Office), Wiesbaden. Stuttgart and Mainz: Verlag W. Kohlhammer, GmbH

G15 *Gehalts- und Lohnstrukturerhebung 1957* (Salary and Wage Levels 1957). Vol. 1: *Verdienste der Arbeiter in der Industrie im Oktober 1957* (Earnings of Industrial Workers in October 1957).

G16 *Statistisches Jahrbuch für die Bundesrepublik Deutschland* (Statistical Yearbook of the Federal Republic of Germany) for the years *1959, 1960,* and *1963.*

G17 *Preise, Löhne, Wirtschaftsrechnungen, Reihe 17* (Prices, Wages, and Economic Accounts, Series 17). Vol. 1: *Gewerbliche Wirtschaft und Dienstleistungsbereich, Arbeiterverdienste, 1962* (Worker Earnings, Manufacturing, and Service Activities, 1962).

G18 *Wirtschaft und Statistik* (Economics and Statistics). Vol. 10, No. 9, September 1958; Vol. 12: No. 1, January 1960, and No. 10, October 1960; Vol. 15: No. 10, October 1963, and No. 12, December 1963; Vol. 16: No. 1, January 1964, and No. 10, October 1964; and Vol. 18, No. 3, March 1966.

Italy

Istituto Centrale di Statistica (ISTAT—Central Institute of Statistics), Rome

G19 *Annali di Statistica* (Statistical Annals)
Agostinelli, Arnando. "Valutazione del capitale fisso interno per settori di attività economica e per ripartizioni territoriali alla fine del 1961" (Valuation of Domestic Fixed Capital by Type of Activity and Regional Breakdown to Year End 1961), Appendix 5 in Guiseppe de Meo, *Produttività e distribuzione del rèddito in Italia nel 1951–1963* (Productivity and Distribution of National Income in Italy Between 1951 and 1963). Anno 94, Series VIII, Vol. 15, 1965.

Ministèro del Bilancio (Ministry of the Budget), Rome

G20 *Relazione Generale.* Presented to Parliament by the Minister of the Budget
Relazione Generale sulla Situazione Economica del Paese, 1961 (General Report on the Economic Situation of the Country for 1961). Vol. 1, 1962.
Relazione Generale sulla Situazione Economica del Paese, 1964 (General Report on the Economic Situation of the Country for 1964). Vol. 2, 1965.

Associazione per lo Sviluppo dell'Industria nel Mezzogiorno, "Centro per gli Studi sullo Sviluppo Economico" (SVIMEZ—Organization for the Development of Industry in Southern Italy, Center for the Study of Economic Growth), Rome: Guiffrè

G21 *L'aumento dell'occupazione in Italia dal 1950 al 1957* (Increase in Employment in Italy from 1950 to 1957). Research Series, No. 1. 1959.

G22 *Stime sui consumi privati in Italia nel prossimo decennio* (Estimates of Private Consumption in Italy During the Next Decade). Research Series, No. 2. 1960.

Netherlands

Centraal Bureau voor de Statistiek (cbs—Central Bureau of Statistics), Zeist: W. de Haan, N.V.

G23 *Jaarcijfers voor Nederland* (Netherlands Statistical Yearbook). Selected issues, 1951–52 to 1963–64.

G24 "Der verdiensten van employes in 1962" (Earnings of Salaried Employees in 1962), *Maandschrift van het Centraal Bureau voor de Statistiek* (Monthly Bulletin of the Central Bureau of Statistics). Vol. 59, No. 6.

G25 *Nationale rekeningen* (National Accounts) for the years *1961, 1962, 1963,* and *1964.*

G26 *Sociale Maandstatistiek* (Monthly Social Statistics). Vol. 6, No. 8, August 1958; Vol. 10, No. 2, February 1962; and Vol. 12, No. 4, April 1964.

G27 "National Vermogen" (National Wealth), *Statistische en econometrische onderzoekingen* (Statistical and Econometric Research). 3rd Quarter 1960.

G28 *Statistical Studies.* No. 11: *National Accounts of the Netherlands, 1960.* December 1961.

Centraal Planbureau (National Planning Bureau), The Hague: Staatsuitgeverij

G29 *Centraal Economisch Plan* (National Economic Plan) for the years *1963, 1964, 1965,* and *1966.*

Norway

Kommunal- og arbeidsdepartementet (Department of Labor and Municipal Affairs), Oslo

G30 *Virkninger av arbeidstidsforkortelsen fra 48 til 45 timer* (Effects of Shortening the Hours of Work from 48 to 45 Hours). 1962.

Statistisk Sentralbyrå (Central Bureau of Statistics of Norway), Norges Offisielle Statistikk (nos—Norway's Official Statistics), Oslo: Grøndahl & Søns

G31 *Jordbruksstatistikk* (Agricultural Statistics). Selected issues, 1951–65.

G32 *Lønnsstatistikk, 1960* (Wage Statistics, 1960). nos Series XII, No. 80, 1961.

G33 *Nasjonalregnskap* (National Accounts)
Nasjonalregnskap, 1865–1960 (National Accounts, 1865–1960). nos Series XII, No. 163, 1965.
Nasjonalregnskap, 1949–1962 (National Accounts, 1949–1962). nos Series A, No. 95, 1964.

G34 *Norges Økonomi etter Krigen* (The Norwegian Postwar Economy). Samfunnøkonomiske Studier Nr. 12 (Economic Studies No. 12). 1965.

G35 *Statistisk Årbok* (Statistical Yearbook for Norway)
Statistisk Årbok for Norge. Selected issues, 1951–64.
Statistisk Årbok, 1965. nos Series XII, No. 170, 1965.

United Kingdom
London: Her Majesty's Stationery Office (hmso)

Central Statistical Office

G36 *Annual Abstract of Statistics* for the years *1955, 1958,* and *1964.*

G37 "The Relationship of Stocks to Production: An Analysis of Stocks/Output Ratios Since 1956," *Economic Trends.* No. 133, November 1964, pp. ii–xxii.

G38 *National Income and Expenditure* for the years *1963, 1964,* and *1965.*

Ministry of Education

G39 *15 to 18.* A Report of the Central Advisory Council for Education (England). Vol. 1, July 24, 1959.

G40 Committee on Higher Education. "Administrative, Financial, and Economic Aspects of Higher Education," Appendix Four of *Higher Education,* Report of the Committee Appointed by the Prime Minister Under the Chairmanship of Lord Robbins, 1961–63. HMSO Cmnd. 2154–IV, 1963.

G41 *Children and Their Primary Schools.* A Report of the Central Advisory Council for Education (England). 2 vols. 1967.

Ministry of Labour

G42 *Ministry of Labour Gazette.* Vol. LXIX: No. 2, February 1961, and No. 9, September 1961; Vol. LXX, No. 2, February 1962; Vol. LXXII, No. 2, February 1964; and Vol. LXXIII, No. 4, April 1964.

National Economic Development Council

G43 *Growth of the United Kingdom Economy, 1961–1966.* 1963.

H. M. Treasury

G44 *The Financial and Economic Obligations of the Nationalised Industries.* HMSO Cmnd. 1337, 1961.

G45 *The National Plan.* Presented to Parliament by the First Secretary of State and Secretary of State for Economic Affairs, September 1965. HMSO Cmnd. 2764.

United States

Washington, D. C.: Government Printing Office

U. S. Congress

G46 Joint Economic Committee. *Inventory Fluctuations and Economic Stabilization.* 87 Cong. 1 sess., 1961.

McGouldrick, Paul F. "The Impact of Credit Cost and Availability on Inventory Investment," in Pt. II, Causative Factors in Movements of Business Inventories, pp. 89–117.

Smith, Mabel A. "Factors Influencing Manufacturers' Inventories," in Pt. I, Postwar Fluctuations in Business Inventories, pp. 149–63.

Terleckyji, Nestor E., assisted by Alfred Tella. "Measures of Inventory Conditions," in Pt. II, Causative Factors in Movements of Business Inventories, pp. 165–94.

G47 Senate Subcommittee on Antitrust and Monopoly of the Committee on the Judiciary. *Antitrust Developments in the European Common Market.* Report. 88 Cong. 2 sess., 1964.

G48 Wason, James R. "Apprenticeship and Youth Employment in Western Europe: An Economic Study," in Senate Subcommittee on Employment and Manpower of the Committee on Labor and Public Welfare, *Selected Readings in Employment and Manpower.* Vol. 3: *The Role of Apprenticeship in Manpower Development: United States and Western Europe.* 88 Cong. 2 sess., 1964, pp. 1275–1357.

G49 House Select Subcommittee on Labor of the Committee on Education and Labor. *Hours of Work.* Hearings, Pt. 1, 88 Cong. 2 sess., 1963.

Statement of Ewan Clague, Commissioner, Bureau of Labor Statistics, accompanied by Peter Henle, Special Assistant to Mr. Clague, pp. 4–104.

Executive Branch

G50 *Manpower Report of the President,* and U. S. Department of Labor, *A Report on Manpower Requirements, Resources, Utilization, and Training.* March 1965.

G51 *Manpower Report of the President,* and U. S. Department of Labor, *A Report on Manpower Requirements, Resources, Utilization, and Training.* March 1966.

G52 *Economic Report of the President* together with *The Annual Report of the Council of Economic Advisers.* January 1966.

Department of Commerce, Bureau of the Census

G53 *Census of Agriculture, 1964.* Preliminary Report, Series AC 64-P1, November 1966.

G54 *Census of Population, 1950: Education.* Special Report, PE NO.5B; *Occupational Characteristics.* Special Report, PE NO.1B.

G55 *Census of Population, 1960: Educational Attainment.* Final Report, PC(2)-5B, 1963.

G56 *Census of Population, 1960: Occupation by Earnings and Education.* Final Report, PC(2)-7B, 1963.

G57 *Current Population Reports.* Series P-50
   14. "School Enrollment and Educational Attainment of Workers in United States, October 1948," May 1949.
   49. "Educational Attainment and Literacy of Workers: October 1952," October 1953.
   78. "Educational Attainment of Workers: March 1957," November 1957.

G58 *Long-Term Economic Growth, 1860–1965.* A Statistical Compendium. ES4-No. 1, October 1966.

G59 *Census of Manufactures, 1954.* 4 vols.

G60 *Statistical Abstract of the United States.* Selected issues, 1951–65.

G61 *Value of New Construction Put in Place, 1946–1963 Revised.* Construction Reports, Construction Activity, C30–61, Supplement, October 1964.

G62 Miller, Herman P. *Trends in the Income of Families and Persons in the United States: 1947 to 1960.* Technical Paper No. 8, 1963.

Department of Commerce, Office of Business Economics

G63 *Survey of Current Business*
   Barnes, Lillian P., George M. Cobren, and Joseph Rosenthal. "State and Local Government Activity: The Postwar Experience Related to the National Economy," Vol. 41, No. 3, March 1961, pp. 12–24.
   Foss, Murray F. "The Utilization of Capital Equipment: Postwar Compared with Prewar," Vol. 43, No. 6, June 1963, pp. 8–16.
   Grose, Lawrence, Irving Rottenberg, and Robert C. Wasson. "New Estimates of Fixed Capital in the United States, 1925–65," Vol. 46, No. 12, December 1966, pp. 34–40.
   Jaszi, George, Robert C. Wasson, and Lawrence Grose. "Expansion of Fixed Business Capital in the United States: Rapid Postwar Growth—Rise Slacker," Vol. 42, No. 11, November 1962, pp. 9–18, 28.
   "National Income and Product of the United States, 1951," National Income Number, Vol. 33, No. 7, July 1953, pp. 6–32.
   "The National Income and Product Accounts of the Revised Estimates, 1929–64," Vol. 45, No. 8, August 1965, pp. 6–56. Data also given in *The National Income and Product Accounts of the United States, 1929–1965: Statistical Tables.* A Supplement to *Survey of Current Business.*
   National Income, 1954 Edition. A Supplement to *Survey of Current Business.*
   U. S. Income and Product. A Supplement to *Survey of Current Business,* 1958.

Department of Health, Education and Welfare, Office of Education

G64 Male, George A. *Education in France.* OE–14091, Bulletin 1963, No. 33, 1963.

Department of the Interior, Bureau of Mines

G65 *Minerals Yearbook, 1962.* Vol. I: *Metals and Minerals.*

Department of Labor, Bureau of Labor Statistics

G66 *Wages and Related Benefits*. Part II: Metropolitan Areas, United States and Regional Summaries, 1963–64. Bulletin No. 1385–82, June 1965.

Wages and Related Benefits. Part II: Metropolitan Areas, United States and Regional Summaries, 1964–65. Bulletin No. 1430–83, May 1966.

G67 *Monthly Labor Review*

Hoover, Ethel D., and Margaret S. Stolz. "Food Distribution Changes and the CPI," Vol. 87, No. 1, January 1964, pp. 58–64.

Johnston, Denis F. "Educational Attainment of Workers, March 1962," Special Labor Force Report, Vol. 86, No. 5, May 1963, pp. 504–15.

Lewis, L. Earl. "Extent of Incentive Pay in Manufacturing," Vol. 83, No. 5, May 1960, pp. 460–63.

Neef, Arthur F. "International Unemployment Rates, 1960–64," Vol. 88, No. 3, March 1965, pp. 256–59.

Schiffman, Jacob. "Marital and Family Characteristics of Workers, March 1960," Special Labor Force Report, Vol. 84, No. 4, April 1961, pp. 355–64.

Stein, Robert L., and Herman Travis. "Labor Force and Employment in 1960," Special Labor Force Report, Vol. 84, No. 4, April 1961, pp. 344–54.

"Supplementary Wage Benefits in Metropolitan Areas, 1959–60," prepared by Otto Hollberg and Alexander Jarrell, Vol. 84, No. 4, April 1961, pp. 379–87.

G68 *Monthly Report on the Labor Force*. Selected issues, 1950–65.

G69 *Population and Labor Force Projections for the United States, 1960 to 1975*. Bulletin 1242. Prepared by the Division of Manpower and Employment Statistics, 1959.

G70 *Special Labor Force Reports*

No. 1. Katz, Arnold. *Educational Attainment of Workers, 1959*. (Also in *Monthly Labor Review*, Vol. 83, No. 2, February 1960, pp. 113–22; Reprint 2333.)

No. 14. Stein, Robert L., and Herman Travis. *Labor Force and Employment in 1960*. (Also in *Monthly Labor Review*, Vol. 84, No. 4, April 1961, pp. 344–54; Reprint 2365.)

No. 30. Johnston, Denis F. *Educational Attainment of Workers, March 1962*. (Also in *Monthly Labor Review*, Vol. 86, No. 5, May 1963, pp. 504–15; Reprint 2416.)

No. 53. Johnston, Denis F. *Educational Attainment of Workers, March 1964*. (Also in *Monthly Labor Review*, Vol. 88, No. 5, May 1965, pp. 517–27; Reprint 2463.)

No. 65. Johnston, Denis F., and Harvey R. Hamel. *Educational Attainment of Workers in March 1965*. (Also in *Monthly Labor Review*, Vol. 89, No. 3, March 1966, pp. 250–57; Reprint 2488.)

Department of Labor, Office of Manpower, Automation and Training

G71 Fabricant, Solomon. *Measurement of Technological Change*. Seminar on Manpower Policy and Program. July 1965.

G72 Gordon, Margaret S. *Retraining and Labor Market Adjustments in Western Europe*. Manpower Automation Research Monograph, No. 4, August 1965.

Department of State, Bureau of Intelligence and Research

Edwards, Corwin D. *Cartelization in Europe*. Policy Research Study, June 1964.

Department of State, International Cooperation Administration

G74 *European Productivity and Technical Assistance Programs. A Summing Up (1947–1958)*. Paris: U. S. Regional Office, Technical Cooperation Division, 1958.

Canada

Ottawa: Queens Printer and Controller of Stationery

G75 *Housing Census, 1961*. 1966.

Dominion Bureau of Statistics, Central Research and Development Staff
  G76 Podoluk, J. R. *Earnings and Education.* Published by authority of the Minister of Trade and Commerce. December 1965.

Series I: Publications of International Organizations

United Nations Publications
United Nations Publishing Service, United Nations, New York. Only English titles are used below. For editions in other languages and bilingual publications, see the United Nations catalogs.

Statistical Office of the United Nations, Department of Economic and Social Affairs, New York
  I1 *Demographic Yearbook, 1964.* Special Topic: Population Census Statistics III.
  I2 *Statistical Yearbook, 1963.* 1964.
  I3 *Monthly Bulletin of Statistics*
      "World Trade: Manufactured Goods Exports," Section C, Vol. XVII, No. 9, September 1963.
      "World Trade: Manufactured Goods Exports," Section D, Vol. XX, No. 6, June 1966.

United Nations Educational, Scientific and Cultural Organization (UNESCO), Paris
  I4 Debiesse, Jean. *Compulsory Education in France, 1951.*
  I5 *The Organization of the School Year: A Comparative Study.* UNESCO Educational Studies and Documents, No. 43, 1962.
  I6 *Pre-school Education.* Document ST/F7. 1963.

Food and Agricultural Organisation (FAO), Rome
  I7 *The State of Food and Agriculture*
     The State of Food and Agriculture, 1964.
     The State of Food and Agriculture, 1965: Review of the Second Postwar Decade.

International Labour Organisation (ILO), International Labour Office, Geneva
  I8 *European Apprenticeship: Effects of Educational, Social and Technical Development on Apprenticeship in Eight Countries.* CIRF Monograph. Report prepared for the United States Department of Labor, Office of Manpower, Automation and Training by the Centre International d'Information et de Recherche sur la Formation Professionelle (CIRF—Information and Research Center for Professional Training). Vol. 2, No. 2, CIRF Publications, 1966.
  I9 *International Labour Review*
      M. Kabaj, "Shift-Work and Employment Expansion," Vol. XCI, No. 1, January 1965, pp. 47–62.
      "An International Survey of Part-time Exployment: I," Vol. LXXXVIII, No. 4, October 1963, pp. 380–407.
  I10 *Hours of Work.* 42nd Session of the International Labour Conference, Report 8, 1965.
  I11 *Payment by Results.* Studies and Reports, New Series, No. 27, 1951.
  I12 *Year Book of Labour Statistics* for the years *1957* and *1963.*

Economic Commission for Europe, Geneva

I13 Department of Economic and Social Affairs, Research and Planning Division. *Economic Survey of Europe*

Economic Survey of Europe in 1955, including "Studies of Investment Problems and Policies of European Countries and Labor Market Problems in Western Europe." New York, 1956.

Economic Survey of Europe in 1961, Part II, "Some Factors in Economic Growth in Europe during the 1950s." New York, 1964.

Economic Survey of Europe in 1965, Part I, "The European Economy in 1965." New York, 1966.

OEEC-OECD Publications

Publications of the Organisation for European Economic Co-operation (OEEC) *and its subsidiary agency, European Productivity Agency* (EPA) *are obtainable from their successor, the Organisation for Economic Co-operation and Development* (OECD), *Paris. Although available in English and French (and, in some instances, in the languages of other member countries), only the English titles of sources cited are given below.*

I14 *Twelfth Annual Economic Review.* OEEC, 1961.

I15 *Statistics of National Product and Expenditure, No. 2, 1938 and 1947 to 1955.* OEEC, 1957.

I16 Gammelgaard, Søren. *Resale Price Maintenance.* Project No. 238. OEEC-EPA, 1958.

I17 Gilbert, Milton, and Associates (Wilfred Beckerman, John Edelman, Stephen Marris, Gerhard Stuvel, and Manfred Teichart). *Comparative National Products and Price Levels: A Study of Western Europe and the United States.* OEEC, 1958.

I18 Gilbert, Milton, and Irving B. Kravis. *An International Comparison of National Products and the Purchasing Power of Currencies: A Study of the United States, the United Kingdom, France, Germany, and Italy.* OEEC, 1954.

I19 Henksmeier, K. H. *The Economic Performance of Self-Service in Europe.* OEEC-EPA Report. 1960.

I20 Jefferys, James B., Simon Hausberger, and Göran Lindblad. *Productivity in the Distributive Trade in Europe, Wholesale and Retail Aspects.* OEEC, 1954.

I21 Massé, Pierre. "Productive Investment," in *Problems of Development: Series of Lectures on Economic Growth.* Lectures given at the University of Madrid. OEEC-EPA, 1961, pp. 71–89.

I22 Paige, Deborah, and Gottfried Bombach. *A Comparison of National Output and Productivity of the United Kingdom and the United States.* OEEC, 1959.

I23 *Productivity Measurement Review.* A publication of European Productivity Agency, OEEC-OECD

Hall, Margaret, and John Knapp. "Productivity in Distribution with Particular Reference to the Measurement of Output," No. 8, February 1957, pp. 22–38.

Bakkenist, S. C., and D. E. Beutick of Bakkenist, Spitz and Co. "An Investigation into the Costs of Distribution in the Grocery Retail Trade in the Netherlands." Special Number, July 1957.

Van der Post, H. J. "Statistics of Operating Costs in the Wholesale Trade in Confectionery and Allied Goods, 1958–59," No. 28, February 1962, pp. 47–48.

Maddison, Angus. "Facts and Observations on Labour Productivity in Western Europe, North America and Japan," No. 33, May 1963, pp. 5–15.

I24 *Demographic Trends*

Demographic Trends 1956–1976 in Western Europe and the United States. OEEC, 1961.

Demographic Trends 1965–1980 in Western Europe and North America. OECD, 1966.

I25 *Active Manpower Policy in the United States, Canada, and Europe.* Report of an International Management Seminar, Brussels, April 14–17, 1963. OECD, 1965.

I26 *Agriculture and Economic Growth: A Report by a Group of Experts* (Mario Bandini, Arthur Hanau, Simon Kuznets, Assar Lindbeck, Louis Malassis, and Brian Reddaway). OECD, 1965.

I27 *Economic Growth, 1960–1970: A Mid-decade Review of Prospects.* OECD, 1966.

I28 *General Statistics.* National Accounts. OECD, January 1965.

I29 *Industrial Statistics, 1900–1962*. OECD, 1964.

I30 *Low Incomes in Agriculture: Problems and Policies*. OECD, 1964.

I31 *Manpower Policy and Programmes in the United States*. OECD, 1964.

I32 *Manpower Statistics*
Manpower Statistics, 1950–1962. OECD, 1963.
Manpower Statistics, 1954–1964. OECD, 1965.

I33 *The Mediterranean Regional Project: Italy*. An Experiment in Planning in Six Countries. *Country Reports*, Education and Development Series. OECD, 1965.

I34 *Modern Cotton Industry: A Capital Intensive Industry*. OECD, 1965.

I35 *National Accounts Statistics, 1955–1964: Expenditure, Product, and Income*. OECD, 1966.

I36 *OECD Observer*

Menge, Franz. "Housing Construction Policies and Techniques in the Federal Republic of Germany," No. 20, February 1966, pp. 13–32.
"Towards a European Market in Electricity," No. 1, November 1962, pp. 10–12.

I37 *Problems of Manpower in Agriculture*. Food and Agriculture Documentation Series, No. 67. OECD, 1964.

I38 *Resources of Scientific and Technical Personnel in the OECD Area*. Statistical Report of the Third International Survey on the Demand for and Supply of Scientific and Technical Personnel. OECD, 1963.

I39 *Statistics of National Accounts, 1950–1961*. OECD, 1964.

I40 *Trade by Commodities* (Commodity Trade). Series B: "Analysis by Main Regions." Series C: "Detailed Analysis by Products." OECD, selected issues, 1963–66.

I41 *Wages and Labour Mobility*. A report by a group of independent experts, foreword by Pieter de Wolff. OECD, 1965.

I42 Beckerman, Wilfred. *International Comparisons of Real Incomes*. Development Centre Studies. OECD, 1966.

I43 Denison, Edward F. "Measuring the Contribution of Education (and the Residual) to Economic Growth" in *The Residual Factor and Economic Growth*. Study Group in the Economics of Education. OECD, 1965, pp. 13–55, 86–100. Comments on this paper by Edmond Malinvaud, pp. 57–66. Reprinted in Robinson and Vaizey (eds.) [B94]. Extracts translated into Italian: "L'insegnamento e la qualità del lavoro: contributo alla crescita economica degli Stati Uniti" in *L'Istruzione come Investimento* (Education as Investment). CENSIS Serie Readings. Rome: Centro Studi Investimenti Sociali, 1966, pp. 148–72.

I44 Freeman, C., and A. Young. *The Research and Development Effort in Western Europe, North America and the Soviet Union*. An experimental international comparison of research expenditures and manpower in 1962. OECD, 1965.

I45 Leicester, Colin. *The Manpower Link Between Economic Growth and Education*. Meeting of the Group of Experts on the Census Study. OECD, 1966 (English only).

I46 Svennilson, Ingvar, in association with Friedrich Edding and Lionel Elvin. *Policy Conference on Economic Growth and Investment*. Vol. II: *Targets for Education in Europe in 1970*. OECD, 1962.

Publications of the European Community

Publications of the European Community are generally available in French, German, Italian, and Dutch, and occasionally in English. French titles are used below unless official English translations are available.

European Community Information Service, Washington, D. C.

I47 "Wage Equality for Women Workers" in *Labor in the European Community*. Vol. 10. November 1965, pp. 2–6.

Office Statistique des Communautés Européennes (OSCE—Statistical Office of the European Communities), Brussels and Luxembourg

I48 *Bulletin Général de Statistiques* (General Statistical Bulletin). No. 12, 1961; No. 12, 1962; No. 11, 1964; Nos. 11 and 12, 1965; No. 11, 1966; and No. 1, 1967.

I49 *Informations Statistiques* (Statistical Information)
Wartna, J. A. "Import Duties Inside and Outside the European Economic Community," in *Quarterly Review of Economic Integration in Europe*. No. 2, 1966 (in English).
Methods of Forecasting Long-Term Economic Growth. No. 6, 1960 (in English).
Cahiers Trimestriels de l'Intégration Economique Européenne: Une Enquête sur les Forces de Travail dans les Pays de la C.E.E. en 1960 (Quarterly Review of Economic Integration in Europe: A Survey of the Labor Force in the EEC Countries in 1960). No. 2 bis, 1963.
La Recherche et la Production de Hydro-carbures Liquides et Gaseux dans les Pays de la Communauté Européenne: Eléments Statistiques (Basic Data Concerning the Search for and Exploitation of Liquid and Gaseous Hydrocarbons in the Countries of the European Community). No. 1 bis, 1965.

I50 *Statistique Agricole* (Agricultural Statistics)
"Utilisation des terres" (Land Use), No. 8, 1964.
"Utilisation des terres" (Land Use), No. 1, 1966.

I51 *Statistiques de Base* (Basic Statistics)
Basic Statistics for Fifteen European Countries: Comparison with the United States and the Union of Soviet Socialist Republics. 1961.
Basic Statistics of the Community: Comparison with Some European Countries, Canada, the United States of America and the Union of Soviet Socialist Republics. 5th ed. 1964.

I52 *Statistiques Sociales* (Social Statistics)
"Prix, taux d'équivalence de pouvoir d'achat à la consommation et revenus réels dans les pays de la C.E.C.A., 1954–1958" (Prices, Consumption Purchasing Power Parities, and Real Incomes in the Countries of the European Coal and Steel Community, 1954–1958), No. 2, 1960.
"Statistiques de l'emploi dans les pays de la Communauté et la Grèce, 1958–1962" (Employment Statistics in the Countries of the Community and Greece, 1958–1962), No. 4, 1963.

Communauté Européenne Economique (EEC—European Economic Community), Brussels

I53 *Exposé sur l'Evolution de la Situation Sociale dans la Communauté en 1963* (Report on Social Developments in the Community in 1963). EEC Commission, 1964.

I54 *Report on the Economic Situation in the Countries of the Community*. EEC Commission, 1958.

I55 *La Formation Professionelle des Jeunes dans les Enterprises Industrielles, Artisanales et Commerciales des Pays de la C.E.E.* (Professional Training of Young People in Industrial, Handicraft, and Commercial Enterprises in the EEC Countries). Social Policy Series No. 1. EEC Commission, 1963.

I56 *Les Perspectives de Développement Economique dans la C.E.E. de 1960 à 1970: Rapport d'un Groupe d'Experts* (The Economic Development Prospects in the EEC from 1960 to 1970: Report of a Group of Experts). EEC Commission, 1962.

I57 *Perspectives de Développement Economique dans la C.E.E. Jusqu'en 1970* (Prospects of Economic Growth in the EEC to 1970). Groupe d'Etudes des Perspectives Economiques à Moyen Terme (Working Party on Medium-Term Economic Prospects). EEC Commission, 1966.

I58 *General Report*
Eighth General Report on the Activities of the Community (1 April 1964–31 March 1965). EEC Commission, 1965.
Ninth General Report on the Activities of the Community (1 April 1965–31 March 1966). EEC Commission, 1966.

I59 Zijlstra, J., with M. B. Goudzwaard. *Politique Economique et Problèmes de la Concurrence dans la C.E.E. et dans les Pays Membres de la C.E.E.* (Economic Policy and Problems of Competition in the EEC and in EEC Member Countries). Competition Series, No. 2. EEC Commission, 1966.

Communauté Européenne du Charbon et de l'Acier (CECA—European Coal and Steel Community), Luxembourg

I60 *C.E.C.A., 1952–1962.* CECA, 1963.

Council of Europe, Strasbourg

Publications of the Council of Europe are generally available in English and French. English titles are used below.

I61 Council for Cultural Co-operation. *School Systems: A Guide. Education in Europe* series, No. 5, Section II, General and Technical Education. 1965.

I62 Wander, Hilde. "Communication on the Origin and Destination of Recent Migration in Western Europe." Paper presented at the European Population Conference, Strasbourg, August 30–September 6, 1966. *Official Documents of the Conference.* Vol. II, C 31, 1966.

Series B: Books and Pamphlets

B1 Abramovitz, Moses. *Resource and Output Trends in the United States since 1870.* Occasional Paper 52. New York: National Bureau of Economic Research, 1956.

B2 Automobile Manufacturers' Association. *Automobile Facts and Figures* for the years *1952, 1964, 1965, 1966.* Detroit: Automobile Manufacturers' Association.

B3 Bain, Joe S. *Barriers to New Competition: Their Character and Consequences in Manufacturing Industries.* Cambridge, Mass.: Harvard University Press, 1956.

B4 Bain, Joe S. *International Differences in Industrial Structure: Eight Nations in the 1950s.* New Haven, Conn.: Yale University Press, 1966.

B5 Balassa, Bela. *The Theory of Economic Integration.* Homewood, Ill.: Richard D. Irwin, 1961.

B6 Barna, Tibor. *Investment and Growth Policies in British Industrial Firms.* Occasional Papers 20. Cambridge, Eng.: Cambridge University Press for National Institute of Economic and Social Research, 1962.

B7 Barna, Tibor. "On Measuring Capital," in F. A. Lutz, and D. C. Hague (ed.), *The Theory of Capital.* Proceedings of a Conference Held by the International Economic Association. London: Macmillan, 1961; New York: St. Martin's Press, 1961, pp. 25–94.

B8 Baum, Warren C. *The French Economy and the French State.* RAND Corporation Research Study. Princeton, N. J.: Princeton University Press, 1958.

B9 Bayliss, Brian T. *European Transport: A Study of Freight Transport in the UK and the EEC with Special Reference to Road Haulage.* London: Kenneth Mason, 1965.

B10 Becker, Gary S. *Human Capital: A Theoretical and Empirical Analysis, with Special Reference to Education.* General Series No. 80. New York: National Bureau of Economic Research, 1964.

B11 Beckerman, W., and Associates. *The British Economy in 1975.* Cambridge, Eng.: Cambridge University Press for National Institute of Economic and Social Research, 1965.

B12 Bignami, Enrico. "Management Growth and Development in the European Economic and Political Climate," in *Proceedings, CIOS XIII International Management Congress*. New York: Council for International Progress in Management, 1963, pp. 406–09.

B13 Serge A. Birn Company, Management Consultants. *A Survey of International Labor Productivity: Are European Labor Costs Really Lower?* New York: Serge A. Birn Company, Inc., 1966.

B14 Brinberg, Herbert R., and Herbert R. Northrup. *Economics of the Work Week*. New York: National Industrial Conference Board, 1950.

B15 Brown, David G. "Hours and Output," in Clyde E. Dankert, Floyd C. Mann, and Herbert R. Northrup (eds.), *Hours of Work*. Publication No. 32. New York: Harper & Row for Industrial Relations Research Association, 1965.

B16 Camacho, Guillermo Franco. *Rendimiento de la Inversión en Educación en Colombia* (Return from Investment in Education in Colombia). Paper presented to the Fourth Commission of the Seventh Latin American Sociological Convention. Bogota: Centro de Estudios sobre Desarrolo Económico (CEDE—Center for Economic Development Studies), Universidad de los Andes (University of the Andes), July 1964.

B17 Cao-Pinna, Vera. "Validité théorique et empirique d'une prévision globale de la croissance de l'économie italienne de 1958 à 1970" (Theoretical and Empirical Validity of an Overall Growth Forecast of the Italian Economy from 1958 to 1970), in R. C. Geary (ed.), *Europe's Future in Figures*. Vol. I. Amsterdam: North-Holland Publishing Co. for ASEPELT (Association Scientifique Européenne pour la Prévision Economique à Moyen et à Long Terme—European Scientific Association for Medium- and Long-Term Forecasting), 1962, pp. 111–61.

B18 Clark, Colin. *Growthmanship: A Study in the Mythology of Investment*. Hobart Paper No. 10. London: Barrie and Rockliff for Institute of Economic Affairs, 1961.

B19 Cole, John. "The Price of Obstinacy: Crises in the Trade Unions," in Arthur Koestler (ed.), *Suicide of a Nation?* London: Hutchinson, 1963, pp. 105–23.

B20 Committee for Economic Development (CED). *Economic Development of Central America. Desarrollo Económico de Centroamerica*. A Statement on National Policy by the Research and Policy Committee of the CED. New York: CED, 1964. (Bilingual, English-Spanish.)

B21 Committee for Economic Development (CED). *The European Common Market and Its Meaning to the United States*. A Statement on National Policy by the Research and Policy Committee of the Committee for Economic Development. New York: CED, 1959.

B22 Correa, H. *The Economics of Human Resources*. Contributions to Economic Analysis XXXIV. Amsterdam: North-Holland Publishing Co., 1963.

B23 Crawley, Aidan. "A Red Under Every Bed?" in Arthur Koestler (ed.), *Suicide of a Nation?* London: Hutchinson, 1963, pp. 94–104.

B24 Denison, Edward F. "Improved Allocation of Labor as a Source of Higher European Growth Rates," in Michael J. Brennan (ed.), *Patterns of Market Behavior: Essays in Honor of Philip Taft*. Providence, R. I.: Brown University Press, 1965, pp. 65–88. Brookings Reprint No. 94.

B25 Denison, Edward F. *The Sources of Economic Growth in the United States and the Alternatives Before Us* (referred to in the text as *Sources of Economic Growth*). Supplementary Paper No. 13. New York: Committee for Economic Development, 1962.

B26 Denison, Edward F. "Theoretical Aspects of Quality Change, Capital Consumption, and Net Capital Formation," in *Problems of Capital Formation: Concepts, Measurement, and Controlling Factors*. Studies in Income and Wealth, Vol. 19. Conference on Research in Income and Wealth. Princeton, N. J.: Princeton University Press for National Bureau of Economic Research, 1957, pp. 215–84.

B27 Denison, Edward F. "Comment" on Edward C. Budd, "Factor Shares, 1850–1910," in *Trends in the American Economy in the Nineteenth Century*. Studies in Income and Wealth, Vol. 24. Conference on Research in Income and Wealth. Princeton, N. J.: Princeton University Press for National Bureau of Economic Research, 1960, pp. 399–403.

B28 Denison, Edward F. "Measurement of Labor Input: Some Questions of Definition and the Adequacy of Data," in *Output, Input, and Productivity Measurement*. Studies in Income and Wealth, Vol. 25. Conference on Research in Income and Wealth. Princeton, N. J.: Princeton University Press for National Bureau of Economic Research, 1961, pp. 347–86.

B29 Despicht, Nigel S. *Policies of Transport in the Common Market*. A Survey of the National Transport Policies of the Six Member States of the European Economic Community and of the Implementation of the Transport Provisions of the Treaty of Rome. Sidcup, Kent: Lambarde Press, 1964.

B30 Deutsches Institut für Wirtschaftsforschung (German Institute for Economic Research). *Produktionsvolumen und Produktionsfaktoren der Industrie im Gebiet der Bundesrepublik Deutschland* (Production Volume and Production Factors in West German Industry), "Statistische Kennziffern 1950 bis 1960, Neuberechnung auf der Basis 1958" (Statistical Indexes 1950 to 1960, Revised Data in 1958 Prices) and "Statistische Kennziffern 1958 bis 1964." Berlin: Dunker and Humblot, September 1964 and November 1965.

B31 Dewhurst, J. Frederick. "Manpower," in J. Frederick Dewhurst, John O. Coppock, P. Lamartine Yates, and Associates, *Europe's Needs and Resources: Trends and Prospects in Eighteen Countries*. New York: Twentieth Century Fund, 1961, pp. 61–106. French edition: *Besoins et Moyens de l'Europe: Tendances et Perspectives de Dix-huit Pays*. Paris: Berger-Levrault, 1962.

B32 Fabricant, Solomon. *Employment in Manufacturing, 1899–1939: An Analysis of Its Relation to the Volume of Production*. New York: National Bureau of Economic Research, 1942.

B33 Fitzgerald, Mark J. *The Common Market's Labor Programs*. Notre Dame, Ind.: University of Notre Dame Press, 1966.

B34 Flanders, Allan. *The Fawley Productivity Agreements: A Case Study of Management and Collective Bargaining*. London: Faber and Faber, 1964.

B35 Forte, Francesco, and Francesco Indovina. "Struttura e dinamica regionale-settoriale dell'economía italiana 1951–61" (The Regional and Sectoral Structure and Dynamics of the Italian Economy 1951–61), in Francesco Forte and S. Lombardini (eds.), *Saggi di Economía* (Economic Essays). Milan: Guiffrè, 1965.

B36 Fourastié, Jean. *Machinisme et Bien-Être*. Paris: Editions de Minuit, 1954. American edition, revised, adapted, and supplemented: Theodore Caplow (ed. and trans.), *The Causes of Wealth*. New York: Free Press of Glencoe, 1960.

B37 Fuà, Giorgio. *Notes on Italian Economic Growth, 1861–1964*. Milan: Giuffrè, 1965.

B38 Fuchs, Victor R. *Productivity Trends in the Goods and Service Sectors, 1929–61: A Preliminary Survey*. Occasional Paper No. 89. New York: National Bureau of Economic Research, 1964.

B39 Fulop, Christina. *Competition for Consumers: A Study of the Changing Channels of Distribution*. London: A. Deutsch for Institute of Economic Affairs, 1964.

B40 Galbraith, J. K., and R. H. Holton, in collaboration with Robert E. Branson, Jean Ruth Robinson, and Caroline Shaw Bell. *Marketing Efficiency in Puerto Rico*. Cambridge, Mass.: Harvard University Press, 1955.

B41 Goldsmith, Raymond W. *The National Wealth of the United States in the Postwar Period*. Princeton, N. J.: Princeton University Press for National Bureau of Economic Research, 1962.

B42 Goldsmith, Raymond W., and Christopher Saunders (eds.). *The Measurement of National Wealth*. Income and Wealth Series VIII. London: Bowes & Bowes for International Association for Research in Income and Wealth, 1963.

B43 Granick, David. *The European Executive*. Garden City, N. Y.: Doubleday, 1962. French edition: *Les Enterprises Européennes. Par Qui et Comment Sont-Elles Dirigées?* Paris: Editions d'Organisation, 1964.

B44 Griliches, Zvi. "Production Functions in Manufacturing: Some Preliminary Results." Paper presented to the Conference on Research in Income and Wealth, October 15–16, 1965. To be published in *The Theory and Empirical Analysis of Production*. Studies in Income and Wealth, Vol. 31. Conference on Research in Income and Wealth. National Bureau of Economic Research.

B45 Habakkuk, N. J. *American and British Technology in the Nineteenth Century: The Search for Labor-Saving Devices*. Cambridge, Eng.: Cambridge University Press, 1962.

B46 Hall, Margaret, John Knapp, and Christopher Winsten. *Distribution in Great Britain and North America: A Study in Structure and Productivity*. London: Oxford University Press, 1961.

B47 Harberger, Arnold C. "Taxation, Resource Allocation, and Welfare," in *The Role of Direct and Indirect Taxes in the Federal Revenue System*. A Conference Report of the National Bureau of Economic Research and the Brookings Institution, Studies of Government Finance. Princeton, N. J.: Princeton University Press for National Bureau of Economic Research and Brookings Institution, 1964.

B48 Henksmeier, K. H. *Self-Service, 1964*. Cologne: International Self-Service Organisation, 1965.

B49 Hennessy, Jossleyn. "A British 'Miracle'?" in *Rebirth of Britain*. A Symposium of Essays by Eighteen Writers. London: Pan Books in Association with Institute of Economic Affairs, 1964, pp. 241–55.

B50 Hildebrand, George H. *Growth and Structure in the Economy of Modern Italy*. Cambridge, Mass.: Harvard University Press, 1965.

B51 Hultgren, Thor, assisted by Maude R. Pech. *Cost, Prices and Profits: Their Cyclical Relations*. New York: Columbia University Press for National Bureau of Economic Research, 1965.

B52 Hutton, Graham. *We Too Can Prosper; The Promise of Productivity*. London: Allen & Unwin for British Productivity Council, formerly Anglo-American Council on Productivity (U. K. Section), 1953.

B53 Janssen, L. H. *Free Trade, Protection, and Customs Union*. Leiden: H. E. Stenfert Kroese N.V. for the Economisch-Sociologisch Instituut—Tilburg, 1961.

B54 Jaszi, George. "The Conceptual Basis of the Accounts: A Re-examination," in *A Critique of the United States Income and Product Accounts*. Studies in Income and Wealth, Vol. 22. Conference on Research in Income and Wealth. Princeton, N. J.: Princeton University Press for National Bureau of Economic Research, 1958, pp. 13–145.

B55 Jefferys, James B., and Derek Knee. *Retailing in Europe: Present Structure and Future Trends*. London: Macmillan, 1962. French edition: *Le Commerce de Détail en Europe*. Paris: Presses Universitaires de France, 1963.

B56 Jewkes, John, and Sylvia Jewkes. *Value for Medicine*. Oxford: Basil Blackwell, 1963.

B57 Kendrick, John W. *Productivity Trends in the United States*. Princeton, N. J.: Princeton University Press for National Bureau of Economic Research, 1961.

B58 Kindleberger, Charles P. *Economic Growth in France and Britain, 1851–1950*. Cambridge, Mass.: Harvard University Press, 1964.

B59 Kindleberger, Charles P. *Europe and the Dollar*. Cambridge, Mass.: M.I.T. Press, 1966.

B60 Kindleberger, Charles P. "The Postwar Resurgence of the French Economy," in Stanley H. Hoffmann and others, *In Search of France*. Cambridge, Mass.: Harvard University Press, 1963, pp. 118–58.

B61 Krause, Lawrence (ed.). *The Common Market: Progress and Controversy*. Modern Economic Issues S-91. Englewood Cliffs, N. J.: Prentice-Hall, 1964.

B62 Krause, Lawrence B. *The Meaning of European Economic Integration for the United States*. Washington, D. C.: Brookings Institution, 1967.

B63 Kravis, Irving B. *The Structure of Income: Some Quantitative Essays*. Based on U. S. Bureau of Labor Statistics, "Study of Consumer Expenditures, Incomes, and Savings." Philadelphia: University of Pennsylvania Press, 1962.

B64 Krengel, Rolf. *Anlagevermögen, Produktion und Beschäftigung der Industrie im Gebiet der Bundesrepublik von 1924 bis 1956* (Capital Structure, Production and Employment in West German Industry from 1924 to 1956). Berlin: Dunker and Humblot for Deutsches Institut für Wirtschaftsforschung (German Institute for Economic Research), 1958.

B65 Krengel, Rolf and others. "Arbeitszeit und Produktivität" (Hours of Work and Productivity), in *Untersuchungsergebnisse wissenschaftlicher Forschungsinstitut*. Vol. 4 (Studies of the Scientific Research Institute). Berlin: Dunker and Humbolt for Deutsches Institut für Wirtschaftsforschung (German Institute for Economic Research), 1962.

B66 Lamfalusy, A. *Investment and Growth in Mature Economies: The Case of Belgium*. London: Macmillan, 1961; New York: St. Martin's Press, 1961.

B67 Lamfalusy, A. *The United Kingdom and the Six: An Essay on Economic Growth in Western Europe*. London: Macmillan, 1963; New York: St. Martin's Press, 1963.

B68 Layton, Christopher. *Trans-Atlantic Investments*. The Atlantic Papers. Boulogne-sur-Seine: The Atlantic Institute, 1966.

B69 Lutz, Vera. *Italy: A Study in Economic Development*. London: Oxford University Press for Royal Institute of International Affairs, 1962.

B70 McClelland, W. G. *Studies in Retailing*. Oxford: Basil Blackwell, 1963.

B71 Maddison, Angus. *Economic Growth in the West: Comparative Experience in Europe and North America*. New York: Twentieth Century Fund, 1964.

B72 Madsen, Finn, Ketty Pedersen, and Hans Elgaard. *Nogle Tabeller om Uddannelse Erhverv og Helbred* (Statistical Data on Occupation and Health). Socialforskningsinstituttets Publikationer 21 (Social Research Institute Publication 21). Copenhagen: I Kommission hos Teknisk Forlag, 1966.

B73 Marchal, Jean, and Jacques Lecaillon. "Les entrepreneurs, agriculteurs, prêteurs, bénéficiares de transferts" (Entrepreneurs, Farmers, Lenders, Beneficiaries of Transfer Payments), in *La Répartition du Revenu National* (The Distribution of National Income). Vol. II. Paris: M-Th. Génin, 1958.

B74 Marris, Robin, assisted by Ian MacLean and Simon Bernau. *The Economics of Capital Utilisation: A Report on Multiple-Shift Work*. Cambridge, Eng.: Cambridge University Press, 1964.

B75 Meade, James E. *UK, Commonwealth and Common Market*. Hobart Paper 17. London: Institute of Economic Affairs, 1962. French edition: "Royaume-Uni, Commonwealth et Marché Commun," in *Bulletin* SEDEIS, No. 816, April 1, 1962, Supplement, pp. 1–49.

B76 Michaely, Michael. *Concentration in International Trade*. Contributions to Economic Analysis XXVIII. Amsterdam: North-Holland Publishing Co., 1962.

B77 Minhas, Bagicha Singh. *An International Comparison of Factor Costs and Factor Use*. Contributions to Economic Analysis XXXI. Amsterdam: North-Holland Publishing Co., 1963.

B78 Mueller, Bernard. *A Statistical Handbook of the North Atlantic Area: Western Europe, Canada, United States*. Captions in English and French. New York: Twentieth Century Fund, 1965.

B79 National Education Association, Educational Policies Commission. *Universal Opportunity for Early Childhood Education*. Washington, D. C.: National Education Association, 1966.

B80 National Bureau of Economic Research. Annual Reports: *The National Bureau Enters Its Forty-fifth Year*, 44th Annual Report, June 1964; *The Task of Economics*, 45th Annual Report, June 1965; and *Anticipating the Nation's Needs for Economic Knowledge*, 46th Annual Report, June 1966. New York: National Bureau of Economic Research.

B81 National Bureau of Economic Research. *A Critique of the United States Income and Product Accounts*. Studies in Income and Wealth, Vol. 22. Conference on Research in Income and Wealth. Princeton, N. J.: Princeton University Press for National Bureau of Economic Research, 1958.

B82 Nelson, Richard R. *Aggregate Production Functions and Medium-Range Growth Projections*. RAND RM-3912-PR. Santa Monica, Calif.: RAND Corporation, December 1962.

B83 Nelson, Richard R., Merton J Peck, and Edward D. Kalachek. *Technology, Economic Growth, and Public Policy.* A RAND Corporation and Brookings Institution Study. Washington, D. C.: Brookings Institution, 1967.

B84 Okun, Arthur M. "Potential GNP: Its Measurement and Significance," in American Statistical Association, *1962 Proceedings of the Business and Economics Statistics Section.* Washington, D. C.: American Statistical Association, 1963, pp. 98–104. Reprinted as Cowles Foundation Paper No. 190. New Haven, Conn.: Yale University Press for Cowles Foundation for Research in Economics, 1963.

B85 Owen, Wilfred. "The Transport Revolution," in J. Frederick Dewhurst, John O. Coppock, P. Lamartine Yates, and Associates, *Europe's Needs and Resources: Trends and Prospects in Eighteen Countries.* New York: Twentieth Century Fund, 1961. French edition available, see [B31]. Brookings Reprint No. 53.

B86 Pedersen, Jørgen. "A Study of Post-war Industrial Fluctuations in Denmark," in Erik Lundberg, assisted by A. D. Knox (eds.), *The Business Cycle in the Post-war World.* Proceedings of a Conference Held by the International Economic Association. London: Macmillan, 1955; New York: St. Martin's Press, 1955.

B87 Poignant, Raymond. *L'Enseignement dans les Pays du Marché Commun* (Education in the Common Market Countries). Paris: Institut Pédagogique National, 1965.

B88 Political and Economic Planning (PEP). *Growth in the British Economy: A Study of Economic Problems and Policies in Contemporary Britain.* London: Allen & Unwin, 1960.

B89 Pratten, C., and R. M. Dean, in collaboration with A. Silberston. *The Economics of Large-Scale Production in British Industry: An Introductory Study.* Cambridge, Eng.: Cambridge University Press, 1965.

B90 Quin, Claude. *Physionomie et Perspectives d'Evolution de l'Appareil Commercial Français, 1950–1970* (The Character and Development Prospects of the French Commercial Network, 1950–1970). Paris: Gauthier-Villars, 1964.

B91 Reader's Digest Association. *The European Common Market and Britain: Basic Report.* A Marketing Survey Sponsored by Reader's Digest Association. New York: Reader's Digest Association, 1963.

B92 Reynolds, Lloyd. *Labor Economics and Labor Relations.* 2nd ed. Englewood Cliffs, N. J.: Prentice-Hall, 1954.

B93 Robinson, E. A. G. (ed.). *Economic Consequences of the Size of Nations.* Proceedings of a Conference Held by the International Economic Association. London: Macmillan for International Economic Association, 1960; New York: St. Martin's Press, 1960.

B94 Robinson, E. A. G., and J. E. Vaizey (eds.). *The Economics of Education.* Proceedings of a Conference Held by the International Economic Association. London: Macmillan for International Economic Association, 1966; New York: St. Martin's Press, 1966.

B95 Salter, W. E. G. *Productivity and Technical Change.* Monograph 6. Cambridge, Eng.: Cambridge University Press, 1960.

B96 Sandee, J. (ed.). *Europe's Future Consumption.* Vol. II. Amsterdam: North-Holland Publishing Co. for ASEPELT (Association Scientifique Européenne pour la Prévision Economique à Moyen et à Long Terme—European Scientific Association for Medium- and Long-Term Forecasting), 1964.

B97 Schmookler, Jacob. *Invention and Economic Growth.* Cambridge, Mass.: Harvard University Press, 1966.

B98 Scitovsky, Tibor. *Economic Theory and Western European Integration.* Stanford Studies in History, Economics, and Political Science 16. Stanford, Calif.: Stanford University Press, 1958; London: Allen & Unwin, 1958.

B99 Shanks, Michael. "The Comforts of Stagnation," in Arthur Koestler (ed.), *Suicide of a Nation?* London: Hutchinson, 1963, pp. 51–69.

B100 Sheahan, John. *Promotion and Control of Industry in Postwar France.* Cambridge, Mass.: Harvard University Press, 1963.

B101 Stacey, Nicholas A. H. *Mergers in Modern Business.* London: Hutchinson, 1966.

B102 Starbuck, William H. "Sales Volume and Employment in British and American Retail Trade," in *Emerging Concepts in Marketing.* Proceedings of the Winter Conference of the American Marketing Association, Pittsburgh, December 27–29, 1962. Chicago, Ill.: American Marketing Association, 1963.

B103 Stigler, George J. "Economic Problems in Measuring Changes in Productivity," in *Output, Input, and Productivity Measurement.* Studies in Income and Wealth, Vol. 25. Conference on Research in Income and Wealth. Princeton, N. J.: Princeton University Press for National Bureau of Economic Research, 1961, pp. 42–63.

B104 Swann, C., and J. McLeachlan. *Competition in the Common Market.* London: PEP (Political and Economic Planning) and Chatham House, 1966.

B105 Tinbergen, Jan. "The European Economic Community: Conservative or Progressive?" in *International Trade and Finance. A Collected Volume of Wicksell Lectures, 1958–1964.* Stockholm: Almqvist & Wiksell, 1965, pp. 221–50.

B106 Vaizey, John. *The Economics of Education.* New York: Free Press of Glencoe, 1962; London: Faber and Faber, 1962.

B107 Webb, R. K. *Britain Faces the Sixties.* Headline Series No. 156. New York: Foreign Policy Association, 1962.

B108 Webb, Sidney, and Harold Cox. *The Eight Hours Day.* London: Walter Scott, 1891.

B109 Williams, Gertrude. *Apprenticeship in Europe; The Lesson of Britain.* London: Chapman and Hall, 1963.

B110 Yamey, B. S. (ed.). *Resale Price Maintenance.* Chicago: Aldine Publishing Co., 1966; London: Weidenfeld & Nicolson, 1966.

B111 Yates, P. Lamartine. *Food, Land and Manpower in Western Europe.* London: Macmillan, 1960; New York: St. Martin's Press, 1960.

Series P: Periodicals

P1 *American Economic Review.* A publication of the American Economic Association, Evanston, Ill.

Abramovitz, Moses. "Economic Growth in the United States," Vol. LII, No. 4, September 1962, pp. 762–82. A Review Article.

Bowen, William G., and T. Aldrich Finegan. "Educational Attainment and Labor Force Participation," Vol. LVI, No. 2, May 1966, pp. 567–82. Papers and Proceedings of the Seventy-eighth Annual Meeting of the American Economic Association.

Denison, Edward F. "The Unimportance of the Embodied Question," Vol. LIV, No. 2, Pt. 1, March 1964, pp. 90–94.

Denison, Edward F. "Capital Theory and the Rate of Return," Vol. LIV, No. 5, September 1964, pp. 721–25. A Review Article.

Miller, Herman P. "Annual and Lifetime Income in Relation to Education: 1939–1959," Vol. L, No. 5, December 1960, pp. 962–86.

Spaventa, Luigi. "Review of *Growth and Structure in the Economy of Modern Italy* by George H. Hildebrand," Vol. LVI, No. 5, December 1966, pp. 1297–1300.

P2 *Amsterdam-Rotterdam Bank N.V., Economic Quarterly Review,* Amsterdam

Haccoû, J. F. "Concentration in Netherlands Manufacturing Industries," No. 2, September 1965, pp. 13–19.

Van Krevelen, D. W. "The Importance of Research for Industrial Development," No. 147, March 1965, pp. 15–19.

P3 *Analyse & Prévision* (Analysis & Forecasting). A publication of Société d'Etudes et de Documentation Economiques, Industrielles et Sociales (SEDEIS—Society for Economic, Industrial, and Social Studies and Documentation), Paris

Houssiaux, J. "L'économie médicale dans la Communauté Economique Européenne: problèmes et perspectives" (Medical Economics in the European Economic Community: Problems and Perspectives), Vol. 1, No. 2, February 1966, pp. 83–102.

P4 *Banca Nazionale del Lavoro Quarterly Review,* Rome

Giannone, A. "Evaluation of Italian National Wealth in the last 50 Years," Vol. XVI, No. 67, December 1963, pp. 421–36.

Holton, Richard H. "Economic Development and the Growth of the Trade Sector in Italy," Vol. XV, No. 62, September 1962, pp. 240–57.

Krengel, Rolf. "Some Reasons for the Rapid Economic Growth of the German Federal Republic," Vol. XVI, No. 64, March 1963, pp. 121–44.

De Meo, Giuseppe. "Productivity and the Distribution of Income to Factors in Italy (1951–63)," Vol. XIX, No. 76, March 1966, pp. 42–71.

Williams, David. "The Anatomy of a Crisis: Investment and Output in Britain 1958–62," Vol. XVI, No. 64, March 1963, pp. 108–20.

P5 *The Banker,* London

Barna, T. "Investment in Industry—Has Britain Lagged?" Vol. CVII, No. 375, April 1957, pp. 219–30.

Barna, T. "Industrial Investment in Britain and Germany," Vol. CVIII, No. 384, January 1958, pp. 12–23.

P6 *Bulletin* SEDEIS (see [P3])

Berger, Guy. "De quelques travaux récents sur la réduction de la durée du travail" (On Several Recent Studies Concerning the Reduction of the Length of the Workweek), No. 924, July 1, 1965, Supplement, pp. 3–13.

De Jouvenel, Bertrand. "Niveau de vie et volume de consommation" (Standard of Living and Consumption Volume), No. 874, January 10, 1964, Supplement I, pp. 1–25.

P7 *Business Horizons.* A publication of the University of Indiana, Bloomington, Ind.

Boyd, Harper W., Jr., and Ivan Piercy. "Marketing to the British Consumer," Vol. 6, No. 1, Spring 1963, pp. 77–86.

P8 *Business Week,* New York

"U. S. Business in the New Europe," A Special Report, No. 1914, May 7, 1966, pp. 94–120.

"Another Trade Wall Crumbles," No. 1925, July 23, 1966, p. 32.

"Three Europes, One Boom," A Special Report, No. 1932, September 10, 1966, pp. 116–38.

P9 *Cahiers Economiques de Bruxelles* (Brussels Economic Papers). A publication of Département d'Economie Appliquée de l'Université Libre de Bruxelles (DULBEA—Department of Applied Economics of the Free University of Brussels)

Duprez, Colette. "Le stock de logement" (The Stock of Dwellings), No. 13, January 1962, pp. 37–100.

Duprez, Colette. "Le stock de logement" (The Stock of Dwellings), No. 14, April 1962, pp. 209–66.

Glesjer, H. "Les revenus des facteurs de production en Belgique" (Income from Factors of Production in Belgium), No. 10, April 1961, pp. 297–308.

Groupe de travail pour l'étude du capital humain (Working Party on the Study of Human Investment). "L'éducation et la croissance économique en Belgique" (Education and Economic Growth in Belgium), No. 24, 4th Quarter 1964, pp. 501–23.

Labeau, Y. "La fortune nationale de la Belgique et son évolution de 1950 à 1962" (The National Wealth of Belgium and Its Growth from 1950 to 1962), No. 25, 1st Quarter 1965, pp. 5–46.

Mendelbaum, S. "Evolution de la quantité et de la durée du travail en Belgique de 1948 à 1962" (Development of Man-Hours and Duration of Work in Belgium from 1948 to 1962), No. 21, 1st Quarter 1964, pp. 77–91.

Winterberg, M. "L'évolution des dépenses de consommation en Belgique de 1948 à 1962" (The Growth of Consumption Expenditures in Belgium from 1948 to 1962), No. 19, 3rd Quarter 1963, pp. 343–57.

P10 *Cahiers de l'*ISEA (Essays of the Institute for Applied Economics). A publication of Institut de Science Economique Appliquée, Paris

Bertrand, R. "Comparison du niveau des tarifs douaniers des pays du Marché Commun" (Comparison of the Level of Custom Tariffs in the Common Market Countries), Series R, No. 64, February 1958.

P11 *The Canadian Journal of Economics and Political Science.* A publication of the Canadian Political Science Association, Toronto

Rozen, Marvin E. "Investment Control in Post-War Britain, 1945–1955," Vol. XXIX, No. 2, May 1963, pp. 185–202.

P12 *Cartel,* Quarterly Review of Monopoly Developments and Restrictive Business Practices, London
"Concentration in the Federal Republic of Germany," Vol. XIV, No. 4, October 1964, pp. 170–72.

P13 *Consommation—Annales du* CREDOC, Centre de Recherches et de Documentation sur la Consommation (Consumption—Annals of the Center for Research and Documentation Relating to Consumption), Paris

Quin, Claude. "L'appareil commercial français en 1960" (The French Commercial Network in 1960), Vol. IX, No. 2, April-June 1962, pp. 15–56.

"Tableau général de la consommation des français de 1950 à 1960" (Statistics on French Consumption from 1950 to 1960), Special Number, Vol. VIII, No. 3–4, July-December 1961, pp. 71–121.

"La consommation des français de 1959 à 1961" (French Consumption from 1959 to 1961), Vol. X, No. 1, January-March 1963, pp. 94–192.

P14 *Econometrica.* A publication of the Econometric Society, New Haven, Conn.

Allais, Maurice. "The Influence of the Capital-Output Ratio on Real National Income," Vol. 30, No. 4, October 1962, pp. 700–28.

Houthakker, H. S. "New Evidence on Demand Elasticities," Vol. 33, No. 2, April 1965, pp. 277–88.

P15 *Economic Bulletin.* An English language publication of Deutsches Institut für Wirtschaftsforschung (German Institute for Economic Research), Berlin

"Wage and Salaries in the Federal Republic of Germany, Fourth Quarter, 1963," New Series, Vol. 1, No. 4, April 1964, pp. 1–4.

P16 *Economic Development and Cultural Change.* A publication of the University of Chicago

Pearson, D. S. "Income Distribution and the Size of Nations," Vol. XIII, No. 4, Pt. 1, July 1965, pp. 472–78.

P17 *Economic Journal.* A publication of the Royal Economic Society, London

Hall, Margaret, and John Knapp. "Numbers of Shops and Productivity in Retail Distribution in Great Britain, the United States and Canada," Vol. LXV, No. 257, March 1955, pp. 72–88.

Hill, T. P. "Growth and Investment According to International Comparisons," Vol. LXXIV, No. 294, pp. 287–304.

P18 *Economica.* A publication of The London School of Economics and Political Science, University of London

Diwan, Romesh K. "Alternative Specifications of Economies of Scale," New Series, Vol. XXXIII, No. 132, November 1966, pp. 442–53.

P19 *The Economist,* London

Macrae, Norman. "The German Lesson," A Special Survey, Vol. CCXXI, No. 6425, October 15, 1966, pp. i-xxxii.

"The Carrot and the Stick," Vol. CL, No. 5366, June 29, 1946, pp. 1033–35.

"Enter Gussie," Vol. CCIV, No. 6210, September 1, 1962, p. 840.

"RPM: The French Way," Vol. CCX, No. 6284, February 1, 1964, p. 429.

"At Half Efficiency?" Vol. CCX, No. 6289, March 7, 1964, pp. 863–65.

"Who Will do the Teaching," Vol. CCXII, No. 6316, September 12, 1964, pp. 996–97.

"Britons Will Be Slaves," Vol. CCXIII, No. 6331, December 26, 1964, pp. 1411–13.

"How Much Does Investment Count?" Vol. CCXIV, No. 6334, January 16, 1965, pp. 233–34.

"Norwegian Shipping: America's Restrictions Bite," Vol. CCXV, No. 6353, May 29, 1965, p. 1064.

"The Purpose of Recession," Vol. CCXVI, No. 6366, August 28, 1965, pp. 759–61.

"Overmuch Overtime," Vol. CCXIX, No. 6405, May 28, 1966, pp. 931–32.

"Productivity Again," Vol. CCXXI, No. 6426, October 22, 1966, p. 410.

P20 *The Educational Record.* A publication of the American Council on Education, Washington, D. C.
Kaulfers, Walter V. "Pitfalls in Comparing Foreign Schools with Ours," Vol. 44, No. 3, July 1963, pp. 275–81.

P21 *Frozen Foods.* Journal of the Refrigeration Press Limited, London. May 1961.

P22 *L'Indùstria: Rivista di economía politica* (Industry: Journal of Political Economy). Under the auspices of Istituto di Politica Economica dell Università Commerciale Luigi Bocconi (Institute of Political Economy of the Commercial University Luigi Bocconi), Milan
Barberi, Benedetto. "Aspetti statistici nelle teorie dello sviluppo economico" (Statistical Aspects of the Theory of Economic Growth), No. 3, 1960, pp. 313–45.

P23 *Industrial and Labor Relations Review.* A publication of Cornell University, Ithaca, N. Y.
Sanborn, Henry. "Pay Differences between Men and Women," Vol. 17, No. 4, July 1964, pp. 534–50.

P24 *Industrial Medicine and Surgery,* The International Journal of Medicine in Industry, Miami
Enterline, Philip E. "Sick Absence in Certain Western Countries," Vol. XXXIII, No. 10, October 1964, pp. 738–41.

P25 *Journal of Political Economy,* Chicago: University of Chicago Press
Balassa, Bela. "Tariff Protection in Industrial Countries: An Evaluation," Vol. LXXIII, No. 6, December 1965, pp. 573–94.

Bowman, Mary Jean. "Schultz, Denison, and the Contribution of 'Eds' to National Income Growth," Vol. LXXII, No. 5, October 1964, pp. 450–64.

Mincer, Jacob. "On-the-Job Training: Costs, Returns, and Some Implications," Vol. LXX, No. 5, Pt. 2, October 1962, Supplement, pp. 50–79.

Mushkin, Selma J. "Health as an Investment," Vol. LXX, No. 5, Pt. 2, October 1962, Supplement, pp. 129–57.

P26 *Journal of the Royal Statistical Society,* London
Armstrong, Alan, and Aubrey Silverston. "Size of Plant, Size of Enterprise and Concentration in British Manufacturing Industry 1935–38," Series A, Vol. 128, Pt. 3, 1965, pp. 395–420.

Dean, Geoffrey. "Fixed Investment in Britain and Norway. An Experiment in International Comparison," Series A, Vol. 127, Pt. 1, 1964, pp. 89–107.

Dean, Geoffrey. "The Stock of Fixed Capital in the United Kingdom in 1961," Series A, Vol. 127, Pt. 3, 1964, pp. 327–51.

Ward, Harry. "Discussion of Mr. Dean's Paper," Series A, Vol. 127, Pt. 3, 1964, pp. 352–58.

P27 *Lloyds Bank Review,* London
Nicolson, R. J. "The Distribution of Personal Income," No. 83, January 1967, pp. 11–21.

P28 *Manchester School of Economic and Social Studies*
Blaug, Mark. "The Rate of Return on Investment in Education in Great Britain," Vol. XXXIII, No. 3, September 1965, pp. 205–61. "Appendix: Estimate of the Rate of Return to Education in Great Britain" by D. Henderson-Stewart, pp. 252–61.

Johnson, Harry G. "The Gains from Freer Trade with Europe: An Estimate," Vol. XXVI, No. 3, September 1958, pp. 247–55.

P29 *Milbank Memorial Fund Quarterly,* New York
Fuchs, Victor R. "The Contribution of Health Services to the American Economy," Vol. 44, No. 4, Pt. 2, October 1966, pp. 65–102.

P30 *National Institute Economic Review.* A publication of the National Institute of Economic and Social Research, London
Gilbert, R. S. "The Fall in Britain's Invisible Earnings," No. 12, November 1960, pp. 45–52.
Godley, W. A. H., and J. R. Shepherd. "Long-Term Growth and Short-Term Policy," No. 29, August 1964, pp. 26–38.

P31 *National Tax Journal.* A publication of the National Tax Association, Columbus, Ohio
Richman, Peggy Brewer. "Depreciation and the Measurement of Effective Profits Tax Rates in the European Common Market and United Kingdom," Vol. XVIII, No. 1, March 1964, pp. 86–91.

P32 *New York Times*
Olsen, Arthur J. "Annual Supplement on the European Economy," January 13, 1965, p. C81.
"Annual Supplement on the European Economy," January 21, 1966, p. C60.

P33 *Oxford Economic Papers,* London
Shepherd, William G. "Changes in British Industrial Concentration, 1951–1958," New Series, Vol. 18, No. 1, March 1966, pp. 126–32.
Wiles, P. J. D. "Notes on the Efficiency of Labor," New Series, Vol. 3, No. 2, June 1951, pp. 158–80.

P34 *Quarterly Journal of Economics,* Cambridge, Mass.: Harvard University Press
Balassa, Bela. "Whither French Planning?" Vol. LXXIX, No. 4, November 1965, pp. 537–54.
Moore, Frederick T. "Economies of Scale: Some Statistical Evidence," Vol. LXXII, No. 2, May 1959, pp. 232–45.
Morgan, James, and Charles Lininger. "Education and Income: Comment," Vol. LXXVIII, No. 2, May 1964, pp. 346–47.

P35 *Recherches Economiques de Louvain* (Louvain Economic Studies). A publication of Catholic University of Louvain
Paelinck, Jean. "Etude comparative sur l'âge de l'équipement industriel dans les pays de la Communaté Economique Européenne" (Comparative Study on the Age of Industrial Equipment in the European Economic Community Countries), Vol. XXVIII, No. 2, March 1962, pp. 43–74.

P36 *Reflets et Perspectives de la Vie Economique* (Reflections and Views on Economic Activities), Brussels
Demeulenaere, Jacques. "La dimension et la concentration des enterprises en Belgique" (The Size and Concentration of Belgian Enterprises), Vol. III, No. 6, December 1964, pp. 431–42.

P37 *The Review of Economics and Statistics,* Cambridge, Mass.: Harvard University Press
Brakel, L. "A Comparison of Productivity and Recent Productivity Trends in Various Countries," Vol. XLIV, No. 2, May 1962, pp. 123–33.
Houthakker, H. S. "Education and Income," Vol. XLI, No. 1, February 1959, pp. 24–28.
Leibenstein, Harvey. "Incremental Capital-Output Ratios and Growth Rates in the Short Run," Vol. XLVIII, No. 1, February 1966, pp. 20–27.
Nelson, Richard R. "The CES Production Function and Economic Growth Projections," Vol. XLVII, No. 3, August 1965, pp. 326–28.
Waldorf, William H. "Labor Productivity in Food Wholesaling and Retailing, 1929–1958," Vol. XLVIII, No. 1, February 1966, pp. 88–93.

P38 *Revue Belge de Sécurité Sociale* (Belgian Journal of Social Security), Brussels
Rogiers, F. "Les prévisions de la population active et de l'emploi dans le cadre de la programmation économique" (Forecast of the Labor Force and Employment in the Framework of an Economic Program), Vol. VII, No. 12, December 1965, pp. 1559–1638.

P39 *Revue d'Economie Politique* (Review of Political Economy), Paris
Dupriez, Léon H. "L'accélération du progrès technique" (The Acceleration of Technical Progress), Congrès des Economistes de Langue Français, Rapport Général (Special Issue on Convention of French-Speaking Economists), May-June 1966.

P40 *Revue Economique* (Economic Review), Paris
Mandy, Paul L., and Guy de Ghelinck. "La structure de la dimension des entreprises dans les pays

du Marché Commun" (The Structure and Size of Enterprises in the Common Market Countries), No. 3, May 1960, pp. 395–413.

Le Thanh, Khoi. "La plus grande industrie du xx siècle" (The Largest Industry of the Twentieth Century), No. 1, January 1966, pp. 1–33.

P41 *Schriften des Vereins für Sozialpolitik* (Review of the Society for Socio-Political Studies), Berlin
Kirner, Wolfgang. "Struktur und Strukturverhanderungen des Anlagevermogens in der Bundesrepublik im Zeitraum von 1950 bis 1960" (Structure and Structural Changes of Capital Stock in the Federal Republic in the Period 1950 to 1960), New Series, Vol. 26, 1962.

P42 *Selbstbedienung und Supermarkt* (Self-Service and Supermarket), Cologne
"Stand der Selbstbedienung in Europa am 1.1. 1965" (Position of Self-Service in Europe on 1.1. 1965), No. 11, 1965, p. 53.

P43 *Statist,* London
Broadway, Frank. "The 'No Ambition Nation?' " Vol. CXL, No. 4586, January 28, 1966, pp. 213–14.
Carpenter, David. "Getting Down to Productivity at Last," Vol. CXC, No. 4599, April 29, 1966, pp. 1057–58.
Carpenter, David. "Behind the Ballyhoo," Vol. CXC, No. 4623, October 14, 1966, pp. 908–09.
Cooper, Bruce. "Management Training: How to Make It Pay," Vol. CXC, No. 4623, October 21, 1966, pp. 982–83.
Fulop, Christina. "An Unconscionable Time A-dying," Vol. CXCI, No. 4608, July 1, 1966, pp. 11–13.
"Britain's Hidden Unemployed," Vol. CXC, No. 4583, January 7, 1966, p. 5.

P44 *The Sunday Times,* London
Allen, William. "Britain in Blinkers," June 12, 1966, p. 49.

P45 *Techniques Marchandes Modernes* (Modern Marketing Techniques), Paris
"La distribution en Scandinavie: Danemark, Norvège" (Distribution in Scandinavia: Denmark, Norway), Vol. 16, No. 187, April 1966, pp. 25, 31.
"Le libre-service en Europe au 1er Janvier 1966" (Self-Service in Europe on January 1, 1966), Vol. 16, No. 192, September 1966, pp. 9–36.
"Développement du libre-service" (Development of Self-Service), Vol. 17, No. 198, March 1967, pp. 25–29.

P46 *Three Banks Review,* London. A publication of The Royal Bank of Scotland, Glyn, Mills & Co., and William Deacon's Bank Limited
Browaldh, Tore. "A Swedish View of Britain's Economy," No. 58, June 1963, pp. 3–16.

P47 *Vierteljahrshefte zur Wirtschaftsforschung* (Economic Research Quarterly). A publication of Deutsches Institut für Wirtschaftsforschung (German Institute for Economic Research), Berlin
Krengel, Rolf. "Produktionsvolumen und Produktionsfaktoren der Industrie im Gebeit der Bundesrepublik Deutschland" (Production Volume and Production Factors in West German Industry), 4th Quarter 1964, pp. 360–80.

P48 *Wall Street Journal*
Bonar, J. Russell. "Productivity Bargains," March 7, 1966.
June 24, 1965.

P49 *Westminister Bank Review,* London
"Wage Policy at Home and Abroad," November 1962, pp. 29–38.

P50 *World Politics. Quarterly Journal of International Relations.* A publication of Princeton University, Princeton, N. J.
Verdoorn, P. J. "A Customs Union for Western Europe: Advantages and Feasibility," Vol. VI, No. 4, July 1954, pp. 482–500.

P51 *Yale Economic Essays,* New Haven, Conn.
Shepherd, William G. "British Nationalized Industry: Performance and Policy," Vol. 4, No. 1, Spring 1964, pp. 183–222.

P52 *The Yale Review. A National Quarterly,* New Haven, Conn.
   Berger, Suzanne. "Edouard Leclerc: Grocer of France," Vol. LV, No. 1, Autumn 1965, pp. 90–106.

P53 *Zeitschrift für die gesamte Staatswissenschaft* (Journal for Public Policy Studies), Tubingen
   Hartog, Floor. "Wirtschaftliche Probleme der Arbeitszeitverkurzung" (Economic Problems of
   Shortening of Hours of Work), Vol. 112, No. 4, 1956, pp. 671–84.

Series S: Supplementary Sources

S1 France. Commissariat Général du Plan d'Equipement et de la Productivité (General Planning Board
   for Equipment and Productivity). *Ve Plan, 1966–1970. Rapport Général de la Productivité* (5th
   Plan, 1966–1970. General Report of the Productivity Commission). Paris: La Documentation
   Française, 1966.

S2 France. Ministère de l'Education. *Encyclopédie de l'Education Française.* "La formation professionnelle" (Encyclopedia of French Education. "Professional Training"). Paris, 1956.

S3 Netherlands. Parliament. *Brief van de Staatssecretaris van Economische Zaken. Enige gegevens over
   de concentratie tendens in het bedrijfsleven* (Statement of the State Secretary of Economic Affairs.
   Some Comments on the Concentration Trends Among Corporations). Parliamentary Session
   1965–66, Doc. 8038. No. 3, January 7, 1966, pp. 3–31.

S4 Divisia, François, Jean Dupin, and René Roy. *Fortune de la France.* Vol. 3: *A la Recherche du
   Franc Perdu* (France's Wealth. Vol. 3: In Search of the Lost France). Paris: Societé d'Edition
   de Revues et de Publications, 1957.

S5 De Ferron, Olivier. *Le Problème des Transports et le Marché Commun* (The Common Market and
   Its Transportation Problem). Geneva: Librairie Droz, 1965.

S6 De Gaay Fortman, Bastiaan. *Theory of Competition Policy: A Confrontation of Economic, Political and Legal Principles.* Amsterdam: North-Holland Publishing Co., 1966.

S7 Szapary, Georges, in Léon Dupriez and others, *Diffusion des Prix et Convergence des Prix* (Diffusion
   and Convergence of Prices). Vol. I: "Europe–Etats-Unis, 1899–1962" (Europe–United States,
   1899–1962). Etudes Internationales (International Studies). Louvain: Editions Nauwelaerts,
   1966; Paris: Béatrice Nauwelaerts, 1966, pp. 259–492.

S8 Van den Beld, C. A. "Short-Term Planning Experience in the Netherlands," in Bert G. Hickman
   (ed.), *Quantitative Planning of Economic Policy.* A Conference of the Social Science Research
   Council Committee on Economic Stability. Washington, D. C.: Brookings Institution, 1965, pp.
   134–62.

S9 Dunning, John H. "U. S. Subsidiaries in Britain and their U. K. Competitors—A Case Study in
   Business Ratios," *Business Ratios,* No. 1 (London: Dun & Bradstreet), Autumn 1966, pp. 5–18.

S10 Fuchs, Victor R. "A Statistical Analysis of Productivity in Selected Service Industries in the United
   States, 1939–63," *Review of Income and Wealth,* No. 3, September 1966, pp. 211–44. Also in
   Productivity Differences Within the Service Sector. Pt. I. Occasional Paper 102. New York: Na-
   tional Bureau of Economic Research, 1967, pp. 3–52.

S11 Italy. Ministèro del Lavoro (Ministry of Labor). *Rassegna di Statistiche del Lavoro* (Review of
   Labor Statistics). Rome. Selected issues, 1951–66.

Index

Index

Abramovitz, Moses, 11*n*, 153, 153*n*, 281*n*
Age of capital stock, *see* Embodiment models
Age-sex composition of the labor force, *see* Earnings; Employment; Hours of work; Labor input; Quality indexes
Agostinelli, Arnando, 422, 422*n*
Agriculture
  Employment, 46–50, 201–02, 211–13
  Fluctuations in output, 277–78
  Fragmentation of farms, 214
  Land utilized by, 181, 184
  Overallocation of resources to, 202–04, 219–24
  Ratio of income per worker to nonagricultural income, 203–04
  Reallocation of resources, 211–15, 322
Alfred Politz Research, Inc., 253*n*
Allais, Maurice, 171*n*
Allen, William W., 113*n*, 294*n*
Allocation of resources, *see* Resources, allocation
Appetito, Alberto, 427
Armed forces, *see* Military personnel
Armstrong, Alan, 270, 271*n*
Arnesen, Anne-Marie, 89*n*, 394, 394*n*
ASEPELT, Association Scientifique Européenne pour la Prévision Economique à Moyen et à Long Terme (European Scientific Association for Medium- and Long-term Forecasting), 240*n*
Aukrust, Odd, 39*n*
Automobile Manufacturers' Association, 253
Automobile ownership, economies of scale in distribution due to, 252–55

Bain, Joe S., 227*n*, 228*n*, 269
Bakkenist, S. C., 434
Balassa, Bela, 226*n*, 228*n*, 237*n*, 257*n*, 267*n*
Barberi, Benedetto, 422, 422*n*
Barna, Tibor, 140*n*, 151*n*, 156*n*, 169*n*, 267*n*
Baum, Warren, 267*n*
Bayliss, Brian T., 263*n*
Becker, Gary S., 84*n*
Beckerman, Wilfred, 113*n*, 243*n*

Belgium
  Agriculture: overallocation of resources to, 206, 211, 215, 219, 223; ratio of income per worker to nonagricultural income, 204
  Automobile ownership, 253
  Capital input: growth rate, 192–94; as percentage o total national income, 38, 42
  Deflation procedures for measuring growth rate, 25, 27, 27*n*
  Depreciation of assets, 120
  Earnings of males by years of education, 378–79
  Economic growth, sources, 300–03, 321–32
  Economies of scale: contribution to growth rate due to growth of national market, 233; contribution due to income elasticities, 249; independent growth of local markets and, 255
  Education: compulsory, 103, 104; number of years of, 93, 107–08, 387; part-time, 403; pre-primary, 97, 97*n*; time spent on, 93, 399–401
  Education quality indexes, 89, 91, 387; adjusted for school leaving age, 95; adjusted for time spent in school, 93, 401; compared with U.S., 105; increase in, 1950–62, 103; projection of, 106
  Employment, 46–50, 355–58; age-sex distribution, 71; changes in, 1950–62, 51; comparison of components, 205–06; growth rate, 52, 320; in manufacturing, by size of unit, 269–70
  Enterprise structures and equipment: age of, 146*n*, 156*n*; construction as percentage of, 168; contribution to difference from U.S. in national income per person employed, 172–73; contribution to growth rate, 140, 141, 142, 192, 194; gross investment in, 160, 164–65, 407, 409; growth rate, 138; growth rate per person employed, 139; indexes of value of gross and net stock of, 136, 137, 416, 423; net stock of, 166–71, 172–73; as percentage of GNP, 138; as percentage of total national income, 38, 42; ratio of prices to GNP prices, 161, 162; shift work and productivity of, 153, 154
  Foreign trade: as percentage of GNP, 231; tariffs, 232
  Gross investment, ratio to gross national product, 118, 119*n*, 120

475